The Best Bed & Breakfast
in England, Scotland & Wales
2000–2001

Sigourney Welles

Jill Darbey

Joanna Mortimer

The finest Bed & Breakfast accommodations in the

British Isles

from the Scottish Hebrides to

London's Belgravia

Country Houses, Town Houses, City Apartments, Manor
Houses, Village Cottages, Farmhouses, Castles

U.K.H.M. Publishing, London, U.K.

The Globe Pequot Press, Guilford, Connecticut, U.S.A.

Library of Congress Catalog Card Number: 91-074158

U.S. ISBN 0-7627-0502-7

Typeset by U.K.H.M. Publishing Ltd., London.
Printed and bound in China.
Produced by Phoenix Offset Ltd.

U.K.H.M. Publishing Ltd. P.O. Box 2070, London W12 8QW, England. U.K.

Contents

Foreword

Bed & Breakfast has suddenly become the fashionable way to travel. The secret has escaped & thousands of people are discovering for themselves that it is possible to combine high quality accommodation with friendly, personal attention at very reasonable prices. The New York Times said about us that "...after an unannounced inspection of rooms booked through The Worldwide Bed & Breakfast Association it is clear that the standards of comfort & cleanliness are exemplary ...at least as good as in a five star hotel & in most cases, better, reflecting the difference between sensitive hosts taking pride in their homes & itinerant hotel staff doing as little as they can get away with..."

Discerning travellers are turning away from the impersonal hotels with the expensive little refridgerators & microwave breakfasts in each room. How much nicer to have a real English breakfast to begin the day, enough to keep you going until evening. Many of our houses will provide dinner too - often the hostess will be a Cordon Bleu cook & the price will be within your range. We try to provide the best accommodation possible within a wide range of prices, some as little as £15.00 per person per night, whilst others will be up to £55.00 per person per night. The choice is yours, but you can be certain that each will be the best available in that particular area of the country at that price.

Our inspectors are out & about visiting our homes to ensure that standards are maintained. We encourage everyone to use the recommendations & complaints page at the back of the book. Let us know your opinion of the accommodation or inform us of any delightful homes you may have come across & would like to recommend for future inclusion.

In order to avoid the classification trap, which we feel is invidious, we encourage you to read about each home, what they offer & their respective price range, so that you find the one that best suits your expectations. Our hosts in turn offer hospitality in their own unique style, so each home naturally retains its individuality & interest. We have found this to be a very successful recipe which often leads to lasting friendships.

Bed & Breakfast really is a marvellous way to travel, meeting a delightful cross section of fellow travellers with whom to exchange information & maybe the address of ...that lovely little place which was discovered by chance and which serves the most delicious dinner or... the best route to take to a particular farmhouse but make sure you get there by 5 o'clock so that you're in time to watch the evening milking...

This is the fun & real pleasure that is part of Bed & Breakfasting. Once you've tried it you will be a dedicated Best Bed & Breakfaster.

How to use this Guide

To get the full benefits of staying at our Bed & Breakfast homes it is important to appreciate how they differ from hotels, so both hosts & guests know what to expect.

Arrival & Departure

These times are more important to a family than to hotel desk clerks, so your time of arrival (E.T.A.) is vital information when making a reservation either with the home directly or with one of our agencies. This becomes even more important to your reception if you intend travelling overnight & will be arriving in the early morning. So please have this information & your flight number ready when you book your rooms. **At most B & Bs the usual check-in time is 6 P.M. & you will be expected to check out by 10 A.M. on the morning of departure.** These arrangements do vary from home to home. The secret to an enjoyable visit is to let your hosts know as much about your plans as possible & they will do their best to meet your requirements.

Other personal requests

There are a few other details that you should let your hosts know when planning your Bed & Breakfast trip that will make everyone much happier during your visit. Do you smoke? Would you prefer to be in a non-smoking home? Do you suffer from any allergies? Some families have cats, dogs, birds & other pets in the house....Can you make it up a flight of stairs? Would you prefer the ground floor? Do you have any special dietary requirements? Will you be staying for dinner?

Do you prefer a private bathroom or are you prepared to share facilities? Do you prefer a shower instead of a bath? The ages of any children travelling.

In all these cases let your host know what you need & the details can be arranged before you arrive rather than presenting a problem when you are shown to your rooms.

Prices

The prices quoted throughout the guide are the *minimum* per person per night for two sharing. Single occupancy usually attracts a supplement. Prices will increase during busy seasons. You should always confirm the prevailing rate when you make a reservation.

Facilities

The bathroom & toilet facilities affect the prices. Sharing is the cheapest, private is a little more costly & en-suite carries a premium.

Descriptions

Rooms are described as follows: Single:1 bed (often quite small). Double:1 large bed (sometimes King or Queensize).
Twin: 2 separate single beds.
Four-poster: a King or Queen size bed with a canopy above supported by four corner posts.
Bathrooms and toilets are described as follows;
Shared: these facilities are shared with some other guests or perhaps the hosts.
Private: for your use only, however they may occasionally be in an adjacent room.
En-suite: private facilities within your bedroom suite.

Making a Reservation

Once you have chosen where you want to stay, have all the following information ready & your reservation will go smoothly without having to run & find more travel documents or ask someone else what they think you should do. Here is a brief check list of what you will probably be asked & examples to illustrate answers:

Dates & number of nights…August 14-19(6 nights).

Estimated time of arrival at the home …7 P.M.(evening) & flight number.

Type & number of rooms…1 Double & 2 Single.

Toilet & Bathroom facilities…1 Double en-suite) & 2 singles (shared)

Smoking or Non-smoking?

Any allergies?

Special dietary requests?

Children in the party & their ages?

Any other preferences… Is a shower preferred to a bath?

Maximum budget per person per night based on all the above details.

The London Reservation Agency

There is a minimum two night consecutive stay at our London homes.

Reservations for London homes can only be made through one of our Worldwide Bed & Breakfast Agencies. They can be contacted by 'phone, fax, e-mail or on-line from our website at www.bestbandb.co.uk.

All reservations must be confirmed with advance payments which are non-refundable in the event of cancellation. You simply pay the balance due after you arrive at the home. The advance payment can be made with major credit & charge cards or by cheque. Cash is the preferred method of paying the balance & always in pounds sterling.

The advance payments confirm each night of your visit, **not just the first one**.

When arriving at a later date or departing at an earlier date than those confirmed, the guest will be liable to pay only the appropriate proportion of the stated balance that is due. For example, staying three nights out of four booked means paying 3/4 of the stated balance due. The advance payment is non-refundable. A minimum of 2 nights will always apply.

Outside London

We encourage you to make use of the information in this guide & contact the homes directly. The hosts may require varying amounts of advance payments & may or may not accept credit & charge cards. Remember, many B&Bs are small, family-run establishments and are unable to accept payment by credit card. The confirmed prices shall be those prevailing on the dates required… as previously mentioned, *the prices shown in this guide are the* **minimum** *& will increase during the busy seasons.*

Alterations

If you wish to alter or change a previously confirmed booking through one of the agencies there will be a further fee of £15 per alteration.

Cancellations

All advance payments for London are non-refundable.

All booking fees outside London are non-refundable.

Notice of cancellation must be given as soon as possible & the following suggested rates shall apply outside London only;

30 - 49 days notice - 80% refund.

10-29 days notice -50% refund.

0 - 9 days notice - No refund.

The Worldwide Bed & Breakfast Agencies reserve the right to alter your accommodation should it be necessary & will inform you of any alteration as soon as possible

London Reservation Agency

Website:http://www.bestbandb.co.uk

We offer an outstanding selection of accommodation in London. As with all our accommodation each one has been personally inspected so you can be sure of the highest standards. We offer an immensely wide range of accommodation. We have a type, style and location to suit everyone. From city apartments close to shops, museums and galleries to spacious homes in leafy residential suburbs near the river, parks and restaurants. No matter what your reason for visiting London we can accommodate you. Whether on business or vacation Best Bed & Breakfast provides great accommodation together with a fast, efficient reservation service. Our helpful staff are always happy to advise you on all your accommodation requirements. We are located in London, we know the city and all our hosts. We know how to provide an enjoyable, affordable, hassle free trip. There are plenty of ways to contact us. To make a reservation simply do one of the following;

Worldwide call Tel: +44 (0)20 8742 9123 (24Hrs.)

North America call Toll Free: 011 800 852 26320

Australia call Toll Free: 0011 800 852 26320

E-mail: bestbandb@atlas.co.uk

Fax: +44 (0)20 8749 7084

The Discount Offer

This offer is made to people who have bought this book & wish to make reservations for Bed & Breakfast in London through our London Reservation Agency. The offer only applies to a minimum stay of three consecutive nights at one of our London homes between the following dates; January 7. 2000 & April 1. 2000 then from September 15. 2000 to December 1. 2000. Only one discount per booking is allowed. Call the reservation office to make your booking in the normal way & tell the clerk that you have bought the book & wish to have the discount. After a couple of questions the discount will be deducted from the advance payment required to confirm the reservation.

Regions

To assist tourists with information during their travels, counties have been grouped together under Regional Tourist Boards that co-ordinate the various efforts of each county.

The British Tourist Authority has designated these areas in consultation with the English, Scottish & Wales Tourist Boards & we have largely adopted these areas for use in this guide

Counties are listed alphabetically throughout our guide & then have a sub-heading indicating which Tourist Region they belong to.

ENGLAND
Cumbria
County of Cumbria
Northumbria.
Counties of Cleveland, Durham, Northumberland, Tyne & Wear.
North West
Counties of Cheshire, Greater Manchester, Lancashire, Merseyside, High Peaks of Derbyshire.
Yorkshire & Humberside
Counties of North Yorkshire, South Yorkshire, West Yorkshire, Humberside.
Heart of England
Counties of Gloucestershire, Herefordshire & Worcestershire, Shropshire, Staffordshire, Warwickshire, West Midlands.
East Midlands
Counties of Derbyshire, Leicestershire, Nottinghamshire, Rutland, Lincolnshire & Northamptonshire,
East Anglia
Counties of Cambridgeshire, Essex, Norfolk, Suffolk.
West Country
Counties of Cornwall, Devon, Dorset (parts of), Somerset, Wiltshire, Isles of Scilly.
Southern
Counties of Hampshire, Dorset (East & North), Isle of Wight.
South East
Counties of East Sussex, Kent, Surrey, West Sussex.

SCOTLAND
The subdivisions of Scottish Regions in this guide differ slightly from the current Marketing Regions of the Scottish Tourist Board.

The Borders, Dumfries & Galloway
Districts & counties of Scottish Borders, Dumfries & Galloway.
Lothian & Strathclyde
City of Edinburgh, Forth Valley, East Lothian, Kirkaldy, St. Andrews & North-East Fife, Greater Glasgow, Clyde Valley, Ayrshire & Clyde Coast, Burns Country.
Argyll & The Isles
Districts & counties of Oban & Mull, Mid Argyll, Kintyre & Islay, Dunoon, Cowal, Rothesay & Isle of Bute, Isle of Arran.
Perthshire, Loch Lommond & The Trossachs
Districts & counties of Perthshire, Loch Lomond, Stirling & Trossachs.
The Grampians
Districts & counties of Banff & Buchan, Moray, Gordon, Angus, City of Aberdeen, Kincardine & Deeside, City of Dundee.
The Highlands & Islands
Districts & counties of Shetland, Orkney, Caithness, Sutherland, Ross & Cromarty, Western Isles, South West Ross & Isle of Skye, Inverness, Loch Ness & Nairn, Aviemore & Spey Valley, Fort William & Lochaber.

WALES
The regions are defined as follows:
North Wales
Counties of Anglesey, Conwy, Denbighshire, Flintshire & Gwynedd.
Mid Wales
Counties of Ceredigion & Powys.
South Wales
Counties of Carmarthenshire, Glamorgan, Monmouthshire, Newport, Pembrokeshire & Swansea.
The photographs appearing in the Introductions & Gazeteers are by courtesy of the appropriate Tourist Board for each county or W.W.B.B.A.

Counties map

Each county has been assigned a page number where a more detailed map can be found. These maps include principal towns, major roads & the location of each Bed & Breakfast establishment.

OUTER HEBRIDES
WESTERN ISLES
INNER HEBRIDES

HIGHLANDS

MORAY

SCOTLAND
502

ABERDEENSHIRE
ABERDEEN

ANGUS
PERTHSHIRE & KINROSS
DUNDEE

ARGYLL & BUTE
STIRLING
FIFE
EAST LOTHIAN

1	INVERCLYDE	7	NORTH LANARKSHIRE
2	DUNBARTON & CLYDEBANK	8	FALKIRK
3	RENFREWSHIRE	9	CLACKMANNAN
4	EAST RENFREWSHIRE	10	WEST LOTHIAN
5	GLASGOW	11	EDINBURGH
6	EAST DUNBARTONSHIRE	12	MID LOTHAIN

NORTH AYRSHIRE
SOUTH LANARKSHIRE
EAST AYRSHIRE
BORDERS

North Sea

SOUTH AYRSHIRE
DUMFRIES & GALLOWAY

NORTHUMBERLAND

TYNE AND WEAR
298

CUMBRIA
85
DURHAM
CLEVELAND

YORKSHIRE

Irish Sea

461 HUMBERSIDE

LANCASHIRE
52

MANCHESTER
MERSEYSIDE

ENGLAND

FLINTSHIRE
DENBIGHSHIRE
ANGLESEY
CONWY
CHESHIRE
52
DERBYSHIRE & STAFFORD-SHIRE
NOTTINGHAM-SHIRE, LEICESTERSHIRE & RUTLAND
270
LINCOLNSHIRE
277

GWYNEDD
WREXHAM

WALES
555
SHROP-SHIRE
323

NORFOLK
285

CEREDIGION
POWYS
HEREFORD & WORCESTER
237
WARWICK-SHIRE
417
CAMBRIDGE-SHIRE & NORTHAMPTON-SHIRE
43
SUFFOLK
379

CARMARTHENSHIRE
MONMOUTH-SHIRE
188
GLOUCESTER-SHIRE
307
OXFORD-SHIRE
BEDFORDSHIRE, BERKSHIRE, BUCKINGHAMSHIRE & HERTFORDSHIRE
32
ESSEX
183

PEMBROKESHIRE
SWANSEA
NEWPORT
LONDON
15

1 BRIDGEND
2 RHONDA CYNON TAFF
3 MERTHYR TYDFIL
4 CAERPHILLY
5 BLAENAU GWENT
6 TORFAEN

NEATH & PORT TALBOT
VALE OF GLAMORGAN
CARDIFF
WILTSHIRE
445
387
SURREY
KENT
250

SOMERSET
336
HAMPSHIRE
220
SUSSEX
395

168
DEVON
134
DORSET

64
CORNWALL

English Channel

9

General Information

To help overseas visitors with planning their trip to Britain, we have compiled the next few pages explaining the basic requirements & customs you will find here.

Before you arrive

Documents you will have to obtain before you arrive;
Valid passports & visas. Citizens of Commonwealth countries or the U.S.A. don't need visas to enter the U.K.
Bring your local Driving Licence.

Medical Insurance.

This is strongly recommended although visitors will be able to receive free emergency treatment. If you have to stay in hospital in the U.K. you will be asked to pay unless you are a citizen of European Community Countries.

Restrictions on arrival

Immigration procedures can be lengthy & bothersome, be prepared for questions like:
a) where are you staying in the U.K.?
b) do you have a round trip ticket?
c) how long do you intend to stay?
d) how much money are you bringing in?
e) do you have a credit card?
Do not bring any animals with you as they are subject to 6 months quarantine & there are severe penalties for bringing in pets without appropriate licences. Do not bring any firearms, prohibited drugs or carry these things for anyone else. If you are in doubt about items in your possession, declare them by entering the Red Channel at Customs & seek the advice of an officer.

After you have arrived

You can bring in as much currency as you like. You can change your own currency or travellers cheques at many places at varying rates.

Airports tend to be the most expensive places to change money & the 'Bureau de Change" are often closed at nights. So bring enough Sterling to last you at least 2 or 3 days. Banks often charge commission for changing money. Some Cashcard machines (or A.T.M.'s) will dispense local currency using your charge card, if they are affiliated systems, & don't charge commissions to your account. Major credit cards/charge cards are widely accepted & you may only need to carry small amounts of cash for "pocket money".

Driving

Don't forget to drive on the Left... especially the first time you get into a car... at the airport car hire parking lot... or from the front of a railway station... or straight after breakfast... old habits are hard to shake off. If you need to know the rules, get a copy of the Highway Code. You must wear a seat belt & so must any other front seat passenger. The speed limits are clearly shown in most areas - generally 30 mph. in residential areas (48 kph) & 70 mph on motorways (113 kph.). Traffic lights are at the side of the road & not hanging overhead. Car hire is relatively expensive in the U.K. & it is often a good idea to arrange this before you arrive. Mileage charges, V.A.T. (Sales Tax) & insurance are usually charged extra & you will need to be over 21 to hire a car in the U.K. Petrol (gas) is also relatively expensive & you may find petrol stations hard to find or closed at night in rural areas... so fill up often. Driving in London is not a recommended experience for newcomers & parking is also a very complex arrangement which can become a nightmare if the car gets "clamped" (immobilised) or towed away.

General Information

Buses & Coaches

If you are not driving & only want to travel 5-10 miles there are good bus services within most towns & cities, however, rural routes have seriously declined over the last few years. There are regular & fast coach services between the major towns which are very popular - so book ahead to be sure of a seat.

Trains

There is an extensive railway system throughout the U.K. which serves the major towns on a fast & frequent basis. These services are relatively expensive & like most railway systems are subject to delays.

Tubes (Subways)

London is the only city with an extensive subway system although some other towns do have "Metro" trains of linked under & overground systems.

The "tube" is a very popular means of getting around London, but it can get very crowded & unpleasant at "rush hours". It is often the preferred way to get into London from say Heathrow Airport in the early morning, when there are long delays on the roads that hold up both buses & taxis with increasingly expensive rides into the city centre, £40 is not unusual for this cab fare, compared with a few pounds on the "tube". The "tube" in London is operated by London Transport which also operates the London bus service ... the famous red buses. They sell tickets which allow you to travel all over London on tubes, buses & trains at very good rates, called Travelcards... a transfer system. Ask your local travel agent about these & other travel passes throughout the U.K.

Telephones

When calling the U.K. from abroad always drop the 0 from the area code.

In the U.K. the only free calls are the operator - 100, enquiries - 192 (international 153) & emergencies - 999.

You may use your calling card to call home which is billed to your account or call collect, ask the operator to "reverse charge" the call. The famous red telephone kiosks are slowly being replaced with new glass booths & they differ in that the old boxes only take 10 & 50 pence pieces & don't give any change, whereas the new ones take many combinations of coins & do give change. Phonecards are becoming more popular as the number of boxes that only accept these cards increases. Cards can be bought at Post Offices & many newsagents & shops.

Doctors/Chemists

All local police stations have lists of chemists & doctors should you need one, at night, for instance.

Voltage

The standard voltage throughout the country is 240v AC.50Hz. If you bring small electrical appliances with you, a converter will be required.

Tipping

Is not obligatory anywhere but a general guide if you wish to leave a tip for service is between 10%-15%.

Pubs

Most open between 11 a.m. & 11 p.m. every day.

You must be over 18 years old to buy & drink alcohol in pubs .

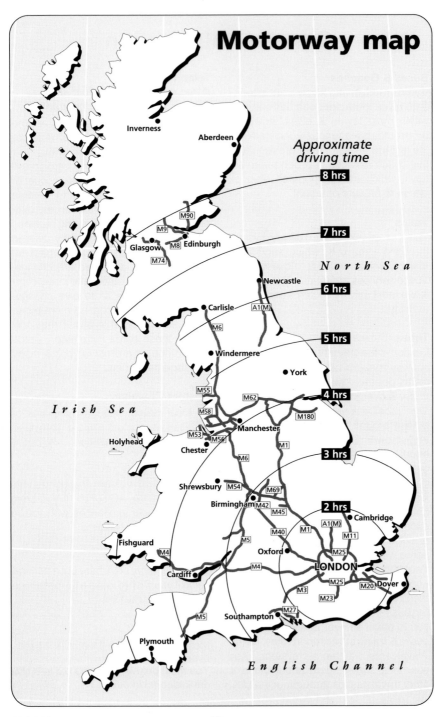

Motorway map

Approximate driving time

8 hrs
7 hrs
6 hrs
5 hrs
4 hrs
3 hrs
2 hrs

Inverness

Aberdeen

North Sea

M90
M9
Glasgow M8 Edinburgh
M74

Newcastle

Carlisle A1(M)
M6

Windermere

York

M55
M62
M58
M180
M53 M56 Manchester
M1
Chester
M6

Irish Sea

Holyhead

Shrewsbury M54 M69
Birmingham M42
M45
M40 M1 A1(M) Cambridge
M5 M11
Fishguard
M4 Oxford M25
Cardiff M4 LONDON
M25 M20 Dover
M3 M23
M5 Southampton M27

Plymouth

English Channel

12

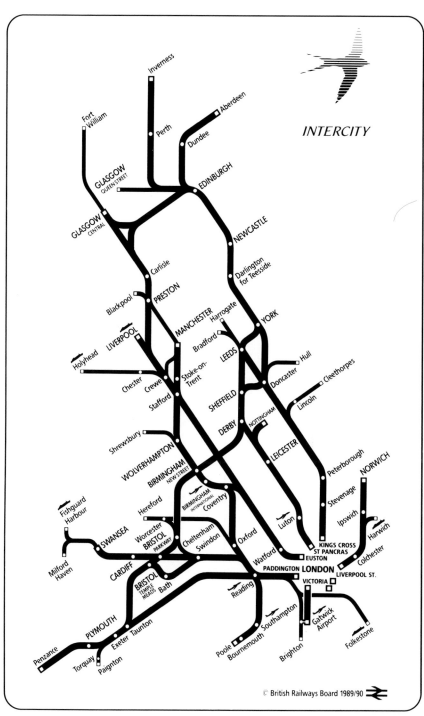

INTERCITY

© British Railways Board 1989/90

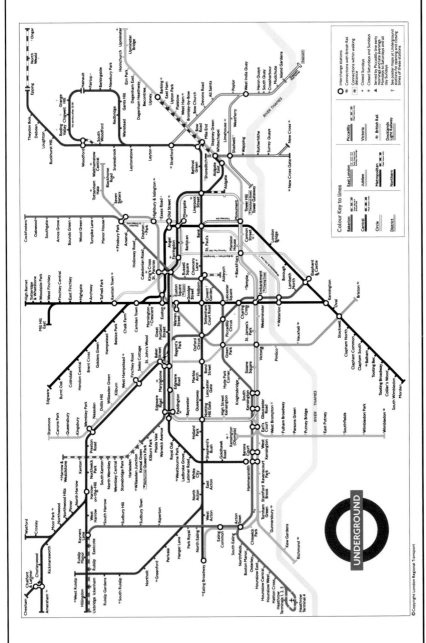

UNDERGROUND

91/1258

©Copyright London Regional Transport

LONDON MAP

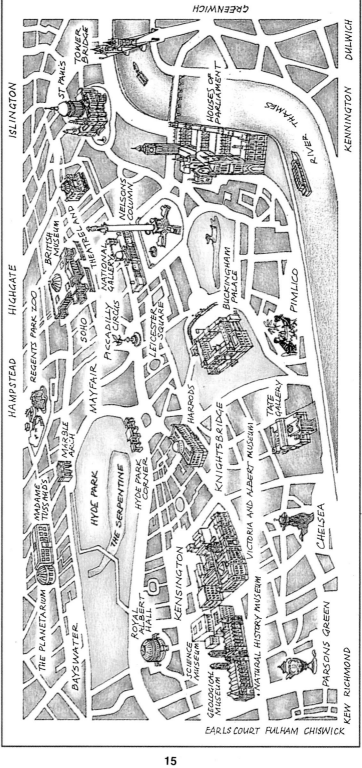

London

Visit our website: www.bestbandb.co.uk

	rate £ from - to per person	children taken	evening meals	animals taken
Home No. 01. London. Tel: +44 (0)20-8742-9123 Fax: +44 (0)20-8749-7084 U.S.A., Canada call: Toll Free 011-800-852-26320 Australia call: Toll Free 0011-800-852-26320 E-mail:bestbandb@atlas.co.uk Nearest Tube: Putney Bridge. An attractive Victorian terraced house, situated in a quiet residential street, yet only 3 mins walk from the station. 1 spacious double-bedded room with an en-suite bathroom & a twin-bedded room with a private bathroom. Each room is tastefully furnished & has tea/coffee facilities. (T.V. available.) Breakfast is served in the pleasant kitchen/dining room. Many good pubs, restaurants & shops locally. An excellent location from which to explore London. Parking. Children over 12. (No smoking)	£29.00 to £50.00	Y	N	N
Home No. 04. London. Tel: + 44 (0)20-8742-9123 Fax: + 44 (0)20-8749-7084 U.S.A., Canada call: Toll Free 011-800-852-26320 Australia call: Toll Free: 0011-800-852-26320 E-mail: bestbandb@atlas.co.uk Nearest Tube: Parsons Green. A lovely Victorian terraced house, set in a quiet street. The delightful host offers 1 extremely attractive, light & airy double-bedded room with T.V., tea/coffee-making facilities & a well-equipped private bathroom. There is also a smaller double room available, making this ideal accommodation for parties of 3 or 4 persons. Breakfast is served in the attractive dining room. A perfect spot for a relaxing break with easy access to central London by both bus & tube. (No smoking)	£29.00 to £50.00	N	N	N
Home No. 06. London. Tel: +44 (0)20-8742-9123 Fax: +44 (0)20-8749-7084 U.S.A, Canada call: Toll Free 011-800-852-26320 Australia call: Toll Free 0011-800-852-26320 E-mail: bestbandb@atlas.co.uk Nearest Tube: East Putney. A Victorian terraced house with a traditional family atmosphere & set in a quiet residential street. The friendly hosts offer 1 comfortable twin-bedded room with T.V., overlooking the rear garden, & with an adjacent private bathroom. A large Continental or Full English breakfast is served. Putney is a delightful area with a variety of good shops & restaurants. Transport facilities are excellent & provide easy access to central London & the attractions.	£26.00 to £40.00	Y	N	N
Home No. 07. London. Tel: +44 (0)20-8742-9123 Fax: +44 (0)20-8749-7084 U.S.A., Canada call: Toll Free 011-800-852-26320 Australia call: Toll Free 0011-800-852-26320 E-mail: bestbandb@atlas.co.uk Nearest Tube: Fulham Broadway. Set in the heart of Fulham, this is an attractive Victorian maisonette which is elegantly furnished throughout with antiques. The charming host, who has an in-depth knowledge of London, offers 2 beautifully furnished double-bedded rooms. Each is attractively decorated & has tea/coffee facilities & an en-suite or private bathroom. In summer, breakfast can be taken in the delightful garden. Only 8 mins' walk from the tube this is an ideal base from which to explore London. Many good restaurants & antique shops close by. (No smoking)	£33.00 to £50.00	N	N	N
Home No. 12. London. Tel: +44 (0)20-8742-9123 Fax: +44 (0)20-8749-7084 U.S.A., Canada call: Toll Free 011-800-852-26320 Australia call: Toll Free 0011-800-852-26320 E-mail:bestbandb@atlas.co.uk Nearest Tube: Parsons Green. Set in a quiet residential street, yet only 5 mins' walk from the station, this is a delightful Victorian terraced house. It has been beautifully decorated & is furnished throughout with antiques. The charming hosts offer 1 attractive King-size double/twin-bedded room with T.V., tea/coffee-making facilities & an en-suite shower room. Breakfast is taken in the elegant dining room which overlooks the garden. There are many antique shops & good restaurants just a short walk away. Easy access to central London & the sights. (No smoking)	£40.00 to £78.00	N	N	N

Home No. 17. London.

London
Visit our website: www.bestbandb.co.uk

	rate £ from - to per person	children taken	evening meals	animals taken
Home No. 17. London. Tel: +44 (0)20-8742-9123 Fax: +44 (0)20-8749-7084 U.S.A, Canada call: Toll Free **011-800-852-26320** Australia call: Toll Free **0011-800-852-26320** E-mail: bestbandb@atlas.co.uk	Nearest Tube: Richmond Situated in an excellent 17th-century terrace, this is an outstanding home, elegantly furnished throughout with antiques. 3 guest rooms: 1 double 4-poster, 1 twin-bedded room & a triple with a 4-poster & a single bed. Each has a super private bathroom. 2 of the bedrooms have French doors leading onto an Italiante garden, the triple room commands views of the Thames. A wealth of riverside shops & restaurants are a few mins walk. Easy access to central London. Waterloo 12 mins by train. Heathrow 20 mins by taxi.	£45.00 to £88.00 🚭 *see PHOTO over p. 17*	N	N	N
Home No. 18. London. Tel: +44 (0)20-8742-9123 Fax: +44 (0 20-8749-7084 U.S.A., Canada call: Toll Free **011-800-852-26320** Australia call: Toll Free **0011-800-852-25320** E-mail: bestbandb@atlas.co.uk	Nearest Tube: High St. Ken. A beautiful house, furnished with many interesting paintings & situated in the heart of Kensington. The charming host offers 1 light & airy, twin-bedded room with a private bathroom. Also another, equally attractive twin-bedded room, is across the hall, & is ideal for a third or fourth member of the party. Each bedroom is well-furnished & a T.V. is available. Only a short walk from the High Street with its many shops & restaurants & within easy reach of Kensington Palace, Knightsbridge & the museums. Children over 12.	£32.00 to £50.00 🚭	Y	N	N
Home No. 19. London. Tel: +44 (0)20-8742-9123 Fax: +44 (0)20-8749-7084 U.S.A, Canada call: Toll Free **011-800-852-26320** Australia call: Toll Free **0011-800-852-26320** E-mail: bestbandb@atlas.co.uk	Nearest Tube: Parsons Green Located in the quiet Parsons Green area of Fulham. This superb house offers accommodation in 1 king-size double-bedded room with private facilities & 2 doubles which share a bathroom. Each room is beautifully decorated & very comfortably furnished. This is a delightful home & the ideal base for visitors to London. Many of the attractions including Buckingham Palace & Knightsbridge are only 15 mins away by tube.	£29.00 to £52.00	N	N	N
Home No. 21. London. Tel: +44 (0)20-8742-9123 Fax: +44 (0)20-8749-7084 U.S.A., Canada call: Toll Free **011-800-852-26320** Australia call: Toll Free **0011-800-852-26320** E-mail: bestbandb@atlas.co.uk	Nearest Tube: Hammersmith This is a charming Victorian terraced house, where the welcoming hosts offer 1 spacious, attractive & comfortably furnished twin-bedded room with sitting area & 1 attractive king-size double/twin room. Each with private facilities, T.V. & tea/coffee. Breakfast is served in the elegant dining room. A delightful family home set in a quiet street, yet only 8 mins walk from the bustle of Hammersmith with its many restaurants etc. Excellent transport facilities providing access to Heathrow, central London & the sights.	£28.00 to £50.00 🚭	Y	N	N
Home No. 24. London. Tel: +44 (0)20-8742-9123 Fax: +44 (0)20-8749-7084 U.S.A., Canada call: Toll Free **011-800-852-26320** Australia call: Toll Free **0011-800-852-26320** E-mail: bestbandb@atlas.co.uk	Nearest Tube: Parsons Green An elegantly furnished Victorian terraced house, set in a quiet street yet only 5 mins walk from the tube. The most charming hosts offer 1 delightful double-bedded room which overlooks the rear garden & an attractive king-size double/twin-bedded room. Each has a private bathroom & tea/coffee facilities, & is beautifully decorated. Parsons Green is perfect for exploring the delights of London & has many excellent restaurants & antique shops. Non-smokers preferred.	£29.00 to £50.00	N	N	N

London
Visit our website: www.bestbandb.co.uk

	rate £ from - to per person	children taken	evening meals	animals taken

Home No. 31. London.
Tel: +44 (0)20-8742-9123
Fax: +44 (0)20-8749-7084
U.S.A, Canada call:
Toll Free 011-800-852-26320
Australia call:
Toll Free 0011-800-852-26320
E-mail: bestbandb@atlas.co.uk

Nearest Tube: Parsons Green
A charming Victorian terraced house, situated only minutes from many excellent shops & restaurants in Fulham. The welcoming host has elegantly furnished this property throughout. Accommodation is in 1 attractive king-size double/twin-bedded room. It is comfortable & has a good private bathroom. Also, a cosy single room for a third member of the party. A large Continental breakfast is served. Situated only a short walk from the station, this is an excellent base from which to explore London. Children over 12.

£30.00 to £50.00 — Y | N | N (non-smoking)

Home No. 35. London.
Tel: +44 (0)20-8742-9123
Fax: +44 (0)20-8749-7084
U.S.A., Canada call:
Toll Free 011-800-852-26320
Australia call:
Toll Free 0011-800-852-26320
E-mail: bestbandb@atlas.co.uk

Nearest Tube: Fulham Broadway
Located in Fulham, this modern townhouse is set in a quiet street & yet is only 5 mins walk from the station. The friendly & very helpful host offers 1 twin-bedded room with an adjacent private bathroom. Also, 1 double room is available for another member of the party. Each room is tastefully furnished & well-appointed with T.V. & tea/coffee-making facilities. A large Continental breakfast is served. A variety of local restaurants offer a wide choice of international cuisine. Children over 12.

£29.00 to £50.00 — Y | N | N (non-smoking)

Home No. 38. London.
Tel: +44 (0)20-8742-9123
Fax: +44 (0)20-8749-7084
U.S.A, Canada call:
Toll Free 011-800-852-26320
Australia call:
Toll Free 0011-800-852-26320
E-mail: bestbandb@atlas.co.uk

Nearest Tube: Earls Court
A lovely apartment situated on the top floor of a Victorian mansion block (with lift access) & only 3 mins walk from Earls Court station. The charming host offers 1 spacious & attractively furnished double bedded room with an en-suite bathroom & T.V. Breakfast is served in the attractive dining area. Easy access to Knightsbridge, South Kensington & the museums & Heathrow. Many good local restaurants.

£30.00 to £50.00 — Y | N | N

Home No. 39. London.
Tel: +44 (0)20-8742-9123
Fax: +44 (0)20-8749-7084
U.S.A, Canada call:
Toll Free 011-800-852-26320
Australia call:
Toll Free 0011-800-852-26320
E-mail: bestbandb@atlas.co.uk

Nearest Tube: Earls Court
A superb home, designer decorated & furnished to the highest standard with antiques throughout. 2 double & 1 twin bedded rooms. Each beautiful bedroom is large & airy with a lovely bathroom en-suite, T.V. & tea/coffee facilities. A large dining room. A delightful garden where breakfast can be served if the weather is good. Guests have their own private entrance. Only 10 mins. to Harrods. Children over 12 years. Parking.

£45.00 to £65.00 — Y | N | N (non-smoking)
see PHOTO over
p. 20

Home No. 40. London.
Tel: +44 (0)20-8742-9123
Fax: +44 (0)20-8749-7084
U.S.A., Canada call:
Toll Free 011-800-852-26320
Australia call: Toll Free
0011-800-852-26320
Email: bestbandb@atlas.co.uk

Nearest Tube: Gunnersbury
A large Victorian residence, with garden, only minutes from the tube station, with easy access to Heathrow, central London, Richmond & beautiful Kew Gardens. The charming host offers 2 spacious guest rooms suitable for doubles or twins & ideal for families. Each room has an en-suite bathroom, T.V., tea/coffee-making facilities & is decorated in natural tones with stripped pine. Children are especially welcome.

£29.00 to £50.00 — Y | N | N (non-smoking)

Home No. 39. London.

London
Visit our website: www.bestbandb.co.uk

	rate £ from - to per person	children taken	evening meals	animals taken

Home No. 44. London.
Tel: +44 (0)20-8742-9123
Fax: +44 (0)20-8749-7084
U.S.A., Canada call:
Toll Free 011-800-852-26320
Australia call:
Toll Free 0011-800-852-26320
E-mail: bestbandb@atlas.co.uk

Nearest Tube: Richmond
Situated in the heart of delightful Richmond this really is the perfect location for a relaxing break in London. The charming host, who is an interior designer has refurbished this Victorian home & offers 1 gorgeous double-bedded room with a private bathroom adjacent. Delicious Continental breakfasts are served in the kitchen/diner which overlooks a pretty garden. Richmond abounds with fashionable shops & restaurants & is within easy reach of several stately homes. Central London 25 mins. Easy access to Heathrow.

£32.00 to £50.00 — N N N (No smoking)

Home No. 48. London.
Tel: +44 (0)20-8742-9123
Fax: +44 (0)20-8749-7084
U.S.A., Canada call:
Toll Free 011-800-852-26320
Australia call:
Toll Free 0011-800-852-26320
E-mail: bestbandb@atlas.co.uk

Nearest Tube: Parsons Green
A beautifully decorated, very stylish late Victorian house, situated in Parsons Green & only 20 mins. from Harrods by tube. Offering 2 double/twin-bedded rooms & 1 single room, all are en-suite & have T.V. & tea/coffee-making facilities. Each room is furnished to the highest standards of comfort. Guests are welcomed with a glass of sherry. A country house breakfast is served. This is a no smoking house.

£38.00 to £60.00 — N N N (No smoking)

Home No. 50. London.
Tel: +44 (0)20-8742-9123
Fax: +44 (0)20-8749-7084
U.S.A., Canada call:
Toll Free 011-800-852-26320
Australia call:
Toll Free 0011-800-852-26320
E-mail: bestbandb@atlas.co.uk

Nearest Tube: Parsons Green
This is a delightful Victorian terraced house which has been beautifully decorated & furnished throughout. The lovely hosts offer 1 very comfort-able king-size double-bedded room & 1 attractive single-bedded room. Each room has a T.V. & bottled water etc. & an excellent private bath-room. There are a variety of good bars, bistros & restaurants nearby. Located only 5 mins' walk from the tube station, this is a perfect spot from which to explore London. A charming home.

£32.00 to £50.00 — N N N (No smoking)

Home No. 51. London.
Tel: +44 (0)20-8742-9123
Fax: +44 (0)20-8749-7084
U.S.A., Canada call:
Toll Free 011-800-852-26320
Australia call:
Toll Free 0011-800-852-26320
E-mail: bestbandb@atlas.co.uk

Nearest Tube: Holland Park
Set in a quiet, secluded street, this is a modern mews house with an original brick kiln which has been converted into an elegant dining room. Only a few minutes walk from fashionable restaurants, antique shops, Portobello Market & beautiful Hol-land Park. It has been attractively furnished throughout by the host who is an interior designer. 1 delightful & spacious en-suite double-bedded room with T.V. etc. & a dressing room. Easy access to many of London's attractions.

£37.00 to £60.00 — N N N (No smoking)

Home No. 52. London.
Tel: +44 (0)20-8742-9123
Fax: +44 (0)20-8749-7084
U.S.A., Canada call:
Toll Free 011-800-852-26320
Australia call:
Toll Free 0011-800-852-26320
E-mail: bestbandb@atlas.co.uk

Nearest Tube: South Kensington
Located in Chelsea, in a quiet residential street yet, only a short walk from many fashionable shops & restaurants. A charming Victorian ter-raced house which has been attractively deco-rated throughout with many interesting prints & artifacts. The friendly hosts offer 1 spacious double-bedded room & a lovely twin-bedded room. Each has an excellent en-suite shower room, T.V. & tea/coffee-making facilities. A delightful home with easy access to the museums at South Kensington, Knightsbridge & Harrods.

£33.00 to £50.00 — Y N N

London

Visit our website: www.bestbandb.co.uk

		rate £ from - to per person	children taken	evening meals	animals taken
Home No. 56. London. **Tel: +44 (0)20-8742-9123** **Fax: +44 (0) 20-8749-7084** **U.S.A., Canada call:** **Toll Free 011-800-852-26320** **Australia call:** **Toll Free 0011-800-852-26320** E-mail: bestbandb@atlas.co.uk	Nearest Tube: Hammersmith A lovely house, pleasantly situated in leafy Brook Green mid-way between Hammersmith & Kensington. Offering a spacious & comfortably furnished double bedded room with private bathroom & tea/coffee making facilities which overlooks the rear garden. A pretty lounge with T.V. is often available & in which guests may choose to relax. An ideal base, with good access to Heathrow & central London.	£32.00 to £50.00	Y	N	N
Home No. 60. London. **Tel: +44 (0)20-8742-9123** **Fax: +44 (0)20-8749-7084** **U.S.A., Canada call:** **Toll Free 011-800-852-26320** **Australia call:** **Toll Free 0011-800-852-26320** E-mail: bestbandb@atlas.co.uk	Nearest Tube: High St. Ken. A beautifully appointed home located in a quiet cul-de-sac, close to Kensington Palace. A lift will take you to the 2nd floor accommodation. A delightful, spacious & elegantly furnished double-bedded room with brass bed, T.V., tea/coffee-making facilities & biscuits are also provided. A delicious varied breakfast is also served. Knightsbridge, Kensington & Hyde Park are all just a short walk from here.	£34.00 to £54.00	N	N	N
Home No. 61. London. **Tel: +44 (0)20-8742-9123** **Fax: +44 (0)20-8749-7084** **U.S.A., Canada call:** **Toll Free 011-800-852-26320** **Australia call:** **Toll Free 0011-800-852-26320** E-mail: bestbandb@atlas.co.uk	Nearest Tube: Holland Park A lovely apartment situated on the 7th floor of an Edwardian mansion block with lift access. Offering 1 spacious & attractive double bedded room with a private bathroom, T.V. & a small balcony with rooftop views. A large Continental breakfast is served. The charming hosts have an extensive knowledge of London & are happy to give advice on what to see do. Their home is ideally situated & has easy access to central London & the sights, beautiful Holland Park & many good shops & restaurants. Heathrow Airbus stops nearby.	£32.00 to £50.00	N	N	N
Home No. 63. London **Tel: +44 (0)20-8742-9123** **Fax: +44 (0)20-8749-7084** **U.S.A., Canada call:** **Toll Free 011-800-852-26320** **Australia call:** **Toll Free 0011-800-852-26320** E-mail: bestbandb@atlas.co.uk	Nearest Tube: Sloane Square An attractive 2-storey penthouse apartment with prize-winning roof garden, situated in the heart of fashionable Chelsea & only minutes from the River Thames & the trendy shops & restaurants of the King's Road. The delightful host, who is an artist, is always happy to advise guests on what to see & do. 1 comfortable en-suite double-bedded room. A large Continental breakfast is served in the attractive dining room which is adorned with many of the hosts interesting pictures.	£32.00 to £50.00	N	N	N
Home No. 64. London. **Tel: +44 (0)20-8742-9123** **Fax: +44 (0)20-8749-7084** **U.S.A., Canada call:** **Toll Free 011-800-852-26320** **Australia call:** **Toll Free 0011-800-852-26320** E-mail: bestbandb@atlas.co.uk	Nearest Tube: Camden Town A unique timber & glass house (designed by the host who is an architect), only mins. from the bustling market & many excellent shops & restaurants. 1 attractive double-bedded room with T.V. & tea/coffee-making facilities & a single room for a third member of the party. Each room is light & airy, very comfortable & modern in design. An excellent private bathroom. Breakfast is served in the lovely open-plan kitchen/dining area which overlooks the pretty garden. Easy access to the West End & theatreland.	£32.00 to £50.00	Y	N	N

London

Visit our website: www.bestbandb.co.uk

	rate £ from - to per person	children taken	evening meals	animals taken
Home No. 65. London. Tel: +44 (0)20-8742-9123 Fax: +44 (0)20-8749-7084 U.S.A., Canada call: Toll Free 011-800-852-26320 Australia call: Toll Free 0011-800-852-26320 E-mail: bestbandb@atlas.co.uk — Nearest Tube: Baker Street. An elegant Georgian townhouse, situated only moments from Baker Street, Regent's Park & Mayfair. It is beautifully decorated throughout & furnished with French antiques. A selection of charming guest rooms including doubles, singles & triples. Each bedroom is spacious, attractive & completely unique & has an en-suite/private bathroom, T.V. & 'phone. An elegant lounge in which guests may relax where tea/coffee is available. A large Continental breakfast is served. A marvellous location only minutes from the West End.	£49.00 to £85.00	N	N	N
Home No. 66. London. Tel: +44 (0)20-8742-9123 Fax: +44 (0)20-8749-7084 U.S.A., Canada call: Toll Free 011-800-852-26320 Australia call: Toll Free 0011-800-852-26320 E-mail: bestbandb@atlas.co.uk — Nearest Tube: Earls Court. A spacious apartment located at garden level offering attractive accommodation in 1 double bedded room with en-suite facilities, T.V. , fridge & 'phone. The friendly host (a fashion designer) has tastefully furnished & decorated this apartment with many interesting paintings. Guests may relax in the garden which is accessible from their room. Situated only a few minutes walk from the underground station, this home is within easy reach of museums, galleries, shops & theatres.	£32.00 to £50.00	N	N	N
Home No. 69. London. Tel: +44 (0)20-8742-9123 Fax: +44 (0)20-8749-7084 U.S.A., Canada call: Toll Free 011-800-852-26320 Australia call: Toll Free 0011-800-852-26320 E-mail: bestbandb@atlas.co.uk — Nearest Tube: South Kensington. A super home from which to explore London, situated only a very short walk from the Natural History & Science Museums & the station. An attractively furnished apartment, located on the 1st floor of an Edwardian conversion, where the friendly host offers 1 light & airy king-size double/twin-bedded room with en-suite bathroom & T.V. A large Continental breakfast is served. A good location with many good restaurants etc.	£32.00 to £50.00	N	N	N
Home No. 72. London. Tel: +44 (0)20-8742-9123 Fax: +44 (0)20-8749-7084 U.S.A., Canada call: Toll Free 011-800-852-26320 Australia call: Toll Free 0011-800-852-26320 E-mail: bestbandb@atlas.co.uk — Nearest Tube: Baker Street. A traditional 4-storey Georgian townhouse in a marvellous location, only moments from Madame Tussauds, the Sherlock Holmes museum, Lord's Cricket Ground & Regents Park. The charming hosts, who are artists, offer 1 king-size double/twin-bedded room& an attractive double-bedded room with low-beamed ceilings. Each has an en-suite bathroom, T.V., tea/coffee facilities & views towards Regents Park. An ideal base for exploring London on foot; the West End, theatreland & Piccadilly are only 10 mins away.	£37.00 to £60.00	Y	N	N
Home No. 73. London. Tel: +44 (0)20-8742-9123 Fax: +44 (0)20-8749-7084 U.S.A., Canada call: Toll Free 011-800-852-26320 Australia call: Toll Free 0011-800-852-26320 E-mail: bestbandb@atlas.co.uk — Nearest Tube: Sloane Square. A delightful Victorian townhouse in fashionable Chelsea, & very close to Harrods, stylishly decorated throughout & offering 2 lovely guest rooms. 1 king-size double/twin-bedded room with en-suite shower room & the other a double with a spacious en-suite bathroom & access to a pretty garden. Each is comfortably furnished & has T.V. & tea/coffee-making facilities. A wonderful location. Only a short walk from Sloane Square, Knightsbridge, the museums at South Kensington, superb restaurants & many tourist attractions.	£37.00 to £60.00	Y	N	N

London
Visit our website: www.bestbandb.co.uk

	rate £ from - to per person	children taken	evening meals	animals taken

Home No. 76. London. Tel: +44 (0)20-8742-9123 Fax: +44 (0)20-8749-7084 U.S.A., Canada call: Toll Free **011-800-852-26320** Australia call: Toll Free **0011-800-852-26320** E-mail: bestbandb@atlas.co.uk	Nearest Tube: Earls Court One king-size double or twin-bedded room with very large en-suite bath & separate shower & 1 king-size double with adjacent private bath & shower. Each room has a T.V. & clock/radio & have been beautifully decorated & furnished by this most helpful host. Close to all the best places for shopping, museums, sight-seeing & within walking distance of many excellent restaurants. Easy access to Gatwick & Heathrow Airports.	**£29.00** to **£60.00** (no smoking)	N	N	N
Home No. 77. London. Tel: +44 (0)20-8742-9123 Fax: +44 (0)20-8749-7084 U.S.A., Canada call: Toll Free **011-800-852-26320** Australia call: Toll Free **0011-800-852-26320** E-mail: bestbandb@atlas.co.uk	Nearest Tube:Clapham Jt.(B.R.) A large Edwardian house built for Earl Spencer backing onto a private park. Breakfast may be served in the dining room or large conservatory. There is 1 double en-suite room, 1 family room en-suite, 1 twin bedded room with private facilities, also, 1 double room with shared bathroom. Plenty of car parking space. There are two cats & a friendly dog. A charming & most friendly host. Smoking permitted on the ground floor.	**£32.00** to **£50.00** *see PHOTO over p. 25*	N	N	N
Home No. 78. London. Tel: +44 (0)20-8742-9123 Fax: +44 (0)20-8749-7084 U.S.A., Canada call: Toll Free **011-800-852-26320** Australia call: Toll Free **0011-800-852-26320** E-mail: bestbandb@atlas.co.uk	Nearest Tube: Parsons Green An impressive Victorian house with pretty garden in a fashionable area facing a park with a public tennis court. Easy access to central London & excellent shops & restaurants nearby. The charming host is a well-travelled author, with 1 cat. 2 bedrooms, each with a double bed, completely private facilities, T.V. & hairdryer. A full English breakfast is served. Charming guest sitting-room (rare in a private home). No business facilities.	**£33.00** to **£50.00** (no smoking)	N	N	N
Home No. 79. London. Tel: +44 (0)20-8742-9123 Fax: +44 (0) 20-8749-7084 U.S.A., Canada call: Toll Free **011-800-852-2632** Australia call: Toll Free **0011-800-852-26320** E-mail: bestbandb@atlas.co.uk	Nearest Tube: East Putney An elegant Victorian house with a pretty garden located in the residential area of Putney. The charming hosts offer 2 stylishly decorated guest rooms, located on the 3rd floor. An attractive & spacious twin room with a lovely private bathroom & one large, sunny double bedroom with shower room en-suite. Each room has colour T.V. Only 25 minutes to central London by tube or 35 mins' to Windsor by train. River trips to Hampton Court & Kew go from Putney Bridge just 10 minutes walk away. Many excellent local restaurants.	**£30.00** to **£45.00** (no smoking)	Y	N	N
Home No. 81. London. Tel: +44 (0)20-8742-9123 Fax: +44 (0)20-8749-7084 U.S.A., Canada call: Toll Free **011-800-852-26320** Australia call: Toll Free **0011-800-852-26320** E-mail: bestbandb@atlas.co.uk	Nearest Tube: Fulham Broadway Situated in Fulham, with many good restaurants, pubs & antique shops nearby. This is a charming Victorian house, standing in a quiet street. The delightful hosts offer 1 spacious King-size double/ twin-bedded room with an exquisite marble en-suite bathroom & another lovely, light & airy twin-bedded room with a beautiful private bathroom adjacent. Each bedroom is well-furnished & has colour T.V., hairdryer & tea/coffee-making facilities. Very good access to central London & the sights by bus or tube.	**£29.00** to **£58.00**	Y	N	N

Home No. 77 . London.

London

Visit our website: www.bestbandb.co.uk

	rate £ from - to per person	children taken	evening meals	animals taken
Home No. 83. London. Tel: +44 (0)20-8742-9123 Fax: +44 (0)20-8749-7084 U.S.A., Canada call: Toll Free 011-800-852-26320 Australia call: Toll Free 0011-800-852-26320 E-mail: bestbandb@atlas.co.uk	Nearest Tube: Stamford Brook A spacious Edwardian house set in a quiet street only 4 mins' walk from the station. The charming hosts offer 1 spacious & beautifully decorated Queen-size double-bedded room with Victorian-style brass bedstead, fridge, T.V., trouser press, tea/coffee-making facilities & an excellent bathroom en-suite. Breakfast is served in the conservatory overlooking the garden. Only 7 mins' walk from the River Thames with its variety of riverside pubs. Easy access to central London & Heathrow Airport. Children over 8.	£29.00 to £50.00	Y	N	N
Home No. 84. London. Tel: +44 (0)20-8742-9123 Fax: +44 (0)20-8749-7084 U.S.A., Canada call: Toll Free 011-800-852-26320 Australia call: Toll Free 0011-800-852-26320 E-mail: bestbandb@atlas.co.uk	Nearest Tube: Parsons Green This is an attractive Victorian terraced house, situated in a quiet street & yet only 5 mins' walk from the tube. The friendly & helpful host, who is an interior decorator, offers 1 light & airy King-size double/twin-bedded room & 1 attractive single room. Each has a private bathroom. T.V. available. Breakfast is served in the country-style kitchen/dining room. The familys' delightful pet dog is a 'furry filmstar'. An ideal base from which to explore London, many attractions are only 20 mins' by tube.	£29.00 to £50.00	N	N	N
Home No. 85. London. Tel: +44 (0)20-8742-9123 Fax: +44 (0)20-8749-7084 U.S.A., Canada call: Toll Free 011-800-852-26320 Australia call: Toll Free 0011-800-852-26320 E-mail: bestbandb@atlas.co.uk	Nearest Tube: Fulham Broadway Situated in the heart of Fulham, this is a delightful 3 storey Victorian house conveniently located only 3 mins' walk from the tube. The very friendly hosts offer 1 double-bedded room with an en-suite bathroom & another double-bedded room with a shower room en-suite. Each bedroom is beautifully decorated & very comfortable. T.V. & tea/coffeee facilities are available. There are many famous bars, bistros & restaurants in Fulham Broadway. Heathrow Airport & Londons' many attractions are easily accessible by tube.	£30.00 to £50.00	N	N	N
Home No. 88. London. Tel: +44 (0)20-8742-9123 Fax: +44 (0)20-8749-7084 U.S.A., Canadacall: Toll Free 011-800-852-26320 Australia call: Toll Free 0011-800-852-26320 E-mail: bestbandb@atlas.co.uk	Nearest Tube: Sloane Square This is an elegantly furnished apartment situated less than 10 mins' walk from the tube. The friendly hosts offer 1 attractive twin-bedded room with a private bathroom. Breakfast is served in the elegant dining room. Situated in the hreat of Chelsea within easy reach of the fashionable shops in the King's Road & good restaurants. London's attractions including Buckingham Palace & the museums at South Kensington are a short distance away by bus or tube.	£36.00 to £60.00	N	N	N

When booking your accommodation please mention
The Best Bed & Breakfast

All the establishments mentioned in this guide are members of the Worldwide Bed & Breakfast Association.

If you have any comments regarding your accommodation please send them to us using the form at the back of the book. We value your comments.

Beds:Berks:Bucks:Herts.

Bedfordshire
(Thames & Chilterns)

The county of Bedfordshire is an area of great natural beauty from the Dunstable Downs in the south to the great River Ouse in the north, along with many country parks & historic houses & gardens.

Two famous wildlife parks are to be found, at Woburn &Whipsnade. The Woburn Wild Animal Kingdom is Britain's largest drive-through safari park, with entrance to an exciting leisure park all included in one admission ticket.

Whipsnade Zoo came into existence in the 1930's as a country retreat for the animals of London Zoo, but is now very much a zoo in its own right & renowned for conservation work.

Woburn Abbey, home of the Dukes of Bedford for three centuries, is often described as one of England's finest showplaces. Rebuilt in the 8th century the Abbey houses an important art collection & is surrounded by a magnificent 3,000 acre deer park.

John Bunyan drew on local Bedfordshire features when writing the Pilgrims Progress, & the ruins of Houghton House, his "House Beautiful" still remain.

Buckinghamshire
(Thames & Chilterns)

Buckinghamshire can be divided into two distinct geographical regions: The high Chilterns with their majestic beechwoods & the Vale of Aylesbury chosen by many over the centuries as a beautiful & accessible place to build their historical homes.

The beechwoods of the Chilterns to the south of the county are crisscrossed with quiet lanes & footpaths., Ancient towns & villages like Amersham & Chesham lie tucked away in the

Rose gardens. St.Albans. Herts.

folds of the hills & a prehistoric track; the Ichnield Way winds on its 85 mile journey through the countryside.

The Rothschild family chose the Vale of Aylesbury to create several impressive homes, & Waddesdon House & Ascott House are both open to the public. Benjamin Disraeli lived at Hughenden Manor, & Florence Nightingale, "the Lady with the Lamp", at Claydon House. Sir Francis Dashwood, the 18th century eccentric founded the bizarre Hellfire Club, which met in the man-made caves near West Wycombe House.

Berkshire
(Thames & Chilterns)

Berkshire is a compact county but one of great variety & beauty.

In the East is Windsor where the largest inhabited castle in the world stands in its majestic hilltop setting. Nine centuries of English monarchy have lived here, & it is home to the present Queen. The surrounding parkland, enormous yards, vast interior & splendour of the State Apartments make a trip to Windsor Castle an unforgettable experience.

To the West are the gently rolling Berkshire Downs where many a champion racehorse has been trained.

Beds:Berks:Bucks:Herts.

To the north of the county, the River Thames dominates the landscape - an opportunity for a river-bank stroll & a drink at a country pub.

In the south is the Kennet & Avon Canal, a peaceful waterway with horse-drawn barges.

Historically, Berkshire has occupied an important place due to its strategic position commanding roads to & from Oxford & the north, & Bath & the west. Roundheads & Cavaliers clashed twice near Newbury during the 17th century English Civil Wars. Their battles are colourfully recreated by historic societies like the Sealed Knot.

The Tudor period brought great wealth from wool-weaving. Merchants built wonderful houses & some built churches but curiously, there is no cathedral in Berkshire.

Hertfordshire
(Thames & Chilterns)

Old & new exist side by side in Hertfordshire. This attractive county includes historic sites, like the unique Roman theatre in St. Albans, as well as new additions to the landscape such as England's first Garden City at Letchworth.

The countryside varies from the chalk hills & rolling downlands of the Chilterns to rivers, lakes, canals & pretty villages. The county remains largely rural despite many large towns & cities. The Grand Union Canal, built at the end of the 18th century to link the Midlands to London, passes through some glorious scenery, particularly at Cassiobury Park in Watford.

Verulamium was a newly-built town of the Roman Empire. It was the first name of Alban, himself a Roman, who became the first Christian to be martyred for his faith in England. The great Abbey church was built by the Normans around his original church, & it was re-established under the Rule of St. Benedict & named St. Albans some 600 years after his death.

Windsor Castle.

29

Beds:Berks:Bucks:Herts.

Bedfordshire
Gazeteer
Area of outstanding natural beauty.
Dunstable Downs, Ivinghoe Beacon.
Historic Houses
Woburn Abbey - house & gardens, extensive art collection, deer park, antiques centre.
Luton Hoo - the Wernher collection of Old Masters, tapestries, furniture, ivories & porcelain, unique collection of Russian Faberge jewellry. Parkland landscaped by Capability Brown.

Other Things to see & do
Woburn Wildlife Park
Whipsnade Zoo-Whipsnade
Old Warden - the village houses a collection of working vintage aeroplanes with flying displays each month from April to October.

Berkshire
Gazeteer
Areas of outstanding natural beauty.
North West Downs.
Historic Houses & Castles
Windsor Castle - Royal Residence at Windsor
State apartments, house, historic treasures. The Cloisters, Windsor Chapel. Mediaeval house.
Basildon Park - Nr. Pangbourne
Overlooking the Thames. 18th century Bath stone building, massive portico & linked pavilions. Painted ceiling in Octagon Room, gilded pier glasses. Garden & wooded walks.
Cliveden - Nr. Taplow
Once the home of Nancy Astor.

Churches
Lambourn (St. Michael & All Saints)
Norman with 15th century chapel. 16th century brasses, glass & tombs.
Padworth (St. John the Baptist)
12th century Norman with plastered exterior, remains of wall paintings, 18th century monuments.
Warfield (St. Michael & All Angels)
14th century decorated style. 15th century wood screen & loft.

Museums
Newbury Museum - Newbury
Natural History & Archaeology - Paleolithic to Saxon & Mediaeval times.
Household Cavalry Museum - Windsor

Other Things to see & do
Racing - at Newbury, Ascot & Windsor
Highlight of the racing year is the Royal Meeting at Ascot each June, attended by the Queen & other members of the Royal Family.
Antiques - Hungerford is a famous centre for antiques.

Buckinghamshire
Gazeteer
Area of outstanding natural beauty.
Burnham Beeches - 70 acres of unspoilt woodlands, inspiration to poet
Thomas Gray.
Historic Houses
Waddesdon Manor & Ascott House - homes of the Rothschilds.
Chalfont St. Giles - cottage home of great English poet John Milton.
Old Jordans & the Meeting House - 17th century buildings associated with William Penn, the founder of Pennsylvania & with the Society of Friends, often called the Quakers.

Things to see & do
Buckinghamshire Railway Centre - at Quainton
Vintage steam train rides & largest private railway collection in Britain.
Chalfont Shire Horse Centre - home of the gentle giants of the horse world.

Beds:Berks:Bucks:Herts.

Hertfordshire
Gazeteer
Areas of outstanding natural beauty.
Parts of the Chilterns.

Historic Houses & Castles
Hatfield House - Hatfield
Home of the Marquess of Salisbury.
Jacobean House & Tudor Palace -
childhood home of Queen Elizabeth I.
Knebworth House - Knebworth
Family home of the Lyttons. 16th century
house transformed into Victorian High
Gothic. Furniture, portraits. Formal
gardens & unique Gertrude Jekyll herb
garden.
Shaw's Corner - Ayot St. Lawrence
Home of George Bernard Shaw.

Cathedrals & Churches
St. Albans Cathedral - St. Albans
9th century foundation, murals, painted
roof over choir, 15th century reredos,
stone rood screen.

Stanstead St. Abbots (St. James)12th
century nave, 13th century chancel, 15th
century tower & porch, 16th century
North chapel, 18th century box pews
& 3-decker pulpit.
Watford (St. Mary)
13 - 15th century. Essex chapel.
Tuscan arcade. Morryson tombs.

Museums
**Rhodes Memorial Museum &
Commonwealth Centre** - at Bishop
Stortford
Zoological Museum - Tring
Gardens
Gardens of the Rose - Chiswell Green
Nr. St Albans
Showgrounds of the Royal National Rose
Society
Capel Manor
Extensive grounds of horticultural
college.
Many fine trees, including the largest
copper beech in the country.

Bledlow Village; Bucks.

BEDS/BUCKS
BERKSHIRE
HERTS

Map reference

02	Wilson	15	Must
03	Cook	16	Codd
05	Power	18	Wallace
05	Rashleigh	19	Kirchner
06	Digby	20	Pibworth
09	Steeds	21	Knowles
09	Sanders-Rose	22	Pollock-Hil
10	Thornely	24	Dunn
12	Barker		

Bedfordshire & Berkshire

rate £ from - to per person
children taken
evening meals
animals taken

		rate £ from - to per person	children taken	evening meals	animals taken
Janet Must **Church Farm** **41 High Street** **Roxton** **Bedford MK44 3EB** **Tel: (01234) 870234** **Fax 01234 870234** **Open: ALL YEAR** **Map Ref No. 15**	Nearest Road: A.1, A.421 Church Farm is an ideal base for those wanting somewhere a little special & a comfortable place to stay. 3 delightful bedrooms (all en-suite) have colour T.V. & welcome tray. A guest lounge with open fire is available for relaxation. Breakfast is served in the beamed 17th-century dining room. There are walks around the village & countryside, & inns for evening meals. A warm welcome awaits you at this lovely home.	£22.50 to £30.00	N	N	Y
Mrs Margaret Codd **Highfield Farm** **Great North Road** **Sandy** **SG19 2AQ** **Tel: (01767) 682332** **Fax 01767 692503** **Open: ALL YEAR** **Map Ref No. 16**	Nearest Road: A.1 A tranquil & very welcoming house with comfort, warmth & a friendly atmosphere in a lovely setting on an arable farm. There are 6 attractive bedrooms, 4 en-suite, including 3 ground-floor rooms in tastefully converted stables. Highfield Farm is set back off the A.1, giving peaceful seclusion & yet easy access to London, Cambridge, Bedford, the Shuttleworth Collection, the R.S.P.B. & the east-coast ports. Ample parking. Most guests return to this lovely home. VISA: M'CARD:	£25.00 to £30.00	Y	N	Y

Berkshire

		rate £ from - to per person	children taken	evening meals	animals taken
Mrs Mary Wilson **Fishers Farm** **Ermin Street** **Shefford Woodlands** **Hungerford** **RG17 7AB** **Tel: (01488) 648466** **Fax 01488 648706** **Open: ALL YEAR** **Map Ref No. 02**	Nearest Road: A.338, M.4 A traditional farmhouse on a working arable & livestock farm with all modern comforts & a beautiful large garden in a secluded & peaceful location, yet only 1 mile from Jt. 14 of the M.4 motorway. 3 large bedrooms with en-suite/private bathrooms. An ideal base for exploring southern England, & within easy reach of Heathrow & Gatwick Airports. A heated indoor swimming pool. Excellent cooking using many home-grown ingredients. Evening meals by arrangement. **E-mail: fishersf@globalnet.co.uk**	£25.00 to £35.00	Y	Y	N
Sally Cook **Lodge Down** **Lambourn** **Hungerford** **RG17 7BJ** **Tel: (01672) 540304** **Fax 01672 540304** **Open: ALL YEAR** **Map Ref No. 03**	Nearest Road: B.4000 A warm welcome is assured at Lodge Down, a country house with superb accommodation & en-suite bathrooms, set in lovely grounds. Excellent & varied dining in surrounding villages. Easy access to the M.4 motorway at Jts 14 & 15. 1 hr or less for Heathrow (60 miles), Bath (43 miles) & Oxford (26 miles). This location provides a central base for excursions to Stonehenge, Salisbury & the Cotswolds, etc., or an easy drive to Heathrow & London. A charming home. *see PHOTO over p. 34*	£22.50 to £30.00	N	N	N

Visit our website at:
http://www.bestbandb.co.uk

Lodge Down. Lambourn.

Berkshire

	Nearest Road			
Michael & Joanna Power **Woodpecker Cottage** **Warren Row** **Nr. Maidenhead** **RG10 8QS** **Tel: (01628) 822772** **Fax 01628 822125** **Open:** ALL YEAR (Excl. Xmas) **Map Ref No. 05**	Nearest Road: A.4 Country cottage set in bluebell woods, yet easy access to motorways, Heathrow, Windsor & London. Double (en-suite), single (en-suite) & twin-bedded room (own bathroom) are all ground-floor rooms & have T.V.s, tea/coffee facilities, hairdryers etc. Breakfast includes home-made bread & jams, & eggs from our own hens. Peaceful retreat, with large garden & croquet lawns. Good choice of pubs & restaurants nearby. Children over 8 years welcome. **E-mail: power@woodpecker.co.uk**	£20.00 to £30.00	Y	N	N
Lavinia Rashleigh **Dumbledore** **Warren Row** **Maidenhead** **RG10 8QS** **Tel: (01628) 822723** **Fax 01628 822723** **Open: ALL YEAR** **Map Ref No. 05**	Nearest Road: A.4 A charming (part-16th-century) Tudor country house, located in the pretty village of Warren Row, close to the picturesque town of Henley-on-Thames. There are 3 elegantly furnished bedrooms, 1 en-suite & each with T.V. & tea/coffee-making facilities. Breakfast is served in the attractive dining room. A residents' lounge is available throughout the day in which guests may choose to relax. Easy access to Windsor, Marlow & Heathrow & Gatwick Airports. Children over 12.	£30.00 to £35.00	Y	N	N
Mrs Charlotte Digby **Rookwood Farmhouse** **Stockcross** **Newbury RG20 8JX** **Tel: (01488) 608676** **Fax 01488 608676** **Open: ALL YEAR** **Map Ref No. 06**	Nearest Road: A.34 This charming & comfortable former farmhouse combines ease of access with rural views & a large garden. The guest bedrooms are in a newly converted coach house which is traditionally furnished & yet affords all modern facilities. In winter, there is a welcoming log fire in the guests' sitting room, while in summer, breakfast is served in the conservatory overlooking the swimming pool. An ideal base for a relaxing break. VISA: M'CARD:	£35.00 to £45.00	Y	N	N
Mrs Jane Steeds **Highwoods** **Hermits Hill** **Burghfield Common** **Reading RG7 3BG** **Tel: (0118) 9832320** **Fax 0118 9831070** **Open: ALL YEAR (Excl.** **Xmas & New Year)** **Map Ref No. 09**	Nearest Road: A.4, M.4 A friendly & relaxing atmosphere at this fine Victorian country house set in 4 acres of attractive grounds, with unspoilt, far-reaching views. 3 spacious, comfortable, attractively furnished rooms (1 en-suite) with all modern amenities & colour T.V.. Guests are welcome to use the garden & hard tennis court. Also, a gallery specialising in English watercolours & prints. Easy access to London, Heathrow Airport, Windsor, Oxford & Bath. Non-smokers preferred. **E-mail: steeds@patrol.i-way.co.uk**	£20.00 to £28.00	Y	N	N
Mrs R. Sanders-Rose **The Old Manor** **Whitehouse Green** **Sulhamstead** **Reading RG7 4EA** **Tel: (0118) 9832423** **Fax 0118 9832423** **Open: ALL YEAR** **Map Ref No. 09**	Nearest Road: A.4 A beautiful country house in 10 acres of secluded grounds yet only 2 miles from Junction 12 on the M.4. Large, elegant, beamed bedrooms with en-suite facilities. The west suite has a 4-poster bed & jacuzzi bath. The east suite has a bath, shower & dressing room. Evening meals are of a high standard & include wine. A beautiful drawing room is available & the dining & morning rooms are furnished with elegance. Relaxation, hospitality & quality are the keynotes at The Old Manor.	£35.00 to £50.00	N	Y	N

Berkshire
& Buckinghamshire

		rate £ from - to per person	children taken	evening meals	animals taken

Mrs Jill Thornely **Bridge Cottage** **Station Road** **Woolhampton** **Reading** **RG7 5SF** **Tel: (0118) 9713138** **Fax 0118 9714331** **Open:** ALL YEAR (Excl. Xmas) **Map Ref No. 10**	Nearest Road: A.4, M.4 A warm welcome awaits the visitor to this delightful 300-year-old riverside cottage, offering 5 attractive & comfortably furnished bedrooms with beamed ceilings including 2 twin-bedded rooms with en-suite facilities. Breakfast is served in a lovely conservatory overlooking the River Kennet, where old narrow boats pass by. It is surrounded by lovely countryside. Close by is the local pub which serves excellent home-cooked suppers. London 1 hr away. Ideal for Heathrow & rail/air connections to Reading & London, etc.	£22.00 to £25.00	Y	N	N
Mrs C. Barker **The Hermitage** **63 London Road** **Twyford** **RG10 9EJ** **Tel: (0118) 9340004** **Fax 0118 9340004** **Open:** ALL YEAR (Excl. Xmas) **Map Ref No. 12**	Nearest Road: A.4 A large, elegant Georgian house with unique Victorian additions. A central village location. An ideal base for exploring the Thames Valley (including Henley, Oxford & Windsor). Convenient for Heathrow Airport. A short walk to the mainline station (London 40 mins). A choice of 5 bedrooms (3 en-suite, including 2 in the recently converted coach house), all with colour T.V. & tea/coffee-making facilities. A spacious dining room overlooking a large established garden, which guests are welcome to use.	£26.00 to £32.00	N	N	N

Buckinghamshire

Wynyard & Julia Wallace **Little Parmoor** **Parmoor Lane** **Frieth** **Henley-on-Thames** **RG9 6NL** **Tel: (01494) 881447** **Fax 01494 883012** **Open:** ALL YEAR **Map Ref No. 18**	Nearest Road: A.40 A pretty Georgian country house surrounded by farmland, situated in the beautiful Chiltern Hills between Henley & Marlow. Within easy reach of Oxford & Windsor, & 40 mins from Heathrow - a perfect & peaceful spot to begin or end a holiday. 2 spacious & attractively furnished double/twin rooms with en-suite facilities & 1 small double with a private bathroom. All rooms have colour T.V. & tea-making facilities. A pretty, panelled drawing room. Ample parking. Evening meals served if ordered in advance. Children over 5.	£26.00 to £28.00	Y	Y	N
Charles & Susie Kirchner **The Old Vicarage** **Mentmore** **Leighton Buzzard** **LU7 0QG** **Tel: (01296) 661243** **Fax 01296 661243** **Open:** ALL YEAR **Map Ref No. 19**	Nearest Road: A.418 Only 45 mins from central London, this imposing Gothic house is set in mature gardens in a picturesque Rothschild estate village. Mentmore boasts a good pub in addition to architectural interest & a fine setting. It is very much a family home with plenty of activity. The guest rooms are spacious with en-suite bathrooms, enjoying uninterrupted views over rolling countryside. Meals are served in the 'William Morris' dining room using garden produce when available.	£25.00 to £30.00	Y	Y	N

Buckinghamshire & Hertfordshire

		rate £ from - to per person	children taken	evening meals	animals taken
Garry & Ruth Pibworth **Home Farm** **Warrington** **Olney** **MK46 4HN** **Tel: (01234) 711655** **Fax 01234 711855** **Open: ALL YEAR** **Map Ref No. 20**	Nearest Road: A.509, A.428 The Pibworths' offer a warm welcome to their stone farmhouse. The 3 individually decorated en-suite rooms offer colour T.V., mini-fridge & tea/coffee facilities. Guests have their own lounge & a traditional breakfast is served in the dining room. A kitchen is also available. Summer use of outdoor heated pool & gardens. Home Farm is an arable farm 1 1/2 miles north of Olney. 10 miles from Bedford, Northampton, Milton Keynes. Central for Cotswolds, Oxford, Cambridge, Stratford-upon-Avon & London. **E-mail: B&B@homefarm.force9.co.uk**	£25.00 to £30.00 🚭 VISA: M'CARD:	Y	N	N

Hertfordshire

		rate £ from - to per person	children taken	evening meals	animals taken
Mrs Alison Knowles **Broadway Farm** **Berkhamsted** **HP4 2RR** **Tel: (01442) 866541** **Fax 01442 866541** **Open: ALL YEAR (Excl. Xmas)** **Map Ref No. 21**	Nearest Road: A.4251 A warm welcome is guaranteed at Broadway, a working arable farm with its own fishing lake. There are 3 comfortable en-suite rooms in a recently converted building adjacent to the farmhouse. Each has tea/coffee-making facilities & colour T.V.. Everything for the leisure or business guest: the relaxation of farm life in an attractive rural setting, yet easy access to London, airports, motorways & mainline rail services. **E-mail: a.knowles@broadway.nildram.co.uk**	£25.00 to £32.00 🚭	Y	N	N
Samantha Pollock-Hill **Homewood** **Knebworth** **SG3 6PP** **Tel: (01438) 812105** **Open: ALL YEAR (Excl. Xmas)** **Map Ref No. 22**	Nearest Road: A.1 M Homewood is a classic blend of comfort & style: an Edwardian country house which is also a well-equipped family home. It has been used as a location for period drama by the B.B.C., & is often sought out by admirers of its designer, the distinguished architect Edwin Lutyens. You will be treated as a member of the family, or your privacy will be respected - whichever you prefer. Additional meals can be arranged, including dinner. Accommodation is in 2 lovely bedrooms, each with an en-suite/private bathroom.	£30.00 to £40.00 🚭 *see PHOTO over* *p.38*	Y	Y	Y
Helen & Dick Dunn **The Old Rectory** **Ayot St. Lawrence** **Welwyn** **AL6 9BT** **Tel: (01438) 820429** **Tel: (01438) 820603** **Fax 01438 821844** **Open: ALL YEAR** **Map Ref No. 24**	Nearest Road: A.1 A Grade II listed rectory built around 1680, surrounded by open countryside yet at the heart of a beautiful conservation village. Ayot was the home of George Bernard Shaw & his house is now owned by the N.T. & open Apr - Oct. Farmhouse breakfasts are served on the terrace or in the 17th-century dining room (Light supper trays are available). Dinner is on request or at the local inn. The 3 charming bedrooms are entered through a cobbled courtyard & unusually, the secluded gardens accommodate a listed squash court for the use of guests. London is 30 mins' away. Easy access to Stansted, Luton & Heathrow Airports. **E-mail: AyotBandB@aol.com**	£25.00 to £35.00	Y	N	N

Homewood. Knebworth.

Cambridge & Northants

Cambridgeshire
(East Anglia)

A county very different from any other, this is flat, mysterious, low-lying Fenland crisscrossed by a network of waterways both natural & man-made.

The Fens were once waterlogged, misty marshes but today the rich black peat is drained & grows carrots, sugar beet, celery & the best asparagus in the world.

Drive north across the Fens & slowly you become aware of a great presence dominating the horizon. Ely cathedral, the "ship of the Fens", sails closer. The cathedral is a masterpiece with its graceful form & delicate tracery towers. Begun before the Domesday Book was written, it took the work of a full century before it was ready to have the timbered roof raised up. Norman stonemasons worked with great skill & the majestic nave is glorious in its simplicity. Their work was crowned by the addition of the Octagon in the 14th century. Despite the ravages of the Reformation, the lovely Lady Chapel survives as one of the finest examples of decorated architecture in Britain with its exquisitely fine stone carving.

To the south, the Fens give way to rolling chalk hills & fields of barley, wheat & rye, & Cambridge. Punts gliding through the broad river, between smooth, lawned banks, under willow trees, past college buildings as extravagant as wedding cakes. The names of the colleges resound through the ages - Peterhouse, Corpus Christi, Kings, Queens, Trinity, Emmanuel. A city of learning & progress, & a city of great tradition where cows graze in open spaces, just 500 yards from the market square.

Northamptonshire
(East Midlands)

Northamptonshire has many features to attract & interest the visitor, from the town of Brackley in the south with its charming buildings of mellow stone, to ancient Rockingham Forest in the north. There are lovely churches, splendid historic houses & peaceful waterways.

The Waterways Museum at Stoke Bruerne makes a popular outing, with boat trips available on the Grand Union Canal beside the museum. Horse-racing at Towcester & motor-racing at Silverstone draws the crowds, but there are quieter pleasures in visits to Canons Ashby, or to Sulgrave Manor, home of George Washington's ancestors.

In the pleasantly wooded Rockingham Forest area are delightful villages, one of which is Ashton with its thatched cottages, the scene of the World Conker Championships each October. Mary Queen of Scots was executed at Fotheringay, in the castle of which only the mound remains.

Rockingham Castle has a solid Norman gateway & an Elizabethan hall; Deene Park has family connections with the Earl of Cardigan who led the Charge of the Light Brigade & Kirby Hall is a dramatic Elizabethan ruin.

The county is noted for its parish churches, with fine Saxon examples at Brixworth & at Earl's Barton, as well as the round Church of the Holy Sepulchre in the county town itself.

Northampton has a fine tradition of shoemaking, so it is hardly surprising that boots & shoes & other leathergoods take pride of place in the town';s museums. The town has one of the country's biggest market squares, an historic Royal Theatre & a mighty Wurlitzer Organ to dance to at Turner's Musical Merry-go-round ! !

Cambridge & Northants

Cambridgeshire Gazeteer

Areas of outstanding natural beauty
The Nene Valley

Historic Houses & Castles

Anglesy Abbey - Nr. Cambridge
Origins in the reign of Henry I. Was redesigned into Elizabethan Manor by Fokes family. Houses the Fairhaven collection of Art treasures - stands in 100 acres of Ground.

Hinchingbrooke House - Huntingdon
13th century nunnery converted mid-16th century into Tudor house. Later additions in 17th & 19th centuries.

King's School - Ely
12th & 14th centuries - original stonework & vaulting in the undercroft, original timbering 14th century gateway & monastic barn.

Kimbolton Castle - Kimbolton
Tudor Manor house - has associations with Katherine of Aragon. Remodelled by Vanbrugh 1700's - gatehouse by Robert Adam.

Longthorpe Tower - Nr. Peterborough
13th & 14th century fortification - rare wall paintings.

Peckover House - Wisbech
18th century domestic architecture - charming Victorian garden.

University of Cambridge Colleges

Peterhouse	1284
Clare	1326
Pembroke	1347
Gonville & Caius	1348
Trinity Hall	1350
Corpus Christi	1352
King's	1441
Queen's	1448
St. Catherine's	1473
Jesus	1496
Christ's	1505
St. John's	1511
Magadalene	1542
Trinity	1546
Emmanuel	1584
Sidney Sussex	1596
Downing	1800

Wimpole Hall - Nr. Cambridge
18th & 19th century - beautiful staterooms - aristocratic house.

Cathedrals & Churches

Alconbury (St. Peter & St. Paul)
13th century chancel & 15th century roof. Broach spire.

Babraham (St. Peter)
13th century tower - 17th century monument.

Ely Cathedral
Rich arcading - west front incomplete. Remarkable interior with Octagon - unique in Gothic architecture.

Great Paxton (Holy Trinity)
12th century.

Harlton (Blessed Virgin Mary)
Perpendicular - decorated transition. 17th century monuments

Hildersham (Holy Trinity)
13th century - effigies, brasses & glass.

Lanwade (St. Nicholas)
15th century - mediaeval fittings

Peterborough Cathedral
Great Norman church fine example - little altered. Painted wooden roof to   nave - remarkable west front - Galilee Porch & spires later additions.

Ramsey (St. Thomas of Canterbury)
12th century arcades - perpendicular nave. Late Norman chancel with Angevin vault.

St. Neots (St. Mary)
15th century

Sutton (St. Andrew)
14th century

Trumpington (St. Mary & St. Nicholas)
14th century. Framed brass of 1289 of Sir Roger de Trumpington.

Westley Waterless (St. Mary the Less)
Decorated. 14th century brass of Sir John & Lady Creke.

Wimpole (St. Andrew)
14th century rebuilt 1749 - splendid heraldic glass.

Yaxley (St. Peter)
15th century chancel screen, wall paintings, fine steeple.

Museums & Galleries

Cromwell Museum - Huntingdon
Exhibiting portraits, documents, etc. of the Cromwellian period.

Fitzwilliam Museum - Cambridge
Gallery of masters, old & modern, ceramics, applied arts, prints & drawing, mediaeval manuscripts, music & art library.

Cambridge & Northants

Scott Polar Research Institute - Cambridge
Relics of expeditions & the equipment used. Current scientific work in Arctic & Antarctic.

University Archives - Cambridge
13th century manuscripts, Charters, Statutes, Royal letters & mandates. Wide variety of records of the University.

University Museum of Archaeology & Anthropology - Cambridge
Collections illustrative of Stone Age in Europe, Africa & Asia.
Britain prehistoric to mediaeval times.
Prehistoric America.

Ethnographic material from South-east Asia, Africa & America.

University Museum of Classical Archaeology - Cambridge
Casts of Greek & Roman Sculpture - representative collection.

Whipple Museum of the History of Science - Cambridge 16th, 17th & 18th century scientific instruments - historic collection.

Other Things to see & do

Nene Valley Railway
Steam railway with locomotives & carriages from many countries.

Caius College; Cambridge.

Cambridge & Northants

Northamptonshire Gazeteer

Historic Houses & Castles

Althorp - Nr. Northampton
Family home of the Princess of Wales, with fine pictures & porcelain.

Boughton House - Nr. Kettering
Furniture, tapestries & pictures in late 17th century building modelled on Versailles, in beautiful parkland.

Canons Ashby House - Nr. Daventry
Small 16th century manor house with gardens & church.

Deene Park - Nr. Corby
Family home for over 4 centuries, surrounded by park, extensive gardens & lake.

Holdenby House - Nr. Northampton
Gardens include part of Elizabethan garden, with original entrance arches, terraces & ponds. Falconry centre. Rare breeds.

Kirby Hall - Nr. Corby
Large Elizabethan mansion with fine gardens.

Lamport Hall - Nr. Northampton
17th & 18th century house with paintings, furniture & china. One of the first garden rockeries in Britain. Programme of concerts & other special events.

Rockingham Castle - Rockingham, Nr. Market Harborough
Norman gateway & walls surrounding mainly Elizabethan house, with pictures & Rockingham china. Extensive gardens with 16th century yew hedge.

Rushton Triangular Lodge - Nr. Kettering
Symbolic of the Trinity, with 3 sides, 3 floors, trefoil windows.

Sulgrave Manor - Nr. Banbury
Early English Manor, home of George Washington's ancestors.

Museums

Abington Museum - Northampton
Domestic & social life collections in former manor house.

Museum of Leathercraft - Northampton
History of leather use, with Queen Victoria's saddle, & Samuel Pepys' wallet.

Waterways Museum - Stoke Bruerne Nr. Towcester
200 years of canal & waterway life, displayed beside the Grand Union Canal.

Cathedrals & Churches

Brixworth Church - Nr. Northampton
One of the finest Anglo-Saxon churches in the country, mostly 7th century.

Earls Barton Church - Nr. Northampton
Fine Anglo-Saxon tower & Norman arch & arcading.

Church of the Holy Sepulchre - Northampton
Largest & best preserved of four remaining round churches in England, dating from 1100.

Other Things to see & do

Billing Aquadrome - Nr. Northampton
Boating, fishing, swimming & amusements.

Wicksteed Park - Kettering
Large playground & variety of amusements for families.

Lilford Park - Nr. Oundle
Birds & farm animals in parkland setting where many special events are held.

Rushton Triangular Lodge.

CAMBRIDGESHIRE & NORTHAMPTONSHIRE

Map reference

01 Percival
02 Hindley
03 Scott
05 Myburgh
06 Nix
07 Bailey
08 Roper
09 Elbourn
10 Barlow
11 Clarke
12 Faulkner

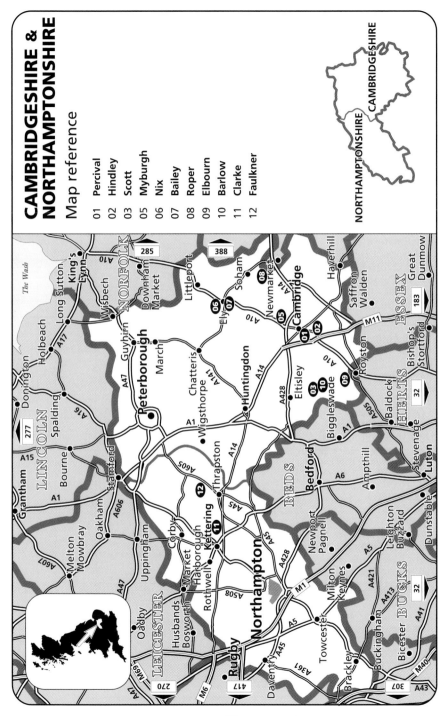

43

Cambridgeshire

		rate £ from - to per person	children taken	evening meals	animals taken
Mrs Alice Percival **46 Panton Street** **Cambridge** **CB2 1HS** **Tel: (01223) 365285** **Fax 01223 461142** **Open: ALL YEAR** **Map Ref No. 01**	Nearest Road: M.11 A 19th-century cottage situated in the historic centre of Cambridge with the great advantage of private parking. An excellent location near the Botanical Gardens & Fitzwilliam Museum, & only 10 mins' walk from the station, Kings College Chapel & the beautiful colleges. 2 very comfortable bedrooms each with a tea tray & T.V.. A full English breakfast is served. A charming home & the perfect location from which to explore Cambridge. Children over 12. Single supplement. VISA: M'CARD:	£32.50 to £32.50	Y	N	N
Olga & David Hindley **Purlins** **12 High Street** **Little Shelford** **Cambridge CB2 5ES** **Tel: (01223) 842643** **Fax (01223) 842643** **Open: FEB - DEC** **Map Ref No. 02**	Nearest Road: A.10 Lovely, individually designed family home, with 2 acres of parkland, situated in a quiet, pretty village on the Cam, 4 miles south of Cambridge. An ideal centre for Colleges, Audley End House, the Imperial War Museum & bird watching. 3 well-appointed double bedrooms (2 ground-floor), all with en-suite bathrooms, T.V. & tea/coffee. Varied breakfasts (special diets by arrangement). Restaurants nearby. Children over 8 welcome. **E-mail: dgallh@ndirect.co.uk**	£22.00 to £36.00	Y	N	N
Peter & Maggie Scott **Church Farm** **Gransden Road** **Caxton** **Cambridge** **CB3 8PL** **Tel: (01954) 719543** **Fax 01954 718999** **Open: ALL YEAR** **Map Ref No. 03**	Nearest Road: A.1198 This elegant & spacious listed farmhouse, which retains original 16th- & 17th-century features with 19th-century additions, is set in over 3 acres of rural peace. A wealth of oak beams, antiques, English watercolours, open log fires, comfortable beds & imaginative country-house cooking make for a relaxing stay. Ely Cathedral, Wimpole Hall, Kings College Chapel, Audley End & the Fitzwilliam Museum are all within easy reach. A delightful home. Children by arrangement. **E-mail: Churchfarm@aol.com** VISA: M'CARD:	£31.00 to £38.50	Y	Y	N
Phil & Sally Myburgh **Berry House** **High Street** **Waterbeach** **Cambridge** **CB5 9JU** **Tel: (01223) 860702** **Fax 01223 570588** **Open: ALL YEAR** **Map Ref No. 05**	Nearest Road: A.14 Berry House is a Grade II listed building built around 1820. The garden still contains a number of fruit trees from the original orchards. The elegant bedrooms have mahogany double beds, Edwardian & Georgian furniture & modern en-suite facilities, including power showers. Tea/coffee facilities & radio/alarms are provided in the rooms, which have a warm, period, cottage style. A beautiful home, perfect for visiting Cambridge & Ely. Dinner by arrangement. **E-mail: sal@BERRYHOUSE.DEMON.CO.UK**	£30.00 to £45.00	Y	Y	N
Mr & Mrs Derek Bailey **Springfields** **Ely Road Little Thetford** **Little Thetford** **Ely CB6 3HJ** **Tel: (01353) 663637** **Fax 01353 663130** **Open: JAN - NOV** **Map Ref No. 07**	Nearest Road: A.10 Award-winning Springfields is an elegant family home set in 1 acre of beautiful gardens, surrounded by mature trees, situated 1 1/2 miles from Ely Cathedral & 11 miles from Cambridge. Offering 3 delightful & tastefully furnished bedrooms, all with en-suite/private facilities, tea/coffee facilities, colour T.V. etc. & all with just that extra flair to make your stay memorable. A perfect base from which to explore the changeless beauty of the Fens. Come - stay awhile & smell the roses!	£25.00 to £££	N	N	N

Cambridgeshire

		rate £ from - to per person	children taken	evening meals	animals taken
Mrs Hilary Nix **Hill House Farm** **9 Main Street** **Coveney** **Ely** **CB6 2DJ** **Tel: (01353) 778369** **Open: ALL YEAR (Excl. Xmas)** **Map Ref No. 06**	Nearest Road: A.142, A.10 A warm welcome awaits you at this spacious Victorian farmhouse, situated in the quiet village of Coveney, 3 miles west of the historic cathedral city of Ely. Open views of the surrounding countryside & easy access to Cambridge, Newmarket & Huntingdon. It is ideally placed for touring Cambridgeshire, Norfolk & Suffolk. Wicken Fen & Welney wildfowl refuge are nearby. 3 tastefully furnished bedrooms, 1 twin & 2 double en-suite rooms, 1 ground floor. All have their own entrance, T.V., clock/radio & tea/coffee facilities. Children over 12 years.	£22.00 to £24.00 🚭	N	N	N
Malcolm & Jan Roper **Queensberry** **196 Carter Street** **Fordham** **CB7 5JU** **Tel: (01638 720916** **Fax 01638 720233** **Open: ALL YEAR** **Map Ref No. 08**	Nearest Road: A.14 A delightful Georgian house set peacefully in large gardens. Queensberry is ideally situated for touring East Anglia - Elys' cathedral 'Ship of the Fens', Bury St Edmunds, the University city of Cambridge & Newmarket, horse racing centre of the world. Rise early to go gallop-watching on the farmhouse heath & return to a hearty breakfast. Accommodation is in 2 attractive bedrooms, each with an en-suite/private bathroom. Fordham is the first village off the A.14 on Newmarket to Ely (A.142) road. Good restaurants are within walking distance. Parking available.	£22.50 to £25.00 🚭	Y	N	Y
John & Bernice Elbourn **Chiswick House** **Meldreth** **Royston** **SG8 6LZ** **Tel: (01763) 260242** **Open: MAR - NOV** **Map Ref No. 09**	Nearest Road: A.10 A beautiful timber-framed farmhouse dating from the 16th century. The royal crest of King James I is found above the fireplace, suggesting this was his hunting lodge in the early 1600s. Jacobean panelling, oak beams & open fireplaces create a wonderful atmosphere. 6 en-suite rooms, with tea/coffee-making facilities. T.V. is available. Many excellent inns nearby. An ideal base for touring Cambridge, Suffolk & Hertfordshire.	£22.50 to £22.50 🚭 *see PHOTO over p. 46*	Y	N	Y
Mrs Sue Barlow **Model Farm** **Little Gransden** **Sandy** **SG19 3EA** **Tel: (01767) 677361** **Fax 01767 677883** **Open: ALL YEAR** **Map Ref No. 10**	Nearest Road: A.1198 A warm & friendly welcome awaits visitors to this traditional 1870s farmhouse situated on a working family farm. The house, providing comfortable accommodation & lovely views, is set in open countryside between the villages of Little Gransden & Longstowe. Guests are welcome to walk around the farm & garden. Cambridge can be reached in 20 mins via the B.1046 which takes the motorist on a picturesque drive through villages. **E-mail: modelfm@globalnet.co.uk**	£20.00 to £25.00 🚭	Y	N	Y

Visit our website at:
http://www.bestbandb.co.uk

Chiswick House. Royston

Northamptonshire

		rate £ from - to per person	children taken	evening meals	animals taken
Mrs Audrey Clarke **Dairy Farm** **Cranford St. Andrew** **Kettering** **NN14 4AQ** **Tel: (01536) 330273** **Open: ALL YEAR** **Map Ref No. 11**	Nearest Road: A.14 Situated in an idyllic Northamptonshire village, Dairy Farm is a charming 17th-century farmhouse, featuring oak beams & inglenook fireplaces. 3 comfortable bedrooms, each with en-suite/private bathroom. Families are well catered for. There is a delightful garden, containing an ancient circular dovecote, for guests to enjoy in a relaxed & friendly atmosphere. Delicious meals, using farmhouse produce.	£22.00 to £30.00 	Y	Y	N
Margaret Faulkner **The Maltings** **96 Main Street** **Aldwincle** **Oundle** **NN14 3EP** **Tel: (01832) 720233** **Fax 01832 720326** **Open: ALL YEAR** **Map Ref No. 12**	Nearest Road: A.605, A.14 There is a warm & friendly welcome with personal attention at this former 16th-century maltings - the Faulkner family home for 25 years. A lovely stone house & charming conversion of a small granary, all bordering a plant lover's garden, in a quiet village setting. Exposed beams, inglenooks & antique furniture complete this period home. 3 cosy bedrooms - all with bathrooms - 24-hour heating & good eating places nearby. Children over 10 please. Local attractions: Burghley House, Rockingham Castle & Rutland Water.	£25.00 to £26.00 VISA: M'CARD:	Y	N	N

All the establishments mentioned in this guide are members of
The Worldwide Bed & Breakfast Association

When booking your accommodation please mention
The Best Bed & Breakfast

Cheshire & Lancashire

Cheshire
(North West)

Cheshire is located between the Peak District & the mountains of North Wales & is easily accessible from three major motorways. It has much to attract long visits but is also an ideal stopping-off point for travellers to the Lake District & Scotland, or to North Wales or Ireland. There is good access eastwards to York & the east coast & to the south to Stratford-upon-Avon & to London.

Cheshire can boast seven magnificent stately homes, the most visited zoo outside London, four of Europe's largest garden centres & many popular venues which feature distinctive Cheshire themes such as silk, salt, cheese, antiques & country crafts.

The Cheshire plain with Chester, its fine county town, & its pretty villages, rises up to Alderley Edge in the east from where there are panoramic views, & then climbs dramatically to meet the heights of the Peaks.

To the west is the coastline of the Wirral Peninsula with miles of sandy beaches & dunes &, of course, Liverpool.

The countryside shelters very beautiful houses. Little Moreton Hall near Congleton, is one of the most perfect imaginable. It is a black & white "magpie" house & not one of its walls is perpendicular, yet it has withstood time & weather for nearly four centuries, standing on the waterside gazing at its own reflection.

Tatton Hall is large & imposing & is splendidly furnished with many fine objects on display. The park & gardens are a delight & especially renowned for the azaleas & rhododendrons. In complete contrast is the enormous radio telescope at Jodrell Bank where visitors can be introduced to planetary astronomy in the planetarium.

Chester is a joy; a walk through its streets is like walking through living history. The old city is encircled by city walls enclosing arcaded streets with handsome black & white galleried buildings that blend well with modern life. There are many excellent shops along these "Rows". Chester Cathedral is a fine building of monastic foundation, with a peaceful cloister & outstanding wood carving in the choir stalls. Boat rides can be taken along the River Dee which flows through the city.

Manchester has first rate shopping, restaurants, sporting facilities, theatres & many museums ranging from an excellent costume museum to the fascinating Museum of Science & Industry.

Little Moreton Hall.

Liverpool grew from a tiny fishing village on the northern shores of the Mersey River, receiving its charter from King John in 1207. Commercial & slave trading with the West Indies led to massive expansion in the 17th & 18th centuries. The Liverpool of today owes much to the introduction of the steam ship in the mid 1900s, which enabled thousands of Irish to emigrate when the potatoe famine was at its height in Ireland. This is a city with a reputation for patronage of art, music & sport.

Cheshire & Lancashire

Lancashire
(North West)

Lancashire can prove a surprisingly beautiful county. Despite its industrial history of cotton production, there is magnificent scenery & there are many fine towns & villages. Connections with the Crown & the clashes of the Houses of Lancaster & York have left a rich heritage of buildings with a variety of architecture. There are old stone cottages & farmhouses, as well as manor houses from many centuries.

For lovers of the countryside, Lancashire has the sweeping hills of Bowland, the lovely Ribble Valley, the moors of Rossendale & one mountain, mysterious Pendle Hill.

The Royal Forest of Bowland is a forest without trees, which has provided rich hunting grounds over the centuries. An old windswept pass runs over the heights of Salter Fell & High Cross Fell from Slaidburn, where the Inn, the "Hark to Bounty", was named after the noisiest hound in the squire's pack & used to be the courtroom where strict forest laws were enforced.

Further south, the Trough of Bowland provides an easier route through the hills, & here is the beautiful village of Abbeystead in Wynesdale where monks once farmed the land. The church has stained glass windows portraying shepherds & their flocks & there are pegs in the porch where shepherds hung their crooks.

Below the dramatic hills of Bowland, the green valley of the Ribble climbs from Preston to the Yorkshire Dales. Hangridge Fell, where the tales of witches are almost as numerous as those of Pendle Hill, lies at the beginning of the valley.

Pendle Hill can be reached from the pretty village of Downham which has Tudor, Jacobean & Georgian houses, village stocks & an old inn. Old Pendle rises abruptly to 1831 feet & is a strange land formation. It is shrouded in legend & stories of witchcraft.

Between Pendle Hill & the moors of Rossendale are the textile towns of Nelson, Colne, Burnley, Accrington & Blackburn. The textile industry was well established in Tudor times & the towns grew up as markets for the trading of the cloth woven in the Piece Halls.

The moors which descend to the very edges of the textile towns are wild & beautiful & have many prehistoric tumuli & earthworks. Through the towns & the countryside, winds the Liverpool & Leeds canal, providing an excellent towpath route to see the area.

Lancaster is an historic city boasting the largest castle in England, dating back to Norman times.

Lancashire's coastal resorts are legendary, & Blackpool is Queen of them all with her miles of illuminations & millions of visitors.

Downham Village.

Cheshire & Lancashire

Lancashire Gazeteer

Areas of outstanding natural beauty.
The Forest of Bowland, Parts of Arnside & Silverdale.

Historic Houses & Castles

Rufford Old Hall - Rufford
15th century screen in half-timbered hall of note. Collection of relics of Lancashire life.
Chingle Hall - Nr. Preston
13th century - small manor house with moat. Rose gardens. Haunted!
Astley Hall - Chorley
Elizabethan house reconstructed in 17th century. Houses pictures, tapestries, pottery & furniture.
Gawthorpe Hall - Padiham
17th century manor house with 19th century restoration. Moulded ceilings & some fine panelling. A collection of lace & embroidery.
Bramall Hall - Bramall
Fine example of half-timbered (black & white) manor house built in 14th century & added to in Elizabethan times. .
Lancaster Castle - Lancaster
Largest of English castles - dates back to Norman era.
Astley Hall - Chorley
16th century half-timbered grouped around central court. Rebuilt in the Jacobean manner with long gallery. Unique furniture.
Hoghton Tower - Nr. Preston
16th century - fortified hill-top mansion - magnificent banquet hall. Dramatic building - walled gardens & rose gardens.
Thurnham Hall - Lancaster
13th century origins. 16th century additions & 19th century facade. Beautiful plasterwork of Elizabethan period. Jacobean staircase.

Cathedrals & Churches

Lancaster (St. Mary)
15th century with 18th century tower. Restored chapel - fine stalls.
Whalley (St. Mary)
13th century with 15th century tower, clerestory & aisle windows. Fine wood carving of 15th century canopied stalls.
Halsall (St. Cuthbert)
14th century chancel, 15th century perpendicular spire. 14th century tomb. Original doors, brasses & effigies. 19th century restoration.
Tarleton (St. Mary)
18th century, part 19th century.
Great Mitton (All Hallows)
15th century rood screen, 16th century font cover, 17th century pulpit.

Museums & Galleries

Blackburn Museum - Blackburn
Extensive collections relating to local history archeology, ceramics, geology & natural history. One of the finest collection of coins & fine collection of mediaeval illuminated manuscripts & early printed books.
Bury Museum & Art Gallery - Bury
Houses fine Victorian oil & watercolours. Turner, Constable, Landseer, de Wint.
City Gallery - Manchester
Pre-Raphaelites, Old Masters, Impressionists, modern painters all represented in this fine gallery; also silver & pottery collections.
Higher Mill Museum - Helmshaw
One of the oldest wool textile finishing mills left in Lancashire. Spinning wheels, Hargreave's Spinning Jenny, several of Arkwrights machines, 20 foot water wheel.
Townley Hall Art Gallery & Museum, & Museum of Local Crafts & Industries -
Burnley.

Cheshire Gazeteer

Area of outstanding natural beauty
Part of the Peaks National Park
Addington Hall - Macclesfield
15th century Elizabethan Black & White half timbered house.
Bishop Lloyd's House - Chester
17th century half timbered house (restored). Fine carvings. Has associations with Yale University & New Haven, USA.
Chorley Old Hall - Alderley Edge
14th century hall with 16th century Elizabethan wing.
Forfold Hall - Nantwich
17th century Jacobean country house, with fine panelling.

Cheshire & Lancashire

Gawsworth Hall - Macclesfield
Fine Tudor Half timbered Manor House.
Tilting ground. Pictures, furniture,
sculptures, etc.
Lyme Park - Disley
Elizabethan with Palladian exterior by
Leoni. Gibbons carvings. Beautiful park
with herd of red deer.
Peover Hall - Over Peover, Knutsford
16th century- stables of Tudor period;
has the famous magpie ceiling.
Tatton Park - Knutsford
Beautifully decorated & furnished
Georgian House with a fine collection of
glass, china & paintings including Van
Dyke & Canaletto. Landscaping by
Humphrey Repton.
Little Moreton Hall - Nr. Congleton
15th century timbered, moated house
with 16th century wall-paintings.

Cathedrals & Churches

Acton (St. Mary)
13th century with stone seating around
walls. 17th century effigies.
Bunbury (St. Boniface)
14th century collegiate church -
alabaster effigy.
Congleton (St. Peter)
18th century - box pews, brass
candelabrum, 18th century glass.
Chester Cathedral - Chester
Subjected to restoration by Victorians -
14th century choir stalls.
Malpas (St. Oswalds)
15th century - fine screens, some old
stalls, two family chapels.
Mobberley (St. Wilfred)
Mediaeval - 15th century rood screen,
wall paintings, very old glass.
Shotwick (St. Michael)
Twin nave - box pews, 14th century
quatre - foil lights, 3 deck pulpit.
Winwick (St. Oswald)
14th century - splendid roof. Pugin
chancel.
Wrenbury (St. Margaret)
16th century - west gallery, monuments
& hatchments. Box pews.
Liverpool Cathedral - the Anglican
Cathedral was completed in 1980 after
76 years of work. It is of massive
proportions, the largest in the U.K. with
much delicate detailed work.

Museums & Galleries

Grosvenor Museum - Chester
Art, folk history, natural history, Roman
antiquities including a special display of
information about the Roman army.
Chester Heritage Centre - Chester
Interesting exhibition of the architectural
heritage of Chester.
Cheshire Military Museum - Chester
The three local Regiments are
commemorated here.
King Charles Tower - Chester
Chester at the time of the Civil War
illustrated by dioramas.
Museum & Art Gallery - Warrington
Anthropology, geology, ethnology, botany
& natural history. Pottery, porcelain,
glass, collection of early English
watercolours.
West Park Museum & Art Gallery -
Macclesfield
Egyptian collection, oil paintings,
watercolours, sketches by Landseer &
Tunnicliffe.
Norton Priory Museum - Runcorn
Remains of excavated mediaeval priory.
Also wildlife display.
Quarry Bank Mill - Styal
The Mill is a fine example of industrial
building & houses an exhibition of the
cotton industry: the various offices retain
their original furnishing, & the turbine
room has the transmission systems &
two turbines of 1903.
Nether Alderley Mill - Nether Alderley
15th century corn mill which was still
used in 1929. Now restored.
The Albert Dock & Maritime Museum
- Liverpool
Housing the Liverpool Tate Gallery, the
Tate of the North.
Walker Art Gallery - Liverpool
Jodrell Bank - radio telescope &
planetarium.

Historic Monuments

Chester Castle - Chester
Huge square tower remaining.
Roman Amphitheatre - Chester
12th legion site - half excavated.
Beeston Castle - Beeston
Remains of a 13th century fort.
Sandbach Crosses - Sandbach
Carved stone crosses date from the 9th C.

CHESHIRE & LANCASHIRE

Map reference

01	**D.Taylor**	07	**Sutcliffe**	14	**Townend**
02	**Ikin**	08	**I.Taylor**	14	**M. Smith**
03	**West**	11	**Butler**	15	**G. Smith**
04	**Read**	12	**Rothwell**		

Longview Hotel. Knutsford.

Cheshire

see PHOTO over p. 53

see PHOTO over p. 55

		rate £ from - to per person	children taken	evening meals	animals taken
David Taylor **Ash Farm** **Park Lane** **Little Bollington** **Altrincham WA14 4TJ** Tel: (0161) 9299290 Fax 0161 9285002 Open: ALL YEAR (Excl. Xmas) Map Ref No. 01	Nearest Road: A.56 Set in beautiful N.T. countryside. David & Janice have renovated this 18th-century farmhouse to a very high standard. Bedrooms are en-suite & have many features to delight the discerning traveller. The lounge & dining area is furnished with an antique oak dining suite & open log fire & is the setting for fine farmhouse food. 5 mins' walk to Dunham Deer Park; 2 miles M.56, 6 miles M.6. Manchester Airport 10 mins. Easy access to Manchester & Chester. Single supplement. VISA: M'CARD: AMEX:	£28.50 to £33.50	N	N	N
Mrs Ann Ikin **Golborne Manor** **Platts Lane** **Hatton Heath** **Chester CH3 9AN** Tel: (01829) 770310 Fax 01829 770370 Open: ALL YEAR Map Ref No. 02	Nearest Road: A.41 Golborne Manor is an elegant 19th-century country residence, with glorious views, renovated to a high standard & set in 3 1/2 acres of gardens & grounds. Beautifully decorated with spacious en-suite bedrooms. Farmhouse breakfasts. Evening meals by arrangement. Piano & croquet set available for guests' use. Large car park. Easy access for motorways. 10 mins' drive south from Chester on the A.41, turning right a few yards after D.P. Motors (on the left).	£33.00 to £36.00	Y	Y	N
Stephen West **Longview Hotel &** **Restaurant** **51-55 Manchester Road** **Knutsford WA16 0LX** Tel: (01565) 632119 Fax 01565 652402 Open: ALL YEAR Map Ref No. 03	Nearest Road: A.50 Set in this pleasant Cheshire market town overlooking the common is this lovely, friendly hotel, furnished with many antiques that reflect the elegance of this Victorian building. Care has been taken to retain its character, while also providing all required comforts for the discerning traveller. The 23 en-suite bedrooms are prettily decorated, giving them that cared-for feeling which is echoed throughout the hotel. E-mail: longview_hotel@compuserve.com VISA: M'CARD: AMEX:	£32.50 to £45.00	Y	Y	Y
Mrs Anne Read **Hardingland Farm** **Macclesfield Forest** **SK11 0ND** Tel: (01625) 425759 Fax 01625 615011 Open: MAR - NOV Map Ref No. 04	Nearest Road: A.537 Enjoy yourself in this early-Georgian farmhouse, lovingly restored & furnished with antiques. In a beautiful position in the Peak National Park, with superb views over the Cheshire Plain. Relax in the delightful lounge, & enjoy delicious meals prepared by Anne, who is renowned for her cooking. There are 3 bedrooms, 2 en-suite & all individually decorated. Ideally situated for the Peak District & Cheshire. E-mail: AnneBandB@aol.com	£20.00 to £25.00	N	Y	N
Mrs Sally Sutcliffe **Roughlow Farm** **Chapel Lane** **Willington** **Tarporley** **CW6 0PG** Tel: (01829) 751199 Fax 01829 751199 Open: ALL YEAR Map Ref No. 07	Nearest Road: A.51, A.54 An 18th-century sandstone farmhouse set in a magnificent position with wonderful views to Shropshire & Wales. An elegantly furnished home, decorated to a high standard. 3 well-equipped en-suite bedrooms (double or twin). 1 has its own private entrance & sitting room. An attractive garden surrounds the cobbled courtyard. A superb home in a peaceful situation. Ideal location for exploring Chester, Welsh castles & lovely gardens & walks close by. Children over 5. E-mail: sutcliffe@roughlow.freeserve.co.uk	£25.00 to £35.00	Y	N	N

Roughlow Farm. Willington.

The Manor. Worthenbury.

Cheshire & Lancashire

	Nearest Road: A.525, A.41			
Ian Taylor	Surrounded by rolling Cheshire Plains, Welsh	£28.00	Y	Y	N
The Manor	Marches & National Trust properties, Worthenbury	to			
Worthenbury	Manor makes the ideal setting for a relaxing	£38.00			
LL13 0AW	break. In this fully restored, Grade II listed				
Tel: (01948) 770342	building with oak panelling & 4-poster beds, you can indulge yourself with an excellent dinner,	*see PHOTO over*			
Open: ALL YEAR	prepared by a qualified Chef using fresh local	*p. 56*			
Map Ref No. 08	produce. Guaranteed to be an experience you will want to repeat again & again. An elegant home. Children over 10 years.	VISA:			

Lancashire

	Nearest Road: A.679, M.65			
Mrs Mavis Butler	Eaves Barn Farm is a working farm situated in a	£25.00	Y	Y	N
Eaves Barn Farm	semi-rural location. Superb accommodation in	to			
Hapton	the luxuriously furnished 18th-century farmhouse.	£30.00			
Burnley	The bedrooms are individually styled, tastefully				
BB12 7LP	furnished & very comfortable, all with en-suite facilities. Excellent dinner by arrangement, using				
Tel: (01282) 771591	fresh local produce. A traditional full English				
Fax 01282 771591	breakfast is served in the conservatory. Winner of				
Open: ALL YEAR (Excl. Xmas & New Year)	major tourism award in Lancashire. Easy access to all Lancashire's tourist attractions & Manchester Airport by using the extensive motorway net-				
Map Ref No. 11	work. Children over 10 years.				

	Nearest Road: A.6			
Mrs S. A. Rothwell	A beautiful, small Georgian country house, set in	£27.00	Y	Y	Y
The Bower	an Area of Outstanding Natural Beauty. Superb	to			
Yealand Conyers	walks right from the door, including to Leighton	£32.00			
Carnforth	Moss RSPB reserve. 2 lovely bedrooms, 1 with a double & single bed & en-suite bathroom, & 1				
LA5 9SF	with double bed & private bathroom. Both have colour T.V., clock radio, hairdryer, electric blan-				
Tel: (01524) 734585	kets & tea/coffee-making facilities. Delicious	*see PHOTO over*			
Fax (01524 730710	home-cooked, 4-course dinners. Perfect for exploring the Lake District & Yorkshire Dales. 10	*p. 58*			
Open: ALL YEAR	mins from M.6. Very peaceful, & ideal for stop-				
Map Ref No. 12	overs to or from Scotland. Children over 12 yrs. **E-mail: thebower@currantbun.com**	VISA: M'CARD:			

	Nearest Road: A.6			
Mrs Melanie Smith	Capernwray House is a tastefully furnished coun-	£21.00	Y	Y	N
Capernwray House	try home set in rolling countryside with panoramic	to			
Borrans Lane	views from all windows. Offering 3 bedrooms, all	£22.50			
Capernwray	with en-suite facilities, tea/coffee, hairdryer etc. There is a comfortable residents' lounge with				
Carnforth	T.V., books, magazines & games, ideal for relax-				
LA6 1AE	ing in after the adventures of the day. Conve-				
Tel: (01524) 732363	niently situated & within easy reach of the Lake District, Yorkshire Dales, the coast, Lancaster &				
Fax 01524 732363	RSPB Leighton Moss. Ideal stop-over en-route				
Open: ALL YEAR (Excl. Xmas & New Year)	North/South. Dinner by arrangement, although there are many traditional pubs & inns serving				
Map Ref No. 14	food close by. Children over 5. **E-mail: capernwray@village2000.co.uk**				

The Bower. Yealand Conyers.

Lancashire

		rate £ from - to per person	children taken	evening meals	animals taken
Sally & Peter Townend **New Capernwray Farm** Capernwray Carnforth LA6 1AD Tel: (01524) 734284 Fax 01524 734284 Open: MAR - OCT Map Ref No. 14	Nearest Road: A.6, M.6 Ex. 35 Ideal stop London-Scotland, 3 miles from Ex. 35, M.6. Ideal, also, for touring the Lake District & Yorkshire Dales. Welcoming, with wonderfully relaxed, friendly atmosphere. Superb accommodation in 17th-century former farmhouse, full of character, in beautiful countryside. Luxuriously equipped king, queen & twin bedrooms with en-suite or private facilities. Excellent, 4-course candle-lit dinners. Drawing room glows with William Morris wallpaper & silky apricot-coloured curtains. Detailed help with routes & individually printed maps. Manchester Airport 1 1/4 hours. Winner Best Bed & Breakfast Award: North-West. Children over 10. **E-mail: info@newcapfarm.co.uk**	£30.00 to £35.00 *see PHOTO over* *p. 60* VISA: M'CARD:	Y	Y	Y
Gordon & Jean Smith **Peter Barn Country House** Cross Lane Waddington Clitheroe BB7 3JH Tel: (01200) 428585 Open: ALL YEAR (Excl. Xmas & New Year) Map Ref No. 15	Nearest Road: A.59 Nestling on the edge of the Forest of Bowland, & surrounded by a beautiful garden with stream & ponds, is the award-winning Peter Barn. Superb accommodation, oak beams & log fires in the 1st-floor sitting room with panoramic views of the glorious Ribble Valley. All 3 bedrooms are most attractive, & each has an en-suite or private bathroom & tea/coffee-making facilities. The home-made marmalade is delicious. Good walking & exploring - Browsholme Hall, Whalley Abbey ... or just relaxing. Children over 12.	£21.00 to £23.00	Y	N	N

All the establishments mentioned in this guide are members of
The Worldwide Bed & Breakfast Association

When booking your accommodation please mention
The Best Bed & Breakfast

New Capernwray Farm. Carnforth.

Cornwall

Cornwall
(West Country)

Cornwall is an ancient Celtic land, a narrow granite peninsula with a magnificent coastline of over 300 miles & wild stretches of moorland.

The north coast, washed by Atlantic breakers, has firm golden sands & soaring cliffs. The magnificent beaches at Bude offer excellent surfing & a few miles to the south you can visit the picturesque harbour at Boscastle & the cliff-top castle at Tintagel with its legends of King Arthur. Newquay, with its beaches stretching for over seven miles, sheltered coves & modern hotels & shops, is the premier resort on Cornwall's Atlantic coast. St. Ives, another surfing resort, has great charm which has attracted artists for so long & is an ideal place from which to explore the Land's End peninsula.

The south coast is a complete contrast - wooded estuaries, sheltered coves, little fishing ports, & popular resorts. Penzance, with its warmth & vivid colours, is an all-the-year-round resort & has wonderful views across the bay to St. Michael's Mount. Here are excellent facilities for sailing & deep-sea fishing, as there are at Falmouth & Fowey with their superb harbours. Mevagissey, Polperro & Looe are fine examples of traditional Cornish fishing villages.

In the far west of Cornwall, you can hear about a fascinating legend: the lost land of Lyonesse - a whole country that was drowned by the sea. The legend goes that the waters cover a rich & fertile country, which had 140 parish churches. The Anglo-Saxon Chronicle records two great storms within a hundred years, which drowned many towns & innumerate people. Submerged forests are known to lie around these coasts - & in Mount's Bay beech trees have been found with the nuts still hanging on the branches, so suddenly were they swamped.

Today, St Michael's Mount & the Isles of Scilly are said to be all that remains of the vanished land. St. Michael's Mount, with its tiny fishing village & dramatic castle, can be visited on foot at low tide or by boat at high water. The Isles of Scilly, 28 miles beyond Land's End, have five inhabited islands, including Tresco with its subtropical gardens. Day trips to the numerous uninhabited islands are a special feature of a Scilly holiday.

Inland Cornwall also has its attractions. To the east of Bodmin, the county town, are the open uplands of Bodmin Moor, with the county's highest peaks at Rough Tor & Brown Willy. "Jamaica Inn", immortalised in the novel by Daphne du Maurier, stands on the lonely road across the moor, & "Frenchman's Creek" is on a hidden inlet of the Helford River.

There is a seemingly endless number & variety of Cornish villages in estuaries, wooded, pastoral or moorland settings, & here customs & traditions are maintained. In Helston the famous "Fleury Dance" is still performed, & at the ancient port of Padstow, May Day celebrating involves decorating the houses with green boughs & parading the Hobby Horse through the street to the tune of St. George's Song.

Helford Creek

Cornwall

Cornwall Gazeteer

Areas of outstanding natural beauty.
Almost the entire county.

Historic Houses & Castles

Anthony House - Torpoint
18th century - beautiful & quite unspoiled Queen Anne house, excellent panelling & fine period furnishings.
Cotehele House - Calstock
15th & 16th century house, still contains the original furniture, tapestry, armour, etc.
Ebbingford Manor - Bude
12th century Cornish manor house, with walled garden.
Godolphin House - Helston
Tudor - 17th century colonnaded front.
Lanhydrock - Bodmin
17th century - splendid plaster ceilings, picture gallery with family portraits 17th/20th centuries.
Mount Edgcumbe House - Plymouth
Tudor style mansion - restored after destruction in 1949. Hepplewhite furniture & portrait by Joshua Reynolds.
St. Michael's Mount - Penzance
Mediaeval castle & 17th century with 18th & 19th century additions.
Pencarrow House & Gardens - Bodmin
18th century Georgian Mansion - collection of paintings, china & furniture - mile long drive through fine woodlands & gardens.
Old Post Office - Tintagel
14th century manor house in miniature - large hall used as Post Office for a period, hence the name.
Trewithen - Probus Nr. Truro
Early Georgian house with lovely gardens.
Trerice - St. Newlyn East
16th century Elizabethan house, small with elaborate facade. Excellent fireplaces, plaster ceilings, miniature gallery & minstrels' gallery.

Cathedral & Churches

Altarnun (St. Nonna)
15th century, Norman font, 16th century bench ends, fine rood screen.
Bisland (St. Protus & St. Hyacinth)
15th century granite tower - carved wagon roofs, slate floor. Georgian wine - glass pulpit, fine screen.
Kilkhampton (St. James)
16th century with fine Norman doorway, arcades & wagon roofs.
Laneast (St. Michael or St. Sedwell)
13th century, 15th century enlargement, 16th century pulpit, some painted glass.
Lanteglos-by-Fowley (St. Willow)
14th century, refashioned 15th century, 13th century font, 15th century brasses & altar tomb, 16th century bench ends.
Launcells (St. Andrew)
Interior unrestored - old plaster & ancient roofs remaining, fine Norman font with 17th century cover, box pews, pulpit, reredos, 3 sided alter rails.
Probus (St. Probus & St. Gren)
16th century tower, splendid arcades, three great East windows.
St. Keverne (St. Keverne)
Fine tower & spire. Wall painting in 15th century interior.
St. Neot (St. Neot)
Decorated tower - 16th century exterior, buttressed & double-aisled. Many windows of mediaeval glass renewed in 19th century.

Museums & Galleries

Museum of Witchcraft - Boscastle
Relating to witches, implements & customs.
Military Museum - Bodmin
History of Duke of Cornwall's Light Infantry.
Public Library & Museum - Cambourne
Collections of mineralogy, archaeology, local antiquities & history.
Cornish Museum - East Looe
Collection of relics relating to witchcraft customs & superstitions. Folk life & culture of district.
Helston Borough Museum - Helston
Folk life & culture of area around Lizard.
Museum of Nautical Art - Penzance
Exhibition of salvaged gold & silver treasures from underwater wreck of 1700's.
Museum of Smuggling - Polperro
Activities of smugglers, past & present.

Cornwall

Penlee House Museum - Penlee, Penzance
Archaeology & local history & tin mining exhibits.
Barbara Hepworth Museum - St. Ives
Sculpture, letters, documents, photographs, etc., exhibited in house where Barbara Hepworth lived.
Old Mariners Church - St. Ives
St. Ives Society of Artists hold exhibitions here.
County Museum & Art Gallery - Truro
Ceramics, art local history & antiquities, Cornish mineralogy.

Historic Monuments

Cromwell's Castle - Tresco (Scilly Isles)
17th century castle.
King Charles' Fort - Tresco (Scilly Isles)
16th century fort.
Old Blockhouse - Tresco (Scilly Isles)
16th century coastal battery.
Harry's Wall - St. Mary's (Scilly Isles)
Tudor Coastal battery
Ballowall Barrow - St. Just
Prehistoric barrow.
Pendennis Castle - Falmouth
Fort from time of Henry VII.

Restormel Castle - Lostwithiel
13th century ruins.
St. Mawes Castle - St. Mawes
16th century fortified castle.
Tintagel Castle - Tintagel
Mediaeval ruin on wild coast, King Arthur's legendary castle.

Things to see & do

Camel trail - Padstow to Bodmin
12 miles of recreation path along scenic route, suitable for walkers, cyclists & horse-riders.
Tresco Abbey Gardens - Tresco
Collection of sub-tropical flora
Trethorne Leisure Farm - Launceston
Visitors are encouraged to feed & stroke the farm animals
Seal sanctuary - Gweek Nr. Helston
Seals, exhibition hall, nature walk, aquarium, seal hospital, donkey paddock.
Dobwalls Theme Park - Nr. Liskeard
2 miles of scenically dramatic miniature railway based on the American railroad.
Padstow tropical bird gardens - Padstow
Mynack Theatre - Porthcurno

Lands End.

CORNWALL

Map reference

02	Purslow	40	Tuckett
04	Crocker	42	Rowe
06	Knight	44	Studley
08	Tremayne	46	Epperson
10	Leith	48	Jackson
12	Griffin	50	Nancarrow
14	Rowe	52	Mason
16	Stanley	52	Sykes
18	Low	56	Semmens
20	Mackenzie	58	Bryant
22	Woodley	58	Devlin
24	Walker	60	Fry
26	Martin	64	Heasman
28	Ferrari	66	Poole
30	Hilder	68	Vichniakov
32	Richards	70	Barstow
34	Mercer	72	A. Tremayne
36	Taylor	74	Dymond
38	Wooldridge		

Manor Farm. Crackington Haven

		rate £ from - to per person	children taken	evening meals	animals taken
W.J. & E. Purslow **Orchard Lodge** **Gunpool Lane** **Boscastle** **PL35 0AT** **Tel: (01840) 250418** **Open: APR - JAN** **Map Ref No. 02**	Nearest Road: A.39, B.3266 Orchard Lodge, set in its own attractive gardens, is a large, delightful base for a relaxing holiday. Offering 6 very pleasant guest rooms, decorated & furnished to a high standard, with modern facilities. A delicious full English or Continental breakfast is served in the pretty dining room, with pine furnishings, which overlooks the garden. Ample parking. An ideal base for touring Cornwall. A warm & friendly welcome awaits you.	£20.00 to £24.00 🚭	N	N	N
Mrs Gayle Crocker **Trevigue** **Trevigue Farm** **Crackington Haven** **Bude EX23 0LQ** **Tel: (01840) 230418** **Fax 01840 230418** **Open: ALL YEAR** **Map Ref No. 04**	Nearest Road: A.39 Trevigue is a 16th-century farmhouse built around an ancient cobbled courtyard, nestled high on the rugged north Cornish cliffs. Take a stroll to the romantic strangles beach, down the cliffs via a meandering donkey path. The house has flagstone slate floors, oak beams, roaring log fires & a wealth of books. The bedrooms are en-suite with antique furniture. 'West Country cooking' award-winning food is served. Trevigue is a highly conservation-conscious farm.	£26.00 to £32.00 🚭 VISA: M'CARD:	N	Y	N
Mrs M. Knight **Manor Farm** **Crackington Haven** **EX23 0JW** **Tel: (01840) 230304** **Open: ALL YEAR (Excl.** **Xmas Day)** **Map Ref No. 06**	Nearest Road: A.39 A really super 11th-century manor house, retaining all its former charm & elegance. Mentioned in the 1086 Domesday book, it belonged to the Earl of Mortain, half-brother to William the Conqueror. Delightfully located in a beautiful & secluded position, & surrounded by both attractive gardens & 40 acres of farmland. Guest rooms have private facilities. Dining at Manor Farm is considered the highlight of the day. Only 1 mile from the beach. Non-smokers only. West Country winner of the Best Bed & Breakfast award.	£30.00 to £35.00 🚭 *see PHOTO over p. 65*	N	Y	N
Mr & Mr T. P. Tremayne **'The Home' Country** **House Hotel** **Penjerrick** **Budock Water** **Falmouth TR11 5EE** **Tel: (01326) 250427** **Fax 01326 250143** **Open: APR - OCT** **Map Ref No. 08**	Nearest Road: A.39 A quiet & charming country house, with views over Maenporth & Falmouth Bay. Accommodation is in 18 comfortable rooms, 17 with a private/en-suite bath/shower. All have tea/coffee-making facilities. A colour-T.V. lounge & bar are available, & guests may relax in the beautiful sheltered garden. A golf course & boating facilities nearby. A friendly host, who prepares delicious meals using local produce. Special diets provided by arrangement. Children over 6 years welcome. Animals by arrangement.	£26.00 to £32.00 VISA: M'CARD:	Y	Y	Y
Mrs Susan L. Leith **The Old Rectory** **Mawgan-in-Meneage** **Helston** **TR12 6AD** **Tel: (01326) 221261** **Fax 01326 221797** **Open: ALL YEAR** **Map Ref No. 10**	Nearest Road: A.3083 Where buzzards mew & curlews call, this 200-year-old, listed former rectory lies hidden in a secluded valley on the upper reaches of the mystical Helford River. The elegant guest rooms with private bathrooms overlook south-facing gardens, bordered by a stream. The surrounding ancient woodland provides enchanting walks leading to the river, whilst the grandeur of the west coast is just 5 mins' drive away. A delightful home. Animals by arrangement.	£32.00 to £36.00 🚭	N	N	Y

Coombe Farm. Widegates.

Cornwall

		rate £ from - to per person	children taken	evening meals	animals taken
Mrs Valerie Griffin **Wheatley Farm** **Maxworthy** **Launceston** **PL15 8LY** **Tel: (01566) 781232** **Fax 01566 781232** **Open: APR - OCT** **Map Ref No. 12**	Nearest Road: A.39 You will be made very welcome at Wheatley, a spacious farmhouse, built by the Duke of Bedford in 1871, which stands in landscaped gardens on a working family farm in the peaceful Cornish countryside. Excellent touring base for exploring Cornwall/Devon. Spectacular coastline nearby. Beautiful accommodation, en-suite bedrooms, 1 with romantic 4-poster; each with T.V. & tea/coffee facilities. Splendid food using local produce. Log fires. Special breaks April, May, Sept. **E-mail: wheatleyfrm@compuserve.com**	£19.00 to £23.00 VISA: M'CARD:	Y	Y	N
Stephanie Rowe **Tregondale Farm** **Menheniot** **Liskeard** **PL14 3RG** **Tel: (01579) 342407** **Fax 01579 342407** **Open: ALL YEAR** **Map Ref No. 14**	Nearest Road: A.390, A.38 Feeling like a break? Relax in style in this charming, elegant farmhouse, beautifully set in an original walled garden. 3 delightful bedrooms, 2 en-suite & 1 with a private bathroom, all with T.V., radio & tea/coffee. Log fires for chilly evenings. Home produce a speciality. Play tennis, explore the woodland trail, through a 200-acre mixed farm. Find award-winning pedigree cattle, lambs in spring. Special rates for golf, cycling, fishing. A warm welcome awaits you. Children over 3.	£20.00 to £22.50	Y	Y	N
Peter & Marion Stanley **Landewednack House** **Church Cove** **The Lizard** **TR12 7PQ** **Tel: (01326) 290909** **Fax 01326 290192** **Open: ALL YEAR** **Map Ref No. 16**	Nearest Road: A.3083 An elegant Grade II listed restored Georgian country house, idyllically positioned overlooking the sea, offering absolute peace & comfort. Delightful sea-view bedrooms, furnished with antiques; 4-poster & half-tester beds with private bathrooms (1 with jacuzzi). Relax in front of log fires, laze in the secluded walled garden by the heated swimming pool, play boules or croquet or just step onto the Heritage coastal footpath of the beautiful Lizard Peninsula. Be utterly spoilt in this delightful home at England's most southerly point.	£38.00 to £44.00 VISA: M'CARD:	N	Y	N
Alexander & Sally Low **Coombe Farm** **Widegates** **Looe** **PL13 1QN** **Tel: (01503) 240223** **Fax 01503 240895** **Open: MAR - NOV** **Map Ref No. 18**	Nearest Road: A.387 A lovely country house, beautifully furnished with antiques, set in 10 acres of lawns, meadows, woods, streams & ponds, with views down a wooded valley to the sea. The atmosphere is delightful, with open log fires, a candlelit dining room (in which to enjoy delicious home-cooking) & an informal, licensed bar. An old barn has been converted for indoor games, including snooker & table tennis. Croquet lawn, a swimming pool & many birds & animals, including peacocks & horses. All bedrooms en-suite. Children over 10.	£28.00 to £35.00 *see PHOTO over* *p. 67* VISA: M'CARD: AMEX:	Y	Y	N
Mac & Jennie Mackenzie **Trenance Lodge Restaurant** **83 Trenance Road** **Newquay TR7 2HW** **Tel: (01637) 876702** **Fax 01637 878772** **Open: ALL YEAR** **Map Ref No. 20**	Nearest Road: A.3075 An attractive house standing in its own grounds, overlooking lakes & gardens of Trenance Valley leading to the Gannel Estuary. The restaurant has a reputation for serving the finest fresh local food in elegant surroundings. Adjoining the restaurant is a spacious, relaxing bar lounge. 5 comfortable bedrooms, en-suite, with colour T.V., radio & tea/coffee facilities. An excellent base for touring, with a warm welcome assured.	£25.00 to £35.00 VISA: M'CARD:	N	Y	N

The Old Mill. Little Petherick.

Cornwall

			rate £ from - to per person	children taken	evening meals	animals taken
Kathy Woodley **Degembris Farmhouse** **St. Newlyn East** **Newquay** **TR8 5HY** **Tel: (01872) 510555** **Fax 01872 510230** **Open: ALL YEAR (Excl. Xmas)** **Map Ref No. 22**	Nearest Road: A.30 The original manor house of Degembris was built in the 16th century & is now used as a barn. The present-day house, surrounded by attractive gardens, was built a 200 years ago, & its slate-hung exterior blends well with the rolling countryside. 5 bedrooms, 3 en-suite, each decorated in a coordinating theme, with dried flowers & stripped pine promoting the country atmosphere. Traditional 4-course evening meals. Degembris is well-situated in superb countryside, yet close to the sea. **E-mail: kathyw@email.infotrade.co.uk**	£20.00 to £22.00 VISA: M'CARD:	Y	Y	N
David & Debbie Walker **The Old Mill Country** **House** **Little Petherick** **Padstow PL27 7QT** **Tel: (01841) 540388** **Fax 0870 0569360** **Open: MAR - OCT** **Map Ref No. 24**	Nearest Road: A.389 This delightful, 16th-century, converted corn mill, complete with water wheel, stands in its own grounds at the head of Little Petherick Creek on the A.389. The house & bedrooms are furnished with antiques & collections of genuine artifacts, & each bedroom has an en-suite/private bathroom & tea/coffee facilities. Licensed, with a T.V. available for guests' use. Also, a terraced sun garden. Light supper available on request. **E-mail: <dwalker@oldmillbandb.demon.co.uk>**	£26.75 to £31.75 *see PHOTO over* *p. 69* VISA: M'CARD: AMEX:	N	N	N
Keith & Fiona Martin **Nanscawen House** **Prideaux Road** **St. Blazey** **Par** **PL24 2SR** **Tel: (01726) 814488** **Fax 01726 814488** **Open: ALL YEAR (Excl. Xmas)** **Map Ref No. 26**	Nearest Road: A.390 A beautiful 15th-century manor house with an elegant, stately Georgian wing, set in 5 acres of grounds with stunning views across a romantic valley. Keith & Fiona offer you a relaxed welcome & friendly hospitality. You can enjoy the heated swimming pool, & the luxurious bedrooms are all en-suite with spa baths. Breakfasts are a treat to the eye & the palette. Ideally situated for visiting the Heligan Gardens, Fowey, Lanhydrock & the future Eden Project. Children over 12. **E-mail: keithmartin@compuserve.com**	£25.00 to £38.00 *see PHOTO over* *p. 71* VISA: M'CARD:	Y	N	N
Maureen & Alan Ferrari **Wheal Henrietta** **Treeshill** **Par PL24 2TX** **Tel: (01726) 816188** **Fax 01726 816188** **Open: ALL YEAR** **Map Ref No. 28**	Nearest Road: A.390 Built in 1837 as an engine house to the Fowey Consul Mines, Wheal Henrietta has been converted to provide comfortable guest accommodation, whilst still retaining the original character of this unique building. Set in 10 acres of grounds in the hamlet of Treeshill, approx. 2 miles from Fowey & beaches. You are assured of a warm welcome, quiet surroundings & a very good breakfast. There are 2 attractive guest bedrooms.	£18.50 to £20.00	N	N	N
Mr & Mrs R. Hilder **Carnson House** **East Terrace** **Penzance** **TR18 2TD** **Tel: (01736) 365589** **Fax 01736 365594** **Open: ALL YEAR (Excl. Xmas)** **Map Ref No. 30**	Nearest Road: A.30 Carnson offers you a Cornish welcome & a friendly atmosphere, with T.V. & tea/coffee makers. Some en-suite. Licensed, with a pleasant lounge. Enjoying one of Penzance's most central positions close to the railway & bus stations. Coach & boat trips, car hire & bus tours are available all year round, & can be arranged by the hotel. Add international recommendations for food, & it all makes for a happy & memorable visit. Children over 12. **E-mail: rhilder@netcomuk.co.uk**	£17.00 to £24.00 VISA: M'CARD: AMEX:	N	Y	N

Nanscawen House. St. Blazey.

Cornwall

		rate £ from - to per person	children taken	evening meals	animals taken
Carol Richards **Con Amore** **38 Morrab Road** **Penzance** **TR18 4EX** Tel: (01736) 363423 Fax 01736 363423 Open: ALL YEAR Map Ref No. 32	Nearest Road: A.30 A warm, friendly welcome awaits you at Con Amore. All of the bedrooms are tastefully decorated, some en-suite & all to a high standard. All have colour T.V. & tea-making facilities. An elegant T.V. lounge just for your relaxation. Breakfast of your choice available throughout the year. Con Amore is ideally situated for visiting the 'island kingdom' of west Cornwall that is among the finest in Europe. **E-mail: krich30327@aol.com**	£16.00 to £22.00 VISA: M'CARD:	Y	N	Y
M. J. & C. J. Mercer **Roseudian** **Crippas Hill** **St. Just** **Penzance** **TR19 7RE** Tel: (01736) 788556 Open: MAR - OCT Map Ref No. 34	Nearest Road: A.3071 A small guest house in a quiet rural setting. An ideal centre for exploring the Land's End area. A traditional Cornish cottage, now comfortably modernised, standing in a 3/4-acre terraced garden for guests to enjoy. 3 attractive en-suite rooms, with tea/coffee-making facilities, delicious home-cooked meals, using seasonal garden produce, a lounge with T.V. & the warmest of welcomes all ensure a friendly, relaxed stay. Children over 10. Dogs by prior arrangement.	£19.50 to £24.50	Y	Y	Y
Christine Taylor **Ednovean Farm** **Perranuthnoe** **Penzance** **TR20 9LZ** Tel: (01736) 711883 Fax 01736 710480 Open: ALL YEAR Map Ref No. 36	Nearest Road: A.394 A small working farm nestling above the peaceful village of Perranuthnoe, with stunning views over Mounts Bay & St. Michael's Mount. A unique 17th-century barn, lovingly renovated, now offers guests the choice of 3 elegant, country-style bedrooms, with en-suite facilities & charmingly decorated with fresh flowers, pretty chintz & stylish bed linen. Stroll across the fields to the village pub, sandy beach, cliff-top paths & secluded coves. Perfect peace!	£20.00 to £30.00	N	N	N
Margaret & Keith Wooldridge **Beach Dunes** **Ramoth Way** **Perranporth** **TR6 0BY** Tel: (01872) 572263 Fax 01872 573824 Open: JAN - OCT incl. Map Ref No. 38	Nearest Road: A.30 A small friendly hotel pleasantly situated in almost an acre of grounds amidst the sand dunes adjoining the golf course, & overlooking Perran Bay with its 3 miles of golden sands & Atlantic beach. 9 bedrooms, 7 en-suite, each with tea/coffee facilities, television/radio & private telephone. Also, 1 with private facilities. Excellent food is freshly prepared. Facilities include an indoor pool, a squash court, a cosy bar & residents' lounge. An excellent touring centre. Children over 4 yrs. **E-mail: beachdunes@thenet.co.uk**	£26.50 to £29.50 VISA: M'CARD: AMEX:	Y	Y	Y
Lynne & Anthony Tuckett **Trenderway Farm** **Pelynt** **Polperro** **PL13 2LY** Tel: (01503) 272214 Fax 01503 272991 Open: ALL YEAR (Excl. Xmas) Map Ref No. 40	Nearest Road: A.387 A warm welcome awaits you at the award-winning Trenderway Farm. Built in the late 16th-century, this attractive farmhouse is set in beautiful countryside at the head of the Polperro valley, 5 mins' from the fishing ports of Looe & Polperro. Bedrooms here are truly superb, individually decorated with the flair of an interior designer. A wide choice of breakfast, including smoked salmon & scrambled egg, is served in the sunny conservatory. Many excellent restaurants & inns nearby. **E-mail: trenderwayfarm@hotmail.com**	£25.00 to £35.00 *see PHOTO over* *p. 73* VISA: M'CARD:	N	N	N

Trenderway Farm. Pelynt.

Landaviddy Manor. Polperro.

		rate £ from - to per person	children taken	evening meals	animals taken
Eric & Meryl Rowe **Landaviddy Manor** **Landaviddy Lane** **Polperro** **PL13 2RT** **Tel: (01503) 272210** **Fax 01503 272210** **Open: Mid MAR - Mid OCT** **Map Ref No. 42**	Nearest Road: A.387 A beautiful, licensed, 18th-century, small manor house built of traditional Cornish stone. Situated in lovely grounds on a hillside above the picturesque fishing village of Polperro, commanding charming views of the bay & surrounding N.T. countryside. Retaining its former character while incorporating modern comforts. Many of the charming bedrooms feature antique furniture incl. 4-poster & Victorian beds. All have private facilities, most are en-suite. Restaurants within 10 mins' walk. Children over 14 years. *see PHOTO over p. 74* VISA: M'CARD:	£24.00 to £34.00	Y	N	N
The Studley Family **Aviary Court** **Mary's Well** **Illogan** **Redruth TR16 4QZ** **Tel: (01209) 842256** **Fax 01209 843744** **Open: ALL YEAR** **Map Ref No. 44**	Nearest Road: A.30 Aviary Court stands in 2 1/2 acres of grounds on the edge of Illogan Woods. This part-300-year-old house offers guests a choice of 6 comfortable bedrooms, all with en-suite facilities, overlooking the gardens. Each has radio, colour T.V., tea/coffee-making facilities & 'phone. The comfortable lounge has a bar &, in winter, a log fire. The restaurant serves delicious food with a selection of wine. Children over 3 yrs welcome. **E-mail: aviarycourt@connexions.co.uk** VISA: M'CARD: AMEX:	£31.00 to £31.00	Y	Y	N
Jane & Steven Epperson **Anchorage House Guest** **Lodge** **Nettles Corner** **Tregrehan** **St. Austell PL25 3RH** **Tel: (01726) 814071** **Open: ALL YEAR** **Map Ref No. 46**	Nearest Road: A.390 Every attention has been paid to the smallest detail in this impressive antique-filled house featured in a national magazine. Guests are treated to heated pool, satellite T.V., large beds & luxurious en-suite rooms & everything to make you very comfortable. A superb breakfast is taken in the grand conservatory. Steven & Jane combine wonderful hospitality & pleasing informality for a special stay. Perfect for visiting historic houses, gardens, Heligan & Eden. Children over 16. *see PHOTO over p. 76* VISA: M'CARD:	£30.00 to £34.00	N	Y	N
Mrs J. Jackson **Polrudden Farm** **Pentewan** **Nr. Mevagissey** **St. Austell PL26 6BJ** **Tel: (01726) 842051** **Fax 01726 842051** **Open: MAR - OCT** **Map Ref No. 48**	Nearest Road: A.30, A.38 Polrudden is a small working farm set in 74 acres of unspoilt coastal farmland with breathtaking views over the bay. A stone's throw from the sea, it is situated centrally between Penzance & Plymouth. 3 bedrooms, each with an en-suite/private bathroom, T.V. & tea/coffee. A friendly, relaxed atmosphere prevails. Polrudden has a small, secluded private beach & is within 5 mins' walk from Pentewan Sands, where there is safe bathing, water skiing & sailing. Children over 12.	£22.50 to £25.00	Y	N	N
Judith Nancarrow **Poltarrow Farm** **St. Mewan** **St. Austell** **PL26 7DR** **Tel: (01726) 67111** **Fax 01726 67111** **Open: ALL YEAR (Excl. Xmas)** **Map Ref No. 50**	Nearest Road: A.390 Set in 45 acres of pastoral farmland, this wisteria-clad farmhouse holds a commanding position, with views across rolling pastures. 5 attractively furnished bedrooms with en-suite/private bathroom, T.V. & tea/coffee. The dining room offers traditional farmhouse fare, with a full English breakfast made using fresh local produce & served in generous Cornish portions. A comfortable sitting room. Log fire. Indoor heated swimming pool. Close to the south coast of Cornwall, yet centrally situated between Plymouth & Penzance. VISA: M'CARD:	£22.00 to £25.00	Y	N	N

Anchorage House Guest Lodge. Tregrehan.

Cornwall

		rate £ from - to per person	children taken	evening meals	animals taken
Diana & Derek Mason **Kandahar** **11 The Warren** **St. Ives** **TR26 2EA** **Tel: (01736) 796183** **Open: Mid FEB - Mid NOV** **Map Ref No. 52**	Nearest Road: A.3074 Kandahar has a unique water's-edge location, lapped by the Atlantic & overlooking the harbour. The town centre, beaches, coach & railway station are all within 150 yds. All 5 rooms have superb sea views, colour T.V., tea/coffee-making facilities & full central heating. There are 2 en-suite bedrooms. English & vegetarian breakfasts served. There are many restaurants close by. Children over 6 years welcome.	£19.00 to £27.00 🚭 VISA: M'CARD:	Y	N	N
Irene & Jack Sykes **Old Vicarage Hotel** **Parc-an-Creet** **St. Ives** **TR26 2ET** **Tel: (01736) 796124** **Fax 01736 796343** **Open: APR - OCT** **Map Ref No. 52**	Nearest Road: A.30 The Old Vicarage Hotel, set in its own wooded grounds, secluded & peaceful, on the edge of the moorlands to the west of St. Ives. Offering 8 comfortable bedrooms, 6 with a private bath/shower, all with colour T.V.. All rooms have tea/coffee makers. Families well catered for. A delightful large garden for guests to relax in, & a safe recreation area for children. Convenient for the beach & other places of interest.	£20.00 to £25.00 VISA: M'CARD:	Y	N	Y
Suzanne Semmens **Beckside Cottage** **Treeve Lane** **Connor Downs** **St. Ives** **TR27 5BN** **Tel: (01736) 756751** **Open: ALL YEAR** **Map Ref No. 56**	Nearest Road: A.30 'Beck' means stream in Celtic, so naturally there's one in the garden of Beckside Cottage, where butterflies visit from the adjacent nature reserve. Nearby, 400 acres of sand dunes nudge the Atlantic coast. Cornish gardens, charming St. Ives, the National Trust beach which inspired Virginia Woolf, helicopters for the Isles of Scilly ... all are accesible from this 200-year-old cottage with its 2 delightful en-suite bedrooms, guests' lounge & genuine friendly feel. Children over 10. **E-mail: enquiry@becksidecottage.demon.co.uk**	£22.50 to £27.50 🚭	Y	N	N
Jim & Suzanne Bryant **The Old Borough House** **Bossiney** **Tintagel** **PL34 0AY** **Tel: (01840) 770475** **Fax 01840 770475** **Open: ALL YEAR (Excl. Xmas)** **Map Ref No. 58**	Nearest Road: A.39 An historic listed 16th-century house formerly the home of J.B. Priestly & the Mayors of Bossiney, now beautifully furnished with country antiques. Close to the coastal path & Bossiney Cove, a sandy sea-washed beach. 3 delightful en-suite rooms with large comfortable beds, guests' lounge & cosy dining room. Freshly prepared meals, cooked on the Aga from the highest quality local ingredients. Children over 12 years.	£25.00 to £29.00 🚭 VISA: M'CARD:	Y	Y	N
Mrs J. A. Fry **Polkerr Guest House** **Molesworth Street** **Tintagel** **PL34 0BY** **Tel: (01840) 770382** **Tel: (01840) 770132** **Open: ALL YEAR (Excl. Xmas Day)** **Map Ref No. 60**	Nearest Road: A.39, B.3263 Polkerr has been converted from a farmhouse to a refurbished guest house of a very high standard. All of the bedrooms have an en-suite or private bathroom & T.V. & tea-making facilities. A recent addition has been a beautifully appointed sun lounge where guests can relax after viewing some of the most impressive coastal views of north Cornwall. Within easy reach of Tintagel village is the King Arthur Castle & other amenities such as golf, gardens, horse riding & much more. Polkerr is a charming home.	£19.00 to £25.00	Y	Y	N

Trebrea Lodge. Trenale.

		rate £ from - to per person	children taken	evening meals	animals taken
John Charlick & Sean Devlin Trebrea Lodge Trenale Tintagel PL34 0HR Tel: (01840) 770410 Fax 01840 770092 Open: MAR - DEC Map Ref No. 58	Nearest Road: A.39 This lovely Grade II listed Georgian house, set in 4 1/2 acres of wooded hillside, has outstanding views of the north Cornish coast. The land was originally granted by the Black Prince to the Bray family, who lived here for 600 years. The beautiful bedrooms are individually decorated with antique furniture, & all have en-suite bathrooms. Award-winning, high-quality cooking, log fires & a relaxed atmosphere. Trebrea Lodge is a truly delightful home. Children over 12.	£34.00 to £47.00 *see PHOTO over p. 78* VISA: M'CARD: AMEX:	Y	Y	Y
Ann Heasman Cliff House Devonport Hill Kingsand Torpoint PL10 1NJ Tel: (01752) 823110 Fax 01752 822595 Open: ALL YEAR Map Ref No. 64	Nearest Road: A.374 Cliff House is a Grade II listed 17th-century building, converted from 2 cottages into 1 house around 150 years ago. Although modernised to include en-suite facilities, it still retains many original features. The drawing room with wonderful views, log fires, T.V. etc., has a large balcony through French windows overlooking Plymouth Sound, Cawsand Bay & the village. Ann is an enthusiastic wholefood cook, & meals (by arrangement) include home-made soups, mousses & bread. E-mail: info@cliffhse.abel.co.uk	£20.00 to £28.00 (no smoking)	Y	Y	N
Button & Clive Poole The Old Rectory St. John-in-Cornwall Torpoint PL11 3AW Tel: (01752) 822275 Fax 01752 823322 Open: ALL YEAR Map Ref No. 66	Nearest Road: A.374 Regency-period country house with subtropical garden & millpond located by tidal creek in this 'forgotten corner of Cornwall'. This home, full of interest, allows guests time to reflect; to enjoy its understated elegance with its beautifully appointed & romantic bedrooms, imaginative breakfasts & relaxing drawing room. Coastal path walks, beaches, moors, golf, sailing & N.T. properties close by. 4 miles from chain ferry.	£30.00 to £45.00 (no smoking) *see PHOTO over p. 80*	Y	N	Y
Sonia & Mikhail Vichniakov Bissick Old Mill Ladock Truro TR2 4PG Tel: (01726) 882557 Fax 01726 884057 Open: ALL YEAR Map Ref No. 68	Nearest Road: A.30, A.390 Bissick Old Mill, formerly a working corn mill, is conveniently situated in the village of Ladock (10 mins' drive from Truro), & provides exceptional standards of comfort, cuisine & hospitality. Its central position makes it an ideal base from which to visit all areas of Cornwall, whether it be on business or purely for pleasure. A chef proprietor (mostly English/French dishes). A residential licence. The perfect spot for a relaxing break.	£29.20 to £39.95 (no smoking) VISA: M'CARD:	N	Y	N
Oliver & Rosemary Barstow Crugsillick Manor Ruan High Lanes St. Mawes Truro TR2 5LJ Tel: (01872) 501214 Fax 01872 501228 Open: ALL YEAR Map Ref No. 70	Nearest Road: A.3078 A hidden treasure of the Roseland Peninsula, one of Cornwall's loveliest areas - meandering lanes, unspoilt fishing villages & sheltered coves. Find Crugsillick, a beautiful Grade II listed Queen Anne manor house offering peace & comfort. Stroll down the smugglers' path below the house to glorious beaches & spectacular coastline, visit the historic houses & famous gardens - returning to dine, if you wish, on freshly caught seafood & home-grown vegetables. Above all, enjoy the tranquillity. Children over 12. E-mail: barstow_crugsillick@csi.com	£35.00 to £48.00 VISA: M'CARD:	Y	Y	Y

The Old Rectory. St. John-in-Cornwall.

		rate £ from - to per person	children taken	evening meals	animals taken
Ann Tremayne **Apple Tree Cottage** **Laity Moor** **Ponsanooth** **Truro** **TR3 7HR** **Tel: (01872) 865047** **Open: ALL YEAR** **Map Ref No. 72**	Nearest Road: A.39 Apple Tree Cottage, set amid rolling countryside with delightful gardens & river, is furnished with country antiques & has a warm, welcoming atmosphere. The large lounge has a log fire, & traditional farmhouse breakfasts, cooked on the Aga, are taken in the sunlit dining room. The attractive bedrooms have pine double beds, tea/coffee-making facilities, washbasins & lovely views. Several N.T. gardens & the famous Trebah Gardens on the Helford River are only 15 mins away. Children over 12 years. **E-mail: raistlin@dial.pipex.com**	£20.00 to £25.00	Y	N	Y
Bridget & Ernie Dymond **Trevispian-Vean Farm** **Guest House** **St. Erme** **Truro TR4 9BL** **Tel: (01872) 279514** **Fax 01872 263730** **Open: ALL YEAR** **Map Ref No. 74**	Nearest Road: A.39 A delightful farmhouse, dating back over 300 years, offering a very warm welcome & good accommodation in 9 pleasant & comfortably furnished en-suite guest rooms. Only 7 miles from the coast, & surrounded by beautiful countryside, it is a perfect base for everyone. Families will particularly enjoy it here, as children can look around the farm, & there are plenty of places to visit & things to do. There's even a donkey for the children. A charming home.	£21.00 to £24.00	Y	Y	N

All the establishments mentioned in this guide are members of
The Worldwide Bed & Breakfast Association

When booking your accommodation please mention
The Best Bed & Breakfast

Cumbria

Cumbria

The Lake District National Park is deservedly famous for its magnificent scenery. Here, England's highest mountains & rugged fells surround shimmering lakes & green valleys. But there is more to Cumbria than the beauty of the Lake District. It also has a splendid coastline, easily accessible from the main lakeland centres, as well as a border region where the Pennines, the backbone of England, reach their highest point, towering over the Eden valley.

Formation of the dramatic Lakeland scenery began in the Caledonian period when earth movements raised & folded the already ancient rocks, submerging the whole mass underseas & covering it with limestone. During the ice age great glaciers ground out the lake beds & dales of todays landscape. There is tremendous variety, from the craggy outcrops of the Borrowdale Volcanics with Skiddaw at 3054 feet, to the gentle dales, the open moorlands & the lakes themselves. Each lake is distinctive, some with steep mountain sides sliding straight to the water's edge, others more open with sloping wooded hillsides. Ellerwater, the enchanting "lake of swans" is surrounded by reed & willows at the foot of Langdale. The charm of Ullswater inspired Wordsworth's famous poem "Daffodils". Whilst many lakes are deliberately left undisturbed for those seeking peace, there are others - notably Windermere - where a variety of water sports can be enjoyed. The changeable weather of the mountainous region can produce a sudden transformation in the character of a tranquil lake, raising choppy waves across the darkened surface to break along the shoreline. It is all part of the fascination of Lakeland.

Fell walking is the best way to appreciate the full beauty of the area. There are gentle walks along the dales, & the tops of the ridges are accessible to walkers with suitable footwear & an eye to the weather.

Ponytrekking is another popular way to explore the countryside & there are many centres catering even for inexperienced riders.

There are steamboats on lakes such as Coniston & Ullswater, where you can appreciate the scenery. On Windermere there are a variety of boats for hire, & facilities for water-skiing.

Traditional crafts & skills are on display widely. Craft centres at Keswick, Ambleside & Grasmere, & the annual exhibition of the Guild of Lakeland Craftsmen held in Windermere from mid-July to early September represent the widest variety of craft artistry.

Fairs & festivals flourish in Lakeland. The famous Appleby Horse Fair, held in June is the largest fair of its kind in the world & attracts a huge gypsy gathering. Traditional agriculture shows, sheep dog trials & local sporting events abound. The Grasmere Sports, held each August include gruelling fell races, Cumberland & Westmoreland wrestling, hound trails & pole-leaping.

The traditional custom of "Rush-bearing" when the earth floors of the churches were strewn with rushes still survives as a procession in Ambleside & Grasmere & many other villages in the summer months

The coast of Cumbria stretches from the estuaries of Grange-over-Sands & Burrow-in-Furness by way of the beautiful beaches between Bootle & Cardurnock, to the mouth of the Solway Firth. The coastal areas, especially the estuaries, are excellent for bird-watching. The sand dunes north of the Esk are famous for the colony of black-headed gulls which can be visited by arrangement, & the colony of seabirds at St. Bees Head is the largest in Britain.

Cumbria

Cumbria

Gazeteer

Area of outstanding natural beauty.
The Lake District National Park.

House & Castles

Carlisle Castle - Carlisle
12th century. Massive Norman keep - half-moon battery - ramparts, portcullis & gatehouse.
Brough Castle - Kirby Stephen
13th century - on site of Roman Station between York & Carlisle.
Dacre Castle - Penrith
14th century - massive pele tower.
Sizergh Castle - Kendal
14th century - pele tower - 15th century great hall. English & French furniture, silver & china - Jacobean relics. 18th century gardens.
Belle Island - Boweness-on-Windermere
18th century - interior by Adams Brothers, portraits by Romney.
Swarthmoor Hall - Ulverston
Elizabethan house, mullioned windows, oak staircase, panelled rooms. Home of George Fox - birthplace of Quakerism - belongs to Society of Friends.
Lorton Hall - Cockermouth
15th century pele tower, priest holes, oak panelling, Jacobean furniture.
Muncaster Castle - Ravenglass
14th century with 15th & 19th century additions - site of Roman tower.
Rusland Hall - Ulveston
Georgian mansion with period panelling, sculpture, furniture, paintings.
Levens Hall - Kendal
Elizabethan - very fine panelling & plasterwork - famous topiary garden.
Hill Top - Sawrey
17th century farmhouse home of Beatrix Potter - contains her furniture, china & some of original drawings for her children's books.
Dove Cottage - Town End, Grasmere
William Wordsworth's cottage - still contains his furnishing & his personal effects as in his lifetime.
Brantwood
The Coniston home of John Ruskin, said to be the most beautifully situated house in the Lake District. Exhibition, gardens, bookshops & tearooms.

Cathedrals & Churches

Carlisle Cathedral - Carlisle
1130. 15th century choir stalls with painted backs - carved misericords, 16th century screen, painted roof.
Cartmel Priory (St. Mary Virgin)
15th century stalls, 17th century screen, large east window, curious central tower.
Lanercost Priory (St. Mary Magdalene)
12th century - Augustinian - north aisle now forms Parish church.
Greystoke (St. Andrew)
14th/15th century. 19th century misericords. Lovely glass in chancel.
Brougham (St. Wilfred)
15th century carved altarpiece.
Furness Abbey
12th century monastery beautiful setting.
Shap Abbey
12th century with 16th century tower.

Museums & Galleries

Abbot Hall - Kendal
18th century, Georgian house with period furniture, porcelain, silver, pictures, etc. Also contains modern galleries with contemporary paintings, sculptures & ceramics. Changing exhibitions on show.
Carlisle Museum & Art Gallery - Carlisle
Archaeological & natural history collections. National centre of studies of Roman Britain. Art gallery principally exhibiting paintings & porcelain.
Hawkshead Courthouse - Kendal
Exhibition of domestic & working life housed in mediaeval building.
Helena Thompson Museum - Workington
displays Victorian family life & objects of the period.
Lakeland Motor Museum - Holker Hall - Grange-over-Sands
Exhibits cars, bicycles, tricycles, motor cycles, etc., & model cars.
Millom Folk Museum - St. George's Road, Millom
Reconstructions of drift in iron ore mine, miner's cottage kitchen, blacksmith's forge & agricultural relics.
Ravenglass Railway Museum - Ravenglass
History of railways relics, models, etc.

Cumbria

Wordsworth Museum - Town End, Grasmere
Personal effects, first editions, manuscripts, & general exhibits from the time of William Wordsworth.
Border Regiment Museum - The Castle, Carlisle.
Collection of uniforms, weapons, trophies, documents, medals from 1702, to the present time.
Whitehaven Museum - Whitehaven
History & development of area show in geology, paleontology, archaeology, natural history, etc. Interesting maritime past.
Fitz Park Museum & Art Gallery - Keswick.

Collection of manuscripts - Wordsworth, Walpole, Coleridge, Southey.
The Beatrix Potter Gallery - Hawkshead

Things to see & do

Fell Walking - there is good walking throughout Cumbria, but check weather reports, clothing & footwear before tackling the heights.
Pony-trekking - opportunities for novice & experienced riders.
Watersports - Windermere is the ideal centre for sailing, waterskiing, windsurfing, scuba-diving.
Golf - championship course to the north at Silloth.

Grasmere.

CUMBRIA

Map reference

01	Seedhouse	27	Lowe
02	Rhone	28	R. Jones
03	Kirby	28	Coy
04	Butcher	28	Russ
05	Hood	29	Miller
07	Stobbart	30	Bryant
08	McKenzie	31	Humphreys
09	Sisson	32	Sanders
10	Hempstead	33	White
11	Cervetti	34	Weightman
12	Hodge	35	Whittam
13	Denman	36	Sowerby
14	Hatch	37	Clowes
15	Semple	38	Casey
16	Wilkinson	38	Tyson
17	Pettit	38	Thomas
18	Clark	38	Butterworth
19	J.Edwards	38	Garside
21	Savasi	38	Price
22	Craig	38	Todd
23	Midwinter	38	Holcroft
26	Briggs		

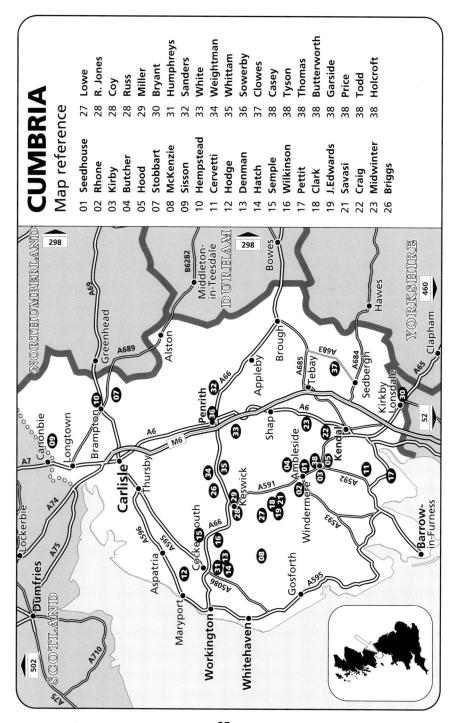

The Fairfield. Bowness-on-Windermere.

Laurel Villa. Ambleside.

			rate £ from - to per person	children taken	evening meals	animals taken

George B. Seedhouse **Laurel Villa Hotel** **Lake Road** **Ambleside** **LA22 0DB** **Tel: (015394) 33240** **Open: ALL YEAR** **Map Ref No. 01**	Nearest Road: A.591 Visited by Beatrix Potter, this charming Victorian residence, now sympathetically restored & refurbished to a very high standard, offers 8 comfortable en-suite bedrooms; 2 of which boast 4-poster beds whilst some at the rear have splendid views over the village & surrounding fells. A residents' lounge in which to relax & an attractive dining room. All major outdoor activities are catered for nearby, including watersports, pony trekking &, of course, fell walking. Car park.	£30.00 to £40.00 🚭 *see PHOTO over* *p. 87* VISA: M'CARD:
Alan Rhone **Riverside Lodge** **Rothay Bridge** **Ambleside** **LA22 0EH** **Tel: (015394) 34208** **Fax 015394 31884** **Open: ALL YEAR** **Map Ref No. 02**	Nearest Road: A.593 Riverside Lodge is a house of immense charm & character, superbly situated in a unique riverside setting, just a few mins' walk from the centre of Ambleside & Lake Windermere. The house has been refurbished throughout in keeping with its beamed ceilings & stone-flagged floors. Guests have access to the house without any restrictions in a very relaxed & informal atmosphere. There are 5 beautifully furnished en-suite bedrooms. **E-mail: riverside@altavista.net**	£25.00 to £31.00 *see PHOTO over* *p. 90* VISA: M'CARD:
Robert & Helen Kirby **Buckle Yeat Guest House** **Nr. Sawrey** **Hawkshead** **Ambleside** **LA22 0LF** **Tel: (015394) 36538** **Tel/Fax 015394 36446** **Open: ALL YEAR** **Map Ref No. 03**	Nearest Road: B.5285, A.590 Buckle Yeat is famous for its connections with Beatrix Potter. Although over 200 years old, it has been sympathetically & tastefully refurbished. A large lounge with log fire & an attractive dining room which also serves morning coffee & afternoon teas. 7 comfortable en-suite bedrooms. Many good local pubs & restaurants offer excellent meals. Buckle Yeat is perfect for touring Lakeland, with walks, fishing & birdwatching all nearby. Animals by arrangement. **E-mail: info@buckle-yeat.co.uk**	£25.00 to £27.00 VISA: M'CARD: AMEX:
Philip & Jane Butcher **Rowanfield Country** **House** **Kirkstone Road** **Ambleside LA22 9ET** **Tel: (015394) 33686** **Fax 015394 31569** **Open: MAR - DEC** **Map Ref No. 04**	Nearest Road: A.591 Set in quiet countryside 3/4 of a mile outside Ambleside, Rowanfield enjoys breathtaking lake & mountain views. Superbly situated for exploring the whole Lake District area. A period house with Laura Ashley style decor. All bedrooms are en-suite with power showers, some have baths, Queen & King-size beds. Certain weeks of the year your chef/patron performs wizardry in the kitchen. His dinners are superb. Unlicensed, but own wine welcome. Children over 8. Parking.	£30.00 to £40.00 🚭 *see PHOTO over* *p. 89* VISA: M'CARD: AMEX:
Ray & Barbara Hood **The Fairfield** **Brantfell Road** **Bowness-on-Windermere** **LA23 3AE** **Tel: (015394) 46565** **Fax 015394 46565** **Open: FEB - NOV** **Map Ref No. 05**	Nearest Road: A.591 Fairfield is a small, friendly, 200-year-old Lakeland hotel found in a peaceful garden setting, 200 metres from Bowness village, 400 metres from the shores of Lake Windermere & at the end of the Dales Way (an 81-mile walk from Ilkley to Bowness). The Beatrix Potter Exhibition is within easy walking distance. 9 tastefully furnished bedrooms with T.V., welcome tray & private showers/bathrooms. Breakfasts are a speciality. Leisure facilities available. **E-mail: Ray&barb@the-fairfield.co.uk**	£25.00 to £32.00 🚭 *see PHOTO over* *p. 86* VISA: M'CARD:

The "children taken", "evening meals", "animals taken" columns:

- George B. Seedhouse: N N N
- Alan Rhone: N N N
- Robert & Helen Kirby: Y N Y
- Philip & Jane Butcher: Y Y N
- Ray & Barbara Hood: Y N N

Rowanfield Country House. Ambleside.

Riverside Lodge Country House. Rothay Bridge.

Wood House. Buttermere.

Cumbria

		rate £ from - to per person	children taken	evening meals	animals taken

Mrs S. R. Stobbart **Hullerbank** **Talkin** **Brampton** **CA8 1LB** **Tel: (016977) 46668** **Fax 016977 46668** **Open: ALL YEAR (Excl.** **Xmas & New Year)** **Map Ref No. 07**	Nearest Road: A.69 A Georgian farmhouse, dated 1635-1751, standing in its own grounds near the picturesque village of Talkin, 2 1/2 miles from Brampton. Superb walking country, central for visiting Hadrian's Wall, the Lake District & the borders. A warm, friendly, relaxed atmosphere awaits. 3 comfortable bedrooms, with private facilities, electric underblankets & tea makers. A comfortable T.V. lounge, & dining room with excellent home cooking, including home-produced lamb & fresh produce. Children over 12 welcome.	£22.00 to £22.50 VISA: M'CARD:	Y	Y	N
Michael & Judy McKenzie **Wood House** **Buttermere** **CA13 9XA** **Tel: (017687) 70208** **Open: MAR - OCT** **Map Ref No. 08**	Nearest Road: A.66 Wood House, near Buttermere village overlooking Crummock Water, stands on one of the outstanding sites in the Lake District. The drawing room, with high-quality furnishings & antiques, spanning the front of the house, has a spellbinding view over the lake, as do each of the 3 spacious & attractively furnished en-suite bedrooms. Freshly prepared food is served in the traditional surroundings of a charming dining room.	£29.00 to £35.00 *see PHOTO over* *p. 91*	N	Y	N
Jack & Margaret Sisson **Bessiestown Farm** **Country Guest House** **Catlowdy** **Longtown** **Carlisle CA6 5QP** **Tel/Fax: (01228) 577219** **Open: ALL YEAR** **Map Ref No. 09**	Nearest Road: A.7 An award-winning farm guest house, overlooking the Scottish borders, where a friendly, relaxing atmosphere is assured. 5 pretty, en-suite rooms with radio, T.V. & tea/coffee-making facilities. Delightfully decorated public rooms & conservatory. Also, ground-floor accommodation in extremely comfortable courtyard cottages. Delicious home cooking. Residential licence. Guests may use the indoor heated swimming pool (May-Sept). Stop-off to/from Scotland & N. Ireland.	£23.50 to £30.00 *see PHOTO over* *p. 93* VISA: M'CARD:	Y	Y	N
Mrs Janet Hempstead **Courtyard Cottages** **Warren Bank Station Road** **Brampton** **Carlisle CA8 1EX** **Tel: (016977) 41818** **Fax 016977 41398** **Open: ALL YEAR (Excl.** **Xmas & New Year)** **Map Ref No. 10**	Nearest Road: A.69 You won't be staying in someone else's home but in a comfortable double-bedded en-suite bedroom in the lovely, but tiny, courtyard cottage of a Victorian mansion with stone steps leading to the upper accommodation, providing total independence & privacy. Breakfast is served in your room. Enjoy Hadrian's Wall, the lakes & Scottish borders, or just stay as a stop-over & be pampered as you travel north or south. (M.6 10 mins.) E-mail: janethempstead@warrenbank.demon.co.uk	£25.00 to £30.00	N	N	N
Mrs E. M. Cervetti **Lightwood Country** **Guest House** **Cartmell Fell** **LA11 6NP** **Tel: (015395) 31454** **Fax 015395 31454** **Open: FEB - DEC** **Map Ref No. 11**	Nearest Road: A.592 Lightwood is a 17th-century farmhouse built in approx. 1650. It possesses all modern amenities whilst retaining the charm of original oak beams & staircase. 2 acres of lovely gardens, with streams running through. Individually decorated rooms, with countryside views. 6 en-suite bedrooms. A cosy lounge with T.V. & log fire. A charming dining room facing the early morning sun. Only 2 miles from the southern end of Lake Windermere. Good English breakfast, with free-range eggs.	£23.00 to £28.00 VISA: M'CARD:	Y	Y	N

Bessiestown Farm. Catlowdy.

New House Farm. Lorton.

Cumbria

		rate £ from - to per person	children taken	evening meals	animals taken
Bob & Pauline Hodge **Sundawn** **Bridekirk** **Cockermouth CA13 0PA** **Tel: (01900) 822384** **Fax 01900 822885** **Open: ALL YEAR (Excl.** **Xmas & New Year)** **Map Ref No. 12**	Nearest Road: A.595 Bob & Pauline offer you a warm & friendly welcome. The emphasis here is on comfort, relaxation, personal service & imaginative home cooking. From the sun lounge, view the panorama of the Lakeland Fells & the historic market town of Cockermouth, birthplace of William Wordsworth. Accommodation is in 4 tastefully decorated rooms, 2 en-suite, all with modern amenities & tea/coffee makers. A charming home. **E-mail: robert.hodge1@virgin.net**	£25.00 to £30.00	Y	N	N
Mary & Derek Denman **Winder Hall** **Low Lorton** **Cockermouth** **CA13 9UP** **Tel: 01900 85107** **Fax 01900 85107** **Open: ALL YEAR** **Map Ref No. 13**	Nearest Road: A.66 This historic manor house has grounds to the River Cocker in possibly the most peaceful valley in the National Park, ideal for the Northern & Western Lakes. Mary & Derek provide 6 luxurious rooms with superb views, 2 with special 4-posters. Guests appreciate the attentive service, the wide breakfast choice & the 4-course dinner featuring local produce. Residential licence. Short breaks available. Children over 8. **E-mail: winderhall@lowlorton.freeserve.co.uk** *see PHOTO over* *p. 96* VISA: M'CARD:	£30.00 to £38.00	Y	Y	N
Hazel Hatch **New House Farm** **Lorton** **Cockermouth CA13 9UU** **Tel: (01900) 85404** **Fax 01900 85404** **Open: ALL YEAR** **Map Ref No. 14**	Nearest Road: A.66 New House Farm is set superbly in the Lorton Vale, has its own 15 acres of fields, ponds, stream & woods & easy access to nearby fells & lakes. All bedrooms are tastefully furnished & en-suite, & there is a comfortable sitting room with open fire & a cosy dining room. Lots of personal attention is offered by the hosts. The cooking is fine traditional fare with a Cumbrian flavour. Children over 10. Animals by arrangement. *see PHOTO over* *p. 94*	£35.00 to £45.00	Y	Y	Y
Steve Semple **Lakeside Guest House** **Dubwath** **Bassenthwaite Lake** **Cockermouth** **CA13 9YD** **Tel: (017687) 76358** **Open: ALL YEAR** **Map Ref No. 15**	Nearest Road: A.66 An elegant country house offering friendly & relaxing hospitality, with superb views across Bassenthwaite Lake to Skiddaw & the surrounding fells. Keswick is only a short drive away. Also, the peaceful western fells & lakes of Buttermere & Crummock Water. There are 8 tastefully furnished bedrooms, 7 en-suite, each with T.V., radio & tea/coffee facilities. Oak floors & a panelled hall. A pleasant lounge in which to relax. A delicious breakfast is served. *see PHOTO over* *p. 97*	£21.00 to £26.00	Y	N	N
Fred & Hazel Wilkinson **Riggs Cottage** **Routenbeck** **Bassenthwaite Lake** **Cockermouth** **CA13 9YN** **Tel: (017687) 76500** **Fax 017687 76580** **Open: ALL YEAR** **Map Ref No. 16**	Nearest Road: A.66 Riggs Cottage is a super 17th-century cottage of great character & charm, with many exposed oak beams, a log-burning inglenook fireplace & period furniture. 3 comfortable & tastefully furnished bedrooms with modern amenities. The cosy lounge is available throughout the day. In the dining room, tasty home-cooked meals are served, using only the best ingredients. Oven-fresh bread & home-made preserves are a speciality. Situated 'off the beaten track', an ideal base for a Lakeland holiday. Children over 5. VISA: M'CARD:	£21.00 to £26.00	Y	Y	N

Winder Hall. Low Lorton.

Lakeside. Bassenthwaite.

Cumbria

			rate £ from - to per person	children taken	evening meals	animals taken
Barbara & Ray Pettit **Greenacres Country Guest House, Lindale** Grange-over-Sands LA11 6LP Tel/Fax: (015395) 34578 Open: ALL YEAR (Excl. Xmas) Map Ref No. 17	Nearest Road: A.590 Greenacres is a charming 19th-century cottage ideally located for exploring the lakes & dales. Situated in the National Park, in the small village of Lindale at the foot of the beautiful Winster Valley, where you can walk in unspoilt country-side. All bedrooms are luxury en-suite. There is a lovely lounge & conservatory, & cosy dining room where excellent home-cooking is served. Friendly & relaxed atmosphere.	£25.00 to £30.00 ⊘ VISA: M'CARD:	Y	Y	N
Martin & Angela Clark **Banerigg Guest House** **Lake Road** **Grasmere** LA22 9PW Tel: (015394) 35204 Open: ALL YEAR Map Ref No. 18	Nearest Road: A.591 Delightfully situated overlooking Grasmere Lake is this small, friendly guest house. The informal hospitality & relaxing atmosphere make this a super base for a holiday. All 7 comfortable rooms have modern amenities. A pleasant lounge with a cosy log fire. A delicious & plentiful breakfast is served. Ideally located for fell walking, sailing, canoeing & fishing. Angela & Martin ensure that guests have a memorable Lakeland holiday.	£20.00 to £26.00 ⊘ *see PHOTO over* *p. 99*	Y	N	N
Mrs Joyce Edwards **Riversdale** **Grasmere** LA22 9RQ Tel: (015394) 35619 Open: ALL YEAR Map Ref No. 19	Nearest Road: A.591 Quiet riverside setting with fine views, a traditional Lakeland stone house of character & charm, built 1830. Fully centrally heated & tastefully fur-nished, Riversdale offers every comfort. 3 guest bedrooms, all double, 2 en-suite & 1 with a private bathroom, each with refreshment trays, hairdryers & toiletries provided. There is a comfortable lounge & your hosts serve an exceptional break-fast, freshly prepared. A warm & friendly wel-come awaits all guests, the majority of whom return time & again. Private parking.	£23.00 to £30.00 ⊘	N	N	N
Mr & Mrs Attilio Savasi **Oak Bank Hotel** **Broadgate** **Grasmere** LA22 9TA Tel: (015394) 35217 Fax 015394 35685 Open: FEB - DEC Map Ref No. 21	Nearest Road: A.591 The Oak Bank Hotel is a little gem one stumbles upon all too rarely, with a new conservatory dining room overlooking the garden, by which the river Rothay flows. An award-winning hotel for cordon-bleu cuisine, hospitality & comfort. Log fires in the lounge/bar & delightful Victorian-style bedrooms complete this restful, owner-run hotel. The Oak Bank Hotel is the perfect spot for a relaxing break or for touring the Lake District. E-mail: grasmereoakbank@btinternet.com	£30.00 to £50.00 VISA: M'CARD:	Y	Y	Y
Alison & Philip Midwinter **Low Jock Scar Country Guest House** **Selside** **Kendal** LA8 9LE Tel: (01539) 823259 Fax 01539 823259 Open: MAR - OCT Map Ref No. 23	Nearest Road: A.6 A charming country guest house. A relaxing & friendly atmosphere with genuine warmth. In an idyllic setting with 6 acres of garden & woodland, it is a peaceful base from which to explore the Lakes & Yorkshire Dales. There are 5 comfort-able bedrooms (3 en-suite, 2 on the ground floor) & a lounge well-stocked with books & maps. Excellent freshly prepared dinners - vegetarians catered for. Residential licence. Single supple-ment. Children over 12. E-mail: philip@low-jock-scar.freeserve.co.uk	£23.00 to £28.50 ⊘ *see PHOTO over* *p. 100*	Y	Y	Y

Banerigg House. Grasmere.

Low Jock Scar. Selside

Cumbria

rate £ from - to per person / *children taken* / *evening meals* / *animals taken*

Establishment	Description	Rate £ from - to	children taken	evening meals	animals taken
Maureen & Jack Craig **Burrow Hall** **Plantation Bridge** **Kendal** **LA8 9JR** **Tel: (01539) 821711** **Open: ALL YEAR** **Map Ref No. 22**	Nearest Road: A.591 Although built in 1648, this delightful guest house offers modern-day comforts. It is situated amidst open countryside, midway between Kendal & Windermere on the A.591, yet only 10 miles from M.6 Jt. 36. All 3 en-suite bedrooms are centrally heated, have colour T.V., tea/coffee-making facilities, radio/alarms & hairdryer & are all tastefully decorated. A well-furnished guest lounge. A warm & friendly welcome is assured.	£22.50 to £25.00 (non-smoking) VISA: M'CARD:	N	N	N
R. Jones **Greystones** **Ambleside Road** **Keswick** **CA12 4DP** **Tel: (017687) 73108** **Open: JAN - NOV** **Map Ref No. 28**	Nearest Road: A.66 Greystones enjoys an enviable position overlooking the grounds of St. John's Church, & has excellent fell views. It is just a short walk to the market square & Lake Derwentwater. There are 8 delightful en-suite rooms, each with T.V., hot drinks tray & a folder of suggested walks & tours. Private parking. An excellent base for a relaxing break. Children over 10. E-mail: greystones@keslakes.freeserve.co.uk	£23.00 to £26.00 (non-smoking) *see PHOTO over* *p. 102* VISA: M'CARD:	Y	N	N
Chris & Caroline Briggs **Scales Farm Country** **Guest House** **Threlkeld** **Keswick** **CA12 4SY** **Tel: (017687) 79660** **Fax 017687 79660** **Open: ALL YEAR** **Map Ref No. 26**	Nearest Road: A.66 Stunning open views & a warm friendly welcome await you at Scales Farm, a traditional 17th-century fells farmhouse sensitively modernised to provide accommodation of the highest standard. All of the bedrooms are en-suite, centrally heated, with tea/coffee facilities, colour T.V. & fridges. Separate entrance from private car park allows guests access to rooms & the traditional lounge. A Lakeland Inn/Restaurant next door. A lovely base for touring or walking. E-mail: scales@scalesfarm.com	£24.00 to £29.00 (non-smoking) VISA: M'CARD:	Y	N	Y
Mr & Mrs Alan Lowe **Dale Head Hall Lakeside** **Hotel** **Lake Thirlmere** **Keswick** **CA12 4TN** **Tel: (017687) 72478** **Fax 017687 71070** **Open: ALL YEAR** **Map Ref No. 27**	Nearest Road: A.591 Lose yourself in the ancient woodlands & mature gardens of an Elizabethan country manor, set serenely on the shores of Lake Thirlmere. Delicious dinners prepared by mother & daughter, using fresh produce from the Victorian kitchen garden, served with fine wines in the oak-beamed dining room. 9 individually decorated bedrooms, some with 4-posters, each with bath/shower rooms. Together with the lounge & bar, there are unspoilt views across lawns, lakes & fells. E-mail: holiday@dale-head-hall.co.uk	£32.50 to £47.50 *see PHOTO over* *p. 103* VISA: M'CARD: AMEX:	Y	Y	N
A. Russ **Ravensworth Hotel** **29 Station Street** **Keswick** **CA12 5HH** **Tel: (017687) 72476** **Fax 017687 75287** **Open: ALL YEAR** **Map Ref No. 28**	Nearest Road: A.591 Ravensworth Hotel is ideally situated near the town centre & all its amenities. The lake & lower fells are just a short walk away. All rooms are tastefully furnished & all are en-suite with colour T.V. & beverage tray. Starting with a wholesome breakfast you may enjoy the lakes by day & then relax in the lounge or enjoy a drink in the Herdwick Bar. (Dinner by arrangement.) Personally run by proprietors Tony & Tina, the Ravensworth is a charming small hotel. Children over 6. E-mail: RAVENSWORTH@btinternet.com	£21.00 to £26.00 (non-smoking) VISA: M'CARD:	Y	N	N

Greystones. Keswick.

Dale Head Hall. Lake Thirlmere

The Grange Country House Hotel. Manor Brow.

		rate £ from - to per person	children taken	evening meals	animals taken
Roger & Irene Coy **Lairbeck Hotel** **Vicarage Hill** **Keswick** **CA12 5QB** **Tel: (017687) 73373** **Fax 017687 73144** **Open: MAR - NOV (& Xmas)** **Map Ref No. 28**	Nearest Road: A.66 On the outskirts of Keswick, yet less than 10 mins' walk from the centre, Lairbeck is a delightful, family-run hotel built in 1875 of Lakeland stone, within a secluded garden setting. All 14 bedrooms are en-suite, non-smoking, each with its own individual character. The atmosphere is welcoming & informal. Featured on a national T.V. programme, Lairbeck offers excellent home-cooking. Log fires, spacious car parking. Children over 5 welcome. **E-mail: rogerc@lairbeck.demon.co.uk**	£29.00 to £37.00 *see PHOTO over* *p. 107* VISA: M'CARD:	Y	Y	N
Duncan & Jane Miller **Grange Country House** **Manor Brow** **Keswick-on-Derwentwater** **CA12 4BA** **Tel: 017687 72500** **Open: FEB - NOV** **Map Ref No. 29**	Nearest Road: A.66 Grange Country House is situated in its own grounds, with excellent parking, overlooking Keswick-on-Derwentwater & the surrounding mountains. Lovely bedrooms with those extra touches together with comfort, care, quality furnishings & relaxed hospitality make this award-winning home a perfect holiday base. The exceptional breakfast menu will give you an ideal start to your day in Lakeland. Somewhere special for lovers of the countryside. Children over 7.	£30.00 to £39.00 *see PHOTO over* *p. 104* VISA: M'CARD:	Y	Y	N
Ian Bryant **Hipping Hall** **Cowan Bridge** **Kirkby Lonsdale** **LA6 2JJ** **Tel: (015242) 71187** **Fax 015242 72452** **Open: MAR - NOV** **Map Ref No. 30**	Nearest Road: A.65 Hipping Hall is a 17th-century country house set in 3 acres of walled gardens on the edge of the Yorkshire Dales National Park, 2 miles from pretty Kirkby Lonsdale & only 30 mins' from Windermere. The 5 bedrooms (all en-suite & for non-smokers) & 2 apartments are attractively furnished & fully equipped. Guests dine in the beautiful Great Hall with a Minstrel's Gallery. All dishes are freshly prepared by from home & local produce. Children over 12. Reduced half-board rates for 3 nights. **E-mail: hippinghal@aol.com**	£44.00 to £53.00 *see PHOTO over* *p. 106* VISA: M'CARD:	Y	Y	Y
Roger & Helen Humphreys **The Old Vicarage** **Church Lane** **Lorton** **CA13 9UN** **Tel: (01900) 85656** **Fax 01900 85656** **Open: FEB - DEC** **Map Ref No. 31**	Nearest Road: A.66 The Old Vicarage is a small, family-run, licensed country guest house in an unspoilt part of the National Park. An elegant property which has stunning views, wooded grounds, log fires & historic charm. Accommodation is in 6 attractive en-suite bedrooms including 4-poster & family suite, each with T.V. & tea/coffee-making facilities. Excellent 4-course dinner & good wine list. Local pub 5 mins' walk. **E-mail: oldvicarage@compuserve.com**	£24.00 to £30.00 *see PHOTO over* *p. 108* VISA: M'CARD:	Y	Y	N
Ros Sanders **Hornby Hall Country** **Guest House** **Brougham** **Penrith CA10 2AR** **Tel: (01768) 891114** **Fax 01768 891114** **Open: ALL YEAR** **Map Ref No. 32**	Nearest Road: A.66 Hornby Hall is a 16th-century farmhouse situated in quiet countryside near the River Eamont. There are 7 tastefully furnished & comfortable guest rooms, with beverage facilities. 2 are en-suite. Dinner is served in the original sandstone-floored dining hall. Advance bookings are essential, as only the freshest local ingredients are used. Special diets catered for. Licensed. An ideal base for touring the Lake District, Dales, North Pennines & Hadrian's Wall. Animals by arrangement.	£25.00 to £35.00 VISA: M'CARD:	Y	Y	Y

Hipping Hall. Kirkby Lonsdale

Lairbeck Hotel. Keswick.

The Old Vicarage. Lorton.

Cumbria

		rate £ from - to per person	children taken	evening meals	animals taken
Lesley White **Beckfoot** **Helton** **Penrith** **CA10 2QB** **Tel: (01931) 713241** Fax 01931 713391 **Open: MAR - NOV** **Map Ref No. 33**	Nearest Road: A.66 A fine old residence featuring a half-panelled hall, staircase & attractive panelled dining room. Set in 3 acres of grounds in the delightful Lake District, it is a quiet, peaceful retreat for a holiday base, & is within easy reach of the many pleasure spots in the area. Offering 6 rooms, all with private shower/bathroom & tea/coffee-making facilities. A dining room, drawing & reading room. This is a delightful base for a touring holiday. **E-mail: beckfoot@aol.com**	£26.00 to £32.00 VISA: M'CARD: AMEX:	Y	Y	Y
Mrs C. A. Weightman **Near Howe** **Mungrisdale** **Penrith** **CA11 0SH** **Tel: (017687) 79678** Fax 017687 79678 **Open: MAR - NOV** **Map Ref No. 34**	Nearest Road: A.66 A comfortable traditional Cumbrian family house, where guests receive a warm, friendly welcome. Standing in 300 acres of rolling moorland, it offers a choice of 5 nice bedrooms (all with en-suite facilities), a colour-T.V. lounge, a games room & a smaller lounge with a well-stocked bar with log fire. In the pleasant, homely dining room, freshly prepared meals are served, using local produce when possible. Close by are golf, fishing, pony trekking, boating & walking.	£22.00 to £22.00	Y	Y	Y
Mrs Marjorie Whittam **Netherdene Guest House** **Troutbeck** **Penrith** **CA11 0SJ** **Tel: (017684) 83475** Fax 017684 83475 **Open: ALL YEAR (Excl.** **Xmas & New Year)** **Map Ref No. 35**	Nearest Road: A.66 A traditional Lakeland house set in its own quiet grounds, with extensive mountain views. Offering a warm welcome & personal attention. Accommodation is in 5 attractively furnished bedrooms, all en-suite, each with central heating, colour T.V. & tea/coffee-making facilities. A cosy lounge with log fire & T.V. is available throughout the day, & a dining room with excellent home cooking. Private parking. An ideal location from which to explore the Lake District. Traditional inns/restaurants close-by. Children over 10 yrs.	£18.50 to £24.00	Y	N	N
Peter Sowerby **& Eileen Reid** **Brandelhow Guest House** **1 Portland Place** **Penrith** **CA11 7QN** **Tel: (01768) 864470** **Open: ALL YEAR** **Map Ref No. 36**	Nearest Road: A.66, M.6 Brandelhow is a very pleasant Victorian house situated in the lovely market town of Penrith. Accommodation is in 5 tastefully decorated & furnished, bright & comfortable rooms, all with modern amenities, central heating, colour T.V. & tea/coffee-making facilities. Penrith is an ideal base for touring the beautiful Lake District & enjoying the usual outdoor sporting activities. A warm & friendly welcome is assured.	£16.50 to £20.00	Y	N	Y
Alan & Chris Clowes **The Cross Keys** **Temperance Inn** **Cautley** **Sedbergh LA10 5NE** **Tel: (015396) 20284** Fax 015396 21966 **Open: ALL YEAR** **Map Ref No. 37**	Nearest Road: A.683 For those looking for an inn full of character situated in one of the most magnificent of Dales settings the Cross Keys offers excellent food & accommodation. The restaurant provides wonderful home-produced food with a wide choice to suit all tastes, and although a Temperance Inn guests are invited to bring along the drink of their choice. The bedrooms, recently totally refurbished, offer full en-suite facilities. VISA: M'CARD:	£29.50 to £34.50	Y	Y	N

Beaumont Hotel. Windermere.

Cumbria

		rate £ from - to per person	children taken	evening meals	animals taken
Vanessa Price **The Archway** **13 College Road** **Windermere** **LA23 1BU** **Tel: (015394) 45613** **Fax 015394 45328** **Open: ALL YEAR** **Map Ref No. 38**	Nearest Road: A.591 An impeccable Victorian home, beautifully furnished throughout with antiques, pictures & fresh flowers, where good food & comfort of guests is the priority. 4 bedrooms, all en-suite, with colour T.V., & beverage tray. A breakfast well worth getting up for includes homemade granola & yoghurt, a selection of dried & fresh fruits, followed by a choice of cooked breakfast, the decision is hard. Superb mountain views, easy access to the lakes & surrounding places of interest. **E-mail: Archway@BTinternet.com**	£22.00 to £30.00 VISA: M'CARD:	N	N	N
Brian & Frances Holcroft **Lynwood Guest House** **Broad Street** **Windermere** **LA23 2AB** **Tel: (015394) 42550** **Fax 015394 42550** **Open: ALL YEAR** **Map Ref No. 38**	Nearest Road: A.591 A Victorian Lakeland stone house built in 1865, offering 9 centrally heated bedrooms, each with en-suite bathrooms, all with modern amenities including colour T.V. & tea/coffee-making facilities. Guests may relax in the T.V. lounge available throughout the day. Centrally located, only 150 yards from village shops & restaurants, & only 5 mins from the bus & railway station. The host is a Lakeland tour guide, & is happy to assist in planning your stay. Children over 5 years.	£15.00 to £24.00	Y	N	N
James & Barbara Casey **The Beaumont** **Holly Road** **Windermere** **LA23 2AF** **Tel: (015394) 47075** **Fax 015394 47075** **Open: JAN - NOV** **Map Ref No. 38**	Nearest Road: A.591 This elegant Victorian house hotel combines all the grace & charm of its time with all the comforts of today. Ideal for Windermere & Bowness, & perfect for touring the lakes. 9 attractive en-suite bedrooms with tea facilities, T.V. & hairdryers. 2 4-poster bedrooms for that special occasion, & a 'Romantic Presentation' of wine, chocolates, fruit & flowers may be ordered. The standards are high, breakfasts are hearty & the hospitality is warm & sincere. Parking. Children over 10. **E-mail: thebeaumonthotel@btinternet.com**	£28.00 to £45.00 *see PHOTO over* *p. 110* VISA: M'CARD:	Y	N	N
Mr Geoffrey Todd **Fir Trees Guest House** **Lake Road** **Windermere** **LA23 2EQ** **Tel: (015394) 42272** **Fax 015394 42272** **Open: ALL YEAR** **Map Ref No. 38**	Nearest Road: A.590 Situated mid-way between Windermere village & the lake & built in the traditional Lakeland style, Fir Trees offers delightful accommodation of exceptional quality & charm. The dining room has been extensively refurbished & similarly, the 8 en-suite bedrooms are now beautifully appointed to offer T.V., clock/radio, tea/coffee facilities, hairdryers & bath robes. A full English breakfast is served using the best of local produce. (Vegetarians catered for.) Parking. Guest e-mailing facilities. **E-mail: firtreeshotel@msn.com**	£22.00 to £32.00 *see PHOTO over* *p. 112* VISA: M'CARD: AMEX:	Y	N	N

Visit our website at:
http://www.bestbandb.co.uk

Fir Trees. Windermere.

Hawksmoor Guest House.   Windermere.

Cumbria

		rate £ from - to per person	children taken	evening meals	animals taken
Barbara & Bob Tyson **Hawksmoor Guest House** **Lake Road** **Windermere** **LA23 2EQ** **Tel: (015394) 42110** **Fax 015394 42110** **Open: FEB - NOV** **Map Ref No. 38**	Nearest Road: A.591 Hawksmoor is situated halfway between the centres of Windermere & Bowness, just 10 mins' walk from the lake. Standing in lovely grounds, this creeper-clad house has 10 charming rooms, all en-suite & with garden views; some also with 4-poster beds, & some strictly no smoking. A residents' lounge with T.V., & a garden for guests' enjoyment. Licensed. Boating, golf, tennis, swimming, fishing & pony trekking nearby. Phone for availability before booking. Children over 6. **E-mail: tyson@hawksmoor.net1.co.uk**	£25.00 to £32.00 *see PHOTO over* *p. 113* VISA: M'CARD:	Y	Y	N
Steve Thomas **& Helen Sowerby** **Rosemount** **Lake Road** **Windermere LA23 2EQ** **Tel: (015394) 43739** **Fax 015394 48978** **Open: ALL YEAR** **Map Ref No. 38**	Nearest Road: A.591 Rosemount is an attractive Victorian house halfway between Windermere & the lake. Accommodation is in 17 comfortable & attractively furnished bedrooms (including 3 singles & 3 spacious family rooms), each with an en-suite or private bathroom, colour T.V. & tea/coffee-making facilities. An excellent breakfast is served. Rosemount is the perfect base for a relaxing break & affords first-class accommodation. **E-mail: ROSEMT3739@AOL.COM**	£20.00 to £28.00 VISA: M'CARD: AMEX:	Y	N	N
Iain & Jackie Garside **Fayrer Garden House Hotel** **Lyth Valley Road** **Bowness-on-Windermere** **Windermere** **LA23 3JP** **Tel: (015394) 88195** **Fax 015394 45986** **Open: ALL YEAR** **Map Ref No. 38**	Nearest Road: A.5074 Beautiful country house hotel, in 5 acres of grounds overlooking Lake Windermere. Award-winning cuisine served in the air-conditioned conservatory restaurant. All of the delightful bedrooms are en-suite with colour T.V., hairdryers etc. Some have 4-poster beds, whirlpool baths & lake views at a supplement. Special breaks, interest weekends & free use of local leisure centre. An ideal spot for a relaxing break. Colour brochure available on request. **E-mail: lakescene@fayrergarden.com**	£32.50 to £65.00 *see PHOTO over* *p. 115* VISA: M'CARD: AMEX:	Y	Y	N
Brenda Butterworth **Orrest Head House** **Kendal Road** **Windermere LA23 IJG** **Tel: (015394) 44315** **Fax 015394 44315** **Open: FEB - DEC** **Map Ref No. 38**	Nearest Road: A.591 Orrest Head House, Windermere, is a charming country house dating back to the 16th century. All of the comfortable bedrooms are en-suite & have colour T.V. & tea/coffee-making facilities. A delicious breakfast is served. The house is is set in 3 acres of garden & woodland & has distant views to mountains & lakes. Close to the station & village with a very homely atmosphere. Children over 6 years welcome.	£22.50 to £25.00 *see PHOTO over* *p. 116*	Y	N	N

When booking your accommodation please mention
The Best Bed & Breakfast

Fayrer Garden House. Bowness-on-Windermere.

Orrest Head House. Windermere.

**All the establishments mentioned in this guide
are members of the
Worldwide Bed & Breakfast Association.**

**If you have any comments regarding your
accommodation please send them to us
using the form at the back of the book.
We value your comments.**

Derbyshire & Staffordshire

Derbyshire
(East Midlands)

A county with everything but the sea, this was Lord Byron's opinion of Derbyshire, & the special beauty of the Peak District was recognised by its designation as Britain's first National Park.

Purple heather moors surround craggy limestone outcrops & green hills drop to sheltered meadows or to deep gorges & tumbling rivers.

Derbyshire's lovely dales have delightful names too - Dove Dale, Monk's Dale, Raven's Dale, Water-cum-Jolly-Dale, & they are perfect for walking. The more adventurous can take up the challenge of the Pennine Way, a 270 mile pathway from Edale to the Scottish border.

The grit rock faces offer good climbing, particularly at High Tor above the River Derwent, & underground there are extensive & spectacular caverns. There are show caves at the Heights of Abraham, which you reach by cable-car, & at Castleton, source of the rare Blue John mineral, & at Pole's Cavern in Buxton where there are remarkable stalactites & stalagmites.

Buxton's splendid Crescent reflects the town's spa heritage, & the Opera House is host to an International Festival each summer.

The waters at Matlock too were prized for their curative properties & a great Hydro was built there in the last century, to give treatment to the hundreds of people who came to "take the waters".

Bakewell is a lovely small town with a fascinating market, some fine buildings & the genuine Bakewell Pudding, (known elsewhere as Bakewell tart).

Well-dressing is a custom carried on throughout the summer in the villages & towns. It is a thanksgiving for the water, that predates the arrival of Christianity in Britain. Flower-petals, leaves, moss & bark are pressed in

Haddon Hall; Derby.

Derbyshire & Staffordshire

intricate designs into frames of wet clay & erected over the wells, where they stay damp & fresh for days.

The mining of lead & the prosperity of the farms brought great wealth to the landowning families who were able to employ the finest of architects & craftsmen to design & build their great houses. Haddon Hall is a perfectly preserved 12th century manor house with with terraced gardens of roses & old-fashioned flowers. 17th century Chatsworth, the "Palace of the Peak", houses a splendid collection of paintings, drawings, furniture & books, & stands in gardens with elaborate fountains.

Staffordshire
(Heart of England)

Staffordshire is a contrast of town & county. Miles of moorland & dramatic landscapes lie to the north of the country, & to the south is the Vale of Trent & the greenery of Cannock Chase. But the name of Staffordshire invokes that of the Potteries, the area around Stoke-on-Trent where the world-renowned ceramics are made.

The factories that produce the Royal Doulton, Minton, Spode & Coalport china will arrange tours for visitors, & there is a purpose-built visitor centre at Barlaston displaying the famous Wedgwood tradition.

The Gladstone Pottery Museum is set in a huge Victorian potbank, & the award-winning City museum in Stoke-on-Trent has a remarkable ceramics collection.

There is lovely scenery to be found where the moorlands of Staffordshire meet the crags & valleys of the Peak District National Park. From the wild & windy valleys of The Roaches (from the French 'roche') you can look across the county to Cheshire & Wales. Drivers can take high moorland roads that are marked out as scenic routes.

The valleys of the Dove & Manifold are beautiful limestone dales & ideal for walking or for cycling. Sir Izzak Walton, author of 'The Compleat Angler', drew his inspiration, & his trout, from the waters here.

The valley of the River Churnet is both pretty & peaceful, being largely inaccessible to cars. The Caldon Canal, with its colourful narrowboats, follows the course of the river & there are canalside pubs, picnic areas, boat rides & woodland trails to enjoy. The river runs through the grounds of mock-Gothic Alton Towers, now a leisure park.

The Vale of Trent is largely rural with small market towns, villages, river & canals.

Cannock Chase covers 20 square miles of heath & woodland & is the home of the largest herd of fallow deer in England. Shugborough Hall stands in the Chase. The ancestral home of Lord Lichfeld, it also houses the Staffordshire County Museum & a farm for rare breeds including the famous Tamworth Pig.

Burton-on-Trent is known as the home of the British brewery industry & there are two museums in the town devoted to the history of beer.

Lichfield is a small & picturesque city with a cathedral which dates from the 12th century & has three graceful spires known as the 'Ladies of the Vale'. Dr. Samuel Johnson was born in the city & his house is now a museum dedicated to his life & work.

One of the Vale's villages retains its mediaeval tradition by performing the Abbot's Bromley Horn Dance every September.

Derbyshire & Staffordshire

Derbyshire

Gazeteer

Areas of outstanding natural beauty.
Peak National Park. The Dales.

Houses & Castles

Chatsworth - Bakewell
17th century, built for 1st. Duke of Devonshire. Furniture, paintings & drawings, books, etc. Fine gardens & parklands.
Haddon Hall - Bakewell
Mediaeval manor house - complete. Terraced rose gardens.
Hardwick Hall - Nr. Chesterfield
16th century - said to be more glass than wall. Fine furniture, tapestries & furnishings. Herb garden.
Kedlestone Hall - Derby
18th century - built on site of 12th century Manor house. Work of Robert Adam - has world famous marble hall. Old Master paintings. 11th century church nearby.
Melbourne Hall - Nr. Derby
12th century origins - restored by Sir John Coke. Fine collection of pictures & works of art. Magnificent gardens & famous wrought iron pagoda
Sudbury Hall - Sudbury
Has examples of work of the greatest craftsmen of the period-Grinling Gibbons,Pierce and Laguerre.
Winster Market House Nr. Matlock
17th century stone built market house.

Cathedrals & Churches

Chesterfield (St. Mary & All Saints)
13th & 14th centuries.
4 chapels, polygonal apse, mediaeval screens, Jacobean pulpit.
Derby (All Saints)
Perpendicular tower - classical style - 17th century plate, 18th century screen.
Melbourne (St. Michael & St. Mary)
Norman with two west towers & crossing tower.
Splendid plate, 18th century screen.
Normbury (St. Mary & St. Barloke)
14th century - perpendicular tower.
Wood carving & brasses.
Wirksworth (St. Mary)
13th century, restored & enlarged.

Staffordshire

Gazeteer

Houses & Castles

Ancient High House - Stafford
16th century - largest timber-framed town house in England.
Shugborough - Nr. Stafford
Ancestral home of the Earl of Lichfield. Mansion house, paintings, silver, ceramics, furniture. County Museum. Rare Breeds Farm.
Moseley Old Hall - Nr. Wolverhampton
Elizabethan house formerly half-timbered.
Stafford Castle
Large & well-preserved Norman castle in grounds with castle trail.
Tamworth Castle
Norman motte & bailey castle with later additions. Museum.

Cathedrals & Churches

Croxden Abbey
12th century foundation Cistercian abbey. Ruins of 13th century church.
Ingestre (St. Mary the Virgin)
A rare Wren church built in1676.
Lichfield Cathedral
Unique triple-spired 12th century cathedral.
Tamworth (St. Editha's)
Founded 963, rebuilt 14th century. Unusual double spiral staircase.
Tutbury (St. Mary's)
Norman church with impressive West front.

Museums & Galleries

City Museum & Art Gallery - Stoke-on-Trent
Modern award-winning museum. Ceramics, decorative arts, etc.
Dr. Johnson Birthplace Museum - Lichfield
Gladstone Pottery Museum - Longton
Izaak Walton Cottage & Museum - Shallowfield, Nr. Stafford
National Brewery Museum & the Bass Museum of Brewing-both in Stoke-on-Trent
Stafford Art Gallery & Craft Shop - Stafford
Major gallery for the visual arts & centre for quality craftsmanship.

DERBYSHIRE & STAFFORDSHIRE

Map reference

02 Chambers		13 Rowlands	
03 Moore		14 Heelis	
04 Tunnicliffe		15 Wilkins	
05 Slack		17 Winterton	
06 Moffett		17 Sutcliffe	
08 Lewis		19 Egerton-Orme	
10 Bailey		19 Ball	
11 Stewart		20 Grey	
12 Singleton		20 White	

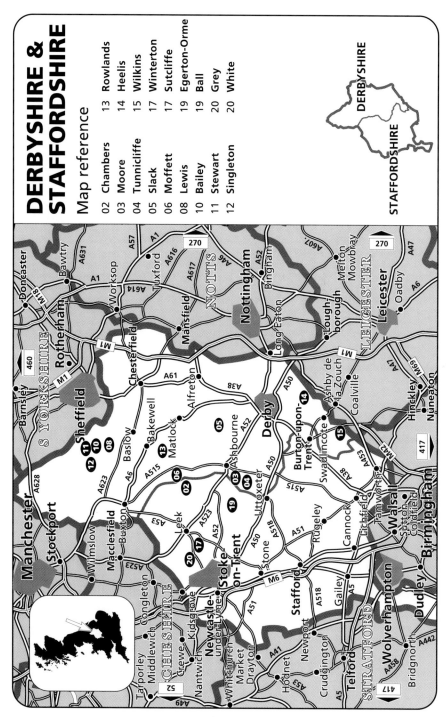

Beeches Farmhouse. Waldley.

Derbyshire

		rate £ from - to per person	children taken	evening meals	animals taken
Naomi Chambers & Nick Lourie Stanshope Hall Stanshope Ashbourne DE6 2AD Tel: (01335) 310278 Fax 01335 310470 Open: ALL YEAR Map Ref No. 02	Nearest Road: A.515 Stanshope Hall, with its informal feel but with every comfort, stands in splendid isolation among the dry stone walls of the southern Peak District. Walks from the door lead to verdant Dovedale or the undiscovered seclusion of the Manifold Valley. The en-suite rooms have hand-painted walls & frescos in the bathrooms. Candle-lit dinners are prepared using uncomplicated but imaginative recipes with local & garden produce. E-mail: naomi@stanshope.demon.co.uk	£25.00 to £40.00 *VISA: M'CARD:*	Y	Y	N
Mrs Cynthia Moore Rose Cottage Snelston Ashbourne DE6 2DL Tel: (01335) 324230 Fax 01335 324651 Open: ALL YEAR Map Ref No. 03	Nearest Road: A.515 A mid-Victorian house in 6 acres, Rose Cottage is a family home in quiet, unspoilt, beautiful & peaceful countryside. Bedrooms have panoramic views over Dove Valley towards Weaver Hills (George Eliot's 'Adam Bede' country). Ideal for visiting Dales, walking, country houses (Chatsworth, Haddon Hall etc.), potteries & Alton Towers (9 miles). Comfortable double rooms, private bathrooms, 1 en-suite, T.V., tea-making facilities in rooms. Children over 12.	£23.00 to £30.00	Y	N	N
Barbara Tunnicliffe Beeches Farmhouse Waldley, Doveridge Ashbourne DE6 5LR Tel: (01889) 590288 Fax 01889 590559 Open: ALL YEAR Map Ref No. 04	Nearest Road: A.50 Relax & unwind in this rural farm retreat after exploring the Derbyshire Dales or the thrills of Alton Towers. Dine in the award-winning 18th-century licensed farmhouse restaurant on fresh English food & home-made desserts. Guests are invited to meet the Shetland pony, pigs, dogs, rabbits & kittens, whilst enjoying the freedom of the gardens, fields & the beautiful countryside. E-mail: BEECHESFA@AOL.COM	£31.00 to £48.00 *see PHOTO over p. 122* *VISA: M'CARD: AMEX:*	Y	Y	N
Joan & Martin Slack Dannah Farm Country House, Dannah Farm Bowmans Lane, Shottle Belper DE56 2DR Tel: (01773) 550273 Fax 01773 550590 Open: ALL YEAR (Excl. Xmas) Map Ref No. 05	Nearest Road: A.517 Superb Georgian farmhouse set on the Chatsworth Estates at Shottle, beautifully furnished with antiques & old pine. En-suite bedrooms, some with private sitting rooms & 4-poster beds, open fires, whirlpool baths & wonderful views. Award-winning, oak-beamed, licensed dining room where guests can enjoy fresh food imaginatively cooked, homemade bread & breakfasts that will 'set you up for the day'. A perfect escape. E-mail: slack@dannah.demon.co.uk	£35.00 to £55.00 *see PHOTO over p. 124* *VISA: M'CARD:*	Y	Y	N
David & Meirlys Lewis Delf View House Church Street Eyam S32 5QH Tel: (01433) 631533 Fax 01433 631972 Open: ALL YEAR Map Ref No. 08	Nearest Road: A.623 Beautiful & tranquil accommodation in an elegant listed Georgian country house in historic Eyam village in the magnificent Peak National Park. Guests are warmly welcomed in the drawing room, delightfully furnished with antiques, pictures & books. 3 superb bedrooms, 1 en-suite, include a Sheraton 4-poster & 18th-century French twin beds. Sumptuous breakfasts served in the oak-beamed dining room. Restaurants nearby, 1 within 3 mins' walk. Ideal for visiting Chatsworth, Haddon & Eyam Hall. E-mail: lewis@delfview.demon.co.uk	£25.00 to £32.00	N	N	N

Dannah Farm Country House. Shottle.

Biggin Hall. Biggin by Hartington.

Derbyshire

		rate £ from - to per person	evening meals children taken	animals taken

			rate £ from - to per person	children taken	evening meals	animals taken
James Moffett **Biggin Hall** **Biggin-by-Hartington** **Buxton** **SK17 0DH** **Tel: (01298) 84451** Fax 01298 84681 **Open: ALL YEAR** **Map Ref No. 06**	Nearest Road: A.515 A delightful 17th-century stone house, completely restored & keeping all the character of its origins, with massive oak beams. 17 comfortable rooms, all charmingly furnished, 1 with a 4-poster bed, all with en-suite facilities & modern amenities. Guests have the choice of 2 sitting rooms, 1 with a log fire, 1 with colour T.V. & library, & there is a lovely garden. The house is beautifully furnished, with many antiques. Non-smoking areas. Children over 12. Animals by arrangement. **E-mail: bigginhall@compuserve.com**	£25.00 to £45.00 *see PHOTO over* *p. 125* VISA: M'CARD:	Y	Y	Y
Mary Bailey **Carr Head Farm** **Church Bank** **Hathersage** **Hope Valley S32 1BR** **Tel: (01433) 650383** Fax 01433 651441 **Open: ALL YEAR** **Map Ref No. 10**	Nearest Road: A.625 In a most peaceful setting high on the hillside above the village of Hathersage, an unusual farmhouse c.1650, full of character & charm. Surrounded by beautiful mature gardens, all rooms have magnificent unspoilt views. 2 spacious & superbly furnished en-suite bedrooms, 1 with 4-poster. Oak-beamed dining room & an elegant drawing room. Decorated throughout in period style. The village offers a wide choice of eating places & has Charlotte Bronte connections.	£27.50 to £45.00	N	N	N
Kath & Ray Stewart **The Old Barn** **Booths Farm** **Booths Edge, Hathersage** **Hope Valley** **S32 1DA** **Tel: (01433) 650667** Fax 01433 650667 **Open: MAR - OCT** **Map Ref No. 11**	Nearest Road: A.6187 The Old Barn, believed to be of 16th-century origin, has been sympathetically restored to retain much of its original character, including exposed beams & flagstone floors. 3 beautifully furnished en-suite bedrooms, 1 with 4-poster. All have T.V. & tea/coffee facilities. Also, a residents lounge which is both comfortable & homely. One of the main features of this house is the splendid view across Hope Valley towards the Pennines. Exactly 1 mile from Hathersage & easy access to Bakewell, the Chatsworth Estate & Sheffield.	£22.50 to £32.50 VISA: M'CARD:	N	N	N
Mrs B. Singleton **Underleigh House** **Edale Road** **Hope** **Hope Valley S33 6RF** **Tel: (01433) 621372** Fax 01433 621324 **Open: ALL YEAR** **Map Ref No. 12**	Nearest Road: A.6187 A 19th-century farmhouse-style home in a superb, secluded hillside position, with beautiful countryside views, in the heart of the National Park. Each of the 6 en-suite rooms is furnished to a high standard, with many extras, & each has a resident teddy bear! Renowned for hearty breakfasts & gourmet house-party dinners prepared by the owner/chef. Ideally situated for walking or exploring the area by car. Children over 12. **E-mail: Underleigh.House@btinternet.com**	£33.00 to £50.00 *see PHOTO over* *p. 127* VISA: M'CARD:	N	Y	N

When booking your accommodation please mention
The Best Bed & Breakfast

Underleigh House. Hope.

Derbyshire & Staffordshire

		rate £ from - to per person	children taken	evening meals	animals taken
Elizabeth & Jonathan Rowlands Uppertown Farmhouse Uppertown Lane Birchover Matlock DE4 2BH Tel: (01629) 650112 Fax 01629 650112 Open: MAR - DEC Map Ref No. 13	Nearest Road: A.6 Uppertown Farmhouse, formerly a 17th-century coaching inn, is a Grade II listed farmhouse complete with its own walled courtyard & village stocks. Standing in the heart of Derbyshire's National Peak Park it commands a panoramic view over the Dales. It is furnished with antiques & retains many original features. All bedrooms are en-suite with modern day comforts. Good pubs, restaurants & antique shops abound in the area together with many historic houses & castles, including Chatsworth House & Haddon Hall. E-mail: jonliz@hudrow.enterprise-plc.com	£30.00 to £40.00 VISA: M'CARD:	N	N	N
Robert & Patricia Heelis Shaw House Robinsons Hill Melbourne DE73 1DJ Tel: (01332) 863827 Fax 01332 863827 Open: ALL YEAR (Excl. Xmas) Map Ref No. 14	Nearest Road: A.514 An elegant 18th-century listed house with Victorian conservatory set on the edge of the historic village of Melbourne. 3 spacious & elegantly appointed bedrooms each with en-suite bath/shower room, T.V. & tea/coffee. A delicious breakfast is served in the antique furnished dining room. Le Patron's vintage cars give added interest. Easy access from M.1 (Jt.23) & M./A.42. (Jt.13). Conveniently placed for visiting Calke Abbey, Staunton Harold, East Midlands Airport & Donington Park, all within 3 miles. Single supplement. Children over 12.	£27.50 to £35.00	Y	N	Y
Mrs Clemency Wilkins The Old Hall Netherseal Swadlincote DE12 8DF Tel: (01283) 760258 Fax 01283 762991 Open: ALL YEAR (Excl. Xmas & New Year) Map Ref No. 15	Nearest Road: A.444, A.42 A particularly peaceful Grade II listed manor house situated in 18 acres of mature gardens & woodland, overlooking a lake. The house, dating from 1644, incorporates part of a medieval monastery & despite all modern conveniences retains its unique character, original features & panelling. 3 comfortable, spacious, attractively furnished bedrooms with en-suite/private bathrooms, colour T.V. & tea/coffee. Traditional English food is served by arrangement. Convenient for Lichfield, Shugborough, Calke Abbey, Kedleston, Castle Donington & the N.E.C..	£27.50 to £35.00	N	Y	N

Staffordshire

		rate £ from - to per person	children taken	evening meals	animals taken
Mrs Elizabeth Winterton Brook House Farm Brook House Lane Cheddleton Leek ST13 7DF Tel: (01538) 360296 Open: ALL YEAR Map Ref No. 17	Nearest Road: A.520 Brook House is a dairy farm in a picturesque valley 1/2 a mile from the A.520, down a private lane. Many pleasant walks locally; convenient for the Peak District, pottery museums and Alton Towers. Comfortable rooms in the farmhouse, and 2 spacious family rooms with patio doors in a tastefully converted annex. All en-suite & centrally heated, with tea/coffee facilities. Good farmhouse breakfast served in a conservatory with magnificent views. A warm welcome assured.	£18.00 to £20.00	Y	N	N

Staffordshire

		rate £ from - to per person	children taken	evening meals	animals taken
William & Elaine Sutcliffe **Choir Cottage** **& Choir House** **Ostlers Lane, Cheddleton** **Leek ST13 7HS** **Tel: (01538) 360561** **Open: ALL YEAR** **Map Ref No. 17**	Nearest Road: A.520 This 17th-century stone cottage, once a resting place for ostlers, now provides beautifully appointed bedrooms, with full en-suite facilities, central heating, colour T.V., tea/coffee tray & 'phone. The Pine Room & Rose Room have 4-poster beds, & 1 is suitable as a family suite. Quiet location convenient for the Peak District, potteries & Alton Towers. Excellent food & careful attention to detail assured. Children over 5 years.	£25.00 to £28.00	Y	N	N
Mrs Muriel Egerton-Orme **Bank House** **Farley Lane** **Oakamoor** **Stoke-on-Trent** **ST10 3BD** **Tel: (01538) 702810** **Fax 01538 702810** **Open: ALL YEAR (Excl. Xmas)** **Map Ref No. 19**	Nearest Road: A.522, A.524 A handsome house, overlooking the picturesque Churnet Valley. This elegantly furnished home provides superb en-suite/private accommodation. All rooms are well-equipped. The aim at Bank House is to create a relaxed & friendly 'house party' ambience for guests, & the facilities are all that one might expect from a friend's country house that has all the comforts of a quality hotel. Excellent 4-course evening meals served on request. Wonderful centre for touring this region. Animals by arrangement. Single supplement. **E-mail: john.orme@dial.pipex.com**	£28.00 to £37.50 VISA: M'CARD:	Y	Y	Y
Mrs I. H. Grey **The Old Vicarage** **The Close** **Endon** **Stoke-on-Trent** **ST9 9JH** **Tel: (01782) 503686** **Open: ALL YEAR** **Map Ref No. 20**	Nearest Road: A.53 A friendly atmosphere is found at this delightful 85-year-old former vicarage. It is situated in a quiet spot in the village of Endon, between the Staffordshire moorlands & Stoke-on-Trent. Accommodation is in 3 rooms, all with modern amenities, T.V. & tea/coffee-making facilities. There is a separate guests' lounge. This makes a good base from which to visit the world-famous potteries, the wonderful countryside & museums.	£17.50 to £20.00	Y	N	N
Mrs Barbara White **Micklea Farm** **Micklea Lane** **Longsdon** **Stoke-on-Trent ST9 9QA** **Tel: (01538) 385006** **Fax 01538 382882** **Open: ALL YEAR** **Map Ref No. 20**	Nearest Road: A.53 Micklea Farm is an 18th-century cottage set in a lovely quiet garden. There are 2 double/twin & 2 single rooms, with cots available. There is also a charming sitting room for guests, with an open fire & colour T.V.. Evening meals are available, using home-grown garden produce & home baking. A choice of English or Continental breakfast; also, packed lunches. Conveniently situated for the potteries, Alton Towers & the Peak District.	£18.00 to £18.00	Y	Y	N
Christopher Ball **Manor House Farm** **Quixhill Lane** **Prestwood, Denstone** **Uttoxeter ST14 5DD** **Tel: (01889) 590415** **Tel: (01335) 343669** **Fax 01335 342198** **Open: ALL YEAR** **Map Ref No. 19**	Nearest Road: A.50 A beautiful Grade II listed farmhouse, set amid rolling hills & rivers. Accommodation is in 3 attractive bedrooms, all with 4-poster beds & an en-suite bathroom. (1 can be used as a twin.) Tastefully furnished with antiques & retaining traditional features including an oak-panelled breakfast room. Guests may relax in the extensive gardens with grass tennis court & Victorian summer house. Ideal for visiting Alton Towers, the Peak District or the potteries.	£20.00 to £25.00 *see PHOTO over* *p. 130* VISA: M'CARD:	Y	N	N

Manor House Farm.   Prestwood.

Devon

Devon
(West Country)

Here is a county of tremendous variety. Two glorious & contrasting coastlines with miles of sandy beaches, sheltered coves & rugged cliffs. There are friendly resorts & quiet villages of cob & thatch, two historic cities, & a host of country towns & tiny hamlets as well as the wild open spaces of two national parks.

From the grandeur of Hartland Point east to Foreland Point where Exmoor reaches the sea, the north Devon coast is incomparable. At Westward Ho!, Croyde & Woolacombe the rolling surf washes the golden beaches & out to sea stands beautiful Lundy Island, ideal for bird watching, climbing & walking. The tiny village of Clovelly with its cobbled street tumbles down the cliffside to the sea. Ilfracombe is a friendly resort town & the twin towns of Lynton & Lynmouth are joined by a cliff railway.

The south coast is a colourful mixture of soaring red sandstone cliffs dropping to sheltered sandy coves & the palm trees of the English Riviera. This is one of England's great holiday coasts with a string of popular resorts; Seaton, Sidmouth, Budleigh Salterton, Exmouth, Dawlish, Teignmouth & the trio of Torquay, Paignton & Brixham that make up Torbay. To the south, beyond Berry Head are Dartmouth, rich in navy tradition, & Salcombe, a premiere sailing centre in the deep inlet of the Kingsbridge estuary. Plymouth is a happy blend of holiday resort, tourist centre, historic & modern city, & the meeting-point for the wonderful old sailing vessels for the Tall Ships Race.

Inland the magnificent wilderness of Dartmoor National Park offers miles of sweeping moorland, granite tors, clear streams & wooded valleys, ancient stone circles & clapper bridges. The tors, as the Dartmoor peaks, are called are easily climbed & the views from the tops are superb. Widecombe-in-the-Moor, with its imposing church tower, & much photographed Buckland-in-the-Moor are only two of Dartmoor's lovely villages.

The Exmoor National Park straddles the Devon/Somerset border. It is a land of wild heather moorland above deep wooded valleys & sparkling streams, the home of red deer, soaring buzzards & of legendary Lorna Doone from R.D. Blackmore's novel. The south west peninsula coastal path follows the whole of the Exmoor coastline affording dramatic scenery & spectacular views, notably from Countisbury Hill.

The seafaring traditions of Devon are well-known. Sir Walter Raleigh set sail from Plymouth to Carolina in 1584; Sir Francis Drake began his circumnavigation of the world at Plymouth in the "Golden Hind" & fought the Spanish Armada off Plymouth Sound. The Pilgrim Fathers sailed from here & it was to here that Sir Francis Chichester returned having sailed around the world in 1967.

Exeter's maritime tradition is commemorated in an excellent museum located in converted riverside warehouses but the city's chief glory is the magnificent 13th century cathedral of St. Mary & St. Peter, built in an unusual decorated Gothic style, with its west front covered in statues.

The River Dart near Dittisham.

Devon

Devon
Gazeteer

Areas of outstanding natural beauty.
North, South, East Devon.

Houses & Castles

Arlington Court - Barnstaple
Regency house, collection of shell, pewter & model ships.

Bickleigh Castle - Nr. Tiverton
Thatched Jacobean wing. Great Hall & armoury. Early Norman chapel, gardens & moat.

Buckland Abbey - Nr. Plymouth
13th century Cistercian monastery - 16th century alterations. Home of Drake - contains his relics & folk gallery.

Bradley Manor - Newton Abbot
15th century Manor house with perpendicular chapel.

Cadhay - Ottery St. Mary
16th century Elizabethan Manor house.

Castle Drogo - Nr.Chagford
Designed by Lutyens - built of granite, standing over 900 feet above the gorge of the Teign river.

Chambercombe Manor - Illfracombe
14th-15th century Manor house.

Castle Hill - Nr. Barnstaple
18th century Palladian mansion - fine furniture of period, pictures, porcelain & tapestries.

Hayes Barton - Nr. Otterton
16th century plaster & thatch house. Birthplace of Walter Raleigh.

Oldway - Paignton
19th century house having rooms designed to be replicas of rooms at the Palace of Versailles.

Powederham Castle - Nr. Exeter
14th century mediaeval castle much damaged in Civil War. Altered in 18th & 19th centuries. Fine music room by Wyatt.

Saltram House - Plymouth
Some remnants of Tudor house built into George II house, with two rooms by Robert Adam. Excellent plasterwork & woodwork.

Shute Barton - Nr. Axminster
14th century battlemented Manor house with Tudor & Elizabethan additions.

Tiverton Castle - Nr. Tiverton
Fortress of Henry I. Chapel of St. Francis. Gallery of Joan of Arc.

Torre Abbey Mansion - Torquay
Abbey ruins, tithe barn. Mansion house with paintings & furniture.

Cathedrals & Churches

Atherington (St. Mary)
Perpendicular style - mediaeval effigies & glass, original rood loft. Fine screens, 15th century bench ends.

Ashton (St. John the Baptist)
15th century - mediaeval screens, glass & wall paintings. Elizabethan pulpit with canopy, 17th century altar railing.

Bere Ferrers (St. Andrew)
14th century rebuilding - 14th century glass, 16th century benches, Norman font.

Bridford (St. Thomas a Becket)
Perpendicular style - mediaeval glass & woodwork. Excellent rood screen c.1530.

Cullompton (St. Andrew)
15th century perpendicular - Jacobean west gallery - fan tracery in roof, exterior carvings.

Exeter Cathedral
13th century decorated - Norman towers. Interior tierceron ribbed vault (Gothic) carved corbels & bosses, moulded piers & arches. Original pulpitum c.1320. Choir stalls with earliest misericords in England c.1260.

Haccombe (St. Blaize)
13th century effigies, 14th century glass, 17th century brasses, 19th century screen, pulpit & reredos.

Kentisbeare (St. Mary)
Perpendicular style - checkered tower. 16th century rood screen.

Ottery St. Mary (St. Mary)
13th century, 14th century clock, fan vaulted roof, tomb with canopy, minstrel's gallery, gilded wooded eagle. 18th century pulpit.

Parracombe (St. Petrock)
Unrestored Georgian - 16th century benches, mostly perpendicular, early English chancel.

Sutcombe (St. Andrew)
15th century - some part Norman. 16th century bench ends, restored rood screen, mediaeval glass & floor tiles.

Swimbrige (St. James)
14th century tower & spire - mediaeval stone pulpit, 15th century rood screen, font cover of Renaissance period.

Devon

Tawstock (St. Peter)
14th century, Italian plasterwork ceiling, mediaeval glass, Renaissance memorial pew, Bath monument.

Buckfast Abbey
Living Benedictine monastery, built on mediaeval foundation. Famous for works of art in church, modern stained glass, tonic wine & bee-keeping.

Museums & Galleries

Bideford Museum - Bideford
Geology, maps, prints, shipwright's tools, North Devon pottery.

Burton Art Gallery - Bideford
Hubert Coop collection of paintings etc.

Butterwalk Museum - Dartmouth
17th century row of half timbered buildings, nautical museum. 140 model ships.

Newcomen Engine House - Nr. Butterwalk Museum
Original Newcomen atmospheric/pressure steam engine c.1725.

Royal Albert Memorial Museum Art Gallery - Exeter
Collections of English watercolours, paintings, glass & ceramics, local silver, natural history & anthropology.

Rougemont House Museum - Exeter
Collections of archaeology & local history. Costume & lace collection.

Guildhall - Exeter
Mediaeval structure with Tudor frontage - City regalia & silver.

Exeter Maritime Museum - Exeter
Largest collection in the world of working boats, afloat, ashore & under cover.

The Steam & Countryside Museum - Exmouth
Very large working layout - hundreds of exhibits.
Including Victorian farmhouse - farmyard pets for children.

Shebbear - North Devon
Alcott Farm Museum with unique collections of agricultural implements & photographs, etc.

The Elizabethan House - Totnes
Period costumes & furnishings, tools, toys, domestic articles, etc.

The Elizabethan House - Plymouth
16th century house with period furnishings.

City Museum & Art Gallery - Plymouth
Collections of pictures & porcelain, English & Italian drawing. Reynolds' family portraits, early printed books, ship models.

Cookworthy Museum - Kingsbridge
Story of china clay. Local history, shipbuilding tools, rural life.

Honiton & Allhallows Public Museum - Honiton
Collection of Honiton lace, implements etc. Complete Devon Kitchen.

Lyn & Exmoor Museum - Lynton
Life & history of Exmoor.

Torquay & Natural History Society Museum - Torquay
Collection illustrating Kent's Cavern & other caves - natural history & folkculture.

Historic Monuments

Okehampton Castle - Okehampton
11th -14th century chapel, keep & hall.

Totnes Castle - Totnes
13th - 14th century ruins of Castle.

Blackbury Castle - Southleigh
Hill fort - well preserved.

Dartmouth Castle - Dartmouth
15th century castle - coastal defence.

Lydford Castle - Lydford
12th century stone keep built upon site of Saxon fortress town.

Hound Tor - Manaton
Ruins of mediaeval hamlet.

Other things to see & do

The Big Sheep - Abbotsham
Sheep-milking parlour, with gallery, dairy & production rooms. Exhibition & play area.

Dartington Crystal - Torrington
Watch skilled craftworkers make lead crystalware. Glass centre & exhibition.

Dartmoor Wildlife Park - Sparkwell Nr. Plymouth
Over 100 species, including tigers, lions, bears, deer, birds of prey & waterfowl.

The Devon Guild of Craftsmen - Riverside Mill, Bovey Tracey
Series of quality exhibitions throughout the year.

Paignton Zoological & Botanical Gardens - Paignton
Third largest zoo in England. Botanical gardens, tropical house, "The Ark" family activity centre.

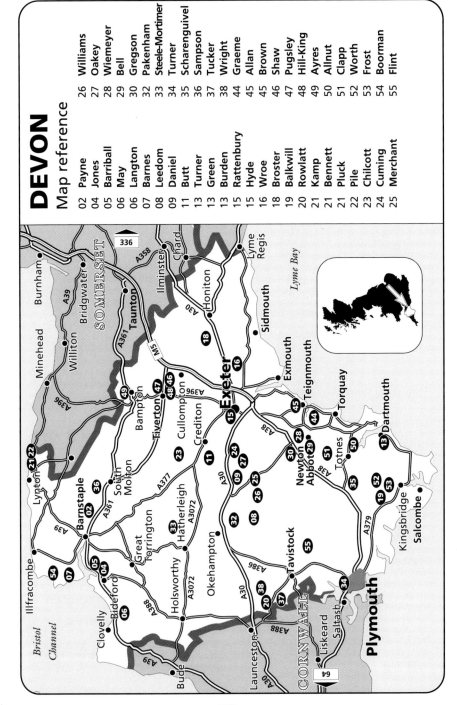

DEVON
Map reference

02	Payne	26	Williams
04	Jones	27	Oakey
05	Barriball	28	Wiemeyer
06	May	29	Bell
06	Langton	30	Gregson
07	Barnes	32	Pakenham
08	Leedom	33	Steele-Mortimer
09	Daniel	34	Turner
11	Butt	35	Scharenguivel
13	Turner	36	Sampson
13	Green	37	Tucker
13	Burden	38	Wright
15	Rattenbury	44	Graeme
15	Hyde	45	Allan
16	Wroe	45	Brown
18	Broster	46	Shaw
19	Balkwill	47	Pugsley
20	Rowlatt	48	Hill-King
21	Kamp	49	Ayres
21	Bennett	50	Allnut
21	Pluck	51	Clapp
22	Pile	52	Worth
23	Chilcott	53	Frost
24	Cuming	54	Boorman
25	Merchant	55	Flint

Lower Waytown. Horns Cross.

Devon

		rate £ from - to per person	children taken	evening meals	animals taken
Jackie & Antony Payne **Huxtable Farm** **West Buckland** **Barnstaple** **EX32 0SR** **Tel: (01598) 760254** **Fax 01598 760254** **Open: FEB - NOV** **& New Year** **Map Ref No. 02**	Nearest Road: A.361 Enjoy a memorable candlelit dinner of farm/local produce with complimentary home-made wine in this wonderful medieval longhouse with original oak panelling, beams & bread ovens. This secluded sheep farm with abundant wildlife & panoramic views is ideally situated on the Tarka Trail for exploring Exmoor & N. Devon's coastline. Tennis court, sauna, fitness & games room. Log fires in winter. 5 en-suite bedrooms & 1 with a private bathroom, each with T.V. & tea/coffee. **E-mail: jpayne@huxhilton.enterprise-plc.com**	£24.00 to £25.00 VISA: M'CARD:	Y	Y	N
Jenny & Barry Jones **The Pines at Eastleigh** **Eastleigh** **Bideford** **EX39 4PA** **Tel: (01271) 860561** **Fax 01271 861248** **Open: Easter - OCT** **& winter weekends** **Map Ref No. 04**	Nearest Road: A.386 Rediscover peace & relaxation at this Grade II listed Georgian home. Set in 7 acres of gardens & paddocks with views of Bideford, Lundy & Hartland Point. Licensed. Books & maps to borrow & an audio system for guest use. Generous farmhouse-style cooking featuring fresh local produce by arrangement. Special diets catered for. 6 attractive bedrooms with en-suite facilities. Colour T.V., 'phones, tea/coffee, hairdryers. Ground-floor courtyard rooms & king-size beds. **E-mail: barry@barpines.demon.co.uk**	£29.00 to £43.00 🚭 VISA: M'CARD:	Y	Y	Y
L. G. & G. I. Barriball **Horwood House** **Horwood** **Bideford** **EX39 4PD** **Tel: (01271) 858231** **Fax 01271 858231** **Open: ALL YEAR** **Map Ref No. 05**	Nearest Road: A.39 Horwood House is a Grade II listed Georgian house of large proportions. Set in 2 acres of landscaped gardens with a large pond, easily viewed from the guest rooms & beyond to lovely rolling countryside. The Barriballs farm around 25 acres surrounding the house plus more off-ground. Horwood is a small hamlet surrounding a medieval church. Only 3 miles from Bideford, 6 from Barnstaple. Ideal for N.T. properties, Rosemoor & the north Devon coastline.	£30.00 to £35.00 🚭	N	N	N
Mrs Caroline May **Lower Waytown** **Horns Cross** **Bideford EX39 5DN** **Tel: (01237) 451787** **Fax 01237 451787** **Open: ALL YEAR (Excl.** **Xmas & New Year)** **Map Ref No. 06**	Nearest Road: A.39 This beautifully converted barn & roundhouse provides a delightful, spacious & comfortable home offering superb accommodation. Extensive grounds with ponds & ornamental waterfowl, & a coastal footpath nearby. The en-suite bedrooms, 2 double (1 ground-floor) & 1 twin-bedded, are tastefully furnished, & each has T.V., hairdryers & tea/coffee facilities. The unique, round, beamed sitting room adjoins the spacious dining room, where breakfast is served. Children over 12.	£24.50 to £28.50 🚭 *see PHOTO over* *p. 135*	Y	N	N
Jean & Jack Langton **The Old Rectory** **Rectory Lane** **Parkham** **Bideford EX39 5PL** **Tel: (01237) 451443** **Open: ALL YEAR (Excl.** **Xmas & New Year)** **Map Ref No. 06**	Nearest Road: A.39 Charming, delightfully furnished country house. Log fires, unique ambience & superb cuisine. 3 en-suite/private-facility bedrooms, very prettily decorated & furnished with every comfort in mind. Dine with your hosts, & enjoy good wine with your excellent evening meal, which, using fresh local produce, is home-cooked by Jean to the highest of standards. Set in an Area of Outstanding Natural Beauty, it is ideally situated for the coast, picturesque Clovelly & Exmoor. Children over 12.	£38.00 to £40.00 🚭 *see PHOTO over* *p. 137*	Y	Y	N

The Old Rectory. Parkham.

Devon

	Nearest Road	rate £ from - to per person	children taken	evening meals	animals taken
Mrs Jean Barnes **Denham Farm** **North Buckland** **Braunton EX33 1HY** **Tel: (01271) 890297** **Fax 01271 890297** **Open: FEB - NOV** **Map Ref No. 07**	Nearest Road: A.361 Denham is beautifully situated in the heart of the countryside, with 160 acres of its own farmland. Only a short drive away are superb beaches, breathtaking scenery & lovely coastal walks. Situated only 3 miles from a championship golf course, this delightful house offers 10 en-suite bedrooms, each with T.V. & tea/coffee-making facilities. The inglenook fireplace & bread oven are a part of the character of this country home, built in the 1700s.	£25.00 to £30.00 VISA: M'CARD:	Y	N	N
Graham & Pauline Leedom **Cherryford House** **Gidleigh** **Chagford** **TQ13 8HS** **Tel: (01647) 433260** **Fax 01647 433637** **Open: ALL YEAR** **Map Ref No. 08**	Nearest Road: A.30 Cherryford is delightfully situated within the Dartmoor National Park approx. 300 yds from the gates leading to Gidleigh Common/Scorhill Down. You can savour gastronomic breakfasts (choice of 5, including full English) using West Country produce where possible, & why not take advantage of the exceptional cuisine served at dinner (2, 3 or 4 courses)? Unfortunately, no liquor licence, so bring your own alcoholic beverage. There are 3 very comfortable en-suite bedrooms. **E-mail: stay@cherryford.freeserve.co.uk**	£27.50 to £37.50	N	Y	N
Tim Daniel **Parford Well** **Sandy Park** **Chagford** **TQ13 8JW** **Tel: (01647) 433353** **Open: ALL YEAR** **Map Ref No. 09**	Nearest Road: A.382 Parford Well is a comfortable & cosy house, surrounded by its own walled garden, set in the tiny hamlet of Sandy Park in the Dartmoor National Park. It is the ideal place to stay if you want to get away from it all, relax & be well looked after. Accommodation is in 3 charming & attractively furnished bedrooms, each with an en-suite/private bathroom. There are wonderful walks on the doorstep both in the wooded valley of the River Teign & on the open moor. Children over 10.	£23.00 to £28.00	Y	N	N
Paul & Irene Butt **The New Inn** **Coleford** **Crediton** **EX17 5BZ** **Tel: 01363 84242** **Fax 01363 85044** **Open: ALL YEAR (Excl. Xmas/Boxing Day)** **Map Ref No. 11**	Nearest Road: A.377 The New Inn is a 13th-century thatched inn nestling in a quiet valley by the side of a brook. Accommodation in this attractive property includes 6 en-suite bedrooms with 'phone, T.V. & tea/coffee-making facilities. There is also an extensive menu, using fresh local produce whenever possible. Local amenities include several golf courses, fishing, horse riding & sport & leisure facilities. Easy access to Dartmoor, Exmoor & the north & south Devon coasts. **E-mail: NEW-INN@EUROBELL.CO.UK**	£30.00 to £35.00 *see PHOTO over* *p. 139* VISA: M'CARD: AMEX:	Y	Y	N
Richard Turner **Ford House** **44 Victoria Road** **Dartmouth** **TQ6 9DX** **Tel: (01803) 834047** **Open: MAR - OCT** **Map Ref No. 13**	Nearest Road: A.3122 Ford House is an attractive Grade II listed Regency house, centrally situated within walking distance of the many shops, restaurants & pubs of Dartmouth. The comfortable, en-suite & individually decorated bedrooms are equipped with either king- or queen-size double beds or twin beds. Each room has a fridge, 'phone, hairdryer, T.V. etc. Breakfast is served from 8 a.m. until 12 noon, & ranges from traditional full English to scrambled eggs & smoked salmon. Parking. Special 'dinner party' weekends can be arranged.	£20.00 to £40.00 VISA: M'CARD: AMEX:	Y	N	Y

The New Inn. Coleford.

The Edwardian. Exeter.

			rate £ from - to per person	children taken	evening meals	animals taken

Robert & Brenda Green **Boringdon House** **1 Church Road** **Dartmouth** **TQ6 9HQ** **Tel: (01803) 832235** **Open: ALL YEAR** **Map Ref No. 13**	Nearest Road: A.3122, A.379 Boringdon is a lovely, welcoming Georgian house in a quiet part of Dartmouth, lying within a large, secluded leafy garden & looking down to the town & river, & sea beyond. Courtyard parking. Only a short, 10-min walk through picturesque lanes down to the historic town. 3 spacious en-suite bedrooms, attractively furnished with Laura Ashley drapes. Comfortable & relaxing, with colour T.V., c/h & tea/coffee facilities.	£22.50 to £27.50	N	N	N
Anthony & Diana Burden **Barnabas House** **57 Above Town** **Dartmouth** **TQ6 9RH** **Tel: (01803) 832885** **Open: ALL YEAR** **Map Ref No. 13**	Nearest Road: A.379 Barnabas House is an attractive Georgian house overlooking the River Dart. 2 very attractive & comfortably furnished bedrooms, each has an en-suite/private bathroom, T.V., tea/coffee & spectacular river views. Breakfast is served in the lovely dining room which has a flagstone floor & antique pine furniture. A short walk via a network of paths & steep steps leads to the town centre with its many shops & restaurants. An ideal base for exploring beautiful Devon. The charming hosts will ensure that your stay is memorable.	£22.50 to £35.00	N	N	N
Michael & Kay Rattenbury **The Edwardian** **30 & 32 Heavitree Road** **Exeter EX1 2LQ** **Tel: (01392) 276102** **Tel: (01392) 254699** **Fax 01392 253393** **Open: ALL YEAR (Excl. Xmas)** **Map Ref No. 15**	Nearest Road: M.5, A.30 Elegant Edwardian townhouses with tasteful, period decor, near Roman walls, cathedral & city centre. Choice of en-suite rooms from singles, twins, doubles (including 3 romantic 4-posters - 1 on the ground floor) & rooms for 3 or 4 persons. Spa bath. English & vegetarian, freshly prepared breakfasts. Local hosts with wide knowledge of the West Country. Large car park opposite. Discounts for stays of 3 nights or more. **E-mail: edwardex@globalnet.co.uk**	£24.00 to £28.00 *see PHOTO over* *p. 140* VISA: M'CARD: AMEX:	Y	N	Y
Richard & Susan Hyde **Raffles** **11 Blackall Road** **Exeter** **EX4 4HD** **Tel: (01392) 270200** **Fax 01392 270200** **Open: ALL YEAR** **Map Ref No. 15**	Nearest Road: M.5 Imagine a large Victorian town house, furnished with antiques, tastefully decorated, a delightful walled garden yet minutes from the town centre, then come to Raffles the home of Richard & Sue. Their aim is to offer high-quality accommodation with friendly personal service. All bedrooms are en-suite with tea/coffee-making facilities, colour T.V. & central heating. Lock-up garages are also available on request. **E-mail: raffleshtl@btinternet.com**	£24.00 to £25.00 VISA: M'CARD: AMEX:	Y	Y	Y
Mrs Sian Wroe **Lower Marsh Farm** **Marsh Green** **Exeter** **EX5 2EX** **Tel: (01404) 822432** **Open: ALL YEAR (Excl. Xmas)** **Map Ref No. 16**	Nearest Road: A.30 Charming 17th-century Grade II listed farmhouse set in 5 acres of gardens & paddocks with orchard, pond, stream & stable courtyard on the edge of a pretty east Devon hamlet. Easy access to Exeter, coast, Exmoor & Dartmoor. Family home, tastefully furnished with antiques. 3 comfortable guest bedrooms (2 en-suite, 1 private bathroom), each with colour T.V. & hospitality tray. Guest sitting room with log fire. Excellent country pubs nearby.	£21.00 to £25.00 *see PHOTO over* *p. 142*	Y	N	N

Lower Marsh Farm. Rockbeare.

Court Barton. Aveton Gifford.

Devon

	rate £ from - to per person	children taken	evening meals	animals taken

Gordon Broster Colestocks Country House Hotel Payhembury Honiton EX14 0JR Tel: (01404) 850633 Fax 01404 850901 Open: APR - OCT Map Ref No. 18	**Nearest Road: A.30** Pink-washed & newly re-thatched, a lovely 16th-century, Grade II listed country house set in 2 acres of gardens. Tranquil rural situation, & well placed for touring the West Country. All rooms have en-suite bath/shower, T.V. & tea facilities. Many antiques, 1 canopied brass bed. Log fires in the huge inglenook fireplace. Excellent restaurant, all home-cooking. Wines personally chosen & imported by the proprietor. Children over 10 years. Reduced rates for 2 nights or more.	£27.50 to £30.00 VISA: M'CARD:	Y	Y	N
Mrs Jill Balkwill Court Barton Aveton Gifford Kingsbridge TQ7 4LE Tel: (01548) 550312 01548 550128 Open: ALL YEAR (Excl. Xmas) Map Ref No. 19	**Nearest Road: A.379** An absolutely delightful 16th-century, listed manor farmhouse situated on a 40-acre farm. 7 comfortable bedrooms, 6 with en-suite facilities & all with T.V. & tea/coffee-making facilities. A comfortable, well-furnished T.V. lounge with lots of books. Delicious country breakfasts are served in the sunny breakfast room. Full central heating & log fires in cooler weather. Close to moorland & beaches. Ideal for walking, sailing & fishing. **E-mail: jill@courtbarton.co.uk**	£24.00 to £30.00 *see PHOTO over* *p. 143* VISA: M'CARD:	Y	N	N
Mrs Maureen Rowlatt Tor Cottage Chillaton Lifton PL16 0JE Tel: (01822) 860248 Fax 01822 860126 Open: FEB - NOV Map Ref No. 20	**Nearest Road: A.30** Award-winning Tor Cottage has a warm & relaxed atmosphere & nestles in its own private valley. 18 acres wildlife hillsides. Lovely gardens & a streamside setting. Beautifully appointed en-suite bedrooms with log fires & a private terrace & gardens. Candlelit dinners or tray suppers. Traditional menus or your hosts' renowned vegetarian cuisine which guests describe as 'inspired'. Heated outdoor pool (summer). Tranquil base adjacent Dartmoor/Tamar Valley. **E-mail: info@torcottage.demon.co.uk.**	£45.00 to £47.00 *see PHOTO over* *p. 145* VISA: M'CARD: AMEX:	N	Y	N
June & Adrian Kamp Southcliffe Lee Road Lynton EX35 6BS Tel: (01598) 753328 Fax 01598 753328 Open: MAR - OCT Map Ref No. 21	**Nearest Road: A.39** A Listed Victorian gentleman's residence with characteristic pitch-pine staircase & doors & Swiss-style balconies. Beautifully appointed bedrooms, all with private bathrooms, colour T.V. & beverage makers. June & Adrian Kamp have been at Southcliffe since 1978, & have a reputation for good food, comfort, cleanliness & value for money. Southcliffe is the perfect spot for a relaxing break. Children over 9 welcome.	£22.00 to £25.00 VISA: M'CARD:	Y	Y	N
Ben & Jane Bennett Victoria Lodge Lee Road Lynton EX35 6BS Tel: (01598) 753203 Fax 01598 753203 Open: FEB - NOV Map Ref No. 21	**Nearest Road: A.39** Lovingly refurbished, Victoria Lodge retains the character & charm of the Victorian era. The interior, with its original fireplaces & antique clocks, creates an atmosphere of elegance & genuine hospitality. All 9 en-suite rooms (some with 4-poster or antique brass beds) are beautifully furnished with the amenities one expects from an award-winning hotel. Dinner is served Thurs-Sun. Enjoy the magic of Exmoor National Park, with its heritage coastline & sweeping moorlands. **E-mail: info@victorialodge.co.uk**	£24.00 to £34.00 *see PHOTO over* *p. 146* VISA: M'CARD:	Y	Y	N

Tor Cottage. Chillaton.

Victoria Lodge Hotel. Lynton.

Devon

		rate £ from - to per person	children taken	evening meals	animals taken
John & Carol Pluck **Longmead House Hotel** **9 Longmead** **Lynton** **EX35 6DQ** Tel: (01598) 752523 Fax 01598 752523 Open: MAR - OCT Map Ref No. 21	Nearest Road: A.39 A haven for good home-cooking, with that little extra flair which makes many guests return. John & Carol offer a warm welcome to their home, & encourage a relaxed, friendly atmosphere. The 7 bedrooms are all individually furnished, comfortable & attractive; 6 are en-suite. Set in a large garden with parking, & close to the Valley of Rocks, Longmead provides an excellent base from which to discover Exmoor.	£20.00 to £23.00 VISA: M'CARD:	Y	Y	N
Susan Pile **Coombe Farm** **Countisbury** **Lynton** **EX35 6NF** Tel: (01598) 741236 Fax 01598 741236 Open: MAR - NOV Map Ref No. 22	Nearest Road: A.39 Coombe is a 365-acre, hill-sheep farm, with an early-17th-century farmhouse set betwixt Lynmouth & the legendary Doone Valley. The coast path runs through the farm at Desolate. All within the spectacular Exmoor National Park. The bedrooms are 2 doubles, en-suite, 1 twin & 2 family. All have hot-drink facilities, shaver points, & bath & hand towels. Central heating. A lounge with woodburner fire & colour T.V..	£19.00 to £25.00	Y	N	N
Stephen & Dawn Chilcott **Wigham** **Morchard Bishop** **EX17 6RJ** Tel: (01363) 877350 Fax 01363 877350 Open: ALL YEAR Map Ref No. 23	Nearest Road: A.377 Wigham is a 16th-century Devon longhouse, with a 30-acre farm which provides fresh fruit, vegetables & dairy produce for imaginative meals. Accommodation is in 5 double rooms, including a 4-poster suite. All with colour T.V. & video & full en-suite bathroom. There are 2 sitting rooms in which guests may relax & a snooker lounge & outdoor heated pool for pleasure. Licensed. Full S.A. organic symbol Sept. 1999. Children over 8. (Please note rates printed include dinner). **E-mail: info@wigham.co.uk**	£49.00 to £85.00 *see PHOTO over* *p. 148* VISA: M'CARD: AMEX:	Y	Y	N
Mrs Mary Cuming **Great Wooston Farm** **Moretonhampstead** **TQ13 8QA** Tel: (01647) 440367 Fax 01647 440367 Open: ALL YEAR Map Ref No. 24	Nearest Road: B.3212, A.30 Wooston, once part of the Manor House Estate owned by Lord Hambledon, is situated high above the Teign Valley in the Dartmoor National Park, with views over open moorland, & plenty of walks, golf, fishing & riding nearby. It is surrounded by a delightful garden of 1/2 an acre. 3 pleasant bedrooms, 2 en-suite, 1 with 4-poster, 1 with private bathroom, with every facility included. Excellent breakfasts are served. Also, a guests' lounge for your relaxation after a day exploring the Devon countryside. Children over 8 years.	£20.00 to £22.00 VISA: M'CARD:	Y	N	N
Mrs Trudie Merchant **Great Sloncombe Farm** **Moretonhampstead** **TQ13 8QF** Tel: (01647) 440595 Fax 01647 440595 Open: ALL YEAR Map Ref No. 25	Nearest Road: A.382 Great Sloncombe Farm is a listed, granite-&-cob-built, 13th-century farmhouse. Set in a peaceful Dartmoor valley, the rambling house has a magical atmosphere, & is furnished with oak & pine, antique china & interesting old photographs. The 3 warm & pleasant bedrooms are all en-suite, with every facility included. Delicious breakfasts, with home-made bread & plentiful Devonshire suppers, are served. Children over 8.	£22.00 to £23.00	Y	Y	Y

Wigham. Morchard Bishop.

Gate House. North Bovey.

Devon

		rate £ from - to per person	children taken	evening meals	animals taken
John & Sheila Williams **Gate House** **The Village** **North Bovey** **Moretonhampstead** **TQ13 8RB** **Tel/Fax: (01647) 440479** **Open: ALL YEAR** **Map Ref No. 26**	Nearest Road: A.30, A.38 North Bovey is an historic village set within the Dartmoor National Park. Gate House, near the village green, is a listed 500-year-old thatched medieval longhouse with beamed ceilings, granite fireplaces & bread oven. An acre of private gardens with a swimming pool. Guest rooms are charmingly furnished, & the bedrooms combine country-style elegance with en-suite/private bathrooms. Lovely walks amidst breathtaking scenery & N.T. properties within easy reach.	£26.00 to £28.00 (non-smoking) *see PHOTO over* *p. 149*	N	Y	Y
Gill & David Oakey **Great Doccombe Farm** **Doccombe** **Moretonhampstead** **TQ13 8SS** **Tel: (01647) 440694** **Open: ALL YEAR** **Map Ref No. 27**	Nearest Road: A.30 Great Doccombe Farm is situated in the pretty hamlet of Doccombe, within the Dartmoor National Park, on the B.3212 from Exeter. An ideal base for walking in the Teign Valley & nearby moors, with golf, riding & fishing nearby. This lovely 16th-century granite farmhouse is surrounded by gardens & fields. The bedrooms (1 ground-floor) are all en-suite, & have shower, T.V. & tea/coffee facilities. A traditional full English breakfast is served.	£18.00 to £19.00 (non-smoking)	Y	N	N
Mrs J. L. Wiemeyer **The Thatched Cottage** **9 Crossley Moor Road** **Kingsteignton** **Newton Abbot TQ12 3LE** **Tel: (01626) 365650** **Fax 07070 660794** **Open: ALL YEAR** **Map Ref No. 28**	Nearest Road: A.380 A beautiful 400-year-old, Grade II listed, thatched longhouse where old oak beams & a large open fireplace lend a cosy & welcoming atmosphere. There are 3 en-suite bedrooms, all with T.V. & tea/coffee-making facilities. A full English breakfast is served. Character bar & restaurant, where table d'hote & a la carte menus are available each evening. A pretty garden for guests' use. An ideal base for touring, with a warm welcome. **E-mail: thatched@globalnet.co.uk**	£22.50 to £22.50 (non-smoking) VISA: M'CARD: AMEX:	Y	Y	N
Nigel Bell **Sampsons Farm** **Accommodation** **Preston** **Newton Abbot** **TQ12 3PP** **Tel: (01626) 354913** **Fax 01626 354913** **Open: ALL YEAR** **Map Ref No. 29**	Nearest Road: A.38, A.380 A super, relaxed, family atmosphere is found at this traditional thatched Devon longhouse. This Grade II listed building, of historical importance, retains much of its original charm & character, with oak beams, panelling & inglenook fireplaces. All rooms have modern amenities, 4-poster & en-suite rooms available. An extensive a la carte & table d'hote menu is offered in the evening. A view of Dartmoor from the windows. A short distance from the coast. Riding, fishing, golf nearby. **E-mail: info@sampsonsfarm.com**	£20.00 to £35.00 *see PHOTO over* *p. 151* VISA: M'CARD: AMEX:	Y	Y	Y
Mrs Madeleine Gregson **Penpark** **Bickington** **Newton Abbot** **TQ12 6LH** **Tel: (01626) 821314** **Fax 01626 821101** **Open: ALL YEAR** **Map Ref No. 30**	Nearest Road: A.38 In the Dartmoor National Park, with secluded, beautiful woodland gardens, tennis court & glorious panoramic views, Penpark is an elegant country house, a gem of its period, designed by Clough Williams Ellis of Portmeirion fame. 3 charming rooms: a spacious double/twin with balcony; a single next door & a further double - all with wonderful views; private facilities; tea/coffee & T.V.. The Gregsons offer you a truly relaxed stay in beautiful & friendly surroundings. **E-mail: Penpark@freeuk.com**	£23.00 to £25.00 (non-smoking) *see PHOTO over* *p. 152*	Y	N	N

Sampsons Farm Restaurant. Newton Abbot

Penpark. Bickington.

Devon

		rate £ from - to per person	children taken	evening meals	animals taken
Maureen & John Pakenham **Tor Down House** **Belstone** **Okehampton** **EX20 1QY** **Tel: (01837) 840731** **Fax 01837 840731** **Open: ALL YEAR (Excl.** **Xmas & New Year)** **Map Ref No. 32**	Nearest Road: A.30 14th-century thatched Dartmoor Longhouse (Grade II) in lovely secluded gardens within Dartmoor National Park. Hidden away from a quiet lane, 100 paces from the moor, but only a mile from the A30 giving fast access to all the West Country. Old oak beams, huge granite fireplaces, cats on Persian rugs, 4-poster beds, en-suite facilities, etc. Sumptuous breakfasts. National Trust properties, famous gardens, Bronze Age stone circles on Dartmoor, character pubs & restaurants. Birdwatchers' & painters' paradise.	£30.00 to £40.00 *see PHOTO over* *p. 154* VISA: M'CARD:	N	N	N
Peter & Sarah Steele- **Mortimer** **Holme Down** **Exbourne** **Okehampton EX20 3QY** **Tel: (01837) 851485** **Fax 01837 851485** **Open: ALL YEAR** **Map Ref No. 33**	Nearest Road: A.30 Situated in 100 acres of private pasture & woodland, Holme Down, a Victorian manor house, offers a tranquil & secluded hide-a-way. The spacious rooms have stunning views over Dartmoor & are attractively furnished throughout. All guests are made to feel very welcome by Peter, Sarah & their young family. Private fishing available on a mile stretch of river plus a stocked lake. Modern equestrian facilities also available. Children over 12.	£30.00 to £35.00 VISA: M'CARD:	Y	Y	N
John & Daphne Turner **Westways** **706 Budshead Road** **Crownhill** **Plymouth** **PL6 5DY** **Tel: (01752) 776617** **Fax 01752 776617** **Open: ALL YEAR** **Map Ref No. 34**	Nearest Road: A.38 Situated approx. 3 1/2 miles from Plymouth city centre, this attractive detached house offers pleasant accommodation in 3 well-furnished rooms, with tea/coffee facilities. Excellent breakfasts are served in the elegant dining room. Guests may choose to relax & plan their excursions in the comfortable sitting room. Also, a small T.V. room. A homely & friendly base both for visitors wishing to make the most of the many attractions in the area, & for touring Devon. Children over 12. **E-mail: westways@cw.com.net**	£20.00 to £££ VISA: M'CARD:	Y	N	N
John & Faith Scharenguivel **Coombe House** **North Huish** **South Brent** **TQ10 9NJ** **Tel: (01548) 821277** **Fax 01548 821277** **Open: ALL YEAR** **Map Ref No. 35**	Nearest Road: A.38 A Georgian house set in a tranquil & beautiful valley. 4 en-suite bedrooms & 1 single with private bathroom. T.V., tea/coffee facilities, radio, hairdryer & trouser press. Elegant dining room & guest lounge. Fresh local produce for meals. The coast, Dartmoor, Totnes, Kingsbridge, Plymouth & Exeter are all within easy reach. 4 barn conversions for self-catering in 4 acres of grounds in an Area of Outstanding Natural Beauty. **E-mail: coombehouse@hotmail.com**	£25.00 to £30.00	Y	Y	N
Mrs Theresa Sampson **Kerscott Farm** **Bishopsnympton** **South Molton** **EX36 4QG** **Tel: (01769) 550262** **Open: FEB - NOV** **Map Ref No. 36**	Nearest Road: A.361 Kerscott Farm offers quality accommodation. This peaceful Exmoor working farm & olde worlde farmhouse is mentioned in the Domesday Book (1086). It has an absolutely fascinating interior with many antiques, pictures & china - a rare find. There are beautiful, extensive views. 3 pretty & tastefully furnished en-suite bedrooms with colour T.V. & tea/coffee facilities. Wholesome country cooking. An elegant home & an ideal base from which to explore glorious Devon.	£20.00 to £25.00	N	Y	N

Tor Down House. Belstone.

Wytchwood. West Buckeridge.

Devon

		rate £ from - to per person	children taken	evening meals	animals taken
Hilary Tucker **Beera Farmhouse** **Milton Abbot** **Tavistock PL19 8PL** **Tel: (01822) 870216** Fax 01822 870216 **Open: ALL YEAR** **Map Ref No. 37**	Nearest Road: A.30 Beera is a large, traditional stone built Victorian farmhouse set in an Area of Outstanding Natural Beauty. The farm is a 160-acre beef & sheep farm on the bank of the river Tamar. 2 attractive bedrooms (1 with 4-poster), each has an en-suite/private bathroom, T.V. & tea/coffee facilities. The delicious evening meals are provided by arrangement. Ideal for touring & within easy reach of the coast, Dartmoor National Park & N.T. properties. **E-mail: robert.tucker@farming.co.uk**	£20.00 to £25.00	Y	Y	N
David & Jill Wright **Quither Mill** **Quither** **Nr. Chillaton** **Tavistock** **PL19 0PZ** **Tel: Tel: (01822) 860160** **Open: ALL YEAR** **Map Ref No. 38**	Nearest Road: A.30 Quither Mill is situated in a sleepy hamlet & is listed as being of architectural & historical interest. Dating from the 18th century, the mill wheel & workings are intact. Guests enjoy the comfort of beamed en-suite bedrooms & full English breakfast. The hosts are proud of their reputation for fine cooking drawn from 20 years in the hotel world, which makes dinner a memorable experience. Animals by arrangement. Children over 7. **E-mail: quither.mill@virgin.net**	£30.00 to £35.00 VISA: M'CARD:	Y	Y	Y
Mrs Jennifer Graeme **Fonthill** **Torquay Road** **Shaldon** **Teignmouth** **TQ14 0AX** **Tel: (01626) 872344** Fax 01626 872344 **Open: MAR - NOV** **Map Ref No. 44**	Nearest Road: A.379 Visitors are warmly welcomed to this lovely Georgian house, for a peaceful holiday in charming & very comfortable accommodation. Fonthill stands in 20 acres of beautiful gardens, woodland & fields on the edge of Shaldon, a pretty village on the South Devon coast. 2 delightful rooms, with en-suite/private bathrooms & every comfort. The lovely garden is for guests' enjoyment, & there is also a tennis court in the grounds. Several sandy beaches nearby & an 18-hole golf course. **E-mail: swanphoto2@aol.com**	£26.00 to £29.00	Y	N	N
Alison & John Allan **Thomas Luny House** **Teign Street** **Teignmouth** **TQ14 8EG** **Tel: (01626) 772976** **Open: ALL YEAR** **Map Ref No. 45**	Nearest Road: A.381 A Grade II listed Georgian house, built by the marine artist Thomas Luny. Tucked away in the old quarter of Teignmouth, it forms a quiet oasis surrounded by its own high walls. Each superb, en-suite bedroom is individual in style, some with views over the River Teign. Alison & John & their family love to share their home, & they spare no effort in preparing the delicious breakfasts & attending to their guests' general well-being. Licensed. Children over 12 yrs.	£30.00 to £35.00 *see PHOTO over* *p. 157* VISA: M'CARD:	Y	N	N
Jenny Richardson Brown **Wytchwood** **West Buckeridge** **Teignmouth** **TQ14 8NF** **Tel: (01626) 773482** **Open: ALL YEAR** **Map Ref No. 45**	Nearest Road: A.381 Award-winning Wytchwood has an outstanding reputation for lavish hospitality & traditional home-cooking. To stay here is to be truly pampered! Panoramic views, beautiful garden, stylish interior design & the prettiest en-suite bedrooms, all combine to fulfil every expectation. Home-made bread & rolls, jams, preserves, orchard honey & garden produce. Delicious Devonshire cream teas, sponges & cakes. Many culinary awards. A warm welcome always. **E-mail: wytchwood@yahoo.com**	£25.50 to £32.50 *see PHOTO over* *p. 155*	Y	N	N

Thomas Luny House. Teignmouth.

Hornhill. Tiverton.

		rate £ from - to per person	evening meals	children taken	animals taken
Mrs Jenny Shaw **Poole Farm** **Ash Thomas** **Tiverton EX16 4NS** **Tel: (01884) 820201** **Open: ALL YEAR** **Map Ref No. 46**	Nearest Road: M.5, A.361 An attractive old farmhouse, recently renovated, with 18 acres & a pretty garden. Set in a peaceful hamlet, Poole Farm has 2 comfortable, en-suite bedrooms, with colour T.V., tea tray & full central heating. There are plenty of good places to eat nearby, but evening meals can usually be provided by prior arrangement. It is an ideal touring base or stop-over en-route.	£24.00 to £24.00	Y	N	Y
Barbara Pugsley **Hornhill** **Exeter Hill** **Tiverton** **EX16 4PL** **Tel: (01884) 253352** **Fax 01884 253352** **Open: ALL YEAR** **Map Ref No. 47**	Nearest Road: A.361 Hornhill, originally a coaching inn, has panoramic views over the beautiful Exe valley. Set in a large garden & surrounded by farmland. The charming hosts offer guests comfort, delicious home-cooking & a happy atmosphere. The house, furnished with antiques, has 3 lovely bedrooms (1 with Victorian 4-poster), each with private bathroom, T.V. & tea/coffee. 1 is suitable for the partially disabled. The elegant drawing room has plenty of books & a log fire on chilly evenings. Children over 10. Animals by arrangement.	£20.00 to £25.00 *see PHOTO over* *p. 158* VISA: M'CARD:	Y	N	Y
Mrs Ruth Hill-King **Little Holwell** **Collipriest** **Tiverton** **EX16 4PT** **Tel: (01884) 257590** **Fax 01884 257590** **Open: ALL YEAR (Excl. Xmas)** **Map Ref No. 48**	Nearest Road: A.361, A.396 A warm welcome awaits you in this 13th-century home, set amidst rolling hills & woodland in the favoured Exe Valley. Offering 3 very comfortable rooms, 2 en-suite, all with tea/coffee facilities. There is an inglenook fireplace, oak beams, a spiral staircase & relaxing views. Home cooking. An ideal centre for touring the coast & moors, all within easy reach. From the A.361, take the B.3391 to the 4th roundabout, proceed for approx. 2 miles & it is the last house on the right. **E-mail: holwellgh@aol.com**	£17.50 to £22.00 VISA: M'CARD:	Y	N	N
Chris & Kathy Ayres **Manor Mill House** **Bampton** **Tiverton** **EX16 9LP** **Tel: (01398) 332211** **Fax 01398 332009** **Open: ALL YEAR** **Map Ref No. 49**	Nearest Road: A.396, B.3227 Manor Mill House is a relaxing & welcoming 17th-century home with inglenooks, beams, log fires & delicious breakfasts using local produce. There are 3 double/twin rooms, 2 with 4-poster beds (1 ground floor) & all are en-suite & have T.V. & tea/coffee-making facilities. A pleasant garden with views over water meadows, yet close to the amenities of historic Bampton. An ideal base for exploring moors, coasts & N.T. properties & walks. Several good places to eat locally. Parking. **E-mail: stay@manormill.demon.co.uk**	£19.50 to £22.50 *see PHOTO over* *p. 160*	N	N	N
Mrs Jeannie Allnutt **The Old Forge at Totnes** **Seymour Place** **Totnes** **TQ9 5AY** **Tel: (01803) 862174** **Fax 01803 865385** **Open: ALL YEAR** **Map Ref No. 50**	Nearest Road: A.381, A.384 A delightfully converted, working, 600-year-old smithy. This family-run hotel, located in the centre of Totnes, offers visitors a choice of 10 comfortable, well-equipped bedrooms, 9 en-suite, all with radio, T.V., 'phone & tea/coffee-making facilities. A cottage suite also available for families. There is a pleasant walled garden for guests' use, where delicious cream teas are served. The Old Forge is ideally located for touring the Torbay coast & Dartmoor. Golf breaks a speciality. Licensed. Leisure lounge with whirlpool spa.	£27.00 to £46.00 *see PHOTO over* *p. 161* VISA: M'CARD:	Y	N	N

Manor Mill House. Bampton.

The Old Forge at Totnes.   Totnes.

Orchard House. Horner.

Devon

		rate £ from - to per person	children taken	evening meals	animals taken
Sarah Clapp **Manor Farm** **Broadhempston** **Totnes** **TQ9 6BD** **Tel: (01803) 813260** **Fax 01803 813260** **Open: ALL YEAR (Excl. Xmas)** **Map Ref No. 51**	Nearest Road: A.381 Manor Farm is an elegant Georgian farmhouse built in 1774 with a walled garden & cider orchard, situated in the picturesque village of Broadhempston, with 2 pubs. Your hosts have a small holding of a few sheep & chickens & family pets roam the house. 2 bedrooms, each with a private bathroom, T.V. & tea/coffee. (No smoking in the house.) Set on the edge of the South Hams & Dartmoor, ideal for walking, sailing, fishing & golf. Children over 12. Animals by arrangement.	£23.00 to £26.00	Y	N	Y
Mrs Helen Worth **Orchard House** **Horner** **Halwell** **Totnes** **TQ9 7LB** **Tel: (01548) 821448** **Open: MAR - NOV** **Map Ref No. 52**	Nearest Road: A.381 Tucked away in a rural hamlet of the South Hams, between Totnes & Kingsbridge, Orchard House nestles within an old cider orchard. It offers superb accommodation: all bedrooms are en-suite with colour T.V., radio, tea/coffee-making facilities & beautiful furnishings. Breakfasts are ample, with cereals, juice, yoghurts & grapefruit, followed by a cooked platter with toast & crois-sants. Also, guests' own sitting & dining room, with a log fire. Large garden & private parking.	£20.00 to £22.00 *see PHOTO over p. 162*	Y	N	N
Petrina & Kevin Frost **Lower Grimpstonleigh** **East Allington** **Totnes** **TQ9 7QH** **Tel: (01548) 521258** **Fax 01548 521258** **Open: ALL YEAR (Excl. Xmas)** **Map Ref No. 53**	Nearest Road: A.381 Idyllic rural retreat situated at the end of a quiet Devon lane, 4 miles from Kingsbridge. The ideal location for both Dartmoor & the south Devon coastline. Old stone house with spacious & very comfortably furnished bedrooms with vaulted ceilings, country antiques & en-suite bath/shower. T.V., tea/coffee facilities, sofas, clock/radios & hairdryers provided. Breakfasts include the Frosts' own free-range eggs, home-made preserves & local produce. Dogs by arrangement. E-mail: Grimpstonleigh@ukgateway.net	£25.00 to £30.00 *see PHOTO over p. 164*	Y	N	N
Jean & Charles Boorman **Sandunes** **Beach Road** **Woolacombe** **EX34 7BT** **Tel: (01271) 870661** **Open: MAR - OCT** **Map Ref No. 54**	Nearest Road: A.361 Sandunes is a very pleasant, most comfortable modern guest house where you are assured of a friendly welcome, a relaxed atmosphere & cour-teous service. Conveniently located for Woolacombe Sands & the village. 7 en-suite bedrooms, many with lovely sea views. The well-appointed guest lounge & sun patio have marvel-lous panoramic views out to sea. This is an ideal base for touring, with sandy beaches, Illfracombe, Lynton, Lynmouth & Exmoor within easy reach.	£20.00 to £25.00	N	Y	N
John & Liz Flint **Burrator House** **Sheepstor** **Yelverton** **PL20 6PF** **Tel: (01822) 855669** **Fax 01822 855669** **Open: ALL YEAR (Excl. Xmas)** **Map Ref No. 55**	Nearest Road: A.386, B.3212 Burrator House, historically connected with the White Rajah of Sarawk, is delightfully situated in a wooded valley within the Dartmoor National Park, adjacent to the picturesque Burrator Reser-voir. Splendid walking country. Your hosts offer a warm welcome into their home, recently taste-fully refurbished. Delightful, fully-equipped en-suite rooms, guest lounge with log fire. Excellent breakfast with local produce. Secluded garden, swimming pool, within 21 acres. Children over 8. E-mail: burratorhouse@compuserve.com	£22.50 to £27.50 VISA: M'CARD:	Y	Y	Y

Lower Grimpstonleigh. East Allington.

Dorset

Dorset
(West Country)

The unspoilt nature of this gem of a county is emphasised by the designation of virtually all of the coast & much of the inland country as an Area of Outstanding Natural Beauty. Along the coast from Christchurch to Lyme Regis there are a fascinating variety of sandy beaches, towering cliffs & single banks, whilst inland is a rich mixture of downland, lonely heaths, fertile valleys, historic houses & lovely villages of thatch & mellow stone buildings.

Thomas Hardy was born here & took the Dorset countryside as a background for many of his novels. Few writers can have stamped their identity on a county more than Hardy on Dorset, forever to be known as the "Hardy Country". Fortunately most of the area that he so lovingly described remains unchanged, including Egdon Heath & the county town of Dorchester, famous as Casterbridge.

In the midst of the rolling chalk hills which stretch along the Storr Valley lies picturesque Cerne Abbas, with its late mediaeval houses & cottages & the ruins of a Benedictine Abbey. At Godmanstone is the tiny thatched "Smiths Arms" claiming to be the smallest pub in England.

The north of the county is pastoral with lovely views over broad Blackmoor Vale. Here is the ancient hilltop town of Shaftesbury, with cobbled Gold Hill, one of the most photographed streets in the country.

Coastal Dorset is spectacular. Poole harbour is an enormous, almost circular bay, an exciting mixture of 20th century activity, ships of many nations & beautiful building of the 15th, 18th & early 19th centuries.

Westwards lies the popular resort of Swanage, where the sandy beach & sheltered bay are excellent for swimming. From here to Weymouth is a marvellous stretch of coast with scenic wonders like Lulworth Cove & the arch of Durdle Door.

Chesil Beach is an extraordinary bank of graded pebbles, as perilous to shipping today as it was 1,000 years ago. It is separated from the mainland by a sheltered lagoon known as the Fleet. From here a range of giant cliffs rises to 617 feet at Golden Gap & stretches westwards to Lyme Regis, beloved by Jane Austen who wrote "Persuasion" whilst living here.

Dorset has many interesting archaeological features. Near Dorchester is Maiden Castle, huge earthwork fortifications on a site first inhabited 6,000 years ago. The Badbury rings wind round a wooded hilltop near Wimborne Minster; legend has it that King Arthur's soul, in the form of a raven, inhabited this "dread" wood. The giant of Cerne Abbas is a figure of a man 180 feet high carved into the chalk hillside. Long associated with fertility there is still speculation about the figures' origins, one theory suggesting it is a Romano-British depiction of Hercules. A Roman amphitheatre can be seen at Dorchester, & today's road still follows the Roman route to Weymouth.

Corfe Castle.

Dorset

Dorset

Gazeteer

Areas of outstanding natural beauty.
The Entire County.

Houses & Castles

Athelthampton
Mediaeval house - one of the finest in all England. Formal gardens.
Barneston Manor - Nr. Church Knowle
13th - 16th century stone built manor house.
Forde Abbey - Nr. Chard
12th century Cistercian monastery - noted Mortlake tapestries.
Manor House - Sandford Orcas
Mansion of Tudor period, furnished with period furniture, antiques, silver, china, glass, paintings.
Hardy's Cottage - Higher Bockampton
Birthplace of Thomas Hardy, author (1840-1928).
Milton Abbey - Nr. Blandford
18th century Georgian house built on original site of 15th century abbey.
Purse Caundle Manor - Purse Caundle
Mediaeval Manor - furnished in style of period.
Parnham House - Beaminster
Tudor Manor - some later work by Nash. Leaded windows & heraldic plasterwork. Home of John Makepeace & the International School for Craftsmen in Wood. House, gardens & workshops.
Sherborne Castle - Sherborne
16th century mansion - continuously occupied by Digby family.
No. 3 Trinity Street - Weymouth
Tudor cottages now converted into one house, furnished 17th century.
Smedmore - Kimmeridge
18th century manor.
Wolfeton House - Dorchester
Mediaeval & Elizabethan Manor. Fine stone work, great stair. 17th century furniture - Jacobean ceilings & fireplaces.

Cathedrals & Churches

Bere Regis (St. John the Baptist)
12th century foundation - enlarged in 13th & 15th centuries.
Timber roof & nave, fine arcades. 16th century seating.

Blandford (St. Peter & St. Paul)
18th century - ashlar - Georgian design. Galleries, pulpit, box pews, font & mayoral seat.
Bradford Abbas (St. Mary)
14th century - parapets & pinnacled tower, panelled roof. 15th century bench ends, stone rood screen. 17th century pulpit.
Cerne Abbas (St. Mary)
13th century - rebuilt 15th & 16th centuries, 14th century wall paintings, 15th century tower, stone screen, pulpit possibly 11th century.
Chalbury (dedication unknown)
13th century origin - 14th century east windows, timber bellcote. Plastered walls, box pews, 3-decker pulpit, west gallery.
Christchurch (Christ Church)
Norman nave - ribbed plaster vaulting - perpendicular spire. Tudor renaissance Salisbury chantry - screen with Tree of Jesse: notable misericord seats.
Milton Abbey (Sts. Mary, Michael, Sampson & Branwaleder)
14th century pulpitum & sedilla, 15th century reredos & canopy, 16th century monument, Milton effigies 1775.
Sherborne (St. Mary)
Largely Norman but some Saxon remains - excellent fan vaulting, of nave & choir. 12th & 13th century effigies - 15th century painted glass.
Studland (St. Nicholas)
12th century - best Norman church in the country. 12th century font, 13th century east windows.
Whitchurch Canonicorum (St. Candida & Holy Cross)
12th & 13th century. 12th century font, relics of patroness in 13th century shrine, 15th century painted glass, 15th century tower.
Wimbourne Minster (St. Cuthberga)
12th century central tower & arcade, otherwise 13th-15th century. Former collegiate church. Georgian glass, some Jacobean stalls & screen. Monuments & famed clock of 14th century.
Yetminster (St. Andrew)
13th century chancel - 15th century rebuilt with embattled parapets. 16th century brasses & seating.

Dorset

Museums & Galleries

Abbey Ruins - Shaftesbury
Relics excavated from Benedictine Nunnery founded by Alfred the Great.

Russell-Cotes Art Gallery & Museum - Bournemouth
17th-20th century oil paintings, watercolours, sculptures, ceramics, miniatures, etc.

Rothesay Museum - Bournemouth
English porcelain, 17th century furniture, collection of early Italian paintings, arms & armour, ethnography, etc.

Bournemouth Natural Science Society's Museum
Archaeology & local natural history.

Brewery Farm Museum - Milton Abbas
Brewing & village bygones from Dorset.

Dorset County Museum - Dorchester
Geology, natural history, pre-history. Thomas Hardy memorabilia

Philpot Museum - Lyme Regis
Old documents & prints, fossils, lace & old fire engine.

Guildhall Museum - Poole
Social & civic life of Poole during 18th & 19th centuries displayed in two-storey Georgian market house.

Scapolen's Court - Poole
14th century house of local merchant exhibiting local & archaeological history of town, also industrial archaeology.

Sherborne Museum - Sherborne
Local history & geology - abbey of AD 705, Sherborne missal AD 1400, 18th century local silk industry.

Gallery 24 - Shaftesbury
Art exhibitions - paintings, pottery, etc.

Red House Museum & Art Gallery - Christchurch
Natural history & antiques of the region. Georgian house with herb garden.

Priest's House Museum - Wimbourne Minster
Tudor building in garden exhibiting local archaeology & history.

Other things to see & do

Abbotsbury Swannery - Abbotsbury
Unique colony of Swans established by monks in the 14th century. 16th century duck decoy, reed walk, information centre.

Dorset Rare Breeds Centre - Park Farm, Gillingham

Poole Potteries - the Quay, Poole

Sea Life Centre - Weymouth
Variety of displays, including Ocean Tunnel, sharks, living "touch" pools.

West Bay.

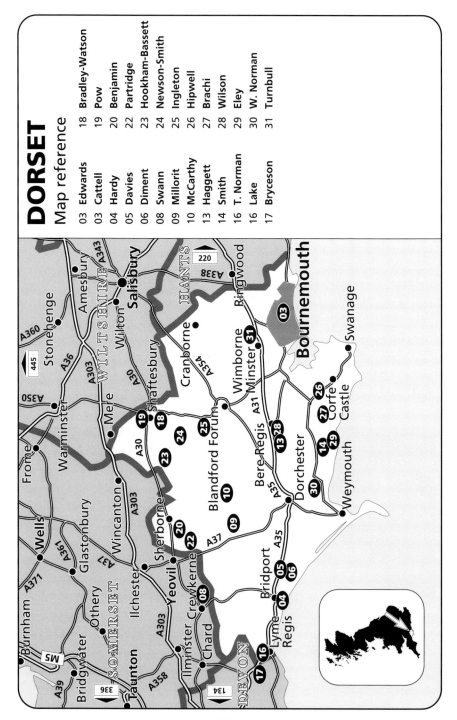

DORSET
Map reference

03	Edwards
03	Cattell
04	Hardy
05	Davies
06	Diment
08	Swann
09	Millorit
10	McCarthy
13	Haggett
14	Smith
16	T. Norman
16	Lake
17	Bryceson
18	Bradley-Watson
19	Pow
20	Benjamin
22	Partridge
23	Hookham-Bassett
24	Newson-Smith
25	Ingleton
26	Hipwell
27	Brachi
28	Wilson
29	Eley
30	W. Norman
31	Turnbull

Dorset

			rate £ from - to per person	children taken	evening meals	animals taken
Alan & Jackie Edwards **Gervis Court Hotel** **38 Gervis Road** **Bournemouth** **BH1 3DH** **Tel: (01202) 556871** **Fax 01202 556871** **Open: ALL YEAR** **Map Ref No. 03**	Nearest Road: A.338 Gervis Court is a charming detached Victorian villa, set in its own grounds amongst the pine trees. Centrally located for all amenities. It is just a very short walk to the beach, shops, theatres, clubs & Conference Centre. Each of the bedrooms are en-suite, tastefully furnished with comfort in mind & all have T.V. & coffee/tea making facilities. Many rooms are on the ground floor. It is ideally located for visiting the beautiful Dorset coast & the New Forest. **E-mail: enquiries@gerviscourthotel.co.uk**	£19.00 to £26.00 VISA: M'CARD:	Y	N	N
Brian & Jane Cattell **Sandhurst Hotel** **16 Southern Road** **Southbourne** **Bournemouth** **BH6 3SR** **Tel: (01202) 423748** **Open: APR - OCT** **Map Ref No. 03**	Nearest Road: A.338 Guests' comfort is a priority at this friendly, welcoming hotel. There's a choice of 5 comfortable rooms (incl. a ground-floor one) each with en-suite facilities. All have colour T.V. & tea/coffee makers. Good home-cooked breakfasts, & evening meals available. Situated 2 mins from the beach in a quiet suburb of Bournemouth. An ideal centre for touring, with Christchurch, Beaulieu, the New Forest, Salisbury & Dorchester a short drive. Private parking. Children over 4.	£20.00 to £25.00	Y	Y	N
Alan & Louisa Hardy **Britmead House** **154 West Bay Road** **Bridport** **DT6 4EG** **Tel: (01308) 422941** **Fax 01308 422941** **Open: ALL YEAR** **Map Ref No. 04**	Nearest Road: A.35 A friendly welcome in a relaxed & comfortable atmosphere. Renowned for good food, a high standard of facilities, personal service & attention to detail. Situated between Bridport, the fishing harbour of West Bay, Chesil Beach & the Dorset Coastal Path. 7 individually decorated en-suite bedrooms, 1 ground-floor, all with T.V., tea facilities & hairdryer. South-facing lounge & dining room overlook the garden & open countryside beyond. Optional dinner, incorporating local fish & produce. Licensed. Parking.	£19.00 to £37.00 VISA: M'CARD:	Y	Y	Y
Sydney & Jayne Davies **Innsacre Farmhouse** **Shipton Gorge** **Bridport DT6 4LJ** **Tel: (01308) 456137** **Fax 01308 456137** **Open: ALL YEAR (Excl.** **Xmas & New Year)** **Map Ref No. 05**	Nearest Road: A.35 17th-century farmhouse & barn in a magical & peaceful setting. Hidden midway between Lyme Regis & Dorchester, 3 miles from the sea & N.T. coastal path. South-facing, 10 acres of spinneys, steep hillsides, orchard & lawns in a beautiful setting. A mix of French rustic style, English comfort & a genuine, warm welcome. All rooms en-suite (with T.V. & tea tray). Large, cosy sitting-room, log fires, beams & delicious breakfasts. Parking. Licensed. Children over 9.	£30.00 to £55.00 VISA: M'CARD:	Y	Y	Y
Sue Diment **Rudge Farm** **Chilcombe** **Bridport DT6 4NF** **Tel: (01308) 482630** **Fax 01308 482635** **Open: ALL YEAR (Excl. Xmas)** **Map Ref No. 06**	Nearest Road: A.35 Rudge Farm is peacefully situated on a gentle south-facing slope overlooking the beautiful Bride Valley, just over 2 miles from the sea. After a day spent exploring the West Dorset countryside, relax in this comfortable Victorian farmhouse before trying one of the excellent pubs or restaurants. The attractively furnished rooms are all en-suite, with T.V., tea tray & far-reaching views. **E-mail: sue@rudge-farm.co.uk**	£24.00 to £26.00 VISA: M'CARD:	Y	N	N

Broadview Gardens. Crewkerne.

Dorset

		rate £ from - to per person	children taken	evening meals	animals taken

Gillian & Robert Swann **Broadview Gardens** **East Crewkerne** **Crewkerne** **TA18 7AG** Tel: (01460) 73424 Fax 01460 73424 Open: **ALL YEAR** Map Ref No. 08	Nearest Road: A.30 Unusual Colonial bungalow built in an era of quality. En-suite rooms overlooking an acre of beautiful secluded gardens. Furnished with your hosts personal collection of antiques. Achieving top quality awards for comfort, friendliness & cleanliness plus special awards given for their full English breakfasts & traditional English home cooking. Rooms with easy chairs, tea & coffee facilities, fresh milk, fridge, elec. fan & colour T.V.. 20 min Dorset coast. Secure parking. **E-mail: broadgdn@eurobell.co.uk**	£25.00 to £30.00 *see PHOTO over* *p. 170* VISA: M'CARD:	Y	Y	Y
Anita & Andre Millorit **Brambles** **Woolcombe** **Melbury Bubb** **Dorchester DT2 0NJ** Tel: (01935) 83672 Open: **ALL YEAR (Excl. Xmas)** Map Ref No. 09	Nearest Road: A.37 Set in beautiful, tranquil countryside, Brambles is a pretty thatched cottage offering every comfort, superb views & a friendly welcome. There is a choice of en-suite twin, double or single rooms, all having colour T.V. & tea/coffee-making facilities. A pretty garden is available for relaxing. A full English or Continental breakfast is served. There are many interesting places to visit & wonderful walks for enthusiasts. A charming home.	£20.00 to £25.00 *see PHOTO over* *p. 172*	Y	N	N
Annette & Rupert McCarthy **Rew Cottage** **Buckland Newton** **Dorchester DT2 7DN** Tel: (01300) 345467 Fax 01300 345467 Open: **ALL YEAR (Excl. Xmas & New Year)** Map Ref No. 10	Nearest Road: A.35, A.37 A warm welcome awaits you in a peaceful cottage in the heart of Hardy's Dorset. Surrounded by green farmland with lovely views on all sides. An ideal centre for walking or touring & within easy reach of Sherborne, Dorchester & the sea. Bedrooms are comfortably furnished; double, twin & single rooms (with tea/coffee facilities & T.V.). 2 private bathrooms adjacent. Attractive pubs within easy reach for evening meals. Children & animals by arrangement.	£20.00 to £25.00	Y	N	Y
Mrs D. M. Haggett **Vartrees House** **Moreton** **Dorchester** **DT2 8BE** Tel: (01305) 852704 Open: **ALL YEAR** Map Ref No. 13	Nearest Road: B.3390 off A.35 Peaceful & secluded character country house set in 3 acres of picturesque woodland gardens. Built by Hermann Lea, friend of Thomas Hardy. Accommodation throughout is spacious & comfortable. Tea/coffee makers in all 3 bedrooms, 1 en-suite. T.V. lounge. Situated near the pretty village of Moreton, with its renowned church & burial place of Lawrence of Arabia. Coast 4 miles. Station 1/4 of mile. Excellent local pubs. Children over 10 years welcome.	£18.00 to £25.00	Y	N	Y
Mrs Jennifer Smith **The Manor House** **Winfrith Newburgh** **Dorchester** **DT2 8JR** Tel: (01305) 854987 Fax 01305 854988 Open: **ALL YEAR** Map Ref No. 14	Nearest Road: A.352 This much-loved manor house with large walled garden is near Lulworth Cove, a spectacular coast path & Hardy Country. A Jacobean staircase ascends to the Green Room with a large double bed, 18th-century panelling & an en-suite bathroom with roll-top bath. The Victorian Room has twin brass beds with a private shower room adjacent. Both have T.V., tea-making facilities & antique furniture. A self-contained wing also available. 2 nearby pubs serve excellent evening meals. Please note 2-night minimum bookings.	£23.00 to £25.00	Y	N	N

Brambles. Woolcombe.

Dorset

			rate £ from - to per person	children taken	evening meals	animals taken
Tony & Vicky Norman **The Red House** **Sidmouth Road** **Lyme Regis** **DT7 3ES** **Tel: (01297) 442055** **Fax 01297 442055** **Open: Mid MAR - Mid NOV** **Map Ref No. 16**	Nearest Road: A.3052 This distinguished house, set in mature grounds, enjoys spectacular coastal views, & yet is only a short walk to the centre of Lyme Regis. The 3 en-suite bedrooms (1 for family use; 2 are especially spacious) are furnished with every comfort, in-cluding tea/coffee makers, T.V., clock-radio, desk, armchairs, a drink refrigerator, central heating & electric heaters. Fresh flowers & magazines are among the little extras. Breakfast can be taken on the garden balcony. Parking. Children over 8. **E-mail: red.house@virgin.net**	£20.00 to £25.00 VISA: M'CARD:	Y	N	N
Mrs Diana Lake **Rashwood Lodge** **Clappentail Lane** **Lyme Regis** **DT7 3LZ** **Tel: (01297) 445700** **Open: FEB - NOV** **Map Ref No. 16**	Nearest Road: A.3052, A.35 Rashwood Lodge is an unusual octagonal house, located on the western hillside with views over Lyme Bay. Just a short walk away is the coastal footpath & Ware Cliff, famed for its part in 'The French Lieutenant's Woman'. The bedrooms have their own facilities & benefit from their south-facing aspect overlooking a large & colourful garden set in peaceful surroundings. Golf course 1 mile. A charming home. Children over 4 years.	£21.00 to £25.00	Y	N	N
Mr & Mrs Andrew Bryceson **Amherst Lodge** **Uplyme** **Lyme Regis** **DT7 3XH** **Tel: (01297) 442773** **Fax 01297 442625** **Open: Easter - Jan 5** **Map Ref No. 17**	Nearest Road: A.35 A small country estate with a casual feel where traditional elegance & comfort border on luxury. Gardens, walks & fly fishing are within the 140-acre grounds whilst the coast, excellent pubs & picturesque villages are nearby. Wake up to the birdsong & finish the day slumped in front of the fire in the ancient oak-panelled lounge. Gourmet meals (available selected nights only) & 30 single malt whiskies. A charming home. **E-mail: stay@amherstlodge.com**	£27.50 to £42.50 VISA: M'CARD:	N	N	N
Richard & Tavy Bradley-Watson **Melbury Mill** **Melbury Abbas** **Shaftesbury** **SP7 0DB** **Tel: (01747) 852163** **Open: ALL YEAR** **Map Ref No. 18**	Nearest Road: A.350, A.30 Mr & Mrs Bradley-Watson offer a warm welcome at this old working mill, set in 9 acres of meadows & overlooking a mill pond abounding with water-fowl. All bedrooms are large & centrally heated, & have en-suite facilities. Located just south of Shaftesbury, famous for its Gold Hill, it is in picturesque Thomas Hardy countryside. Ideal for walkers, with N.T. downland & the properties of Stourhead & Kingston Lacy close by. 3-course dinners are provided using fresh local produce.	£25.00 to £27.50 *see PHOTO over* *p. 174*	Y	Y	N
J. Benjamin **Munden House** **Mundens Lane** **Alweston** **Sherborne** **DT9 5AU** **Tel: (01963) 23150** **Fax 01963 23153** **Open: ALL YEAR** **Map Ref No. 20**	Nearest Road: A.3030 The main part of Munden House dates back to the 17th century & over the past year it has been beautifully restored. There are 6 attractively decorated & tastefully furnished bedrooms & a studio annexe with its own kitchenette & bath-room. Each room has its own bathroom, 'phone, colour T.V., tea/coffee facilities, books & maga-zines. The guests drawing room & dining room are particularly attractive. Munden House is the perfect spot from which to explore this beautiful region. (Single occupancy supplement.)	£25.00 to £35.00 VISA: M'CARD:	Y	N	N

Melbury Mill. Melbury Abbas.

**All the establishments mentioned in this guide
are members of the
Worldwide Bed & Breakfast Association.**

**If you have any comments regarding your
accommodation please send them to us
using the form at the back of the book.
We value your comments.**

Manor Farmhouse. Yetminster.

Dorset

			rate £ from - to per person	children taken	evening meals	animals taken

David & Diana Pow **Cliff House** **Breach Lane** **Shaftesbury** **SP7 8LF** **Tel: (01747) 852548** Fax 01747 852548 **Open: ALL YEAR** **Map Ref No. 19**	Nearest Road: A.30, A.350 A fine example of a spacious Grade II listed period property with quiet rooms. Within walking distance of the ancient Saxon hilltop town which is one of the oldest & highest in southern England, having magnificent views & the famous Gold Hill. An ideal central position for visiting the surrounding countryside of Wessex which abounds with historic country houses, cathedrals & abbeys. Good pubs & restaurants locally. 2 bedrooms, each with an en-suite bathroom. Children over 5. **E-mail: dpow@dial.pipex.com**	£25.00 to £27.50 🚭 **Y N N**
Mrs A. C. Partridge **Manor Farmhouse** **High Street** **Yetminster** **Sherborne DT9 6LF** **Tel: (01935) 872247** Fax 01935 872247 **Open: ALL YEAR** **Map Ref No. 22**	Nearest Road: A.37 This 17th-century farmhouse, with oak panelling, beams & inglenook fireplaces, offers every comfort to the discerning visitor. 4 bedrooms, all with en-suite facilities & modern amenities, including T.V. & tea/coffee. Delicious meals served, made from traditional recipes & using fresh local produce. The village is described as the best 17th-century stone-built village in the south of England. An excellent centre for visiting Sherborne, Glastonbury, New Forest & Hardy's Dorset.	£30.00 to £30.00 🚭 *see PHOTO over* p. 176 VISA: M'CARD: **N Y N**
Jill & Ken Hookham-Bassett **Stourcastle Lodge** **Gough's Close** **Sturminster Newton** **DT10 1BU** **Tel: (01258) 472320** Fax 01258 473381 **Open: ALL YEAR** **Map Ref No. 23**	Nearest Road: A.357 Stourcastle Lodge is a family-run business, offering a very high standard of accommodation, with personal service & excellent cuisine. A superb breakfast is served in the attractive dining room. All the elegant bedrooms are south-facing & overlook the delightful garden, which is stocked full of herbaceous & perennial borders. Stourcastle Lodge is a beautiful home, & an ideal base for exploring Dorset & its many attractions. **E-mail: jillyhb@talk21.com**	£28.50 to £36.00 *see PHOTO over* p. 178 VISA: M'CARD: **Y Y N**
Mary-Ann Newson-Smith **Lovells Court** **Marnhull** **Sturminster Newton** **DT10 1JJ** **Tel: (01258) 820652** Fax 01258 820487 **Open: ALL YEAR** **Map Ref No. 24**	Nearest Road: A.30 Lovells Court is a rambling old house of character, set in the delightful countryside of Thomas Hardy, & with fine views across the Blackmore Vale. The market town of Sturminster Newton & the Abbeys of Sherborne & Milton Abbas are nearby. An excellent base for enjoying rural Dorset & its many N.T. properties. There are 2 en-suite rooms & 1 with private bathroom, all with colour T.V., radio & tea-making facilities. 2 excellent village inns for food all year round. Children over 12.	£23.00 to £26.00 🚭 **Y N N**
A. & J. Ingleton **Fiddleford Mill House** **Fiddleford** **Sturminster Newton** **DT10 2BX** **Tel: (01258) 472786** **Open: ALL YEAR** **Map Ref No. 25**	Nearest Road: A.357 An idyllically situated, Grade I listed 16th-century farm/manor house of great architectural interest overlooking the River Stour in peacefully secluded countryside. A beautifully furnished & decorated family home. 3 comfortable bedrooms, 1 with a 16th-century moulded plaster ceiling & en-suite bathroom, the other 2 sharing a bathroom. All have tea-making facilities & T.V.. A beautiful garden with a sitting area. 2 pubs within walking distance. Country pursuits available locally. Children over 12. Animals by arrangement.	£20.00 to £27.50 **Y N Y**

Stourcastle Lodge. Sturminster Newton.

Dorset

		rate £ from - to per person	children taken	evening meals	animals taken
Anthea & Michael Hipwell **Gold Court House** **St. John's Hill** **Wareham** **BH20 4LZ** **Tel: (01929) 553320** **Fax 01929 553320** **Open: ALL YEAR (Excl. Xmas & New Year)** **Map Ref No. 26**	Nearest Road: A.351 Gold Court House is a charming Georgian house with walled garden on a small garden on the south-side of Wareham. Offering 3 light & airy double or twin rooms with private bathrooms & all facilities at hand, at your request. Wareham is ideally situated for exploring the magnificent coast-line of South Dorset & the Isle of Purbeck. Anthea & Michael are always pleased to help & advise on the many places of interest, sporting activities & where to dine. (Evening meals are available during the winter only.) Children over 10 years.	£22.50 to £30.00	Y	Y	N
Rachel & Peter Brachi **West Coombe Farmhouse** **Coombe Keynes** **Wareham** **BH20 5PS** **Tel: (01929) 462889** **Fax 01929 405863** **Open: ALL YEAR (Excl. Xmas)** **Map Ref No. 27**	Nearest Road: A.352 Discover a peaceful way of life when you stay at this restored Georgian farmhouse in the delightful village of Coombe Keynes. In summer unwind in the beautiful garden & in winter linger by the open fire in the private sitting room. There are 3 attractive guest bedrooms. Lulworth is only 3 miles away & many traditional outdoor activities can be found locally, or explore the glorious countryside on your hosts mountain bikes. Children over 12 years welcome.	£20.00 to £22.00	Y	N	N
Mrs Beryl Wilson **Appletree Cottage** **12 Shitterton** **Bere Regis** **Wareham BH20 7HU** **Tel: (01929) 471686** **Open: ALL YEAR** **Map Ref No. 28**	Nearest Road: A.31, A.35 Appletree Cottage is a pretty 17th-century thatched cottage in a peaceful hamlet on the edge of Bere Regis in Hardy country, 20 mins from Lulworth Cove & centrally placed for exploring Dorset's beautiful coast, countryside & towns. 2 village pubs 1/2 a mile away serve lunches & evening meals. Guests have their own bathroom, stair-case & cosy sitting room with beams, inglenook fireplace & woodburner.	£19.00 to £20.00	Y	N	N
Tony & Mary Eley **Gatton House** **West Lulworth** **BH20 5RU** **Tel: (01929) 400252** **Fax 01929 400252** **Open: MAR - OCT** **Map Ref No. 29**	Nearest Road: A.352 Spectacularly positioned, quiet & comfortable, this small hotel is set amongst the Purbeck Hills, yet only a strolling distance from famous Lulworth Cove. The house has a spacious breakfast room, 8 attractive en-suite bedrooms & a lounge with colour T.V.. Outside, the terrace provides a perfect venue for morning coffee or afternoon tea. Gatton House is an ideal location for walking or touring Dorset's beauty spots, & it is within easy reach of Bournemouth, Poole, Swanage, Dorchester & Weymouth. VISA: M'CARD:	£23.50 to £30.50	Y	N	Y
Joyce & Bill Norman **Dingle Dell** **Church Lane** **Osmington** **Weymouth DT3 6EW** **Tel: (01305) 832378** **Fax 01305 832378** **Open: MAR - OCT** **Map Ref No. 30**	Nearest Road: A.353 Dingle Dell is situated on the edge of the village of Osmington, in its own charming garden, with roses covering the mellow stone walls. 2 spa-cious & comfortable bedrooms (1 en-suite), fur-nished to the highest of standards, & with each overlooking the garden & countryside. Both rooms have T.V. & tea/coffee facilities. A hearty English breakfast is served. Dingle Dell provides a truly peaceful spot to rest & relax, & is a convenient base for exploring the many attractions of Dorset.	£21.00 to £22.00	N	N	N

Dorset

		rate £ from - to per person	children taken	evening meals	animals taken
John & Sara Turnbull **Thornhill** **Holt** **Wimborne** **BH21 7DJ** **Tel: (01202) 889434** **Open: ALL YEAR** **Map Ref No. 31**	Nearest Road: A.31 Visitors are warmly welcomed to this large, thatched family house located in rural surroundings 3 1/2 miles from Wimborne. Large garden. Hard tennis court available. Double, twin & single rooms. 1 private bathroom, & another which may be shared. Sitting room with colour T.V. & coffee/tea-making & laundry facilities. Plenty of good local pubs. Well situated for exploring the coast, New Forest & Salisbury area.	£22.00 to £25.00	N	N	N

**All the establishments mentioned in this guide
are members of
The Worldwide Bed & Breakfast Association**

**When booking your accommodation please
mention
The Best Bed & Breakfast**

Essex

Essex
(East Anglia)

Essex is a county of commerce, busy roads & busier towns, container ports & motorways, yet it is also a landscape of mudflats & marshes, of meadows & leafy lanes, villages & duckponds. Half timbered buildings & thatched & clapboard cottages stand among rolling hills topped by orange brick windmills.

The coast on the east, now the haunt of wildfowl, sea-birds, sailors & fishermen has seen the arrival of Saxons, Romans, Danes, Vikings & Normans. The names of their settlements remain - Wivenhoe, Layer-de-la-Haye, Colchester & Saffron Walden - the original Saxon name was Walden, but the Saffron was added when the crocus used for dyes & flavouring was grown here in the 15th century.

The seaside resorts of Southend & Clacton are bright & cheery, much-loved by families for safe beaches. Harbours here are great favourites with anglers & yachtsmen.

Inland lie the watermeadows & windmills, willows & cool green water which shaped the life & work of John Constable, one of the greatest landscape painters. Scenes are instantly recognisable today as you walk to Dedham along the banks of the swiftly flowing River Stour.

Colchester is England's oldest recorded town, once the Roman capital of Britain trading in corn & cattle, slaves & pearls. Roman remains are still to be seen & their original street plan is the basis of much of modern Colchester. A great feast is held here annually to celebrate the famous oyster - the "Colchester native".

South Essex, though sliced through by the M.25 motorway is still a place of woodland & little rivers. The ancient trees of Epping Forest, hunting ground for generations of monarchs, spread 6,000 acres of leafy glades & heathland into the London suburbs.

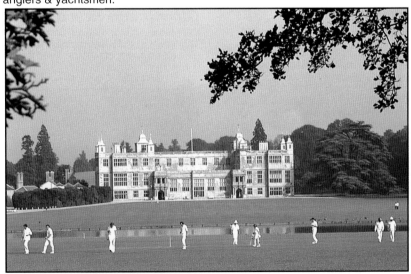

Audley End. Saffron Walden.

Essex

Essex

Gazeteer

Areas of outstanding natural beauty.
Dedham Vale (part), Epping Forest.

Houses & Castles

Audley End House - Saffron Walden
1603 - Jacobean mansion on site of
Benedictine Abbey. State rooms & Hall.
Castle House - Dedham
Home of the late Sir A. Munnings.
President R.A. Paintings & other works.
Hedingham Castle - Castle Hedingham
Norman keep & Tudor bridge.
Layer Marney Tower - Nr. Colchester
1520 Tudor brick house. 8 storey gate
tower. Formal yew hedges & lawns.
Payecock's - Coggeshall
1500 - richly ornamented - merchant's
house - National Trust.
St. Osyth's Priory - St. Osyth
Was Augustinian Abbey for 400 years until
dissolution in 1537, 13th-18th century
buildings. 13th century chapel. Wonderful
gatehouse containing works of art
including ceramics & Chinese Jade.
Spains Hall - Finchingfield
Elizabethan Manor incorporating parts of
earlier timber structure. Paintings,
furniture & tapestries.

Cathedrals & Churches

Brightlingsea (All Saints)
15th century tower - some mediaeval
painting fragments. Brasses.
Castle Hedingham (St. Nicholas)
12th century doorways, 14th century rood
screen, 15th century stalls, 16th century
hammer beams, altar tomb.
Copford (St. Michael & All Angels)
12th century wall paints. Continuous
vaulted nave & chancel
.**Finchingfield** (St. John the Baptist)
Norman workmanship. 16th century tomb
-18th centuary tower & cupola.
Layer Marney (St. Mary)
Tudor brickwork, Renaissance
monuments, mediaeval screens, wall
paintings.
Little Maplestead (St. John the Baptist)
14th century, one of the five round
churches in England, having hexagonal
nave, circular aisle, 14th century arcade.
Newport (St. Mary the Virgin)
13th century. Interesting 13th century
altar (portable) with top which becomes
reredos when opened. 15th century
chancel screen. Pre-Reformation Lectern.
Some old glass.

Museums & Galleries

Dutch Cottage Museum - Canvey Island
17th century thatched cottage of octagonal
Dutch design. Exhibition of models of
shipping used on the Thames through the
ages.
Ingatestone Hall - Ingatestone
Documents & pictures of Essex.
The Castle - Colchester
Norman Keep now exhibiting
archeological material from Essex &
especially Roman Colchester.
Southchurch Hall - Southend-on-Sea
14th century moated & timber framed
manor house - Tudor wing, furnished as
meiaeval manor.
Thurrock - Grays
Prehistoric, Romano-British & pagan
Saxon archaeology.

Other things to see & do

Colchester Oyster Fishery - Colchester
Tour showing cultivating, harvesting,
grading & packing of oysters. Talk, tour
& sample.

Burnham on Crouch.

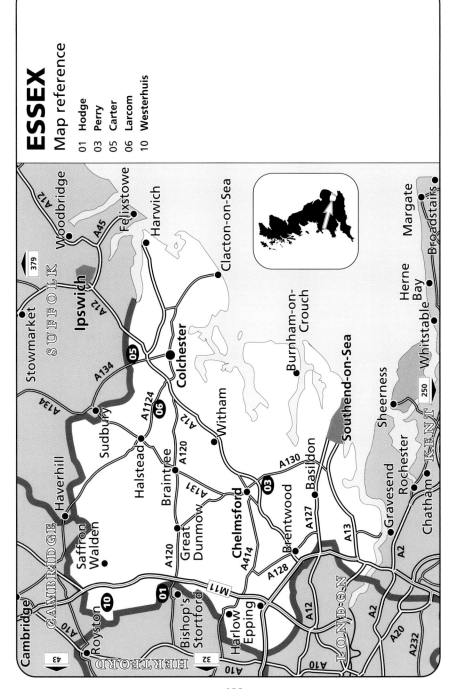

ESSEX

Map reference

01 Hodge
03 Perry
05 Carter
06 Larcom
10 Westerhuis

Essex

	rate £ from - to per person	evening meals children taken	animals taken
John & Angela Hodge **The Cottage** **71 Birchanger Lane** **Birchanger** **Bishop's Stortford** CM23 5QA **Tel: (01279) 812349** **Fax 01279 815045** **Open:** ALL YEAR (Excl. Xmas) **Map Ref No. 01**	Nearest Road: A.120, M.11 Situated within a quiet village, this charming 17th-century listed house offers 15 comfortable en-suite bedrooms, all with colour T.V. & tea/coffee makers. Oak-panelled reception rooms with log burners, & a conservatory/dining room looking onto mature gardens. A convenient base for trips to Cambridge, London & East Anglia, & within easy reach of Stansted Airport & Bishops Stortford. Private parking available. A delightful home, ideal for a relaxing short break. VISA: M'CARD:	£25.00 to £45.00	Y N N
Mrs Glen Perry **Little Sir Hughes** **West Hanningfield Road** **Great Baddow** **Chelmsford** **CM2 7SZ** **Tel: (01245) 471701** **Fax 01245 478023** **Open: ALL YEAR** **Map Ref No. 03**	Nearest Road: A.1114, A.12 Little Sir Hughes is a 300-year-old Grade II listed country house set in a 2 1/2 acre formal garden. Set in a very peaceful location, yet only 5 mins from A.12, 10 mins from Chelmsford & 35 mins by rail from London. All rooms are beautifully furnished. 2 double bedrooms & 1 twin, all en-suite & each with hairdryer, T.V. & tea/coffee. Delightful guests' drawing room with log fire. Superb breakfasts with home-made preserves a speciality. Dinner on request. Parking. Children over 10. **E-mail: accom@englishlive.co.uk**	£27.50 to £55.00	Y Y N
Col. & Mrs Jeremy Carter **Round Hill House** **Parsonage Hill** **Boxted** **Colchester** **CO4 5ST** **Tel: (01206) 272392** **Fax 01206 272392** **Open: ALL YEAR** **Map Ref No. 05**	Nearest Road: A.134 Round Hill House is an attractive, comfortable house with en-suite bedrooms, beautiful views & delightful gardens set in Constable country on the edge of the Dedham Vale. Tennis & coarse fishing are on the premises. Rural East Anglia is on the doorstep with its medieval villages, churches, antique shops, music festivals, art galleries, stately homes & gardens. Walking, racing at Newmarket, golf, riding, trout fishing & safe beaches are all within easy distance. Evening meals by arrangement.	£22.50 to £30.00	Y Y Y
Lady Larcom **Elm House** **14 Upper Holt Street** **Earls Colne** **Colchester** **CO6 2PG** **Tel: (01787) 222197** **Open:** ALL YEAR (Excl. Xmas) **Map Ref No. 06**	Nearest Road: A.1124 A comfortable & welcoming 18th-century family home in a village of great architectural interest, & with a delightful, secluded garden. Imaginative cuisine using local produce. Evening meals available on request. There are 3 charming bedrooms, 2 with en-suite/private bathroom. Within easy reach of Colchester (Roman walls, Norman castle), Dedham Vale (immortalised by Constable's paintings), Cambridge, Long Melford & Beth Chatto's gardens.	£19.00 to £25.00	Y Y Y
Mrs Tineke Westerhuis **Rockells Farm** **Duddenhoe End** **Saffron Walden CB11 4UY** **Tel: (01763) 838053** **Fax 01763 837001** **Open:** ALL YEAR (Excl. Xmas) **Map Ref No. 10**	Nearest Road: A.14, A.120 Rockells is an arable farm in a beautiful corner of Essex. The Georgian house has a large garden with a 3-acre lake for coarse fishing. All 3 rooms have en-suite facilities. 1 room is on the ground floor. On the farm are several footpaths. Beautiful villages in the area. Within easy reach are Audley End House, Duxford Air Museum & Cambridge. London is approx. 1 hour by car or train. Stansted Airport 30 mins by car.	£20.00 to £25.00	Y N N

Gloucestershire

Gloucestershire
(Heart of England)

The landscape is so varied the people speak not of one Gloucestershire but of three - Cotswold, Vale & Forest. The rounded hills of the Cotswolds sweep & fold in graceful compositions to form a soft & beautiful landscape in which nestle many pretty villages. To the east there are wonderful views of the Vale of Berkeley & Severn, & across to the dark wooded slopes of the Forest of Dean on the Welsh borders.

Hill Forts, ancient trackways & long barrows of neolithic peoples can be explored, & remains of many villas from late Roman times can be seen. A local saying "Scratch Gloucester & find Rome" reveals the lasting influence of the Roman presence. Three major roads mark the path of invasion & settlement. Akeman street leads to London, Ermine street & the Fosse Way to the north east. A stretch of Roman road with its original surface can be seen at Blackpool Bridge in the Forest of Dean, & Cirencester's museum reflects its status as the second most important Roman city in the country.

Offa's Dyke, 80 miles of bank & ditch on the Welsh border was the work of the Anglo-Saxons of Mercia who invaded in the wake of the Romans. Cotswold means "hills of the sheepcotes" in the Anglo-Saxon tongue, & much of the heritage of the area has its roots in the wealth created by the wool industry here.

Fine Norman churches such as those at Tewkesbury & Bishops Cleeve were overshadowed by the development of the perpendicular style of building made possible by the growing prosperity. Handsome 15th century church towers crown many wool towns & villages as at Northleach, Chipping Camden & Cirencester, & Gloucester has a splendid 14th century cathedral. Detailing on church buildings gives recognition to the source of the wealth-cloth-workers shears are depicted on the north west buttresses of Grantham church tower & couchant rams decorate church buttresses at Compton Bedale.

Wool & cloth weaving dominated life here in the 14th & 15th centuries with most families dependent on the industry. The cottage craft of weaving was gradually overtaken by larger looms & water power. A water mill can be seen in the beautiful village of Lower Slaughter & the cottages of Arlington Row in Bibury were a weaving factory.

The Cotswold weaving industry gave way to the growing force of the Lancashire mills but a few centres survive. At Witney you can still buy the locally made blankets for which the town is famous.

From the 16th century the wealthy gentry built parks & mansions. Amongst the most notable are the Jacobean Manor house at Stanway & the contrasting Palladian style mansion at Barnsley Park. Elizabethan timber frame buildings can be seen at Didbrook, Dymock & Deerhurst but houses in the local mellow golden limestone are more common, with Chipping Camden providing excellent examples.

Cheltenham was only a village when, in 1716 a local farmer noticed a flock of pigeons pecking at grains of salt around a saline spring in his fields. He began to bottle & sell the water & in 1784 his son-in-law, Henry Skillicorne, built a pump room & the place received the name of Cheltenham Spa. Physicians published treatises on the healing qualities of the waters, visitors began to flock there & Cheltenham grew in style & elegance.

Gloucestershire

Gloucestershire Gazeteer

Areas of outstanding natural beauty
The Cotswolds, Malvern Hills & the
Wye Valley.

Houses & Castles

Ashleworth Court - Ashleworth
15th century limestone Manor house.
Badminton House - Badminton
Built in the reign of Charles II.
Stone newel staircase.
Berkeley Castle - Berkeley
12th century castle - still occupied by the
Berkeley family. Magnificent collections of
furniture, paintings, tapestries & carved
timber work. Lovely terraced gardens &
deer park.
Chavenage - Tetbury
Elizabethan Cotswold Manor house,
Cromwellian associations.
Clearwell Castle - Nr. Coleford
A Georgian neo-Gothic house said to be
oldest in Britain, recently restored.
Court House - Painswick
Cotswold Manor house - has original court
room & bedchamber of Charles I.
Splendid panelling & antique furniture.
Dodington House - Chipping Sodbury
Perfect 18th century house with superb
staircase. Landscape by
Capability Brown.
Horton Court - Horton
Cotswold manor house altered & restored
in 19th century.
Kelmscott Manor - Nr. Lechlade
16th century country house - 17th century
additions. Examples of work of William
Morris, Rosetti & Burne-Jones.
Owlpen Manor - Nr. Dursley
Historic group of traditional Cotswold
stone buildings. Tudor Manor house with
church, barn, court house & a grist mill.
Holds a rare set of 17th century painted
cloth wall hangings.
Snowshill Manor - Broadway
Tudor house with 17th century facade.
Unique collection of musical instruments &
clocks, toys, etc. Formal garden.
Sudeley Castle - Winchcombe
12th century - home of Katherine Parr, is
rich in historical associations, contains art
treasures & relics of bygone days.

Cathedrals & Churches

Bishops Cleeve (St. Michael & All Saints)
12th century with 17th century gallery.
Magnificent Norman west front & south
porch. Decorated chancel.   Fine
window.
Bledington (St.Leonards)
15th century glass in this perpendicular
church, Norman bellcote. Early English
east window.
Buckland (St. Michael)
13th century nave arcades. 17th century
oak panelling, 15th century glass.
Cirencester (St. John the Baptist)
A magnificent church - remarkable
exterior, 3 storey porch, 2 storey oriel
windows, traceries & pinnacles. Wine-
glass pulpit c.1450. 15th century glass in
east window, monuments in Lady chapel.
Gloucester Cathedral
Birthplace of Perpendicular style in 14th
century. Fan vaulting, east windows
commemorate Battle of Crecy - Norman
Chapter House.
Hailes Abbey - Winchcombe
14th century wall paintings, 15th century
tiles, glass & screen, 17th century pulpit.
Elizabethan benches.
Iron Acton (St. James the Less)
Perpendicular - 15th century memorial
cross. 19th century mosaic floors,
Laudian alter rails, Jacobean pulpit,
effigies.
Newland (All Saints)
13th century, restored 18th century.
Pinnacled west tower, effigies.
Prinknash Abbey - Gloucester
14th & 16th century - Benedictine Abbey.
Tewkesbury Abbey - Tewkesbury
Dates back to Norman times, contains
Romanesque & Gothic styles. 14th
century monuments.
Yate (St. Mary)
Splendid perpendicular tower.

Museums & Galleries

Bishop Hooper's Lodgings - Gloucester
3 Tudor timber frame buildings - museum
of domestic life & agriculture in Gloucester
since 1500.
Bourton Motor Museum - Bourton-on-
the-Water
Collection of cars & motor cycles.
Cheltenham Art Gallery - Cheltenham.

Gloucestershire

Lower Slaughter.

Gallery of Dutch paintings, collection of oils, watercolours, pottery, porcelain, English & Chinese; furniture.
City Wall & Bastion - Gloucester
Roman & mediaeval city defences in an underground exhibition room.
Stroud Museum - Cirencester
Depicts earlier settlements in the area & has a very fine collection of Roman antiquities.

Historic Monuments
Chedworth Roman Villa - Yanworth
Remains of Romano-British villa.
Belas Knap Long Barrow - Charlton Abbots
Neolithic burial ground - three burial chambers with external entrances.
Hailes Abbey - Stanway
Ruins of beautiful mediaeval abbey built by son of King John, 1246.
Witcombe Roman Villa - Nr. Birdlip

Large Roman villa - Hypocaust & mosaic pavements preserved.
Ashleworth Tithe Barn - Ashleworth
15th century tithe barn - 120 feet long - stone built, interesting roof timbering.
Odda's Chapel - Deerhurst
Rare Saxon chapel dating back to 1056.
Hetty Pegler's Tump - UleLong Barrow-fairly complete, chamber is 120 feet long.

Other things to see & do
Cheltenham International Festival of Music & Literature - Annual event.
Cotswolds Farm Park - dozens of rare breeds of farm animals.
The Three Choirs Festival - music festival staged in alternating years at Gloucester, Hereford & Worcester Cathedrals.
Slimbridge - Peter Scott's Wildfowl Trust.

GLOUCESTERSHIRE

Map reference

01	Nesbitt	18	Keyser
01	Bolton	19	Cassidy
01	Wright	20	Parsons
01	Adams	21	Sayers
02	Thornely	22	Beer
03	Moodie	23	Annis
04	Paz	24	Parkes
05	N.Brown	25	Helm
06	Hazell	26	Smalley
07	Beauvoisin	27	Anderson
09	Cittadino	28	Dean
09	Berg	29	Dare
09	Stone	30	Peacock
10	Tracey	31	Reeves
11	Minchin	32	Walsh
12	Burrough	33	Brunsdon
13	Whent	34	Tremellen
14	Carey-Wilson	35	Herford
15	Wilson	36	M.Brown
16	Holdsworth-Hunt		
17	Langton		

Clapton Manor. Clapton on the Hill.

Gloucestershire

		rate £ from - to per person	children taken	evening meals	animals taken
Mrs Caroline Nesbitt **Church House** **Clapton-on-the-Hill** **Bourton-on-the-Water** **GL54 2LG** **Tel: (01451) 822532** **Fax 01451 822472** **Open: ALL YEAR** **Map Ref No. 01**	Nearest Road: A.429 This completely restored 17th-century family house offers seclusion & privacy to its guests in elegant surroundings. Bedrooms are very comfortable with sloping ceilings, beams & T.V.. The tastefully furnished drawing room is available for guests' use & breakfast is served in a galleried dining room. Wonderful views over the church & the Windrush Valley complete the recipe for a delightful stay in Church House.	£30.00 to £35.00	Y	N	N
Mrs Karin Bolton **Clapton Manor** **Clapton-on-the-Hill** **Bourton-on-the-Water** **GL54 2LG** **Tel: (01451) 810202** **Fax 01451 821804** **Open: ALL YEAR (Excl.** **Xmas & New Year)** **Map Ref No. 01**	Nearest Road: A.40, A.429 Clapton Manor is an impressive 17th-century stone house standing at the top of a quiet village with stunning views across the Windrush Valley. The garden is planted with peonies, old-fashioned shrub roses & many unusual plants. The house is an elegant & informal family home. A sitting room for the guests' use & 2 delightful en-suite bedrooms with comfortable beds. Situated in the heart of the Cotswolds, it is ideal for visiting the well-known local gardens & within easy reach of Warwick, Stratford, Oxford & Blenheim Palace.	£30.00 to £32.50 🚭 *see PHOTO over* *p. 189* VISA: M'CARD:	Y	N	N
Julia Wright **Farncombe** **Clapton-on-the-Hill** **Bourton-on-the-Water** **GL54 2LG** **Tel: (01451) 820120** **Fax 01451 820120** **Open: ALL YEAR** **Map Ref No. 01**	Nearest Road: A.429 Come & share the peace, tranquillity & superb views of Farncombe, & eat, drink & sleep - smoke-free - 700ft above sea level & only 2 miles from Bourton-on-the-Water. 2 attractive doubles, with showers, & 1 twin en-suite. A spacious dining room, with tea/coffee-making facilities, & a comfortable T.V. lounge. Tourist information, maps & books & current menus for your choice when eating out. Numerous walks & drives, with easy access to all attractions & places of interest.	£19.50 to £22.00 🚭	N	N	N
Mrs Helen Adams **Upper Farm** **Clapton-on-the-Hill** **Bourton-on-the-Water** **GL54 2LG** **Tel: (01451) 820453** **Fax 01451 810185** **Open: MAR - NOV** **Map Ref No. 01**	Nearest Road: A.40, A.429 If peace & tranquillity is what you require, then this charming undiscovered village 2 miles from Bourton is certainly the spot. Clapton enjoys one of the finest Cotswold views from its hill position. Here, you will find Upper Farm, with its 17th-century stone farmhouse lovingly restored & yet retaining a wealth of original charm. Delightful accommodation, commanding views & personal attention are complemented with fresh farmhouse fayre. Children over 6 yrs welcome.	£19.00 to £22.50 🚭	Y	N	N
Mrs Ann Thornely **Eastcote Cottage** **Knapp Road East** **Thornbury** **Bristol BS35 2HJ** **Tel: (01454) 413106** **Fax 01454 281812** **Open: ALL YEAR (Excl. Xmas)** **Map Ref No. 02**	Nearest Road: A.38 Eastcote is a charming 200-year-old stone house located in a lovely rural setting, with splendid views across open countryside. Guests have a choice of 4 comfortable bedrooms with modern amenities. A colour-T.V. lounge is available for guests' use. Conveniently situated for the M.4/ M.5 interchange for the Cotswolds, with Bristol, Bath, Cheltenham & the Wye Valley easily accessible. Private parking available.	£24.00 to £26.00	Y	N	N

The Elms. Olveston.

The Malt House. Broad Campden.

Gloucestershire

		rate £ from - to per person	children taken	evening meals	animals taken
Mr & Mrs David Moodie **The Elms** **Olveston** **Bristol** **BS35 4DR** **Tel: (01454) 614559** Fax 01454 618607 **Open: ALL YEAR** **Map Ref No. 03**	Nearest Road: A.38 An elegant Grade II listed village house set in 2 acres with a stable conversion providing a comfortable suite (with its own access) & a self-contained cottage. Great attention is paid to guests' comfort. The owners are very allergy conscious & whenever possible, organic food is served in the beautifully furnished dining room. Ample private parking. Thornbury Castle Restaurant is only 3 miles away. Ideally situated close to M4/M5 interchange for Bristol, (Aztec Business Park), Cheltenham & the Cotswolds.	£35.00 to £40.00 *see PHOTO over* p. 191	N	N	N
John & Daphne Paz **Dornden Guest House** **15 Church Lane** **Old Sodbury** **Bristol BS37 6NB** **Tel: (01454) 313325** Fax 01454 312263 **Open: ALL YEAR (Excl. Xmas & New Year)** **Map Ref No. 04**	Nearest Road: A.432 Dornden, built of local Cotswold stone, stands in a beautiful garden enjoying the peace of the countryside & magnificent views to the west. 9 attractive rooms, 6 en-suite, overlooking the garden & the open country beyond. Delicious meals are prepared, using home-made produce (where possible) and free-range eggs. There is also a grass tennis court available to guests. A delightful home, with a warm, friendly atmosphere, ideal for exploring the beautiful West Country.	£28.00 to £38.00	Y	Y	Y
Mr Nick Brown **The Malt House** **Broad Campden** **GL55 6UU** **Tel: (01386) 840295** Fax 01386 841334 **Open: ALL YEAR (Excl. Xmas)** **Map Ref No. 05**	Nearest Road: A.44 Nick & Jean Brown have achieved a blend of relaxed & yet professional service, welcoming guests as part of an extended house party. This 17th-century former malting house is set in extensive gardens, with an orchard & croquet lawn. Public rooms are furnished with antiques. Bedrooms are en-suite, individually decorated & overlook the gardens. The Windrush Suite has an 18th-century 4-poster bed. Family & private garden suites. Excellent table d'hote evening meals. **E-mail: nick@the-malt-house.freeserve.co.uk**	£39.50 to £52.50 *see PHOTO over* p. 192 VISA: M'CARD: AMEX:	Y	Y	Y
Andrea Hazell **Laverton Meadow House** **Broadway** **WR12 7NA** **Tel: (01386) 584200** Fax 01386 584612 **Open: ALL YEAR** **Map Ref No. 06**	Nearest Road: A.44 Laverton Meadows is a beautiful Cotswold house & stables set in 22 acres with stunning views & lovely gardens. Romantic rooms with canopied beds, antiques & spacious bathrooms make this luxury accommodation. Full English breakfast served in the farmhouse kitchen warmed by the Aga. Gourmet candlelit dinners in sumptous private dining room. A log fire in the delightful sitting room offers you the perfect retreat.	£35.00 to £45.00 *see PHOTO over* p. 194	Y	Y	N
Mrs Elizabeth Beauvoisin **The Old Rectory** **Church Street** **Willersey** **Broadway WR12 7PN** **Tel: (01386) 853729** Fax 01386 858061 **Open: ALL YEAR (Excl. Xmas)** **Map Ref No. 07**	Nearest Road: A.44 Hidden at the end of a lane, opposite the 11th-century church, this old Georgian rectory, built of Cotswold stone, is very quiet & comfortable. Superb en-suite/private, spacious rooms, 4-posters. In winter, a roaring log fire greets you at breakfast, in the elegant dining room, & in summer the walled garden, with its 300-year-old Mulberry tree, offers tranquillity. Only 300 yards to the super 13th-century Bell Inn. Children over 8. **E-mail: beauvoisin@btinternet.com**	£35.00 to £52.50 *see PHOTO over* p. 195 VISA: M'CARD: AMEX:	Y	N	N

Laverton Meadow House. Broadway.

The Old Rectory. Willersey.

Georgian House. Cheltenham.

Gloucestershire

			rate £ from - to per person	children taken	evening meals	animals taken
Penny & Alex Gamez **Georgian House** **77 Montpellier Terrace** **Cheltenham GL50 3AY** **Tel: (01242) 515577** **Fax 01242 545929** **Open: ALL YEAR (Excl. Xmas & New Year)** **Map Ref No. 09**	Nearest Road: A.40	Take 3 beautiful bedrooms in an elegant Georgian home, set them among the charming terraces of Montpellier, only 5 mins' from the Promenade, add a warm welcome from your hosts, Penny & Alex, & there you have Georgian House. Each en-suite room has T.V. with satellite, 'phone with modem socket, ironing facilities, trouser press & fridge. The delicious English breakfasts include fresh fruit - the perfect combination! Parking. *see PHOTO over p. 196* VISA: M'CARD: AMEX:	£27.50 to £35.00 (non-smoking)	N	N	N
Claude Cittadino **Milton House Hotel** **12 Royal Parade** **Bayshill Road** **Cheltenham GL50 3AY** **Tel: (01242) 582601** **Fax 01242 222326** **Open: ALL YEAR** **Map Ref No. 09**	Nearest Road: A.40	Milton House stands in a quiet tree-lined avenue of elegant Regency homes. Situated a 4-min' stroll from the promenade, restaurants & the Imperial Gardens. There are 8 tastefully furnished en-suite bedrooms providing all the comforts & amenities. Elegant drawing room, dining room & inviting conservatory facing an attractive garden. Staying at Milton House is the perfect way to enjoy the many attractions of Cheltenham & the Cotswolds. Children over 6. VISA: M'CARD: AMEX:	£30.00 to £38.50	Y	Y	N
Mr R. Tracey **Cleeve Hill Hotel** **Cleeve Hill** **Cheltenham GL52 3PR** **Tel: (01242) 672052** **Fax 01242 679969** **Open: ALL YEAR (Excl. Xmas)** **Map Ref No. 10**	Nearest Road: B.4632	Situated in an Area of Outstanding Natural Beauty, Cleeve Hill has the friendly, relaxed atmosphere of a family home. All bedrooms have superb views, some to the Malvern Hills, & all are en-suite & equipped to the highest standards with 'phone, T.V., radio/alarm & beverage facilities. The excellent breakfasts are generous, & provide the perfect start to the day. Located in the heart of the Cotswolds, it is ideally placed for visiting Bath, Oxford, Stratford, Warwick. Children over 8. *see PHOTO over p. 198* VISA: M'CARD:	£32.50 to £40.00 (non-smoking)	Y	N	N
Juergen & Annette Berg **Hollington House Hotel** **115 Hales Road** **Cheltenham GL52 6ST** **Tel: (01242) 256652** **Fax 01242 570280** **Open: ALL YEAR** **Map Ref No. 09**	Nearest Road: A.40, M.5	An elegant Victorian house, easy to find off the London Road/A.40, with a large garden, croquet lawn & ample parking. Spacious bedrooms, with en-suite/private facilities, tea/coffee trays & colour T.V.. Good food for breakfast & dinner, with a choice of menu. (Evening meals by arrangement). A pleasant, relaxed atmosphere, with proprietors' personal attention, & a comfortable lounge with a bar. The perfect location, within easy driving distance of Oxford, Bath, Stratford-upon-Avon & the Cotswolds. Children over 3. VISA: M'CARD: AMEX:	£25.00 to £35.00	Y	N	N
Mera & Bev Stone **Charlton House** **18 Greenhills Road** **Charlton Kings** **Cheltenham GL53 9EB** **Tel: (01242) 238997** **Fax 01242 238997** **Open: ALL YEAR** **Map Ref No. 09**	Nearest Road: A.435	Charlton House is a friendly, family-run guest house located in a good residential area of Cheltenham with views of the Cotswold Hills. This comfortable home is fully double-glazed & centrally heated, with good-quality fitments & furnishings throughout. Excellent home-cooking. Your special dietary requirements provided for by a trained nutritionist. Reductions for extended stays. Ample off-road parking. Charlton House is completely non-smoking. Children over 8 years. *see PHOTO over p. 199*	£25.00 to £35.00 (non-smoking)	Y	Y	N

Cleeve Hill Hotel. Cleeve Hill.

Charlton House.   Charlton Kings.

Halewell Close. Withington.

Gloucestershire

		rate £ from - to per person	children taken	evening meals	animals taken
Michael & Pamela Minchin **The Ridge** **Whiteshoots Hill** **Bourton-on-the-Water** **Cheltenham GL54 2LE** Tel: **(01451) 820660** Fax 01451 822448 Open: **ALL YEAR** Map Ref No. 11	Nearest Road: A.429 The Ridge stands in 2 acres of beautiful secluded grounds just 1 mile from the centre of Bourton-on-the-Water. A large country house with 4 individually decorated, centrally heated bedrooms, most with en-suite facilities. 1 is on the ground floor. This house provides an extremely pleasant & comfortable base for touring the Cotswolds. A delicious full English breakfast is served. Good restaurants & pubs nearby serve excellent evening meals. Children over 6 years welcome.	£20.00 to £22.50	Y	N	N
David & Jenny Burrough **Windrush Farm** **Bourton-on-the-Water** **Cheltenham** **GL54 3BY** Tel: **(01451) 820419** Fax 01451 820446 Open: **MAR - NOV** Map Ref No. 12	Nearest Road: A.436 This 150-acre farm is situated in the heart of the glorious Cotswolds, renowned for its beauty & interest. The traditional, stone-mullioned farmhouse has a lovely garden & commands superb views, & yet is only 2 miles from Bourton. The guest rooms are tastefully furnished, & comprise 1 twin-bedded & 1 double room, with en-suite bathrooms & beverage-making facilities. A delicious English breakfast is served. Jenny & David enjoy helping to plan your day.	£20.00 to £££	N	N	N
Graham & Elaine Whent **Cotteswold House** **Market Place** **Northleach** **Cheltenham GL54 3EG** Tel/Fax: **(01451) 860493** Open: **ALL YEAR (Excl.** **Xmas & New Year)** Map Ref No. 13	Nearest Road: A.40, A.429 Relax in this 400-year-old Cotswold-stone wealthy wool merchant's home with beamed ceilings, original panelling & Tudor archway. Offering the choice of a luxury private suite or en-suite double or twin rooms - all spacious, elegant & well-equipped. Enjoy traditional English food & a friendly welcome. Cotteswold House is in the centre of this ancient market town of Northleach in the centre of the Cotswolds - an ideal base from which to tour this region.	£22.50 to £35.00 VISA: M'CARD:	N	Y	N
Mrs E. J. Carey-Wilson **Halewell Close** **Withington** **Cheltenham** **GL54 4BN** Tel: **(01242) 890238** Fax 01242 890332 Open: **ALL YEAR** Map Ref No. 14	Nearest Road: A.40 Halewell is a Cotswold stone house dating back in parts to the early 15th century. Situated on the edge of the very quiet & pretty village of Withington in a glorious setting in the hills. There are 6 superb, large, well-equipped double & twin-bedded en-suite rooms of individual character. 1 twin is located at ground level. An outstanding country home with easy access to the delights of the Cotswolds & surrounding area. Children & animals by arrangement.	£55.00 to £70.00 *see PHOTO over* *p. 200* VISA: M'CARD: AMEX:	Y	N	Y
Susie & Jim Wilson **Westward** **Sudeley** **Winchcombe** **Cheltenham GL54 5JB** Tel: **(01242) 604372** Fax 01242 604372 Open: **ALL YEAR (Excl. Xmas)** Map Ref No. 15	Nearest Road: A.40 The Wilson families share this beautiful Georgian house on the scarp of the Cotswolds above Sudeley Castle, sitting within its own 600-acre estate with spectacular views to the Malverns. The heart of the Cotswolds is very close, with Broadway, Oxford & Stratford within easy reach. The Wilsons combine good food - Susie trained at Prue Leith's - with elegance & comfort in a relaxed family home. 2 delightful en-suite rooms available. Children over 10 years welcome.	£35.00 to £35.00 *see PHOTO over* *p. 202* VISA: M'CARD:	N	Y	Y

Westward. Sudeley.

Lady Lamb Farm. Meysey Hampton.

Gloucestershire

		rate £ from - to per person	children taken	evening meals	animals taken
Mr & Mrs C. Holdsworth Hunt **The Kettle House** **Leysbourne** **Chipping Camden** **GL55 6HN** **Tel: (01386) 840328** **Fax 01386 841740** **Open: ALL YEAR** **Map Ref No. 16**	Nearest Road: A.44 A Grade II listed building of great historical importance. The Kettle House, which was built in 1640, offers exclusive & original accommodation which includes 2 double bedrooms with en-suite bathrooms & 2 twin-bedded rooms with a shared bathroom. Guests' have their own sitting room with T.V. & refreshment bar, together with paved courtyard & sun balcony approached from their own private entrance. A delightful home. Children over 12. Animals by arrangement. E-mail: info@kettlehouse.co.uk	£25.00 to £30.00 (non-smoking) VISA: M'CARD:	Y	Y	Y
Stephen & Anna Langton **Cripps House** **51 Coxwell Street** **Cirencester** **GL7 2BQ** **Tel: (01285) 653164** **Fax 01285 642803** **Open: ALL YEAR (Excl. Xmas)** **Map Ref No. 17**	Nearest Road: A.419, A.417 Cripps House is a fascinating 17th-century mansion in the tranquil medieval centre of Cirencester. Close to the beautiful Parish Church & only 3 mins' walk from shops & restaurants & the 3,000 acres of Cirencester Park for walking & watching polo. The house has been restored beautifully, & offers 3 double bedrooms, each with their own bathroom & T.V.. Breakfast in the panelled dining room or in the garden in summer. Parking. E-mail: langton@cripps.force9.co.uk	£30.00 to £35.00 (non-smoking) VISA:	Y	N	N
Mrs J. Keyser **Lady Lamb Farm** **Meysey Hampton** **Cirencester** **GL7 5LH** **Tel: (01285) 712206** **Fax 01285 712206** **Open: ALL YEAR** **Map Ref No. 18**	Nearest Road: A.417 Lady Lamb Farm is a Cotswold-stone farmhouse, surrounded by countryside & situated less than a mile from the small market town of Fairford. 2 attractively furnished bedrooms, each with T.V. & tea/coffee. (1 is en-suite.) A swimming pool & tennis court. Set on the edge of the Cotswolds, Bath, Oxford & Cotswold towns & lovely gardens are within easy reach. Cotswold Water Park offers a range of watersports, & golf, riding & fishing are nearby. Animals by arrangement. E-mail: jekeyser1@aol.com	£30.00 to £30.00 *see PHOTO over* *p. 203* VISA: M'CARD:	Y	N	Y
Ian & Mary Cassidy **Waterton Garden Cottage** **Ampney Crucis** **Cirencester** **GL7 5RX** **Tel: (01285) 851303** **Open: ALL YEAR** **Map Ref No. 19**	Nearest Road: A.417 Situated in the heart of the Cotswolds, Waterton Garden Cottage, part of a late-Victorian stable block, has been sympathetically converted, & retains many original features. A high standard of comfort, & an ambience which would match many small country houses All bedrooms are en-suite, & one can expect fine cuisine, comfort & attention to detail without unnecessary formality. Every effort is made to ensure that your stay is both memorable & enjoyable. Children over 9.	£22.50 to £30.00	N	Y	N
Shaun & Susanna Parsons **Winstone Glebe** **Winstone** **Cirencester** **GL7 7JL** **Tel: (01285) 821451** **Fax 01285 821451** **Open: ALL YEAR (Excl. Xmas)** **Map Ref No. 20**	Nearest Road: A.417 A small Georgian rectory overlooking a Saxon church in a Domesday-listed village, with spectacular rural views. Ideal for exploring Cotswold market towns, with their medieval churches, antique shops & rich local history. 3 delightful rooms, each with private/en-suite bathroom. Being an Area of Outstanding Natural Beauty, there are well-signposted walks. The more energetic can borrow a bicycle & explore, or just enjoy warm hospitality & delicious food . Single supplement.	£29.00 to £33.00 *see PHOTO over* *p. 205* VISA: M'CARD:	Y	Y	Y

Winstone Glebe. Winstone.

Gloucestershire

		rate £ from - to per person	children taken	evening meals taken	animals taken
Mrs Marie-Teresa Sayers **The Old Rectory** **Didmarton** **GL9 1DS** Tel: **(01454) 238233** Open: **ALL YEAR (Excl. Xmas)** Map Ref No. **21**	Nearest Road: A.433 The Old Rectory (Grade II listed) is a charming home, where a happy & relaxed atmosphere prevails. The friendly hosts offer very comfortable accommodation in 3 attractive bedrooms, each with an en-suite/private bathroom & T.V.. Also, a cosy lounge with T.V. & a pretty garden in which guests may choose to relax. A delicious breakfast is served. An ideal base from which to explore this beautiful region. Children over 12.	£21.00 to £22.50	N	N	N
Jenny Beer **Gilbert's** **Gilbert's Lane** **Brookthorpe** **Gloucester GL4 0UH** Tel: **(01452) 812364** Fax 01452 812364 Open: **ALL YEAR** Map Ref No. **22**	Nearest Road: A.4173 Gilbert's, a 16th-century, half-timbered listed gem, snuggles beneath the dramatic western escarpment of the Cotswolds. The highly acclaimed delicious British breakfast is largely home-produced & as organic, fresh & local as possible. With a relaxed, caring atmosphere, comfortable, comprehensive accommodation (all 4 rooms with bathrooms & other comforts) & plenty of literature to study by the log fire, guests soon feel at home. E-mail: Jenny@gilbertsbb.demon.co.uk	£26.50 to £29.50 (no smoking)	Y	N	N
Keith & Joyce Annis **Evington Hill Farm** **Tewkesbury Road** **Leigh (The)** **GL19 4AQ** Tel: **(01242) 680255** Open: **ALL YEAR** Map Ref No. **23**	Nearest Road: A.38 Crown your Gloucestershire visit at this lovely 16th-century house. Take tea & homemade cake in the sunny conservatory, stay in the antique pine furnished bedrooms with their beautiful new spacious bathrooms. 1 has a 4-poster, all have T.V. & hostess tray. The old beamed sitting room with log burning fire is perfect for a relaxing drink. Set in 4 acres with ample parking. Licensed bar. Games room. Evening meals by arrangement. 2 holiday cottages available for extending stays.	£28.00 to £35.00 (no smoking)	Y	N	N
Alan & Christine Parkes **Edale House** **Folly Road** **Parkend** **Lydney GL15 4JF** Tel: **(01594) 562835** Fax 01594 564488 Open: **ALL YEAR** Map Ref No. **24**	Nearest Road: A.48 Edale House is a fine Georgian residence facing the cricket green in the village of Parkend at the heart of the Royal Forest of Dean. Once the home of local G.P. Bill Tandy, author of 'A Doctor in the Forest', the house has been tastefully restored to provide comfortable en-suite accommodation with every facility for guests. Enjoy delicious & imaginative cuisine prepared by your hosts. Fully licensed. Animals by arrangement. E-mail: edale@lineone.net	£22.50 to £27.50 VISA: M'CARD:	N	Y	Y
Margaret & Peter Helm **Hunters Lodge** **Dr Browns Road** **Minchinhampton** **GL6 9BT** Tel: **(01453) 883588** Fax 01453 731449 Open: **ALL YEAR (Excl. Xmas)** Map Ref No. **25**	Nearest Road: A.46 A friendly and helpful welcome is assured for guests at this beautifully furnished Cotswold stone country house situated adjoining 600 acres of N.T. common land and golf course. Central heating throughout. All bedrooms have T.V., tea/coffee facilities & en-suite/private bathrooms. A visitors' lounge, with colour T.V., adjoins a delightful conservatory overlooking a large garden. An ideal centre for Bath, Cheltenham, Cirencester & the Cotswolds. Peter is a registered tourist guide. Children over 10 years.	£20.00 to £25.00 (no smoking) *see PHOTO over p. 207*	Y	N	N

Hunters Lodge. Minchinhampton.

Gunn Mill House. Mitcheldean.

Gloucestershire

		rate £ from - to per person	children taken	evening meals	animals taken
Sue Smalley **Foresters House** **Chapel Lane** **Minchinhampton GL6 9DL** **Tel: (01453) 882106** **Fax 01453 882106** **Open: ALL YEAR** **Map Ref No. 26**	Nearest Road: A.419 An old Cotswold stone house set in 12 acres within a secret valley. Secluded, yet not remote, within walking distance of the village & 5 pubs. Spacious & attractive accommodation with stylish antique furniture & brass beds. Large luxurious bathrooms with separate shower & bidet. A host of attractions nearby. Close to Gatcombe Park & Badminton. Convenient for Bath, Bristol & Cheltenham. Children over 5.	£45.00 to £50.00	Y	N	Y
David & Caroline Anderson **Gunn Mill House** **Lower Spout Lane** **Mitcheldean** **GL17 0EA** **Tel: (01594) 827577** **Fax 01594 827577** **Open: ALL YEAR** **Map Ref No. 27**	Nearest Road: A.4136, A.48 Bounded by its mill stream & the Royal Forest of Dean, the Andersons' Georgian home stands in 5 acres of gardens & meadows. Refurbished to a high standard, the galleried sitting room & 8 large en-suite bedrooms & suites (4-poster, doubles, twins, family) are filled with antiques & collectables from around the world. Share your hosts' love of good food, home-made breads & preserves. Vegetarians catered for. Liquor licence. Overseas visitors especially welcomed. **E-mail: info@gunnmillhouse.co.uk**	£22.50 to £35.00 *see PHOTO over* *p. 208* VISA: M'CARD: AMEX:	Y	Y	Y
Mrs Elizabeth Dean **Treetops Guest House** **London Road** **Moreton-in-Marsh** **GL56 0HE** **Tel/Fax: (01608) 651036** **Tel: (01608) 651362** **Open: ALL YEAR** **Map Ref No. 28**	Nearest Road: A.44 A beautiful family home offering traditional Bed & Breakfast. 6 attractive bedrooms, all with a bathroom en-suite, & 2 of which are on the ground floor and thus suitable for disabled persons or wheelchair users. All rooms have T.V., radio and tea/coffee facilities. Cots and high chairs available. Delightful secluded gardens to relax in. Ideally situated for exploring the Cotswolds. A warm and homely atmosphere awaits you here. **E-mail: dean@treetops1.freeserve.co.uk**	£21.00 to £22.50 VISA: M'CARD:	Y	N	Y
Mrs W. V. Dare **Mill Dene** **Blockley** **Moreton-in-Marsh** **GL56 9HN** **Tel: (01386) 700457** **Fax 01386 700526** **Open: ALL YEAR** **Map Ref No. 29**	Nearest Road: A.44 A Cotswold stone water mill, mostly 17th-century but with parts dating back to 1086, now beautifully converted. Barry & Wendy offer a warm welcome to their home which is set in an award-winning 2 1/2 acre garden. Sights & sounds of the mill pool & stream surround the house, which is set on the edge of the peaceful & delightfully hidden village of Blockley. There are good eating places nearby. Each bedroom has tea-making facilities & T.V. & wonderful views. Children over 5. **E-mail: wendydare@cableinet.co.uk**	£22.00 to £35.00	Y	N	N
Gillie Peacock **Cinderhill House** **St. Briavels** **GL15 6RH** **Tel: (01594) 530393** **Fax 01594 530098** **Open: ALL YEAR** **Map Ref No. 30**	Nearest Road: A.466 A pretty, 14th-century house tucked into the hill below the castle in St. Briavels, with magnificent views across the Wye Valley to the Brecon Beacons & Black Mountains. A lovingly restored & tastefully furnished house with 5 beautiful bedrooms (& 2 4-posters), each with a private or en-suite bathroom. Gillie is a professional cook, & takes delight in ensuring that all meals are well cooked using local produce. 3 self-catering cottages, 1 for the disabled. Licensed.	£31.00 to £38.00 *see PHOTO over* *p. 210*	Y	Y	N

Cinderhill House. St. Briavels.

The Grey Cottage. Leonard Stanley.

Hope Cottage Guest House. Box.

Gloucestershire

		rate £ from - to per person	children taken	evening meals	animals taken
Andrew & Rosemary Reeves **The Grey Cottage** **Bath Road** **Leonard Stanley** **Stonehouse** **GL10 3LU** **Tel: (01453) 822515** **Fax 01453 822515** **Open: ALL YEAR** **Map Ref No. 31**	Nearest Road: A.419 Andrew & Rosemary welcome you to their Cotswold stone home where the ambience is anything but 'grey'! They aim to ensure your stay is hasslefree & memorable. Enclosed parking. A pretty flower garden. All bedrooms are individually & comfortably furnished with many extras. Log fires in season. Home cooking using the highest quality regional ingredients. Evening meals by arrangement. Licensed. Ideal base for a relaxing break. Prior booking essential. Children over 10 years welcome.	£35.00 to £55.00 *see PHOTO over* *p. 211*	Y	Y	N
Carol & Gerry Walsh **The Firs** **Selsey Road** **North Woodchester** **Stroud** **GL5 5NQ** **Tel: (01453) 873088** **Fax 01453 873053** **Open: ALL YEAR (Excl. Xmas)** **Map Ref No. 32**	Nearest Road: A.46 The Firs is set in a quiet village location. A fine Georgian house with many period features & panoramic views over the Cotswold escarpment. Within walking distance of several pubs & restaurants. Ideally situated for exploring the north Cotswolds, Bath, Cheltenham, Westonbirt Arboretum, Gatcomb, Badminton, Cirencester, Gloucester Docks & Bristol. Accommodation is in 2 attractive en-suite rooms. Your hosts put great emphasis on guest comfort & strive to make each guest's stay memorable. E-mail: CWalsh3088@aol.com	£20.00 to £26.00	Y	N	N
Sheila & Garth Brunsdon **Hope Cottage** **Box** **Stroud** **GL6 9HD** **Tel: (01453) 832076** **Open: JAN - NOV** **Map Ref No. 33**	Nearest Road: A.46, A.419 For peace & tranquillity, this charming, undiscovered village 10 miles from Cirencester is unrivalled. Box is in an Area of Outstanding Natural Beauty enjoying glorious Cotswold views. Here, you can savour the charm of this delightful country house, set in 3 acres of landscaped gardens & with a heated pool. A lovely en-suite room with T.V. & hospitality tray. Sumptuous traditional English breakfasts. Good local restaurants & pubs. Strategic base for walking & touring.	£20.00 to £25.00 *see PHOTO over* *p. 212*	Y	N	N
Janet & Tim Tremellen **Tavern House** **Willesley** **Tetbury** **GL8 8QU** **Tel: (01666) 880444** **Fax 01666 880254** **Open: ALL YEAR** **Map Ref No. 34**	Nearest Road: A.433 A Grade II listed, part-17th-century, former staging post that has been sympathetically refurbished to provide an exceptionally high standard of accommodation. All rooms have bath/shower en-suite, 'phones, T.V., etc. Delightful, secluded, walled gardens in which to relax. Ideally situated for Westonbirt Arboretum, & convenient for Bath, Cheltenham & Gloucester. A genuine country-house atmosphere, & an excellent base from which to explore the Cotswolds. Charming inns offering dinner close by. Children over 10.	£30.50 to £35.00 *see PHOTO over* *p. 214* VISA: M'CARD	Y	N	N

Visit our website at:
http://www.bestbandb.co.uk

Tavern House.   Willesley.

Upper Court. Kemerton.

Gloucestershire

		rate £ from - to per person	children taken	evening meals	animals taken
H. W. Herford **Upper Court** **Kemerton** **Tewkesbury** **GL20 7HY** **Tel: (01386) 725351** **Fax 01386 725472** **Open: ALL YEAR (Excl. Xmas)** **Map Ref No. 35**	Nearest Road: A.438, M.5 This fine Georgian manor (c. 1760) is in one of the prettiest villages on Bredon Hill in the north Cotswolds. The 15 acres of garden & grounds are idyllic, with a lake, tennis & croquet. Riding, walking, golf & clay shooting nearby. Stay in a 4-poster or twin room. The Garden Room & the Coach House are ideal for family or disabled guests. The house is filled with pieces from the Herford's antique stock. Only 4 miles from M.5 & ideal for visiting gardens, castles & antique shops. Cheltenham, Broadway, Oxford, Stratford & Bath are all within easy reach. Dinner by arrangement. **E-mail: UpperCourt@compuserve.com**	£37.50 to £60.00 *see PHOTO over* *p. 215* VISA: M'CARD:	Y	Y	N
Matthew Brown **Wesley House** **High Street** **Winchcombe** **GL54 5LJ** **Tel: (01242) 602366** **Fax 01242 602405** **Open: ALL YEAR** **Map Ref No. 36**	Nearest Road: A.4 Wesley House is a delightful mediaeval half-timbered house dating from c.1435. John Wesley the Methodist, is believed to have stayed here in 1779. There are 5 cosy en-suite bedrooms which have been individually designed & decorated, each with modern facilities. An elegant lounge with log fire which conveys a sense of old world intimacy. Jonathan Lewis has acquired an excellent reputation for fine cuisine at Wesley House. A perfect spot from which to explore the Cotswolds; Cheltenham, Oxford & Stratford are all within easy reach by car.	£30.00 to £40.00 *see PHOTO over* *p. 217* VISA: M'CARD: AMEX:	Y	Y	N

All the establishments mentioned in this guide are members of
The Worldwide Bed & Breakfast Association

When booking your accommodation please mention
The Best Bed & Breakfast

Wesley House. Winchcombe.

Hampshire & Isle of Wight

Hampshire (Southern)

Hampshire is located in the centre of the south coast of England & is blessed with much beautiful & unspoilt countryside. Wide open vistas of rich downland contrast with deep woodlands. Rivers & sparkling streams run through tranquil valleys passing nestling villages. There is a splendid coastline with seaside resorts & harbours, the cathedral city of Winchester & the "jewel" of Hampshire, the Isle of Wight.

The north of the county is known as the Hampshire Borders. Part of this countryside was immortalised by Richard Adams & the rabbits of 'Watership Down'. Beacon Hill is a notable hill-top landmark. From its slopes some of the earliest aeroplane flights were made by De Haviland in 1909. Pleasure trips & tow-path walks can be taken along the restored Basingstoke Canal.

The New Forest is probably the area most frequented by visitors. It is a landscape of great character with thatched cottages, glades & streams & a romantic beauty. There are herds of deer & the New Forest ponies wander at will. To the N.W. of Beaulieu are some of the most idyllic parts of the old forest, with fewer villages & many little streams that flow into the Avon. Lyndhurst, the "capital" of the New Forest offers a range of shops & has a contentious 19th century church constructed in scarlet brickwork banded with yellow, unusual ornamental decoration, & stained glass windows by William Morris.

The Roman city of Winchester became the capital city of Saxon Wessex & is today the capital of Hampshire. It is famous for its beautiful mediaeval cathedral, built during the reign of William the Conquerer & his notorious son Rufus. It contains the great Winchester Bible.

William completed the famous Domesday Book in the city, & Richard Coeur de Lion was crowned in the cathedral in 1194.

Portsmouth & Southampton are major ports & historic maritime cities with a wealth of castles, forts & Naval attractions from battleships to museums.

The channel of the Solent guarded by Martello towers, holds not only Southampton but numerous yachting centres, such as Hamble, Lymington & Bucklers Hard where the ships for Admiral Lord Nelson's fleet were built.

The River Test.

The Isle of Wight

The Isle of Wight lies across the sheltered waters of the Solent, & is easily reached by car or passenger ferry. The chalk stacks of the Needles & the multi-coloured sand at Alum Bay are among the best known of the island's natural attractions & there are many excellent beaches & other bays to enjoy. Cowes is a famous international sailing centre with a large number of yachting events throughout the summer. Ventnor, the most southerly resort is known as the "Madeira of England" & has an exotic botanic garden. Inland is an excellent network of footpaths & trails & many castles, manors & stately homes.

Hampshire & Isle of Wight

Hampshire

Gazeteer

Areas of outstanding natural beauty.
East & South Hampshire, North Wessex Downs & Chichester Harbour.

Houses & Castles

Avington Park - Winchester
16th century red brick house, enlarged in 17th century by the addition of two wings & a classical portico. Stateroom, ballroom with wonderful ceiling. Red drawing room, library, etc.

Beaulieu Abbey & Palace House - Beaulieu
12th century Cistercian abbey - the original gatehouse of abbey converted to palace house 1538. Houses historic car museum.

Breamore House - Breamore
16th century Elizabethan Manor House, tapestries, furniture, paintings. Also museum.

Jane Austen's Home - Chawston
Personal effects of the famous writer.

Broadlands - Romsey
16th century - park & garden created by Capability Brown. Home of the Earl Mountbatten of Burma.

Mottisfont Abbey - Nr. Romsey
12th century Augustinian Priory until Dissolution. Painting by Rex Whistler trompe l'oeil in Gothic manner.

Stratfield Saye House - Reading
17th century house presented to the Duke of Wellington 1817. Now contains his possessions - also wild fowl sanctuary.

Sandham Memorial Chapel - Sandham, Nr. Newbury
Paintings by Stanley Spencer cover the walls.

The Vyne - Sherbourne St. John
16th century red brick chapel with Renaissance glass & rare linenfold panelling. Alterations made in 1654 - classical portico. Palladian staircase dates form 1760.

West Green House - Hartley Wintney
18th century red brick house set in a walled garden.

Appuldurcombe House - Wroxall, Isle of Wight
The only house in the 'Grand Manner' on the island. Beautiful English baroque east facade. House now an empty shell standing in fine park.

Osbourne House - East Cowes, Isle of Wight
Queen Victoria's seaside residence.

Carisbrooke Castle - Isle of Wight
Oldest parts 12th century, but there was a wooden castle on the mound before that. Museum in castle.

Cathedrals & Churches

Winchester Cathedral
Largest Gothic church in Europe. Norman & perpendicular styles, three sets of mediaeval paintings, marble font c.1180. Stalls c.1320 with 60 misericords. Extensive mediaeval tiled floor.

Breamore (St. Mary) - Breamore
10th century Saxon. Double splayed windows, stone rood.

East Meon (All Saints)
15th century rebuilding of Norman fabric. Tournai marble front.

Idsworth (St. Hubert)
16th century chapel - 18th century bell turret. 14th century paintings in chancel.

Pamber (dedication unknown)
Early English - Norman central tower, 15th central pews, wooden effigy of knight c.1270.

Romsey (St. Mary & St. Ethelfleda)
Norman - 13th century effigy of a lady - Saxon rood & carving of crucifixion, 16th century painted reredos.

Silchester (St. Mary)
Norman, perpendicular, 14th century effigy of a lady, 15th century screen, Early English chancel with painted patterns on south window splays, Jacobean pulpit with domed canopy.

Winchester (St. Cross)
12th century. Original chapel to Hospital. Style changing from Norman at east to decorated at west. Tiles, glass, wall painting.

HAMPSHIRE
Map reference

01 Humphryes		17 Cutmore	
02 Mason		17 Gallagher	
03 Mallam		17 Thompson	
04 Biddolph		17 Messenger	
05 Hicks		18 Ames	
06 Whitaker		20 Baigent	
07 Beachamp		22 Taylor	
08 Buckley		23 Sherwood	
08 Ford		24 Yates	
09 Twine		25 Hayles	
10 Tose		26 Chivers	
11 Cadman		27 Talbot	
12 Ratcliffe		28 Parker	
13 Watling		28 Pollock	
14 Pritchett			
15 Poulter			
16 Barnfield			

English Channel

Malt Cottage. Upper Clatford.

Hampshire

		rate £ from - to per person	children taken	evening meals	animals taken
Adam & Laraine Humphryes **Belmont House** **Gilbert Street** **Ropley** **Alresford SO24 0BY** **Tel: (01962) 772344** **Open: ALL YEAR** **Map Ref No. 01**	Nearest Road: A.31 An attractive Georgian house dating back to the 18th century, set in a pretty acre of garden with rural views. Offering 1 comfortably furnished twin-bedded room with tea/coffee-making facilities & use of study with colour T.V. A short walk to the village, ancient church, shop, 2 pubs & the famous Watercress Steam Railway. It is within easy reach of Winchester, Salisbury & 1 hour (approx.) from London airports.	£22.50 to £24.00 🚭	N	N	N
Mrs P. Mason **Malt Cottage** **Upper Clatford** **Andover** **SP11 7QL** **Tel: (01264) 323469** **Fax 01264 334100** **Open: ALL YEAR** **Map Ref No. 02**	Nearest Road: A.303 Walk around the beautiful 6-acre garden with chalk stream & lakes, or sit by the fire in the charming beamed sitting room. Malt Cottage, an ideal stop en-route from London Heathrow to the West Country, is situated in a picturesque village with many thatched cottages & offers 3 bedrooms with en-suite/private facilities. During the summer, evening barbecues are held. Places to visit include Stonehenge, Salisbury & Winchester. Fly fishing & airport collection can be arranged. **E-mail: rooms@maltcottage.co.uk**	£25.00 to £35.00 🚭 *see PHOTO over* *p. 221*	Y	Y	N
Mrs Carolyn Mallam **Broadwater** **Amport** **Andover** **SP11 8AY** **Tel: (01264) 772240** **Fax 01264 772240** **Open: ALL YEAR** **Map Ref No. 03**	Nearest Road: A.303 Broadwater is a 17th-century, listed, thatched cottage situated in a peaceful unspoilt village just off the A.303. It is an ideal base for sightseeing in Hampshire, with easy access to the West Country & London. The cottage offers 2 delightful, double/twin-bedded rooms, both with en-suite facilities. Guests have a private & very comfortable sitting/dining room with an open log fire & a pretty garden to enjoy. Homemade bread. T.V.. **E-mail: carolyn@dmac.co.uk**	£25.00 to £35.00 VISA: M'CARD:	Y	N	N
Tom & Fiona Biddolph **May Cottage** **Thruxton** **Andover SP11 8LZ** **Tel: (01264) 771241** **Fax 01264 771770** **Mobile 0468 242166** **Open: ALL YEAR (Excl. Xmas)** **Map Ref No. 04**	Nearest Road: A.303 May Cottage dates back to 1740 & is situated in the heart of this picturesque tranquil village with Post Office & old inn. A most comfortable home with 1 single & 3 twin rooms with en-suite/private bathrooms, 1 on the ground floor. All with T.V. & tea trays. Guests' sitting/dining room with T.V.. An ideal base for visiting ancient cities, stately homes & gardens, yet within easy reach of ports & airports. Excellent home-cooking & dinner by prior arrangement. Parking. Children over 6.	£25.00 to £££ 🚭 *see PHOTO over* *p. 223*	Y	N	N
Angela Hicks **Lains Cottage** **Quarley** **Andover** **SP11 8PX** **Tel: (01264) 889697** **Fax 01264 889227** **Open: ALL YEAR** **Map Ref No. 05**	Nearest Road: A.303 Lains Cottage is a charming thatched house set in an acre of cottage garden. An ideal base for exploring Stonehenge, Salisbury & Winchester. The A.303 is less than a mile away providing excellent road access to London & the West Country. The house has been carefully restored to combine modern comforts with traditional country style. There are 3 very attractive bedrooms, each with en-suite facilities, T.V. & beverage tray. Children over 8 years. **E-mail: lains-cott-hols@dial.pipex.com**	£23.00 to £28.00 🚭	Y	N	N

May Cottage. Thruxton.

Hampshire

		rate £ from - to per person	children taken	evening meals	animals taken
Jeremy & Philippa Whitaker **Land of Nod** **Headley** **Bordon** **GU35 8SJ** Tel: **(01428) 713609** Fax 01428 717698 Open: **ALL YEAR (Excl. Xmas)** Map Ref No. 06	Nearest Road: A.3 A large neo-Georgian house set in 7 acres of garden in the centre of 100 acres of a private woodland estate. This attractive home affords 3 twin-bedded rooms with private or en-suite bathroom, T.V. & tea/coffee-making facilities. Situated just 1 hour from London, Heathrow, Gatwick & Portsmouth, & within easy reach of some of the finest gardens & historic houses in the south of England, the Land of Nod is the perfect spot for a relaxing break. A car, though, is essential for maximum enjoyment. Children over 12.	£30.00 to £37.50 🚭 *see PHOTO over* *p. 225*	Y	Y	N
Kim & David Beauchamp **Old Oak** **Meerut Road** **Brockenhurst SO42 7TD** Tel: **(01590) 623735** Fax 01590 623735 Open: **APR - OCT** Map Ref No. 07	Nearest Road: A.337 Set in quiet surroundings this charming studio summer house, which is detached from the main house, offers luxurious accommodation for up to 3 people. Brockenhurst is situated in the centre of the New Forest & is ideal for visiting Beaulieu, the Isle of Wight, Exbury Gardens & Lymington. The coast is only 6 miles away. Riding & golf are close at hand. A super Continental breakfast is served in the summer house. Children over 12.	£25.00 to £30.00 🚭	Y	N	N
Robin & Mary Ford **Holmans** **Bisterne Close** **Burley** **Burley BH24 4AZ** Tel/Fax: **(01425) 402307** Open: **ALL YEAR** Map Ref No. 08	Nearest Road: A.35, A.31 Holmans is a charming country house in the heart of the New Forest, set in 4 acres with stabling available for guests' own horses. Superb walking, horse riding & carriage driving, with a golf course nearby. A warm, friendly welcome is assured. All bedrooms are tastefully furnished & en-suite with tea/coffee-making facilities, radio & hairdryers. Colour T.V. in guests' lounge with adjoining orangery & log fires in winter.	£25.00 to £30.00 🚭	Y	N	Y
Mrs Wendy Buckley **Tothill House** **Black Lane** **Thorney Hill** **Bransgore** **Christchurch** **BH23 8DZ** Tel: **(01425) 674414** Fax 01425 672235 Open: **JAN - NOV** Map Ref No. 08	Nearest Road: A.35 An Edwardian country house set in 12 acres of woodland. An Area of Outstanding Natural Beauty noted for its flora & fauna. 5 mins from Burley village, a popular New Forest tourist attraction. Offering good food & 3 attractive rooms, 2 with en-suite facilities & 1 with a private bathroom. Each individually decorated, with T.V. & tea-making facilities. Very secluded, with peace & tranquillity. Local sporting & recreational activities, & a variety of places to visit. The perfect spot for a relaxing break. E-mail: tothill@abc-123.co.uk	£25.00 to £30.00	N	N	N
Lorraine Twine **Merry Hall Hotel** **73 Horndean Road** **Emsworth** **PO10 7PU** Tel: **(01243) 431377** Fax 01243 431411 Open: **ALL YEAR** Map Ref No. 09	Nearest Road: A.27 Merry Hall is situated in a delightful fishing village, set midway between Chichester & Portsmouth. Although a modern hotel, there are log fires & a very cosy, relaxed atmosphere. The 9 attractive bedrooms are well-equipped & have T.V. & tea/coffee facilities; 6 are en-suite. Some bedrooms & the conservatory overlook the pretty garden, which has an abundance of birdlife. Emsworth is well placed for exploring Hampshire & has a number of good local restaurants & pubs.	£24.00 to £35.00 VISA: M'CARD:	Y	N	Y

Land of Nod. Headley.

Hampshire

		rate £ from – to per person	children taken	evening meals	animals taken

		rate £ from – to per person	children taken	evening meals	animals taken
Nigel & Sandra Tose **Rudge House** **Itchel Lane** **Crondall** **Farnham** **GU10 5PR** **Tel: (01252) 850450** **Fax 01252 850829** **Open: ALL YEAR** **Map Ref No. 10**	Nearest Road: A.287 Elegant, spacious family home, dating from the 1850s, featuring a 4-acre garden with tennis court & croquet lawn. Edging an historic village, the house is quiet & secluded, bordering farmland, yet within 45 mins of Heathrow, Gatwick & London. Windsor, Ascot, Winchester & Oxford highly accessible. Extremely comfortable accommodation, offering en-suite/private facilities & pump showers, plus T.V. lounge & tea/coffee. Evening meal & packed lunches by arrangement. Children over 12 years.	£30.00 to £36.00 *see PHOTO over* *p. 227*	Y	Y	N
Mrs G. Cadman **Cottage Crest** **Castle Hill** **Woodgreen** **Fordingbridge SP6 2AX** **Tel: (01725) 512009** **Open: ALL YEAR** **Map Ref No. 11**	Nearest Road: A.338 Woodgreen is a typical New Forest village, with cottages surrounded by thick hedges to keep out the cattle & ponies. Cottage Crest is a Victorian drover's cottage set high in its own 4 acres, & enjoying superb views of the River Avon & valley below. The bedrooms are attractive & spacious & are decorated to a very high standard. All have an en-suite bathroom/shower & w.c.. Children over 8 years welcome.	£21.00 to £22.00	Y	N	N
Mrs P. A. Ratcliffe **Hendley House** **Rockbourne** **Fordingbridge** **SP6 3NA** **Tel: (01725) 518303** **Fax 01725 518546** **Open: FEB - NOV** **Map Ref No. 12**	Nearest Road: A.338, A.354 Overlooking water meadows, a beautiful, south-facing, 16th-century house with a wealth of beams, elegantly decorated & a relaxed family atmosphere. So much to visit & do in surrounding countryside & south coast. Walking & cycling in New Forest, returning to relax by log fires in winter or swimming pool in garden in summer. Riding, fishing, golf & racing nearby. Discounts for 3 nights plus. 2 charming bedrooms with en-suite shower or private bathroom. Children over 10.	£25.00 to £££	Y	N	N
Mrs Geraldine Watling **The Grange** **Alverstone** **Sandown** **Isle of Wight PO36 0EZ** **Tel: (01983) 403729** **Fax 01983 403729** **Open: FEB - NOV** **Map Ref No. 13**	Nearest Road: A.3056, A.3055 Enjoy a peaceful stay at The Grange. Set in a large garden beneath the Downs, it is ideally situated for all aspects of the island. A nature trail passes through the village, & there are sandy beaches just 2 miles away. 7 tastefully furnished bedrooms with en-suite facilities. The house is centrally heated, & there is a comfortable lounge with a log fire. A traditional English breakfast is served to start the day. E-mail: Grange_Alverstone@compuserve.com	£21.00 to £30.00	Y	N	N
James Pritchett **Under Rock Country** **House B & B** **Shore Road, Bonchurch** **Ventnor** **Isle of Wight PO38 1RF** **Tel: (01983) 855274** **Open: FEB - NOV** **Map Ref No. 14**	Nearest Road: A.3055 Historical Georgian house set in large secluded gardens near Horseshoe Bay & southern coastal paths, with isolated coves, narrow ravines or chines, soaring cliffs & high chalk downland, country walks. 3 rooms - single/double, double & twin. T.V., tea/coffee trays. Most have their own bath/shower & W.C.. Guest lounge & terrace, a peaceful, relaxed setting. Picturesque Bonchurch village has literary associations including Thackeray, Dickens & Swinburne.	£19.00 to £25.00	N	N	N

Rudge House. Crondall.

Hampshire

		rate £ from - to per person	children taken	evening meals	animals taken
Mrs Sylvia Poulter Quinces Cranmore Avenue Yarmouth Isle of Wight PO41 OXS Tel: (01983) 760080 Open: ALL YEAR (Excl. Xmas) Map Ref No. 15	Nearest Road: A.3054 An attractive cedar house, centrally heated throughout, peacefully set between a vineyard & a dairy farm on a private road 2 miles from Yarmouth. 2 delightful bedrooms, with tea/coffee facilities. Also available to guests is a comfortable living room with T.V. & log fires in season. The Poulters offer an ideal base for exploring the lovely countryside & coastline of the West Wight, as well as the option of wildlife holidays tailored to your interests. Children over 6 years.	£20.00 to £22.00	Y	N	Y
Mrs Jan Messenger Mulberries 6 West Hayes Lymington SO41 3RL Tel: (01590) 679549 Open: ALL YEAR (Excl. Xmas) Map Ref No. 17	Nearest Road: A.337, M.27 An elegant detached house situated in a quiet cul-de-sac only 5 mins' walk from the high street, quay & marinas. Secluded south-facing walled garden, full of choice plants. Heated outdoor pool for guests' use in the summer. There are 2 large double en-suite bedrooms & 1 single en-suite, all with tea/coffee-making facilities. Comfortable drawing room with T.V.. Ideal base for exploring the New Forest, I.O.W. & surrounding area. Children over 12 years.	£27.00 to £29.00	Y	N	N
R. A. Barnfield The Nurse's Cottage Station Road Sway Lymington SO41 6BA Tel: (01590) 683402 Fax 01590 683402 Open: XMAS - Mid NOV Map Ref No. 16	Nearest Road: A.337 Renowned for warmth of hospitality & first-class cuisine, this former District Nurse's cottage on the edge of the historic New Forest provides an ideal touring centre. Lovingly refurbished in recent years by Tony Barnfield, this award-winning licensed guest house offers reduced-price short breaks for stays of 2+ nights, with over 70 wines to accompany your selection from the 3-course dinner menu. 3 en-suite ground-floor bedrooms with T.V., fridge, 'phone etc. Children over 10. E-mail: nurses.cottage@lineone.net	£45.00 to £62.50 see PHOTO over p. 229 VISA: M'CARD: AMEX:	Y	Y	Y
Peter & Jennifer Cutmore Wheatsheaf House Gosport Street Lymington SO41 9BG Tel: (01590) 679208 Open: ALL YEAR Map Ref No. 17	Nearest Road: A.337 A beautifully appointed early-17th-century former tavern, Wheatsheaf House is close to the centre of this charming Georgian market town, & only 3 mins' walk from the historic town quay. Tea/coffee is available on request in a choice of 3 large comfortable rooms with either en-suite or private facilities. Ideally placed for sailing, the New Forest & for touring the whole region. You are assured of a warm welcome. Animals by arrangement. (Reduced rates for longer stays.)	£27.00 to £33.00	Y	N	Y
Mrs Wendy M. Gallagher Albany House 3 Highfield Lymington SO41 9GB Tel: (01590) 671900 Open: ALL YEAR (Excl. Xmas) Map Ref No. 17	Nearest Road: A.337 This fine Regency house, built in 1842, provides a warm welcoming atmosphere in a traditionally furnished home. There are views over the town of Solent & the Isle of Wight. 3 comfortably furnished bedrooms, with en-suite facilities, T.V. & tea/coffee. Super meals are served in the elegant dining room using freshly prepared ingredients. In season, shellfish & New Forest game are provided. Dinner, children & animals by arrangement. (Supplement for Sat. night bookings.)	£24.00 to £33.00	Y	Y	Y

The Nurse's Cottage. Sway.

Hampshire

			rate £ from - to per person	children taken	evening meals	animals taken
Mrs P. A. Thomson **St. Mary's Lodge** **Captains Row** **Lymington** **SO41 9RR** **Tel: (01590) 678576** Fax 01590 678576 **Open: ALL YEAR** **Map Ref No. 17**	Nearest Road: A.37 A superbly furnished, gracious Georgian house, Grade II listed, in a splendid position with lovely views over the Lymington River, Solent & Isle of Wight beyond. Close to the Old Town quay & marinas. Good restaurants & pubs, & Lymington town with its famous Saturday market & shops. 4 delightful bedrooms, with en-suite/private facilities. The New Forest, walks, cycling, golf, riding, a ferry to I.o.W., within 5 mins' walk. Enviable comfort for a memorable stay. Children over 12.	£25.00 to £35.00	Y	N	N
Paul Ames **Ormonde House Hotel** **Southampton Road** **Lyndhurst** **SO43 7BT** **Tel: (023) 8028 2806** Fax 023 8028 2004 **Open: ALL YEAR** **Map Ref No. 18**	Nearest Road: A.35 Ormonde House is set back from the main road opposite the open forest; easy for an early morning walk. Lyndhurst village is just 5 mins' walk & Exbury Gardens & the National Motor Museum, Beaulieu 20 mins' drive. The popular licensed restaurant offers freshly prepared dishes. 19 pretty en-suite bedrooms, all with satellite T.V., 'phone & tea facilities. Lovely rooms with king-size beds & whirlpool baths for a special treat. **E-mail: info@ormondehouse.co.uk**	£28.00 to £43.00 *see PHOTO over* *p. 231* | | | VISA: M'CARD: AMEX:	Y |	Y |	Y |
Mrs J. E. Baigent **Trotton Farm** **Trotton** **Rogate (Nr.)** **Petersfield GU31 5EN** **Tel: (01730) 813618** Fax 01730 816093 **Open: ALL YEAR** **Map Ref No. 20**	Nearest Road: A.272 This charming home, set in 200 acres of farmland, offers comfortable accommodation in 2 twin-bedded rooms & 1 double-bedded room each with en-suite shower & modern amenities, including tea/coffee-making facilities. Residents' lounge is available throughout the day. Games room & pretty garden for guests' relaxation. Ideally situated for visiting many local, historical & sporting attractions, & 1 hour from Gatwick & Heathrow. Single supplement.	£17.50 to £30.00	Y	N	Y
Dr. & Mrs A. Taylor **11 Clarence Parade** **Southsea** **Portsmouth PO5 3NU** **Tel: (02392) 736510** Fax 02392 736510 Mobile (0402) 986145 **Open: ALL YEAR** **Map Ref No. 22**	Nearest Road: A.27 This elegant, Georgian-style house overlooks Southsea Common, with magnificent views across the Solent & the Isle of Wight. Convenient for the Continental Ferry Port, I.O.W. ferries & ancient ships. Parking in front of house. 2 large, beautifully decorated & comfortable en-suite bedrooms, each with T.V., coffee/tea-making facilities, etc.. The seafront, tennis courts, shops & restaurants are all within 2 mins' walk. A warm welcome awaits you. German is spoken. Children over 12.	£22.50 to £25.00	Y	N	N
Mrs C. Sherwood **Roughwood House** **Highwood** **Ringwood** **BH24 3LE** **Tel: (01425) 474977** Fax 01425 471005 **Open: ALL YEAR** **Map Ref No. 23**	Nearest Road: A.31, A.338 Roughwood House is an elegant country house set in 20 acres of garden, pasture & woodland with stunning views. It is very secluded & has direct access to the New Forest for walking, riding & cycling. Stabling for guests' horses. Accommodation is in a self-contained annexe adjoining the main house & comprises 2 en-suite rooms, with T.V. & tea/coffee facilities. Within easy reach of Bournemouth, Poole, Lymington, Salisbury, Winchester, Dorchester & Southampton. **E-mail: tallyho@bigfoot.com**	£20.00 to £25.00	Y	N	Y

Ormonde House Hotel. Lyndhurst.

Hampshire

	Nearest Road	rate £ from - to per person	children taken	evening meals	animals taken
Jane Yates **Plantation Cottage** **Mockbeggar** **Ringwood** **BH24 3NQ** **Tel: (01425) 477443** **Fax 01425 477443** **Open: ALL YEAR** **Map Ref No. 24**	Nearest Road: A.338 Plantation Cottage is a charming 200-year-old Grade II listed house set in 3 acres in a New Forest hamlet where wild horses graze by the roadside. Ideally situated for exploring the forest, riding stables & cycle hire. Excellent pubs & restaurants are close by, & Bournemouth, Salisbury, Poole & Portsmouth are within easy reach. En-suite rooms with colour T.V., tea/coffee, hairdryer & radios. Choice of delicious breakfast from an extensive menu.	£25.00 to £35.00	N	N	N
David & Carole Hayles **Burbush Farm** **Pound Lane** **Burley** **Ringwood** **BH24 4EF** **Tel/Fax: (01425) 403238** **Open: ALL YEAR** **Map Ref No. 25**	Nearest Road: A.31 David & Carole Hayles welcome you to their beautiful farmhouse nestling in 12 acres of peace & tranquillity in the heart of the New Forest. The fine Spode china sets off a hearty & delicious aga-cooked English breakfast with award-winning New Forest sausages, free-range eggs & home-made marmalade. There are comfortable, spacious king-size beds in well-decorated en-suite/private bedrooms with tea/coffee facilities & colour T.V..	£25.00 to £30.00 VISA: M'CARD:	N	N	N
Mrs Y. M. Chivers **Montrose** **Solomons Lane** **Shirrell Heath** **Southampton** **SO32 2HU** **Tel: (01329) 833345** **Fax 01329 833345** **Open: ALL YEAR** **Map Ref No. 26**	Nearest Road: A.32, A.334 Montrose offers accommodation of a high standard in tasteful surroundings. 3 delightful bedrooms, 1 en-suite. Comfort & personal attention has helped to build a superb reputation. Situated in the Meon Valley between the historical villages of Wickham & Bishops Waltham, & yet close to the M.27, M.3 & continental ferry ports, thus providing an ideal base for exploring the towns of Winchester, Portsmouth & Southampton, & the lovely Hampshire countryside & coastline.	£25.00 to £30.00 VISA: M'CARD:	N	N	N
James & Jean Talbot **Church Farm** **Barton Stacey** **Winchester** **SO21 3RR** **Tel: (01962) 760268** **Fax 01962 761825** **Open: ALL YEAR** **Map Ref No. 27**	Nearest Road: A.303, A.30 Church Farm is a 15th-century tithe barn with Georgian & modern additions. It features an adjacent coach house & groom's cottage, recently converted, where guests may be totally self-contained, or be welcomed to the log-fired family drawing room & dine on locally produced fresh food. 6 beautiful bedrooms for guests, all with a private bathroom, T.V. & tea/coffee-making facilities. Horses are kept. Swimming pool & croquet. Tennis court adjacent.	£20.00 to £35.00 VISA: M'CARD:	Y	Y	Y
Mrs E. Kathy Pollock **Shawlands** **46 Kilham Lane** **Winchester** **SO22 5QD** **Tel: (01962) 861166** **Fax 01962 861166** **Open: ALL YEAR** **Map Ref No. 28**	Nearest Road: A.3090 Shawlands is situated on the edge of Winchester (1 mile from the centre), in a quiet lane overlooking fields. The bedrooms are spotlessly clean, bright & attractively decorated. There is a cosy lounge & the breakfast room overlooks the garden. Kathy & Bill Pollock ensure a warm welcome & the inviting breakfasts include homemade bread & preserves with fruit from their large garden. An excellent base from which to explore Hampshire.	£22.50 to £30.00 *see PHOTO over* *p. 233* VISA: M'CARD:	Y	N	Y

Shawlands. Winchester.

Hampshire

		rate £ from - to per person	evening meals children taken	animals taken	

Judy & John Parker
East View
16 Clifton Hill
Winchester
SO22 5BL
Tel: (01962) 862986
Open: ALL YEAR (Excl.
Xmas & New Year)
Map Ref No. 28

Nearest Road: A.34, A.3090
This Victorian townhouse is set in its own secluded, landscaped garden, & yet is only 5 mins
from the city centre.   East View has splendid
views over the city & cathedral to the South
Downs beyond. 3 attractive bedrooms, each with
en-suite/private facilities, T.V., radio, tea/coffee
trays. Elegant sitting room & dining room furnished with antiques. In summer, breakfast is
served in the conservatory. Private car park.

£24.00
to
£40.00

VISA: M'CARD:

N N N

All the establishments mentioned in this guide
are members of
The Worldwide Bed & Breakfast Association

When booking your accommodation please
mention
The Best Bed & Breakfast

Hereford & Worcester

Hereford & Worcester
(Heart of England)

Hereford is a beautiful ancient city standing on the banks of the River Wye, almost a crossing point between England & Wales. It is a market centre for the Marches, the border area which has a very particular history of its own.

Hereford Cathedral has a massive sandstone tower & is a fitting venue for the Three Choirs festival which dates from 1727, taking place yearly in one or the other of the three great cathedrals of Hereford, Worcester & Gloucester.

The county is fortunate in having many well preserved historic buildings. Charming "black & white" villages abound here, romantically set in a soft green landscape.

The Royal Forest of Dean spreads its oak & beech trees over 22,000 acres. When people first made their homes in the woodlands it was vaster still. There are rich deposits of coal & iron mined for centuries by the foresters, & the trees have always been felled for charcoal. Ancient courts still exist where forest dwellers can & do claim their rights to use the forest's resources.

The landscape alters dramatically as the land rises to merge with the great Black Mountain range at heights of over 2,600 feet. It is not possible to take cars everywhere but a narrow mountain road, Gospel Pass, takes traffic from Hay-on-Wye to Llanthony with superb views of the upper Wye Valley.

The Pre-Cambrian Malvern Hills form a natural boundary between Herefordshire & Worcestershire & from the highest view points you can see over 14 counties. At their feet nestle pretty little villages such as Eastonor with its 19th century castle in revived Norman style that looks quite mediaeval amongst the parklands & gardens.

There are, in fact, five Malverns. The largest predictably known as Great Malvern was a fashionable 19th century spa & is noted for the purity of the water which is bottled & sold countrywide.

The Priory at Malvern is rich in 15th century stained glass & has a fine collection of mediaeval tiles made locally. William Langland, the 14th century author of "Piers Ploughman", was educated at the Priory & is said to have been sleeping on the Malvern Hills when he had the visionary experience which led to the creation of the poem. Sir Edward Elgar was born, lived & worked here & his "Dream of Gerontius" had its first performance in Hereford Cathedral in 1902.

In Worcestershire another glorious cathedral, with what remains of its monastic buildings, founded in the 11th century, stands beside the River Severn. College Close in Worcester is a lovely group of buildings carefully preserved & very English in character.

The Severn appears to be a very lazy waterway but flood waters can reach astonshing heights, & the "Severn Bore" is a famous phenomenon.

A cruise along the river is a pleasant way to spend a day seeing villages & churches from a different perspective, possibly visiting a riverside inn. To the south of the county lie the undulating Vales of Evesham & Broadway - described as the show village of England.

The Malvern Hills.

Hereford & Worcester

Hereford & Worcester Gazeteer

Areas of outstanding natural beauty.
The Malvern Hills, The Cotswolds, The Wye Valley.

Historic Houses & Castles

Berrington Hall - Leominster
18th century - painted & plastered ceilings. Landscape by Capability Brown.

Brilley - Cwmmau Farmhouse - Whitney-on-Wye
17th century timber-framed & stone tiled farmhouse.

Burton Court - Eardisland
14th century great hall. Exhibition of European & Oriental costume & curios. Model fairground.

Croft Castle - Nr. Leominster
Castle on the Welsh border - inhabited by Croft family for 900 years.

Dinmore Manor - Nr. Hereford
14th century chapel & cloister.

Eastnor Castle - Nr. Ledbury
19th century - Castellated, containing pictures & armour. Arboretum.

Eye Manor - Leominster
17th century Carolean Manor house - excellent plasterwork, paintings, costumes, books, secret passage. Collection of dolls.

Hanbury Hall - Nr. Droitwich
18th century red brick house - only two rooms & painted ceilings on exhibition.

Harvington Hall - Kidderminster
Tudor Manor house with moat, priest's hiding places.

The Greyfriars - Worcester
15th century timber-framed building adjoins Franciscan Priory.

Hellen's - Much Marcle
13th century manorial house of brick & stone. Contains the Great hall with stone table - bedroom of Queen Mary. Much of the original furnishings remain.

Kentchurch Court - Hereford
14th century fortified border Manor house. Paintings & Carvings by Grinling Gibbons.

Moccas Court - Moccas
18th century - designed by Adam - Parklands by Capability Brown - under restoration.

Pembridge Castle - Welsh Newton
17th century moated castle.

Sutton Court - Mordiford
Palladian mansion by Wyatt, watercolours, embroideries, china.

Cathedrals & Churches

Amestry (St. John the Baptist & St.Alkmund)
16th century rood screen.

Abbey Dore (St. Mary & Holy Trinity)
17th century glass & great oak screen - early English architecture.

Brinsop (St. George)
14th century, screen & glass, alabaster reredos, windows in memory of Wordsworth, carved Norman tympanum.

Bredon (St. Giles)
12th century - central tower & spire. Mediaeval heraldic tiles, tombs & early glass.

Brockhampton (St. Eadburgh)
1902. Central tower & thatched roof.

Castle Frome (St. Michael & All Angles)
12th century carved font, 17th century effigies in alabaster.

Chaddesley Corbett (St. Cassian)
14th century monuments, 12th century font.

Elmley (St. Mary)
12th century & 15th century font, tower, gargoyles, mediaeval.

Great Witley (St. Michael)
Baroque - Plasterwork, painted ceiling, painted glass, very fine example.

Hereford (All Saints)
13th-14th centuries, spire, splendid choir stalls, chained library.

Hereford Cathedral
Small cathedral.
Fine central tower c.1325, splendid porch, brasses, early English Lady Chapel with lancet windows. Red sandstone.

Kilpeck (St. Mary & St. David)
Romanesque style - mediaeval windows - fine carvings.

Leominster (St. Peter & St. Paul)
12th century doorway, fine Norman arches, decorated windows.

Much Marcle (St. Bartholomew)
13th century. 14th & 17th century monuments.

HEREFORD & WORCESTER

Map reference

01 Ailesbury
02 Bengry
03 Lee
04 Watson
07 Conolly
08 Fothergill
09 Allen
10 Robertson
12 Kemp
13 Meekings
16 Rowan
17 J. Williams
19 Lloyd

237

Herefordshire

		rate £ from - to per person	children taken	evening meals	animals taken
Caroline Ailesbury **The Old Rectory** **Garway** **HR2 8RH** **Tel: (01600) 750363** Fax 01600 750364 **Open: ALL YEAR (Excl.** **Xmas & New Year)** **Map Ref No. 01**	Nearest Road: A.466 Flowers, ticking clocks, log fires & Aga cooking all make you feel welcome here. Beautiful views towards the Black Mountains & Brecon Beacons. The Blue Bedroom with 4-poster, & the Pink Room with twin beds, have handbasins & T.V.s & share a bathroom. Also a shower room & separate W.C.s. Dinner by arrangement. The delicious breakfast sets you up for the day. Hereford Cathedral with Mappa Mundi & Chained Library, Monmouth & Hay-on-Wye are within easy reach. Children over 8. Single supplement.	£20.00 to £22.50 🚭 VISA: M'CARD:	Y	Y	N
Mr & Mrs J. Bengry **The Vauld Farm** **The Vauld** **Marden** **Hereford** **HR1 3HA** **Tel: (01568) 797898** **Open: ALL YEAR** **Map Ref No. 02**	Nearest Road: A.49 The Vauld Farm is a delightful 16th-century black-&-white former farmhouse, set in a beautiful garden. It retains many period features throughout & affords attractive accommodation. 3 charming & elegantly furnished bedrooms, each with an en-suite bathroom, T.V. & tea/coffee-making facilities. (1 with 4-poster.) Hearty breakfasts & delicious evening meals are served in the tastefully decorated dining room. A beautiful home & the perfect location for a relaxing break.	£25.00 to £30.00	N	Y	N
Mrs G. W. Lee **Cwm Craig Farm** **Little Dewchurch** **Hereford HR2 6PS** **Tel: (01432) 840250** Fax 01432 840250 **Open: ALL YEAR** **Map Ref No. 03**	Nearest Road: A.49 Spacious Georgian farmhouse, surrounded by superb unspoilt countryside. Situated between the cathedral city of Hereford & Ross-on-Wye, & just a few mins' drive from the Wye Valley. Ideal base for touring the Forest of Dean. All 3 bedrooms have modern amenities, shaver points & tea/coffee facilities. 2 are en-suite. There is a lounge & separated dining room, both with colour T.V.. A full English breakfast is served.	£17.00 to £18.00	Y	N	N
Grace Watson **Hall's Mill House** **Huntington** **Kington** **HR5 3QA** **Tel: (01497) 831409** **Open: ALL YEAR (Excl. Xmas)** **Map Ref No. 04**	Nearest Road: A.438, A.44 Hall's Mill House has recently been restored & is situated in peaceful, idyllic countryside overlooking the River Arrow. 3 attractively furnished bedrooms with en-suite/private bathrooms. A comfortable lounge in which guests may choose to relax. Easy access to Offa's Dyke, the Black Mountains, Hay-on-Wye, black-&-white villages, Welsh border country, churches & castles. Many excellent pubs & restaurants locally. Evening meals by prior arrangement. Children over 4.	£18.00 to £20.00	Y	Y	N
Peter & Jane Conolly **The Hills Farm** **Leysters** **Leominster** **HR6 0HP** **Tel: (01568) 750205** Fax 01568 750306 **Open: MAR - OCT** **Map Ref No. 07**	Nearest Road: A.4112 Magnificent views & a splendid welcome await you at this 15th-century farmhouse on the edge of the village of Leysters betwixt Ludlow & Leominster. Delightful en-suite bedrooms have T.V.s & beverage facilities. 3 are in charming barn conversions offering complete seclusion. Scrumptious dinners, traditional or vegetarian, are available in the individually tabled dining room - the dairy in days gone by - which is unlicensed, so bring your own wine. A wonderful escape.	£25.00 to £27.00 🚭 *see PHOTO over* *p. 239* VISA: M'CARD:	N	Y	Y

The Hills Farm. Leystors.

Broxwood Court. Broxwood.

Herefordshire & Worcestershire

		rate £ from - to per person	children taken	evening meals	animals taken
Catherine & Marguerite Fothergill **Highfield** **Newtown** **Ivington Road** **Leominster HR6 8QD** **Tel: (01568) 613216** **Open: ALL YEAR** **Map Ref No. 08**	Nearest Road: A.44, A.49 Twins Catherine & Marguerite are eager to make you feel welcome & at home in their elegant Edwardian house, set in a rural, tranquil location. You will be very comfortable in any of the 3 attractive bedrooms, all with a bathroom (1 being en-suite) & tea/coffee-making facilities. There is a large garden & a T.V. lounge with a crackling fire in which guests may relax, & the home-made food is absolutely delicious. Residential licence.	£18.00 to £22.00	N	Y	N
Mike & Anne Allen **Broxwood Court** **Broxwood** **Leominster** **HR6 9JJ** **Tel: (01544) 340245** **Fax 01544 340573** **Open: ALL YEAR (Excl. Xmas & New Year)** **Map Ref No. 09**	Nearest Road: A.4112 Elegant manor house with superb views & stunning 30 acre garden; sweeping lawns, specimen trees & trout lake with numerous white & coloured peacocks who roam the grounds. For the energetic there is a 40 ft heated swimming pool in the rose garden & an all-weather tennis court. The delightful bedrooms all have en-suite bathrooms. Anne is an excellent cook whose delicious dinners include fruit & vegetables from the organic kitchen garden. A warm welcome awaits you.	£33.00 to £48.00 *see PHOTO over* *p. 240* VISA: M'CARD:	Y	Y	N
Mrs D. Robertson **Sunnymount Hotel** **Ryefield Road** **Ross-on-Wye** **HR9 5LU** **Tel: (01989) 563880** **Open: ALL YEAR** **Map Ref No. 10**	Nearest Road: A.40 Quietly situated on the edge of the town, this attractive Edwardian house is warm & inviting. Offering 6 well-appointed bedrooms, with en-suite bathrooms & tea/coffee-making facilities. The sitting rooms (1 with colour T.V.) & dining room overlook the pretty garden. A wide choice of breakfasts using home & local produce freshly prepared for each meal. English/French cooking. Licensed. Ample private parking. An ideal base from which to explore this fascinating area.	£22.00 to £27.00 VISA: M'CARD:	Y	Y	N

Worcestershire

		rate £ from - to per person	children taken	evening meals	animals taken
Mrs Mary Kemp **Cowley House** **Church Street** **Broadway** **WR12 7AE** **Tel: (01386) 853262** **Open: ALL YEAR** **Map Ref No. 12**	Nearest Road: A.44 Cowley House is a delightful 17th-century Cotswold stone house set in a 3/4-acre garden, situated just off Broadways village green in a central but secluded position. It has beautiful antiques, and a wealth of charm & character with exposed stone walls, stone-flagged floors & ceiling beams. Bedrooms have private facilities & hairdryers. Complementary beverages are available. Ample car parking. Children over 5.	£25.00 to £35.00 *see PHOTO over* *p. 242*	Y	N	N

Visit our website at:
http://www.bestbandb.co.uk

Cowley House. Broadway.

Leasow House. Broadway.

		rate £ from - to per person	children taken	evening meals	animals taken
Mrs Barbara Meekings **Leasow House** **Laverton Meadow** **Broadway** **WR12 7NA** **Tel: (01386) 584526** Fax 01386 584596 **Open: ALL YEAR** **Map Ref No. 13**	Nearest Road: A.44 Leasow is a charming 17th-century Cotswold stone farmhouse. Recently renovated, it offers 7 delightful spacious bedrooms, with shower/bath en-suite, T.V. & tea/coffee-making facilities. Set in the peaceful tranquillity of the open countryside, it is only 2 1/2 miles from Broadway village. The house has wonderful panoramic views of the Cotswold escarpment. Ideally situated for touring the Cotswolds & the Vale of Evesham. A warm welcome from the friendly hosts is assured. E-mail: Leasow@clara.net	£28.00 to £45.00 *see PHOTO over* *p. 243* VISA: M'CARD: AMEX:	Y	N	Y
Barbara & Richard Rowan **The Red Gate** **32 Avenue Road** **Malvern** **WR14 3BJ** **Tel: (01684) 565013** Fax 01684 565013 **Open: ALL YEAR** **Map Ref No. 16**	Nearest Road: A.449 Situated in a tree-lined avenue within walking distance of the town centre & hills. This late-Victorian house has retained much of its traditional charm, which is matched by the courtesy & hospitality you would expect from a friendly family-run hotel. Each of the 6 bedrooms is quite different, some high & spacious, some cottagey with stripped pine furniture. All are non-smoking, have en-suite bathrooms, colour T.V., tea/coffee & the small comforts one would like to find when away from home. The Red Gate is a very special place. Children over 8 years.	£25.00 to £30.00 VISA: M'CARD:	Y	N	N
Judith & Jon Williams **Wyche Keep** **22 Wyche Road** **Malvern** **WR14 4EG** **Tel: (01684) 567018** Fax 01684 892304 **Open: ALL YEAR** **Map Ref No. 17**	Nearest Road: B.4218, A.449 Wyche Keep is a unique arts-&-crafts castle-style house, perched high on the Malvern Hills, built by the family of Sir Stanley Baldwin, Prime Minister, to enjoy spectacular 60-mile views, & having a long history of elegant entertaining. 3 large double suites, including a 4-poster. Traditional English cooking is a speciality, & guests can savour memorable 4-course candle-lit dinners, served in a 'house party' atmosphere in front of a log fire. A magical setting with private parking. Home of Brother John Medieval Britain Tours, acclaimed in USA for scholarship. Fully licensed. E-mail: wyche-keep-tours@england.com	£25.00 to £30.00 *see PHOTO over* *p. 246*	N	Y	N
Mrs Val Lloyd **40 Britannia Square** **Worcester** **WR1 3DN** **Tel: (01905) 611920** Fax 01905 27152 **Open: ALL YEAR** **Map Ref No. 19**	Nearest Road: A.449, A.38 Brittannia Square, Worcester's most prestigious area, is a quiet, park-like square of outstanding Georgian houses. Its close proximity to restaurants, station & the city centre make it an ideal place to stay. Featured on T.V. & in interior-design magazines, this handsome house is superbly decorated; the bedrooms have en-suite bathrooms, T.V. & tea/coffee trays. English breakfast is served in the impressive dining room. The garden is a special feature with plenty to interest the keen plantsman. E-mail: valuloyd@aol.com	£30.00 to £45.00 *see PHOTO over* *p. 245* VISA: M'CARD: AMEX:	Y	N	N

When booking your accommodation please mention
The Best Bed & Breakfast

40 Britannia Square. Worcester.

Wyche Keep. Malvern.

Kent

Kent
(South East)

Kent is best known as "the garden of England". At its heart is a tranquil landscape of apple & cherry orchards, hop-fields & oast-houses, but there are also empty downs, chalk sea-cliffs, rich marshlands, sea ports, castles & the glory of Canterbury Cathedral.

The dramatic chalk ridgeway of the North Downs links the White Cliffs of Dover with the north of the county which extends into the edge of London. It was a trade route in ancient times following the high downs above the Weald, dense forest in those days. It can be followed today & it offers broad views of the now agricultural Weald.

The pilgrims who flocked to Canterbury in the 12th-15th centuries, (colourfully portrayed in Chaucer's Canterbury Tales), probably used the path of the Roman Watling Street rather than the high ridgeway.

Canterbury was the cradle of Christianity in southern England & is by tradition the seat of the Primate of All England. This site, on the River Stour, has been settled since the earliest times & became a Saxon stonghold under King Ethelbert of Kent. He established a church here, but it was in Norman times that the first great building work was carried out, to be continued in stages until the 15th century. The result is a blending of styles with early Norman work, a later Norman choir, a vaulted nave in Gothic style & a great tower of Tudor design. Thomas Becket was murdered on the steps of the Cathedral in 1170. The town retains much of its mediaeval character with half-timbered weavers' cottages, old churches & the twin towers of the west gate.

Two main styles of building give the villages of Kent their special character. The Kentish yeoman's house was the home of the wealthier farmers & is found throughout the county. It is a timber-frame building with white lath & plaster walls & a hipped roof of red tiles. Rather more modest in style is a small weatherboard house, usually painted white or cream. Rolvenden & Groombridge have the typical charm of a Kentish village whilst Tunbridge Wells is an attractive town, with a paved parade known as the Pantiles & excellent antique shops.

There are grand houses & castles throughout the county. Leeds Castle stands in a lake & dates back to the 9th century. It has beautifully landscaped parkland. Knowle House is an impressive Jacobean & Tudor Manor House with rough ragstone walls, & acres of deer-park & woodland.

Kent is easily accessible from the Channel Ports, Gatwick Airport & London.

Leeds Castle.

Kent

Kent
Gazeteer

Areas of outstanding natural beauty.
Kent Downs.

Historic Houses & Castles

Aylesford, The Friars - Nr. Maidstone
13th century Friary & shrine of Our Lady, (much restored), 14th century cloisters - original.

Allington Castle -Nr. Maidstone
13th century. One time home of Tudor poet Thomas Wyatt. Restored early 20th century. Icons & Renaissance paintings.

Black Charles - Nr. Sevenoaks
14th century Hall house - Tudor fireplaces, beautiful panelling.

Boughton Monchelsea Place - Nr. Maidstone
Elizabethan Manor House - grey stone battlements - 18th century landscaped park, wonderful views of Weald of Kent.

Chartwell - Westerham
Home of Sir Winston Churchill.
Chiddingstone Castle - Nr. Edenbridge
18th century Gothic revival building encasing old remains of original Manor House - Royal Stuart & Jacobite collection.
 Ancient Egyptian collection - Japanese netsuke, etc.

Eyehorne Manor - Hollingbourne
15th century Manor house with 17th century additions.

Cobham Hall - Cobham
16th century house - Gothic & Renaissance - Wyatt interior. Now school for girls.

Fairfield - Eastry, Sandwich
13th-14th centuries - moated castle. Was home of Anne Boleyn. Beautiful gardens with unique collection of classical statuary.

Knole - Sevenoaks
15th century - splendid Jacobean interior - 17th & 18th century furniture. One of the largest private houses in England.

Leeds Castle- Nr. Maidstone
Built in middle of the lake, it was the home of the mediaeval Queens of England.

Lullingstone Castle - Eynsford
14th century mansion house - frequented by Henry VIII & Queen Anne.
Still occupied by descendants of the original owners

Long Barn - Sevenoaks
14th century house - said to be home of William Caxton. Restored by Edwin Lutyens; 16th century barn added to enlarge house. Galleried hall - fine beaming & fireplaces. Lovely gardens created by Sir Harold Nicholson & his wife Vita Sackville-West.

Owletts - Cobham
Carolean house of red brick with plasterwork ceiling & fine staircase.

Owl House - Lamberhurst
16th century cottage, tile hung; said to be home of wool smuggler. Charming gardens.

Penshurst Place - Tonbridge
14th century house with mediaeval Great Hall perfectly preserved.English Gothic. Birthplace of Elizabethan poet, Sir Philip Sidney
Fine staterooms, splendid picture gallery, famous toy museum. Tudor gardens & orchards.

Saltwood Castle - Nr. Hythe
Mediaeval - very fine castle & is privately occupied. Was lived in by Sir Ralph de Broc, murderer of Thomas a Becket.

Squerreys Court - Westerham
Manor house of William & Mary period, with furniture, paintings & tapestries of time. Connections with General Wolfe.

Stoneacre - Otham
15th century yeoman's half-timbered house.

Cathedrals & Churches

Brook (St. Mary)
11th century paintings in this unaltered early Norman church.

Brookland (St. Augustine)
13th century & some later part. Crown-post roofs, detached wooden belfry with conical cap. 12th century lead font.

Canterbury Cathedral
12th century wall paintings, 12th & 13th century stained glass. Very fine Norman crypt. Early perpendicular nave & cloisters which have heraldic bosses. Wonderful central tower.

Charing (St. Peter & St. Paul)
13th & 15th century interior with 15th century tower. 17th century restoration.

Kent

Cobham (St. Mary)
16th century carved & painted tombs - unequalled collection of brasses in county.
Elham (St. Mary the Virgin)
Norman wall with 13th century arcades, perpendicular clerestory. Restored by Eden.
Lullingstone (St. Botolph)
14th century mainly - 16th century wood screen. Painted glass monuments.
Newington-on-the-Street (St. Mary the Virgin)
13th & 14th century - fine tower. 13th century tomb. Wall paintings.
Rochester Cathedral
Norman facade & nave, otherwise early English.
12th century west door. 14th century doorway to Chapter room.
Stone (St. Mary)
13th century - decorated - paintings, 15th century brass, 16th century tomb.
Woodchurch (All Saints)
13th century, having late Norman font & priest's brass of 1320. Arcades alternating octagonal & rounded columns. Triple lancets with banded marble shafting at east end.

Museums & Galleries

Royal Museums - Canterbury
Archaeological, geological, mineralogical exhibits, natural history, pottery & porcelain. Engravings, prints & pictures.
Westgate - Canterbury
Museum of armour, etc. in 14th century gatehouse of city.
Dartford District Museum - Dartford
Roman, Saxon & natural history.
Deal Museum - Deal
Prehistoric & historic antiquities.
Dicken's House Museum - Broadstairs
Personalia of Dickens; prints, costume & Victoriana.
Down House - Downe
The home of Charles Darwin for 40 years, now his memorial & museum.
Dover Museum - Dover
Roman pottery, ceramics, coins, zoology, geology, local history, etc.
Faversham Heritage Society - Faversham
1000 years of history & heritage.
Folkestone Museum & Art Gallery - Folkestone
Archeology, local history & sciences.

Herne Bay Museum - Herne Bay
Stone, Bronze & Early Iron Age specimens. Roman material from Reculver excavations. Items of local & Kentish interest.
Museum & Art Gallery - Maidstone
16th century manor house exhibiting natural history & archaeolgical collections. Costume Gallery, bygones, ceramics, 17th century works by Dutch & Italian painters. Regimental museum

Historic Monuments

Eynsford Castle - Eynsford
12th century castle remains.
Rochester Castle - Rochester
Storied keep - 1126-39
Roman Fort & Anglo-Saxon Church - Reculver
Excavated remains of 3rd century fort & Saxon church.
Little Kit's Coty House - Aylesford
Ruins of burial chambers from 2 long barrows.
Lullingstone Roman Villa - Lullingstone
Roman farmstead excavations.
Roman Fort & Town - Richborough
Roman 'Rutupiae' & fort
Tonbridge Castle - Tonbridge
12th century curtain walls, shell of keep & 14th century gatehouse.
Dover Castle - Dover
Keep built by Henry II in 1180. Outer curtain built 13th century.

Gardens

Chilham Castle Gardens - Nr. Canterbury
25 acre gardens of Jacobean house, laid out by Tradescant.
Lake garden, fine trees & birds of prey. Jousting & mediaeval banquets.
Great Comp Gardens - Nr. Borough Green
Outstanding 7 acre garden with old brick walls.
Owl House Gardens - Lamberhurst
16th century smugglers cottage with beautiful gardens of roses, daffodils & rhododendrons.
Sissinghurst Castle Gardens - Sissinghurst
Famous gardens created by Vita Sackville-West around the remains of an Elizabethan mansion.

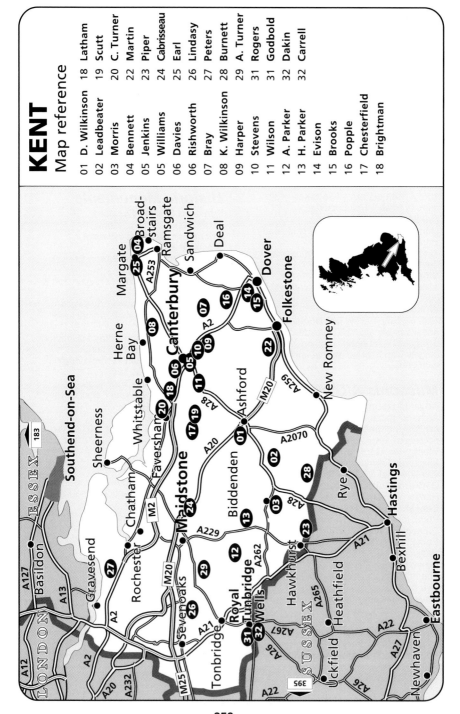

KENT
Map reference

01	D. Wilkinson	18	Latham
02	Leadbeater	19	Scutt
03	Morris	20	C. Turner
04	Bennett	22	Martin
05	Jenkins	23	Piper
05	Williams	24	Cabrisseau
06	Davies	25	Earl
06	Rishworth	26	Lindsay
07	Bray	27	Peters
08	K. Wilkinson	28	Burnett
09	Harper	29	A. Turner
10	Stevens	31	Rogers
11	Wilson	31	Godbold
12	A. Parker	32	Dakin
13	H. Parker	32	Carrell
14	Evison		
15	Brooks		
16	Popple		
17	Chesterfield		
18	Brightman		

250

Thanington Hotel. Canterbury.

Kent

		rate £ from - to per person	children taken	evening meals	animals taken
Denise & Charles Wilkinson **Worten House** **Great Chart** **Ashford TN23 3BU** **Tel: (01233) 622944** **Fax 01233 662249** **Open: ALL YEAR** **Map Ref No. 01**	Nearest Road: A.20, A.28 A beautiful 18th-century farmhouse set in a large garden in the heart of the beautiful Kent countryside. Offering 2 very comfortable twin-bedded rooms, each with tea/coffee-making facilities. Denise & Charles Wilkinson & their family assure the visitor of a warm welcome. Plenty of parking space. Within easy reach of the Channel Tunnel & Dover. Evening meals by arrangement. An excellent base for explore this delightful region.	£22.50 to £28.00	Y	Y	N
Mrs Tessa Leadbeater **Shirkoak Farm** **Bethersden Road** **Woodchurch** **Ashford** **TN26 3PZ** **Tel: (01233) 860056** **Fax 01233 861402** **Open: ALL YEAR** **Map Ref No. 02**	Nearest Road: A.28 Lovingly restored 18th-century Georgian farmhouse in 2 acres of beautiful gardens with tennis court. 3 bedrooms, all en-suite (2 queen-size doubles & 1 twin). All with T.V. & tea/coffee tray. Elegant dining-room overlooking small lake, drawing-room with oak beams & an inglenook fireplace. Furnished with antiques. Situated in quiet rural setting ideal for Kentish Weald, Sissinghurst Castle, Tenterden, Canterbury & Dover. (M.20 at Ashford only 10 mins' drive.) Children over 10. **E-mail: ShirkoakFm@aol.com**	£22.50 to £25.00	Y	N	N
Mrs Susan Morris **Tudor Cottage** **25 High Street** **Biddenden** **Ashford TN27 8AL** **Tel: (01580) 291913** **Open: ALL YEAR** **Map Ref No. 03**	Nearest Road: A.262 Tudor Cottage is a beautiful 15th-century house in the centre of the charming & historic village of Biddenden, with 2 good restaurants nearby. Accommodation is in 3 delightful double bedrooms, 2 en-suite, 1 with private facilities, each well-equipped with colour T.V. & tea/coffee-making facilities. Children over 10 welcome. Tudor Cottage is an ideal location from which to explore beautiful Kent & East Sussex. Children over 10.	£20.00 to £25.00	Y	N	N
Mrs Judith Bennett **North Goodwin House** **Cliff Promenade** **Broadstairs** **CT10 3QY** **Tel: (01843) 864128** **Open: ALL YEAR** **Map Ref No. 04**	Nearest Road: A.253, A.256 A substantial cliff-top residence overlooking the English Channel on a private estate 1 mile east of Broadstairs. 1 en-suite double bedroom & 1 double & 1 single bedroom with private bathroom. All with sea views, T.V. & tea/coffee facilities. Full English breakfast. Excellent restaurants nearby. Beaches/golf course 5 mins. 12 other courses within 45 mins. Convenient for channel ports, tunnel & Canterbury.	£22.50 to £28.00	Y	N	N
Jill & David Jenkins **Thanington Hotel** **140 Wincheap** **Canterbury** **CT1 3RY** **Tel: (01227) 453227** **Fax 01227 453225** **Open: ALL YEAR** **Map Ref No. 05**	Nearest Road: A.28 Spacious Georgian hotel, ideally situated 10 mins' stroll from the city centre. 15 en-suite bedrooms, beautifully decorated & furnished, all in immaculate condition with modern-day extras. King-size 4-poster beds, antique bedsteads & 2 large family rooms. Walled garden with patio, indoor heated swimming pool, bar, guest lounge & snooker/games room. Delicious breakfast served in the elegant dining room. Car park. An oasis in a busy tourist city, convenient for channel ports, tunnel & historic houses of Kent. Gatwick 60 mins. **E-mail: thanington_hotel@compuserve.com**	£34.00 to £44.00 *see PHOTO over* *p. 251* VISA: M'CARD: AMEX:	Y	N	Y

Magnolia House. Canterbury.

Kent

		rate £ from - to	children taken	evening meals	animals taken
Mrs Loraine Williams **Clare Ellen Guest House** **9 Victoria Road** **Canterbury** **CT1 3SG** **Tel: (01227) 760205** **Fax 01227 784482** **Open: ALL YEAR** **Map Ref No. 05**	Nearest Road: A.28 A warm welcome & bed & breakfast in style. Large, elegant en-suite/private bedrooms, all with colour T.V., clock/radio, hairdryer & tea/coffee-making facilities. Ironing centre with trouser press for guests' convenience. Vegetarians & special diets catered for on request. Cosy residents' lounge. Numerous restaurants/pubs close by. Only 6 mins' walk to the town centre/cathedral. 4 mins' walk to Canterbury East Station. Private car park & garage available. **E-mail: loraine.williams@virgin.net** VISA: M'CARD:	£23.00 to £26.00	Y	N	N
Ann & John Davies **Magnolia House** **36 St Dunstan's Terrace** **Canterbury CT2 8AX** **Tel: (01227) 765121/** **Mobile 07885 595970** **Fax 01227 765121** **Open: ALL YEAR** **Map Ref No. 06**	Nearest Road: A.2 Magnolia House is a charming, detached late-Georgian house situated in a quiet, residential street a 10-min walk from the city centre. The 7 bedrooms are individually coordinated to a high standard, & have every facility for an enjoyable stay. A varied breakfast menu is served in the dining room overlooking the attractive walled garden, where you are welcome to relax after a busy day's sightseeing. Evening meals available Nov - Feb. Children over 12. *see PHOTO over* *p. 253* VISA: M'CARD: AMEX:	£35.00 to £47.50 (non-smoking)	Y	N	N
Keith & Anthea Rishworth **Oriel Lodge** **3 Queens Avenue** **Canterbury** **CT2 8AY** **Tel: (01227) 462845** **Fax 01227 462845** **Open: ALL YEAR** **Map Ref No. 06**	Nearest Road: A.2 In a tree-lined residential avenue, 5 mins' walk from the city centre & restaurants, Oriel Lodge is an attractive Edwardian detached house, retaining a warm & restful period character. There are 6 well-furnished bedrooms with clean, up-to-date facilities. Afternoon tea is served in the garden, or in the lounge, with a log fire in winter. Smoking in lounge area only. Private parking. Children over 6 years welcome. VISA: M'CARD:	£21.00 to £31.00	Y	N	N
Rosemary Bray **Ratling House** **Ratling** **Canterbury** **CT3 3HL** **Tel: (01304) 842200** **Open: ALL YEAR** **Map Ref No. 07**	Nearest Road: A.2 A comfortable 18th-century country house in a quiet rural setting near the A.2. Off the B.2046 approx. 1 mile east of Adisham, & 1 mile north of Aylesham. Centrally heated & attractively furnished double bedrooms, 1 with en-suite facilities, T.V., etc., 2 with an adjacent bathroom. Large gardens of 2 acres. Ample private parking. Convenient for Channel ports & Tunnel. Dover & Canterbury 9 miles.	£21.00 to £27.00 (non-smoking)	Y	N	N
Kathy & Mike Wilkinson **Chislet Court Farm** **Chislet** **Canterbury** **CT3 4DU** **Tel: (01227) 860309** **Fax 01227 860444** **Open: ALL YEAR (Excl. Xmas)** **Map Ref No. 08**	Nearest Road: A.28 A listed Queen Anne farmhouse, set in mature gardens with views overlooking the surrounding countryside & the ancient village church. The 2 double bedrooms (1 en-suite) are large & comfortable with tea/coffee-making facilities & colour T.V.. Guests are welcome to wander round the garden or relax in the conservatory - where breakfast is served. An ideal base for exploring Canterbury & the Kent countryside. Children over 12. **E-mail: chisletcourtfarm@dial.pipex.com**	£20.00 to £30.00 (non-smoking)	Y	N	N

Iffin Farmhouse. Canterbury.

Kent

		rate £ from - to per person	children taken	evening meals	animals taken
Hilary Harper **East Bridge Country Hotel** **Bridge Hill** **Bridge** **Canterbury CT4 5AS** **Tel: (01227) 830808** **Fax 01227 832181** **Open: ALL YEAR** **Map Ref No. 09**	Nearest Road: A.2 A friendly, elegant & comfortable Georgian house in a pretty village. 15 mins from the sea ports of Dover & Folkestone. Overlooking open country-side of outstanding beauty, the house offers ac-commodation in 8 comfortable rooms, 4 en-suite, all with modern amenities, T.V. & tea/coffee-making facilities. Ideal for walking, riding, fishing. Close to Kent's historic castles. Tasty English breakfasts. A licensed restaurant available to residents & non-residents. VISA: M'CARD:	£22.00 to £45.00	Y	Y	N
Rosemary Stevens **Iffin Farmhouse** **Iffin Lane** **Canterbury** **CT4 7BE** **Tel: (01227) 462776** **Fax 01227 462776** **Open: ALL YEAR** **Map Ref No. 10**	Nearest Road: A.2 A warm welcome awaits you in this old 18th-century farmhouse, renovated to a very high standard. 3 large double bedrooms, each with views to the garden & orchards, T.V., tea/coffee facilities & an en-suite/private bathroom. Enjoy a full English breakfast, served in a lovely dining room. Set in 10 acres of gardens, paddocks & orchards, the house (only 6 mins' drive from Canterbury) is a delightful spot for touring Kent. Children over 5. Dinner is available Nov - Mar. *see PHOTO over* *p. 255*	£27.50 to £30.00	Y	N	N
Mrs Jane Wilson **Stour Farm** **Riverside** **Chartham** **Canterbury CT4 7NX** **Tel: (01227) 731977** **Fax 01227 731977** **Open: MAR - OCT** **Map Ref No. 11**	Nearest Road: A.28 Jane & Jeremy welcome you to their delightful barn conversion overlooking the River Stour on the edge of Chartham village, 3 miles from Can-terbury. 2 en-suite double bedrooms each with T.V. & tea/coffee facilities. Breakfast is served in the dining room or, weather permitting, on the sun terrace overlooking the river. Good restaurants & pubs nearby. Parking. Convenient for ferry & channel tunnel ports. Many gardens, walks & golf courses within easy reach. Children over 12. **E-mail: jjwilson@adept.co.uk** VISA: M'CARD:	£23.00 to £35.00	Y	N	N
Jeremy & Annie Parker **West Winchet** **Winchet Hill, Goudhurst** **Cranbrook TN17 1JX** **Tel: (01580) 212024** **Fax 01580 212250** **Open: ALL YEAR (Excl.** **Xmas & New Year)** **Map Ref No. 12**	Nearest Road: A.262 West Winchet is the west wing of a Victorian mansion surrounded by parkland in a secluded & peaceful setting. 2 beautifully decorated rooms, 1 double with private bathroom & 1 twin with en-suite shower. Each with T.V., tea/coffee etc. Both rooms are on the ground floor, & the twin room has French windows onto the terrace & into the garden. A magnificent drawing room. Ideal for touring Kent & East Sussex. 2 1/2 miles mainline station (London 55 mins). Children over 5.	£25.00 to £35.00	Y	N	Y
Heather & Kenneth Parker **Maplehurst Mill** **Mill Lane** **Frittenden** **Cranbrook TN17 2DT** **Tel: (01580) 852203** **Fax 01580 852117** **Open: ALL YEAR** **Map Ref No. 13**	Nearest Road: A.229 Maplehurst Mill is a beautiful water mill, attached to a medieval mill house & standing in 11 acres of landscaped gardens. 3 attractively furnished bedrooms (incl. 1 4-poster), with en-suite bath-room, T.V., etc. & views over the water & the surrounding countryside. A breakfast & candlelit dinner are served in the medieval miller's house, in a beautiful beamed dining room with inglenook & antiques. A warm welcome awaits you. **E-mail: maplehurst@clara.net** VISA: M'CARD:	£30.00 to £37.00	N	Y	N

The Old Vicarage. Chilverton Elms.

	rate £ from - to per person	children taken	evening meals	animals taken
Mrs Judy Evison **The Old Vicarage** **Chilverton Elms** **Hougham** **Dover** **CT15 7AS** Tel: (01304) 210668 Fax 01304 225118 **Open: ALL YEAR** **Map Ref No. 14**	Nearest Road: A.20, M.20 Many guests are totally surprised by the peaceful atmosphere & commanding position of this house, given its closeness to Dover. This is a beautiful country house built around 1870 & now totally restored, yet retaining many original features. It is elegantly furnished with antiques & provides everything for your stay to the very highest standards, 2 en-suite bedrooms & 1 with private bathroom. Excellent base for touring east Kent. 2 miles ferry ports/9 miles Channel Tunnel. Parking. Dinner by arrangement only. **E-mail: vicarage@esi.com**	£30.00 to £35.00 *see PHOTO over* *p. 257* VISA: M'CARD:	Y	Y	N
Diana Brooks **Rose Hill Farm** **Mill Lane** **West Hougham** **Dover CT15 7BD** Tel: (01304) 240609 **Open: ALL YEAR** **Map Ref No. 15**	Nearest Road: A.20, M.20 A sympathetically restored 17th-century farmhouse in peaceful, unspoilt countryside. 1 1/2 acres of beautiful gardens, croquet lawn, swimming pool - a joy for garden lovers & an excellent centre for touring, walking, sailing, golf & visiting the numerous castles, historic houses & gardens of Kent. 10 mins' drive to Dover/Channel Tunnel. Comfortable en-suite bedrooms with colour T.V. & tea/coffee-making facilities.	£22.50 to £25.00	Y	N	N
Barry & Lyn Popple **Sunshine Cottage** **The Green, Mill Lane** **Shepherdswell** **Dover CT15 7LQ** Tel: (01304) 831359/ 831218 **Open: ALL YEAR** **Map Ref No. 16**	Nearest Road: A.2 A 17th-century, Grade II listed cottage, overlooking Shepherdswell village green, with a wealth of beams, an inglenook fireplace & 2 lounges. Tastefully furnished, & with a homely atmosphere. 6 attractive bedrooms. A pretty garden & courtyard available to guests. Good home-cooking & home-made preserves. Good food also available at a nearby pub. Shepherdswell is situated halfway between Canterbury & Dover, 25 mins from the Channel Tunnel. BR station 5 mins' walk.	£21.00 to £23.00 VISA: M'CARD:	Y	N	N
Mr & Mrs M. Chesterfield **Frith Farm House** **Otterden** **Faversham** **ME13 0DD** Tel: (01795) 890701 Fax 01795 890009 **Open: ALL YEAR** **Map Ref No. 17**	Nearest Road: A.20 A warm welcome awaits guests at this restored Georgian farmhouse, surrounded by lovely cherry trees. It stands in an Area of Outstanding Natural Beauty. Accommodation is in a choice of 3 comfortable en-suite rooms with radio, T.V. & tea/coffee-making facilities. This makes a pleasant base from which to tour the whole of Kent. Leeds Castle, Rochester, Chilam & Canterbury are nearby. A delightful home. **E-mail: markham@frith.force9.co.uk**	£23.00 to £29.00 *see PHOTO over* *p. 259* VISA: M'CARD:	N	Y	N
Mr & Mrs A. Brightman **The Granary** **Plumford Lane,** **Off Brogdale Road** **Faversham** **ME13 0DS** Tel: (01795) 538416 Fax 01795 538416 **Open: ALL YEAR** **Map Ref No. 18**	Nearest Road: A.2 Set deep in apple-orchard country, The Granary - recently part of a working farm - has been tastefully & beautifully converted to provide an interesting & spacious home. All rooms are delightfully furnished to a high standard, whilst retaining a rustic charm. 3 charming bedrooms with en-suite/private bathrooms. The guests' lounge, with balcony, overlooks the surrounding countryside. Good local pubs offering food. Ideal for touring historic Kent. Children over 12. **E-mail: annette@the-granary.co.uk**	£24.50 to £24.50 VISA: M'CARD:	Y	N	N

Frith Farm House. Otterden.

Kent

	rate £ from - to per person	children taken	evening meals	animals taken

Mrs Corrine Scutt Leaveland Court Leaveland Faversham ME13 0NP Tel: (01233) 740596 Fax 01233 740015 Open: FEB - NOV Map Ref No. 19	Nearest Road: A.251 Guests are warmly welcomed to this enchanting 15th-century timbered farmhouse, & its delightful gardens with heated swimming pool. Situated in a quiet rural setting, between 13th-century Leaveland church & woodlands, & surrounded by a 300-acre downland farm. All of the attractive bedrooms have en-suite facilities, colour T.V. & tea/coffee tray. Conveniently placed only 5 mins from M.2 & Faversham, 20 mins Canterbury & 30 mins Channel ports. A charming home.	£22.50 to £25.00 VISA: M'CARD:	Y	N	N
Alan & Catherine Turner Preston Lea Canterbury Road Faversham ME13 8XA Tel: (01795) 535266 Fax 01795 533388 Open: ALL YEAR Map Ref No. 20	Nearest Road: A.2 A warm welcome & tea on arrival are guaranteed in this beautiful, elegant house, set in secluded gardens on the edge of Faversham. Spacious en-suite, sunny bedrooms with garden views & antique furniture & offering every comfort. The drawing-rooms, pannelled dining-room & gardens are available to guests. Help & advice is on hand from your caring hosts. Delicious breakfasts. Good restaurants nearby, beautiful countryside, beaches & places of interest to visit. **E-mail: preston.lea@which.net**	£25.00 to £27.50 VISA: M'CARD:	Y	N	N
Prudence Latham Tenterden House 209 The Street Boughton Faversham ME13 9BL Tel: (01227) 751593 Open: ALL YEAR Map Ref No. 18	Nearest Road: A.2, M.2 The renovated gardener's cottage of this listed 16th-century Yeoman's house provides 2 en-suite bedrooms (1 double, 1 twin), used separately or together for families. Situated in the village, close to Canterbury, the ferry ports & Euro-Tunnel, it makes an ideal base for day-trips to France & for touring historic Kent. Off-road parking is provided. Tea/coffee-making facilities & T.V.. A full English breakfast is served in the main house & excellent pub or restaurant food is within easy walking distance.	£20.00 to £30.00	Y	N	N
Mary Martin Pigeonwood House Grove Farm Arpinge Folkestone CT18 8AQ Tel: (01303) 891111 Fax 01303 891019 Open: MAR - OCT Map Ref No. 22	Nearest Road: A.260 Pigeonwood House is the original, 18th-century farmhouse of the surrounding area, positioned in rural tranquillity in chalk downland. The 2 guest bedrooms have beautiful panoramic views over the surrounding countryside & many guests return for the homely, relaxing atmosphere. Pigeonwood House is ideally situated for touring historic Kent as well as having the channel tunnel & ports close by. Children over 1. **E-mail: samandmary@aol.com**	£20.00 to £24.00 VISA: M'CARD:	Y	N	N
Mrs Rosemary Piper Conghurst Farm Hawkhurst TN18 4RW Tel: (01580) 753331 Fax 01580 754579 Open: FEB - NOV Map Ref No. 23	Nearest Road: A.268 Set in peaceful, totally unspoilt countryside, Conghurst Farm offers a perfect spot for a restful holiday. Within easy reach of all the marvellous houses & gardens that this part of the country has to offer. Accommodation is in 3 very comfortable bedrooms, all with en-suite/private bathrooms. There is a drawing room, a separate T.V. room &, in the summer, a delightful garden for guests to enjoy. An ideal base from which to explore Kent.	£25.00 to £30.00 VISA: M'CARD:	N	Y	N

Jordans.　Plaxtol.

Kent

		rate £ from - to per person	evening meals	children taken	animals taken
Sylvette Cabrisseau **Willington Court** **1 Willington Street** **Bearstead** **Maidstone ME15 8JW** **Tel: (01622) 738885** Fax 01622 631790 **Open: ALL YEAR** **Map Ref No. 24**	Nearest Road: A.20 Willington Court is a Grade II listed Waldean/ Tudor building offering elegant accommodation, fine food & congenial hosts. 8 bedrooms, 7 are en-suite & all are well-equipped. Meals are prepared using only the best ingredients (organic when possible). Dinner is complemented by wine from the reputed cellar. Easy access to London, Dover & the Channel Tunnel. Conducted tours in luxury of London, Calais, Lille & Paris available. **E-mail: willington@maidstone.prestel.co.uk**	£27.50 to £32.50 VISA: M'CARD: AMEX:	Y	Y	N
Mrs Ann Earl **The Greswolde Hotel** **20 Surrey Road** **Cliftonville** **Margate CT9 2LA** **Tel: (01843) 223956** Fax 01843 223956 **Open: ALL YEAR** **Map Ref No. 25**	Nearest Road: A.28 The Greswolde is a 6-bedroomed Victorian hotel retaining much of its original character & charm. All rooms have en-suite facilities, with colour T.V. & tea makers. There is a quiet, relaxing lounge/ reading room. Located 100 yds from the prom- enade, & close to championship indoor & outdoor bowling greens. Many golf courses also within easy reach. Pubs & eating places are nearby. Ideal for touring, with Channel ports close by. Children over 8 years welcome.	£20.00 to £26.00 VISA: M'CARD:	Y	N	Y
Mrs Jo Lindsay N.D.D., A.T.D. **Jordans** **Sheet Hill** **Plaxtol** **Sevenoaks** **TN15 0PU** **Tel: (01732) 810379** **Open: Mid JAN - Mid DEC** **Map Ref No. 26**	Nearest Road: A.25 Beautiful, picture-postcard, 15th-century Tudor house (awarded a 'Historic Building of Kent' plaque) in the picturesque village of Plaxtol, among orchards & parkland. It is beautifully furnished, & has leaded windows, inglenook fireplaces, mas- sive oak beams & an enchanting old English garden with roses & espalier trees. Within easy reach are Ightham Mote, Leeds & Hever Castle, Penshurst, Chartwell & Knole. 3 lovely rooms, 2 with en-suite/private facilities. London 35 mins by train, & easy access to airports. Children over 12.	£26.00 to £35.00 *see PHOTO over* *p. 261*	Y	N	N
Mrs Valerie Peters **Gardeners Cottage** **Puckle Hill** **Shorne** **DA12 3LB** **Tel: (01474) 823269** Fax 01474 823269 **Open: ALL YEAR** **Map Ref No. 27**	Nearest Road: A.2 Gardeners Cottage is an attractive house set in 5 acres of gardens with a bluebell wood, a magnifi- cent ancient lime tree, croquet lawn & rhododen- dron-lined driveway. 3 attractively furnished bed- rooms, each with an en-suite/private bathroom, tea/coffee & T.V.. It retains many original features including oak beams, inglenooks & wood-burning stoves. Close to the A.2/M.2 & M.25 & ideal for touring Kent & for visiting London. Bluewater - Europes largest shopping centre - only 10 mins'. **E-mail: aegc@compuserve.com**	£25.00 to £27.50	Y	Y	N
Mrs Eve Burnett **Oxney Farm** **Moons Green** **Wittersham** **Tenterden TN30 7PS** **Tel: (01797) 270558** Fax 01797 270958 **Open: ALL YEAR** **Map Ref No. 28**	Nearest Road: A.28, B.2082 A warm welcome awaits you at award-winning Oxney Farm. Convenient for the Channel Tunnel, ports & Gatwick Airport. The spacious, well- furnished farmhouse, with luxurious indoor pool, lies between Tenterden & Rye (2km from B.2082) in peaceful surroundings. The area is steeped in history, scenery & culture. The miniature ponies add their charm to the friendly country house atmosphere. Dinner & children by arrangement. **E-mail: oxneyf@globalnet.co.uk**	£25.00 to £30.00 VISA: M'CARD:	Y	N	N

The Old Parsonage. Frant.

Kent

Anne Turner **Leavers Oast** **Stanford Lane** **Hadlow** **Tonbridge TN11 0JN** **Tel: (01732) 850924** **Fax 01732 850924** **Open: ALL YEAR** **Map Ref No. 29**	Nearest Road: A.26 A warm, friendly welcome & imaginative cooking is to be found in this beautiful 19th-century oast. An en-suite bedroom in the barn & 2 roundel bedrooms provide comfortable accommodation. The house is furnished with interesting antiques, & the lovely garden overlooks open country. Excellent communications make it an ideal base for visiting many historic houses & gardens. London 40 mins by rail. Children over 12 years. Evening meals by arrangement.	£27.50 to £32.00	N	N	N
Richard & Sue Rogers **Ash Tree Cottage** **7 Eden Road** **Tunbridge Wells TN1 1TS** **Tel: (01892) 541317** **Fax 01892 616770** **Open: ALL YEAR (Excl.** **Xmas & New Year)** **Map Ref No. 31**	Nearest Road: A.21 Ashtree Cottage is situated in a quiet private road just above the famous Pantiles, & within a few minutes' walk of the high street & station. There are 2 charming & attractively furnished bedrooms with en-suite bathrooms, radio, T.V., tea/coffee-making facilities & plenty of tourist information. There is an excellent choice of restaurants & country pubs nearby, & many places of interest are within easy reach. Children over 8.	£22.50 to £25.00	Y	N	N
Mary & Tony Dakin **The Old Parsonage** **Church Lane** **Frant** **Tunbridge Wells** **TN3 9DX** **Tel: (01892) 750773** **Fax 01892 750773** **Open: ALL YEAR** **Map Ref No. 32**	Nearest Road: A.267 This award-winning country house is peacefully situated by the church in pretty Frant village with its 2 character pubs & restaurant. Overlooking Lord Abergavenny's deer park on one side & the church on the other, this Georgian house provides superb accommodation including en-suite bedrooms, antique-furnished reception rooms & a flower-filled conservatory. Short drive to 15 historic houses & gardens. Gatwick 40 mins. Heathrow 70 mins. London 45 mins by train. **E-mail: oldparson@aol.com**	£32.00 to £37.00 *see PHOTO over* *p. 263* VISA: M'CARD:	Y	N	Y
Carolyn Carrell **Rowden House Farm** **Frant** **Tunbridge Wells** **TN3 9HS** **Tel: (01892) 750259** **Open: APR - OCT** **Map Ref No. 32**	Nearest Road: A.267 A delightful Elizabethan house, listed as of architectural interest, standing in 20 acres, with sheep, horses, dogs & chickens. Surrounded by the beautiful, rolling, wooded countryside of Sussex, it is perfectly placed for visiting the stately homes & towns of Kent & Sussex. 1 twin-bedded room, with private bathroom, & 2 singles with washbasins. All have tea/coffee-making facilities. An attractive drawing room, with T.V.. Gatwick 1 hour, London 1 1/4 hours. Children over 10.	£22.50 to £25.00	Y	N	N
Angela & Michael Godbold **Danehurst House** **41 Lower Green Road** **Rusthall** **Tunbridge Wells TN4 8TW** **Tel: (01892) 527739** **Fax 01892 514804** **Open: ALL YEAR (Excl. Xmas)** **Map Ref No. 31**	Nearest Road: A.264 Danehurst is a charming gabled house in a village setting in the heart of Kent. The tastefully furnished bedrooms afford excellent accommodation, & a delicious breakfast is served in the Victorian conservatory. Angela & Michael are delighted to welcome you to their home & will ensure that your stay is relaxing & enjoyable. Private parking available. Children over 8 years welcome. (Please note Danehurst is closed during the last week in August.)	£39.50 to £49.50 *see PHOTO over* *p. 265* VISA: M'CARD: AMEX:	Y	N	N

Danehurst. Rustall.

Leicestershire, Nottinghamshire & Rutland

Leicestershire
(East Midlands)

Rural Leicestershire is rich in grazing land, a peaceful, undramatic landscape broken up by the waterways that flow through in the south of the county.

The River Avon passes on its way to Stratford, running by 17th century Stanford Hall & its motorcycle museum. The Leicester section of the Grand Union Canal was once very important for the transportation of goods from the factories of the Midlands to London Docks. It passes through a fascinating series of multiple locks at Foxton. The decorative barges, the 'narrow boats' are pleasure craft these days rather than the lifeblood of the closed community of boat people who lived & worked out their lives on the canals.

Rutland was formerly England's smallest county, but was absorbed into East Leicestershire in the 1970's. Recently, once again, it has become a county in its' own right. Rutland Water, is one of Europe's largest reservoirs & an attractive setting for sailing, fishing or enjoying a trip on the pleasure cruiser. There is also the Rutland Theatre at Tolethorpe Hall, where a summer season of Shakespeare's plays is presented in the open air.

Melton Mowbray is famous for its pork pies & it is also the centre of Stilton cheese country. The "King of Cheeses" is made mainly in the Vale of Belvoir where Leicestershire meets Nottinghamshire, & the battlements & turrets of Belvoir Castle overlook the scene from its hill-top.

To the north-west the Charnwood Forest area is pleasantly wooded & the deer park at Bradgate surrounding the ruined home of Lady Jane Grey, England's nine-day queen, is a popular attraction.

Nottinghamshire
(East Midlands)

Nottinghamshire has a diversity of landscape from forest to farmland, from coal mines to industrial areas.

The north of the county is dominated by the expanse of Sherwood Forest, smaller now than in the time of legendary Robin Hood & his Merry Men, but still a lovely old woodland of Oak & Birch.

The Dukeries are so called because of the numerous ducal houses built in the area & there is beautiful parkland on these great estates that can be visited. Clumber Park, for instance has a huge lake & a double avenue of Limes.

Newstead Abbey was a mediaeval priory converted into the Byron family home in the 16th century. It houses the poet Byron's manuscripts & possessions & is set in wonderful gardens.

More modest is the terraced house in Eastwood, where D.H. Lawrence was born into the mining community on which his novels are based.

Nottingham was recorded in the Domesday Book as a thriving community & that tradition continues. It was here that Arkwright perfected his cotton-spinning machinery & went on to develop steam as a power source for industry.

Textiles, shoes, bicycles & tobacco are all famous Nottingham products, & the story of Nottingham Lace can be discovered at the Lace Hall, housed in a former church.

Nottingham Castle, high on Castle Rock, was built & destroyed & rebuilt many times during its history. It now houses the city's Art Gallery & Museum. The Castle towers over the ancient 'Trip to Jerusalem' Inn, said to be so named because crusaders stopped there for a drink on their way to fight in the Holy Land.

Leicestershire, Nottinghamshire & Rutland

Leicestershire Gazeteer

Areas of outstanding natural beauty.
Charnwood Forest, Rutland Water.

Historic Houses & Castles

Belvoir Castle - Nr. Grantham
Overlooking the Vale of Belvoir, castle rebuilt in 1816, with many special events including jousting tournaments. Home of the Duke of Rutland since Henry VIII. Paintings, furniture, historic armoury, military museums, magnificent stateroom.

Belvoir Castle

Belgrave Hall - Leicester
18th century Queen Anne house - furnishing of 18th & 19th centuries.
Langton Hall - Nr. Market Harborough
Privately occupied - perfect English country house from mediaeval times - drawing rooms have 18th century Venetian lace.

Oakham Castle - Oakham
Norman banqueting hall of late 12th C.
Stanford Hall - Nr Lutterworth
17th century William & Mary house - collection of Stuart relics & pictures, antiques & costumes of family from Elizabeth I onward. Motor cycle museum.
Stapleford Park - Nr. Melton Mowbray
Old wing dated 1500, restored 1663. Extended to mansion in 1670. Collection of pictures, tapestries, furniture & Balston's Staffordshire portrait figures of Victorian age.

Cathedrals & Churches

Breedon-on-the-Hill (St. Mary & St. Hardulph)
Norman & 13th century. Jacobean canopied pew, 18th century carvings.
Empingham (St. Peter)
14th century west tower, front & crocketed spire. Early English interior - double piscina, triple sedilla.
Lyddington (St. Andrew)
Perpendicular in the main - mediaeval wall paintings & brasses.
Staunton Harol (Holy Trinity)
17th century - quite unique Cromwellian church - painted ceilings.

Museums & Galleries

Bosworth Battlefield Visitor Centre - Nr Market Bosworth
Exhibitions, models, battlefield trails at site of 1485 Battle of Bosworth where Richard III lost his life & crown to Henry.
Leicestershire Museum of Technology - Leicester
Beam engines, steam shovel, knitting machinery & other aspects of the county's industrial past.
Leicester Museum & Art Gallery - Leicester
Painting collection.
18th & 19th century, watercolours & drawings, 20th century French paintings, Old Master & modern prints. English silver & ceramics, special exhibitions.
Jewry Wall Museum & Site - Leicester
Roman wall & baths site adjoining museum of archaeology.

Leicestershire, Nottinghamshire & Rutland

Melton Carnegie Museum-Melton Mowbray
Displays of Stilton cheese, pork pies & other aspects of the past & present life of the area.
Rutland County Museum - Oakham
Domestic & agricultural life of Rutland, England's smallest county.
Donnington Collection of Single-Seater Racing Cars - Castle Donington
Large collection of grand prix racing cars & racing motorcycles, adjoining Donington Park racing circuit..
Wygson's House Museum of Costume - Leicestershire
Costume, accessories & shop settings in late mediaeval buildings.
The Bellfoundry Museum - Loughborough
Moulding, casting, tuning & fitting of bells, with conducted tours of bellfoundry.

Historic Monuments

The Castle - Ashby-de-la-Zouch
14th century with tower added in 15th century.
Kirby Muxloe Castle - Kirby Muxloe
15th century fortified manor house with moat ruins.

Other things to see & do

Rutland Farm Park - Oakham
Rare & commercial breeds of livestock in 18 acres of park & woodland, with early 19th century farm buildings.
Stoughton Farm Park - Nr. Leicester
Shire horses, rare breeds, small animals & modern 140 dairy herd. Milking demonstrations, farm museum, woodland walks. Adventure playground.
Twycross Zoo - Nr. Atherstone
Gorillas, orang-utans, chimpanzees, gibbons, elephants, giraffes, lions & many other animals.
The Battlefield Line Nr. Market Bosworth
Steam railway & collection of railway relics, adjoining Bosworth Battlefield.
Great Central Railway - Loughborough
Steam railway over 5-mile route in Charnwood Forest area, with steam & diesel museum.
Rutland Railway Museum - Nr. Oakham
Industrial steam & diesel locomotives.

Nottinghamshire Gazeteer

Historic Houses & Castles

Holme Pierrepont Hall - Nr. Nottingham
Outstanding red brick Tudor manor, in continuous family ownership, with 19th century courtyard garden.
Newark Castle - Newark
Dramatic castle ruins on riverside site, once one of the most important castles of the north.
Newstead Abbey - Nr. Mansfield
Priory converted to country mansion, home of poet Lord Byron with many of his possessions & manuscripts on display. Beautiful parkland, lakes & gardens.
Nottingham Castle - Nottingham
17th century residence on site of mediaeval castle.
Fine collections of ceramics, silver, Nottingham alabaster carvings, local historical displays. Art gallery. Special exhibitions & events.
Wollaton Hall - Nottingham
Elizabethan mansion now housing natural history exhibits. Stands in deer park, with Industrial Museum in former stables, illustrating the city's bicycle, hosiery, lace, pharmaceutical & other industries.

Cathedrals & Churches

Egmanton (St. Mary)
Magnificent interior by Comper. Norman doorway & font. Canopied rood screen, 17th century altar.
Newark (St. Mary Magdalene)
15th century. 2 painted panels of "Dance of Death". Reredos by Comper.
Southwell Cathedral
Norman nave, unvaulted, fine early English choir. Decorated pulpitum, 6 canopied stalls, fine misericords. Octagonal chapter house..
Terseval (St. Catherine)
12th century - interior 17th century unrestored.

Museums & Galleries

Castlegate Museum - Nottingham
Row of Georgian terraced houses showing costume & textile collection.
Lace making equipment & lace collection.

Leicestershire, Nottinghamshire & Rutland

Nottingham Castle Museum - Nottingham
Collections of ceramics, glass & silver. Alabaster carvings.

D.H. Lawrence Birthplace - Eastwood
Home of the novelist & poet, as it would have been at time of his birth, 1885.

Millgate Museum of Social & Folk Life - Newark
Local social & folk life, with craft workshops.

Brewhouse Yard Museum - Nottingham
Daily life in Nottingham, displayed in 17th century cottages & rock-cut cellars.

The Lace Hall - Nottingham
The story of Nottingham Lace audio-visual display & exhibition with lace shops, in fine converted church.

Museum of Costume & Textiles - Nottingham
Costumes, lace & textiles on display in fine Georgian buildings.

Bassetlaw Museum - Retford
Local history of north Nottinghamshire.

Canal Museum - Nottinghamshire
History of the River Trent & canal history, in former canal warehouse.

Ruddington Framework Knitters' Museum - Ruddington
Unique complex of early 19th-century framework knitters' buildings with over 20 hand frames in restored workshop.

Other things to see & do

The Tales of Robin Hood - Nottingham
A 'flight to adventure' from mediaeval Nottingham to Sherwood Forest through the tales of the world's most famous outlaw.

Clumber Park - Nr. Worksop
Landscaped parkland, with double avenue of limes, lake, chapel. One of the Dukeries' estates, though the house no longer remains.

Rufford - Nr. Ollerton
Parkland, lake & gallery with fine crafts, around ruin of Cistercian abbey.

Sherwood Forest Visitor Centre - Nr. Edwinstowe
Robin Hood exhibition.
450 acres of ancient oak woodland associated with the outlaw & his merry men.

Sherwood Forest Farm Park - Nr. Edwinstowe
Rare breeds of cattle, sheep, pigs & goats. Lake with wildfowl.

White Post Farm Centre - Farnsfield, Nr Newark
Working modern farm with crops & many animals, including cows, sheep, pigs, hens, geese, ducks, llamas, horses. Indoor displays & exhibits.

Newark Castle.

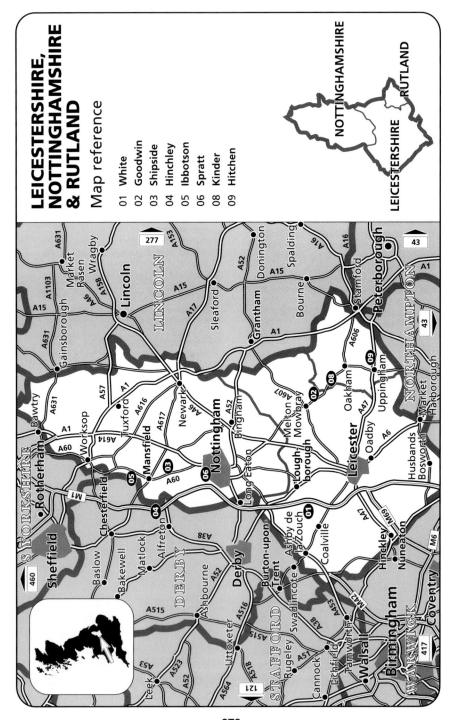

LEICESTERSHIRE, NOTTINGHAMSHIRE & RUTLAND

Map reference

01 White
02 Goodwin
03 Shipside
04 Hinchley
05 Ibbotson
06 Spratt
08 Kinder
09 Hitchen

NOTTINGHAMSHIRE
RUTLAND
LEICESTERSHIRE

Holly Lodge. Blidworth.

Leicestershire & Nottinghamshire

		rate £ from - to per person	children taken	evening meals	animals taken
Bill, Audrey & Carolyn White **Abbots Oak Country House** **Warren Hills Road** **Greenhill** **Coalville** **LE67 4UY** **Tel: (01530) 832328** **Fax 01530 832328** **Open: ALL YEAR** **Map Ref No. 01**	Nearest Road: A.511, M.1 A Grade II listed building with a wealth of oak panelling, & including the staircase reputedly from Nell Gwynn's town house. Set in mature gardens & woodland, with natural granite outcrops. 4 delightful rooms, all with en-suite/private bathroom. Open fires create a warm & welcoming atmosphere, & Carolyn's superb dinners are served in the candlelit dining room. Stratford, Belvoir Castle & Rutland Water can all be reached within the hour. Tennis court, billiard room. Children over 6 years welcome.	£30.00 to £60.00	Y	Y	Y
Jacqueline Goodwin **Hillside House** **27 Melton Road** **Burton Lazars** **Melton Mowbray LE14 2UR** **Tel: (01664) 566312** **Fax 01664 501819** **Open: ALL YEAR (Excl.** **Xmas & New Year)** **Map Ref No. 02**	Nearest Road: A.606 Charmingly converted farm buildings with superb views over open countryside, in the small village of Burton Lazars. Comfortable accommodation is offered in 1 double & 2 twin-bedded rooms, each with an en-suite/private bathroom. All have tea/coffee-making facilities & colour T.V.. A pleasant garden to relax in on sunny days. Close to Melton Mowbray, famous for its pork pies & Stilton cheese, & with Burghley House, Belvoir Castle & Rutland Water within easy reach. Children over 10 years welcome. Single supplement.	£17.00 to £20.00	Y	N	N

Nottinghamshire

		rate £ from - to per person	children taken	evening meals	animals taken
Mrs Ann Shipside **Holly Lodge** **Ricket Lane** **Ravenshead** **Blidworth NG21 0NQ** **Tel: (01623) 793853** **Fax 01623 490977** **Open: ALL YEAR** **Map Ref No. 03**	Nearest Road: A.60 Holly Lodge is situated just off the A.60, 9 miles north of Nottingham. This attractive former hunting lodge stands in 15 acres of grounds. The 4 comfortable & attractive, en-suite guest rooms are housed within the converted stables. There are panoramic countryside views on all sides, with woodland walks, tennis, golf & riding nearby. Ideally situated for a peaceful, rural holiday base with a relaxed & friendly atmosphere.	£24.00 to £34.00 *see PHOTO over* *p. 271* VISA: M'CARD: AMEX:	Y	N	N
Betty Hinchley **Titchfield Guest House** **300/302 Chesterfield Road** **North** **Mansfield NG19 7QU** **Tel: (01623) 810921** **Tel/Fax: (01623) 810356** **Open: ALL YEAR** **Map Ref No. 04**	Nearest Road: A.617 This is 2 houses converted into 1 family-run guest house, offering 8 comfortable rooms, a lounge with T.V., a kitchen for guests' use, a bathroom & showers. It also has an adjoining garage. Near to Mansfield, which is a busy market town. Sherwood Forest & the Peak District are both easily accessible. Titchfield Guest House is a very handy location for touring this lovely area, & for onward travel. A warm & friendly welcome is assured at this charming home.	£17.00 to £18.00 VISA: M'CARD: AMEX:	Y	N	Y

Visit our website at:
http://www.bestbandb.co.uk

Nottinghamshire & Rutland

	Nearest Road	Rate £ from - to per person	children taken	evening meals	animals taken
June M. Ibbotson **Blue Barn Farm** **Langwith** **Mansfield NG20 9JD** **Tel: (01623) 742248** **Fax 01623 742248** **Open: ALL YEAR (Excl. Xmas & New Year's Day)** **Map Ref No. 05**	Nearest Road: A.616 An enjoyable visit is guaranteed at this family-run, 250-acre farm, set in tranquil countryside on the edge of Sherwood Forest (Robin Hood country). 3 guest bedrooms, each with modern amenities including h&c, tea/coffee-making facilities & a guest bathroom with shower. 1 bedroom is en-suite. A colour-T.V. lounge & garden are also available. Guests are very welcome to walk around the farm. Many interesting places, catering for all tastes, only a short journey away.	£18.00 to £24.00	Y	N	N
Sheila & Michael Spratt **Greenwood Lodge City** **Guest House** **Third Avenue** **Sherwood Rise** **Nottingham NG7 6JH** **Tel: (0115) 9621206** **Fax 0115 9621206** **Open: ALL YEAR** **Map Ref No. 06**	Nearest Road: A.60 A warm, welcoming Victorian house situated in a quiet cul-de-sac, 1 mile from the city centre. The home of Sheila & Michael Spratt, The Lodge is furnished mainly with antiques, & boasts a fine 4-poster bed. All rooms are en-suite & individually decorated & furnished to a high standard, with T.V., hairdryer, trouser press & hospitality tray. Evening meals are by prior arrangement. An ideal base from which to explore Nottingham & its many places of interest. **E-mail: coolspratt@aol.com**	£28.00 to £35.00 VISA: M'CARD:	Y	Y	Y

Rutland

	Nearest Road	Rate £ from - to per person	children taken	evening meals	animals taken
Mrs Georgiana Kinder **Torr Lodge** **Main Street** **Barrow** **Oakham** **LE15 7PE** **Tel: (01572) 813396** **Fax 01572 813396** **Open: ALL YEAR** **Map Ref No. 08**	Nearest Road: A.1 Torr Lodge, Barrow is in the heart of scenic Rutland, England's smallest county, but one with the biggest welcome! Oakham, Stamford & Melton Mowbray are within easy access, as is Rutland Water with sailing, fishing & walking. Golf courses also are nearby. Georgiana has been in the hospitality business for 10 years, & offers guests tastefully furnished en-suite accommodation, home-cooking on an aga & farmhouse breakfast. Crown Derby & crystal dinner is an optional choice for the evening. Children over 12.	£18.00 to £25.00	Y	Y	Y
Jenny Hitchen **Rutland House** **61 High Street East** **Uppingham LE15 9PY** **Tel: (01572) 822497** **Fax 01572 820065** **Open: ALL YEAR** **Map Ref No. 09**	Nearest Road: A.47 Rutland House offers excellent accommodation in 5 delightful guest rooms. All rooms are en-suite, with central heating, colour T.V., radio/alarms & tea/coffee facilities. Being a small establishment, the rooms are quiet & homely. Full English or Continental breakfast served. Close to Rutland Water, Burghley House & Geoff Hamiltons' famous gardens. Children over 5 yrs. A lovely home well-placed for touring.	£21.00 to £21.00 VISA: M'CARD:	Y	N	Y

When booking your accommodation please mention
The Best Bed & Breakfast

Lincolnshire

Lincolnshire (East Midlands)

Lincolnshire is an intriguing mixture of coast & country, of flat fens & gently rising wolds.

There are the popular resorts of Skegness & Mablethorpe as well as quieter coastal regions where flocks of wild birds take food & shelter in the dunes. Gibraltar Point & Saltfleetby are large nature reserves.

Fresh vegetables for much of Britain are produced in the rich soil of the Lincolnshire fens, & windmills punctuate the skyline. There is a unique 8-sailed windmill at Heckington. In spring the fields are ablaze with the red & yellow of tulips. The bulb industry flourishes around Spalding & Holbeach, & in early May tulip flowers in abundance decorate the huge floats of the Spalding Flower Parade.

The city of Lincoln has cobbled streets & ancient buildings & a very beautiful triple-towered Cathedral which shares its hill-top site with the Castle, both dating from the 11th century. There is a 17th century library by Wren in the Cathedral, which has amongst its treasures one of the four original copies of Magna Carta.

Boston has a huge parish church with a distincive octagonal tower which can be seen for miles across the surrounding fenland, & is commonly known as the 'Boston Stump'. The Guildhall Museum displays many aspects of the town's history, including the cells where the early Pilgrim Fathers were imprisioned after their attempt to flee to the Netherlands to find religious freedom. They eventually made the journey & hence to America.

One of England's most outstanding towns is Stamford. It has lovely churches, ancient inns & other fine buildings in a mellow stone.

Sir Isaac Newton was born at Woolsthorpe Manor & educated at nearby Grantham where there is a museum which illustrates his life & work.

The poet Tennyson was born in the village of Somersby, where his father was Rector.

Lincoln Cathedral.

274

Lincolnshire

Lincolnshire Gazeteer

Areas of outstanding natural beauty.
Lincolnshire Wolds.

Historic Houses & Castles

Auborn House - Nr. Lincoln
16th century house with imposing carved staircase & panelled rooms.

Belton House - Grantham
House built 1684-88 - said to be by Christopher Wren - work by Grinling Gibbons & Wyatt also. Paintings, furniture, porcelain, tapestries, Duke of Windsor mementoes. A great English house with formal gardens & extensive grounds with orangery.

Doddington Hall - Doddington, Nr. Lincoln
16th century Elizabethan mansion with elegant Georgian rooms & gabled Tudor gatehouse. Fine furniture, paintings, porcelain, etc. Formal walled knot gardens, roses & wild gardens.

Burghley House - Stamford
Elizabethan - England's largest & grandest house of the era. Famous for its beautiful painted ceilings, silver fireplaces & art treasures.

Gumby Hall - Burgh-le-Marsh
17th century manor house. Ancient gardens.

Harrington Hall - Spilsby
Mentioned in the Domesday Book - has mediaeval stone base - Carolinean manor house in red brick. Some alterations in 1678 to mullioned windows. Panelling, furnishings of 17th & 18th century.

Marston Hall - Grantham
16th century manor house. Ancient gardens.

The Old Hall - Gainsborough
Fine mediaeval manor house built in 1480's with original kitchen, rebuilt after original hall destroyed during Wars of the Roses. Tower & wings, Great Hall. It was the first meeting place of the "Dissenters", later known as the Pilgrim Fathers.

Woolsthorpe Manor - Grantham
17th century house. Birthplace of Sir Isaac Newton.

Fydell House - Boston
18th century house, now Pilgrim College.

Lincoln Castle - Lincoln
William the Conqueror castle, with complete curtain wall & Norman shell keep. Towers & wall walk. Unique prisoners' chapel.

Tattershall Castle - Tattershall
100 foot high brick keep of 15th century moated castle, with fine views over surrounding country.

Cathedrals & Churches

Addlethorpe (St. Nicholas)
15th century - mediaeval stained glass - original woodwork.

Boston (St. Botolph)
14th century decorated - very large parish church. Beautiful south porch, carved stalls.

Brant Broughton (St. Helens)
13th century arcades - decorated tower & spire - perpendicular clerestory. Exterior decoration.

Ewerby (St. Andrew)
Decorated - splendid example of period - very fine spire. 14th century effigy.

Fleet (St. Mary Magdalene)
14th century - early English arcades - perpendicular windows - detached tower & spire.

Folkingham (St. Andrew)
14th century arcades - 15th century windows - perpendicular tower - early English chancel.

Gedney (St. Mary Magdalene)
Perpendicular spire (unfinished). Early English tower. 13th-14th century monuments, 14th-15th century stained glass.

Grantham (St. Wulfram)
14th century tower & spire - Norman pillars - perpendicular chantry - 14th century vaulted crypt.

Lincoln Cathedral - Lincoln
Magnificent triple-towered Gothic building on fine hill-top site.
Norman west front,
13th century - some 14th century additions. Norman work from 1072. Angel choir - carved & decorated pulpitum - 13th century chapter house - 17th century library by Wren (containing one of the four original copies of Magna Carta).

Lincolnshire

St. Botolph's Church - Boston
Fine parish church, one of the largest in the country, with 272 foot octagonal tower dominating the surrounding fens.
Long Sutton (St. Mary)
15th century south porch, mediaeval brass lectern, very fine early English spire.
Louth (St. James)
Early 16th century - mediaeval Gothic - wonderful spire.
Scotter (St. Peter)
Saxon to perpendicular - early English nave - 15th century rood screen.
Stow (St. Mary)
Norman - very fine example, particularly west door. Wall painting.
Silk Willoughby (St. Denis)
14th century - tower with spire & flying buttresses. 15th-17th century pulpit.
Stainfield (St. Andrew)
Queen Anne - mediaeval armour & early needlework.
Theddlethorpe (All Saints)
14th century - 15th century & reredos of 15th century, 16th century parcloses, 15th century brasses - some mediaeval glass.
Wrangle (St. Mary the Virgin & St. Nicholas)
Early English - decorated - perpendicular - Elizabethan pulpit. 14th century east window & glass.

Museums & Galleries

Alford Manor House - Alford
Tudor manor house - thatched - folk museum. Nearby windmill.
Boston Guildhall Museum - Boston
15th century building with mayor's parlour, court room & cells where Pilgrim Fathers were imprisoned in 1607. Local exhibits.
Lincoln Cathedral Library - Lincoln
Built by Wren housing early printed books & mediaeval manuscripts.
Lincoln Cathedral Treasury - Lincoln
Diocesan gold & silver plate.
Lincoln City & Country Museum - Lincoln
Prehistoric, Roman & mediaeval antiquities with local associations. Armour & local history.
Museum of Lincolnshire Life - Lincoln
Domestic, agricultural, industrial & social history of the county. Edwardian room settings, shop settings, agricultural machinery.

Usher Gallery - Lincoln
Paintings, watches, miniatures, porcelain, silver, coins & medals. Temporary exhibitions. Tennyson collection. Works of English watercolourist Peter de Wint.
Grantham Museum - Grantham
Archeology, watches, miniatures, Saxon & Roman. Local history with special display about Sir Isaac Newton, born nearby & educated in Grantham.
Church Farm Museum - Skegness
Farmhouse & buildings with local agricultural collections & temporary exhibitions & special events.
Stamford Museum - Stamford
Local history museum, with temporary special exhibitions.
Battle of Britain Memorial Flight - Coningsby
Lancaster bomber, five Spitfires & two Hurricanes with other Battle of Britain memorabilia.
National Cycle Museum - Lincoln
Development of the cycle.
Stamford Steam Brewery Museum - Stamford
Complete Victorian steam brewery with 19th century equipment.

Other things to see & do

Springfield - Spalding
Show gardens of the British bulb industry, & home of the Spalding Flower Parade each May. Summer bedding plants & roses.
Butlins Funcoast World - Skegness
Funsplash Water World with amusements & entertainments
Castle Leisure Park - Tattershall
Windsurfing, water-skiing, sailing, fishing & other sports & leisure facilities.
Long Sutton Butterfly Park - Long Sutton
Walk-through tropical butterfly house with outdoor wildflower meadows & pets corner.
Skegness Natureland Marine Zoo - Skegness
Seal sanctuary with aquaria, tropical house, pets corner & butterfly house.
Windmills - at Lincoln (Ellis Mill - 4 sails), Boston (Maud Foster - 5 sails), Burgh-le-Marsh (5 sails), Alford (5 sails), Sibsey (6 sails), Heckington (8 sails).

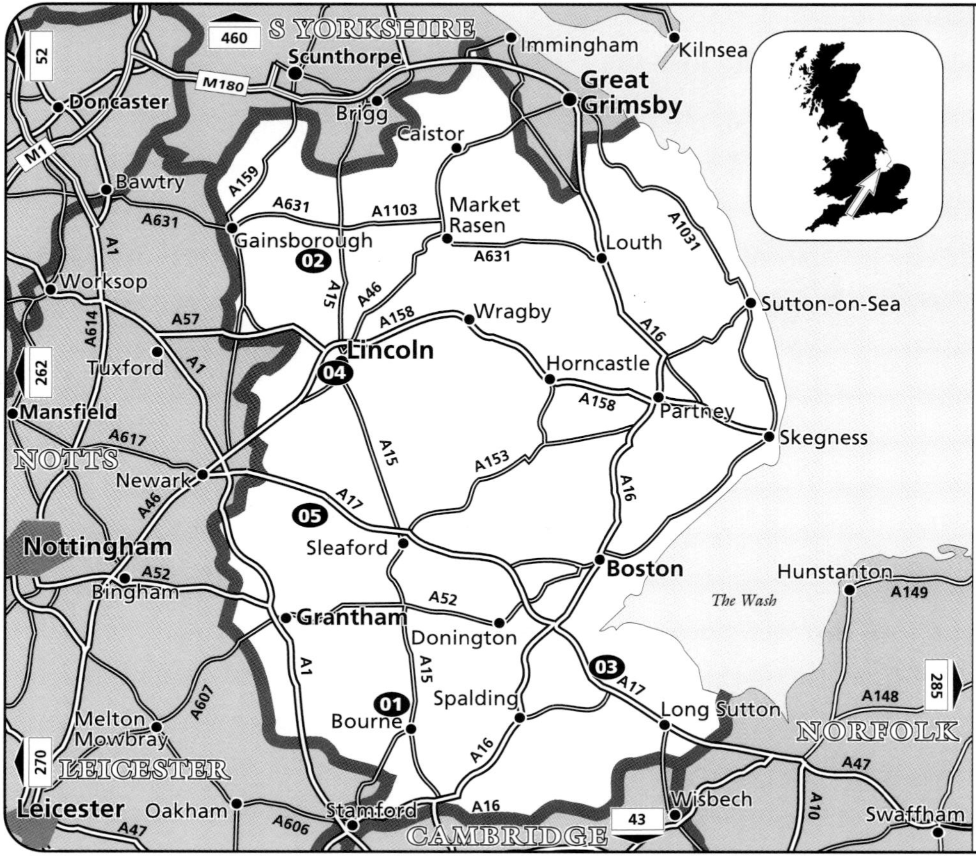

LINCOLNSHIRE
Map reference

01 Armstrong
02 Ramsay
03 Honnor
04 Pritchard
04 Baumber
05 Rook

277

Pipwell Manor. Saracens Head.

Lincolnshire

		rate £ from - to per person	children taken	evening meals	animals taken
Mrs Chantal Armstrong **Cawthorpe Hall** Cawthorpe Bourne PE10 0AB Tel: (01778) 423830 Fax 01778 426620 Open: ALL YEAR Map Ref No. 01	Nearest Road: A.15 This fine, old, listed house is surrounded by a large pretty garden & fields of roses supplying the rose distillery with fragrant blooms. The rooms are bright, spacious & comfortably furnished & have a bathroom en-suite. A full English breakfast will be served in a family country kitchen. Country lovers can enjoy beautiful woodland walks. Horse riding or golf, Grimsthorpe Castle & Park are all within easy reach. A charming home.	£25.00 to £30.00	Y	N	Y
Christine B. Ramsay **Church Farm** Fillingham Gainsborough DN21 5BS Tel: (01427) 668279 Fax 01427 668025 Open: ALL YEAR (Excl. Xmas) Map Ref No. 02	Nearest Road: A.15 Tucked away in unspoilt countryside, the Ramsays guarantee you a friendly welcome. Expect to enjoy good food, conversation, laughter & log fires on chilly evenings. Walk around the beautiful village lake or relax in the garden on sunny days & listen to the birdsong. Hemswell Antique Centre, Lincolnshire Showground, Lincoln & Gainsborough are nearby. Evening meals by arrangement & afternoon teas served. There are 2 attractive bedrooms with en-suite/private facilities & wonderful views. Children over 5.	£22.50 to £30.00	Y	Y	N
Mrs Lesley Honnor **Pipwell Manor** Washway Road Saracens Head Holbeach PE12 8AL Tel: (01406) 423119 Fax 01406 423119 Open: ALL YEAR (Excl. Xmas) Map Ref No. 03	Nearest Road: A.17 Pipwell Manor is a Grade II listed Georgian manor house, built in around 1740, set in paddocks & gardens in a small quiet village in the Lincolnshire Fens, just off the A.17. Beautifully restored & decorated in English-country style, but retaining many original features, Pipwell Manor is a delightful place to stay. There are 4 comfortably furnished & attractive bedrooms, each with an en-suite/private bathroom & tea/coffee-making facilities. Guests are welcomed with tea & home-made cake. Parking.	£22.00 to £30.00 *see PHOTO over p. 278*	N	N	N
Gillian Pritchard **Carline Guest House** 1-3 Carline Road Lincoln LN1 1HL Tel: (01522) 530422 Fax 01522 530422 Open: ALL YEAR (Excl. Xmas & New Year) Map Ref No. 04	Nearest Road: A.57, A.15 Gill & John Pritchard extend a warm welcome. Excellent accommodation, in 12 attractively furnished bedrooms, each with en-suite facilities, colour T.V., radio, beverage facilities, hairdryers & trouser press. The Carline is a short, pleasant stroll from the Lawns Tourism & Conference Centre, & from the historic Uphill area of Lincoln. There are several restaurants & public houses nearby for your lunch or evening meal. Ask your hosts for recommendations.	£21.00 to £30.00	Y	N	N
John & Margaret Baumber **Minster Lodge Hotel** 3 Church Lane Lincoln LN2 1QJ Tel: (01522) 513220 Fax 01522 513220 Open: ALL YEAR Map Ref No. 04	Nearest Road: A.15 A delightful family-run hotel, refurbished to a high standard. This lovely Victorian residence offers 6 attractive en-suite bedrooms with radio, colour T.V., 'phone & beverage facilities. Ideally situated within 50 yds of the only remaining Roman arch still in use & 5 mins' walk from historic Lincoln's major attractions of cathedral, castle & colourful mixture of restaurants & antique & gift shops. John & Margaret extend a very warm welcome! **E-mail: minsterlodge@compuserve.com**	£30.00 to £45.00 *see PHOTO over p. 280* VISA: M'CARD: AMEX:	Y	N	N

Minster Lodge Hotel. Lincoln.

Lincolnshire

		rate £ from - to per person	children taken	evening meals	animals taken
Michael & Elaine Rook **Stragglethorpe Hall** **Stragglethorpe** **LN5 0QZ** **Tel: (01400) 272308** **Fax 01400 273816** **Open: ALL YEAR (Excl.** **Xmas & New Year)** **Map Ref No. 05**	Nearest Road: A.17 Situated just off the A.1, Stragglethorpe Hall is a haven of peace between Cambridge & York, offering unique Tudor elegance & modern amenities. Furnished with antiques & Grade II listed, its stone-mullioned windows & leaded windows over-look formal gardens with ancient yew hedges surrounded by open countryside. The large, elegant double bedrooms are all en-suite, one is a 4-poster. Evening meals by arrangement. **E-mail: stragglethorpe@compuserve.com**	£25.00 to £50.00	Y	N	N

All the establishments mentioned in this guide are members of
The Worldwide Bed & Breakfast Association

When booking your accommodation please mention
The Best Bed & Breakfast

Norfolk

Norfolk
(East Anglia)

One of the largest of the old counties, Norfolk is divided by rivers from neighbouring counties & pushes out into the sea on the north & east sides. This is old East Anglia.

Inland there is great concentration on agriculture where fields are hedged with hawthorn which blossoms like snow in summer. A great deal of land drainage is required & the area is crisscrossed by dykes & ditches - some of them dating back to Roman times.

Holkham Hall.

The Norfolk Broads were formed by the flooding of mediaeval peat diggings to form miles & miles of inland waterways, navigable & safe. On a bright summer's day, on a peaceful backwater bounded by reed & sedge, the Broads seem like paradise. Here are hidden treasures like the Bittern, that shyest of birds, the Swallowtail butterfly & the rare Marsh orchid.

Contrasting with the still inland waters is a lively coastline which takes in a host of towns & villages as it arcs around The Wash. Here are the joys of the seaside at its best, miles of safe & sandy golden beaches to delight children, dunes & salt marshes where birdlife flourishes, & busy ports & fishing villages with pink-washed cottages.

Cromer is a little seaside town with a pier & a prom, cream teas & candy floss, where red, white & blue fishing boats are drawn up on the beach. Hunstanton is more decorous, with a broad green sweeping down to the cliffs. Great Yarmouth is a boisterous resort. It has a beach that runs for miles, with pony rides & almost every amusement imaginable.

It is possible to take a boat into the heart of Norwich, past warehouses, factories & new penthouses, & under stone & iron bridges. Walking along the riverbank you reach Pulls Ferry where a perfectly proportioned grey flint gateway arcs over what was once a canal dug to transport stone to the cathedral site. Norwich Cathedral is magnificent, with a sharply soaring spire, beautiful cloisters & fine 15th century carving preserved in the choir stalls. Cathedral Close is perfectly preserved, as is Elm Hill, a cobbled street from mediaeval times. There are many little shops & narrow alleys going down to the river.

Norfolk is a county much loved by the Royal family & the Queen has a home at Sandringham. It is no castle, but a solid, comfortable family home with red brick turrets & French windows opening onto the terrace.

Norfolk

Norfolk Gazeteer

Areas of outstanding beauty.
Norfolk coast (part)

Historic Houses & Castles

Anna Sewell House - Great Yarmouth
17th century Tudor frontage. Birthplace of writer Anna Sewell.
Blicking Hall - Aylsham
Great Jacobean house. Fine Russian tapestry, long gallery with exceptional ceiling. Formal garden.
Felbrigg Hall - Nr. Cromer
17th century, good Georgian interior. Set in wooded parklands.
Holkham Hall - Wells
Fine Palladian mansion of 1734. Paintings, statuary, tapestries, furnishings & formal garden by Berry.
Houghton Hall - Wells
18th century mansion. Pictures, china & staterooms.
Oxburgh Hall - Swafftham
Late 15th century moated house. Fine gatehouse tower. Needlework by Mary Queen of Scots.
Wolterton Hall - Nr. Norwich
Built in 1741 contains tapestries, porcelain, furniture.
Trinity Hospital - Castle Rising
17th century, nine brick & tile almshouses, court chapel & treasury.

Cathedrals & Churches

Attleborough (St. Mary)
Norman with late 14th century. Fine rood screen & frescoes.
Barton Turf (St. Michael & All Angles)
Magnificent screen with painting of the Nine Orders of Angles.
Beeston-next-Mileham (St. Mary)
14th century. Perpendicular clerestory tower & spire. Hammer Beam roof, parclose screens, benches, front cover. Tracery in nave & chancel windows.
Cawston (St. Agnes)
Tower faced with freestone. Painted screens, wall paintings, tower, screen & gallery. 15th century angel roof.
East Harding (St. Peter & St. Paul)
14th century, some 15th century alterations. Monuments of 15th-17th century. Splendid mediaeval glass.

Erpingham (St. Mary)
14th century military brass to John de Erpingham, 16th century Rhenish glass. Fine tower.
Gunton (St. Andrew)
18th century. Robert Adam - classical interior in dark wood - gilded.
King's Lynn (St. Margaret)
Norman foundation. Two fine 14th century Flemish brasses, 14th century screens, reredos by Bodley, interesting Georgian pulpit with sounding board.
Norwich Cathedral
Romanesque & late Gothic with 15th century spire. Perpendicular lierne vaults in nave, transeptsand presbytery.
Ranworth (St. Helens)
15th century screen, very fine example. Sarum Antiphoner, 14th century illuminated manuscript - East Anglian work.
Salle (St. Peter & St. Paul)
15th century. Highly decorated west tower & porches. Mediaeval glass, pulpit with 15th century panels & Jacobean tester. Stalls, misericords, brasses & monuments, sacrament font.
Terrington (St. Clement)
Detached perpendicular tower. Western front has fire-light window & canopied niches. Georgian panelling west of nave. 17th century painted font cover. Jacobean commandment boards.
Trunch (St. Botolph)
15th century screen with painted panels, mediaeval glass, famous font canopy with fine carving & painting, ringer's gallery, Elizabethan monument.
Wiggenhall (St. Germans)
17th century pulpit, table, clerk's desk & chair, bench ends 15th century.
Wymondham (St. Mary & St. Thomas of Canterbury)
Norman origins including arcades & triforium windows, 13th century font fragments, complete 15th century font. 15th century clerestory & roof. Comper reredos, famous Corporas Case, rare example of 13th century Opus Anglicanum.

Museums & Galleries

Norwich Castle Museum
Art collection, local & natural history,

Norfolk

Strangers Hall - Norwich
Mediaeval mansion furnished as museum of urban domestic life in 16th-19th centuries.

St. Peter Hungate Church Museum - Norwich
15th century church for the exhibition of ecclesiastical art & East Anglican antiquities.

Sainsbury Centre for Visual Arts - University, Norwich
Collection of modern art, ancient, classical & mediaeval art, Art Nouveau, 20th century constructivist art.

Bridewell Museum of Local Industries - Norwich
Crafts, industries & aspects of city life.

Museum of Social History - King's Lynn
Exhibition of domestic life & dress, etc., noted glass collection.

Bishop Bonner's Cottages
Restored cottages with coloured East Anglia pargetting, c. 1502, museum of archaeological discoveries, exhibition of rural crafts.

The Guildhall - Thetford
Duleep Singh Collection of Norfolk & Suffolk portraits.

Shirehall Museum - Walsingham
18th century court room having original fittings, illustrating Walsingham life.

Historic Monuments

Binham Priory & Cross - Binham
12th century ruins of Benedictine foundation.

Caister Castle - Great Yarmouth
15th century moated castle - ruins. Now motor museum.

The Castle - Burgh Castle
3rd century Saxon fort - walls - ruin.

Mannington Hall - Saxthorpe
Saxon church ruin in gardens of 15th century moated house.

Castle Rising - Castle Rising
Splendid Norman keep & earthworks.

Castle Acre Priory & Castle Gate - Swaffham

Other things to see & do

African Violet Centre - Terrington St. Clements.
60 varieties of African Violets. Talks & Tours.

Norfolk Lavender Centre - Heacham
Open to the public in July & August. Demonstrations of harvesting & distilling the oil.

Thetford Forest
Forest walks, rides & picnic places amongst conifers, oak, beech & birch.

The Broads.

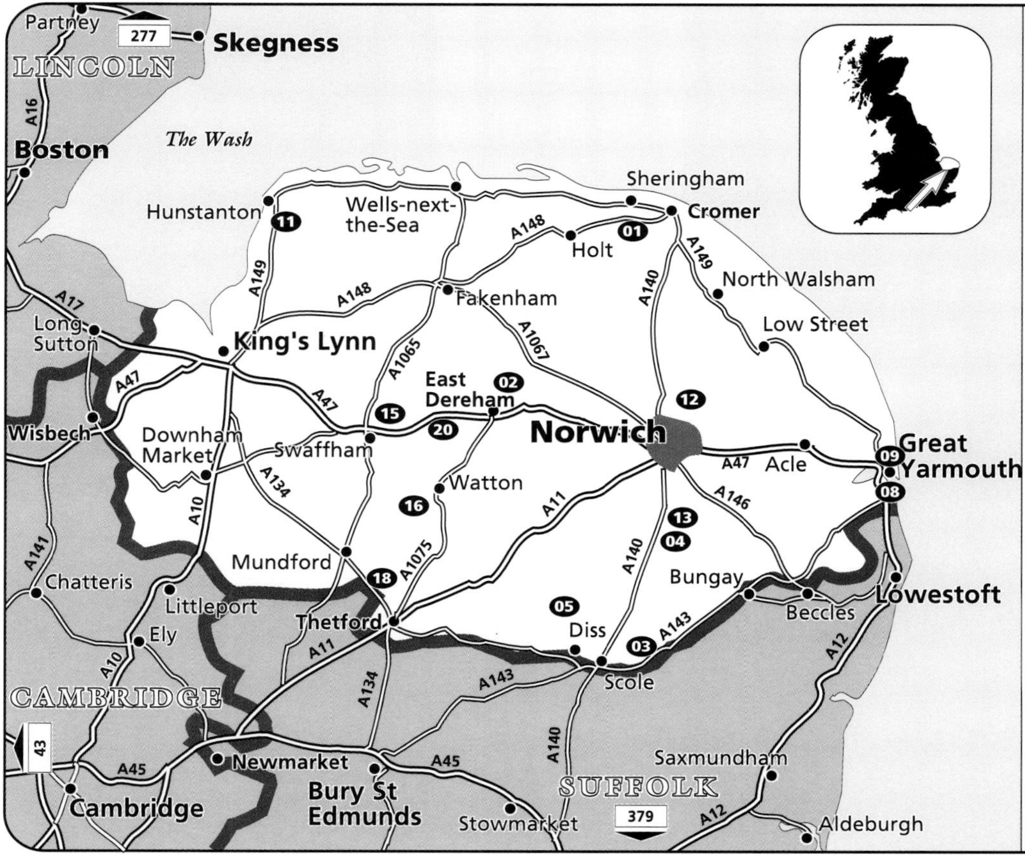

NORFOLK
Map reference

01 Gillam
02 Bartlett
03 Morrish
04 Croft
05 Webb
08 Wells
09 Norris
11 Tweedy Smith
12 Parker Brown
13 Douglas
15 Hickey
16 Garnier
18 Collins
20 Lock

Skegness

Partney 277 LINCOLN
A16

Boston
A17
The Wash
Long Sutton
Wisbech
A47
A141
Chatteris
A10
Littleport
Ely
A45
Cambridge
A45
Newmarket
A134
Bury St Edmunds
A45
Stowmarket
A143
CAMBRIDGE 43

Hunstanton
A149
King's Lynn
A47
Downham Market
A10
Mundford
Thetford
A11
A1075
A134

Wells-next-the-Sea
A148
Swaffham
A1065

Sheringham
Cromer
A148
Holt
A149
Fakenham
A1067
A140
East Dereham
Watton
A11

North Walsham
Low Street
Acle
A47
A146
Norwich
A140
A11
Bungay
A143
Diss
Scole
A140
SUFFOLK
379
Saxmundham
A12
Aldeburgh

Great Yarmouth
Lowestoft
A12
Beccles
A143

01 Holt
12 Norwich
13 / 04 Norwich
03 Scole
05 Diss
02 East Dereham
20 / 15 Swaffham
16 Watton
18 Thetford
11 Hunstanton
08 / 09 Great Yarmouth
20 Lowestoft

285

Felbrigg Lodge. Aylmerton.

		rate £ from - to per person	children taken	evening meals	animals taken

Jill & Ian Gillam **Felbrigg Lodge** **Aylmerton** **NR11 8RA** **Tel: (01263) 837588** Fax 01263 838012 **Open: ALL YEAR** **Map Ref No. 01**	Nearest Road: A.148, A.140 Set in beautiful countryside 2 miles from the coast, Felbrigg Lodge is hidden in 8 acres of spectacular woodland gardens. Time has stood still since Edwardian ladies came here in their carriages to take tea & play croquet. Great care has been taken to preserve this atmosphere with large en-suite rooms all luxuriously decorated with every facility. A true haven of peace & tranquillity. Candlelit dinners & copious breakfast. Indoor heated pool/gym. Children over 8.	**£30.00** to **£55.00** 🚭 *see PHOTO over* *p. 286* VISA: M'CARD:	Y	Y	N
David & Annie Bartlett **Bartles Lodge** **Church Street** **Elsing** **Dereham NR20 3EA** **Tel: (01362) 637177** **Open: ALL YEAR** **Map Ref No. 02**	Nearest Road: A.47, A.1067 Bartles Lodge is in the peaceful, unspoilt village of Elsing, set in 12 acres of landscaped meadows inhabited by plenty of wildlife. The rooms, centred around the patio, pond & fountain, are beautifully furnished in country style, & most overlook the Bartletts' own lakes. All of the bedrooms are en-suite with colour T.V.s, tea/coffee-making facilities etc. Although Bartles Lodge is licensed, the local village inn is nearby.	**£21.00** to **£35.00** VISA: M'CARD:	N	N	Y
Angela & John Morrish **Grove Thorpe** **Grove Road** **Brockdish** **Diss** **IP21 4JE** **Tel: (01379) 668305** Fax 01379 668305 **Open: ALL YEAR** **Map Ref No. 03**	Nearest Road: A.143 Grove Thorpe is a Grade II listed 17th-century farmhouse which has been beautifully renovated to a very high standard, with inglenook fireplaces & beamed rooms. Set in mature, secluded gardens & grounds of 6 acres with livery facilities available for horses. All bedrooms are en-suite & have beverage facilities. Laze around log fires in winter or sit in the gardens through the summer. Excellent evening meals. Conveniently situated for Norfolk, Suffolk, Bressingham, Norwich, Norfolk Broads & the Otter Trust. Children over 12.	**£24.00** to **£30.00** 🚭 *see PHOTO over* *p. 288*	Y	Y	N
Martin & Jean Croft **The Old Bakery** **Church Walk** **Pulham Market** **Diss** **IP21 4SJ** **Tel: (01379) 676492** Fax 01379 676492 **Open: ALL YEAR** **Map Ref No. 04**	Nearest Road: A.140 The Old Bakery is a 16th-century oak-framed house on a private road in the centre of an award-winning conservation village among thatched period houses. All 3 double rooms are fully en-suite & have colour T.V., clock/radio & hospitality tray. The Old Bakery is licensed, & offers excellent traditional meals prepared by Martin, a Master Chef. These are served in the beamed & log-fired dining room, which glows with warmth & history. Situated near Bressingham, Norwich, the Broads & the Heritage Coast.	**£25.00** to **£27.00** 🚭 *see PHOTO over* *p. 289*	N	Y	N
K. Webb **Strenneth** **Airfield Road** **Fersfield** **Diss** **IP22 2BP** **Tel: (01379) 688182** Fax 01379 688260 **Open: ALL YEAR** **Map Ref No. 05**	Nearest Road: A.1066 Strenneth is situated in unspoilt countryside a short drive from Bressingham Gardens & the picturesque market town of Diss. The original 17th-century building has been carefully renovated to a high standard with a wealth of oak beams & a newer single-storey courtyard wing. Parking & plenty of walks nearby. All 6 bedrooms, including a 4-poster & an executive, are en-suite & tastefully arranged with period furniture & distinctive beds, each having T.V. & hospitality tray. **E-mail: ken@mainline.co.uk**	**£23.00** to **£32.50** VISA: M'CARD:	Y	N	Y

Grove Thorpe. Brockdish.

The Old Bakery. Pulham Market.

Norfolk

		Rate £ from - to per person	Children taken	Evening meals	Animals taken
Mrs Barbara Wells **Spindrift Private Hotel** **36 Wellesley Road** **Great Yarmouth** **NR30 1EU** **Tel: (01493) 858674** **Fax 01493 858674** **Open: ALL YEAR (Excl. Xmas)** **Map Ref No. 08**	Nearest Road: A.47, A.12 Good food & comfortable accommodation are the by-words at 'Spindrift'. Attractively situated adjacent to the sea front, the Golden Mile, bowling greens, tennis courts & the water ways. Easygoing atmosphere, with keys provided for access at all times. 8 bedrooms, the front bedrooms overlooking the gardens & sea, & 6 bedrooms with en-suite facilities. All with modern amenities, T.V. & tea/coffee-making facilities. Good on road parking; public car park at rear. Children over 3.	£16.50 to £22.50 VISA: M'CARD: AMEX:	Y	N	N
Jill & Andrew Norris **Barnard House** **2 Barnard Crescent** **Great Yarmouth** **NR30 4DR** **Tel: (01493) 855139** **Fax 01493 843143** **Open: ALL YEAR (Excl. Xmas & New Year)** **Map Ref No. 09**	Nearest Road: A.12, A.47 A welcoming family home in a peaceful residential area of Great Yarmouth. A short distance to the sea, race course & golf links, with the picturesque Norfolk Broads on the doorstep. Barnard House is the perfect place to stay, whether for business or pleasure. 3 comfortable bedrooms (2 double en-suite & 1 twin with private bathroom), all equipped with T.V., clock/radio, hairdryer & hospitality tray. An attractive sitting room with an open fire in winter, or pretty garden with conservatory for summer, all available for guests' use. E-mail: BARNARDHOUSE@BTINTERNET.COM	£20.00 to £24.00 🚭	Y	Y	Y
Sheila & John Tweedy **Smith** **Fieldsend** **26 Homefields Road** **Hunstanton PE36 5HL** **Tel: (01485) 532593** **Fax 01485 532593** **Open: ALL YEAR** **Map Ref No. 11**	Nearest Road: A.149 Come & stay at Fieldsend & enjoy the comfort of a large Edwardian carrstone house, close to the town centre & the sea with panoramic views over the Wash. Guests have a choice of 3 rooms, 2 en-suite, 1 with a private bathroom, all individually decorated by the owner who specialises in rag rolling & making the drapes & pelmets, as well as upholstery & collecting coloured glass. 1 bedroom has a 4-poster. Delicious breakfasts are served by a Cordon Bleu cook. Parking.	£22.50 to £25.00 *see PHOTO over* *p. 291*	Y	N	N
P. M. Parkerbrown **Elm Farm Country House** **55 Norwich Road** **St. Faith** **Norwich NR10 3HH** **Tel: (01603) 898366** **Fax 01603 897129** **Open: ALL YEAR** **Map Ref No. 12**	Nearest Road: A.140 Elm Farm Country House is situated in the attractive village of St. Faith, 4 miles from the city of Norwich, 5 miles from the Norfolk Broads & within easy reach of the Norfolk & Suffolk coasts. Each of the 14 comfortable en-suite bedrooms has T.V., radio, 'phone, hairdryer & tea/coffee-making facilities. Some are non-smoking. Licensed. Ample parking. Attractive gardens with duck pond. Reduced rates for 2 nights or more.	£31.00 to £36.00 VISA: M'CARD: AMEX:	Y	N	N
Joanna Douglas **Greenacres Farmhouse** **Woodgreen** **Long Stratton** **Norwich NR15 2RR** **Tel: (01508) 530261** **Fax 01508 530261** **Open: ALL YEAR** **Map Ref No. 13**	Nearest Road: A.140 A period 17th-century farmhouse on a 30-acre common with ponds & wildlife, only 10 miles from Norwich. All of the en-suite/private bedrooms (2 double/1 twin) are tastefully furnished to complement the oak beams & period furniture, with tea/coffee facilities & T.V.. The beamed sitting room with inglenook fireplace invites you to relax. A sunny dining room encourages you to enjoy a leisurely breakfast. Snooker table & tennis court. Enjoy the peace & tranquillity of this home.	£20.00 to £27.50 🚭	Y	Y	Y

Fieldsend House. Hunstanton.

Norfolk

		rate £ from - to per person	evening meals children taken		animals taken
Linda & Martin Hickey **Corfield House** **The Street** **Sporle** **Swaffham** **PE32 2EA** **Tel: (01760) 723636** **Open: APR - Mid DEC** **Map Ref No. 15**	Nearest Road: A.47 Corfield House is an attractive brick-built house standing in 1/2 an acre of lawned gardens in the peaceful village of Sporle near Swaffham, an ideal base for touring Norfolk. Some of the 4 comfortable & attractive en-suite bedrooms (1 ground-floor) have fine views across open fields, & all have T.V., clock/radio & a fact-file on places to visit. Good home-cooked food using excellent local produce. Licensed. **E-mail: corfield.house@virgin.net**	£19.50 to £23.50 VISA: M'CARD:	Y	Y	N
Lavender Garnier **College Farm** **Thompson** **Thetford** **IP24 1QG** **Tel: (01953) 483318** **Fax 01953 483318** **Open: ALL YEAR** **Map Ref No. 16**	Nearest Road: A.1075 Built 600 years ago as a College of Priests, & became a manor house when Henry VIII dissolved the monasteries. College Farm has been modernised to provide 3 comfortable rooms, 2 en-suite & all with T.V. & superb views over farmland & mature trees. Delicious breakfasts are served in the panelled dining room. An excellent thatched pub in the village offers tasty meals. Norfolk coast, Norwich, Cambridge & Sandringham within easy reach by car. Children over 7.	£19.00 to £19.00	Y	N	N
Mrs Christine Collins **Cedar Lodge** **West Tofts** **Thetford IP26 5DB** **Tel: (01842) 878281** **Fax 01842 878281** **Open: ALL YEAR** **Map Ref No. 18**	Nearest Road: A.134 A warm welcome awaits you at Cedar Lodge, which stands on the edge of Thetford Forest. There are 2 double bedrooms overlooking farmland & big log fires in a lovely sitting room. Food is the password - Christine owns a useful catering company & is a member of The Master Chefs of Great Britain & delights in preparing candlelit dinners for her guests. Children over 12 years welcome. Animals by arrangement.	£20.00 to £22.00	Y	Y	Y
Jennie Lock **Greenbanks Country** **Hotel & Restaurant** **Wendling** **NR19 2AB** **Tel: (01362) 687742** **Open: ALL YEAR** **Map Ref No. 20**	Nearest Road: A.47 Charming, small, 18th-century hotel, with delightful country restaurant, situated in 9 acres of meadows & lakes. Spectacular gardens. Elegant & attractive en-suite rooms, offering peace & comfort. Superb cuisine, with excellent choice from varied menu: special diets catered for. Greenbanks is 15 mins from the fine city of Norwich, & within easy reach of the coast, the Broads & many stately homes. Walking, fishing & golfing breaks available.	£28.00 to £48.00 *see PHOTO over* *p. 293* VISA: M'CARD:	Y	Y	Y

When booking your accommodation please mention
The Best Bed & Breakfast

Greenbanks Country Hotel. Wendling.

Northumbria

Northumbria

Mountains & moors, hills & fells, coast & country are all to be found in this Northern region which embraces four counties - Northumberland, Durham, Cleveland & Tyne & Wear.

Saxons, Celts, Vikings, Romans & Scots all fought to control what was then a great wasteland between the Humber & Scotland.

Northumberland

Northumberland is England's Border country, a land of history, heritage & breathtaking countryside. Hadrian's Wall, stretching across the county from the mouth of the Tyne in the west to the Solway Firth, was built as the Northern frontier of the Roman Empire in 122 AD. Excavations along the Wall have brought many archaeological treasures to light. To walk along the wall is to discover the genius of Roman building & engineering skill. They left a network of roads, used to transport men & equipment in their attempts to maintain discipline among the wild tribes.

Through the following centuries the Border wars with the Scots led to famous battles such as Otterburn in 1388 & Flodden in 1513, & the construction of great castles including Bamburgh & Lindisfarne. Berwick-on-Tweed, the most northerly town, changed hands between England & Scotland 13 times.

Northumberland's superb countryside includes the Cheviot Hills in the Northumberland National Park, the unforgettable heather moorlands of the Northern Pennines to the west, Kielder Water (Western Europe's largest man-made lake), & 40 miles of glorious coastline.

Holy Island, or Lindisfarne, is reached by a narrow causeway that is covered at every incoming tide. Here St. Aidan of Iona founded a monastery in the 7th century, & with St. Cuthbert set out to Christianise the pagan tribes. The site was destroyed by the Danes, but Lindisfarne Priory was built by the monks of Durham in the 11th century to house a Benedictine community. The ruins are hauntingly beautiful.

Durham

County Durham is the land of the Prince Bishops, who with their armies, nobility, courts & coinage controlled the area for centuries. They ruled as a virtually independent State, holding the first line of defence against the Scots.

In Durham City, the impressive Norman Castle standing proudly over the narrow mediaeval streets was the home of the Prince Bishops for 800 years.

Durham Cathedral, on a wooded peninsula high above the River Wear, was built in the early 12th century & is undoubtably one of the world's finest buildings, long a place of Christian pilgrimage.

The region's turbulent history led to the building of forts & castles. Some like Bowes & Barnard Castle are picturesque ruins whilst others, including Raby, Durham & Lumley still stand complete.

The Durham Dales of Weardale, Teesdale & the Derwent Valley cover about one third of the county & are endowed with some of the highest & wildest scenery. Here are High Force, England's highest waterfall, & the Upper Teesdale National Nature Reserve.

The Bowes Museum at Barnard Castle is a magnificent French-style chateau & houses an important art collection.

In contrast is the award-winning museum at Beamish which imaginatively recreates Northern life at the turn of the century.

Northumbria

Cleveland

Cleveland, the smallest 'shire' in England, has long been famous for its steel, chemical & shipbuilding industries but it is also an area of great beauty. The North Yorkshire National Park lies in the south, & includes the cone-shaped summit of Roseberry Topping, "Cleveland's Matterhorn".

Cleveland means 'land of cliffs', & in places along the magnificent coastline, cliffs tower more than 600 feet above the sea, providing important habitat for wild plants & sea-birds.

Pretty villages such as Hart, Elwick & Staithes are full of steep, narrow alleys. Marton was the birthplace of Captain James Cook & the museum there traces the explorer's early life & forms the start of the 'Cook Heritage Trail'.

The Tees estuary is a paradise for birdwatchers, whilst walkers can follow the Cleveland Way or the 38 miles of the Langbaurgh Loop. There is surfing, windsurfing & sailing at Saltburn, & for the less energetic, the scenic Esk Valley Railway runs from Middlesbrough to Whitby.

Tyne & Wear

Tyne & Wear takes its name from the two rivers running through the area, & includes the large & lively city of Newcastle-on-Tyne.

Weardale lies in a beautiful valley surrounded by wild & bleak fells. Peaceful now, it was the setting for a thriving industry mining coal & silver, zinc & lead. Nature trails & recreation areas have been created among the old village & market towns.

The county was the birthplace of George Stephenson, railway engineer, who pioneered the world's first passenger railway on the Stockton to Darlington Line in 1825.

Durham Cathedral.

Northumbria

Northumbria Gazeeter

Areas of Outstanding Natural Beauty
The Heritage Coast, the Cheviot Hills, the North Pennine chain.

Historic Houses & Castles

Alnwick Castle - Alnwick
A superb mediaeval castle of the 12th century.
Bamburgh Castle-Bamburgh
A restored 12th century castle with Norman keep.
Callaly Castle - Whittingham
A 13th century Pele tower with 17th century mansion. Georgian additions.
Durham Castle - Durham
Part of the University of Durham - a Norman castle.
Lindisfarne Castle - Holy Island
An interesting 14th century castle.
Ormesby Hall - Nr. Middlesbrough
A mid 18th century house.
Raby Castle - Staindrop, Darlington
14th century with some later alteration . Fine art & furniture. Large gardens.
Wallington Hall -Combo
A 17th century house with much alteration & addition.
Washington Old Hall-Washington
Jacobean manor house, parts of which date back to 12th century.

Cathedrals & Churches

Brancepeth (St. Brandon)
12th century with superb 17th century woodwork. Part of 2 mediaeval screens. Flemish carved chest.
Durham Cathedral
A superb Norman cathedral. A unique Galilee chapel & early 12th century vaults.
Escombe
An interesting Saxon Church with sundial.
Hartlepool (St. Hilda)
Early English with fine tower & buttresses.
Hexham (St. Andrews)
Remains of a 17th century church with Roman dressing. A unique night staircase & very early stool. Painted screens.
Jarrow (St. Pauls)
Bede worshipped here. Strange in that it was originally 2 churches until 11th century. Mediaeval chair.

Newcastle (St. Nicholas)
14th century with an interesting lantern tower.
Heraldic font. Roundel of 14th century glass.
Morpeth (St. Mary the Virgin)
Fine mediaeval glass in east window - 14th century.
Pittington (St. Lawrence)
Late Norman nave with wall paintings. Carved tombstone - 13th century.
Skelton (St. Giles)
Early 13th century with notable font, gable crosses, bell-cote & buttresses.
Staindrop (St. Mary)
A fine Saxon window.
Priests dwelling.
Neville tombs & effigies.

Museums & Galleries

Aribea Roman Fort Museum - South Shields
Interesting objects found on site.
Berwick-on-Tweed Museum - Berwick
Special exhibition of interesting local finds.
Bowes Museum - Bernard Castle
European art from mediaeval to 19th century.
Captain Cook Birthplace Museum - Middlesbrough
Cook's life & natural history relating to his travels.
Clayton Collection - Chollerford
A collection of Roman sculpture, weapons & tools from forts.
Corbridge Roman Station - Corbridge
Roman pottery & sculpture.
Dormitory Musuem - Durham Cathedral
Relics of St. Cuthbert.
Mediaeval seats & manuscripts.
Gray Art Gallery - Hartlepool
19th-20th century art & oriental antiquities.
Gulbenkian Museum of Oriental Art - University of Durham
Chinese pottery & porcelain, Chinese jade & stone carvings, Chinese ivories, Chinese textiles, Japenese & Tibetan art. Egyptian & Mesopotamian antiquities.
Jarrow Hall - Jarrow
Excavation finds of Saxon & mediaeval monastery.
Fascinating information room dealing with early Christian sites in England.

Northumbria

Keep Museum - Newcastle-upon-Tyne
Mediaeval collection.
Laing Art Gallery - Newcastle-upon-Tyne
17th-19th century British arts, porcelain,
glass & silver.
National Music Hall Museum -
Sunderland
19th-20th century costume & artefacts
associated with the halls.
Preston Hall Museum - Stockton-on-Tees
Armour & arms, toys, ivory period room
University - New Castle -Upon -Tyne
The Hatton Gallery - housing a fine
collection of Italian paintings.
Museum of Antiquities
Prehistoric, Roman & Saxon collection
with an interesting reconstruction of a
temple.
**Beamish North of England Open Air
Museum** - European Museum of the Year
Chantry Bagpipe Museum - Morpeth
Darlington Museum & Railway Centre.

Historic Monuments

Ariiea Roman Fort - South Shields
Remains which include the gateways &
headquarters.
Barnard Castle - Barnard Castle
17th century ruin with interesting keep.
Bowes Castle - Bowes
Roman Fort with Norman keep.
The Castle & Town Walls - Berwick-on-
Tweed
12th century remains, reconstructed later.
Dunstanburgh Castle - Alnwick
14th century remains.
Egglestone Abbey - Barnard Castle
Remains of a Poor House.
Finchdale Priory - Durham
13 th century church with much
remaining.
Hadrian's Wall - Housesteads
Several miles of the wall including castles
& site museum.
Mithramic Temple - Carrawbrough
Mithraic temple dating back to the 3rd
century.
Norham Castle - Norham
The partial remains of a 12th century
castle.
Prudhoe Castle - Prudhoe
Dating from the 12th century with
additions. Bailey & gatehouse well
preserved.

The Roman Fort - Chesters
Extensive remains of a Roman bath
house.
Tynemouth Priory & Castle - Tynemouth
11th century priory - ruin - with 16th
century towers & keep.
Vindolanda - Barton Mill
Roman fort dating from 3rd century.
Warkworth Castle - Warkworth
Dating from the 11th century with
additions.
A great keep & gatehouse.
Warkworth Hermitage - Warkworth
An interesting 14th century Hermitage.
Lindisfarne Priory - Holy Island
(Lindisfarne)
11th century monastery. Island accessible
only at low tide.

Other things to see & do

Botanical Gardens - Durham University
Bird & Seal Colonies - Farne Islands
Conducted tours by boat
Marine Life Centre & Fishing Museum -
Seahouses
Museum of sealife, & boat trips to the
Farne Islands.
Tower Knowe Visitor Centre - Keilder
Water

Saltburn Victorian Festival.

NORTHUMBERLAND, DURHAM & TYNE & WEAR

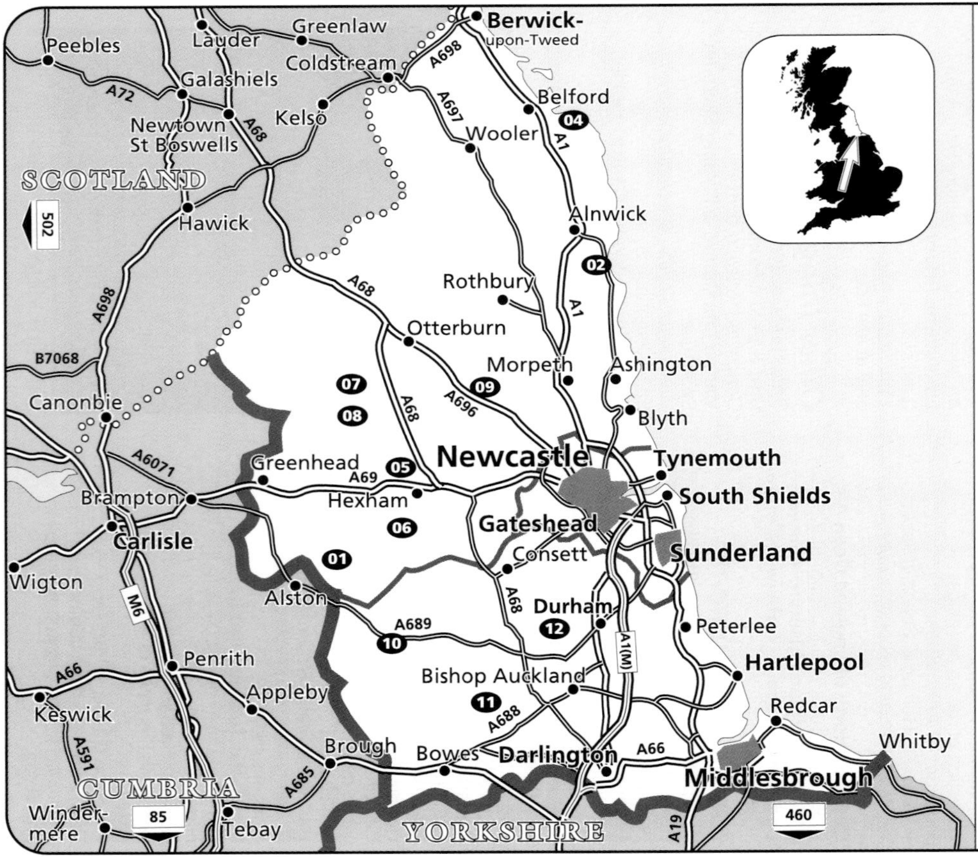

Map reference

01 Finn
02 Jackson
04 Laverack
05 Weightman
06 Courage
07 Minchin
08 Peel
09 Gay
10 Reed
11 Close
12 Booth

NORTHUMBERLAND

TYNE & WEAR

DURHAM

Northumberland

		rate £ from - to per person	children taken	evening meals	animals taken
Eileen Finn **Thornley House** **Allendale** **NE47 9NH** **Tel: (01434) 683255** **Open: ALL YEAR** **Map Ref No. 01**	Nearest Road: A.69 A beautiful country house set in spacious grounds surrounded by a field & woodland, 1 mile from Allendale. Accommodation is in 3 attractive bedrooms, all with tea-makers & private facilities. 2 lounges, 1 with Steinway grand piano, 1 with T.V.. Fine collection of original feline paintings. Georgeous walks - guided available sometimes. Ample maps, books & games. Hadrian's Wall, stately homes & castles nearby. Guests are welcome to bring their own wine.	£39.00 to £39.00	Y	Y	Y
Mrs Dorothy Jackson **Bilton Barns Farmhouse** **Alnmouth** **Alnwick** **NE66 2TB** **Tel: (01665) 830427** **Fax 01665 830063** **Open: MAR - Mid OCT** **Map Ref No. 02**	Nearest Road: A.1 This spacious & well-furnished farmhouse has beautiful, panoramic views over Alnmouth & Warkworth Bay, only 1 1/2 miles away. Set in lovely countryside, & well-situated for the many magnificent beaches, castles, walks & recreational activities. All rooms are centrally heated, & large bedrooms have their own washbasin, T.V. & tea/coffee facilities, 3 with private bathroom. Dorothy makes many dishes with a distinctly local flavour. Brian is pleased to show any interested visitors around the farm. (Animals by arrangement.)	£23.50 to £25.00	Y	Y	Y
Anita & Peter Laverack **Waren House Hotel** **Waren Mill** **Bamburgh** **NE70 7EE** **Tel: (01668) 214581** **Fax 01668 214484** **Open: ALL YEAR** **Map Ref No. 04**	Nearest Road: A.1 Lovingly restored traditional country house set in 6 acres of wooded grounds on the edge of Budle Bay, overlooking the Holy Island of Lindisfarne. Beautiful bedrooms, some with 4-poster, all with both spacious bathrooms & all the facilities you would expect from one of Northumbria's premier award-winning hostelries. Magnificent dining room offering excellent food. 200-plus bin wine list. No smoking except in library. Bamburgh Castle 2 miles. Children over 14. (Rate includes dinner.) **E-mail: enquiries@warenhousehotel.co.uk**	£57.50 to £92.50 VISA: M'CARD: AMEX:	N	Y	Y
Margaret & Bill Weightman **The Courtyard** **Mount Pleasant, Sandhoe** **Corbridge NE46 4LX** **Tel: (01434) 606850** **Fax 01434 607962** **Open: ALL YEAR** **Map Ref No. 05**	Nearest Road: A.69, A.68 A warm family welcome greets visitors to this award-winning lovingly restored & beautifully furnished country house, dating from 1730. Surrounded by open countryside, with wonderful panoramic views over Corbridge & Corstopitum Roman Fort, both 1 1/2 miles away, & the Tyne Valley. All rooms have exposed oak beams, en-suite bath/shower rooms, T.V. & tea/coffee. 1 has an antique 4-poster bed. Licensed.	£30.00 to £40.00 *see PHOTO over* *p. 300*	N	N	N
Elizabeth Courage **Rye Hill Farm** **Slaley** **Hexham** **NE47 OAH** **Tel: (01434) 673259** **Fax 01434 673259** **Open: ALL YEAR** **Map Ref No. 06**	Nearest Road: A.68 Rye Hill Farm dates back some 300 years & is a traditional livestock unit in beautiful countryside just 5 miles south of Hexham. Recently, some of the stone barns adjoining the farmhouse have been converted into superb modern guest accommodation. There are 6 bedrooms, all with private facilities, & all have radio, T.V. & tea/coffee-making facilities. Delicious home-cooked meals. Perfect for a get-away-from-it-all holiday. **E-mail: enquiries@consult-courage.co.uk**	£20.00 to £25.00 VISA: M'CARD:	Y	Y	Y

see PHOTO over p. 300

The Courtyard. Sandhoe.

Northumberland & Durham

		rate £ from - to per person	children taken	evening meals	animals taken
David & June Minchin **Westfield Guest House** **Bellingham** **Hexham** **NE48 2DP** **Tel: (01434) 220340** Fax 01434 220694 **Open: ALL YEAR** **Map Ref No. 07**	Nearest Road: A.68 Westfield is a truly hospitable home. Built as an elegant but cosy Victorian gentleman's residence, with nearly an acre of gardens. The 5 bedrooms, including 4 en-suite & a 4-poster, are all totally comfortable, with more than a touch of luxury. Breakfast & dinner are superb, with traditional cooking at its best. Wonderful countryside - an ideal touring spot - Roman Wall, castles & N.T. properties, so come & bide awhile & be spoilt. Animals by arrangement. **E-mail: westfield.house@virgin.net**	£25.00 to £28.00 VISA: M'CARD:	Y	Y	Y
David & Sally Peel **Low Stead** **Wark** **Hexham** **NE48 3DP** **Tel: (01434) 230352** **Open: APR - OCT** **Map Ref No. 08**	Nearest Road: A.69 The unspoilt countryside of Northumberland's National Park surrounds Low Stead. A 16th-century 'bastle house' built to repel border reivers, its present tranquillity & solitude provide a haven for walkers, wildlife enthusiasts & country lovers. 2 delightful en-suite bedrooms. Imaginatively presented meals using local produce are served in the log-fired oak-beamed dining room. Peace, history & total comfort combine to make Low Stead's unique atmosphere. Children over 9. **E-mail: peel@lowstead.freeserve.co.uk**	£26.50 to £31.50 *see PHOTO over p. 302*	Y	Y	N
Stephen & Celia Gay **Shieldhall** **Wallington by Kirkharle** **Morpeth** **NE61 4AQ** **Tel: (01830) 540387** Fax 01830 540490 **Open: MAR - NOV** **Map Ref No. 09**	Nearest Road: A.696 Within acres of well-kept gardens, offering unimpeded views & overlooking the N.T.'s Wallington estate, this meticulously restored 18th-century farmhouse is built around a pretty courtyard. All of the 3 bedrooms are beautifully furnished & have en-suite facilities & T.V.. There are very comfortable lounges & an extremely charming inglenooked dining room where home produce is often used for delicious meals which are specially prepared when booked in advance. **E-mail: Robinson.Gay@btinternet.com**	£20.00 to £30.00 VISA: M'CARD:	N	Y	N

Durham

Mrs B. Reed **Lands Farm** **Westgate-in-Weardale** **Bishop Auckland** **DL13 1SN** **Tel: (01388) 517210** **Open: MAR - OCT** **Map Ref No. 10**	Nearest Road: A.689 You will be warmly welcomed to Lands Farm, an old stone-built farmhouse within walking distance of Westgate village. A walled garden with stream meandering by. Accommodation is in centrally heated double & family rooms with luxury en-suite facilities, T.V., tea/coffee making. Full English breakfast or Continental alternative served in an attractive dining room. This is an ideal base for touring (Durham, Hadrian's Wall, Beamish Museum, etc.) & for walking.	£22.00 to £27.00	Y	N	N

Visit our website at:
http://www.bestbandb.co.uk

Low Stead. Wark.

Durham

		rate £ from - to per person	evening meals / children taken	animals taken
Helene Close **Grove House** **Hamsterley Forest** **Bishop Auckland** **DL13 3NL** **Tel: (01388) 488203** **Fax 01388 488174** **Open: ALL YEAR** **Map Ref No. 11**	Nearest Road: A.68 Grove House, once an aristocrat's shooting lodge, is tastefully furnished throughout, & is situated in an idyllic setting in the middle of Hamsterley Forest. A spacious lounge with log fire gives a warm & comfortable country-house atmosphere. The grandeur & fineness of the dining room reminds one of an age gone by. (Take note of the door handles!) 3 bedrooms, all en-suite or with private bathrooms, which are well-appointed. Helene does all the cooking herself to ensure freshness & quality to her evening meals. A delightful home & a wonderful base for exploring this little-known region. Children over 8. **E-mail: xov47@dial.pipex.com**	£20.00 to £28.50 🚭	Y Y	N
Roger & Pauline Booth **Ivesley** **Waterhouses** **Durham** **DH7 9HB** **Tel: (0191) 3734324** **Fax 0191 3734757** **Open: ALL YEAR (Excl. Xmas Day)** **Map Ref No. 12**	Nearest Road: A.68 Ivesley is an elegantly furnished country house set in 220 acres. Each of the 3 bedrooms is decorated to a high standard. All are en-suite & have T.V. & tea/coffee-making facilities . Ivesley is adjacent to an equestrian centre with first-class facilities. An ideal centre for walking, sight-seeing & mountain biking. Collection can be arranged from Durham Station & Newcastle Airport. Durham 7 miles. Wine cellar. Dogs by arrangement. Children over 8 years welcome. **E-mail: ivesley@msn.com**	£29.00 to £33.50 VISA: M'CARD:	Y Y	Y

All the establishments mentioned in this guide are members of
The Worldwide Bed & Breakfast Association

When booking your accommodation please mention
The Best Bed & Breakfast

Oxfordshire

Oxfordshire
(Thames & Chilterns)

Oxfordshire is a county rich in history & delightful countryside. It has prehistoric sites, early Norman churches, 15th century coaching inns, Regency residences, distinctive cottages of black & white chalk flints & lovely Oxford, the city of dreaming spires.

The countryside ranges from lush meadows with willow-edged river banks scattered with small villages of thatched cottages, to the hills of the Oxfordshire Cotswolds in the west, the wooded Chilterns in the east & the distinctive ridge of the Berkshire Downs in the south. "Old Father Thames" meanders gently across the county to Henley, home of the famous regatta.

The ancient track known as the Great Ridgeway runs across the shire, & a walk along its length reveals barrows, hill forts & stone circles. The 2,000 year old Uffington Horse cut into the chalk of the hillside below an ancient hill fort site, is some 360 feet in length & 160 feet high.

The Romans built villas in the county & the remains of one, including a magnificent mosaic can be seen at North Leigh. In later centuries lovely houses were built. Minster Lovell stands beside the Windrush; Rousham house with its William Kent gardens is situated near Steeple Aston & beside the Thames lies Elizabethan Mapledurham House with its working watermill.

At Woodstock is Blenheim Palace, the largest private house in Britain & birthplace of Sir Winston Churchill. King Alfred's statue stands at Wantage, commemorating his birth there, & Banbury has its cross, made famous in the old nursery rhyme.

Oxford is a town of immense atmosphere with fine college buildings around quiet cloisters, & narrow cobbled lanes. It was during the 12th century that Oxford became a meeting place for scholars & grew into the first established centre of learning, outside the monasteries, in England.

The earliest colleges to be founded were University College, Balliol & Merton. Further colleges were added during the reign of the Tudors, as Oxford became a power in the kingdom. There are now 35 university colleges & many other outstanding historic buildings in the city . Christ Church Chapel is now the Cathedral of Oxford, a magnificent building with a deservedly famous choir.

St. Mary's Church.

Oxfordshire

Oxfordshire Gazeteer

Areas of Oustanding Natural Beauty
The North Wessex Downs. The Chiltern Hills. The Cotswolds.

Historic Houses & Castles

Ashdown House - Nr. Lambourn
17th century, built for Elizabeth of Bohemia, now contains portraits associated with her. Mansard roof has cupola with golden ball.

Blenheim Palace - Woodstock
Sir John Vanbrugh's classical masterpiece. Garden designed by Vanbrugh & Henry Wise. Further work done by Capability Brown who created the lake. Collection of pictures & tapestries.

Broughton Castle- Banbury.
14th century mansion with moat - interesting plaster work fine panelling & fire places

Chaselton House-Morton in Marsh
17th century,fine examples of plaster work & panelling.Still has original furniture & tapestries. topiary garden from1700.

Grey Court - Henly-on-Thames
16th century house containing 18th century plasterwork & furniture. Mediaeval ruins. Tudor donkey-wheel for raising water from well.

Mapledurham House - Mapledurham
16th century Elizabethan house. Oak staircase, private chapel, paintings, original moulded ceilings. Watermill nearby.

Milton Manor House - Nr. Abingdon
17th century house designed by Inigo Jones - Georgian wings, walled garden, pleasure grounds.

Rousham House - Steeple Ashton
17th century - contains portraits & miniatures.

University of Oxford Colleges

University college ------------------1249
Balliol--------------------------------1263
Merton--------------------------------1264
Hertford------------------------------1284
Oriel----------------------------------1326
New-----------------------------------1379
All Souls-----------------------------1438
Brasenose----------------------------1509
Christ Church----------------------1546
St. John's---------------------------1555
Pembroke--------------------------1624
Worcester--------------------------1714
Nuffield ----------------------------1937
St. Edmund Hall-------------------1270
Exeter------------------------------1314
The Queen's----------------------1340
Lincoln-----------------------------1427
Magdalen --------------------------1458
Corpus Christi --------------------1516
Trinity------------------------------1554
Jesus-------------------------------1571
Wadham----------------------------1610
Keble-------------------------------1868

Cathedrals & Churches

Abingdon (St. Helen)
14th-16th century perpendicular. Painted roof. Georgian stained & enamelled glass.

Burford (St. John the Baptist)
15th century. Sculptured table tombs in churchyard.

Chislehampton (St. Katherine)
18th century. Unspoilt interior of Georgian period. Bellcote.

Dorchester (St. Peter & St. Paul)
13th century knight in stone effigy. Jesse window.

East Hagbourne (St. Andrew)
14th -15th century. Early glass, wooden roofs, 18th century tombs.

North Moreton (All Saints)
13th century with splendid 14th century chantry chapel - tracery.

Oxford Cathedral
Smallest of our English cathedrals. Stone spire form 1230. Norman arcade has double arches, choir vault.

Ryecote (St. Michael & All Angels)
14th century benches & screen base. 17th century altar-piece & communion rails, old clear glass, good ceiling.

Stanton Harcourt (St. Michael)
Early English - old stone & marble floor. Early screen with painting, monuments of 17th -19th century.

Yarnton (St. Bartholomew)
13th century - late perpendicular additions. Jacobean screen. 15th century alabaster reredos.

Oxfordshire

Museums & Galleries

The Ashmolean Museum of Art & Archaeology - Oxford
British ,European ,Mediterranean, Egyptian & Near Eastern archaeology. Oil paintings of Italian, Dutch, Flemish, French & English schools. Old Master watercolours, prints, drawings, ceramics, silver, bronzes & sculptures. Chinese & Japanese porcelain, lacquer & painting, Tibetan, Islamic & Indian art.

Christ Church Picture Gallery - Oxford
Old Master drawings & paintings.

Museum of Modern Art - Oxford
Exhibitiors of contemporary art.

Museum of Oxford
Many exhibits depicting the history of Oxford & its University.

The Rotunda - Oxford
Privately owned collection of dolls' houses 1700-1900, with contents such as furniture, china, silver, dolls, etc.

Oxford University Museum
Entomological, zoological, geological & mineralogical collections.

Pendon Museum of Miniature Landscape & Transport - Abingdon.
Showing in miniature the countryside & its means of transport in the thirties, with trains & thatched village. Railway relics.

Town Museum - Abingdon
17th century building exhibiting fossil, archaeological items & collection of charters & documents.

Tolsey Museum - Burford
Seals, maces, charters & bygones - replica of Regency room with period furnishings & clothing.

Historic Monuments

Uffington Castle & White Horse - Uffington
White horse cut into the chalk - iron age hill fort.

Rollright Stones - Nr. Chipping Norton
77 stones placed in circle - an isolated King's stone & nearby an ancient burial chamber.

Minster Lovell House - Minster Lovell
15th century mediaeval house - ruins.

Deddington Castle - Deddington

Other things to see & do

Didcot railway centre -a large collection of locomotives etc., from Brunel's Great Western Railway.

Filkins -a working wool mill where rugs & garments are woven in traditional way.

Blenheim Palace. Woodstock.

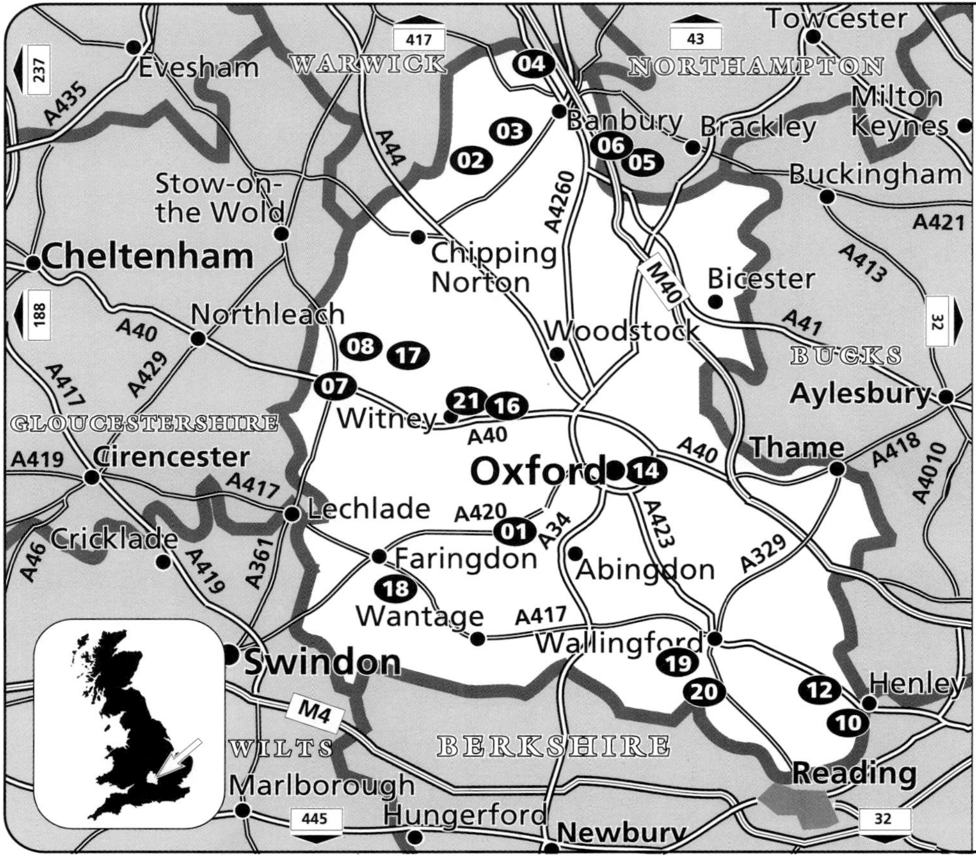

OXFORDSHIRE
Map reference

01 Lloyd
02 Hitching
03 Canning
04 Prickett
05 Grove-White
06 Allday
07 Hicks
08 Jones
10 Talfourd-Cook
12 Fulford-Dobson
14 Price

14 Tompkins
14 Trafford
14 Anderson
14 Edwards
16 Crofts
17 Hill
18 Wadsworth
19 Alexander
20 Watsham
21 Simpson

Fallowfields.   Abingdon.

	rate £ from - to per person	children taken	evening meals	animals taken
Peta Lloyd **Fallowfields** **Faringdon Road** **Kingston Bagpuize with** **Southmoor** **Abingdon OX13 5BH** Tel: (01865) 820416 Fax 01865 821275 Open: ALL YEAR Map Ref No. 01 Nearest Road: A.420 Fallowfields, the former home of Begum Aga Khan, is a delightful 300-year-old Gothic style manor house. Beautifully furnished, with the emphasis on gracious elegance. The 2 lounges are spacious & comfortable. The pleasant bedrooms have pretty linens, tea/coffee, hairdryer, radio, 'phone & valet press. The elegant dining room befits the super cuisine served. Guests are also encouraged to use the tennis court, croquet lawn & swimming pool. Children over 10 years. **E-mail: STAY@FALLOWFIELDS.COM**	£64.00 to £70.00 (non-smoking) *see PHOTO over* *p. 308* VISA: M'CARD: AMEX:	Y	Y	Y
Mrs Judith Hitching **Gowers Close** **Main Street** **Sibford Gower** **Banbury OX15 5RW** Tel: (01295) 780348 Open: ALL YEAR (Excl. Xmas) Map Ref No. 02 Nearest Road: B.4035 Set in a quiet village, within easy reach of Stratford-upon-Avon, the Cotswolds & Oxford, this beautiful beamed & thatched village house was built around 1600, & is the comfortable home of Judith Hitching - gardener, writer & gourmet cook. There are 2 attractive bedrooms with en-suite/private facilities. Expect to enjoy a relaxed atmosphere, good conversation, log fires, music & laughter. Children over 10. Single supplement.	£32.00 to £32.00	Y	Y	N
Patti Ritter & Mike Canning **La Madonette Country** **Guest House** **North Newington** **Banbury** **OX15 6AA** Tel: (01295) 730212 Fax 01295 730363 Open: ALL YEAR Map Ref No. 03 Nearest Road: A.4260 A peacefully situated 17th-century millhouse set in rural surroundings, where Patti & Michael offer a warm welcome to their guests. The 5 spacious double en-suite bedrooms are comfortably furnished with full facilities & are attractively decorated. Well located for the Cotswolds, Stratford-upon-Avon, Oxford & Blenheim. Good local pubs & restaurants offering evening meals nearby. An attractive lounge, gardens & swimming pool for guests' use. Licensed. **E-mail: lamadonett@aol.com**	£28.00 to £35.00 VISA: M'CARD:	Y	N	N
Alan & Yvonne Prickett **Sorbrook House Farm** **Horley** **Banbury** **OX15 6BL** Tel: (01295) 738121 Open: ALL YEAR Map Ref No. 04 Nearest Road: B.4100, M.40 Located in a delightful Oxfordshire village on the edge of the Cotswolds & close to Oxford, Blenheim Palace, Stratford-upon-Avon & Warwick Castle. This attractive stone built farmhouse with inglenook log fires & exposed beams offers charming bedrooms, 1 twin en-suite & 1 double en-suite, each with radio, T.V. & tea/coffee-making facilities. Drawing room & dining room for guests use only. Friendly hosts who offer tea & homemade cakes on arrival. Large gardens. Children over 7.	£27.00 to £35.00	Y	N	N
Col. & Mrs Grove-White **Home Farmhouse** **Charlton** **Banbury** **OX17 3DR** Tel: (01295) 811683 Fax 01295 811683 Open: ALL YEAR Map Ref No. 05 Nearest Road: A.43 This charming, listed stone house dating from 1637, with its attractive, colourful, paved courtyard, provides an excellent base for visiting Oxford, Blenheim, Stratford-upon-Avon, Warwick & the beautiful Cotswold villages. Mrs Grove-White has used her expertise as a professional interior designer to ensure that the 3 double/twin-bedded rooms, with en-suite/private bathroom & T.V., are comfortable & elegantly furnished. Evening meals by arrangement only. Children over 12 years.	£27.00 to £29.00 (non-smoking) *see PHOTO over* *p. 310* VISA: M'CARD:	Y	Y	N

Home Farmhouse. Charlton.

College Farmhouse. King Sutton.

Holmwood. Binfield Heath.

Oxfordshire

	Description	rate £ from - to per person	children taken	evening meals	animals taken
Stephen & Sara Allday **College Farmhouse** **Kings Sutton** **Banbury** **OX17 3PS** **Tel: (01295) 811473** **Fax 01295 812505** **Open: ALL YEAR** **Map Ref No. 06**	Nearest Road: A.43, M.40 Fine period farmhouse, with lovely views, set in its own secluded grounds, which include a lake, tennis court & organic vegetable garden. Ideally located for visits to Oxford, Warwick, Stratford-upon-Avon & the Cotswolds. Excellent home-produced food - special diets catered for. Stephen & Sara have considerable local knowledge. They enjoy gardening, bridge & racing. You will be sure of a very comfortable & peaceful stay. Evening meals by arrangement. **E-mail: SAllday@compuserve.com**	£26.00 to £28.00 *see PHOTO over* *p. 311*	Y	Y	N
Judith Hicks **Glenthorne House** **174 The Hill** **Burford** **OX18 4QY** **Tel: (01993) 822418** **Open: ALL YEAR** **Map Ref No. 07**	Nearest Road: A.40 Situated in the heart of Burford, one of the Cotswolds' most picturesque & historic towns, Glenthorne House is a Grade II listed, 14-century town house with many medieval features, centrally heated throughout & beautifully furnished with antiques. The Hicks family welcome guests to their home & are happy to recommend the many restaurants within a few minutes' walk. Parking. The garden is available for guests' use.	£25.00 to £30.00	N	N	N
Mrs Wendy Jones **Hillborough House** **The Green, Shipton Road** **Milton-under-Wychwood** **Chipping Norton** **OX7 6JH** **Tel: (01993) 830501** **Fax 01993 832005** **Open: ALL YEAR (Excl. Xmas)** **Map Ref No. 08**	Nearest Road: A.361 An elegant Victorian house facing the village green in this delightful Cotswold village. The 4 bedrooms are en-suite, spacious, warm & cheerful, each with its own individual charm, & all enjoy beautiful views overlooking the village green. Breakfast is served in the conservatory leading out onto the patio & gardens. Comfortable lounge with books & games. 2 well-known restaurants in the next village, with the local village pub serving a variety of bar meals just a stroll away. Self-catering Wystaria Cottage is also available.	£25.00 to £25.00 VISA: M'CARD:	Y	N	N
Mr & Mrs A. L. Talfourd-Cook **Holmwood** **Shiplake Row** **Binfield Heath** **Henley RG9 4DP** **Tel: (0118) 9478747** **Fax 0118 9478637** **Open: ALL YEAR (Excl. Xmas)** **Map Ref No. 10**	Nearest Road: A.4155 Holmwood is a large elegant Georgian country house, Grade II listed, furnished with antique, period furniture. There is a galleried hall, coved mahogany doors & marble fireplaces (wood fires in winter). All bedrooms are spacious & have en-suite facilities. The beautiful gardens extend to 3 1/2 acres & have extensive views over the Thames Valley. A good base for London & the South East. Heathrow Airport 30 mins, Reading 4 miles, Henley 2 1/2 miles. Children over 12 years.	£30.00 to £40.00 *see PHOTO over* *p. 312* VISA: M'CARD:	N	N	N
Mrs Sue Fulford-Dobson **Shepherds** **Shepherds Green** **Rotherfield Greys** **Henley-on-Thames** **RG9 4QL** **Tel: (01491) 628413** **Fax 01491 628413** **Open: ALL YEAR (Excl. Xmas)** **Map Ref No. 12**	Nearest Road: A.4130 A warm & welcoming country home (part-18th-century), covered in roses, wisteria, clematis & jasmine. Shepherds stands on a peaceful village green on its own 8-acre grounds. The 4 pretty bedrooms all have en-suite or private facilities, T.V. & tea/coffee trays. Delightful drawing room for guests with antiques & wood fire. An ideal centre from which to explore the Thames Valley, Chilterns, Windsor & Oxford. Heathrow 35 mins, Gatwick 1 1/4 hrs. Children over 12 welcome. Many pubs & restaurants within easy reach.	£21.00 to £34.00 *see PHOTO over* *p. 314* VISA: M'CARD:	Y	N	N

Shepherds. Rotherfield Greys.

Oxfordshire

Mr & Mrs L. S. Price **Arden Lodge** **34 Sunderland Avenue** **Off Woodstock Road** **Oxford OX2 8DX** **Tel: (01865) 552076** **Tel: (01865) 512265** **Open: ALL YEAR** **Map Ref No. 14**	Nearest Road: A.40 A modern detached house, set in a tree-lined avenue, in one of Oxford's most select areas. Offering 3 attractively furnished bedrooms, with private facilities, colour T.V. & beverage tray. An excellent base for touring: within easy reach of London, the Cotswolds, Stratford & Warwick. Convenient for the city centre, parks, river, meadows, golf course & country inns, including the world-famous 'Trout Inn'. Children over 3.	£23.00 to £25.00	Y	N	N
Sally & Tony Tompkins **Gables Guest House** **6 Cumnor Hill** **Oxford** **OX2 9HA** **Tel: (01865) 862153** **Fax 01865 864054** **Open: ALL YEAR (Excl.** **Xmas & New Years Eve)** **Map Ref No. 14**	Nearest Road: A.34 Gables is an excellent award-winning guest house. The property is detached with a conservatory lounge overlooking the beautiful garden. Ideally situated close to the city centre, bus & railway stations. Easy access to A.34 & equally for the Cotswolds & London. A large private car park. The 6 high-quality rooms are fully equipped with satellite T.V., 'phones, hairdryer, tea/coffee facilities & clock/radio. Full range of English, Continental & vegetarian breakfasts available. **E-mail: stay@gables-oxford.co.uk**	£22.00 to £25.00 VISA: M'CARD:	Y	N	N
Mr & Mrs Trafford **Tilbury Lodge Private Hotel** **5 Tilbury Lane** **Eynsham Rd, Botley** **Oxford OX2 9NB** **Tel: (01865) 862138** **Fax 01865 863700** **Open: ALL YEAR** **Map Ref No. 14**	Nearest Road: A.420 Tilbury Lodge is a pleasant, family-run private hotel situated in a quiet residential area. Offering 9 en-suite bedrooms with radio, T.V., 'phone, hairdryer & tea/coffee-making facilities. 1 4-poster & 2 ground-floor rooms. A pleasant jacuzzi bath is also available. Ample parking. Residents' lounge & garden in which guests may choose to relax. Located 2 miles west of the city centre, with good pubs & restaurants a few minutes' walk away. Good bus service.	£31.00 to £35.00 VISA: M'CARD:	Y	N	N
Dr. B. & Mrs A. C. Anderson **Sandfield Guest House** **19 London Road** **Headington** **Oxford** **OX3 7RE** **Tel: (01865) 762406** **Fax 01865 762406** **Open: ALL YEAR (Excl. Xmas)** **Map Ref No. 14**	Nearest Road: A.40 A family-run guest house offering a high standard of comfort to guests preferring personal service & attention. Quiet & attractive accommodation which is tastefully decorated. The well-proportioned rooms are all en-suite or have a private bathroom, T.V., hospitality tray & hairdryer. Guest lounge & gardens. Convenient for city-centre buses. Easy walking distance to Radcliffe Hospital Complex & Oxford Brookes University. On direct coach routes to London and Heathrow & Gatwick Airports. Ample on-site parking. Children over 6.	£28.00 to £32.00 VISA: M'CARD: AMEX:	Y	N	N
Mrs D. Edwards **Highfield House** **91 Rose Hill** **Oxford OX4 4HT** **Tel: (01865) 774083** **Fax 01865 774083** **Open: ALL YEAR** **Map Ref No. 14**	Nearest Road: A.4158 A pleasing & friendly house, with good access to the city centre & ring road. Accommodation is in 7 spacious bedrooms, all attractively furnished & with matching decor. 5 with en-suite bathroom. All have colour T.V. & tea/coffee-making facilities. A short walk brings you to the old attractive village of Iffley. An excellent base for exploring the historic delights of Oxford.	£20.00 to £40.00 VISA: M'CARD:	Y	Y	N

Shipton Grange House. Shipton–under–Wychwood.

Oxfordshire

		rate £ from - to per person	children taken	evening meals	animals taken
Jean A. Crofts **Crofters Guest House** **29 Oxford Hill** **Witney** **Oxford OX8 6JU** **Tel: (01993) 778165** **Fax 01993 778165** **Open: ALL YEAR** **Map Ref No. 16**	Nearest Road: A.40 Situated in a lively market town, 10 miles from Oxford, on the edge of the Cotswolds, Blenheim Palace & Burford, & within easy reach of Stratford. Guests are accommodated in comfortable family, double & twin rooms, all with excellent facilities. En-suite & ground-floor available. Your hosts Jean & Peter will make your stay a memorable experience. Arrive as a guest, leave as a friend. **E-mail: crofters.ghouse@virgin.net**	£20.00 to £30.00	Y	N	N
Mrs Veronica Hill **Shipton Grange House** **Shipton-under-Wychwood** **OX7 6DG** **Tel: (01993) 831298** **Fax 01993 832082** **Open: ALL YEAR (Excl. Xmas)** **Map Ref No. 17**	Nearest Road: A.361 A unique conversion of a Georgian coach house & stabling situated in the former grounds of Shipton Court. Secluded in its own walled garden, & approached by a gated archway. There are 3 elegantly furnished guest rooms, each with an en-suite/private bathroom, colour T.V. & beverage facilities. Delicious breakfasts served in the attractive dining room. The friendly hosts are animal lovers & have a number of pet dogs. Shipton Grange is a delightful house, & ideal for visiting Oxford, Blenheim, etc. Children over 12.	£26.00 to £33.00 *see PHOTO over p. 316*	Y	N	N
Mrs Carol Wadsworth **The Craven** **Fernham Road** **Uffington** **SN7 7RD** **Tel: (01367) 820449** **Open: ALL YEAR** **Map Ref No. 18**	Nearest Road: A.420 An extremely attractive 17th-century thatched farmhouse with exposed beams & open log-burning fire. Accommodation is very comfortable, & comprises 5 bedrooms, 1 with 4-poster bed & private bathroom. Good home cooking with fresh local produce. The Craven offers a friendly, relaxed atmosphere. The perfect base for touring this fascinating area. **E-mail: carol.wadsworth@cw.com.net**	£21.00 to £35.00 *see PHOTO over p. 318* VISA: M'CARD: AMEX:	Y	Y	N
Mrs Joanna Alexander **The Well Cottage** **Caps Lane** **Cholsey** **Wallingford** **OX10 9HQ** **Tel: (01491) 651959** **Mobile 07887 958920** **Open: ALL YEAR** **Map Ref No. 19**	Nearest Road: A.329 The Well Cottage is situated in a pretty garden, close to the River Thames, the historic town of Wallingford, the Berkshire Downs & the Ridgway. The cottage has been extended & now offers a secluded garden flat with 2 double/twin-bedded rooms, each with an en-suite bathroom, T.V. & tea/coffee-making facilities. Each room has its own private entrance. A charming home for a relaxing break. Within easy reach of Oxford & Henley-on-Thames.	£15.00 to £25.00	Y	N	Y
Maria Watsham **White House** **Moulsford On Thames** **Wallingford** **OX10 9JD** **Tel: (01491) 651397** **Fax 01491 652560** **Open: ALL YEAR (Excl. Xmas)** **Map Ref No. 20**	Nearest Road: A.339 White House is an attractive, detached family home in the picturesque Thameside village of Moulsford on the edge of the Berkshire Downs, close to the Ridgeway & Thames Paths. The accommodation is at ground-floor level with its own separate front door, making access easy for disabled guests. Each room is very comfortable. There is a large garden with croquet lawn, which guests are welcome to enjoy. A delightful home.	£22.50 to £30.00	Y	N	N

The Craven.   Uffington.

Oxfordshire

		rate £ from - to per person	evening meals children taken	animals taken	

		rate £ from - to per person	children taken	evening meals	animals taken
Liz & John Simpson **Field View** **Wood Green** **Witney** **OX8 6DE** **Tel: (01993) 705485** **Mobile 0468 614347** **Open:** ALL YEAR (Excl. Xmas) **Map Ref No. 21**	Nearest Road: A.40, A.4095 An attractive Cotswold stone house set in 2 acres, situated on picturesque Wood Green, midway between Oxford University & the Cotswolds. It is an ideal centre for touring, yet only 8 mins' walk from the centre of this lively Oxfordshire market town. A peaceful setting & a warm, friendly atmosphere await you. Accommodation is in 3 comfortable en-suite rooms with modern amenities & tea/coffee-making facilities. **E-mail: Jsimpson@netcomuk.co.uk**	£22.00 to £28.00	N	N	N

All the establishments mentioned in this guide are members of
The Worldwide Bed & Breakfast Association

When booking your accommodation please mention
The Best Bed & Breakfast

Shropshire

Shropshire
(Heart of England)

Shropshire is a borderland with a very turbulent history. Physically it straddles highlands & lowlands with border mountains to the west, glacial plains, upland, moorlands & fertile valleys & the River Severn cutting through. It has been quarrelled & fought over by rulers & kings from earliest times. The English, the Romans & the Welsh all wanted to hold Shropshire because of its unique situation. The ruined castles & fortifications dotted across the county are all reminders of its troubled life. The most impressive of these defences is Offa's Dyke, an enormous undertaking intended to be a permanent frontier between England & Wales.

Shropshire has great natural beauty, countryside where little has changed with the years. Wenlock Edgè & Clun Forest, Carding Mill Valley, the Long Mynd, Caer Caradoc, Stiperstones & the trail along Offa's Dyke itself, are lovely walking areas with magnificent scenery.

Shrewsbury was & is a virtual island, almost completely encircled by the Severn River. The castle was built at the only gap, sealing off the town. In this way all comings & goings were strictly controlled. In the 18th century two bridges, the English bridge & the Welsh bridge, were built to carry the increasing traffic to the town but Shrewsbury still remains England's finest Tudor city.

Massive Ludlow Castle was a Royal residence, home of Kings & Queens through the ages, whilst the town is also noted for its Georgian houses.

As order came out of chaos, the county settled to improving itself & became the cradle of the Industrial Revolution. Here Abraham Darby discovered how to use coke (from the locally mined coal) to smelt iron. There was more iron produced here in the 18th century than in any other county. A variety of great industries sprang up as the county's wealth & ingenuity increased. In 1781 the world's first iron bridge opened to traffic.

There are many fine gardens in the county. At Hodnet Hall near Market Drayton, the grounds cover 60 acres & the landscaping includes lakes & pools, trees, shrubs & flowers in profusion. Weston Park has 1,000 acres of parkland, woodland gardens & lakes landscaped by Capability Brown.

The house is Restoration period & has a splendid collection of pictures, furniture, china & tapestries.

Shrewsbury hosts an annual poetry festival & one of England's best flower shows whilst a Festival of Art, Music & Drama is held each year in Ludlow with Shakespeare performed against the castle ruins.

Coalbrookedale Museum.

Shropshire

Shropshire Gazeteer

Areas of Outstanding Natural Beauty
The Shropshire Hills.

Historic Houses & Castles

Stokesay Castle - Craven Arms
13th century fortified manor house. Still occupied - wonderful setting - extremely well preserved. Fine timbered gatehouse.
Weston Park - Nr. Shifnal
17th century - fine example of Restoration period - landscaping by Capability Brown. Superb collection of pictures.
Shrewsbury Castle - Shrewsbury
Built in Norman era - interior decorations - painted boudoir.
Benthall Hall - Much Wenlock
16th century. Stone House - mullioned windows. Fine wooden staircase - splendid plaster ceilings.
Shipton Hall - Much Wenlock
Elizabethan. Manor House - walled garden - mediaeval dovecote.
Upton Cressett Hall - Bridgnorth
Elizabethan. Manor House & Gatehouse. Excellent plaster work. . 14th century great hall.

Cathedrals & Churches

Ludlow (St. Lawrence)
14th century nave & transepts. 15th century pinnacled tower. Restored extensively in 19th century. Carved choir stalls, perpendicular chancel - original glass. Monuments.
Shrewsbury (St. Mary)
14th, 15th, 16th century glass. Norman origins.
Stottesdon (St. Mary)
12th century carvings.Norman font. Fine decorations with columns & tracery.
Lydbury North (St. Michael)
14th century transept, 15th century nave roof, 17th century box pews and altar rails. Norman font.
Longor (St. Mary the Virgin)
13th century having an outer staircase to West gallery.
Cheswardine (St. Swithun)
13th century chapel - largely early English. 19th century glass and old brasses. Fine sculpture.

Tong (St. Mary the Virgin with St. Bartholomew)
15th century. Golden chapel of 1515, stencilled walls, remains of paintings on screens, gilt fan vaulted ceiling. Effigies, fine monuments

Museums & Galleries

Clive House - Shrewsbury
Fine Georgian House - collection of Shropshire ceramics. Regimental museum of 1st Queen's Dragoon Guards.
Rowley's House Museum - Shrewsbury
Roman material from Viroconium and prehistoric collection.
Coleham Pumping Station - Old Coleham
Preserved beam engines
Acton Scott Working Farm Museum - Nr. Church Stretton
Site showing agricultural practice before the advent of mechanization.
Ironbridge Gorge Museum - Telford
Series of industrial sites in the Severn Gorge.
CoalBrookdale Museum & Furnace Site
Showing Abraham Darby's blast furnace history. Ironbridge information centre is next to the world's first iron bridge.
Mortimer Forest Museum - Nr. Ludlow
Forest industries of today and yesterday. Ecology of the forest.
Whitehouse Museum of Buildings & Country life - Aston Munslow
4 houses together in one, drawing from every century 13th to 18th, together with utensils and implements of the time.
The Buttercross Museum - Ludlow
Geology, natural & local history of area.
Reader's House-Ludlow
Splendid example of a 16th century town house. 3 storied porch.
Much Wenlock Museum.-Much Wenlock
Geology, natural & local history.
Clun Town Museum - Clun
Pre-history earthworks, rights of way, commons & photographs.

Historic Monuments

Acton Burnell Castle - Shrewsbury
13th century fortified manor house - ruins only.

Shropshire

Boscobel House - Shifnal
17th century house.
Bear Steps - Shrewsbury
Half timbered buildings. Mediaeval.
Abbot's House - Shrewsbury
15th century half-timbered.
Buildwas Abbey - Nr. Telford
12th century - Savignac Abbey - ruins.
The church is nearly complete with 14
Norman arches.
Haughmond Abbey - Shrewsbury
12th century - remains of house of
Augustinian canons.
Wenlock Priory - Much Wenlock
13th century abbey - ruins.
Roman Town - Wroxeter
2nd century - remains of town of
Viroconium including public baths and
colonnade.
Moreton Corbet Castle - Moreton Corbet
13th century keep, Elizabethan features -

gatehouse altered 1519.
Lilleshall Abbey
12th century - completed 13th century,
West front has notable doorway.
Bridgnorth Castle - Bridgnorth
Ruins of Norman castle whose angle of
incline is greater than Pisa.
Whiteladies Priory - Boscobel
12th century cruciform church - ruins.
Old Oswestry - Oswestry
Iron age hill fort covering 68 acres; five
ramparts and having an elaborate western
portal.

Other things to see & do

Ludlow Festival of Art and Drama -
annual event
Shrewsbury Flower Show - every August
Severn Valley Railway - the longest full
guage steam railway in the country

Kings Head Inn. Shrewsbury.

SHROPSHIRE

Map reference

Upper Buckton Farm. Leintwardine.

Shropshire

		rate £ from - to per person	children taken	evening meals	animals taken
Mary A. Rowlands **Middleton Lodge** **Middleton Priors** **Bridgnorth** **WV16 6UR** **Tel: (01746) 712228** **Open: ALL YEAR (Excl. Xmas)** **Map Ref No. 02**	Nearest Road: B.4268 Middleton Lodge is set in 20 acres of beautiful rural Shropshire countryside overlooking Brown Clee Hill. Accommodation is in 3 extremely attractive bedrooms, each with a private bathroom, 1 with a 4-poster. There are many places of interest within easy reach of Middleton: the scenic Severn Valley Railway, Ironbridge, Stokesay Castle, the breathtaking beauty of the Long Mynd & the picturesque Carding Mill Valley.	£25.00 to £30.00 🚭	N	N	N
Hayden & Yvonne Lloyd **Upper Buckton** **Leintwardine** **Craven Arms** **SY7 0JU** **Tel: (01547) 540634** **Open: ALL YEAR** **Map Ref No. 05**	Nearest Road: A.4113, A.4110 Set amidst the beautiful unspoilt Teme Valley, a delightful riverside farm situated in the secluded hamlet of Buckton. The Georgian house is surrounded by an attractive garden, millstream & a 12th-century motte. The well-appointed rooms with many antiques & paintings make this a lovely home. 3 elegant bedrooms with private bathrooms & tea/coffee. Cordon bleu dinners. Guests' own wine welcome. In the centre of the Welsh Marches with much of scenic & historic interest. Ludlow, Offa's Dyke, N.T. properties & gardens.	£28.00 to £30.00 🚭 *see PHOTO over* *p. 324*	Y	Y	N
Mrs Anne Prytz **Knock Hundred Cottage** **Abcott** **Clungunford** **Craven Arms** **SY7 0PX** **Tel: (01588) 660594** **Fax 01588 660594** **Open: ALL YEAR** **Map Ref No. 07**	Nearest Road: A.49 Knock Hundred Cottage is believed to originate from the 16th century & enjoys an open aspect with extensive views. 1 double bedroom with a private bathroom & 1 en-suite twin-bedded room. Each room is comfortably furnished & has a T.V.. Early morning tea/coffee is served in your room & breakfast is provided in the dining room. Evening meals by arrangement. Places of interest include Ludlow, the Long Mynd, Offa's Dyke, the beautiful Corve Dale & various National Trust/English Heritage properties & gardens. Children over 14.	£22.50 to £25.00 🚭	Y	Y	N
Mrs Pauline Hannigan **The Severn Trow** **Church Road** **Jackfield** **Ironbridge** **TF8 7ND** **Tel: (01952) 883551** **Open: JAN - OCT** **Map Ref No. 08**	Nearest Road: A.442 The Severn Trow is a wonderful place which has seen the hand of hospitality extended by successive occupants for many centuries. It stands on the riverbank where originally travellers would berth their trows before retiring to recuperate. It has been renovated, & yet it has retained many original features which enhance its character, such as an inglenook & a Jackfield mosaic tile floor. Rooms are delightful: each is en-suite (1 ground-floor) & well-appointed. A choice of eating houses nearby.	£21.00 to £30.00 🚭	N	N	N
Mrs R. C. Woodward **Cleeton Court** **Cleeton St. Mary** **Kidderminster DY14 0QZ** **Tel/Fax: (01584) 823379** **Open: ALL YEAR (Excl.** **Xmas & New Year)** **Map Ref No. 09**	Nearest Road: A.49 Cleeton Court is an attractive old farmhouse part-dating from the 14th century, completely renovated in 1997 it is now a comfortable & attractive home. The 2 bedrooms are en-suite, 1 with 4-poster & a huge bathroom. Breakfast is served in a sunny oak-beamed dining room & a beautiful drawing room with log fire is available for guests. Ludlow with its Michelin starred restaurants is 8 miles away. Children over 5.	£27.50 to £32.50	Y	N	N

The Moor Hall. Ludlow.

Shropshire

	rate £ from - to per person	children taken	evening meals	animals taken

Patricia & Philip Ross **Number Twenty Eight** **28 Lower Broad Street** **Ludlow** **SY8 1PQ** **Tel: (01584) 876996** **Fax 01584 876860** **Open: ALL YEAR** **Map Ref No. 10**	Nearest Road: A.49 A warm welcome awaits you in this guest house which now comprises 3 period houses, in this historic street. Snug sitting rooms, book-lined walls, pictures & open fires make for a relaxing atmosphere. Bedrooms are en-suite & individually furnished. Tea/coffee & T.V.. Many excellent eating houses, all within walking distance. Riverside & hill walks, castles & many book & antique shops to explore in this lovely of Tudor & Georgian market town, near the Welsh border. **E-mail: ross.no28@btinternet.com**	£32.50 to £40.00 VISA: M'CARD:	Y	N	Y
Judith Sanders **Middleton Court** **Middleton** **Ludlow** **SY8 2DZ** **Tel: (01584) 872842** **Open: APR - OCT** **Map Ref No. 11**	Nearest Road: A.49 Middleton Court is a fine country house on a working farm, only 2 1/2 miles from Ludlow. 1 en-suite bedroom, with a double & single bed, & 1 double & 1 twin-bedded room each with a private bathroom. All are comfortably furnished with antiques, & have views over the terraced gardens & woods beyond. Sitting room with T.V. & log fires. Super breakfasts & traditional 4-course evening meals. Ideal for exploring Shropshire & the Welsh border country. Children over 8.	£22.00 to £30.00	Y	Y	N
Mrs B. M. Chivers **The Moor Hall** **Clee Downton** **Ludlow** **SY8 3EG** **Tel: (01584) 823209** **Fax 01584 823387** **Open: ALL YEAR** **Map Ref No. 11**	Nearest Road: A.4117 The atmosphere at The Moor Hall is relaxed & friendly; guests often comment that it's like being at a country house party with friends. The house was built by Lord Boyne in 1789 & is a lovely example of the Georgian Palladian style. The gardens extend to 5 acres & look out over miles of unspoilt countryside. Great cooking, a licensed bar & the opportunity to fish in the small lake complete the experience. **E-mail: info@moorhall.co.uk**	£23.00 to £32.00 *see PHOTO over* *p. 326*	Y	Y	Y
Mrs Pauline Williamson **Mickley House** **Faulsgreen** **Tern Hill** **Market Drayton TF9 3QW** **Tel: (01630) 638505** **Fax 01630 638505** **Open: ALL YEAR (Excl. Xmas)** **Map Ref No. 13**	Nearest Road: A.41, A.53 When visiting Ironbridge, Shrewsbury or Chester, your hosts offer peace, quiet & comfort in their tastefully restored farmhouse, retaining many internal Victorian features. The tranquillity of the house spills out into landscaped gardens. Relax or meander through rose-scented pergolas to pools & a trickling waterfall. Restaurants/pubs nearby. En-suite bedrooms of different style/decor, with all facilities. 1 bedroom with authentic Louis XV king-size bed. Also, ground-floor room.	£22.00 to £32.00	N	N	N
Miles & Audrey Hunter **Pen-Y-Dyffryn Country** **Hotel** **Rhydycroesau** **Oswestry** **SY10 7JD** **Tel: (01691) 653700** **Fax 01691 653700** **Open: ALL YEAR** **Map Ref No. 14**	Nearest Road: A.5 Peace, comfort & a warm welcome await you in this former Georgian rectory, splendidly situated in the Shropshire/Welsh hills just 3 miles west of Oswestry. An ideal base for exploring Chester, Shrewsbury & North Wales. Delicious home-cooked evening meals using English & Welsh local produce. Fully licensed. Log fires in the lounge & restaurant. All bedrooms beautifully furnished, en-suite, colour T.V.. 5 acres of grounds. 1 ground-floor bedroom available. **E-mail: penydyffryn@go2.co.uk**	£34.00 to £47.00 *see PHOTO over* *p. 328* VISA: M'CARD: AMEX:	Y	Y	Y

Pen–Y–Dyffryn Hall. Rhydycroesau.

Shropshire

		rate £ from - to per person	children taken	evening meals	animals taken
Mrs Mair Harris **Tudor House** **2 Fish Street** **Shrewsbury** **SY1 1UR** **Tel: (01743) 351735** **Open: ALL YEAR** **Map Ref No. 16**	Nearest Road: A.5 This Grade II listed building is centrally situated in a quiet medieval street in picturesque & historic Shrewsbury (Brother Cadfael country). Dating from 1450, it has a wealth of oak beams, & has been tastefully redecorated & refurbished. Some rooms have en-suite facilities; all have washbasins, colour T.V. & central heating. Special diets available in non-smoking dining room. Drinks are served in residents' licensed lounge.	£21.00 to £25.00	N	N	N
Mrs C. H. Yates-Roberts **Upper Brompton Farm** **Cross Houses** **Shrewsbury** **SY5 6LE** **Tel: (01743) 761629** **Fax 01743 761679** **Open: ALL YEAR** **Map Ref No. 17**	Nearest Road: A.458 This delightful Georgian farmhouse with extensive lawns & gardens is a haven of peace, comfort & elegance. 5 mins' from Shrewsbury & 15 mins' from Ironbridge & ideal for exploring Houseman's Shropshire. The en-suite bedrooms are furnished with either 4-poster or antique brass or mahogany beds. T.V.'s & hospitality trays. The drawing-room is elegantly furnished with an open fire. Yor hosts will ensure that your experience is one of sensuous enjoyment, whether it be a delicious breakfast, or a feast of traditional British fayre. **E-mail: upper-brompton.farm@dial.pipex.com**	£32.50 to £££ *see PHOTO over* *p. 330* VISA: M'CARD: AMEX:	Y	Y	N
Mike & Gill Mitchell **The White House** **Hanwood** **Shrewsbury** **SY5 8LP** **Tel: (01743) 860414** **Fax 01743 860414** **Open: ALL YEAR** **Map Ref No. 18**	Nearest Road: A.488, A.5 A lovely, 16th-century, black-and-white, half-timbered guest house with nearly 2 acres of gardens & river, 3 miles south-west of medieval Shrewsbury. Ironbridge, Mid-Wales & the Long Mynd within a 30 mins' drive. 6 bedrooms, some en-suite, each with tea/coffee etc. 2 sitting rooms, 1 with T.V.. Car parking. The dining room offers a fresh, varied menu supplemented by vegetables and herbs from the garden, and the house hens provide your breakfast eggs! Children over 12. **E-mail: mgm@whitehousehanwood.freeserve.co.uk**	£25.00 to £30.00	Y	Y	N
Charles & Jane Bebbington **Dearnford Hall** **Tilstock Road** **Whitchurch** **SY13 3JJ** **Tel: (01948) 662319** **Fax 01948 666670** **Open: ALL YEAR (Excl. Xmas)** **Map Ref No. 21**	Nearest Road: A.41, A.49 'Country House hospitality at its best' at this magnificent family home. Cosy sofas, log fires, music & memorable breakfasts in a relaxed & friendly atmosphere. Beautiful en-suite bedrooms & drawing room overlook sweeping lawns & walled garden. Paradise for garden enthusiasts, N.T. visitors, antique browsers, golfers & lovers of country pursuits, with fly-fishing on the Bebbingtons' own trout lake. Business visitors welcome. Strategically placed for Chester, Shrewsbury, the Potteries & the Welsh Borders.	£40.00 to £50.00	N	N	Y

Visit our website at:
http://www.bestbandb.co.uk

Upper Brompton Farm. Cross Houses.

Somerset, Bath & Bristol

Somerset
(West Country)

Fabulous legends, ancient customs, charming villages, beautiful churches, breathtaking scenery & a glorious cathedral, Somerset has them all, along with a distinctively rich local dialect. The essence of Somerset lies in its history & myth & particularly in the unfolding of the Arthurian tale.

Legend grows from the bringing of the Holy Grail to Glastonbury by Joseph of Arimathea, to King Arthur's castle at Camelot, held by many to be sited at Cadbury, to the image of the dead King's barge moving silently through the mists over the lake to the Isle of Avalon. Archaeological fact lends support to the conjecture that Glastonbury, with its famous Tor, was an island in an ancient lake. Another island story surrounds King Alfred, reputedly sheltering from the Danes on the Isle of Athelney & there burning his cakes.

Historically, Somerset saw the last battle fought on English soil, at Sedgemoor in 1685. The defeat of the Monmouth rebellion resulted in the wrath of James II falling on the West Country in the form of Judge Jeffreys & his "Bloody Assize".

To the west of the county lies part of the Exmoor National Park, with high moorland where deer roam & buzzards soar & a wonderful stretch of cliffs from Minehead to Devon. Dunster is a popular village with its octagonal Yarn market, & its old world cottages, dominated at one end by the castle & at the other by the tower on Conygar Hill.

To the east the woods & moors of the Quantocks are protected as an area of outstanding natural beauty. The Vale of Taunton is famous for its apple orchards & for the golden cider produced from them.

The south of the county is a land of rolling countryside & charming little towns, Chard, Crewkerne, Ilchester & Ilminster amongst others.

To the north the limestone hills of Mendip are honeycombed with spectacular caves & gorges, some with neolithic remains, as at Wookey Hole & Cheddar Gorge.

Wells is nearby, so named because of the multitude of natural springs. Hardly a city, Wells boasts a magnificent cathedral set amongst spacious lawns & trees. The west front is one of the glories of English architecture with its sculptured figures & soaring arches. A spectacular feature is the astronomical clock, the work of 14th century monk Peter Lightfoot. The intricate face tells the hours, minutes, days & phases of the moon. On the hour, four mounted knights charge forth & knock one another from their horses.

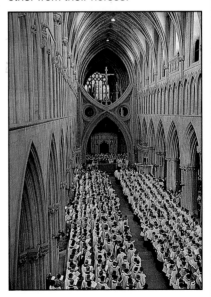

Wells Cathedral Choir.

Somerset, Bath & Bristol

Bath is one of the most loved historic cities in England. It owes its existence to the hot springs which bubble up five hundred thousand gallons of water a day at a temperature of some 120' F. According to legend, King Bladud appreciated the healing qualities of the waters & established his capital here, calling it Aquae Sulis. He built an elaborate healing & entertainment centre around the springs including reservoirs, baths & hypercaust rooms.

The Roman Baths, not uncovered until modern times, are on the lowest of three levels. Above them came the mediaeval city & on the top layer at modern street level is the elegant Georgian Pump Room.

Edward was crowned the first King of all England in 973, in the Saxon Abbey which stood on the site of the present fifteenth century abbey. This building, in the graceful perpendicular style with elegant fan vaulting, is sometimes called the "lantern of the West", on account of its vast clerestories & large areas of glass.

During the Middle Ages the town prospered through Royal patronage & the development of the wool industry. Bath became a city of weavers, the leading industrial town in the West of England.

The 18th century gave us the superb Georgian architecture which is the city's glory. John Wood, an ambitious young architect laid out Queen Anne's Square in the grand Palladian style, & went on to produce his masterpiece, the Royal Crescent. His scheme for the city was continued by his son & a number of other fine architects, using the beautiful Bath stone. Bath was a centre of fashion, with Beau Nash the leader of a glittering society.

In 1497 John & Sebastian Cabot sailed from the Bristol quayside to the land they called Ameryke, in honour of the King's agent in Bristol, Richard Ameryke. Bristol's involvement in the colonisation of the New World & the trade in sugar, tobacco & slaves that followed, made her the second city in the kingdom in the 18th century. John Cabot is commemorated by the Cabot Tower on grassy Brandon Hill - a fine vantage point from which to view the city. On the old docks below are the Bristol Industrial Museum & the SS Great Britain, Brunel's famous iron ship. Another achievement of this master engineer, the Clifton Suspension Bridge, spans Bristol's renowned beauty spot, the Clifton Gorge. For a glimpse of Bristol's elegant past, stroll through Clifton with its stately terraces & spacious Downs.

A short walk from the busy city centre & modern shopping area, the visitor in search of history will find cobbled King Street with its merchant seamen's almshouses & The Theatre Royal, the oldest theatre in continuous use in England, & also Llandoger Trow, an ancient inn associated with Treasure Island & Robinson Crusoe.

Bath Abbey.

Somerset, Bath & Bristol

Somerset, Bath & Bristol Gazeteer

Areas of Outstanding Natural Beauty
Mendip Hills. Quantock Hills. National Park - Exmoor. The Cotswolds.

Historic Houses & Castles

Abbot's Fish House - Meare
14th century house.
Barrington Court - Illminster
16th century house & gardens.
Blaise Castle House - Henbury Nr. Bristol
18th century house - now folk museum, extensive woodlands.
Brympton D'Evercy - Nr. Yeovil
Mansion with 17th century front & Tudor west front. Adjacent is 13th century priest's house & church. Formal gardens & vineyard.
Claverton Manor - Nr. Bath
Greek revival house - furnished with 17th, 18th, 19th century American originals.
Clevedon Court - Clevedon
14th century manor house, 13th century hall, 12th century tower. Lovely garden with rare trees & shrubs. This is where Thackerey wrote much of 'Vanity Fair'.
Dyrham Park - Between Bristol & Bath
17th century house - fine panelled rooms, Dutch paintings, furniture.
Dunster Castle - Dunster
13th century castle with fine 17th century staircase & ceilings.
East Lambrook Manor - South Petherton
15th century house with good panelling.
Gaulden Manor - Tolland
12th century manor. Great Hall having unique plaster ceiling & oak screen. Antique furniture.
Halsway Manor - Crowcombe
14th century house with fine panelling.
Hatch Court - Hatch Beauchamp
Georgian house in the Palladian style with China room.
King John's Hunting Lodge - Axbridge
Early Tudor merchant's house.
Lytes Carry - Somerton
14th & 15th century manor house with a chapel & formal garden.
Montacute House - Yeovil
Elizabethan house with fine examples of Heraldic Glass, tapestries, panelling &
furniture. Portrait gallery of Elizabethan & Jacobean paintings.
Tintinhull House - Yeovil
17th century house with beautiful gardens.
Priory Park College - Bath
18th century Georgian mansion, now Roman Catholic school.
No. 1 Royal Crescent - Bath
An unaltered Georgian house built 1767.
Red Lodge - Bristol
16th century house - period furniture & panelling.
St. Vincent's Priory - Bristol
Gothic revival house, built over caves which were sanctuary for Christians.
St Catherine's Court - Nr. Bath
Small Tudor house - associations with Henry VIII & Elizabeth I.

Cathedrals & Churches

Axbridge (St. John)
1636 plaster ceiling & panelled roofs.
Backwell (St. Andrew)
12th to 17th century, 15th century tower, repaired 17th century. 15th century tomb & chancel, 16th century screen, 18th century brass chandelier.
Bath Abbey
Perpendicular - monastic church, 15th century foundation. Nave finished 17th century, restorations in 1674.
Bishop's Lydeard (St. Mary)
15th century. Notable tower, rood screen & glass.
Bristol Cathedral
Mediaeval. Eastern halfnave Victorian. Chapterhouse richly ornamented. Iron screen, 3 fonts, "fairest parish church in all England".
Bristol (St. Mary Radcliffe)
Bristol (St. Stephens')
Perpendicular - monuments, magnificent tower.
Bruton (St. Mary)
Fine 2 towered 15th century church. Georgian chancel, tie beam roof, Georgian reredos. Jacobean screen. 15th century embroidery.
Chewton Mendip (St. Mary Magdalene)
12th century with later additions. 12th century doorway, 15th century bench ends, magnificent 16th century tower & 17th century lecturn.

Somerset, Bath & Bristol

Crewkerne (St. Bartholomew)
Magnificent west front & roofs, 15th & 16th century. South doorway dating from 13th century, wonderful 15th century painted glass & 18th century chandeliers.

East Brent (St. Mary)
Mainly 15th century. Plaster ceiling, painted glass & carved bench ends.

Glastonbury (St. John)
One of the finest examples of perpendicular towers. Tie beam roof, late mediaeval painted glass, mediaeval vestment & early 16th century altar tomb.

High Ham (St. Andrew)
Sumptuous roofs & vaulted rood screen. Carved bench ends. Jacobean lectern, mediaeval painted glass. Norman font.

Kingsbury Episcopi (St. Martin)
14th-15th century. Good tower with fan vaulting. Late mediaeval painted glass.

Long Sutton (Holy Trinity)
15th century with noble tower & magnificent tie beam roof. 15th century pulpit & rood screen, tower vaulting.

Martock (All Saints)
13th century chancel. Nave with tie beam roof, outstanding of its kind. 17th century paintings of Apostles.

North Cadbury (St. Michael)
painted glass.

Pilton (St. John)
12th century with arcades. 15th century roofs.

Taunton (St. Mary Magdalene)
Highest towers in the county. Five nave roof, fragments of mediaeval painted glass.

Trull (All Saints)
15th century with many mediaeval art treasures & 15th century glass.

Wells Cathedral-Wells
Magnificent west front with carved figures. Splendid tower. Early English arcade of nave & transepts. 60 fine misericords c.1330. Lady chapel with glass & star vault. Chapter House & Bishop's Palace.

Weston Zoyland (St. Mary)
15th century bench ends. 16th century heraldic glass. Jacobean pulpit.

Wrington (All Souls)
15th century aisles & nave; font, stone pulpit, notable screens.

Museums & Galleries

Admiral Blake Museum - Bridgewater
Exhibits relating to Battle of Sedgemoor, archaeology.

American Museum in Britain - Claverton Nr. Bath
American decorative arts 17th to 19th century displayed in series of furnished rooms & galleries of special exhibits. Paintings, furniture, glass wood & metal work, textiles, folk sculpture, etc.

Borough Museum - Hendford Manor Hall, Yeovil
Archaeology, firearms collections & Bailward Costume Collection.

Bristol Industrial Museum - Bristol
Collections of transport items of land, sea & air. Many unique items.

Burdon Manor - Washford
14th century manor house with Saxon fireplace & cockpit.

City of Bristol Art Gallery - Bristol
Permanent & loan collections of paintings, English & Oriental ceramics.

Glastonbury Lake Village Museum - Glastonbury
Late prehistoric antiquities.

Gough's Cave Museum - Cheddar
Upper Paleolithic remains, skeleton, flints, amber & engraved stones.

Holburne of Menstrie Museum - Bath
Old Master paintings, silver, glass, porcelain, furniture & miniatures in 18th century building. Work of 20th century craftworkers.

Hinton Priory - Hinton Charterhouse
13th century - ruins of Carthusian priory.

Kings Weston Roman Villa - Lawrence Weston
3rd & 4th centuries - mosaics of villa - some walls.

Museum of Costume - Bath
Collection of fashion from 17th century to present day.

Roman Baths - Bath
Roman Museum - Bath
Material from remains of extensive Roman baths & other Roman sites.

Stoney Littleton Barrow - Nr. Bath
Neolithic burial chamber - restoration work 1858.

St. Nicholas Church & City Museum - Bristol
Mediaeval antiquities relating to local

Somerset, Bath & Bristol

history, Church plate & vestments. Altarpiece by Hogarth.

Temple Church - Bristol
14th & 15th century ruins.

Victoria Art Gallery - Bath
Paintings, prints, drawings, glass, ceramics, watches, coins, etc. Bygones - permanent & temporary exhibitions. Geology collections.

Wookey Hole Cave Museum - Wookey Hole
Remains from Pliocene period. Relics of Celtic & Roman civilization. Exhibition of handmade paper-making.

Historic Monuments

Cleeve Abbey - Cleeve
Ruined 13th century house, with timber roof & wall paintings.

Farleigh Castle - Farleigh Hungerford
14th century remains - museums in chapel.

Glastonbury Abbey - Glastonbury
12th & 13th century ruins of St. Joseph's chapel & Abbot's kitchen.

Muchelney Abbey - Muchelney
15th century ruins of Benedictine abbey.

Other things to see & do

Black Rock Nature Reserve - Cheddar
Circular walk through plantation woodland, downland grazing.

Cheddar Caves
Show caves at the foot of beautiful Cheddar Gorge.

Clifton Zoological Gardens - Bristol
Flourishing zoo with many exhibits - beautiful gardens.

Clifton Suspension Bridge - Bristol
Designed by Isambard Kingdom Brunel, opened in 1864. Viewpoint & picnic spot Camera Obscura.

Cricket St. Thomas Wildlife Park - Nr. Chard
Wildlife park, heavy horse centre, countryside museum, etc.

The Pump Room - Bath
18th century neo-classical interior. Spa.

Clifton Suspension Bridge. Bristol.

SOMERSET, BATH & BRISTOL

Map reference

00	Johnson	05	Holder
00	Youngs	06	Henry
01	Dodd	08	Hoose
01	Besley	09	Healey
01	Lanz	10	Shellard
01	Poole	11	Gallannaugh
01	Ford	12	Tasker
01	Beckett	13	Newman-Coburn
01	Addison		
01	Napier	14	Gregory
01	Kitching	15	Bale
01	Cox	16	Bradshaw
01	Stabbins	17	Redmond
01	Huxley	18	Vicary
01	Gaunt	21	Brewer
01	Wroe-Parker	22	Dearden
01	Hugh	24	Copeland
01	King	26	Mitchem
01	Lanz	29	Eyre
01	Femor	30	Muers-Raby
01	Bryan	31	Trotman
01	Seymour	33	Thompson
01	Thwaites	34	Frost
01	Selby	35	Nowell
02	Keeling	37	Durbin
01	Westlake		
04	Priddle		
04	Graham		
04	Walker		

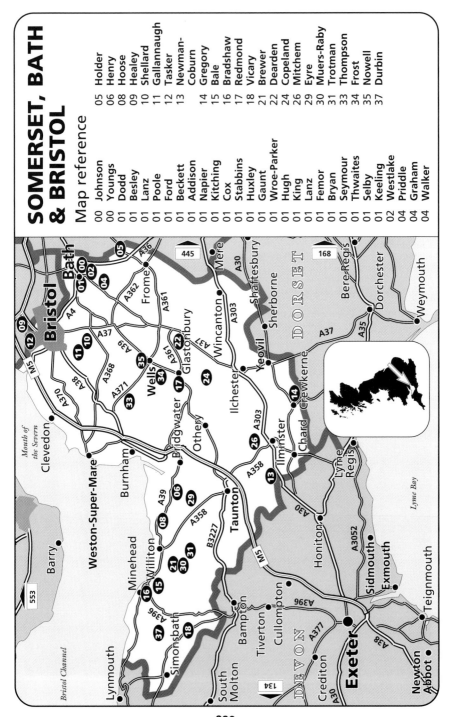

336

Apsley House Hotel. Bath.

The Old Red House. Bath.

Somerset
Bath & Bristol

Marion Dodd **Brocks** **32 Brock Street** **Bath** **BA1 2LN** Tel: (01225) 338374 Fax (01225) 334245 Open: ALL YEAR Map Ref No. 01	Nearest Road: A.4 Brocks is a beautiful Georgian town house situated between the Circus and Royal Crescent. Very close to the Roman Baths, Assembly Rooms, etc. This really is a wonderful part of Bath. This historic house has all modern conveniences, & all of the comfortable bedrooms have en-suite facilities. The aim here is to offer guests the highest standards, and personal attention. A delightful base from which to explore beautiful Bath. E-mail: marion@brocks.force9.net	£30.00 to £36.00 VISA: M'CARD:	Y	N	N
Mrs Chrissie Besley **The Old Red House** **37 Newbridge Road** **Bath BA1 3HE** Tel: (01225) 330464 Fax 01225 331661 Open: FEB - NOV Map Ref No. 01	Nearest Road: A.4 This charming Victorian Gingerbread House is colourful, comfortable & warm; full of unexpected touches & intriguing little curiosities. Its leaded & stained glass windows are now double-glazed to ensure a peaceful stay. The extensive breakfast menu, a delight in itself, is served in a sunny conservatory. Parking. Special rates for 3 or more nights. Dinner available at a local riverside pub. A brochure on request. Children over 4 yrs.	£21.00 to £33.00 see PHOTO over p. 338 VISA: M'CARD: AMEX:	Y	N	Y
David & Annie Lanz **Apsley House Hotel** **141 Newbridge Hill** **Bath** **BA1 3PT** Tel: (01225) 336966 Fax 01225 425462 Open: ALL YEAR (Excl. Xmas) Map Ref No. 01	Nearest Road: A.341 An elegant Georgian country house built for the Duke of Wellington in 1830, situated just over 1 mile from the city centre with private parking. A small privately-run hotel, guests are offered a warm welcome & personal care. The interior includes many period features, the house is furnished with fine antiques & oil paintings. A sumptuous breakfast is served in the delightful dining room. Children over 5. E-mail: apsleyhouse@easynet.co.uk	£32.50 to £55.00 see PHOTO over p. 337 VISA: M'CARD: AMEX:	Y	N	N
Tony & Jan Poole **Cranleigh** **159 Newbridge Hill** **Bath** **BA1 3PX** Tel: (01225) 310197 Fax 01225 423143 Open: ALL YEAR Map Ref No. 01	Nearest Road: A.431 Situated in a quiet residential area, this comfortable Victorian house has great character, with exceptionally spacious, stylish en-suite bedrooms. Most have lovely views across the Avon Valley. You are welcome to relax in the garden. Breakfast includes such choices as fresh-fruit salad & scrambled eggs with smoked salmon. Easy access to the heart of Bath. Parking. The Pooles have a wealth of information to help you make the most of your stay in Bath. Children over 4. E-mail: cranleigh@btinternet.com	£34.00 to £40.00 see PHOTO over p. 340 VISA: M'CARD:	Y	N	N
Mrs Anna Ford **Gainsborough Hotel** **Weston Lane** **Bath** **BA1 4AB** Tel: (01225) 311380 Fax 01225 447411 Open: ALL YEAR Map Ref No. 01	Nearest Road: A.4 The Gainsborough is a large country-house hotel, comfortably furnished & set in its own grounds near the Botanical Gardens & Victoria Park. Offering 17 attractive en-suite bedrooms, each with colour T.V., direct-dial telephone, tea/coffee-making facilities & hairdryer. The dining room & small cocktail bar overlook the lawns, where guests often relax during the summer on the sun terrace. Private parking available. Children over 5. E-mail: gainsborough_hotel@compuserve.com	£28.00 to £45.00 see PHOTO over p. 341 VISA: M'CARD: AMEX:	Y	N	N

Cranleigh. Bath.

Gainsborough Hotel. Bath.

Bailbrook Lodge. Bath.

Somerset
Bath & Bristol

		rate £ from - to per person	children taken	evening meals	animals taken
Derek & Maria Beckett **Cedar Lodge** **13 Lambridge** **London Rd** **Bath** **BA1 6BJ** **Tel: (01225) 423468** **Open: ALL YEAR** **Map Ref No. 01**	Nearest Road: A.4, A.46 Within easy level walk to the historic city centre, this beautiful, detached Georgian house offers period elegance with modern amenities. 3 lovely bedrooms (1 with 4-poster, 1 half-tester, 1 twin), all with en-suite/private bathrooms. Delightful gardens & comfortable drawing room, with fire, to relax in. Ideally situated for excursions to Avebury, Stonehenge, Salisbury, Longleat, Wells, Cotswolds, Wales & many other attractions. Secure private parking. Children over 10.	£25.00 to £35.00 🚭	Y	N	N
Mr & Mrs R.N. Addison **Bailbrook Lodge Hotel** **35/37 London Road West** **Bath** **BA1 7HZ** **Tel: (01225) 859090** **Fax 01225 852299** **Open: ALL YEAR** **Map Ref No. 01**	Nearest Road: A.4, A.46 Bailbrook Lodge is an imposing Grade II listed Georgian house located 1 mile east of Bath. There is a choice of 12 elegantly furnished en-suite bedrooms (some 4-posters), all with T.V. & hospitality tray. Evening meals with traditional English cuisine are provided. The lounge bar & dining room overlook the garden. Bailbrook Lodge is an ideal base for exploring Bath & touring the beautiful surrounding countryside. Parking. **E-mail: hotel@bailbrooklodge.demon.co.uk**	£29.00 to £40.00 *see PHOTO over* *p. 342* VISA: M'CARD: AMEX:	Y	Y	N
John & Rosamund Napier **Eagle House** **Church Street** **Bathford** **Bath BA1 7RS** **Tel: (01225) 859946** **Fax 01225 859430** **Open: ALL YEAR** **Map Ref No. 01**	Nearest Road: A.363, A.4 Eagle House is a fine Georgian Grade II listed house set in 2 acres of garden in the heart of picturesque Bathford. There are 8 comfortable, en-suite bedrooms with 'phone, T.V. & tea/coffee-making facilities, plus spacious public rooms - the drawing room has a 16-ft ceiling, as well as views over the garden down the valley. The house is elegant, yet the atmosphere is informal, & all are welcome. Also, a lovely cottage for 4. **E-mail: jonap@eagleho.demon.co.uk**	£34.00 to £47.00 *see PHOTO over* *p. 344* VISA: M'CARD:	Y	N	Y
Mary & Keith Johnson **The Lodge Hotel** **Bathford Hill** **Bathford** **Bath** **BA1 7SL** **Tel: (01225) 858575** **Tel: (01225) 858467** **Fax 01225 858172** **Open: ALL YEAR** **Map Ref No. 00**	Nearest Road: A.4 The Lodge Hotel is located in a beautiful, quiet village only 2 1/2 miles from the centre of Bath & is set in 2 acres of landscaped gardens with swimming pool. Keith & Mary Johnson consider it a priority to help guests with their itineraries & as local people, have an intimate knowledge of the area & its history. The 6 en-suite bedrooms are spacious & well-appointed with 'phone, T.V. & tea/coffee-making facilities. The Lodge Hotel is an excellent base from which to explore Bath & the glorious surrounding countryside. **E-mail: lodgethe@aol.com**	£27.50 to £55.00 *see PHOTO over* *p. 345* VISA: M'CARD:	Y	N	Y

Visit our website at:
http://www.bestbandb.co.uk

Eagle House. Bathford.

The Lodge Hotel. Bathford.

Bloomfield House. Bath.

Somerset
Bath & Bristol

	Nearest Road	rate £ from - to per person	children taken	evening meals	animals taken
Geoff & Avril Kitching **Wentworth House Hotel** 106 Bloomfield Road Bath BA2 2AP Tel: (01225) 339193 Fax 01225 310460 Open: ALL YEAR (Excl. Xmas) Map Ref No. 01	Nearest Road: A.367 Stay 3 nights & receive a 10% discount. Built as a family home in 1887, Wentworth House is an imposing Victorian mansion enjoying a peaceful location in secluded gardens with stunning views. The Abbey & Roman Baths are within walking distance of the hotel. Each room is individually decorated, most with antique beds, & offers colour T.V., alarm calls, 'phones, hairdryers & tea/coffee. Luscious breakfasts with buffet bar. Private car park, free for all guests. Children over 5. **E-mail: wentworthhouse@dial.pipex.com** VISA: M'CARD: AMEX:	£30.00 to £47.50	Y	N	N
C. M. Cox **Bloomfield House** 146 Bloomfield Rd Bath BA2 2AS Tel: (01225) 420105 Fax 01225 481958 Open: ALL YEAR Map Ref No. 01	Nearest Road: A.367 An elegant Georgian country house in a sylvan setting with stunning views over the city. Antique furniture, French crystal chandeliers, silver-service breakfast & open fires. All rooms have an en-suite/private bath/shower, 'phone, T.V. & canopied or 4-poster beds. Also, the lavish principal bedroom of the Mayor & Mayoress of Bath (1902/3). Bloomfield House offers the finest, the friendliest, the best. Car park. (Also a 2-bed flat.) **E-mail: bloomfieldhouse@compuserve.com** *see PHOTO over* *p. 346* VISA: M'CARD: AMEX:	£35.00 to £47.50	N	N	N
Mrs Nicky Stabbins **The Hollies** Hatfield Road Bath BA2 2BD Tel: (01225) 313366 Fax 01225 313366 Open: FEB - Mid DEC Map Ref No. 01	Nearest Road: A.367 The Hollies is a lovely old Victorian, Grade II listed house situated within walking distance of the city. With just 3 pretty guest rooms, personal attention and hospitality are assured. Each room has en-suite or private facilities, T.V., beverage-making facilities, hairdryer & radio/alarm clock. A wide breakfast menu is served. Private parking is available. Rooms overlook the secluded garden of apple trees, herbs & roses. This is a charming home, ideal for exploring Bath. Children over 5. VISA: M'CARD:	£23.00 to £28.00	Y	N	N
Carol Huxley **Lavender House** 17 Bloomfield Park Bath BA2 2BY Tel: (01225) 314500 Fax 01225 448564 Open: ALL YEAR Map Ref No. 01	Nearest Road: A.367 Set in a quiet conservation area, within easy reach of Bath city centre. Lavender House is an Edwardian house which affords 5 lovely bedrooms. Each is individually designed & has a luxurious bathroom, T.V. & hospitality tray. In addition to serving a traditional English breakfast, using free-range & fresh local produce, there are Vegetarian Cordon Vert options. Evening meals by arrangement. Lavender House is a special place to unwind, relax & be spoiled. Parking. **E-mail: Lavenderhouse@btinternet.com** *see PHOTO over* *p. 348* VISA: M'CARD:	£30.00 to £40.00	Y	N	N
Berkeley & Moira Gaunt **Oldfields Hotel** 102 Wells Road Bath BA2 3AL Tel: (01225) 317984 Fax 01225 444471 Open: FEB - DEC Map Ref No. 01	Nearest Road: A.367 Elegant & traditional bed & breakfast at this beautiful bath stone Victorian house, 10 mins from the city centre. 14 rooms with colour T.V., direct-dial 'phone, hairdryer & tea/coffee-making facilities. All rooms are equipped with a private bath or shower. Experience the true ambience of the 19th century; beautiful antique furniture, rich fabrics & warm decor. A full English breakfast is served, or select from the extensive buffet. **E-mail: info@oldfields.co.uk** *see PHOTO over* *p. 349* VISA: M'CARD: AMEX:	£29.00 to £50.00	Y	N	N

Lavender House. Bath.

Oldfields Hotel. Bath.

Cheriton House. Bath.

Somerset
Bath & Bristol

Mr J. Chiles **& Mrs I. Wroe-Parker** **Cheriton House** **9 Upper Oldfield Park** **Bath BA2 3JX** **Tel: (01225) 429862** **Fax 01225 428403** **Open: ALL YEAR** **Map Ref No. 01**	Nearest Road: A.367 Situated on the southern slope of Bath with splendid views of the city, Cheriton House has been carefully restored & redecorated, & the rooms are attractively furnished. All of the bedrooms have private bathrooms (en-suite), colour T.V. & hot-drink-making facilities. There is a choice of delicious breakfasts including traditional English & Continental. Guests are welcome to enjoy the beautiful, peaceful garden. Children over 12. **E-mail: cheriton@which.net**	£32.00 to £45.00 *see PHOTO over* *p. 350* VISA: M'CARD: AMEX:	Y	N	N
Tim & Kathryn Hugh **Dorian House** **1 Upper Oldfield Park** **Bath BA2 3JX** **Tel: (01225) 426336** **Fax 01225 444699** **Open: ALL YEAR** **Map Ref No. 01**	Nearest Road: A.367 A warm welcome and an aura of nostalgic luxury await every guest at this gracious Victorian house. Accommodation is in 8 charming bedrooms, all en-suite, fully appointed, with tea/coffee trays, hairdryers, telephones and colour T.V.. There is a lounge & a small licensed bar, and a full English breakfast menu is served. Parking available, and only a 10-min. stroll to the city centre. Dorian House is ideal for a relaxing break.	£34.00 to £40.00 *see PHOTO over* *p. 352* VISA: M'CARD: AMEX:	Y	N	N
Jenny King **Oakleigh House** **19 Upper Oldfield Park** **Bath** **BA2 3JX** **Tel: (01225) 315698** **Fax 01225 448223** **Open: ALL YEAR** **Map Ref No. 01**	Nearest Road: A.367 Your comfort is assured at Oakleigh House, quietly situated only 10 mins from the city centre. Oakleigh combines Victorian elegance with today's comforts to make your stay that extra bit special. All of the 4 bedrooms are attractively furnished & have an en-suite bath/shower & w.c., hairdryers, colour T.V., clock radios & tea/coffee-making facilities. A private car park. Oakleigh is an ideal base for beautiful Bath and beyond. **E-mail: oakleigh@which.net**	£30.00 to £35.00 VISA: M'CARD: AMEX:	N	N	N
David & Annie Lanz **Paradise House** **Holloway** **Bath** **BA2 4PX** **Tel: (01225) 317723** **Fax 01225 482005** **Open: ALL YEAR (Excl. Xmas)** **Map Ref No. 01**	Nearest Road: A.367 Paradise House was built in the 1720s, on the ancient Roman Fosse Way. The Fosse Way, now a cul-de-sac, is one of the quietest streets in Bath & provides easy access to the city centre. (The Roman Baths are only 7 mins' walk away.) 10 attractively furnished & well-appointed bedrooms, each with an en-suite bathroom etc. The house enjoys fine views over the Georgian city & has over 1/2 an acre of walled gardens which compete with the golden splendour of the city below. **E-mail: paradise@apsleyhouse.easynet.co.uk**	£32.50 to £55.00 VISA: M'CARD: AMEX:	Y	N	N
Ms E. R. Fermor **Devonshire House** **143 Wellsway** **Bath** **BA2 4RZ** **Tel: (01225) 312495** **Fax 01225 335534** **Open: ALL YEAR** **Map Ref No. 01**	Nearest Road: A.367 Devonshire House was built in 1880 on the site of a 19th-century Boy's Academy. Your host's aim is to make your stay as pleasant & comfortable as possible. The guest bedrooms are well-appointed with en-suite facilities, tea/coffee tray & T.V. Breakfast is served in the comfortable Victorian dining room & special diets are catered for. Devonshire House offers you all the comforts of home combined with the beauty & elegance of Bath. (Babies & children over 7 welcome).	£27.50 to £37.50 VISA: M'CARD: AMEX:	Y	N	N

Dorian House. Bath

Somerset House. Bath.

Ravenscroft. Bath.

Somerset
Bath & Bristol

		rate £ from - to per person	children taken	evening meals	animals taken
Mr P. C. Bryan **Ravenscroft** **North Road** **Bathwick** **Bath BA2 6HZ** **Tel: (01225) 461919** **Fax 01225 461919** **Open: ALL YEAR** **Map Ref No. 01**	Nearest Road: A.36 Built in 1876, Ravenscroft is an elegant Victorian residence with a wealth of period features. Its elevated position provides spectacular views over the city of Bath & countryside beyond. Only a few minutes from the city centre, it is surrounded by an acre of secluded, mature gardens which offer guests peace & tranquillity. 4 lovely bedrooms with colour T.V., tea/coffee & hair-drying facilities. Private parking. Children over 12. **E-mail: ravenscroft@compuserve.com**	£27.50 to £27.50 🚭 *see PHOTO over* *p. 354*	Y	N	Y
Malcolm & Jean Seymour **Somerset House Hotel &** **Restaurant** **35 Bathwick Hill** **Bath** **BA2 6LD** **Tel: (01225) 466451** **Fax 01225 317188** **Open: ALL YEAR** **Map Ref No. 01**	Nearest Road: A.36 Somerset House is an elegant Georgian townhouse from which guests may enjoy fine views across the city of Bath as well as walks into adjacent N. T. fields. To convey the emphasis your hosts place on the food, the hotel is described as a restaurant with rooms. All the rooms have retained their comfortable dimensions. Your hosts can welcome just a few guests & enjoy their company informally. Children over 6. (Dinner, bed & breakfast from £48.00 p.p.p.n.). **E-mail: somersethouse@compuserve.com**	£28.50 to £35.00 🚭 *see PHOTO over* *p. 353* VISA: M'CARD: AMEX:	Y	Y	Y
Roy & Lois Thwaites **Villa Magdala Hotel** **Henrietta Road** **Bath BA2 6LX** **Tel: (01225) 466329** **Fax 01225 483207** **Open: ALL YEAR** **Map Ref No. 01**	Nearest Road: A.4 Ideally situated, this charming Victorian townhouse hotel enjoys a peaceful location overlooking Henrietta Park, only 5 mins' level walk to the city centre & the famous Roman Baths. All of the 17 spacious & comfortable bedrooms have an en-suite bathroom, T.V., direct-dial 'phone, refreshment tray & pleasant views. Private parking is available for guests in the hotel grounds. **E-mail: villa@btinternet.com**	£30.00 to £50.00 🚭 *see PHOTO over* *p. 356* VISA: M'CARD: AMEX:	Y	N	N
David & Sue Selby **Brompton House** **St. John's Road** **Bath** **BA2 6PT** **Tel: (01225) 420972** **Fax 01225 420505** **Open: ALL YEAR (Excl.** **Xmas & New Year)** **Map Ref No. 01**	Nearest Road: A.4, A.36 Built as a rectory in 1777, Brompton House is an elegant Georgian residence with a car park & beautiful mature gardens. Only 5 mins' walk from many of Bath's historic sights, it is run by the Selbys who offer every comfort & service to their guests. The attractive sitting room is furnished with antiques, & the tastefully decorated en-suite bedrooms offer T.V., radio/alarm, 'phone & tea/coffee. Breakfast is a delicious choice of full English, Continental or wholefood. **E-mail: bromptonhouse@btinternet.com**	£30.00 to £45.00 🚭 *see PHOTO over* *p. 357* VISA: M'CARD: AMEX:	N	N	N
David & Susan Keeling **Bath Tasburgh Hotel** **Warminster Road** **Bath** **BA2 6SH** **Tel: (01225) 425096** **Fax 01225 463842** **Open: ALL YEAR** **Map Ref No. 01**	Nearest Road: A.36 Built in 1890, this lovely Victorian residence provides ideal country comfort in a city setting. The hotel sits in 2 acres of beautiful gardens overlooking the Avon Valley, with the adjacent canal towpath providing an idyllic walk into Bath. The 12 en-suite bedrooms (incl. 4-posters) are tastefully furnished, offering many comforts & amenities. Elegant drawing room, dining room & stunning conservatory/terrace. Parking. Licensed. Every effort is made to ensure a memorable stay. **E-mail: hotel@bathtasburgh.demon.co.uk**	£36.00 to £60.00 🚭 *see PHOTO over* *p. 358* VISA: M'CARD: AMEX:	Y	Y	N

Villa Magdala. Bath.

Brompton House. Bath.

Bath Tasburgh Hotel. Bath.

Somerset
Bath & Bristol

		rate £ from - to per person	children taken	evening meals	animals taken
Joan Youngs **Lindisfarne** **41a Warminster Road** **Bathampton** **Bath BA2 6XJ** **Tel: (01225) 466342** **Fax 01225 444062** **Open: ALL YEAR** **Map Ref No. 00**	Nearest Road: A.36 Situated just 1 1/2 miles from the city centre. Lindisfarne is a lovely home offering comfortable en-suite accommodation with colour T.V. & refreshment facilities. Many good eating venues within walking distance. A large private car park & a frequent bus service to Bath centre. The perfect place from which to explore this beautiful city. A warm welcome & personal attention guaranteed by the resident owners. Children over 3. **E-mail: brain.youngs@virgin.net**	£20.00 to £27.50	Y	N	Y
Mr & Mrs M. J. Westlake **Monkshill Guest House** **Shaft Road** **Monkton Combe** **Bath** **BA2 7HL** **Tel: (01225) 833028** **Fax 01225 833028** **Open: ALL YEAR** **Map Ref No. 02**	Nearest Road: A.36 This distinguished Edwardian house is set in its own beautiful gardens, on an English-country hilltop commanding spectacular countryside views, & yet lies only 5 mins from the centre of Bath. Stroll through the small medieval village of Monkton Combe, at the valley's base, & return to tea amid the elegant antiques, fireplace & grand piano that complement the drawing room. The bedrooms are elegant, with colourful flowing drapes, charming brass beds, bath/shower & fine views over the gardens & valley below.	£30.00 to £37.50 *see PHOTO over* *p. 360* VISA: M'CARD:	Y	N	Y
Sarah Priddle & John Webster **The Plaine** **Norton St. Philip** **Bath BA3 6LE** **Tel: (01373) 834723** **Fax 01373 834101** **Open: ALL YEAR** **Map Ref No. 04**	Nearest Road: A.36 The Plaine is a delightful listed building, dating from the 16th century & situated in the heart of an historic conservation village. There are 3 beautiful en-suite rooms, all with 4-poster beds. Opposite is the famous George Inn - one of the oldest hostelries in England. Delicious breakfasts are prepared with local produce and free-range eggs. A convenient location for Bath, Wells, Longleat and the Cotswolds. Parking. Children over 3.	£27.00 to £34.00 *see PHOTO over* *p. 361* VISA: M'CARD: AMEX:	Y	N	N
Leslie & Traudle Graham **Monmouth Lodge** **Norton St. Philip** **Bath** **BA3 6LH** **Tel: (01373) 834367** **Open: ALL YEAR** **Map Ref No. 04**	Nearest Road: A.36, A.366 Set in an acre of attractive garden, looking on to the Somerset Hills surrounding this historic village. 3 attractively furnished ground-floor en-suite bedrooms, with colour T.V., tea/coffee facilities, king-size beds & own patio doors, which offer space & comfort. In the charming sitting room & stylish dining room, there is the same attention to detail & quality, where a good choice of excellent breakfast is served. Ideally situated for Bath, Wells, Stonehenge etc. Private parking. Famous 13th-century pub nearby. Children over 5.	£29.00 to £33.00 VISA: M'CARD:	Y	N	N
Graham & Nicola Walker **Bath Lodge Hotel** **Warminster Road** **Nr. Norton St. Philip** **Bath** **BA3 6NH** **Tel: (01225) 723040** **Fax 01225 723737** **Open: ALL YEAR** **Map Ref No. 04**	Nearest Road: A.36 Bath Lodge is a superbly converted, Heritage Grade II listed, former gatehouse to Farleigh Castle, with both the alterations & landscaping having been completed within the last few years. All of the rooms are beautifully located & have many castellated features within them. Private balconies from 3 of the rooms overlook the natural gardens & adjacent deer forest. Bath Lodge is situated just 7 miles south of Bath on the A.36. Children over 10 years welcome. **E-mail: walker@bathlodge.demon.co.uk**	£30.00 to £50.00 *see PHOTO over* *p. 362* VISA: M'CARD: AMEX:	Y	N	Y

Monkshill. Monkton Combe.

The Plaine. Norton St. Philip.

Bath Lodge. Norton St. Philip.

Somerset
Bath & Bristol

		rate £ from - to per person	children taken	evening meals	animals taken
Jayne & Oliver Holder **Irondale House** **67 High Street** **Rode** **Bath** **BA3 6PB** **Tel: (01373) 830730** Fax 01373 830730 **Open: ALL YEAR** **Map Ref No. 05**	Nearest Road: A.36 A warm welcome awaits you by Jayne & Oliver to their elegant 18th-century Georgian home, set in a quiet village 10 mins' drive from Bath. The house is decorated to the highest standard. Bedrooms are en-suite with hairdryers, tea/coffee, T.V. & king-size beds. Breakfast is a delicious meal in the family dining room. The family suite has a sitting room which leads straight into the lovely walled garden from a patio door. There is a wonderful drawing room which overlooks the garden with amazing views. Ideal for sightseeing in Bath, Wells, Longleat, Lacock & Stonehenge.	£30.00 to £45.00 *see PHOTO over* *p. 364* VISA: M'CARD:	Y	N	N
Mr & Mrs Michael Henry **Brook House** **2 Castle Street** **Nether Stowey** **Bridgwater TA5 1LN** **Tel: (01278) 732881** **Open: ALL YEAR (Excl.** **Xmas & New Year)** **Map Ref No. 06**	Nearest Road: A.39 A warm welcome awaits the discerning visitor at Brook House, an elegant & lovingly restored Georgian house, situated in the centre of this beautiful historic village at the foot of the Quantocks where Coleridge once lived. Hearty breakfasts & tastefully furnished en-suite rooms with colour T.V. & tea/coffee-making facilities. Good local pubs within walking distance. Wonderful coastal & hill walks in an Area of Outstanding Natural Beauty. (M.5 8 miles Junction 23.)	£25.00 to £30.00	N	N	N
Dr & Mrs L. Hoose **Honeymead** **Holford** **Bridgwater TA5 1RZ** **Tel: (01278) 741668** Fax 01278 741668 **Open:** ALL YEAR (Excl. Xmas) **Map Ref No. 08**	Nearest Road: A.39 Warm & welcoming Honeymead, an arts-&-crafts-style house nestles at the foot of the Quantock Hills. Walk in the footsteps of Coleridge & Wordsworth, through moorland & secluded combes, on cliff paths with views of the Welsh coast. Beautiful & tranquil rooms with en-suites, a selection of refreshments; T.V., radio, books & maps. Guest conservatory & beautiful gardens. 10% off bookings of 3 nights & over	£22.00 to £29.00 *see PHOTO over* *p. 365*	Y	Y	N
Christine Healey **The Old Bakery** **The Street, Olveston** **Bristol BS35 4DR** **Tel/Fax: (01454) 616437** **Open: ALL YEAR (Excl.** **Xmas & New Year)** **Map Ref No. 09**	Nearest Road: A.38 The Old Bakery is situated in the centre of the village of Olveston, just 12 miles north of Bristol. This lovely 200-year-old cottage provides comfortable accommodation in 1 attractive twin-bedded room ,1 double-bedded room & 2 single rooms A lounge with colour T.V./video is provided exclusively for guests which overlooks a pretty walled garden. Easy access to Bath, Forest of Dean, South Cotswolds & M.4/M.5.	£23.00 to £25.00	Y	N	Y
Ruth Shellard **Overbrook** **Stowey Bottom** **Bishop Sutton** **Bristol BS39 5TN** **Tel: (01275) 332648** Fax 01275 332648 **Open:** ALL YEAR (Excl. Xmas) **Map Ref No. 10**	Nearest Road: A.368 Overbrook is a charming wisteria-clad house, tastefully furnished, with a lovely garden by a brook. Situated in rural seclusion in a quiet & peaceful lane, with a little ford by the front gate. Breakfast is taken in the conservatory overlooking the garden. 2 beautifully furnished bedrooms, each with en-suite/private facilities. Overbrook is only 1/2 mile from the village & close to the beautiful Chew Valley Lake. Cheddar Gorge, Bath, Wells & Bristol are within easy reach.	£18.00 to £20.00	Y	N	N

Irondale House. Rode.

Honeymead. Holford.

Somerset
Bath & Bristol

		rate £ from - to per person	evening meals children taken	animals taken
Mrs Judy Gallannaugh **Spring Farm** **The Street** **Regil** **Bristol** **BS40 8BB** **Tel: (01275) 472735** **Open: ALL YEAR** **Map Ref No. 11**	Nearest Road: A.38 A cosy informal farmhouse set in a peaceful garden, Spring Farm has views across fields to the Mendip Hills. 2 comfortable double-bedded rooms, each with an en-suite/private bathroom & tea/coffee facilities. The guest sitting/breakfast room has an open fire in winter. A good choice of pubs for an evening meal. Within easy reach by car are Chew Magna, Bristol, Bath & Wells. An excellent base for exploring Somerset & fishing on the Chew & Blagdon lakes. Children over 3.	£20.00 to £25.00	Y N	Y
Mrs Philippa Tasker **Downs Edge** **Saville Road, Stoke Bishop** **Bristol BS9 1JD** **Tel/Fax: (0117) 9683264** **Mobile 0585 866463** **Open: ALL YEAR (Excl.** **Xmas & New Year)** **Map Ref No. 12**	Nearest Road: A.4018 Downs Edge is situated in a superb position on the very edge of Bristol's famous Downs - an open park of some 450 acres. Furnished with fine period furniture, the house is set in magnificent gardens close to the spectacular Avon Gorge & its breathtaking views. This uniquely peaceful location is ideally situated for the city centre, Clifton & the university. Downs Edge is served by an excellent public transport system with easy access to the motorway network.	£29.00 to £33.00 VISA: M'CARD: AMEX:	Y N	N
Sarah & Roger Newman- **Coburn** **Hawthorne House** **Bishopswood** **Chard TA20 3RS** **Tel: (01460) 234482** **Fax 01460 234482** **Open: ALL YEAR** **Map Ref No. 13**	Nearest Road: A.303 Hawthorne House is a cosy 19th-century stone house set in the Blackdown Hills, an Area of Outstanding Natural Beauty. It is ideally situated for an overnight stay en-route to Cornwall, & for visiting N.T. properties & the many other attractions in Somerset & Devon. Each of the 3 comfortable bedrooms has an en-suite/private bathroom & tea/coffee-making facilities. The attractive dining room has panoramic views over the extensive gardens & surrounding hills. Children over 12.	£19.50 to £££	Y Y	Y
John & Sally Gregory **Dryclose** **Newbery Lane** **Misterton** **Crewkerne TA18 8NE** **Tel: (01460) 73161** **Open: ALL YEAR (Excl.** **Xmas & New Year)** **Map Ref No. 14**	Nearest Road: A.30, A.303 Dryclose is an attractive, 16th-century, listed, beamed & panelled former farmhouse, set in 2 acres of lovely garden, with an outdoor swimming pool. There are 3 charming bedrooms, 1 twin, 1 single & 1 twin en-suite. All have hot-drinks facilities. There are 2 sitting rooms, each with T.V., for guests. The area abounds with beautiful gardens & historic houses, & the coast is only 15 miles away. An ideal spot for a relaxing break & for exploring Somerset. Children over 8.	£18.50 to £27.00	Y N	N
Major & Mrs G. H. Bradshaw **Dollons House** **Church Street** **Dunster** **TA24 6SH** **Tel: (01643) 821880** **Fax 01643 822016** **Open: ALL YEAR (Excl.** **Xmas/Boxing Days)** **Map Ref No. 16**	Nearest Road: A.396 17th-century Dollons House nestles beneath the castle in this delightful medieval village in the Exmoor National Park. 3 attractive & very comfortable en-suite rooms, each with its own character & special decor. 100 years ago, the local pharmacist had his shop in Dollons, & in the back he made marmalade for the Houses of Parliament. A delightful home. Dunster is ideal for touring. Pull up outside the front door to unload & get instructions for parking. **E-mail: hannah.bradshaw@virgin.net**	£27.50 to £30.00 *see PHOTO over* p. 367 VISA: M'CARD:	N N	N

Dollons House. Dunster.

Somerset
Bath & Bristol

		rate £ from - to per person	children taken	evening meals	animals taken
Mrs B. Bale **Conygar House** **2A The Ball** **Dunster** **TA24 6SD** **Tel: (01643) 821872** **Fax 01643 821872** **Open: FEB - NOV** **Map Ref No. 15**	Nearest Road: A.39 Conygar House is situated in a quiet road just off the main street of medieval Dunster village. Restaurants, bars & shops are all within 1 mins' walking distance. Wonderful views of castle & moors. Delightful sunny garden & patio for guests' use. Ideal for exploring Exmoor & coast. All rooms decorated & furnished to a high standard. Personal service & your comfort is guaranteed. Dunster Beach is 1 1/2 miles away, Minehead 2 1/2 miles & Porlock 8 miles. E-mail: bale.dunster@virgin.net	£22.00 to £26.00	Y	N	N
Mrs Pat Redmond **Number Three** **3 Magdalene Street** **Glastonbury BA6 9EW** **Tel: (01458) 832129** **Fax 01458 834227** **Open: FEB - NOV** **Map Ref No. 17**	Nearest Road: M.5 Ex. 23, A.39 An attractive Grade II listed Georgian house adjoining the Abbey ruins where the tomb of King Arthur & Guinevere is said to have been discovered in the 13th century. 4 very attractive rooms, each with private facilities, telephone, radio, T.V. & a hostess tray. There is a beautiful walled garden, floodlit at night, & cars are parked here behind security gates. Pat Redmond is here to make your stay at No. 3 as happy as possible.	£35.00 to £50.00 VISA: M'CARD: AMEX:	Y	N	N
Mrs V. A. Vicary **Larcombe Foot** **Winsford** **Minehead** **TA24 7HS** **Tel: (01643) 851306** **Open: APR - DEC** **Map Ref No. 18**	Nearest Road: A.358 Larcombe Foot, a comfortable old country house set in the beautiful & tranquil Upper Exe Valley, is an ideal base for walking, riding, fishing & touring Exmoor. Guests' comfort is paramount. There are 3 bedrooms, 2 with private bathroom & tea/coffee makers in all rooms. A comfortable sitting room with log fire & T.V., plus a pretty garden to relax in. Evening meals by prior arrangement. Winsford is considered one of the prettiest villages on the moor. Children over 8 years.	£20.00 to £20.00	Y	Y	Y
Diana Brewer **Wood Advent Farm** **Roadwater** **TA23 0RR** **Tel: (01984) 640920** **Fax 01984 640920** **Open: ALL YEAR** **Map Ref No. 21**	Nearest Road: A.39 Peace & tranquillity. Discover this listed farmhouse in the Exmoor countryside. Well-marked footpaths go for miles. 4 bedrooms with en-suite/private facilities, T.V. & hospitality trays, & glorious views from all windows. 2 large reception rooms & dining room, where delicious Exmoor dishes are served with good wines. Relax by the heated pool, enjoy afternoon tea in the gardens. Wonderful base for the West Country. Your hosts look forward to welcoming you. Children over 10. E-mail: jddibrewer@aol.com	£22.00 to £25.50 VISA: M'CARD:	Y	Y	N
Mr & Mrs M. Dearden **Pennard House** **East Pennard** **Shepton Mallet** **BA4 6TP** **Tel: (01749) 860266** **Fax 01749 860266** **Open: ALL YEAR** **Map Ref No. 22**	Nearest Road: A.37 Pennard House is a beautiful Grade II listed Georgian house situated on the last south-facing slope of the Mendip Hills, in secluded gardens & surrounded by meadows, woodlands & cider orchards. Furnished throughout with antiques & offering 5 attractive bedrooms, 3 with en-suite/private facilities. Tennis court & Victorian spring fed swimming pool. Ideally situated for visiting Glastonbury, Wells, Bath & historic houses & gardens of Stourhead, Longleat & Montacute . E-mail: m.dearden@uk.online	£25.00 to £30.00 VISA: M'CARD:	Y	N	Y

The Lynch Country House Hotel.   Somerton.

Somerset
Bath & Bristol

	Nearest Road	rate £ from - to per person	children taken	evening meals	animals taken
Roy Copeland **The Lynch Country House** **4 Behind Berry** **Somerton** **TA11 7PD** **Tel: (01458) 272316** **Fax 01458 272590** **Open: ALL YEAR (Excl. Xmas)** **Map Ref No. 24**	Nearest Road: A.372 The Lynch is a charming small hotel, standing in acres of carefully tended, wonderfully mature grounds. Beautifully refurbished & decorated to retain all its Georgian style & elegance, it now offers 5 attractively presented rooms, some with 4-posters, others with Victorian bedsteads, all with thoughtful extras including bathrobes & magazines. Each room is en-suite with 'phone, T.V. & tea/coffee. The dining room overlooks the lawns & lake. Single supplement. Children over 10.	£24.50 to £37.50 *see PHOTO over* *p. 369* VISA: M'CARD: AMEX:	Y	N	Y
Mrs Claire Mitchem **Whittles Farm** **Beercrocombe** **Taunton** **TA3 6AH** **Tel: (01823) 480301** **Fax 01823 480301** **Open: FEB - NOV** **Map Ref No. 26**	Nearest Road: A.358 Guests at Whittles Farm can be sure of a high standard of accommodation & service. A superior 16th-century farmhouse set in 200 acres of pastureland, it is luxuriously carpeted & furnished in traditional style. Inglenook fireplaces & log-burners. 3 en-suite bedrooms, individually furnished, with T.V. & tea/coffee facilities. Super farmhouse food, using own meat, eggs & vegetables, & local Cheddar cheese & butter. Evening meals by prior arrangement. Table licence.	£23.00 to £26.00	N	Y	N
Martin & Marise Eyre **Higher House** **West Bagborough** **Taunton** **TA4 3EF** **Tel: (01823) 432996** **Fax 01823 433568** **Open: ALL YEAR** **Map Ref No. 29**	Nearest Road: A.358 Higher House is set 650 feet up on the southern slopes of the Quantock Hills. The views from the house & gardens are exceptional. The principal part of the house is 17th-century, built around 2 courtyards, 1 with a heated pool. Each bedroom has its own bathroom, 'phone, T.V., tea/coffee facilities, books, magazines. There is a beautifully presented drawing room. An all-weather tennis court & 2 well-appointed cottages, are also available. Evening meals by prior arrangement. **E-mail: eyre@bagborough.u-net.com**	£25.00 to £27.00 🚭 *see PHOTO over* *p. 371*	Y	Y	N
Elizabeth & Brian Totman **Redlands House** **Trebles Holford** **Combe Florey** **Taunton** **TA4 3HA** **Tel: (01823) 433159** **Open: ALL YEAR** **Map Ref No. 31**	Nearest Road: A.358 Originally a barn, Redlands is now a lovely family home, which offers a warm & friendly welcome. It nestles in the sheltered, peaceful hamlet of Trebles Holford with views to the surrounding Quantock Hills. The area is renowned for its beautiful walks, picturesque villages & wildlife. An excellent base for exploring the region, Exmoor, Dartmoor & the beaches of North & South Devon. 2 attractive en-suite guest rooms, one of which is downstairs & converted with the disabled in mind. **E-mail: redlandshouse@hotmail.com**	£25.00 to £27.00 🚭	Y	N	Y

Visit our website at:
http://www.bestbandb.co.uk

Higher House. West Bagborough.

Stoneleigh House. Westbury- sub- Mendip.

Somerset
Bath & Bristol

		rate £ from - to per person	children taken	evening meals	animals taken
Nigel & Finny Muers-Raby **Higher Vexford House** **Higher Vexford** **Lydeard St. Lawrence** **Taunton** **TA4 3QF** **Tel: (01984) 656267** Fax 01984 656707 **Open: ALL YEAR** **Map Ref No. 30**	Nearest Road: A.358 A lovely English country house, some parts dating from the 17th century & added to at various times over the next 200 years, set in stunning, unspoilt countryside between the Quantock & Brendon Hills & Exmoor. Lovely walled gardens, plant & flower-filled cobblestone courtyards & stunning views. Antiques, pictures, books & magazines fill the large flagstone-floored hall, drawing room, dining room & bedrooms. Log fires in winter, pool in summer & hearty breakfasts all year round! **E-mail: highervexford@csl.com**	£30.00 to £38.00 🚭 *see PHOTO over* *p. 374*	Y	N	N
Wendy & Tony Thompson **Stoneleigh House** **Westbury-sub-Mendip** **Wells** **BA5 1HF** **Tel: (01749) 870668** Fax 01749 870668 **Open: ALL YEAR (Excl. Xmas)** **Map Ref No. 33**	Nearest Road: A.371 A beautiful 18th-century farmhouse (flagstone floors, beams, crooked walls) situated between Wells & Cheddar. Wonderful southerly views over unspoilt countryside to Glastonbury Tor from the bedrooms & guests' lounge. The bedrooms are prettily furnished with country antiques & the en-suite bath/shower rooms work properly. Round this off with a delicious breakfast, Wendy's decorative needlework, Tony's classic cars, the old forge, a cottagey garden & friendly cats. Children over 10 welcome. Excellent pubs nearby.	£23.00 to £28.00 🚭 *see PHOTO over* *p. 372*	Y	N	N
Anita Frost **Southway Farm** **Polsham** **Wells** **BA5 1RW** **Tel: (01749) 673396** Fax 01749 670373 **Open: FEB - NOV** **Map Ref No. 34**	Nearest Road: A.39 Southway Farm is a Grade II listed Georgian farmhouse situated halfway between Glastonbury & Wells. Accommodation is in 3 comfortable & attractively furnished bedrooms, 1 en-suite & 2 with a private bathroom. A delicious full English breakfast is served, although vegetarians are also catered for. Guests may relax in the cosy lounge, with colour T.V., or in the pretty, tranquil garden. An ideal location for a restful holiday, or for touring the glorious West Country.	£20.00 to £25.00 🚭	Y	N	N
Eddie & Holly Nowell **Beryl** **Off Hawkers Lane** **Wells BA5 3JP** **Tel: (01749) 678738** Fax 01749 670508 **Open: ALL YEAR (Excl. Xmas)** **Map Ref No. 35**	Nearest Road: A.371 Beryl is a precious gem in a perfect setting, situated 1 mile from the cathedral city of Wells. This striking 19th-century Gothic mansion has beautifully furnished en-suite bedrooms, interesting views & all the accoutrements of luxury living. Dinner is available by prior arrangement & is served in the exquisite dining room. Eddie & Holly are charming hosts, & your stay at their home is sure to be memorable.	£35.00 to £47.50 VISA: M'CARD:	Y	Y	Y
Ann Durbin **Cutthorne** **Luckwell Bridge** **Wheddon Cross** **TA24 7EW** **Tel: (01643) 831255** Fax 01643 831255 **Open: ALL YEAR** **Map Ref No. 37**	Nearest Road: A.396 Tucked away in the heart of Exmoor National Park, Cutthorne offers a quiet & relaxing haven for country lovers. It is situated in an Area of Outstanding Natural Beauty, & walking & riding are unrivalled, whether by the coast or on the moors. Nearby are Lynton & Lynmouth, Tarr Steps & Dunster. The pretty bedrooms all have bathrooms & 1 has a 4-poster bed. The cuisine is traditional or vegetarian, using the finest local meat & organic vegetables.	£25.00 to £31.00 🚭 *see PHOTO over* *p. 375*	N	Y	Y

Higher Vexford House. Lydeard St. Lawrence.

Cutthorne. Luckwell Bridge.

Suffolk

Suffolk
(East Anglia)

In July, the lower reaches of the River Orwell hold the essence of Suffolk. Broad fields of green and gold with wooded horizons sweep down to the quiet water. Orwell Bridge spans the wide river where yachts and tan-sailed barges share the water with ocean-going container ships out of Ipswich. Downstream the saltmarshes echo to the cry of the Curlew. The small towns and villages of Suffolk are typical of an area with long seafairing traditions. This is the county of men of vision; like Constable and Gainsborough, Admiral Lord Nelson and Benjamin Britten.

The land is green and fertile and highly productive. The hedgerows shelter some of our prettiest wild flowers, & the narrow country lanes are a pure delight. Most memorable is the ever-changing sky, appearing higher and wider here than elsewhere in England. There is a great deal of heathland, probably the best known being Newmarket where horses have been trained and raced for some hundreds of years. Gorse-covered heath meets sandy cliffs on Suffolks Heritage Coast. Here are bird reserves and the remains of the great mediaeval city of Dunwich, sliding into the sea.

West Suffolk was famous for its wool trade in the Middle Ages, & the merchants gave thanks for their good fortune by building magnificent "Wool Churches". Much-photographed Lavenham has the most perfect black & white timbered houses in Britain, built by the merchants of Tudor times. Ipswich was granted the first charter by King John in 1200, but had long been a trading community of seafarers. Its history can be read from the names of the streets - Buttermarket, Friars Street, Cornhill, Dial Lane & Tavern Street. The latter holds the Great White Horse Hotel mentioned by Charles Dickens in Pickwick Papers. Sadly not many ancient buildings remain, but the mediaeval street pattern and the churches make an interesting trail to follow. The Market town of Bury St. Edmunds is charming, with much of its architectural heritage still surviving, from the Norman Cornhill to a fine Queen Anne House. The great Abbey, now in ruins, was the meeting place of the Barons of England for the creation of the Magna Carta, enshrining the principals of individual freedom, parliamentary democracy and the supremacy of the law. Suffolk has some very fine churches, notably at Mildenhall, Lakenheath, Framlingham, Lavenham & Stoke-by-Nayland, & also a large number of wonderful houses & great halls, evidence of the county's prosperity.

Lavenham.

Suffolk

Suffolk Gazeteer

Areas of Outstanding Natural Beauty
Suffolk Coast. Heathlands. Dedham Vale.

Historic Houses & Castles

Euston Hall - Thetford
18th century house with fine collection of pictures. Gardens & 17th century Parish Church nearby.

Christchurch Mansion - Ipswich
16th century mansion built on site of 12th century Augustinian Priory. Gables & dormers added in 17th century & other alteration & additions made in 17th & 18th centuries.

Gainsborough's House - Sudbury
Birthplace of Gainsborough, well furnished, collection of paintings.

The Guildhall - Hadleigh
15th century.

Glemham Hall - Nr Woodbridge
Elizabethan house of red brick - 18th century alterations. Fine stair, panelled rooms with Queen Anne furniture.

Haughley Park - Nr. Stowmarket
Jacobean manor house.

Heveningham Hall - Nr. Halesworth
Georgian mansion - English Palladian - Interior in Neo-Classical style. Garden by Capability Brown.

Ickworth - Nr. Bury St. Edmunds
Mixed architectural styles - late Regency & 18th century. French furniture, pictures & superb silver. Gardens with orangery.

Kentwell Hall - Long Melford
Elizabethan mansion in red brick, built in E plan, surrounded by moat.

Little Hall - Lavenham
15th century hall house, collection of furniture, pictures, china, etc.

Melford Hall - Nr. Sudbury
16th century - fine pictures, Chinese porcelain, furniture. Garden with gazebo.

Somerleyton Hall - Nr. Lowestoft
Dating from 16th century - additional work in 19th century. Carving by Grinling Gibbons. Tapestries, library, pictures.

Cathedrals & Churches

Bury St. Edmunds (St. Mary)
15th century. Hammer Beam roof in nave, wagon roof in chancel. Boret monument 1467.

Bramfield (St. Andrew)
Early circular tower. Fine screen & vaulting. Renaissance effigy.

Bacton (St. Mary)
15th century timbered roof. East Anglian stone & flintwork.

Dennington (St. Mary)
15th century alabaster monuments & bench ends. Aisle & Parclose screens with lofts & parapets.

Earl Stonhay (St. Mary)
14th century - rebuilt with fine hammer roof & 17th century pulpit with four hour-glasses.

Euston (St. Genevieve)
17th century. Fine panelling, reredos may be Grinling Gibbons.

Framlingham (St. Michael)
15th century nave & west tower, hammer beam roof in false vaulting. Chancel was rebuilt in 16th century for the tombs of the Howard family, monumental art treasures. Thamar organ. 1674.

Fressingfield (St. Peter & St. Paul)
15th century woodwork - very fine.

Lavenham (St. Peter & St. Paul)
15th century. Perpendicular. Fine towers. 14th century chancel screen. 17th century monument in alabaster.

Long Melford (Holy Trinity)
15th century Lady Chapel, splendid brasses. 15th century glass of note. Chantry chapel with fine roof. Like cathedral in proportions.

Stoke-by-Nayland (St. Mary)
16th-17th century library, great tower. Fine nave & arcades. Good brasses & monuments.

Ufford (St. Mary)
Mediaeval font cover - glorious.

Museums & Galleries

Christchurch Mansion - Ipswich
Country house, collection of furniture, pictures, bygones, ceramics of 18th century. Paintings by Gainsborough, Constable & modern artists.

Ipswich Museum - Ipswich
Natural History; prehistory, geology & archaeology to mediaeval period.

Suffolk

Moyse's Hall Musuem - Bury St. Edmunds
12th century dwelling house with local antiquities & natural history.
Abbot's Hall Museum of Rural Life - Stowmarket
Collections describing agriculture, crafts & domestic utensils.
Gershom-Parkington Collection - Bury St. Edmunds
Queen Anne House containing collection of watches & clocks.
Dunwich Musuem - Dunwich
Flora & fauna; local history.

Historic Monuments

The Abbey - Bury St. Edmunds
Only west end now standing.

Framlingham Castle
12th & 13th centuries - Tudor almshouses.
Bungay Castle - Bungay
12th century. Restored 13th century drawbridge & gatehouse.
Burgh Castle Roman Fort - Burgh
Coastal defences - 3rd century.
Herringfleet Priory - Herringfleet
13th century - remains of small Augustinian priory.
Leiston Abbey - Leiston
14th century - remains of cloisters, choir & trancepts.
Orford Castle - Orford
12th century - 18-sided keep - three towers.

The House in the Clouds. Thorpeness.

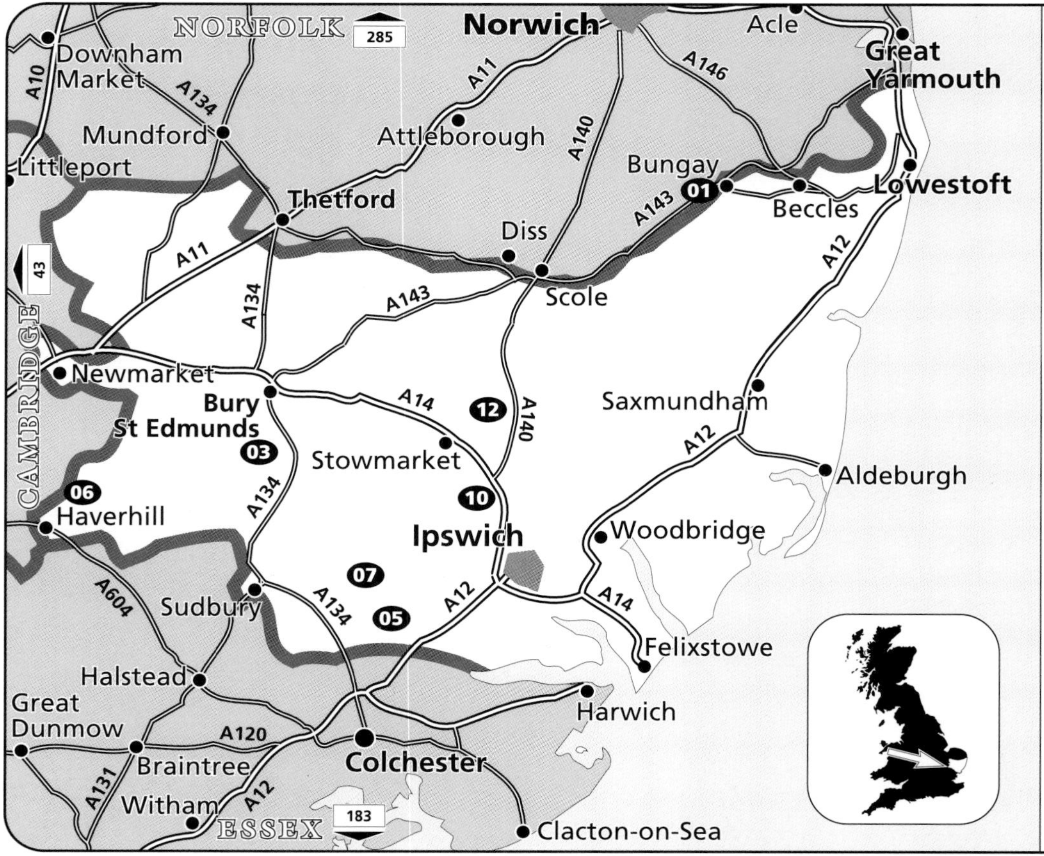

SUFFOLK
Map reference

01 Watchorn
03 Oaten
05 Watkins
06 Sheppard
07 Rolfe
10 Hackett-Jones
12 Ridsdale

The Old Vicarage. Great Thurlow.

Suffolk

		rate £ from - to per person	children taken	evening meals	animals taken
Mrs Bobbie Watchorn **Earsham Park Farm** **Harleston Road** **Earsham** **Bungay NR35 2AQ** **Tel: (01986) 892180** **Fax 01986 892180** **Open: ALL YEAR** **Map Ref No. 01**	Nearest Road: A.143 A Victorian farmhouse set on a hill overlooking the Waveney Valley, with superb views. Park Farm offers 3 really delightful guest rooms, all furnished to a high standard. Each is en-suite, & well-equipped with T.V., radio/alarm & tea/coffee facilities. 1 4-poster. Breakfast is served in the lovely dining room. Within easy reach of Norwich, Lowestoft & Southwold. A wonderful home, where comfort & a relaxed atmosphere prevail.	£20.00 to £35.00 🚭 VISA: M'CARD:	Y	N	N
Bridget & Robin Oaten **The Hatch** **Pilgrims Lane** **Cross Green, Hartest** **Bury St. Edmunds** **IP29 4ED** **Tel: (01284) 830226** **Fax 01284 830226** **Open: ALL YEAR** **Map Ref No. 03**	Nearest Road: A.134 The Hatch is a gorgeous Grade II listed thatched house, peacefully situated just outside the attractive 'High Suffolk' village of Hartest. Surrounded by farmland, with a lovely rose-filled garden for guests to enjoy. Inside are gleaming antiques & fine fabrics. Bedrooms are comfortably furnished with large beds & many extras. Log fires. Home-baked bread, cakes & preserves. Evening meals by arrangement. The Oatens were formerly at Hancocks Farmhouse in Kent. (Babies & children over 9 years welcome.)	£28.00 to £35.00 🚭	Y	Y	Y
Nowell & Penny Watkins **The Bauble** **Higham** **Colchester** **CO7 6LA** **Tel: (01206) 337254** **Fax 01206 337263** **Open: ALL YEAR** **Map Ref No. 05**	Nearest Road: A.12 The Bauble is a delightful house offering accommodation in 3 attractively furnished bedrooms, with modern amenities including T.V. & tea/coffee-making facilities. A delicious full English breakfast is served. Lounge, garden, heated pool & tennis court available for guests' use. Higham lies in the heart of Constable country & is within easy reach of many wool villages, with their churches, antiques shops & N.T. properties. Children over 12 years welcome.	£25.00 to £30.00 🚭	Y	N	N
Mrs Jane Sheppard **The Old Vicarage** **Great Thurlow** **Haverhill** **CB9 7LE** **Tel: (01440) 783209** **Open: ALL YEAR** **Map Ref No. 06**	Nearest Road: A.1307 Set in mature grounds & woodlands, this delightful old vicarage has a friendly family atmosphere. Complete peace & comfort are assured. Wonderful views of the Suffolk countryside. Open log fires welcome you in winter. Perfectly situated for Newmarket, Cambridge, Long Melford & Constable country, the attractively furnished bedrooms have en-suite or private facilities, & tea & coffee trays. (No smoking in bedrooms.) Evening meals are available at prior notice. Children over 7 welcome, & pets by arrangement.	£24.00 to £25.00 *see PHOTO over* *p. 380*	Y	Y	Y
Angela & Rodney Rolfe **Edgehill** **2 High Street, Hadleigh** **Ipswich IP7 5AP** **Tel: (01473) 822458** **Fax 01473 827751** **Open: ALL YEAR (Excl. Xmas)** **Map Ref No. 07**	Nearest Road: A.12 Edgehill is a family-run Georgian house in central Hadleigh. It has been beautifully restored & tastefully modernised, & the hotel offers the ultimate in accommodation. Particular attention is paid to friendly service & traditional home cooking with organic vegetables. Edgehill is situated in the most picturesque part of Suffolk, it is a good base from which to explore the surrounding towns & pretty villages of East Anglia.	£25.00 to £40.00 *see PHOTO over* *p. 382*	Y	Y	Y

Edgehill Hotel. Hadleigh.

Suffolk

		rate £ from - to per person	evening meals children taken	animals taken

Mrs Raewyn Hackett-Jones **Pipps Ford** **Needham Market** **IP6 8LJ** **Tel: (01449) 760208** **Fax 01449 760561** **Open: Mid JAN - Mid DEC** **Map Ref No. 10**	Nearest Road: A.140, A.14 A beautiful, Tudor, beamed guest house in a pretty, old-fashioned garden by the Gipping river. 6 very attractive bedrooms, with private bathrooms & tea/coffee-making facilities. A very extensive breakfast menu & delicious 4-course evening meals, served in the delightful conservatory. Licensed. Colour T.V. & tennis court. Winner of The Best Bed & Breakfast award for East Anglia. A good central position for touring all of East Anglia. Children over 5 years welcome. Animals by arrangement. **E-mail: pippsford@aol.com**	£23.50 to £43.50 *see PHOTO over* *p. 384*	Y	Y	N
Martin & Diana Ridsdale **Cherry Tree Farm** **Mendlesham Green** **Stowmarket** **IP14 5RQ** **Tel: (01449) 766376** **Open: ALL YEAR (Excl.** **Xmas & New Year)** **Map Ref No. 12**	Nearest Road: A.140 Traditional timber-framed farmhouse, standing in three quarters of an acre of garden, with orchard & duck ponds, in a peaceful Suffolk village. 3 bedrooms, each with en-suite facilities. A spacious & comfortable lounge, inglenook fireplaces with log fire. Hearty English breakfast served in the oak-beamed dining room. Home-baked bread, own preserves & honey. Imaginative evening meals, with garden & local produce, good cheeses & fine English wines.	£24.00 to £28.00 🚭	N	Y	N

All the establishments mentioned in this guide are members of
The Worldwide Bed & Breakfast Association

When booking your accommodation please mention
The Best Bed & Breakfast

Pipps Ford. Needham Market.

Surrey

Surrey
(South East)

One of the Home Counties, Surrey includes a large area of London, south of the Thames. Communications are good in all directions so it is easy to stay in Surrey & travel either into central London or out to enjoy the lovely countryside which, despite urban development, survives thanks to the 'Green Belt' policy. The county is also very accessible from Gatwick Airport.

The land geographically, is chalk sandwiched in clay, & probably the lack of handy building material was responsible for the area remaining largely uninhabited for centuries. The North Downs were a considerable barrier to cross, but gradually settlements grew along the rivers which were the main routes through. The Romans used the gap created by the River Mole to build Stane Street between London & Chichester, this encouraged the development of small towns. The gap cut by the passage of the River Wey allows the Pilgrims Way to cross the foot of the Downs. Dorking, Reigate & Farnham are small towns along this route, all with attracitve main streets & interesting shops & buildings.

Surrey has very little mention in the Domesday Book, &, although the patronage of the church & of wealthy families established manors which developed over the years, little happened to disturb the rural tranquility of the region. As a county it made little history but rather reflected passing times, although Magna Carta was signed at Egham in 1215.

The heathlands of Surrey were a Royal playground for centuries. The Norman Kings hunted here & horses became part of the landscape & life of the people, as they are today on Epsom Downs.

Nearness to London & Royal patronage began to influence the area, & the buildings of the Tudor period reflect this. Royal palaces were built at Hampton Court & Richmond, & great houses such as Loseley near Guildford often using stone from the monasteries emptied during the Reformation. Huge deer parks were enclosed & stocked. Richmond, described as the "finest village in the British Dominions", is now beset by 20th century traffic but still has a wonderful park with deer, lakes & woodland that was enclosed by Charles I. The terraces & gardens of such buildings as Trumpeters House & Asgill House on the slopes of Richmond overlooking the Thames, have an air of spaciousness & elegance & there are lovely & interesting riverside walks at Richmond.

Polesden Lacey.

Surrey

Surrey Gazeteer

Historic Houses & Castles

Albury Park - Albury, Nr. Guildford
A delightful country mansion designed by Pugin.

Clandon Park - Guildford
A fine house in the Palladian style by Leoni. A good collection of furniture & pictures. The house boasts some fine plasterwork.

Claremont - Esher
A superb Palladian house with interesting interior.

Detillens - Limpsfield
A fine 15th century house with inglenook fireplaces & mediaeval furniture. A large, pleasant garden.

Greathed Manor- Lingfield
An imposing Victorian manor house.

Hatchlands - East Clandon
A National Trust property of the 18th century with a fine Adam interior.

Loseley House - Guildford
A very fine Elizabethan mansion with superb panelling, furniture & paintings.

Polesden Lacy - Dorking
A Regency villa housing the Grevill collection of tapestries, pictures & furnishings. Extensive gardens.

Cathedrals & Churches

Compton (St. Nicholas)
The only surviving 2-storey sanctuary in the country. A fine 17th century pulpit.

Esher (St. George)
A fine altar-piece & marble monument.

Hascombe (St. Peter)
A rich interior with much gilding & painted reredos & roofs.

Lingfield (St. Peter & St. Paul)
15th century. Holding a chained bible.

Ockham (St. Mary & All Saints)
Early church with 13th century east window.

Stoke D'Abernon (St. Mary)
Dating back to Pre-conquest time with additions from the 12th-15th centuries. A fine 13th century painting. Early brasses.

Museums & Galleries

Charterhouse School Museum - Godalming
Peruvian pottery, Greek pottery, archaeology & natural history.

Chertsey Museum - Chertsey
18th-19th century costume & furnishing displayed & local history.

Guildford House - Guildford
The house is 17th century & of architectural interest housing monthly exhibitions.

Guildford Museum - Guildford
A fine needlework collection & plenty on local history.

Old Kiln Agricultural - Tilford
A very interesting collection of old farm implements.

Watermill Museum - Haxted
A restored 17th century mill with working water wheels & machinery.

Weybridge Museum - Weybridge
Good archaeological exhibition plus costume & local history.

The Gardens. Wisley

SURREY
Map reference

01 McCarthy
02 Franklin-Adams
03 Hill
04 Wallis
05 Travers
06 Carmichael
07 Lees
07 Blok
08 Grinsted
09 Dale
10 Warren
11 Wolf
12 Leeper
13 Carey
14 Rowse

Maidenhead • Slough
LONDON
Reading Windsor
Staines
Richmond
BERKSHIRE
M4
Croydon A232
Wokingham
A2
A3
Camberley 01 14 12
13
Woking
Leatherhead
Farnborough
M3
Guildford
A23
Aldershot
Dorking
M25
A25
KENT
Farnham
Reigate
10
A31
09
Milford
04
A24
Warren
Hindhead
02
03
07
08
11
A22
HANTS
A281
Gatwick
Airport
M23
05
A3
06
Crawley
East
Haslemere
A264
Grinstead
Horsham
A23
Petersfield
Billingshurst
Haywards
Heath
Petworth
A272 Cowfold
Midhurst
Burgess
Pulborough
Hill
A272
SUSSEX
A24
395

Surrey

		rate £ from - to per person	children taken	evening meals	animals taken
Tommy & Ann McCarthy **Pineleigh** **10 Castle Road** **Off Waverley Drive** **Camberley** **GU15 2DS** **Tel/Fax: (01276) 64787** **Open: ALL YEAR** **Map Ref No. 01**	Nearest Road: A.325 Pineleigh is a spacious Edwardian house, built in 1906 & set in half an acre of mature garden in a very quiet area. Accommodation is in 4 comfortable guest rooms, all en-suite with telephone, T.V. & hospitality tray. Attractively furnished in Victorian style with many old prints & pictures. A full English breakfast is served, evening meals by arrangement. Pineleigh is conveniently located for Heathrow Airport & London. VISA: M'CARD: AMEX:	£30.00 to £45.00	N	N	N
Mrs Carol Franklin-Adams **High Edser** **Shere Road** **Ewhurst** **Cranleigh GU6 7PQ** **Tel: (01483) 278214** **Fax 01483 278200** **Open: ALL YEAR** **Map Ref No. 02**	Nearest Road: A.25 A large, handsome Grade II listed home, the earliest part built in the 16th century, situated in an Area of Outstanding Natural Beauty. There are three attractively furnished rooms available: two doubles and one twin. Residents' lounge and T.V.. Tennis court in grounds, and golf nearby. 35 minutes to Gatwick and London Airports. Approximately an hour's drive to London. A delightful home, ideal for a relaxing break.	£25.00 to £30.00	Y	N	Y
Mrs Gill Hill **Bulmer Farm** **Holmbury St. Mary** **Dorking** **RH5 6LG** **Tel: (01306) 730210** **Open: ALL YEAR** **Map Ref No. 03**	Nearest Road: A.25 Enjoy a warm welcome at this delightful 17th-century farmhouse, complete with many beams & an inglenook fireplace. Offering 3 charming bedrooms, all with h/c & tea/coffee-making facilities. Adjoining the house around a courtyard are 5 attractive barn-conversion en-suite bedrooms for non-smokers. Farm produce & home-made preserves are provided. Situated in a picturesque village, it is convenient for London airports. Children over 12 years welcome.	£21.00 to £34.00	N	N	N
Ann & Peter Wallis **Park House** **Abinger Common** **Dorking** **RH5 6LW** **Tel: (01306) 730101** **Fax 01306 730643** **Open: ALL YEAR** **Map Ref No. 04**	Nearest Road: A.25 A delightful large family home, tastefully furnished with many antiques. Accommodation is very comfortable with en-suite/private facilities, satellite T.V., tea/coffee etc.. It is set in 25 acres in an Area of Outstanding Natural Beauty within easy reach of Heathrow & Gatwick Airports, many gardens & N.T. properties. Good train service to London. Ideal walking country, with many village pubs for food. Children over 12. **E-mail: Peterwallis@msn.com**	£20.00 to £30.00	Y	N	N
Mrs L. Travers **Chesham Cottage** **Highercombe Road** **Haslemere** **GU27 2LP** **Tel: (01428) 642712** **Fax 01428 642712** **Open: MAR - NOV** **Map Ref No. 05**	Nearest Road: A.286 A charming late Victorian cottage, carefully & tastefully restored, yet retaining many original period features & set in a mature garden. There are 2 prettily decorated, well-furnished bedrooms & every care has been taken to ensure guests comfort. (En-suite/private bathrooms, T.V. etc.) Within easy reach are the Blackdown Forest, Goodwood, Petworth, Farnham & Winchester. Good places to eat nearby. Children over 10. A warm welcome awaits you.	£25.00 to £25.00	Y	N	N

Surrey

		rate £ from - to per person	children taken	evening meals	animals taken
Mrs Elizabeth Carmichael **Deerfell** **Blackdown Park** **Fernden Lane** **Haslemere GU27 3LA** **Tel: (01428) 653409** **Fax 01428 656106** **Open: ALL YEAR** **Map Ref No. 06**	Nearest Road: A.286 A warm welcome at a spacious & comfortable stone-built home set in downland countryside, with breathtaking views to the hills & valleys of Surrey/Sussex. Offering 2 pretty en-suite rooms which are very comfortable & have tea/coffee facilities & T.V.. Wonderful walks right on door-step. Light suppers available on request. Close by - Haslemere station (4 miles), London (45 mins), Guildford/Chichester (20 miles), Heathrow/Gatwick Airports 1 hour. Children over 6 years.	£25.00 to £30.00	Y	Y	N
David Lees **Latchetts Cottage** **Norwood Hill** **Horley RH6 0ET** **Tel: (01293) 862831** **Fax 01293 862831** **Open: ALL YEAR** **Map Ref No. 07**	Nearest Road: A.217 Latchetts Cottage is situated in the small hamlet of Norwood Hill, yet is less than 10 mins from Gatwick Airport & the station. This cosy cottage has comfortable accommodation, with a warm welcome & homely atmosphere. All bedrooms have fine views over interrupted countryside. The village pub offers a varied menu, & is within walking distance. N.T. properties & walks nearby. Parking & courtesy transport available.	£19.50 to £27.00	Y	N	N
Mrs G. Blok **Crutchfield Farm** **Crutchfield Lane** **Hookwood** **Horley** **RH6 0HT** **Tel: (01293) 863110** **Fax 01293 863233** **Open: ALL YEAR** **Map Ref No. 07**	Nearest Road: A.217 Gatwick is only 3 miles from Crutchfield Farm, a listed 15th-century timber-framed farmhouse in an exquisite setting overlooking its own lake, in landscaped gardens with swimming pool & tennis court, hidden away down a country lane. Its many period features, combined with en-suite, beauti-fully furnished bedrooms equipped with T.V.s & many other delightful touches, make this a fasci-nating place to stay. London & the south coast 30 mins. Rates include airport transfer. Parking. **E-mail: TonyBlok@compuserve.com**	£30.00 to £45.00	Y	N	Y
Carole & Adrian Grinsted **The Lawn Guest House** **30 Massetts Road** **Horley** **RH6 7DE** **Tel: (01293) 775751** **Fax 01293 821803** **Open: ALL YEAR** **Map Ref No. 08**	Nearest Road: A.23 A well-appointed Victorian house 4 mins from Gatwick & 25 miles to London or Brighton. Very useful as a base for travelling, it is close to the rail station & town centre. There are 10 bedrooms, all with en-suite facilities & very comfortable & well decorated, with colour T.V. & tea/coffee-making facilities. Also, a pleasant breakfast room & a garden for guests' use. There is a supplement payable for single use of rooms. Parking. **E-mail: info@lawnguesthouse.co.uk**	£23.00 to £25.00 VISA: M'CARD: AMEX:	Y	N	Y
Ann & David Dale **Herons Head Farm** **Mynthurst** **Leigh** **RH2 8QD** **Tel: (01293) 862475** **Fax 01293 863350** **Open: ALL YEAR** **Map Ref No. 09**	Nearest Road: A.217 A charming, quintessentially British Grade II listed beamed farmhouse set in 5 acres of gardens & paddocks, with a small lake, tennis court & swim-ming pool. The house boasts many original features: antique furnishings, a farmhouse kitchen, inglenook & log fires, & a conservatory overlook-ing the lake & ducks. Close to Dorking & Reigate, Leigh is a picturesque village with inns/restau-rants. Gatwick Airport 10 mins. London 33 mins. **E-mail: heronshead@clara.net**	£25.00 to £50.00	Y	N	Y

Surrey

		rate £ from - to per person	children taken	evening meals	animals taken
Michael & Jill Warren **Ashleigh House Hotel** **39 Redstone Hill** **Redhill RH1 4BG** **Tel: (01737) 764763** **Fax 01737 780308** **Open:** ALL YEAR (Excl. Xmas) **Map Ref No. 10**	Nearest Road: A.25 An Edwardian merchant's house situated within 600 yds of Redhill centre with rail links to Gatwick (15 mins) & London (30 mins) & 4 miles from M.25 motorway with many historic houses within easy reach. The house is comfortably furnished & offers 8 bedrooms, 6 en-suite. The breakfast room overlooks an English garden. Jill & Michael extend a very hospitable welcome to all their guests from around the world. Parking.	£27.00 to £48.00 VISA: M'CARD:	Y	N	N
Philip & Judy Wolf **The Old Farmhouse** **Wasp Green Lane** **Outwood** **Redhill** **RH1 5QE** **Tel: (01342) 842313** **Fax 01342 844744** **Open:** ALL YEAR (Excl. Xmas) **Map Ref No. 11**	Nearest Road: A.25 An early-15th-century medieval 4-bay hall house, which is little altered & retains many original features, including the diamond mullions for the hall window & fine panelling. It also has one of the longest unsupported crossing beams in Surrey. 2 of the attractively furnished bedrooms have brass bedsteads, & 1 has an original oak 4-poster bed. A delightful home. The Old Farmhouse is perfect for exploring the south-east of England & many places of historic interest. Children over 10. **E-mail: <philip@theoldfarmhouse.demon.co.uk>**	£25.00 to £25.00	Y	Y	N
Teresa & Kevin Leeper **Knaphill Manor** **Carthouse Lane** **Woking** **GU21 4XT** **Tel: (01276) 857962** **Fax 01276 855503** **Open: ALL YEAR (Excl. Xmas & Easter)** **Map Ref No. 12**	Nearest Road: M.25 Jt. 11 A delightful, large family home, dating back to the 1700s, set in 6 acres of grounds, with a tennis court & croquet lawn. Located in a farming area, the house is quiet & secluded, yet Heathrow & Gatwick Airports are only a 35-min. drive away. Accommodation is very comfortable, with en-suite facilities plus T.V. & tea/coffee makers. A guests' colour-T.V. lounge is also available. Early-morning arrivals are welcome. London 25 mins. Ascot, Windsor & Oxford are also easily reached. Children over 8 yrs.	£35.00 to £35.00 *see PHOTO over* *p. 391* VISA: M'CARD:	Y	N	N
Joan & David Carey **Swallow Barn** **Chobham** **Woking** **GU24 8AU** **Tel: (01276) 856030** **Fax 01276 856030** **Open: ALL YEAR** **Map Ref No. 13**	Nearest Road: A.3046 Situated in quiet secluded surroundings on the edge of Chobham, attractively converted out-buildings & stables with swimming pool. 3 bed-rooms with an en-suite/private bathroom, T.V. & tea/coffee. Ideal for golf courses: Sunningdale, Wentworth & Foxhills. For garden lovers, Wisley & Savill Gardens are within easy reach. Conve-nient for M.3, M.25, Heathrow Airport, Windsor & Ascot. Woking station 2 miles - London 25 mins by train. Single supplement. Children over 8. **E-mail: swallowbarn@compuserve.com**	£32.50 to £47.50	Y	N	N
Tony & Susie Rowse **Pankhurst** **Bagshot Road, West End** **Woking GU24 9QR** **Tel: (01276) 858149** **Fax 01276 858149** **Open:** ALL YEAR (Excl. Xmas) **Map Ref No. 14**	Nearest Road: A.319 Pankhurst is an attractive & historic Grade II listed country house, set in a walled garden amid 8 acres of gardens & woods. Situated close to the picturesque village of Chobham, it has 3 beautiful guest rooms, each equipped with T.V., radio & tea/coffee, etc. There is also a tennis court & heated outdoor swimming pool. Close to Heathrow & Gatwick Airports, Ascot, Windsor, Sunningdale & Wentworth. 3 miles M.3., 7 miles M.25.	£32.50 to £45.00	N	N	N

Knaphill Manor.   Knaphill.

Sussex

Sussex
(South East)

The South Downs of Sussex stretch along the coast, reflecting the expanse of the North Downs of Kent, over the vast stretches of the Weald.

The South Downs extend from dramatic Beachy Head along the coast to Chichester & like the North Downs, they are crossed by an ancient trackway. There is much evidence of prehistoric settlement on the Downs. Mount Caburn, near Lewes, is crowned by an iron age fort, & Cissbury Ring is one of the most important archaeological sites in England. This large earthwork covers 80 acres & must have held a strategic defensive position. Hollingbury Fort carved into the hillside above Brighton, & the Trundle (meaning circle) date from 300-250 B.C., & were constructed on an existing neolithic settlement. The Long Man of Wilmington stands 226 feet high & is believed to be Nordic, possibly representing Woden, the God of War.

Only two towns are located on the Downs but both are of considerable interest. Lewes retains much of its mediaeval past & there is a folk museum in Ann of Cleves' house, which itself is partly 16th century. Arundel has a fascinating mixture of architectural styles, a castle & a superb park with a lake, magnificent beech trees & an unrivalled view of the Arun valley.

The landscape of the inland Weald ranges from bracken-covered heathlands where deer roam, to the deep woodland stretches of the Ashdown Forest, eventually giving way to soft undulating hills & valleys, patterned with hop-fields, meadows, oast houses, windmills & fruit orchards. Originally the whole Weald was dense with forest. Villages like Midhurst & Wadhurst hold the Saxon suffix "hurst" which means wood. As the forests were cleared for agriculture the names of the villages changed & we find Bosham & Stedham whose suffix "ham" means homestead or farm.

Battle, above Hastings, is the site of the famous Norman victory & 16th century Bodiam Castle, built as defence against the French in later times, has a beautiful setting encircled by a lily-covered moat.

Sussex has an extensive coastline, with cliffs near Eastbourne at Beachy Head, & at Hastings. Further east, the great flat Romney Marshes stretch out to sea, & there is considerable variety in the coastal towns.

Chichester has a magnificent cathedral & a harbour reaching deep into the coastal plain that is rich in archaeological remains. The creeks & mudflats make it an excellent place for bird watching.

Brighton is the most famous of the Sussex resorts with its Pier, the Promenade above the beaches, the oriental folly of George IV's Royal Pavilion & its Regency architecture. "The Lanes" are a maze of alleys & small squares full of fascinating shops, a thriving antique trade, & many good pubs & eating places. Hastings to the east preserves its "Old Town" where timbered houses nestle beneath the cliffs & the fishing boats are drawn up on the shingle whilst the nets are hung up to dry in curious tall, thin net stores. Winchelsea stands on a hill where it was rebuilt in the 13th century by Edward I when the original town was engulfed by the sea. It is a beautiful town with a fine Norman church, an excellent museum in the Town Hall, & many pretty houses. Across the Romney Marshes on the next hill stands Rye, its profile dominated by its church. It is a fascinating town with timbered houses & cobbled streets.

Sussex

Sussex Gazeteer

Areas of Outstanding Natural Beauty
The Sussex Downs. Chichester Harbour.

Historic Houses & Castles

Arundel Castle - Arundel
18th century rebuilding of ancient castle, fine portraits, 15th century furniture.

Cuckfield Park - Cuckfield
Elizabethan manor house, gatehouse. Very fine panelling & ceilings.

Danny - Hurstpierpoint
16th century - Elizabethan .

Goodwood House - Chichester
18th century - Jacobean house - Fine Sussex flintwork, paintings by Van Dyck, Canaletto & Stubbs, English & French furniture, tapestries & porcelain.

Newtimber Place - Newtimber
Moated house - Etruscan style wall paintings.

Purham - Pulborough
Elizabethan house containing important collection of Elizabethan, Jacobean & Georgian portraits, also fine furniture.

Petworth House - Petworth
17th century - landscaped by Capability Brown - important paintings - 14th century chapel.

St. Mary's - Bramber
15th century timber framed house - rare panelling.

Tanyard - Sharpthorne
Mediaeval tannery - 16th & 17th century additions.

The Thatched Cottage - Lindfield
Close-studded weald house - reputedly Henry VII hunting lodge.

Uppark - Petersfield
17th century - 18th century interior decorations remain unaltered.

Alfriston Clergy House - Nr. Seaford
14th century parish priest's house - pre-reformation.

Battle Abbey - Battle
Founded by William the Conqueror.

Charleston Manor - Westdean
Norman, Tudor & Georgian architectural styles - Romanesque window in the Norman wing.

Bull House - Lewes
15th century half-timbered house - was home of Tom Paine.

Bateman's - Burwash
17th century - watermill - home of Rudyard Kipling.

Bodiam Castle - Nr. Hawkshurst
14th century - noted example of mediaeval moated military architecture.

Great Dixter - Northiam
15th century half-timbered manor house - great hall - Lutyens gardens

Glynde Place - Nr. Lewes
16th century flint & brick - built around courtyard-collection of paintings by Rubens, Hoppner, Kneller, Lely, Zoffany.

Michelham Priory - Upper Dicker, Nr. Hailsham
13th century Augustinian Priory - became Tudor farmhouse - working watermill, ancient stained glass, etc., enclosed by moat.

Royal Pavilion - Brighton
Built for Prince Regent by Nash upon classical villa by Holland. Exotic Building - has superb original works of art lent by H.M. The Queen. Collections of Regency furniture also Art Nouveau & Art Deco in the Art Gallery & Museum.

Sheffield Park - Nr. Uckfield
Beautiful Tudor House - 18th century alterations - splendid staircase.

Cathedrals & Churches

Alfriston (St. Andrew)
14th century - transition from decorated style to perpendicular, Easter sepulchre.

Boxgrove (St. Mary & St. Blaise)
13th century choir with 16th century painted decoration on vaulting. Relic of Benedictine priory. 16th century chantry. Much decoration.

Chichester Cathedral
Norman & earliest Gothic. Large Romanesque relief sculptures in south choir aisle.

Etchingham (St. Mary & St. Nicholas)
14th century. Old glass, brasses, screen, carved stalls.

Hardham (St. Botolph)
11th century - 12th century wall paintings.

Rotherfield (St. Denys)
16th century font cover, 17th century canopied pulpit, glass by Burne-Jones, wall paintings, Georgian Royal Arms.

Sussex

Sompting (St. Mary)
11th century Saxon tower - Rhenish Helm
Spire - quite unique.
Worth (St. Nicholas)
10th century - chancel arch is the largest
Saxon arch in England. German carved
pulpit c.1500 together with altar rails.
Winchelsea (St. Thomas the Apostle)
14th century - choir & aisles only.
Canopied sedilia & piscina.

Museums & Galleries

Barbican House Museum - Lewes
Collection relating to pre-historic, Romano-
British & , mediaeval antiquities of the
area. Prints & water colours of the area.
Battle Museum-Battle
Remains from archeological sites in area.
Diorama of Battle of Hastings.
Bignor Roman Villa Collection - Bignor
4th century mosaics, Samian pottery,
hypocaust, etc.
Brighton Museum & Art Gallery -
Brighton
Old Master Paintings, watercolours,
ceramics, furniture. Surrealist paintings,
Art Nouveau & Art Deco applied art,
musical instruments & many other
exhibits.

Marlipins Museum - Shoreham
12th century building housing collections
of ship models, photographs, old maps,
geological specimens, etc.
**Royal National Lifeboat Institution
Museum** - Eastbourne
Lifeboats of all types used from earliest
times to present.
Tower 73 - Eastbourne
Martello tower restored to display the
history of these forts. Exhibition of
equipment, uniforms & weapons of the
times.
The Toy Museum - Rottingdean, Brighton
Toys & playthings from many countries -
children's delight.

Other things to see & do

Bewl Water - Nr. Wadhurst
Boat trips, walks, adventure playground
Chichester Festival Theatre - Chichester
Summer season of plays from May to
September.
Goodwood Racecourse

The Royal Pavilion. Brighton.

SUSSEX

Map reference

01	Fuente	20	Thomas
02	Richards	21	Fowler
03	Earlam	22	Cox
04	Buxton	23	P. Cooper
04	Hansell	24	Skinner
05	Birchell	26	Mulcare
06	Burford	28	Costaras
07	Davis	30	Field
08	Field	31	Francis
08	Waller	32	Steele
10	Blencowe	33	Apperly
11	Dridge	33	Brinkhurst
12	Steward	33	Hadfield
13	Salmon	34	Woods
14	Burgoyne	34	Jempson
15	Pyemont	35	Woodhams
16	Gittoes	36	Warton
17	D. Cooper	37	Carver
18	Scull		
19	Kent		

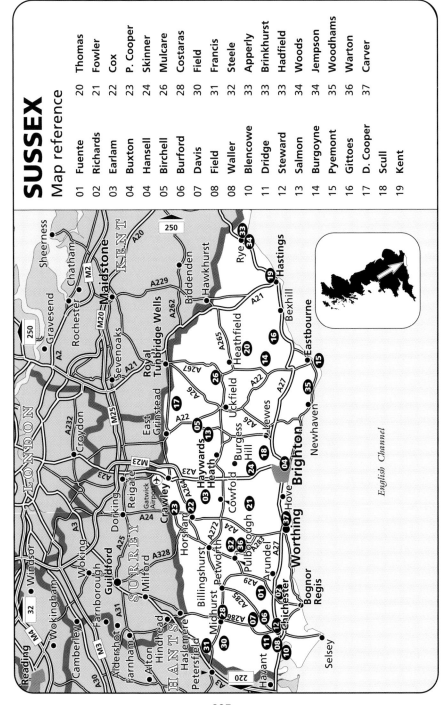

English Channel

		rate £ from - to per person	children taken	evening meals	animals taken
Peter & Sarah Fuente **Mill Lane House** **Slindon** **Arundel** **BN18 0RP** **Tel: (01243) 814440** **Fax 01243 814436** **Open: ALL YEAR** **Map Ref No. 01**	Nearest Road: A.27, A.29 Mainly 17th-century house in beautiful N.T. downland village with magnificent views to the coast. 7 en-suite rooms, each with T.V.. Superb local hill walking & bird-watching from Pulborough Brooks to Pagham Harbour. Within easy reach of Arundel Castle, Fishbourne Roman Palace, Goodwood & Chichester, the cathedral & the Festival Theatre. Beaches 6 miles. Excellent pubs within easy walking distance. Evening meals are available on request.	£21.50 to £21.50	Y	Y	Y
Vicki Richards **Woodacre** **Arundel Lane** **Fontwell** **Arundel BN18 0SD** **Tel: (01243) 814301** **Fax 01243 814344** **Open: ALL YEAR** **Map Ref No. 02**	Nearest Road: A.27 Bed & Breakfast in a traditional family home with accommodation in a separate cottage joining the main house. Rooms are attractive & spacious (2 are on the ground floor) with T.V.'s & tea/coffee-making facilities. Guests are welcome to use the garden & there is plenty of parking space. Woodacre is easy to find from the A.27 & is conveniently located for Chichester, Arundel, Goodwood & Bognor Regis. **E-mail: woodacre@hotelline.co.uk**	£18.00 to £22.50 VISA: M'CARD:	Y	N	Y
Sally & Geoffrey Earlam **Timbers Edge** **Longhouse Lane (off** **Spronketts Lane)** **Warninglid** **Bolney** **RH17 5TE** **Tel: (01444) 461456** **Open: ALL YEAR** **Map Ref No. 03**	Nearest Road: A.272, A.23 This beautiful Sussex country house, set in spacious formal gardens & surrounded by woodlands, is extremely peaceful & quiet. Located within easy reach of Hickstead Showjumping Ground (10 mins), Nymans & Leonardslee Gardens (10 mins), South of England Showground (25 mins), Gatwick Airport (20 mins) & Brighton (30 mins). The bedrooms have a T.V., a private bathroom & beverage facilities. Breakfast is served in the conservatory overlooking the pool. **E-mail: Gearlam@aol.com**	£25.00 to £30.00	N	N	N
Clive Buxton **Adelaide Hotel** **51 Regency Square** **Brighton** **BN1 2FF** **Tel: (01273) 205286** **Fax 01273 220904** **Open: ALL YEAR** **Map Ref No. 04**	Nearest Road: A.259 A warm welcome, friendly service, comfort & delicious food are the hallmarks of this elegant Grade II listed Regency town-house hotel, modernised but retaining the charm of yester-year. Centrally situated in Brighton's premier sea-front square with NCP parking beneath. There are 12 peaceful en-suite bedrooms, tastefully furnished & equipped with 'phone, colour T.V., etc. A beautiful 4-poster bedroom available. Easy access to A.23, 30 mins Gatwick. **E-mail: adelaide@pavilion.co.uk**	£32.50 to £41.00 VISA: M'CARD: AMEX:	Y	N	N
John & Daphne Hansell **Trouville Hotel** **11 New Steine** **Brighton** **BN2 1PB** **Tel: (01273) 697384** **Open: FEB - DEC** **Map Ref No. 04**	Nearest Road: A.259 The Trouville is a Regency, Grade II listed townhouse, tastefully restored & furnished. Accommodation is in 8 attractive rooms, each with colour T.V. & tea/coffee-making facilities. En-suite & 4-poster rooms available. Situated in a charming sea-front square, the Trouville is convenient for shopping, the Lanes, the Pavilion, Marina & Conference Centre & the many restaurants which are all within walking distance.	£25.00 to £28.50 VISA: M'CARD: AMEX:	Y	N	N

Critchfield House. Bosham.

Sussex

rate £ from - to per person
evening meals taken
children taken
animals taken

		rate £ from - to per person	evening meals taken	children taken	animals taken
Mrs Deirdre Birchell **Holly House** **Beaconsfield Road** **Chelwood Gate** **RH17 7LF** **Tel: (01825) 740484** Fax 01825 740172 **Open: ALL YEAR** **Map Ref No. 05**	Nearest Road: A.275 Holly House, an early-Victorian forest farmhouse with character, offers a warm, friendly welcome to visitors. A 1-acre garden with long views. Situated in an Ashdown Forest village & ideal for touring Sussex, with many N.T. properties nearby. A comfortable lounge is available, & breakfast is taken in the conservatory overlooking the garden. The 5 pleasant rooms, 3 en-suite, have tea-making facilities & T.V.. A small swimming pool heated during the summer. Animals welcome. E-mail:deebirchell@hollyhousebnb.demon.co.uk	£22.00 to £30.00	Y	Y	Y
Mr A.C. Bruford **The Bruford** **66 The Street** **Boxgrove** **Chichester PO18 0EE** **Tel: (01243) 774085** Fax 01243 781235 **Open: ALL YEAR** **Map Ref No. 06**	Nearest Road: A.27 Opposite Boxgrove Priory (c. 1105 A.D.) & 1 mile from Goodwood. This turn-of-the-century village house, with rear annex accommodation, offers en-suite twin & 4-poster bedrooms, both with r/c colour T.V., radio/alarm & tea/coffee-making facilities. Trouser press in 4-poster bedroom. Approached through the quiet garden, & with its own private breakfast room, this accommodation is renowned for its sumptuous English breakfasts, & features beamed & flint walls.	£22.50 to £35.00	N	N	N
Alan & Iris Davis **The Old Store Guest House** **Stane Street** **Halnaker** **Chichester PO18 0QL** **Tel/Fax: (01243) 531977** **Open: ALL YEAR** **Map Ref No. 07**	Nearest Road: A.285 A lovely 18th-century Grade II listed house offering 7 comfortable rooms with a choice of single, double or family accommodation. All rooms are en-suite & have colour T.V., tea/coffee trays, hairdryer & trouser press. A full English breakfast is served in the charming breakfast room. Guest lounge. Private car park. Good pub/restaurant close by. Adjacent to Goodwood Estate & ideal for Chichester, Petworth & Arundel. VISA: M'CARD:	£27.50 to £35.00	Y	N	N
Mrs Janetta Field **Critchfield House** **Bosham Lane** **Old Bosham** **Chichester PO18 8HG** **Tel: (01243) 572370** Fax 01243 572370 **Open: MAR - OCT** **Map Ref No. 08**	Nearest Road: A.259 Critchfield dates from the early 18th century & is in a lovely peaceful location, 5 mins' walk from the harbour. It has a large garden with putting green & sun terrace. The house is beautifully furnished with many antiques, & the charming bedrooms all have private or en-suite bathrooms. Breakfast is served in the oak-beamed dining room. Excellent hotel/restaurant & 2 village pubs within easy walking distance. Children over 8 years. E-mail: janetta@critchfield.demon.co.uk see PHOTO over p. 397	£25.00 to £35.00	Y	N	N
Mrs Mary Waller **Hatpins** **Bosham Lane** **Old Bosham** **Chichester PO18 8HG** **Tel/Fax: (01243) 572644** **Open: ALL YEAR** **Map Ref No. 08**	Nearest Road: A.259 Situated in the charming, picturesque harbour village of Old Bosham, 3 miles west of Chichester, & near to Goodwood House, H.M.S. Victory & the Mary Rose, this elegant property offers luxurious & inviting interior-designed decor & antiques, including a half-tester & Victorian brass beds, & a sauna. Suitable, & welcoming, for honeymoon couples. All rooms have private/en-suite bathrooms. A charming home. see PHOTO over p. 399	£30.00 to £45.00	N	N	N

Hatpins. Old Bosham.

Sliders Farm. Furners Green.

Sussex

		rate £ from - to per person	children taken	evening meals	animals taken
Peter & Anna Blencowe **The Old Rectory** **Cot Lane** **Chidham** **Chichester PO18 8TA** **Tel: (01243) 572088** **Fax 01243 572088** **Open: ALL YEAR** **Map Ref No. 10**	Nearest Road: A.259 The Old Rectory is a large, comfortable period house, set in a country lane in the quiet village of Chidham. 5 charming bedrooms, 3 with private facilities, a colour T.V., tea-making facilities, a radio & electric underblankets. There is a delightful lounge, with a colour T.V. & grand piano, & a large garden with a swimming pool. Opposite the Saxon church, & close to the village pub serving excellent meals. Chichester Harbour is nearby. **E-mail: peter.blencowe@lineone.net**	£23.00 to £27.00	Y	N	Y
Jeannette Dridge **Chichester Lodge** **Oakwood** **Chichester** **PO18 9AL** **Tel: (01243) 786560** **Open: ALL YEAR** **Map Ref No. 11**	Nearest Road: B.2178 A picturesque, Grade II listed 1840s Gothic Lodge set in very quiet country surroundings, yet only 4 mins' drive from the city centre and the Festival Theatre. Accommodation is in 2 comfortable & tastefully furnished bedrooms with 4-poster beds & en-suite bathrooms. An adjoining garden room has tea-making facilities & a cosy log-burning fire. You are assured of a warm and friendly welcome at this charming home.	£25.00 to £30.00	N	N	N
Mrs Victoria Steward **Litten House** **148 St Pancras** **Chichester** **PO19 1SH** **Tel: (01243) 774503** **Fax 01243 539187** **Open: ALL YEAR** **Map Ref No. 12**	Nearest Road: A.27 Litten House is an 18th-century Georgian house, set in the city centre & with a warm welcoming atmosphere. It is spacious & peaceful & offers 3 comfortable bedrooms with shared bathroom facilities, 1 with a private balcony overlooking the garden. Each has T.V. & tea/coffee. A full English breakfast is served & includes homemade bread & jams. It is a perfect spot from which to explore Chichester & is close to the museums, theatre, cathedral & shops. Portsmouth is 30 mins by car. **E-mail: b&b@littenho.demon.co.uk**	£20.00 to £30.00	Y	N	N
David & Jean Salmon **Sliders Farm** **Furners Green** **Danehill** **TN22 3RT** **Tel: (01825) 790258** **Fax 01825 790258** **Open: ALL YEAR (Excl. Xmas)** **Map Ref No. 13**	Nearest Road: A.275 A listed 16th-century farmhouse, with a wealth of oak beams & inglenook fireplaces, in a secluded setting on the Sussex Weald. All rooms are en-suite, with T.V. & tea/coffee Home-grown produce & home-cooking. Dining room & lounge with inglenooks & billiard table. An outdoor pool, tennis court & private trout fishing. Ideal for Ardingly Showground, Sheffield Park Gardens, Bluebell Railway & N.T. properties. Coast & Gatwick 30 mins (car). London 45 mins (train). Dinner by arrangement for parties of 4 plus.	£22.00 to £40.00 *see PHOTO over* *p. 400*	Y	N	N
Sarah Burgoyne **Old Whyly** **East Hoathly** **BN8 6EL** **Tel: (01825) 840216** **Fax 01825 840738** **Open: ALL YEAR** **Map Ref No. 14**	Nearest Road: A.22 Old Whyly is a listed Grade II 17th-century manor house & offers charming accommodation with beautiful antiques, pictures, a magical garden, lake, country walks, swimming pool & tennis court. 2 bedrooms with en-suite/private facilities. The house has a romantic history through the Civil War & connections with the early settlers in America. Dinner is a treat, as Sarah offers outstanding food. Glyndebourne is 10 mins away & N.T. houses & gardens are close by. Easy access to Brighton & Lewes. Gatwick Airport 45 mins.	£40.00 to £45.00	N	Y	N

Pinnacle Point. Meads Village.

	Nearest Road	rate £ from - to per person	children taken	evening meals	animals taken
Mrs E. Pyemont **Pinnacle Point** **Foyle Way** **Upper Duke's Drive** **Meads Village** **Eastbourne BN20 7XL** Tel: (01323) 726666 Fax 01323 643946 Open: ALL YEAR Map Ref No. 15	Nearest Road: A.22, A.23 Pinnacle Point is a secluded house with unrivalled views over the English Channel. It occupies an idyllic & unique position on the cliffs near the foot of the South Downs in Eastbourne. It is very modern with 3 designer decorated en-suite bedrooms. All rooms have a T.V. & hot drinks tray. Close to all the facilities in Eastbourne & excellent pubs & restaurants. The host encourages guests to take early morning Downland walks with him before breakfast! A must for bird lovers. Children over 12. Dinner by prior arrangement.	£30.00 to £40.00 🚭 *see PHOTO over* *p. 402* M'CARD:	Y	Y	N
Barry & Rowena Gittoes **Wartling Place** **Wartling** **Herstmonceux** **Hailsham BN27 1RY** Tel: (01323) 832590 Fax 01323 832590 Open: ALL YEAR Map Ref No. 16	Nearest Road: A.271, A.27 A superb listed Georgian country house set in 2 acres of mature secluded gardens. Beautifully restored with period furnishings offering luxurious, individual bedrooms & romantic 4-posters for that special occasion. Each room is en-suite with bath & shower, T.V. & courtesy tray. Ideal for visiting the many National Trust houses, castles & gardens of Sussex & Kent. Private parking. Self-catering lodge cottage available. **E-mail: accom@wartlingplace.prestel.co.uk**	£30.00 to £40.00 🚭 *see PHOTO over* *p. 404* VISA: M'CARD: AMEX:	Y	N	N
Mr David Cooper **Bolebroke Water Mill** **Perry Hill** **Edenbridge Road** **Hartfield** **TN7 4JP** Tel: (01892) 770425 Fax 01892 770425 Open: FEB - DEC Map Ref No. 17	Nearest Road: A.264 A magical watermill, first recorded in 1086 A.D., & an Elizabethan miller's barn offer 5 en-suite rooms of genuine, unspoilt rustic charm, set amid woodland, water & pasture, & used as the idyllic setting for the film 'Carrington'. The mill is complete with machinery, trap doors & very steep stairs. The barn has low doors & beamed ceilings, & includes the enchanting honeymooners' hayloft with a 4-poster bed. Light supper trays are available, & award-winning breakfasts are served in the adjoining mill-house. Children over 8 years.	£31.00 to £39.00 🚭 *see PHOTO over* *p. 405* VISA: M'CARD: AMEX:	Y	N	N
Robert & Helen Scull **Longcroft House** **Beacon Road** **Ditchling** **Hassocks BN6 8UZ** Tel: (01273) 842740 Fax 01273 841935 Open: ALL YEAR Map Ref No. 18	Nearest Road: A.273 Longcroft House is situated in 2 1/2 acres of garden & meadow, near the foot of the Ditchling Beacon, & within easy walking distance of the ancient village centre. 3 prettily furnished bedrooms (including 1 with 4-poster). Each has a colour T.V.. (Complementary morning tea in bed.) Helen is an excellent cook, & meals are delicious. Home-made bread, preserves & afternoon tea served by the log fire are available. A charming home & an ideal base for exploring this region.	£26.00 to £44.00 🚭	Y	Y	N
Brian W. Kent **Parkside House** **59 Lower Park Road** **Hastings** **TN34 2LD** Tel: (01424) 433096 Fax 01424 421431 Open: ALL YEAR Map Ref No. 19	Nearest Road: A.21 Located in a quiet residential conservation area, & set in an elevated position opposite a beautiful park. This elegant Victorian house retains all its original features, but with every modern facility. High standards of hospitality, comfort & good home-cooking are provided, creating an informal, friendly & welcoming atmosphere. Bedrooms are en-suite & offer every luxury. The 'Apricot' room has an antique French bed. A quiet location only 15 mins' walk from the town centre & sea front.	£25.00 to £28.00 🚭 VISA: M'CARD:	Y	N	N

Wartling Place. Wartling.

Bolebroke Watermill.   Hartfield.

Sussex

		rate £ from - to per person	children taken	evening meals	animals taken
Mrs Ruth Thomas **Great Crouch's** **Rushlake Green** **Heathfield** **TN21 9QD** **Tel: (01435) 830145** **Open: ALL YEAR** **Map Ref No. 20**	Nearest Road: A.265, A.267 This Grade II country house is set in the conservation village of Rushlake Green, an Area of Outstanding Natural Beauty, in the heart of rural East Sussex. Oak beams, original doors & antiques furnish the house, whilst the bedrooms, both with en-suite or private bathroom, have T.V., books, magazines & tea/coffee-making facilities. 15 acres of garden & pasture, an indoor heated swimming pool, plus a warm & friendly welcome, make this a great place to relax & unwind.	£27.50 to £37.50	N	N	N
Mrs Sylvia Fowler **Frylands** **Frylands Lane** **Henfield BN5 9BP** **Tel: (01403) 710214** **Fax 01403 711449** **Open: ALL YEAR (Excl. Xmas & New Year)** **Map Ref No. 21**	Nearest Road: A.272 Frylands is a timber-framed Tudor farmhouse in a quiet setting of farmland, woods & river. There are 3 lovely bedrooms, 1 with private facilities, & all with colour T.V., radio & tea/coffee tray with home-made biscuits. A traditional breakfast, cooked to order, is served with a selection of home-made preserves & local honey. Large garden with heated swimming pool. Good pubs & food nearby. 20 mins Gatwick & Brighton. **E-mail: fowler@pavilion.co.uk**	£20.00 to £22.50	Y	N	N
Mrs E. A. Cox **Glebe End** **Church Street** **Warnham** **Horsham** **RH12 3QW** **Tel: (01403) 261711** **Fax 01403 257572** **Open: ALL YEAR** **Map Ref No. 22**	Nearest Road: A.24 Glebe End is a fascinating medieval house, with a secluded, sunny, walled garden, in the heart of Warnham village. It retains many original features, including heavy flagstones, curving ships' timbers & an inglenook fireplace. 4 single, twin or king-sized en-suite rooms, charmingly furnished with antiques & each with T.V. & hot-drink trays. Mrs Cox is an excellent cook, & meals (by arrangement) are delicious & include home-grown produce. Tennis & golf nearby. 20 mins to Gatwick Airport. Animals by arrangement.	£18.00 to £30.00	Y	N	Y
Peggy Cooper **Blackfriars** **Friday Street** **Rusper** **Horsham RH12 4QA** **Tel/Fax: (01293) 871263** **Open: ALL YEAR (Excl. Xmas & New Year)** **Map Ref No. 23**	Nearest Road: A.24, A.264 Blackfriars is a charming country house set in its own 4 acres. Although reputedly dating back to Jacobean days, Blackfriars offers every modern amenity including a swimming pool & tennis court which guests may use. The accommodation in the adjacent guest cottage offers comfortable bedrooms, a sitting room & a fridge. Convenient for Gatwick & central London. A warm welcome from Peggy & John awaits all guests. Children over 2 years welcome.	£24.00 to £30.00	Y	N	N
Mike & Susie Skinner **Clayton Wickham** **Farmhouse** **Belmont Lane** **Hurstpierpoint** **BN6 9EP** **Tel: (01273) 845698** **Fax 01273 846546** **Open: ALL YEAR** **Map Ref No. 24**	Nearest Road: A.23 A delightful, secluded 16th-century farmhouse with lovely views, set amidst the beautiful Sussex countryside. The friendly hosts have refurbished their home to a high standard, yet have retained many original features, hence there are a wealth of beams & a huge inglenook fireplace in the drawing room. There are also a variety of tastefully furnished & well-appointed bedrooms, including a super 4-poster en-suite. Excellent 4-course candlelit dinner by arrangement, & lovely 3-acre grounds with tennis court. Ample parking.	£30.00 to £45.00	Y	Y	Y

Huggetts Furnace Farm. Five Ashes.

Sussex

		rate £ from - to per person	children taken	evening meals taken	animals taken
Gillian & John Mulcare **Huggetts Furnace Farm** **Stonehurst Lane** **Five Ashes** **Mayfield** **TN20 6LL** **Tel: (01825) 830220** **Fax 01825 830722** **Open: ALL YEAR** **Map Ref No. 26**	Nearest Road: A.272 A beautiful medieval farmhouse (Grade II listed) set well off the beaten track in tranquil countryside. 3 attractive bedrooms, all with en-suite/private facilities, radio & tea/coffee trays. The oak-beamed guests' room has an inglenook fireplace (log fires on chilly evenings) & a T.V.. Super dinners & breakfasts use the best home-grown & local produce. Heated outdoor swimming pool, & 120 acres of grounds. Self-catering cottage (non-smokers). Gatwick 45 mins. 30 mins coast. Nearby, many N.T. properties. Children over 7.	£27.50 to £35.00 *see PHOTO over* *p. 407*	Y	Y	N
Alex & Annabelle Costaras **Amberfold** **Heyshott** **Midhurst** **GU29 0DA** **Tel: (01730) 812385** **Open: ALL YEAR** **Map Ref No. 28**	Nearest Road: A.286 Amberfold is a charming 17th-century listed cottage, situated in quiet, idyllic countryside yet only 5 mins drive from Midhurst. 2 self-contained annexes with access all day. 1 is situated on the ground floor. Each annex is comfortably furnished & has private facilities, T.V., clock/radio, hairdryer, fridge etc. To allow you complete freedom & privacy, a large Continental breakfast is self-service & is taken in your room. An attractive garden in which to relax. Parking. An ideal base from which to explore the local attractions of Goodwood, Singleton, Chichester & the coast.	£25.00 to £££	N	N	N
John & Lois Field **Mill Farm** **Trotton** **Petersfield** **GU31 5EL** **Tel: (01730) 813080** **Fax 01730 815080** **Open: ALL YEAR** **Map Ref No. 30**	Nearest Road: A.272 A Sussex country house set in 15 acres of pasture. A large garden, with a grass tennis court. Delightful accommodation in 4 pleasant rooms, 1 en-suite, each with superb views over the South Downs. Colour T.V.s & tea-making facilities. Log fires in the hall & drawing room. Lovely walks & excellent pubs. Chichester, Goodwood & Petworth Houses, Arundel Castle, Heathrow & Gatwick Airports & the coast are within easy reach. Ideal as a holiday base.	£17.50 to £25.00	Y	N	N
Mr & Mrs J. C. Francis **Mizzards Farm** **Rogate** **Petersfield GU31 5HS** **Tel: (01730) 821656** **Fax 01730 821655** **Open: ALL YEAR (Excl. Xmas)** **Map Ref No. 31**	Nearest Road: A.272 This beautifully modernised farmhouse is set in gardens & farmland by the River Rother. All of the bedrooms have en-suite facilities & colour T.V.. There is an elegant drawing room, & breakfast is served in a magnificent vaulted hall dating from the 16th century. There is a covered swimming pool, for guests' use, & beautiful gardens. Situated close to the South Downs, the coast & several N.T. houses.	£28.00 to £32.00 *see PHOTO over* *p. 409*	N	N	N
Alma Steele **New House Farm** **Broadford Bridge Road** **West Chiltington** **Pulborough RH20 2LA** **Tel: (01798) 812215** **Fax 01798 813209** **Open: ALL YEAR** **Map Ref No. 32**	Nearest Road: A.29 A lovely 15th-century house with oak beams & inglenook fireplaces. Situated in a village with a 12th-century church. 3 delightful rooms, 2 with en-suite facilities. T.V. & tea/coffee makers. A pleasant lounge with T.V. & a lovely garden. Gatwick Airport is easily reached. Parham Gardens, W. Sussex golf course, Amberley Wild Brooks, Arundel Castle, Petworth House. Polo at Cowdray Park. Good evening meals available at local inns. W. Chiltington golf course nearby.	£22.50 to £27.50	N	N	N

Mizzards Farm. Rogate.

Jeake's House.   Rye.

Sussex

		rate £ from - to per person	children taken	evening meals	animals taken
Jane Apperly **Cadborough Farm** **Udimore Road** **Rye TN31 6AA** **Tel: (01797) 225426** **Fax 01797 224097** **Open: ALL YEAR (Excl. Xmas & New Year)** **Map Ref No. 33**	Nearest Road: B.2089 Cadborough is a lovely country house set in 24 acres with outstanding views towards the sea, Camber Castle, Rye & Winchelsea. The spacious sunny bedrooms have en-suite facilities & sea views. Drawing room with log fire. Superb English or vegetarian breakfast served in the dining room. Short stay self-catering - 2 studio suites in converted dairy in the grounds with own courtyard. Short walk from town. Children over 8. **E-mail: cadfarm@marcomm.co.uk**	£24.00 to £27.50 (no smoking) VISA: M'CARD:	Y	N	Y
Sara Brinkhurst **Little Orchard House** **West Street** **Rye** **TN31 7ES** **Tel: (01797) 223831** **Fax 01797 223831** **Open: ALL YEAR** **Map Ref No. 33**	Nearest Road: A.259, A.268 This charming Georgian townhouse, with traditional walled garden & Smuggler's Watchtower, is at the heart of ancient Rye. Whilst a perfect touring base, it retains many original features. Open fires, antique furnishings & books ensure a peaceful, relaxed atmosphere. Generous country breakfasts feature organic & free-range local products. 3 lovely en-suite bedrooms - 1 with 4-poster - have T.V. & hot-drinks tray. A romantic suite with kitchen facilities in the detached Tower offers real seclusion. Children over 12.	£32.00 to £42.00 VISA: M'CARD:	Y	N	N
Mrs J. Hadfield **Jeake's House** **Mermaid Street** **Rye** **TN31 7ET** **Tel: (01797) 222828** **Fax 01797 222623** **Open: ALL YEAR** **Map Ref No. 33**	Nearest Road: A.259 Jeakes House is an outstanding 17th-century listed building. Retaining original features, including oak beams & wood panelling, & decorated throughout with antiques. 12 comfortable rooms overlook the gardens, en-suite/private facilities, T.V. etc. 4-poster available. Dine in the galleried former Baptist chapel, where a choice of full English, wholefood vegetarian or Continental breakfast is served. Located in one of Britain's most picturesque medieval streets. Parking. **E-mail: jeakeshouse@btinternet.com**	£33.50 to £££ *see PHOTO over* *p. 410* VISA: M'CARD:	N	N	Y
Geoff & Gillian Woods **The Strand House** **Tanyard's Lane** **Winchelsea** **Rye TN36 4JT** **Tel: (01797) 226276** **Fax 01797 224806** **Open: ALL YEAR** **Map Ref No. 34**	Nearest Road: A.259 Nestling at the foot of the cliffs beneath the 13th-century Strand Gate lies The Strand House, full of atmosphere with oak beams & inglenook fireplaces. Without a level floor or wall, the bedrooms have their own individual charm. (4-poster available.) A traditional English breakfast, using local fresh produce, is served in the heavily beamed dining room. Log fires in season. Pretty gardens. Children over 2 years.	£22.00 to £32.00 (no smoking) VISA: M'CARD:	Y	N	N
Mr & Mrs R. Woodhams **The Old Parsonage** **West Dean** **Alfriston** **Seaford BN25 4AL** **Tel/Fax: (01323) 870432** **Open: ALL YEAR (Excl. Xmas & New Year)** **Map Ref No. 35**	Nearest Road: A.259 The Old Parsonage, built in 1280 & reputed to be the oldest continually inhabited small house in England, is situated in a hamlet in the Friston Forest, 1 mile from the Seven Sisters coastline. With chalk & flint walls 2 1/2 feet thick, massive oak beams, stone spiral staircases, log fires & extensive gardens, the house beautifully combines an antique setting with modern comforts. Eastbourne, Brighton & Glyndebourne nearby. Children over 12 yrs.	£30.00 to £48.00 (no smoking) *see PHOTO over* *p. 412*	Y	N	N

The Old Parsonage. West Dean.

		rate £ from - to per person	children taken	evening meals	animals taken
Mrs Fiona Warton **No. 1 Lime Chase** **Storrington** **RH20 4LX** **Tel: (01903) 740437** **Fax 01903 740437** **Open: ALL YEAR** **Map Ref No. 36**	Nearest Road: A.283 Quiet, secluded village location in the South Downs, an Area of Outstanding Natural Beauty with woodland/hilltop walks. Elegant twin & double rooms with antiques, T.V., beverage facilities & superior bathrooms including en-suite. Enjoy afternoon tea in the ambience of the conservatory or by the log fire. Traditional English breakfast with home-made bread. Romantic breaks a speciality. Excellent restaurants/pubs within walking distance. Good touring location: Arundel, Goodwood, Chichester, Brighton. Gatwick 35 mins. Heathrow 75 mins. Children over 10 years.	£29.00 to £39.00 🚭 *see PHOTO over p. 414*	Y	N	N
Mrs Sarah Jempson **Cleveland House** **Winchelsea** **TN36 4EE** **Tel: (01797) 226256** **Fax 01797 226256** **Open: ALL YEAR** **Map Ref No. 34**	Nearest Road: A.259 A beautiful listed 18th-century house in the centre of historic Winchelsea, completely quiet & peaceful & with wonderful sea views. Magnificent 1 1/2 acre walled garden with heated swimming pool featured on T.V. & in magazines. 1 double room with sea view & private bathroom, 1 twin room overlooking the rose garden with en-suite shower room. Both rooms have colour T.V. & tea/coffee-making facilities. 2 miles from Rye. 3 mins' walk from 2 inns serving lunchtime & evening meals.	£30.00 to £60.00 🚭 VISA: M'CARD:	Y	N	N
John & Doreen Carver **Bonchurch House** **1 Winchester Road** **Worthing** **BN11 4DJ** **Tel: (01903) 202492** **Fax 01903 202492** **Open: ALL YEAR** **Map Ref No. 37**	Nearest Road: A.259 Bonchurch is a home-from-home guest house where a warm welcome is extended to all guests by John & Doreen Carver, resident proprietors for 26 years. There are 6 bedrooms, all well-equipped with shaver points & an en-suite/private shower/bathroom, colour T.V., easy chairs & tea/coffee-making facilities. Home cooking is a speciality. Ideally situated in a picturesque setting, yet close to the sea front, shops & entertainment. Children over 3 years welcome.	£22.00 to £26.00 VISA: M'CARD:	Y	N	N

WORLDWIDE BED & BREAKFAST ASSOCIATION

When booking your accommodation please mention
The Best Bed & Breakfast

1 Lime Chase. Storrington.

Warwickshire

Warwickshire (Heart of England)

Warwickshire contains much that is thought of as traditional rural England, but it is a county of contradictions. Rural tranquillity surrounds industrial towns, working canals run along with meandering rivers, the mediaeval splendour of Warwick Castle vies with the handsome Regency grace of Leamington Spa.

Of course, Warwickshire is Shakespeare's county, with his birthplace, Stratford-upon-Avon standing at the northern edge of the Cotswolds. You can visit any of half a dozen houses with Shakespearian associations, see his tomb in the lovely Parish church or enjoy a performance by the world famous Royal Shakespeare Company in their theatre on the banks of the River Avon.

Warwickshire was created as the Kingdom of Mercia after the departure of the Romans. King Offa of Mercia left us his own particular mark - a coin which bore the imprint of his likeness known as his "pen" & this became our penny. Lady Godiva was the wife of an Earl of Mercia who pleaded with her husband to lessen the taxation burden on his people. He challenged her to ride naked through the streets of Coventry as the price of her request. She did this knowing that her long hair would cover her nakedness, & the people, who loved her, stayed indoors out of respect. Only Peeping Tom found the temptation irresistible.

The 15th, 16th, & 17th centuries were the heyday of fine building in the county, when many gracious homes were built. Exceptional Compton Wynyates has rosy pink bricks, twisted chimney stacks, battlements & moats & presents an unforgettably romantic picture of a perfect Tudor House.

Coventry has long enjoyed the reputation of a thriving city, noted for its weaving of silks and ribbons, learned from the refugee Huguenots. When progress brought industry, watches, bicycles & cars became the mainstay of the city. Coventry suffered grievously from aerial bombardment in the war & innumerable ancient & treasured buildings were lost.

A magnificent new Cathedral stands besides the shell of the old. Mystery plays enacting the life of Christ are performed in the haunting ruin.

Warwick Castle.

Warwickshire

Warwickshire Gazeteer

Areas of Outstanding Natural Beauty
The Edge Hills

Historic Houses & Castles

Arbury Hall - Nuneaton
18th century Gothic mansion - made famous by George Elliot as Cheverel Manor - paintings, period furnishings, etc.
Compton Wynyates
15th century - famous Tudor house - pink brick, twisted chimneys, battlemented walls. Interior almost untouched - period furnishing.
Coughton Court - Alcester
15th century - Elizabethan half-timbered wings. Holds Jacobite relics.
Harvard House - Stratford-upon-Avon
16th century - home of mother of John Harvard, University founder.
Homington Hall - Shipston-on-Stour
17th century with fine 18th century plasterwork.
Packwood House - Hockley Heath
Tudor timber framed house - with 17th century additions. Famous yew garden.
Ragley Hall - Alcester
17th century Palladian - magnificent house with fine collection of porcelain, paintings, furniture, etc. & a valuable library.
Shakespeare's Birthplace Trust Properties - Stratford-upon-Avon
Anne Hathaway's Cottage - Shottery
The thatched cottage home of Anne Hathaway.
Hall's Croft - Old Town
Tudor house where Shakespeare's daughter Susanna lived.
Mary Arden's House - Wilmcote
Tudor farmhouse with dovecote. Home of Shakespeare's mother.
New Place - Chapel Street
Shakespeare's last home - the foundations of his house are preserved in Elizabethan garden.
Birthplace of Shakespeare - Henley Street
Many rare Shakespeare relics exhibited in this half-timbered house.
Lord Leycester Hospital - Warwick
16th century timber framed group around courtyard - hospital for poor persons in the mediaeval guilds.
Upton House - Edge Hill
Dating from James II reign - contains Brussels tapestries, Sevres porcelain, Chelsea figurines, 18th century furniture & other works of art, including Old Masters.
Warwick Castle - Warwick
Splendid mediaeval castle - site was originally fortified more than a thousand years ago. Present castle 14th century. Armoury.

Cathedrals & Churches

Astley (St. Mary the Virgin)
17th century - has remains of 14th century collegiate church. 15th century painted stalls.
Beaudesert (St. Nicholas)
Norman with fine arches in chancel.
Brailes (St. George)
15th century - decorated nave & aisles - 14th century carved oak chest.
Crompton Wynyates
Church of Restoration period having painted ceiling.
Lapworth (St. Mary)
13th & 14th century - steeple & north aisle connected by passage.
Preston-on-Stour (The Blessed Virgin Mary)
18th century. Gilded ceiling, 17th century glass
Tredington (St. Gregory)
Saxon walls in nave - largely14th century, 17th century pulpit. Fine spire.
Warwick (St. Mary)
15th century Beauchamp Chapel, vaulted choir, some 17th century Gothic.
Wooten Wawen (St. Peter)
Saxon, with remnants of mediaeval wall painting, 15th century screens & pulpit: small 17th century chained library.

Museums & Galleries

The Royal Shakespeare Theatre Picture Gallery - Stratford-upon-Avon
Original designs & paintings, portraits of famous actors, etc.
Motor Museum - Stratford-upon-Avon
Collection of cars, racing, vintage, exotic, replica of 1930 garage. Fashions, etc. of 1920's era.

WARWICKSHIRE
Map reference

00 May	13 Castelli
01 Wilson	13 Harvard
02 Shorthouse	13 M. Evans
03 Lawson	13 Machin
03 Powell	13 Wootton
04 Lea	13 Everitt
05 Walliker	13 Andrews
06 Parkinnen	13 P. Evans
07 Mills	13 Spencer
08 Moses	13 Tozer
09 Lowe	13 Mander
10 Vernon-Miller	14 Crook
10 Smith	15 Lyon
11 Mawle	16 Draisey
13 S. Evans	17 Stanton
13 Pettitt	18 Hutsby
13 Workman	

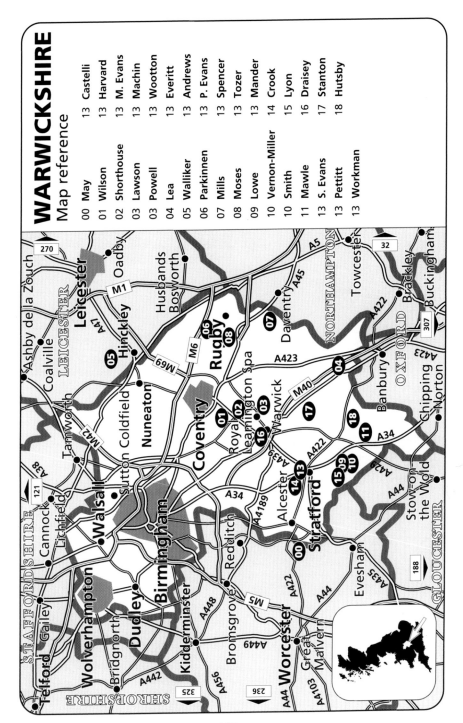

8 Clarendon Crescent. Leamington Spa.

Warwickshire

	rate £ from - to per person	children taken	evening meals	animals taken

		rate £ from - to per person	children taken	evening meals	animals taken
Clive & Sue May **Little Knighton Farm** Alcester B49 5LT Tel: (01386) 793650 Open: ALL YEAR (Excl. Xmas) Map Ref No. 00	Nearest Road: A.442 Standing in 15 acres on the Warwickshire/ Worcestershire borders, Little Knighton Farm is a Grade II listed farmhouse in a charming rural setting. Accommodation is in 1 twin room en-suite & 1 double room with private bathroom. Each room has colour T.V., radio/alarm & tea/ coffee-making facilities. A comfortable guests lounge. Ideal central location for Stratford, Warwick & Worcester area. Animals by arrangement. Children over 10 years.	£25.00 to £25.00	Y	N	Y
Joan Wilson **Ferndale Guest House** 45 Priory Road Kenilworth CV8 1LL Tel: (01926) 853214 Fax 01926 858336 Open: ALL YEAR Map Ref No. 01	Nearest Road: A.46 You are assured of a warm welcome in this family-run, spacious Victorian house situated in a quiet tree-lined avenue only 5 mins' walk from the town centre. All 7 bedrooms are en-suite & tastefully decorated & include T.V. & coffee/tea-making facilities. A guests' T.V. lounge is available throughout the day. Ideally located for Warwick, Coventry, Leamington Spa, the N.E.C., Stoneleigh Agricultural Centre & Warwick University.	£20.00 to £25.00 VISA: M'CARD: AMEX:	Y	N	N
David, Brian & Roma **Shorthouse** **Comber House** 2, Union Road Leamington Spa CV32 5LT Tel: (01926) 421332 Fax 01926 313930 Open: Mid JAN - Mid DEC Map Ref No. 02	Nearest Road: A.452, M.40 Built in the early 1800s Comber House has been lovingly converted into a welcoming guest house, catering both for the tired executive & the inquisitive tourist. You can relax in the spacious lounge, walk in the private garden or try your hand in the billiards room. All of the 5 bedrooms have en-suite facilities & offer an overall feeling of luxury & individuality. Comber House is the perfect spot for a relaxing break. Children over 12. E-mail: b-b@comberhouse.freeserve.co.uk	£28.00 to 32.50 *see PHOTO over* *p. 420* VISA: M'CARD:	Y	N	N
Christine & David Lawson 8 Clarendon Crescent Leamington Spa CV32 5NR Tel: (01926) 429840 Open: ALL YEAR Map Ref No. 03	Nearest Road: A.452 A Grade II listed Regency house overlooking a private dell. Situated in a quiet backwater of Leamington. Elegantly furnished with antiques, & offering accommodation in 5 tastefully furnished bedrooms, 4 en-suite. A delicious full English breakfast is served. Only 5 mins' walk from the town centre. Very convenient for Warwick, Stratford, Stoneleigh Agricultural Centre, Warwick University & the N.E.C.. Children over 3 yrs.	£25.00 to £40.00 *see PHOTO over* *p. 418*	Y	N	N
Bill & Barbara Powell **Flowerdale House** 58 Warwick New Road Leamington Spa CV32 6AA Tel: (01926) 426002 Open: ALL YEAR Map Ref No. 03	Nearest Road: A.452 Flowerdale House, a Victorian building, stands back from the main road midway between Leamington & Warwick. Offering a warm welcome, the 6 bedrooms all have en-suite facilities, T.V. & tea/coffee trays. A residential licence, with several lounging areas creating an informal atmosphere. The dining room can spill over into a plant-filled conservatory with a very inviting garden beyond. Ideally located for Warwick Castle, Stratford-upon-Avon, Warwick University, the N.A.C. & the N.E.C.	£20.00 to £25.00 VISA: M'CARD:	Y	N	N

Comber House. Leamington Spa.

Warwickshire

Listing	Description	rate £ from - to per person	children taken	evening meals	animals taken
Deborah Lea **Crandon House** **Avon Dassett** **Leamington Spa** **CV33 0AA** **Tel: (01295) 770652** **Fax 01295 770632** **Open: ALL YEAR (Excl. Xmas)** **Map Ref No. 04**	Nearest Road: M.40, A.423 Crandon House offers an especially warm welcome & a high standard of accommodation & comfort. Set in 20 acres of beautiful countryside. 5 pretty bedrooms (1 ground-floor) with en-suite/private bathroom, T.V. & tea/coffee. Log fire. Extensive breakfast menu. A tranquil rural retreat, yet within easy reach of Stratford, Warwick, Oxford & the Cotswolds. Located between the M.40 Jts 11 & 12 (4 miles). Animals by arrangement. Children over 10. Special winter breaks. **E-mail: crandonhouse@talk21.com**	£20.00 to £28.00 VISA: M'CARD:	Y	N	Y
John & Wendy Walliker **Ambion Court Hotel** **The Green** **Nuneaton** **CV13 6JB** **Tel: (01455) 212292** **Fax 01455 213141** **Open: ALL YEAR** **Map Ref No. 05**	Nearest Road: A.5, M.69 A charming, modernised Victorian farmhouse, overlooking Dadlington's village green, set in rolling countryside 2 miles north of Hinckley. Rustic character abounds, & each room is well-appointed with en-suite bathroom, T.V., radio, 'phone & hospitality tray. The Pine Room is particularly imposing. A lounge, cocktail bar & excellent restaurant. Comfort, hospitality & exceptional tranquillity for those seeking complete relaxation. No smoking in restaurant/bnedrooms. **E-mail: hotel@ambion.freeserve.co.uk**	£25.00 to £35.00 see PHOTO over p. 422 VISA: M'CARD: AMEX:	Y	Y	Y
Eric & Jan Parkinnen **The Old Rectory** **Main Street** **Rugby** **CV23 0HS** **Tel: (01788) 833151** **Fax 01788 833151** **Open: ALL YEAR (Excl. Xmas)** **Map Ref No. 06**	Nearest Road: A.425 This Victorian rectory is situated in a peaceful village in 1/2 an acre of walled garden. Offering a relaxed & friendly atmosphere with spacious public areas. Tastefully furnished bedrooms (non-smoking) with all amenities & views over the surrounding countryside. Breakfast can be served on the patio. Ideal for touring the Cotswolds & Shakespeare country with easy access to motorway links, including the N.E.C. at Birmingham. Good local pubs. Children over 10.	£25.00 to £35.00	Y	N	Y
C. Alison Mills **Tibbits** **Nethercote** **Rugby** **CV23 8AS** **Tel: (01788) 890239** **Open: ALL YEAR** **Map Ref No. 07**	Nearest Road: A.45, A.425 Retreat along the pretty country lanes on the border of Warwickshire & Northamptonshire to the haven of this totally secluded 17th-century house, beautifully furnished with antiques, where superb accommodation is offered. The spacious & pretty bedrooms have books, tea/coffee facilities, T.V. & en-suite bathroom. Idyllically situated within acres of rolling countryside, providing an ideal base for exploring an area rich in places of historical, scenic & cultural interest.	£25.00 to £28.00	Y	N	N
Don & Susan Moses **Lawford Hill Farm** **Lawford Heath Lane** **Rugby CV23 9HG** **Tel: (01788) 542001** **Fax 01788 537880** **Open: ALL YEAR (Excl. Xmas & New Year)** **Map Ref No. 08**	Nearest Road: A.428 Gardens surround this Grade II listed Georgian farmhouse in an acre of formal lawns, herbaceous borders, shrubberies & a traditional walled vegetable & herb garden. The bedrooms, 3 in the main house & 3 in the converted stables are charmingly decorated & comfortably furnished. Mostly en-suite, colour T.V. & all with tea/coffee tray. Perfectly placed for touring Stratford-upon-Avon, Warwick & the lovely Cotswolds.	£22.50 to £28.00	Y	N	Y

Ambion Court Hotel. Dadlington.

Blackwell Grange. Shipston-on-Stour.

Warwickshire

	rate £ from - to per person	children taken	evening meals	animals taken

Malcolm & Sheila Lowe **Folly Farm Cottage** **Back Street** **Shipston-on-Stour** **CV36 4LJ** **Tel: (01608) 682425** **Fax 01608 682425** **Open: ALL YEAR** **Map Ref No. 09**	Nearest Road: A.3400 Large country cottage in delightful undiscovered quiet Cotswold village with country pubs & pretty cottages within easy reach of Stratford-upon-Avon or Warwick. Offering outstanding accommodation for that special occasion. Romantic en-suite double or 4-poster rooms with T.V. & hospitality tray. Honeymoon apartment suite with whirlpool bath. All rooms overlooking large cottage gardens. Sorry, no family rooms. **E-mail: slowe@cwcom.net**	£26.00 to £38.00 *see PHOTO over* *p. 425*	N	N	N
Mrs Liz Vernon Miller **Blackwell Grange** **Blackwell** **Shipston-on-Stour** **CV36 4PF** **Tel: (01608) 682357** **Fax 01608 682856** **Open: ALL YEAR** **Map Ref No. 10**	Nearest Road: A.3400, A.429 Blackwell Grange is a Grade II listed farmhouse, part of which dates from 1603. It is situated on the edge of a peaceful village, with views of the Ilmington Hills & surrounding countryside. Comfortable rooms & log fires make this an ideal place to relax in. Accommodation includes a ground-floor en-suite bedroom suitable for guests with disabilities. Ideal for touring the Cotswolds, N.T. properties & gardens. 7 miles from Stratford-upon-Avon, 8 miles from Moreton-in-Marsh. Children over 12. Dinner by arrangement. **E-mail: blackwell.grange@saqnet.co.uk**	£28.00 to £35.00 *see PHOTO over* *p. 423* VISA: M'CARD: AMEX:	Y	Y	N
Jackie Smith **Lower Farm** **Shipston-on-Stour** **CV36 4PN** **Tel: (01608) 682750** **Fax 01608 682750** **Open: ALL YEAR** **Map Ref No. 10**	Nearest Road: A.429 On the edge of the Cotswolds, just off the Fosse Way in the pretty, unspoilt hamlet of Darlingscott stands this fine, 18th-century, listed farmhouse. The accommodation comprises 2 attractive double rooms & 1 twin-bedded room, each with an en-suite bathroom, T.V. & tea-making facilities. This is the perfect location from which to visit Chipping Campden. The magnificent gardens of Hidcote & Kiftsgate are just 5 miles away, & Stratford-upon-Avon only 9 miles. Children over 8.	£22.50 to £30.00	Y	N	N
Rebecca & Fred Mawle **Lower Farm Barn** **Great Wolford** **Shipston-on-Stour** **CV36 5NQ** **Tel: (01608) 674435** **Open: ALL YEAR** **Map Ref No. 11**	Nearest Road: A.3400, A.44 This lovely, 100-year-old, converted barn stands in the small, peaceful Warwickshire village of Great Wolford. The property retains much of its original form, including exposed beams & ancient stone work. Now tastefully modernised, it makes a very comfortable home. 2 beautifully furnished double rooms with en-suite facilities. A delightful base from which to explore this fascinating area, & within easy reach of Stratford-upon-Avon.	£19.50 to £21.50	Y	N	N
S. A. Evans **Oxstalls Farm** **Warwick Road** **Stratford-upon-Avon** **CV37 0NS** **Tel: (01789) 205277** **Fax 01789 205277** **Open: ALL YEAR** **Map Ref No. 13**	Nearest Road: A.439 This charming, thoroughbred stud farm overlooks the beautiful Welcombe Hill & golf course. It provides excellent accommodation for touring or relaxing in peaceful surroundings. 24 bedrooms, many with en-suite facilities, T.V. & tea/coffee makers & some with 4-poster. For the keen fisherman there is also a well-stocked trout pond. A guided tour of the farm to see the animals is also available. 1 mile from Stratford town centre & the Royal Shakespeare Theatre. Dinner is available at the local pub. Children over 5 years.	£20.00 to £32.00	Y	N	N

Folly Farm Cottage. Ilmington.

Burton Farm. Bishopston.

Warwickshire

		rate £ from - to per person	children taken	evening meals	animals taken
Eileen Crook **Burton Farm** Stratford-upon-Avon CV37 0RW Tel: (01789) 293338 Fax 01789 262877 Open: ALL YEAR Map Ref No. 14	Nearest Road: A.46 Burton Farm is a 140-acre working farm only 1 1/2 miles from Stratford-upon-Avon. The farmhouse & barns date from Tudor times & are steeped in the character for which the area is world famous. The accommodation, has en-suite/private facilities, is quietly situated & enjoys an environment of colourful gardens & pools which support wildlife & a collection of rare birds & plants. The friendly atmosphere & quiet retreat will ensure a pleasant stay. A charming home.	£25.00 to £30.00 *see PHOTO over* *p. 426*	Y	N	N
Roger & Joanna Pettitt **Parkfield** 3 Broad Walk Stratford-upon-Avon CV37 6HS Tel: (01789) 293313 Fax 01789 293313 Open: ALL YEAR Map Ref No. 13	Nearest Road: A.46 A delightful Victorian house, in a quiet location in Old Town just 5 mins' walk to the town centre & the Royal Shakespeare Theatre. Ideally situated for touring the Cotswolds, Warwick Castle, etc.. 7 spacious & comfortable rooms, 5 en-suite, all with colour T.V. & tea/coffee-making facilities. Excellent breakfasts. Private parking. Lots of tourist information available. Guests can be collected from the station. Children over 5 yrs. **E-mail: Parkfield@btinternet.com**	£21.00 to £23.00 VISA: M'CARD:	Y	N	N
Richard Workman **Ravenhurst** 2 Broad Walk Stratford-upon-Avon CV37 6HS Tel: (01789) 292515 Fax 01789 292515 Open: ALL YEAR Map Ref No. 13	Nearest Road: A.4390, B.439 A Victorian town house with a warm & friendly atmosphere. Ideally situated on the edge of the old town & only a few mins' walk from the Shakespeare Theatre, town centre & places of historical interest. Enjoy the comfort & quiet of this family-run guest house, where all bedrooms have colour T.V. & tea/coffee facilities. Special double en-suite rooms available with 4-poster beds. The Workmans are Stratfordians, therefore local knowledge is a speciality. Children over 5. **E-mail: ravaccom@waverider.co.uk**	£21.00 to £25.00 VISA: M'CARD:	Y	N	N
Mr & Mrs Castelli **Minola House** 25 Evesham Place Stratford-upon-Avon CV37 6HT Tel: (01789) 293573 Open: ALL YEAR Map Ref No. 13	Nearest Road: B.439 A comfortable house with a relaxed atmosphere, offering good accommodation in 5 rooms, 1 with private shower, 3 en-suite; all have T.V. & tea/coffee makers. Stratford offers a myriad of delights for the visitor, including the Royal Shakespeare Theatre. Set by the River Avon, this makes a lovely place for a picnic lunch or early evening meal before the performance. Cots are provided. Children under 2 or over 10 welcome. Italian & French spoken.	£20.00 to £25.00	Y	N	N
Margaret Harvard **Twelfth Night** Evesham Place Stratford-upon-Avon CV37 6HT Tel: (01789) 414595 Open: ALL YEAR Map Ref No. 13	Nearest Road: B.439 Somewhere special - once owned for almost a quarter of a century by the Royal Shakespeare Company as a pied a terre for actors. Delightfully refurbished, this Victorian villa, built in 1897, has retained its character. Providing modern comforts, it includes central heating, en-suite bedrooms with pocket spring beds, brass bedsteads, canopies & half testers plus many other personal touches. Centrally placed with private parking.	£23.00 to £30.00 *see PHOTO over* *p. 428* VISA: M'CARD:	N	N	N

Twelfth Night. Stratford-upon-Avon.

Kawartha House. Stratford-upon-Avon.

Stretton House. Stratford-upon-Avon.

Warwickshire

		rate £ from - to per person	children taken	evening meals	animals taken
Mrs Mavis Evans **Kawartha House** **39 Grove Road** **Stratford-upon-Avon** **CV37 6PB** **Tel: (01789) 204469** **Fax 01789 292837** **Open: ALL YEAR** **Map Ref No. 13**	Nearest Road: A.439 Kawartha House is a well-appointed town house with a friendly atmosphere, overlooking the 'old town' park. It is located just a few mins' walk from the town centre & is ideal for visiting the places of historic interest. Private parking is available. With pretty en-suite/private bedrooms & quality food, these are the ingredients for a memorable stay. This is a delightful base from which to explore Warwickshire, & is within easy reach of the Cotswolds with its many attractive villages. *see PHOTO over* *p. 429* VISA: M'CARD:	£15.00 to £26.00	Y	N	Y
Michael & Yvonne Machin **Stretton House** **38 Grove Road** **Stratford-upon-Avon** **CV37 6PB** **Tel/Fax: (01789) 268647** **Open: ALL YEAR** **Map Ref No. 13**	Nearest Road: A.439 Stretton House is a 'home from home' where a warm & friendly welcome awaits you. Very comfortable accommodation at reasonable prices. Pretty, full en-suite bedrooms & standard rooms, all having T.V. & tea/coffee facilities. Excellent full English breakfast, vegetarians catered for. Limited car parking. Situated opposite lovely Fir Park, within easy reach of the country, yet only 3 mins' walk from the town centre. Children over 8. *see PHOTO over* *p. 430*	£15.00 to £26.00	Y	N	Y
Drenagh & Simon Wootton **Hardwick House** **1 Avenue Road** **Stratford-upon-Avon** **CV37 6UY** **Tel: (01789) 204307** **Fax 01789 296760** **Open: ALL YEAR (Excl. Xmas)** **Map Ref No. 13**	Nearest Road: A.439 Hardwick House is situated in a quiet, residential area of Stratford-upon-Avon, away from main roads yet only a 5-min. walk into the town. All 14 bedrooms are non-smoking, clean & comfortable, with tea/coffee-making facilities & T.V.. Resident proprietors ensure a warm welcome & attention to detail. There is an on-site car park. Directions from M.40: on the A.439, take the first right turn past the 30-mph sign into St. Gregory's Road, & Hardwick House is 200 yds on the right. **E-mail: hardwick@wavender.co.uk** *see PHOTO over* *p. 432* VISA: M'CARD: AMEX:	£21.00 to £29.00	Y	N	N
Mr G. D. Everitt **Eastnor House Hotel** **33 Shipston Road** **Stratford-upon-Avon** **CV37 7LN** **Tel: (01789) 268115** **Fax 01789 266516** **Open: ALL YEAR** **Map Ref No. 13**	Nearest Road: A.3400 By the River Avon, 125 metres from Clopton Bridge, with private parking & just a stroll from theatres & birthplace. This large Victorian townhouse, built for a wealthy draper, offers excellent accommodation, with oak panelling, central open staircase, a pleasant breakfast room & an elegant lounge. 9 spacious, tastefully furnished bedrooms with private bathrooms, T.V. & welcome tray. Breakfast is individually prepared, completing a comfortable & restful stay. **E-mail: eastnor.house@tesco.net** *see PHOTO over* *p. 433* VISA: M'CARD: AMEX:	£25.00 to £35.00	Y	N	N
Patricia Andrews **Melita Private Hotel** **37 Shipston Road** **Stratford-upon-Avon** **CV37 7LN** **Tel: (01789) 292432** **Fax 01789 204867** **Open: ALL YEAR (Excl. Xmas)** **Map Ref No. 13**	Nearest Road: A.3400 An extremely friendly family-run hotel. Offering pleasant service, good food & accommodation in 12 excellent bedrooms, all en-suite/private facilities, T.V., tea/coffee & 'phones. A comfortable lounge/bar & pretty, award-winning garden for guests' use. Parking. A pleasant 5-min. walk to Shakespearian properties/theatres, shopping centre & riverside gardens. Superbly situated for Warwick Castle, Coventry & the Cotswolds. **E-mail: Melita37@email.msn.com** *see PHOTO over* *p. 434* VISA: M'CARD: AMEX:	£33.00 to £39.50	Y	N	Y

Hardwick House.   Stratford-upon-Avon.

Eastnor House Hotel. Stratford-upon-Avon.

Melita Hotel. Stratford-upon-Avon.

		rate £ from - to per person	children taken	evening meals	animals taken

Philip & Jean Evans Sequoia House 51-53 Shipston Road Stratford-upon-Avon CV37 7LN Tel: (01789) 268852 Fax 01789 414559 Open: ALL YEAR Map Ref No. 13	Nearest Road: A.3400 A beautifully appointed private hotel situated across the River Avon from the Royal Shakespeare Theatre. 26 bedrooms (mostly en-suite), a cocktail bar, a cottage annex & an air-conditioned dining room. It is comfortably furnished, & decorated in a warm & restful style, with many extra touches. The garden overlooks the town cricket ground & the old tramway. Lovely walks along the banks of the River Avon opposite the Theatre & Holy Trinity Church. Children over 5. E-mail: info@sequoiahotel.co.uk	£34.50 to £59.00 (non-smoking) see PHOTO over p. 436 VISA: M'CARD: AMEX:	Y	N	N
Mrs G. Lyon Winton House The Green Stratford-upon-Avon CV37 8SX Tel: (01789) 720500 Mobile 0831 485483 Open: ALL YEAR Map Ref No. 15	Nearest Road: B.4632 Built in 1856, this Victorian farmhouse is situated in a peaceful hamlet in an Area of Outstanding Natural Beauty. The bedrooms, 2 en-suite & 1 with a private bathroom, are furnished with antique wrought iron 4-posters, a pine cupboard bed, old lace & hand-made quilts. Award-winning breakfasts with home-made jam & a 'Winton House Special' that changes daily. Log fires. 2 village pubs. Ideally situated for touring, walking (3000 way) & cycling. Children welcome. E-mail: lyong@ibm.net	£27.50 to £30.00 (non-smoking)	Y	N	N
Michael & Maureen Spencer Moonraker House 40 Alcester Road Stratford-upon-Avon CV37 9DB Tel: (01789) 267115 Tel: (01789) 299346 Fax 01789 295504 Open: ALL YEAR (Excl. Xmas) Map Ref No. 13	Nearest Road: A.422 Pretty hanging baskets adorn Moonraker, which is situated on the north-west side of town - an easy 5-10 mins' stroll from the city centre. Moonraker is 2 separate buildings offering 19 beautifully decorated en-suite rooms with T.V. & tea/coffee-making facilities. The charming 4-poster rooms also have a garden terrace. Moonraker II has the advantage of a spacious sun lounge. An excellent location from which to explore Stratford & its many attractions. Children over 10. E-mail: moonraker.spencer@virgin.net	£23.50 to £36.00 see PHOTO over p. 437 VISA: M'CARD:	Y	N	Y
Paul & Dreen Tozer Victoria Spa Lodge Bishopton Lane Stratford-upon-Avon CV37 9QY Tel: (01789) 267985 Fax 01789 204728 Open: ALL YEAR Map Ref No. 13	Nearest Road: A.3400, A.46 Large 19th-century house in country setting, overlooking Stratford canal, with ample parking. A royal coat of arms was built into the gables (with the permission of Queen Victoria) of this Grade II listed building. 7 attractive & comfortable en-suite bedrooms, each with a hostess tray, T.V., hairdryer etc. 1 1/2 miles from the centre of town. Victoria Spa Lodge is an ideal base for the Cotswolds & Shakespearian properties. Pleasant walks along the tow path to Stratford & Wilmcote. E-mail: PTOZER@VICTORIASPALODGE.DEMON.CO.UK	£27.50 to £32.50 (non-smoking) see PHOTO over p. 438 VISA: M'CARD:	Y	N	N

Visit our website at:
http://www.bestbandb.co.uk

Sequoia House. Stratford-upon-Avon.

Moonraker House. Stratford-upon-Avon.

Victoria Spa Lodge. Stratford-upon-Avon.

Pear Tree Cottage. Wilmcote.

Warwickshire

		rate £ from - to per person	children taken	evening meals	animals taken
Mrs Margaret Mander **Pear Tree Cottage** **7, Church Road** **Stratford-upon-Avon** **CV37 9UX** **Tel: (01789) 205889** **Fax 01789 262862** **Open: ALL YEAR** **Map Ref No. 13**	Nearest Road: A.3400 A delightful half-timbered 16th-century house located in the Shakespeare village of Wilmcote. It retains all its original charm & character, with oak beams, flagstone floors, inglenook fireplaces, thick stone walls with deep-set windows & antiques. Offering 7 very comfortable en-suite rooms, all with tea/coffee-making facilities & colour T.V.. A delicious breakfast is served each morning in the dining room. A comfortable lounge is also provided. Children over 3 yrs. A lovely base from which to tour the whole region.	£24.00 to £25.00 🚭 *see PHOTO over* *p. 439*	Y	N	N
Mrs Elizabeth Draisey **Forth House** **44 High Street** **Warwick** **CV34 4AX** **Tel: (01926) 401512** **Fax 01926 490809** **Open: ALL YEAR** **Map Ref No. 16**	Nearest Road: A.429 This rambling Georgian family home in the centre of Warwick provides 2 peaceful guest suites hidden away at the back. 1 family-sized ground-floor suite with en-suite bathroom, sitting room (with T.V.), fridge & drink facilities opens onto the garden, whilst the other room, also en-suite, overlooks the garden. Forth House is ideally situated for holidays or business. Junction 15 (M.40), 2 miles away, brings Oxford, Birmingham (Airport & N.E.C.), Stratford-upon-Avon & the Cotswolds are within easy reach.	£24.00 to £30.00 🚭	Y	N	N
Mrs Judith Stanton **Redlands Farm** **Banbury Road** **Warwick CV35 0AH** **Tel: (01926) 651241** **Fax 01926 651241** **Open: APR - OCT** **Map Ref No. 17**	Nearest Road: B.4100 A lovely 16th-century farmhouse in 2 acres of garden, with a swimming pool. A quiet location, with delightful views over open countryside. Large, beamed bedrooms are tastefully decorated, 1 en-suite with Victorian brass bed. All centrally heated, with tea/coffee facilities. There is a comfortable guests' lounge with T.V., log fires & homely atmosphere. Ideal for Warwick, Stratford, Cotswolds & Motor Heritage Museum. Parking.	£20.00 to £23.00	Y	N	N
Sue Hutsby **Nolands Farm** **Warwick** **CV35 0RJ** **Tel: (01926) 640309** **Fax 01926 641662** **Open: Mid JAN - Mid DEC** **Map Ref No. 18**	Nearest Road: A.422 A working farm situated in a tranquil valley 8 miles from Stratford-upon-Avon. All bedrooms are annexed, some on the ground floor, overlooking either the old stableyard or fields. A selection of 4-posters, king-size doubles, twins, family & single rooms are available. All en-suite with T.V., tea tray, hairdryers, clock/radios & much more. Large gardens. Your hosts also offer clay pigeon shooting, fishing & bicycles. Horse riding nearby. Parking. Dinner by arrangement. Children over 12. **E-mail: nolandsfm@compuserve.com**	£18.00 to £24.00 *see PHOTO over* *p. 441* VISA: M'CARD:	N	Y	N

When booking your accommodation please mention
The Best Bed & Breakfast

Nolands Farm. Oxhill.

Wiltshire

Wiltshire
(West Country)

Wiltshire is a county of rolling chalk downs, small towns, delightful villages, fine churches & great country houses. The expanse of Salisbury Plain is divided by the beautiful valleys of Nadder, Wylye, Ebble & Avon. In a county of open landscapes, Savernake Forest, with its stately avenues of trees strikes a note of contrast. In the north west the Cotswolds spill over into Wiltshire from neighbouring Gloucestershire.

No other county is so rich in archaeological sites. Long barrows and ancient hill forts stand on the skylines as evidence of the early habitation of the chalk uplands. Many of these prehistoric sites are at once magnificent and mysterious. The massive stone arches and monoliths of Stonehenge were built over a period of 500 years with stones transported over great distances. At Avebury the small village is completely encircled by standing stones and a massive bank and ditch earthwork. Silbury Hill is a huge, enigmatic man-made mound. England's largest chambered tomb is West Kennet Long Barrow and at Bush Barrow, finds have included fine bronze and gold daggers and a stone sceptre-head similar to one found at Mycenae in Greece.

Some of England's greatest historic houses are in Wiltshire. Longleat is an Elizabethan mansion with priceless collections of paintings, books & furniture. The surrounding park was landscaped by Capability Brown and its great fame in recent years has been its Safari Park, particularly the lions which roam freely around the visiting cars. Stourhead has celebrated 18th century landscaped gardens which are exceptional in spring when rhododendrons bloom.

Two delightful villages are Castle Combe, nestling in a Cotswold valley, &

Lacock where the twisting streets hold examples of buildings ranging from mediaeval half-timbered, to Tudor & Georgian. 13th century Lacock Abbey, converted to a house in the 16th century, was the home of Fox Talbot, pioneer of photography.

There are many notable churches in Wiltshire. In Bradford-on-Avon, a fascinating old town, is the church of St. Lawrence, a rare example of an almost perfect Saxon church from around 900. Farley has an unusual brick church thought to have been designed by Sir Christopher Wren, & there is stained glass by William Morris in the church at Rodbourne.

Devizes Castle

Salisbury stands where three rivers join, on a plain of luxuriant water-meadows, where the focal point of the landscape is the soaring spire of the Cathedral; at 404 feet, it is the tallest in England. The 13th century cathedral has a marvellous & rare visual unity. The body of the building was completed in just 38 years, although the spire was added in the next century. Salisbury, or "New Sarum" was founded in 1220 when the Bishop abandoned the original cathedral at Old Sarum, to start the present edifice two miles to the south. At Old Sarum you can see the foundation of the old city including the outline of the first cathedral.

Wiltshire

Wiltshire Gazeteer

Area of Outstanding Natural Beauty
The Costwolds & the North Wessex Downs.

Historic Houses & Castles

Corsham Court - Chippenham
16th & 17th centuries from Elizabethan & Georgian periods. 18th century furniture, British, Flemish & Italian Old Masters. Gardens by Capability Brown.

Great Chalfield Manor - Melksham
15th century manor house - moated.

Church House - Salisbury
15th century house.

Chalcot House - Westbury
17th century small house in Palladian manner.

Lacock Abbey - Nr. Chippenham
13th century abbey. In 1540 converted into house - 18th century alterations. Mediaeval cloisters & brewery.

Longleat House - Warminster
16th century - early Renaissance, alterations in early 1800's. Italian Renaissance decorations. Splendid state rooms, pictures, books, furniture. Victorian kitchens. Game reserve.

Littlecote - Nr. Hungerford
15th century Tudor manor. Panelled rooms, moulded plaster ceilings.

Luckington Court - Luckington
Queen Anne for the most part - fine ancient buildings.

Malmesbury House - Salisbury
Queen Anne house - part 14th century. Rococo plasterwork.

Newhouse - Redlynch
17th century brick Jacobean trinity house - two Georgian wings,

Philips House - Dinton
1816 Classical house.

Sheldon Manor - Chippenham
13th century porch & 15th century chapel in this Plantagenet manor.

Stourhead - Stourton
18th century Palladian house with framed landscape gardens.

Westwood Manor - Bradford-on-Avon
15th century manor house - alterations in 16th & 17th centuries.

Wardour Castle - Tisbury
18th century house in Palladian manner.

Wilton House - Salisbury
17th century - work of Inigo Jones & later of James Wyatt in 1810. Paintings, Kent & Chippendale furniture.

Avebury Manor - Nr Malborough
Elizabethan manor house - beautiful plasterwork, panelling & furniture. Gardens with topiary.

Bowood - Calne
18th century - work of several famous architects. Gardens by Capability Brown - famous beechwoods.

Mompesson House - Salisbury
Queen Anne town house - Georgian plasterwork.

Cathedrals & Churches

Salisbury Cathedral
13th century - decorated tower with stone spire. Part of original stone pulpitum is preserved. Beautiful large decorated cloister. Exterior mostly early English.

Salisbury (St. Thomas of Canterbury)
15th century rebuilding - 12th century font, 14th & 15th century glass, 17th century monuments. 'Doom' painting over chancel & murals in south chapel

Amesbury (St. Mary & St. Melor)
13th century - refashioned 15th & restored in 19th century. Splendid timber roofs, stone vaulting over chapel of north transept, mediaeval painted glass, 15th century screen, Norman font.

Bishops Cannings (St. Mary the Virgin)
13th-15th centuries. Fine arcading in transept - fine porch doorway.
17th century almsbox, Jacobean Holy table.

Bradford-on-Avon (St. Lawrence)
Best known of all Saxon churches in England.

Cricklade (St. Sampson)
12th -16th century. Tudor central tower vault, 15th century chapel.

Inglesham (St. John the Baptist)
Mediaeval wall paintings, high pews, clear glass, remains of painted screens.

Malmesbury (St. Mary)
Norman - 12th century arcades, refashioning in 14th century with clerestory, 15th century stone pulpitum added. Fine sculpture.

Wiltshire

Tisbury (St. John the Baptist)
14th-15th centuries. 15th-17th century roofing to nave & aisles. Two storeyed porch & chancel.
Potterne (St. Mary)
13th,14th,15th centuries. Inscribed Norman tub font. Wooden pulpit.

Museums & Galleries

Salisbury & South Wiltshire Museum - Salisbury
Collections showing history of the area in all periods. Models of Stonehenge & Old Sarum - archaeologically important collection.
Devizes Museum - Devizes
Unique archaeological & geological collections, including Sir Richard Colt-Hoare's Stourhead collection of prehistoric material.
Alexander Keiller Museum - Avebury
Collection of items from the Neolithic & Bronze ages & from excavations in district.
Athelstan Museum - Malmesbury
Collection of articles referring to the town - household, coin, etc.
Bedwyn Stone Museum - Great Bedwyn
Open-air museum showing where Stonehenge was carved.
Lydiard Park - Lydiard Tregoze
Parish church of St. Mary & a splendid Georgian mansion standing in park & also permanent & travelling exhibitions.

Borough of Thamesdown Museum & Art Gallery - Swindon
Natural History & Geology of Wiltshire, Bygones, coins, etc. 20th century British art & ceramic collection.
Great Western Railway Museum - Swindon
Historic locomotives.

Historic Monuments

Stonehenge - Nr. Amesbury
Prehistoric monument - encircling bank & ditch & Augrey holes are Neolithic. Stone circles possibly early Bronze age.
Avebury
Relics of enormous circular gathering place B.C. 2700-1700.
Old Sarum - Nr. Salisbury
Possibly first Iron Age camp, later Roman area, then Norman castle.
Silbury Hill - Nr. Avebury
Mound - conical in shape - probably a memorial c.3000-2000 B.C.
Windmill Hill - Nr. Avebury
Causewayed camp c.3000-2300 B.C.
Bratton Camp & White Horse - Bratton
Hill fort standing above White Horse.
West Kennet Long Barrow
Burial place c.4000-2500 B.C.
Ludgershall Castle - Lugershall
Motte & bailey of Norman castle, earthworks, also flint walling from later castle.

Castle Combe.

WILTSHIRE
Map reference

01	Venables	17	Roe
02	Roberts	18	Ross
02	Litherland	19	Gore
03	Denning	20	Brandon
04	Lippiatt	20	Fairbrother
05	R. Sexton	21	Robathan
05	Eldred	24	Sykes
06	Harvey	25	Gifford-Mead
07	Sewell	26	Robertson
08	Steed	27	Lanham
09	P. Sexton	28	Hunt
10	Budden	29	Threlfall
11	Stafford	30	Greathead
12	Daniel	34	Singer
13	O'Flynn		
15	Eavis		
16	Davies		

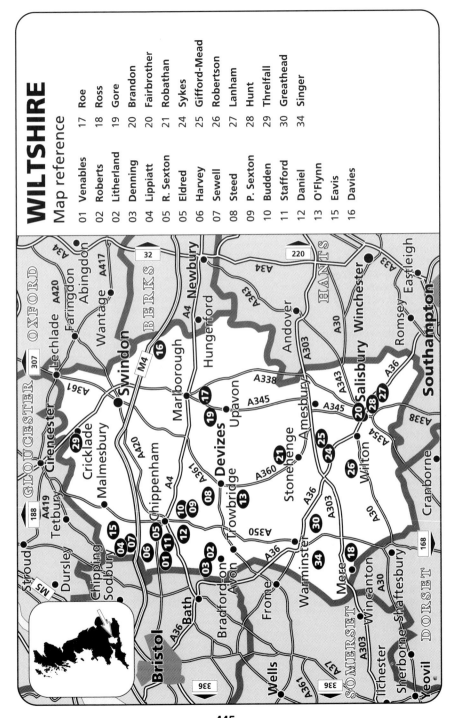

445

Wiltshire

		rate £ from - to per person	children taken	evening meals	animals taken
David & Helga Venables **The Coach House** **Bath** **SN14 7AG** **Tel: (01225) 891026** **Fax 01225 892355** **Open: ALL YEAR** **Map Ref No. 01**	Nearest Road: A.420 A tranquil & attractive Cotswold stone barn conversion with a spacious, elegant interior creating a comfortable, relaxed atmosphere. Set in a large landscaped garden with tennis court & croquet lawn as well as an informal parkland. 2 pretty bedrooms have their own private bathroom, T.V. & tea/coffee makers. (8 miles north-east of Bath, near Jt. 17 or 18 of the M.4.) Close to many delightful Cotswold villages. Children over 8. Evening meals by arrangement only. **E-mail: venables@compuserve.com**	£25.00 to £35.00	Y	Y	N
Priscilla & Peter Roberts **Bradford Old Windmill** **4 Masons Lane** **Bradford-on-Avon** **BA15 1QN** **Tel: (01225) 866842** **Fax 01225 866648** **Open: MAR - DEC** **Map Ref No. 02**	Nearest Road: A.363 A cosy, relaxed atmosphere greets you at this converted windmill high on the hill above the town. The old stone tower overflows with character, & with the many finds picked up by Peter & Priscilla on their backpacking trips around the world. All of the unusually shaped bedrooms have their own distinctive en-suite bathrooms. Imaginative breakfasts are served beneath the massive grain weighing scales. 5 mins' walk from the town centre. Children over 6 years. VISA: M'CARD: AMEX:	£25.00 to £49.90	Y	Y	N
Rob & Barbara Litherland **Hillcrest** **Bradford Road** **Bradford-on-Avon** BA15 2HN **Tel: (01225) 868677** **Fax 01225 868655** **Open: ALL YEAR (Excl.** **Xmas & New Year)** **Map Ref No. 02**	Nearest Road: A.36 Only 6 miles from Bath & 2 miles from Bradford-on-Avon at the southern edge of the Cotswold Hills, Hillcrest is surrounded by old dry stone walls with magnificent views across the Avon Valley. Both bedrooms are en-suite. Your hosts pride themselves on the quality of their food. The a la carte breakfast menu offers an excellent choice. A quaint 17th-century village pub serving excellent food is only 10 mins' walk. Children over 7. **E-mail: hillcrest@b-on-a.freeserve.co.uk**	£25.00 to £27.50 VISA: M'CARD:	Y	Y	N
Elizabeth & John Denning **Burghope Manor** **Winsley** **Bradford-on-Avon BA15 2LA** **Tel: (01225) 723557** **Fax 01225 723113** **Open: ALL YEAR (Excl.** **Xmas & New Year)** **Map Ref No. 03**	Nearest Road: A.36 This historic 13th-century family home is set in beautiful countryside on the edge of the village of Winsley - overlooking the Avon Valley - 5 miles from Bath & 1 1/2 miles from Bradford-on-Avon. Although steeped in history, this family home, has been carefully modernised so that the wealth of historical features complement the present-day comforts, which include en-suite bathrooms. A village pub & restaurant locally. (Dinner for groups only.) Children over 10. Single supplement. **E-mail: burghope.manor@virgin.net**	£40.00 to £45.00 *see PHOTO over* *p. 447* VISA: M'CARD: AMEX:	Y	N	N
Mr & Mrs R. Sexton **Elm Farm House** **The Green** **Chippenham** **SN14 7DG** **Tel: (01249) 713354** **Fax 01249 713354** **Open: ALL YEAR** **Map Ref No. 05**	Nearest Road: A.4, A.420 Elm Farmhouse is located in the centre of beautiful Biddestone & is a fine Grade II listed building retaining many original features. 3 large double bedrooms are offered (2 double, 1 family), each with private facilities, tea/coffee & T.V.. Built in 1778, the house is situated opposite a pond & is close to 2 village pubs. The charming rooms have views overlooking the pond & walled garden. Biddestone is between Lacock & Castle Combe & is only 9 miles from Bath.	£20.00 to £25.00	Y	N	Y

Burghope Manor. Bradford-upon-Avon.

Wiltshire

		rate £ from - to per person	children taken	evening meals	animals taken
Mrs Victoria Lippiatt **Manor Farm** **Chippenham** **SN14 6NL** **Tel: (01666) 840271** **Fax 01666 840271** **Open: ALL YEAR** **Map Ref No. 04**	Nearest Road: A.46 This is a beautiful 17th-century Cotswold family home & working farm, where super hospitality is assured, coupled with high standards in all respects. Alderton is peaceful & completely unspoiled, yet it is only 20 mins by car from Bath, Bristol & Swindon. There are, within a short drive away, many delightful villages to visit & excellent country pubs from which to choose. Children over 12 years welcome. **E-mail: J.Lippiatt@farmline.com**	£28.00 to £30.00 *see PHOTO over p. 449*	Y	N	N
M. & A. Harvey **Goulters Mill** **Chippenham** **SN14 7LL** **Tel: (01249) 782555** **Open: ALL YEAR** **Map Ref No. 06**	Nearest Road: A.420 This is an utterly individual house with a French feel about it, full of pictures & books, set in its own 26-acre (originally farmed) valley with woods, wild flower meadows & a trout stream meandering through it. The walled garden is a sheer delight, particularly in June, with floods of colour & secret paths. Within easy reach of Castle Combe, Bath & the Cotswolds, yet a world apart. There are 3 attractive en-suite rooms. Evening meals & animals by arrangement.	£25.00 to £40.00	Y	Y	Y
Mrs C. M. Sewell **Southview Cottage** **Chippenham** **SN14 7NB** **Tel: (01249) 782908** **Fax 01249 782908** **Open: ALL YEAR** **Map Ref No. 07**	Nearest Road: A.46 Southview is a 300-year-old cottage which is ideally situated for exploring Wiltshire & Gloucestershire & is within easy reach of Castle Combe, Bath & Badminton Park. 3 spacious & well-furnished bedrooms, 2 with en-suite/private facilities & all with tea/coffee tray & T.V.. Log fires & home-cooking in a relaxed country atmosphere. (Dinner by arrangement). Local activities include riding, polo, theatre, motor racing & golf. A beautiful corner of England. Children over 10.	£25.00 to £30.00	Y	Y	Y
Richard & Gloria Steed **The Cottage** **Westbrook** **Chippenham** **SN15 2EE** **Tel: (01380) 850255** **Open: ALL YEAR** **Map Ref No. 08**	Nearest Road: A.342, A.3102 This delightful cottage is reputed to have been a coaching inn, & dates back to 1450. There are 3 charming bedrooms, all with private shower, T.V. & tea/coffee makers, in a beautifully converted barn. Also, many exposed beams that were once ships' timbers. Breakfast is served in the old beamed dining room. A lovely garden & paddock for guests' use. An ideal centre for visiting Bath, Bristol, Devizes, Marlborough, Avebury, Stonehenge, Longleat, Castle Combe & Lacock. **E-mail: RJSteed@cottage16.freeserve.co.uk**	£22.50 to £25.00	Y	N	N

Visit our website at:
http://www.bestbandb.co.uk

Manor Farm. Alderton.

Wiltshire

		rate £ from - to per person	children taken	evening meals	animals taken
Mr & Mrs P. Sexton **The Old Rectory** **Cantax Hill** **Chippenham SN15 2JZ** **Tel: (01249) 730335** **Fax 01249 730166** **Open: ALL YEAR (Excl. Xmas)** **Map Ref No. 09**	Nearest Road: A.350 Situated in the medieval village of Lacock, The Old Rectory, built in 1866, is a fine example of Victorian Gothic architecture, with creeper-clad walls & mullioned windows. It stands in 12 acres of its own carefully tended grounds, which include a tennis court & croquet lawn. The Old Rectory offers 3 very attractive bedrooms, all with en-suite facilities. An excellent base from which to explore the glorious West Country.	£20.00 to £25.00 🚭 *see PHOTO over* *p. 451*	Y	N	Y
Mrs Gill Stafford **Pickwick Lodge Farm** **Guyers Lane** **Corsham** **SN13 0PS** **Tel: (01249) 712207** **Fax 01249 701904** **Open: ALL YEAR (Excl.** **Xmas & New Year)** **Map Ref No. 11**	Nearest Road: A.4 A delightful 17th-century Cotswold stone farmhouse, set in peaceful surroundings. 3 well-appointed, comfortable & tastefully furnished bedrooms, each with an en-suite/private bathroom, radio, T.V. & tea/coffee facilities. Hearty & delicious breakfasts served. Ideally situated for visiting many sites of historical interest, such as the Wiltshire White Horses, Avebury & Stonehenge; stately homes & N.T. properties within easy reach. Ample parking. Children by arrangement. **E-mail: BandB@pickwickfarm.freeserve.co.uk**	£20.00 to £25.00 🚭	Y	N	N
Peter & Jenny Daniel **Heatherly Cottage** **Ladbrook Lane** **Corsham** **SN13 9PE** **Tel: (01249) 701402** **Fax 01249 701412** **Open: FEB - DEC** **Map Ref No. 12**	Nearest Road: A.4 Heatherly Cottage was built in the 17th century & has a large garden with plenty of parking space & beautiful views towards the Westbury White Horse. Each of the 3 attractive bedrooms is well-equipped & has a T.V., tea/coffee facilities & an en-suite bathroom. In nearby Lacock & Gastard, there are traditional English pubs which serve excellent lunches & evening meals. The hosts aim to ensure that you enjoy your stay, & are happy to advise of local attractions etc. Children over 10. **E-mail: ladbrook1@aol.com**	£21.00 to £24.00	Y	N	N
Mrs Jeannie O'Flynn **Wyneshore House** **Devizes** **SN10 4LW** **Tel: (01380) 818180** **Fax 01380 818180** **Open: ALL YEAR (Excl.** **Xmas & New Year)** **Map Ref No. 13**	Nearest Road: A.360 Wyneshore House is set in 3 acres of delightful, recently created gardens with views to Salisbury Plain. Only 10 miles from Stonehenge & well-positioned for Bath, Salisbury, Avebury & other historic houses & gardens, it offers spacious & elegant accommodation with a galleried hall. The 2 twin bedrooms have private bath/shower rooms, & the guest sitting room has a T.V.. There are 3 pubs offering good evening meals in the village. Children over 12.	£21.00 to £24.00 🚭	Y	N	N
Mr & Mrs J. Eldred **The Old Rectory** **Luckington** **SN14 6PH** **Tel: (01666) 840556** **Fax 01666 840989** **Open: ALL YEAR** **Map Ref No. 05**	Nearest Road: A.46 A Regency country house situated in an Area of Outstanding Natural Beauty on the Avon, here just a brook. The house stands in 10 acres with a large garden, stables, tennis court & swimming pool & is peacefully situated at the end of a long private drive. The comfortable en-suite bedrooms, 1 double, 1 twin, overlook beautiful countryside. Delightful reception rooms furnished with antiques. Excellent pubs & restaurants nearby. Children over 10. Animals by arrangement.	£34.00 to £40.00 🚭	Y	N	Y

Old Rectory. Lacock.

	rate £ from - to per person	children taken	evening meals	animals taken
Mrs Ross Eavis **Manor Farm** **Malmesbury SN16 0HF** **Tel: (01666) 822148** **Fax 01666 826565** **Open: ALL YEAR (Excl.** **Xmas & New Year)** **Map Ref No. 15** Nearest Road: A.429 Sample 'home from home' comforts in this award-winning 17th century Cotswold farmhouse on a working dairy/arable farm. 6 tastefully furnished bedrooms, 4 en-suite, all with tea/coffee facilities, radio & T.V.. Meals available in local pub within walking distance. Situated on the edge of the Cotswolds convenient for Bath & just 3 miles north of Junction 17 of the M.4. Manor Farm is ideal for 1 night or longer stays. Children over 12. (non-smoking) VISA: M'CARD:	£20.00 to £27.00	Y	N	N
Mrs Judy Davies **Marridge Hill House** **Marlborough** **SN8 2HG** **Tel: (01672) 520237** **Fax 01672 520053** **Open: ALL YEAR (Excl. Xmas)** **Map Ref No. 16** Nearest Road: M.4, B.4192 The house originated in 1750 & is set in glorious countryside, only 1 hrs. drive from Heathrow Airport. You will be warmly welcomed into the relaxed, informal atmosphere of this home, with its lovely sitting & dining rooms, books galore & an acre of garden. 3 comfortable & attractive twin bedrooms (1 en-suite). Both bathrooms have power showers. Ideal base for visiting Avebury, Salisbury, Bath, Oxford & the Cotswolds. Good pubs & restaurants nearby. Children over 5. E-mail: dando@impedaci.demon.co.uk (non-smoking) VISA: M'CARD:	£19.00 to £22.50	Y	N	Y
Clarissa Roe **Clench Farmhouse** **Marlborough** **SN8 4NT** **Tel: (01672) 810264** **Mobile 0374 784601** **Fax 01672 811458** **Open: ALL YEAR** **Map Ref No. 17** Nearest Road: A.345, A.346 A warm & friendly atmosphere awaits guests when they arrive at this attractive 18th-century farmhouse, which is set in its own grounds & surrounded by lovely countryside. There are 2 double bedrooms & 1 twin bedroom, each with either an en-suite or private bathroom. All well decorated & furnished. Delicious dinners are also served. There is a tennis court & outdoor heated swimming pool. Well situated for Bath, Stonehenge & Salisbury. Ample parking.	£24.00 to £30.00	Y	Y	Y
Colin & Susan Ross **Chetcombe House Hotel** **Chetcombe Road** **Mere** **BA12 6AZ** **Tel: (01747) 860219** **Fax 01747 860111** **Open: ALL YEAR** **Map Ref No. 18** Nearest Road: A.303 Chetcombe is a country-house hotel set in an acre of lovely garden in the picturesque little town of Mere. Accommodation is in 5 attractively furnished rooms with en-suite facilities & modern amenities, including T.V., 'phone & tea/coffee makers. Delicious meals are served. Guests may relax in the comfortable lounge or enjoy the pretty garden. Ideal as a stop-over en-route to the West Country, or as a base for exploring the delights of Wiltshire. (non-smoking) VISA: M'CARD: AMEX:	£26.50 to £35.00	Y	Y	Y
Mrs Serena Gore **St. Cross** **Pewsey** **SN9 5PL** **Tel: (01672) 851346** **Open: ALL YEAR (Excl. Xmas)** **Map Ref No. 19** Nearest Road: A.4 St. Cross is a 17th-century thatched cottage in a quiet village close to the Downs & Kennet & Avon Canal. Also, Salisbury, Bath & Devizes are all close by. The cottage is decorated to a high standard throughout & has a very friendly atmosphere. 2 comfortable bedrooms, each with tea/coffee-making facilities. All food is fresh, the breakfast is delicious & dinner can be arranged. Also, some good pubs in the village serving food. An ideal base for exploring this beautiful county. Dogs are welcome. Children over 6.	£25.00 to £25.00	Y	Y	Y

Wiltshire

	Nearest Road	rate £ from - to per person	children taken	evening meals	animals taken
Mrs Sue Brandon **Griffin Cottage** **10 St. Edmunds Church Street** **Salisbury SP1 1EF** **Tel: (01722) 328259** **Mobile 0467 395898** **Fax 01722 328259** **Open: ALL YEAR (Excl. Xmas)** **Map Ref No. 20**	Nearest Road: A.36, A.30 Within 3 mins of the market square. The house was built 300/500 years ago. Central heating & a real fire greet you in winter. Organic home-produced food where possible, including the bread. Antique furniture mixed with modern comforts to give a warm & informal welcome. The 2 guest rooms have recently been refurbished with comfortable beds, a must when staying away from home. Your hosts look forward to meeting you in their charming home. Single supplement. E-mail: mark@brandonasoc.demon.co.uk	£19.00 to £20.00	N	N	N
Patrick Fairbrother **Glen Lyn House** **6 Bellamy Lane** **Salisbury** **SP1 2SP** **Tel: (01722) 327880** **Fax 01722 327880** **Open: ALL YEAR** **Map Ref No. 20**	Nearest Road: A.36 Situated in a quiet tree-lined lane, 5 mins' walk from the city centre, Glen Lyn is an elegant Victorian house offering 7 individually appointed bedrooms, 4 en-suite & all with colour T.V.. Enjoy a great English breakfast & superb home-produced dinner, then relax in the lounge or listen to birdsong in the beautiful garden. The ideal tranquil base for visiting the cathedral & Stonehenge, & for exploring the New Forest. Parking. Children over 12. Evening meals by prior arrangement. E-mail: glen.lyn@btinternet.com VISA: M'CARD: AMEX:	£20.75 to £30.00	Y	Y	Y
Dick & Joan Robathan **Maddington House** **Maddington Street** **Salisbury SP3 4JD** **Tel/Fax: (01980) 620406** **Open: ALL YEAR** **Map Ref No. 21**	Nearest Road: A.360 Maddington House is the family home of Dick & Joan Robathan. An elegant 17th-century Grade II listed house in the centre of the pretty village of Shrewton - about 2 1/2 miles from Stonehenge & 11 miles from Salisbury. 3 attractive guest rooms, 2 with en-suite facilities. The village has 4 pubs, all within easy walking distance. A delightful home, & the perfect base for a relaxing break.	£20.00 to £25.00	Y	N	N
Mrs Christine Sykes **Elm Tree Cottage** **Chain Hill** **Salisbury** **SP3 4LH** **Tel: (01722) 790507** **Open: MAR - OCT** **Map Ref No. 24**	Nearest Road: A.36, A.303 Elm Tree Cottage is a 17th-century character cottage with inglenook & beams & a lower garden to relax in. The bedrooms, each with an en-suite/private bathroom, are light & airy, are attractively decorated & have T.V. & tea/coffee facilities. The atmosphere is relaxed & warm, & breakfast is served as required. Situated in a picturesque village, there are views across various valleys, & it is a good centre for Salisbury, Wilton, Longleat, Stonehenge, Avebury, etc.	£24.00 to £25.00	Y	N	N
Ian & Rosie Robertson **Wyndham Cottage** **St. Mary's Road** **Salisbury** **SP3 5HH** **Tel: (01722) 716343** **Open: FEB - NOV** **Map Ref No. 26**	Nearest Road: A.36, A.303 A charming 18th-century thatched stone cottage, lovingly restored & set in magnificent N.T. countryside on the edge of a picturesque village. Bluebells, lambs & calves in Spring, delightful walks with marvellous views of the surrounding area. The cottage garden has many interesting plants. Good pubs nearby. Ideally situated for several days sight-seeing: Stonehenge, Avebury, Salisbury, Bath, Wells, Wilton House, Stourhead & Longleat. 2 double bedrooms with en-suite bathrooms, tea/coffee & T.V.. Children over 12.	£23.00 to £27.00	Y	N	N

Wiltshire

		rate £ from - to per person	children taken	evening meals	animals taken
Diana Gifford Mead **The Mill House** **Salisbury** **SP3 4TS** **Tel: (01722) 790331** **Open: ALL YEAR** **Map Ref No. 25**	Nearest Road: A.36, A.303 Stonehenge - a lovely walk - is 3 1/2 miles from Mill House built by the Miller in 1785 & set in a Nature Reserve surrounded by water, abounding in old-fashioned roses, wild flowers & birds. Diana & Michael welcome you to share the idyllic peace, the wonderful walks, English pubs, antiquities, historic houses, fishing & healthy eating. Golf & riding available. Help with your itinerary. Children over 5 years welcome.	£23.00 to £30.00 *see PHOTO over* *p. 455*	Y	N	N
Suzi Lanham **Newton Farmhouse** **Southampton Road** **Salisbury** **SP5 2QL** **Tel: (01794) 884416** **Fax 01794 884416** **Open: ALL YEAR** **Map Ref No. 27**	Nearest Road: A.36 This historic listed 16th-century farmhouse, on the borders of the New Forest, was formerly part of the Trafalgar Estate & is situated 8 miles south of Salisbury, convenient for Stonehenge, Romsey, Winchester & Portsmouth. All rooms are en-suite, 3 with genuine period 4-poster beds. The beamed dining room houses a collection of Nelson memorabilia & antiques & has flagstone floors & an inglenook fireplace. The superb English breakfast includes home-made breads & preserves. (Dinner by arrangement.) Swimming pool. **E-mail: newton.farmhouse.b-b@lineone.net**	£19.00 to £25.00	Y	Y	N
Mrs Norma Hunt **Bridge Farm** **Lower Road** **Salisbury SP5 4DY** **Tel: (01722) 332376** **Fax 01722 332376** **Open: ALL YEAR** **Map Ref No. 28**	Nearest Road: A.338 A warm welcome & a hearty English breakfast are assured at this charming 18th-century farmhouse on a working farm on the southern edge of Salisbury. The 2 double & 1 twin en-suite rooms are spacious & individually & tastefully furnished. Within easy walking distance of the cathedral, & has famous views of the spire along the River Avon that flows alongside the beautiful gardens.	£22.50 to £25.00	Y	N	N
Mrs Valerie Threlfall **1 Cove House** **Swindon** **SN6 6NS** **Tel: (01285) 861226** **Open: ALL YEAR** **Map Ref No. 29**	Nearest Road: A.419 Southern half of a beautiful 17th-century manor house in a pretty Cotswold village. 1 double & 1 twin-bedded room, elegantly decorated & each with en-suite/private facilities. The guests' sitting room is located in the beamed attic, whose interior reflects the hosts' joint hobbies of vintage-car & costume collection. A walled garden/garden room is reached via a recently renovated ball-room. 3 local hostelries offering meals within easy walking distance.	£25.00 to £26.00	Y	N	N
Joy Greathead **Deverill End** **Deverill Road** **Warminster** **BA12 7BY** **Tel: (01985) 840356** **Open: ALL YEAR** **Map Ref No. 30**	Nearest Road: A.36, A.350 Notable for its informality & comfort, Deverill End lies midway between Bath & Salisbury. Longleat, Stonehenge, Stourhead & many other places of historical interest are easily accessible. Joy & Sim have recently retired from a lifetime's farming in Southern Africa. The garden with its panoramic view is a place to relax. The house is tastefully furnished, all 3 bedrooms are en-suite. A variety of excellent pubs nearby. Children over 12.	£20.00 to £30.00	Y	N	N

The Mill House. Berwick St. James

Wiltshire

		rate £ from - to per person	children taken	evening meals	animals taken
Rachel & Colin Singer **Springfield House** **Crockerton** **Warminster** **BA12 8AU** **Tel: (01985) 213696** **Fax 01985 213696** **Open: ALL YEAR** **Map Ref No. 34**	Nearest Road: A.350, A.36 Situated in the beautiful Wylye Valley, on the edge of the famous Longleat Estate, Springfield House is a charming village house dating from the 17th century. Rachel & Colin welcome you to their home, with its beams, open fires, fresh flowers & sunny en-suite rooms, overlooking the garden & grass tennis court. This is a marvellous base for touring, walking or relaxing. Bath, Salisbury, Wells, Stonehenge, Stourhead are all easily reached. Single supplement.	£25.00 to £29.00	Y	N	N

All the establishments mentioned in this guide are members of
The Worldwide Bed & Breakfast Association

When booking your accommodation please mention
The Best Bed & Breakfast

All the establishments mentioned in this guide are members of the Worldwide Bed & Breakfast Association.

If you have any comments regarding your accommodation please send them to us using the form at the back of the book. We value your comments.

Yorkshire

Yorkshire & Humberside

England's largest county is a region of beautiful landscapes, of hills, peaks, fells, dales & forests with many square miles of National Park. It is a vast area taking in big industrial cities, interesting towns & delightful villages. Yorkshire's broad rivers sweep through the countryside & are an angler's paradise. Cascading waterfalls pour down from hillside & moorland.

The North sea coast can be thrilling, with wild seas & cliff-top walks, or just fun, as at the many resorts where the waves break on long beaches & trickle into green rock-pools. Staithes & Robin Hoods Bay are fascinating old fishing villages. Whitby is an attractive port where, Abbey, the small town tumbles in red-roofed tiers down to the busy harbour from which Captain Cook sailed.

The Yorkshire Dales form one of the finest landscapes in England. From windswept moors to wide green valleys the scenery is incomparable. James Herriot tells of of the effect that the broad vista of Swaledale had on him. "I was captivated", he wrote, "completely spell-bound....". A network of dry stone walls covers the land; some are as old as the stone-built villages but those which climb the valley sides to the high moors are the product of the 18th century enclosures, when a good wall builder would cover seven meters a day.

Each of the Dales has a distinctive character; from the remote upper reaches of Swaledale & Wensleydale, where the air sings with the sound of wind, sheep, & curlew, over to Airedale & the spectacular limestone gorges of Malham Cove & Gordale Scar, & down to the soft meadows & woods of Wharfedale where the ruins of Bolton Priory stand beside the river.

To the east towards Hull with its mighty River Humber crossed by the worlds largest single-span suspension bridge, lie the Yorkshire Wolds. This is lovely countryside where villages have unusual names like Fridaythorpe & Wetwang. Beverley is a picture-postcard town with a fine 13th century Minster.

The North Yorks National Park, where the moors are ablaze with purple fire of heather in the late summer, is exhilarating country. There is moorland to the east also, on the Pennine chain; famous Ilkley Moor with its stone circle known as the twelve apostles, & the Haworth Moors around the plain Yorkshire village where the Bronte sisters lived; "the distant dreamy, dim blue chain of mountains circling every side", which Emily Bronte describes in Wuthering Heights.

The Yorkshire Pennines industrial heritage is being celebrated in fascinating museums, often based in the original Woolen Mills & warehouses, which also provide workshop space for skilled craftspeople.

Yorkshires Monastic past is revealed in the ruins of its once great Abbeys. Rievaulx, Jervaux & Fountains, retain their tranquil beauty in their pastoral settings. The wealth of the county is displayed in many historic houses with glorious gardens, from stately 18th Century Castle Howard of 'Brideshead Revisited' fame to Tudor Shibden Hall, portrayed in Wuthering Heights.

York is the finest mediaeval city in England. It is encircled by its limestone city walls with four Great Gates. Within the walls are the jumbled roof line, dog-leg streets & sudden courtyards of a mediaeval town. Half timbered buildings with over-sailing upper storeys jostle with Georgian brick houses along the network of narrow streets around The Shambles & King Edward Square.

Yorkshire

Yorkshire Gazeteer

Areas of Outstanding Natural Beauty.
 The North Yorkshire Moors & The Yorkshire Dales.

Historic Houses & Castles.

Carlton Towers
17th century, remodelled in later centuries. paintings, silver, furniture, pictures. Carved woodwork, painted decorations, examples of Victorian craftmanship.

Castle Howard - Nr. York
18th century - celebrated architect, Sir John Vanbrugh - paintings, costumes, furniture by Chippendale, Sheraton, Adam. Not to be missed.

East Riddlesden Hall - Keighley
17th century manor house with fishponds & historic barns, one of which is regarded as very fine example of mediaeval tithe barn.

Newby Hall - Ripon
17th century Wren style extended by Robert Adam. Gobelins tapestry, Chippendale furniture, sculpture galleries with Roman rotunda, statuary. Award-winning gardens.

Nostell Priory - Wakefield
18th century, Georgian mansion, Chippendale furniture, paintings.

Burton Constable Hall - Hull
16th century, Elizabethan, remodelled in Georgian period. Stained glass, Hepplewhite furniture, gardens by Capability Brown.

Ripley Castle - Harrogate
14th century, parts dating during 16th & 18th centuries. Priest hole, armour & weapons, beautiful ceilings.

The Treasurer's House - York
17th & 18th centuries, splendid interiors, furniture, pictures.

Harewood House - Leeds
18th century - Robert Adam design, Chippendale furniture, Italian & English paintings. Sevres & Chinese porcelain.

Benningbrough Hall - York
18th century. Highly decorative woodwork, oak staircase, friezes etc. Splendid hall.

Markenfield Hall - Ripon
14th to 16th century - fine Manor house surrounded by moat.

Heath Hall - Wakefield

18th century, palladian. Fine woodwork & plasterwork, rococo ceilings, excellent furniture, paintings & porcelain

Bishops House - Sheffield
16th century. Only complete timber framed yeoman farmhouse surviving. Vernacular architecture. Superb

Skipton Castle- Skipton
One of the most complete & well preserved mediaeval castles in England.

Cathedral & Churches

York Minster
13th century. Greatest Gothic Cathedral north of the Alps. Imposing grandeur - superb Chapter house, contains half of the mediaeval stained glass of England. Outstandingly beautiful.

York (All Saints, North Street)
15th century roofing in parts - 18th century pulpit wonderful mediaeval glass.

Ripon Cathedral
12th century - though in some parts Saxon in origin. Decorated choir stalls - gables buttresses. Church of 672 preserved in crypt, , Caxton Book, ecclesiastic treasures.

Bolton Percy (All Saints)
15th century.
Maintains original glass in east window. Jacobean font cover. Georgian pulpit. Interesting monuments.

Rievaulx Abbey
12th century, masterpiece of Early English architecture.
One of three great Cistercian Abbeys built in Yorkshire.
Impressive ruins.

Campsall (St. Mary Magdalene)
Fine Norman tower - 15th century rood screen, carved & painted stone altar.

Fountains Abbey - Ripon
Ruins of England's greatest mediaeval abbey - surrounded by wonderful landscaped gardens. Enormous tower, vaulted cellar 300 feet long.

Whitby (St. Mary)
12th century tower & doorway, 18th century remodelling - box pews much interior woodwork painted - galleries. High pulpit. Table tombs.

Yorkshire

Whitby Abbey - Whitby (St. Hilda)
7th century superb ruin - venue of Synod of 664. Destroyed by Vikings, restored 1078 - magnificent north transept.
Halifax (St. John the Baptist)
12th century origins, showing work from each succeeding century - heraldic ceilings. Cromwell glass.
Beverley Minster - Beverley
14th century. Fine Gothic Minster - remarkable mediaeval effigies of musicians playing instruments. Founded as monastery in 700.
Bolton Priory - Nr. Skipton
Nave of Augustinian Priory, now Bolton's Parish Church, amidst ruins of choir & transepts, in beautiful riverside setting.
Selby Abbey - Selby
11th century Benedictine abbey of which the huge church remains. Roof & furnishings are modern after a fire of 1906, but the stonework is intact.

Museums & Galleries

Aldborough Roman Museum - Boroughbridge
Remnants of Roman period of the town - coins, glass, pottery, etc.
Great Ayton
Home of Captain Cook, explorer & seaman. Exhibits of maps, etc.
Art Gallery - City of York
Modern paintings, Old Masters, watercolours, prints, ceramics.
Lotherton Hall - Nr. Leeds
Museum with furniture, paintings, silver, works of art from the Leeds collection & oriental art gallery.
National Railway Museum - York
Devoted to railway engineering & its development.
York Castle Museum
The Kirk Collection of bygones including cobbled streets, shops, costumes, toys, household & farm equipment - fascinating collection.
Cannon Hall Art Gallery - Barnsley
18th century house with fine furniture & glass, etc. Flemish & Dutch paintings. Also houses museum of the 13/18 Royal Hussars.
Mappin Art Gallery - Sheffield
Works from 18th,19th & 20th century.

Graves Art gallery-Sheffield.
British portraiture. European works, & examples of Asian & African art. Loan exhibitions are held there.
Royal Pump Room Museum - Harrogate
Original sulphur well used in the Victorian Spa. Local history costume & pottery.
Bolling Hall - Bradford
A period house with mixture of styles - collections of 17th century oak furniture, domestic utensils, toys & bygones.
Georgian Theatre - Richmond
Oldest theatre in the country - interesting theatrical memorabilia.
Jorvik Viking Centre - York
Recently excavated site in the centre of York showing hundreds of artifacts dating from the Viking period. One of the most important archaeological discoveries this century.
Abbey House Museum - Kirkstall, Leeds
Illustrated past 300 years of Yorkshire life. Shows 3 full streets from 19th century with houses, shops & workplaces.
Piece Hall - Halifax
Remarkable building - constructed around huge quadrangle - now Textile Industrial Museum, Art Gallery & has craft & antique shops.
National Museum of Photography, Film & Television - Bradford
Displays look at art & science of photography, film & T.V. Britain's only IMAX arena.
The Colour Museum - Bradford
Award-winning interactive museum,which allows visitors to explore the world of colour & discover the story of dyeing & textile printing.
Calderdale Industrial Museum - Halifax
Social & industrial Museum of the year 1987
Shibden Hall & Folk Museum of Halifax
Half-timbered house with folk museum, farmland, miniature train & boating lake.
Leeds City Art Gallery & Henry Moore Sculpture Gallery
Yorkshire Sculpture Park - Wakefield
Yorkshire Museum of Farming - Murton
Award-winning museum of farming & the countryside.

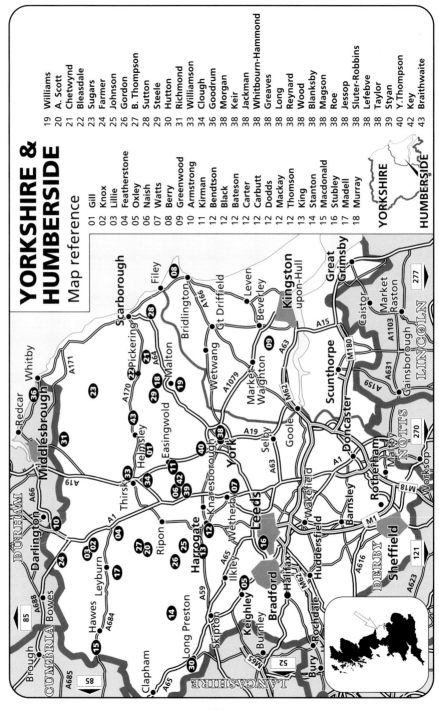

YORKSHIRE & HUMBERSIDE

Map reference

01 Gill	19 Williams	
02 Knox	20 A. Scott	
03 Lillie	21 Chetwynd	
04 Featherstone	22 Bleasdale	
05 Oxley	23 Sugars	
06 Naish	24 Farmer	
07 Watts	25 Johnson	
08 Berry	26 Gordon	
09 Greenwood	27 B. Thompson	
10 Armstrong	28 Sutton	
11 Kirman	29 Steele	
12 Bendtson	30 Hutton	
12 Black	31 Richmond	
12 Bateson	33 Williamson	
12 Carter	34 Clough	
12 Carbutt	36 Goodrum	
12 Dodds	38 Morgan	
12 Mackay	38 Keir	
12 Thomson	38 Jackman	
13 King	38 Whitbourn-Hammond	
14 Stanton	38 Greaves	
15 Macdonald	38 Long	
16 Stubley	38 Reynard	
17 Madell	38 Wood	
18 Murray	38 Blanksby	
	38 Magson	
	38 Roe	
	38 Jessop	
	38 Sluter-Robbins	
	38 Lefebve	
	38 Taylor	
	39 Styan	
	40 Y.Thompson	
	42 Key	
	43 Braithwaite	

YORKSHIRE

HUMBERSIDE

Yorkshire

		rate £ from - to per person	children taken	evening meals	animals taken
P. Gill & A. Van Der Horst **Shallowdale House** **West End** **Ampleforth YO62 4DY** **Tel: (01439) 788325** Fax 01439 788885 **Open: ALL YEAR (Excl.** **Xmas & New Year)** **Map Ref No. 01**	Nearest Road: A.170, A.19 This is an outstanding modern country house, with 2 acres of hillside garden, on the southern edge of the North York Moors National Park. All of the spacious rooms enjoy stunning views of unspoilt countryside & are furnished with style & attention to detail. 3 guest bedrooms (with bath & shower) & 2 sitting rooms. Meals are imaginatively prepared from fresh seasonal ingredients. Licensed. A perfect place to unwind when exploring Herriot country & York. Children over 12.	£32.50 to £40.00 VISA: M'CARD:	Y	Y	N
Mrs Patricia Knox **Mill Close Farm** **Patrick Brompton** **Bedale** **DL8 1JY** **Tel: (01677) 450257** Fax 01677 450585 **Open: MAR - NOV** **Map Ref No. 02**	Nearest Road: A.684 A 17th-century working farm surrounded by beautiful rolling countryside at the foothills of the Yorkshire Dales & Herriot country. Exceptional views yet only 3 miles from A1(M). Lovely en-suite bedrooms with many extras - jacuzzi, super king-size bed, toiletries, hairdryers, T.V. with choice of videos. Highland cattle, sheep, calves roam the grounds amongst wild flowers. Enchanting garden with pond & waterfall. Sumptuous breakfasts. Excellent local pubs. Ideal stopover for Scotland. Animals by arrangement.	£20.00 to £25.00	Y	N	Y
Edith & Jim Lillie **Elmfield Country House** **Arrathorne** **Bedale** **DL8 1NE** **Tel: (01677) 450558** Fax 01677 450557 **Open: ALL YEAR** **Map Ref No. 03**	Nearest Road: A.684 Located in its own grounds in the country. Enjoy a relaxed, friendly atmosphere in spacious surroundings, with a high standard of furnishings. 9 en-suite bedrooms comprising twin-bedded, double & family rooms. 2 rooms have been adapted for disabled guests & another has a 4-poster bed. All rooms have satellite colour T.V., 'phone, radio/alarm & tea/coffee makers. A games room & solarium are also available. Excellent farmhouse cooking. Residential licence. A delightful home. **E-mail: bed@elmfieldhouse.freeserve.co.uk**	£25.00 to £35.00 *see PHOTO over* *p. 463* VISA: M'CARD:	Y	Y	N
Oriella Featherstone **The Hall** **Newton-le-Willows** **Bedale** **DL8 1SW** **Tel: (01677) 450210** Fax 01677 450014 **Open: ALL YEAR** **Map Ref No. 04**	Nearest Road: A.684, A.1 Come stay awhile in this glorious listed Georgian hide-away with secluded gardens & aged copper beeches. Your hosts aim to offer only the best to provide you with comfort & joy. Try the luxurious main suite & its 7ft square bed with a duvet which holds the down of 226 ducks, or sample one of the other exquisitely furnished bedrooms. Experience delightful cuisine served in the opulent dining room. Visit the Dales, Moors, castles & ruins. Make yourselves feel at home. Children over 13.	£40.00 to £50.00	Y	Y	Y
Mrs Pat Oxley **Five Rise Locks Hotel** **Beck Lane** **Bingley** **BD16 4DD** **Tel: (01274) 565296** Fax 01274 568828 **Open: ALL YEAR** **Map Ref No. 05**	Nearest Road: A.650 Tranquil rural setting in the canal conservation area, minutes walk from the Five Rise Locks with panoramic views of the Aire Valley. Visit Haworth, Esholt, Saltaire, the Dales & even spend a day working sheep dogs. Originally a wealthy Victorian mill-owners house, each en-suite bedroom is individually designed & tastefully furnished. Delicious home-cooking is complimented by an imaginative wine list in elegant surroundings. **E-mail: 101731.2134@compuserve.com**	£25.00 to £30.00 VISA: M'CARD:	Y	Y	Y

Elmfield Country House. Arrathorne.

Yorkshire

			rate £ from - to per person	children taken	evening meals	animals taken
Rowena Naish **Prospect Farm** **Marton-cum-Grafton** **Boroughbridge YO51 9QJ** Tel: (01423) 322045 Fax 01423 322045 Open: ALL YEAR Map Ref No. 06	Nearest Road: A.1, B.6265 Prospect Farm is a beautiful 18th-century family farmhouse retaining many original features & with traditional furnishings. This working farm is in a pretty village & has spectacular views over the Vale of York. There are farm cottages & 2 very comfortable bedrooms available to guests with en-suite facilities. Residents' lounge, garden, private fishing lakes. Easy access to York, Harrogate, Dales, Moors & coast.	£17.00 to £20.00	Y	N	N
David Watts **Four Gables** **Oaks Lane** **Boston Spa** **LS23 6DS** Tel: (01937) 849031 Tel: (01937) 845592 Open: ALL YEAR Map Ref No. 07	Nearest Road: A.659 Visitors will love this special Art-and-Craft movement house with its wealth of original features, stripped oak & terracotta floors, fireplaces & beautiful ceilings, & gardens of over 1/2 acre which contains many interesting plants & a croquet lawn. Enjoy the peaceful setting, down a private lane, yet only 3 mins' walk from the Georgian stone village of Boston Spa with all its facilities, shops & restaurants etc. 3 attractive en-suite bedrooms. Log fires in winter. Children over 7. **E-mail: fourgables@wetherby.co.uk**	£25.00 to £28.00	Y	N	N
Lesley Berry **& Geoffrey Miller** **The Manor House** **Flamborough** **Bridlington** **YO15 1PD** Tel: (01262) 850943 Fax 01262 850943 Open: ALL YEAR (Excl. Xmas) Map Ref No. 08	Nearest Road: A.165, A.166 A manor of Flamborough is recorded in the Domesday Book. The current Georgian house is a handsomely proportioned family home offering spacious & comfortable accommodation in well-appointed rooms. Historic Flamborough Head is designated a Heritage Coast, with many interesting walks & a nearby bird reserve. Ideally placed for exploration of North & East Yorkshire. Dinner, by arrangement, features local seafood when available. Children over 8 years. **E-mail: manorhouse@clara.co.uk**	£31.00 to £39.00 VISA: M'CARD: AMEX:	Y	Y	N
Mr Charles Greenwood **Rudstone Walk** **South Cave** **Brough** **HU15 2AH** Tel: (01430) 422230 Fax 01430 424552 Open: ALL YEAR Map Ref No. 09	Nearest Road: A.1034 Rudstone Walk is renowned for its hospitality & good food. Accommodation is in the very tastefully converted farm buildings, adjacent to the main farmhouse where meals are served. Each of the attractive bedrooms has en-suite facilities, T.V., 'phone, hairdryer etc. Rudstone provides a peaceful retreat after a tiring day. It is ideal for a relaxing break, & is within easy reach of York & many other attractions. Animals by arrangement. **E-mail: OFFICE@rudstone-walk.co.uk**	£29.00 to £45.00 VISA: M'CARD: AMEX:	Y	Y	Y
David & Heather Armstrong **Clow Beck House** **Monk End Farm** **Croft-on-Tees** **Darlington** **DL2 2SW** Tel: (01325) 721075 Fax 01325 720419 Open: ALL YEAR Map Ref No. 10	Nearest Road: A.1, A.167 Clow Beck House is decorated with some flamboyance - chandeliers, antiques & Adam-style panels. This award-winning country house exudes warmth, friendliness & relaxation with a tinge of luxury. 14 beautiful rooms with en-suite/private facilities & many extras. Excellent for Herriot country, York & the Dales - route planning is your hosts' speciality. Facilities available for families & those with impaired mobility. Be pampered with old-fashioned hospitality & service. **E-mail: clow.beck.house@dial.pipex.com**	£35.00 to £45.00 *see PHOTO over* p. 465 VISA: M'CARD: AMEX:	Y	Y	N

Clow-beck House. Croft-on-Tees.

Yorkshire

	rate £ from - to per person	children taken	evening meals	animals taken

Christine & John Kirman **The Old Vicarage** **Market Place** **Easingwold YO61 3AL** **Tel: (01347) 821015** **Fax 01347 823465** **Open: FEB - NOV** **Map Ref No. 11**	Nearest Road: A.19 A listed property of immense character built in the 18th century & thoughtfully brought up to modern standards, & yet still retaining many delightful features. Now offering 5 en-suite rooms with T.V. & tea/coffee makers. Standing in extensive lawned gardens, overlooking the market square, & with a croquet lawn & a walled rose garden, it is an ideal touring centre for York, the Dales, the Yorkshire Moors & 'Herriot' countryside. Parking.	£25.00 to £30.00 *see PHOTO over* *p. 467* VISA: M'CARD:	Y	N	N
Gill & Kristian Bendtson **Ashwood House** **7 Spring Grove** **Harrogate HG1 2HS** **Tel: (01423) 560081** **Fax 01423 527928** **Open: ALL YEAR (Excl.** **Xmas & New Year)** **Map Ref No. 12**	Nearest Road: A.61 A charming 9-bedroomed Edwardian house retaining many of its original features. Situated in a quiet, residential cul-de-sac mins from the town centre. The attractive en-suite bedrooms are spacious, some with 4-poster beds, all with hospitality tray, T.V., hairdryer & toiletries. A delicious breakfast is served from lovely Royal Copenhagen china in the elegant dining room. A high standard of service & a warm welcome is assured. Scandinavian languages spoken.	£27.50 to £33.00	N	N	N
Mr & Mrs John Black **Alexa House Hotel &** **Stable Cottages** **26 Ripon Road** **Harrogate HG1 2JJ** **Tel: (01423) 501988** **Fax 01423 504086** **Open: ALL YEAR** **Map Ref No. 12**	Nearest Road: A.61 Built in 1830 for Baron de Ferrier, Alexa House & Stable Cottages is now an elegant & welcoming small hotel. It is conveniently situated within 5 mins' walk of the town centre where the many restaurants are a gourmet's delight. With its tasteful decoration, warm hospitality & a breakfast that's second to none, it offers 13 en-suite bedrooms, a bar, car park & a chance to unwind at one of the north's finest health & fitness spas.	£30.00 to £35.00 VISA: M'CARD: AMEX:	Y	Y	N
Dee & Peter Bateson **Acacia Lodge** **21 Ripon Road** **Harrogate** **HG1 2JL** **Tel: (01423) 560752** **Fax 01423 503725** **Open: ALL YEAR** **Map Ref No. 12**	Nearest Road: A.61 Acacia Lodge is a warm, lovingly restored & charming small family-run hotel with pretty gardens in a select central conservation area a short stroll from Harrogate's fashionable shops, restaurants & attractions. It retains all its original character with fine furnishings, antiques & old paintings. Bedrooms are en-suite & well-furnished with every comfort. Award-winning breakfasts served in the oak-furnished dining room, & guests can relax in the lounge with open fire & library of books. Private floodlit car park. Children over 10.	£27.00 to £34.00	Y	N	N
Ms Denise Carter **The Ruskin Hotel** **1 Swan Road** **Harrogate** **HG1 2SS** **Tel: (01423) 502045** **Fax 01423 506131** **Open: ALL YEAR** **Map Ref No. 12**	Nearest Road: A.61 A truly outstanding small Victorian hotel, set in lovely lawned grounds (with a car park). In a quiet conservation area only mins' stroll from the town, theatres & gardens. Spacious en-suite bedrooms, antique furnished & offering every facility. Superior beds including 4-poster. Charming drawing room with open fire, antique furniture & books create a relaxed atmosphere. Renowned for superb breakfasts & English cuisine served in the Victorian-style dining room. Licensed. **E-mail: ruskin.hotel@virgin.net**	£39.00 to £50.00 VISA: M'CARD: AMEX:	Y	Y	N

The Old Vicarage. Easingwold.

Yorkshire

		rate £ from - to per person	children taken	evening meals	animals taken
Peter & Gill Carbutt **Daryl House Hotel** **42 Dragon Parade** **Harrogate** **HG1 5DA** **Tel: (01423) 502775** **Fax 01423 502775** **Open: ALL YEAR** **Map Ref No. 12**	Nearest Road: A.59 A small, friendly, family-run house offering excellent accommodation in 5 most pleasant rooms with every modern comfort. Tea/coffee makers & T.V. in all rooms. An attractive lounge with colour T.V. & garden for guests' enjoyment. Home-cooked food & personal attention are the hallmarks of Daryl House. Close to the town centre with its conference facilities. A very warm welcome awaits all visitors. Children over 10.	£19.00 to £30.00	Y	N	N
Carol & Jim Dodds **Shannon Court Hotel** **65 Dragon Avenue** **Harrogate** **HG1 5DS** **Tel: (01423) 509858** **Fax 01423 530606** **Open: ALL YEAR** **Map Ref No. 12**	Nearest Road: A.59 Charming Victorian house hotel overlooking the 'stray' in High Harrogate. Enjoy real home cooking in this family-run hotel. Accommodation is in 8 delightful bedrooms, all of which are en-suite & have every modern comfort including radio, colour T.V. & tea/coffee-making facilities. Licensed for residents & their guests. Close to town centre, railway station & conference centre, with easy parking, & direct to main routes for moors & dales. Shannon Court Hotel is an excellent touring base. **E-mail: shannon@hotel.harrogate.com**	£25.00 to £35.00 VISA M'CARD	Y	Y	Y
Mrs Jennifer Mackay **Franklin View** **19 Grove Road** **Harrogate** **HG1 5EW** **Tel: (01423) 541388** **Fax 01423 547872** **Open: ALL YEAR** **Map Ref No. 12**	Nearest Road: A.1 A warm & friendly welcome awaits guests in this fine Edwardian house standing in attractive rockery gardens. The accommodation has been carefully refurbished to a high standard & the bedrooms have private facilities, colour T.V. & tea/coffee makers. A short walk takes you into the famous spa town centre with superb shopping & restaurant facilities. Ideal touring base for historical interests & the wonderful scenery of the Yorkshire Dales. Children over 5 yrs.	£21.00 to £23.00	Y	N	N
Peter & Marion Thomson **Knox Mill House** **Knox Mill Lane** **Killinghall** **Harrogate HG3 2AE** **Tel/Fax: (01423) 560650** **Open: ALL YEAR (Excl.** **Xmas & New Year)** **Map Ref No. 12**	Nearest Road: A.61 Built in 1785, this lovely old millhouse stands on the banks of a stream in a quiet rural setting, & yet is only 1 1/2 miles from the centre of Harrogate. Beautifully renovated, it still retains all its original features: oak beams, an inglenook fireplace & stone arches. There are 3 delightful rooms, attractively & comfortably furnished. 2 are en-suite, & all have tea/coffee makers & views over the stream & fields. A delightful lounge with colour T.V., & a garden for guests' enjoyment.	£21.00 to £21.00	N	N	N
Clive & Gill King **High Winsley Cottage** **Burnt Yates** **Harrogate** **HG3 3EP** **Tel: (01423) 770662** **Open: MAR - DEC** **Map Ref No. 13**	Nearest Road: A.61 Traditional Dales cottage in Nidderdale, situated well off the road in peaceful countryside, with lovely views all around, & ideally placed for both town & country. 2 twin & 2 double rooms, well-appointed & all with en-suite facilities. 2 large sitting rooms, with guide books, games, T.V., etc. Imaginative home cooking using produce from the extensive kitchen garden, complemented by wines from an interesting list. Children over 11.	£24.00 to £27.00 *see PHOTO over* *p. 469*	N	Y	N

High Winsley Cottage. Burnt Yates.

Yorkshire

		rate £ from - to per person	children taken	evening meals	animals taken
Mr & Mrs Nigel Stanton **Knottside Farm** **Pateley Bridge** **Harrogate** **HG3 5DQ** **Tel: (01423) 712927** **Fax 01423 712927** **Open: ALL YEAR** **Map Ref No. 14**	Nearest Road: A.59 Knottside Farm, a beautiful 17th-century farmhouse, is in Nidderdale, an Area of Outstanding Natural Beauty. Ideal for walking, fishing, pony trekking & bird-watching or visiting the Moors, Dales, Harrogate & York. The guest's rooms are delightfully furnished to a very high standard & have wonderful views over this peaceful dale. Nigel creates mouth-watering Cordon Bleu dinners which include local lamb & trout. A charming home & a perfect spot for a relaxing break.	£20.00 to £25.00 🚭	N	Y	Y
Gail Ainley **& Ann Macdonald** **Brandymires** **Muker Road** **Hawes** **DL8 3PR** **Tel: (01969) 667482** **Open: FEB - OCT** **Map Ref No. 15**	Nearest Road: A.684 A warm welcome awaits you in this comfortable mid-19th-century stone house in a tranquil rural setting. Every room has a splendid view over the fells. 4 spacious & attractive double bedrooms, 2 with 4-poster beds, full central heating. Good home cooking, including home-made bread, is an important feature, & dinner is available with prior notice, except on Thursdays. Brandymires is an ideal centre for exploring both the glorious countryside of the Yorkshire Dales & the historic surrounding towns. No T.V.. Ample parking.	£19.00 to £20.00 🚭	N	Y	Y
Charles & Wendy Stubley **Pinewood Hotel** **78 Potternewton Lane** **Chapel Allerton** **Leeds LS7 3LW** **Tel/Fax: (0113) 2622561** **Open: ALL YEAR (Excl.** **Xmas & New Year)** **Map Ref No. 16**	Nearest Road: A.61 Pinewood Hotel is attractively furnished & decorated, with many extra touches enhancing guests comfort. There are 10 well-equipped & comfortably furnished en-suite bedrooms. The hotel is conveniently situated for shopping, theatre, the famous Yorkshire Dales & Moors & a host of other attractions. Special weekend rates are available. A most warming welcome in a small hotel of distinction awaits you.	£22.50 to £37.00 VISA: M'CARD: AMEX:	Y	Y	N
Everyl & Brian Madell **Waterford House** **Kirkgate** **Middleham** **Leyburn** **DL8 4PG** **Tel: (01969) 622090** **Fax 01969 624020** **Open: ALL YEAR** **Map Ref No. 17**	Nearest Road: A.1 A beautiful, traditional stone-built Georgian residence overlooking the market square of Middleham. Once the centre of government in medieval England & featuring the ruins of Richard III's castle. There are 5 spacious en-suite bedrooms, some beamed, including 2 4-posters, & exquisitely decorated in keeping with the period atmosphere. The restaurant has an a la carte menu that changes daily & over 900 wines, many of them from the '50s, '60s & '70s. Ideal base for the Dales & Herriot country.	£35.00 to £45.00 *see PHOTO over* *p. 471* VISA: M'CARD:	Y	Y	Y
Mrs Judith M. Murray **Manor Farm** **Little Barugh** **Malton** **YO17 6UY** **Tel: (01653) 668262** **Fax 01653 668600** **Open: ALL YEAR** **Map Ref No. 18**	Nearest Road: A.169 A charming Georgian manor house set in spacious grounds with hard tennis court, croquet lawn & views to the Howardian Hills. Accommodation is in 3 attractive bedrooms, with either an en-suite or a private bathroom. Excellent cooking caters for all tastes. Manor Farm is within easy reach of York, Scarborough, the Moors, Castle Howard & Flamingoland. Dogs & children are most welcome. **E-mail: cphmurray@compuserve.com**	£22.50 to £25.00	Y	Y	Y

Waterford House. Middleham.

Newstead Grange. Norton.

Yorkshire

	Nearest Road	rate £ from - to per person	children taken	evening meals	animals taken
Paul & Pat Williams **Newstead Grange** **Beverley Road** **Norton** **Malton YO17 9PJ** Tel: (01653) 692502 Fax 01653 696951 Open: Mid MAR - Mid OCT Map Ref No. 19	Nearest Road: A.64, B.1248 An elegant Georgian country house set in 2 1/2 acres of gardens & grounds with delightful views of the North Yorkshire moors & wolds. The style of the house is tastefully enhanced by antique furniture, open log fires burn in cooler weather, & the bedrooms are individually furnished. The proprietors personally prepare the meals to a very high standard from vegetables & fruit in the organic kitchen garden & fresh local produce. Totally non-smoking. Children over 9.	£31.00 to £40.00 🚭 *see PHOTO over* *p. 472* VISA: M'CARD:	Y	Y	N
Avril Scott **Pasture House** **Healey** **Masham HG4 4LJ** Tel: (01765) 689149 Fax 01765 689990 Open: ALL YEAR Map Ref No. 20	Nearest Road: A.6108 Pasture House is a large, comfortable house providing guests with pleasant accommodation in the quiet of the lovely Yorkshire Dales. A perfect centre for walkers & horse-racing enthusiasts, with several courses & Middleham training gallops nearby. 4 comfortable rooms with T.V. & tea/coffee makers. A residents' lounge & large garden are also available. Pony trekking, golf & fishing locally. Children & pets welcome. Facilities for babies. A lovely home.	£18.00 to £18.00 🚭	Y	Y	Y
Mr & Mrs R. Chetwynd **Manor House** **Allerston** **Pickering** **YO18 7PF** Tel: (01723) 850112 Open: ALL YEAR Map Ref No. 21	Nearest Road: A.170 Manor House is quietly placed on the edge of the village bordering the North Yorkshire Moors National Park with views across the Vale of Pickering to the Wolds beyond. Reconstructed in the 18th century around a 14th-century Knights Templar Hall, now lovingly restored preserving old features & adding modern comforts! A warm & friendly home, very well-positioned to explore the famous sights of this beautiful region. Children over 12 years welcome.	£30.00 to £35.00 🚭 VISA: M'CARD:	Y	Y	N
Mrs E. Bleasdale **The Old Manse** **19 Middleton Road** **Pickering YO18 8AL** Tel: (01751) 476484 Fax 01751 477124 Open: FEB - DEC Map Ref No. 22	Nearest Road: A.170 The Old Manse, a former home of Methodist ministers, is a fine Edwardian house in its own grounds in the picturesque market town of Pickering. There are 8 en-suite rooms, a large secluded garden, orchard & private car park. Pickering - gateway to the North Yorkshire Moors & 'Heartbeat' country, is the start of 18 miles of the scenic North York Moors steam railway & an ideal location for touring & walking. Children over 10.	£20.00 to £23.00 🚭	Y	N	Y
Linda Sugars **Sevenford House** **Thorgill** **Rosedale Abbey** **Pickering YO18 8SE** Tel: (01751) 417283 Fax 01751 417505 Open: ALL YEAR Map Ref No. 23	Nearest Road: A.170 Originally a vicarage, & built from the stones of Rosedale Abbey, Sevenford House stands in 4 acres of lovely gardens in the heart of the beautiful Yorkshire Moors National Park. 3 tastefully furnished, en-suite bedrooms, with T.V., radio & tea/coffee, offer wonderful views overlooking valley & moorland. A lounge/library with open fire. Ideal for exploring the region. Riding & golf locally. Also, ruined abbeys, Roman roads, steam railways, the beautiful coastline & pretty fishing towns. **E-mail: sevenford@aol.com**	£22.50 to £22.50 🚭 *see PHOTO over* *p. 474*	Y	N	N

Sevenford House. Rosedale Abbey.

	rate £ from - to per person	children taken	evening meals	animals taken
Mrs Christina Farmer **Hill Top** **Newsham** **Richmond DL11 7QX** **Tel: (01833) 621513** **Fax 01833 621513** **Open: ALL YEAR** **Map Ref No. 24**	Nearest Road: A.66 Hill Top is a lovely Grade II listed house in a rural setting with panoramic views. The charming hosts offer 1 twin-bedded suite which is attractively furnished with antiques & a host of extras including books, magazines, tea/coffee-making facilities, biscuits etc. There is a good en-suite bathroom. Hill Top is an ideal base for a relaxing break & is a perfect spot from which to explore the many delights of Yorkshire.	£25.00 to £25.00 🚭	N	N	N
Mrs Maggie Johnson **Mallard Grange** **Aldfield** **Nr. Fountains Abbey** **Ripon HG4 3BE** **Tel: (01765) 620242** **Fax 01765 620242** **Open: ALL YEAR (Excl. Xmas)** **Map Ref No. 25**	Nearest Road: A.61, B.6265 Rambling 16th-century farmhouse full of character & charm in glorious countryside near Fountains Abbey. Offering superb quality & comfort, spacious rooms furnished with care & some lovely antique pieces. En-suite bedrooms have large comfortable beds, warm towels, colour T.V., hairdryer & refreshments tray. Delicious breakfasts with homemade preserves. Pretty walled garden tended by enthusiastic amateur. Safe parking. Excellent evening meals locally.	£22.50 to £25.00 🚭	N	N	N
Mrs Sandra Gordon **St. George's Court** **Old Home Farm** **Grantley** **Ripon** **HG4 3EU** **Tel: (01765) 620618** **Fax 01765 620618** **Open: ALL YEAR** **Map Ref No. 26**	Nearest Road: A.1 St. George's Court is beautifully situated in peaceful countryside & provides comfortable ground-floor rooms in renovated farm buildings. All modern facilities whilst retaining much charm & character. Delicious breakfasts are served in the conservatory dining room, with views, in the delightful listed farmhouse. Peace & tranquillity is the password here. St. George's Court is near Fountains Abbey & Brimham Rocks. Ripon, Harrogate & York are all within easy reach. Children over 2 years welcome.	£22.50 to £25.00 *see PHOTO over* *p. 476* VISA: M'CARD:	Y	N	Y
Bobby & Lucy Thomson **Bank Villa** **The Avenue** **Masham** **Ripon HG4 4DB** **Tel/Fax: (01765) 689605** **Open: ALL YEAR (Excl. Xmas)** **Map Ref No. 27**	Nearest Road: A.6108, A.1 Set in half an acre of terraced garden, this welcoming Grade II listed home has recently been renovated & refurbished to a high standard. It offers guests 2 delightful lounges & 6 double bedrooms, 4 with en-suite or private facilities, 2 with private shower. Bank Villa is an ideal base from which to explore the Yorkshire Dales, tour around, walk, horse-ride or fish. Children over 5. Animals by arrangement.	£20.00 to £25.00	Y	Y	Y
Mrs Virginia Sutton **Willerby Wold Farm** **Staxton** **Scarborough** **YO12 4TF** **Tel: (01944) 710747** **Fax 01944 710281** **Open: ALL YEAR (Excl. Xmas)** **Map Ref No. 28**	Nearest Road: A.64 Peacefully situated on an 800-acre farm on the edge of the Yorkshire Wolds, Willerby Wold Farm has been in the Sutton family for 3 generations. The elegant Victorian country house is spacious & comfortable & ideally located for exploring the east coast, the North York Moors & York. The 3 attractive double bedrooms have private bathrooms, T.V.s & tea & coffee facilities. Guests are welcome to use the garden & all-weather tennis court. Evening meals by arrangement. A delightful family home.	£20.00 to £25.00 🚭	Y	Y	N

St. Georges Court. Grantley.

Yorkshire

	Nearest Road	rate £ from - to per person	children taken	evening meals	animals taken
Chris & Malcolm Steele **Wildsmith House** **Marton** **Sinnington** **YO62 6RD** **Tel: (01751) 432702** **Open: APR - OCT** **Map Ref No. 29**	Nearest Road: A.170 A former farmhouse, originating from 1720, Wildsmith House is full of character & charm. Set on the village green, at the edge of the North Yorkshire Moors. 2 spacious en-suite bedrooms, decorated & furnished to a high standard, with colour T.V. & tea/coffee-making facilities. Elegant guest sitting room with log fires. Ideally situated for exploring the region with its historic houses, abbeys, unspoilt village & city of York. Children over 12 years. E-mail: pgrms@easynet.co.uk	£20.00 to £25.00	Y	N	N
Mrs D. Hutton **The Country House Hotel** **Long Preston** **Skipton BD23 4NJ** **Tel: (01729) 840246** **Fax 01729 840246** **Open: FEB - DEC** **Map Ref No. 30**	Nearest Road: A.65 An elegant Victorian country house, situated in its own grounds in the Yorkshire Dales. There are 7 attractively furnished bedrooms with en-suite/private bathroom, colour T.V. & tea/coffee-making facilities. Drawing room with log fire & extensive library. A sauna & spa bath are also provided for relaxation. Delightful house, offering a personal service in homely, informal & restful surroundings. Children over 4 years.	£29.00 to £££	Y	N	Y
Carol Richmond **Red Hall** **Ingleby Road** **Great Broughton** **Stokesley TS9 7ET** **Tel: (01642) 712300** **Fax 01642 714023** **Open: ALL YEAR** **Map Ref No. 31**	Nearest Road: A.170, A.172 Warmly welcoming Red Hall is an elegant Grade II listed early Georgian small country house with a marvellous atmosphere, set in its own grounds at the foot of the North York Moors National Park & surrounded by tranquil meadows & woodland. It has been painstakingly modernised, preserving many classic internal features, & has tastefully appointed bedrooms, including a family suite. Meals are served in the dining room opening onto the secluded south-facing walled garden.	£35.00 to £55.00 *see PHOTO over* *p. 478* M'CARD: AMEX:	Y	Y	Y
David & Tess Williamson **Thornborough House Farm** **South Kilvington** **Thirsk** **YO7 2NP** **Tel: (01845) 522103** **Fax 01845 522103** **Open: ALL YEAR** **Map Ref No. 33**	Nearest Road: A.19 A warm welcome awaits you at this 200-year-old farmhouse, set in lovely countryside. Only 1 1/2 miles north of Thirsk, this working farm is situated in the town made famous by James Herriot. 3 comfortable rooms, each with en-suite/private shower room, all with tea/coffee facilities. Guests have their own sitting/dining room with T.V. & open fire. Home cooking a speciality. Conveniently located for York, Ripon, the Pennine Dales & the East Coast. Animals by arrangement. E-mail: williamson@thornboroughhousefarm.freeserve.co.uk	£15.00 to £19.00 VISA: M'CARD:	Y	Y	Y
Robin & Ann Clough **Spital Hill** **York Road** **Thirsk** **YO7 3AE** **Tel: (01845) 522273** **Fax 01845 524970** **Open: ALL YEAR** **Map Ref No. 34**	Nearest Road: A.19 Quiet, peaceful & relaxing, Spital Hill is set in 1 1/2 acres of secluded garden surrounded by parkland, yet only 10 mins from the A.1. Originally a Georgian farmhouse, it was extended in 1884, & is now a lovely home from which to explore York, Harrogate, the Moors, the Dales & Herriot Country. Dinner is en-famille, & includes ingredients from the kitchen garden. Licensed. Bedrooms are delightfully furnished & the bathrooms are well-provisioned. Children over 12. E-mail: wolsey@wolseylo.demon.co.uk	£30.00 to £44.00 VISA: M'CARD: AMEX:	Y	Y	N

Red Hall. Great Broughton.

Yorkshire

	rate £ from - to per person	children taken	evening meals	animals taken
Mrs Ashley Goodrum **Cliffemount Hotel** **Runswick Bay** **Whitby TS13 5HU** **Tel: (01947) 840103** Fax 01947 841025 **Open: ALL YEAR (Excl. Xmas)** **Map Ref No. 36** Nearest Road: A.174 As the name implies, this privately-run hotel is situated on a clifftop with panoramic views over Runswick Bay. Built in the 1920s with later additions, the hotel is tastefully decorated throughout. 12 of the 13 comfortably furnished bedrooms are en-suite, & the majority have spectacular sea views. Cliffemount, with its warm & friendly atmosphere, also enjoys a good reputation for its high standard of food. Licensed. Log fires in winter.	£28.00 to £46.00 VISA: M'CARD:	Y	Y	Y
Michael & Juliet Morgan **Barbican House** **20 Barbican Road** **York** **YO10 5AA** **Tel: (01904) 627617** Fax 01904 647140 **Open: ALL YEAR (Excl.** **Xmas & New Year)** **Map Ref No. 38** Nearest Road: A.19 The Barbican House is a Victorian residence of individual charm & character, overlooking the medieval city walls. Leave your car in the floodlit car park & enjoy a 10 minute walk to all the city centre attractions. All bedrooms have en-suite/private facilities & are attractively furnished with T.V., 'phone, tea/coffee facilities & hairdryer etc. Enjoy a full English breakfast & more, in the lovely dining room. A friendly Yorkshire welcome always assured. Children over 10 years. **E-mail: barbican@thenet.co.uk**	£23.00 to £28.00 VISA: M'CARD: AMEX:	Y	N	N
Lynn M. Keir **Easton's** **90 Bishopthorpe Road** **York** **YO23 1JS** **Tel: (01904) 626646** Fax 01904 626165 **Open: ALL YEAR (Excl. Xmas)** **Map Ref No. 38** Nearest Road: A.64 Award-winning accommodation at a sympathetically & beautifully restored Victorian wine-merchant's residence, centrally situated just 300 yds from the medieval city walls. The period furniture, William Morris decor, open fires & fully equipped bedrooms are in accord with the character of the building, & with the standard of excellence that the owners strive for. The Victorian sideboard breakfast menu follows the same theme of quality, & includes a selection of tradi-tional & vegetarian dishes. Children over 5 yrs.	£24.50 to £36.00 *see PHOTO over* *p. 480*	Y	N	N
Keith Jackman **Dairy Guest House** **3 Scarcroft Road** **York** **YO23 1ND** **Tel: (01904) 639367** **Open: FEB - DEC** **Map Ref No. 38** Nearest Road: A.64 The Dairy is a tastefully renovated Victorian house within walking distance of the city centre & 200 yards from the medieval city walls. Decorated & furnished in the styles of Habitat, Sanderson's & Laura Ashley, with the emphasis on pine & plants. 5 bedrooms, some en-suite (& 4-poster available), each with modern amenities, T.V., hot-drink facilities & information on York & Yorkshire. A lovely enclosed courtyard. Breakfast choices are from English to wholefood vegetarian.	£20.00 to £££	Y	N	Y
Russell & Cherry **Whitbourn-Hammond** **Nunmill House** **85 Bishopthorpe Road** **York** **YO23 1NX** **Tel: (01904) 634047** Fax 01904 655879 **Open: FEB - NOV** **Map Ref No. 38** Nearest Road: A.64, A.59 A warm friendly welcome awaits you at Nunmill House, a delightful late-Victorian house, taste-fully restored throughout with Laura Ashley fur-nishings to enhance the original architectural features. Offering 8 delightful bedrooms, each with en-suite or private facilities. Ideally situated just outside the medieval walls, & a 10-minute walk to all the historic attractions of the city. Complimentary tea & coffee are available, & special diets can be catered for by arrangement. **E-mail: b&b@nunmill.co.uk**	£25.00 to £28.00	Y	N	N

Easton's. York.

Grasmead House Hotel. York.

Yorkshire

		rate £ from - to per person	children taken	evening meals	animals taken
Malcolm & Elizabeth Greaves **Carlton House Hotel** **134 The Mount** **York** **YO24 1AS** **Tel: (01904) 622265** **Fax 01904 637157** **Open: ALL YEAR (Excl. Xmas & New Year)** **Map Ref No. 38**	Nearest Road: A.1036 Each & every guest will receive a warm & friendly welcome from proprietors Liz & Malcolm Greaves. This pleasant, family-run hotel offers guests a choice of 13 en-suite rooms, all with colour T.V., radio & tea/coffee-making facilities. The spacious lounges are comfortable & pleasantly furnished. A traditional English breakfast is cooked to order. Light refreshments are available at most times throughout the day. Nearby are York race course & the resplendent Minster. **E-mail: wwbba@carltonhouse.co.uk**	£27.00 to £30.00	Y	N	N
Mr & Mrs S. Long **Grasmead House Hotel** **1 Scarcroft Hill** **York** **YO24 1DF** **Tel: (01904) 629996** **Fax 01904 629996** **Open: ALL YEAR** **Map Ref No. 38**	Nearest Road: A.1036 An attractive, small, family-run hotel, situated within easy walking distance of the city centre. The charming bedrooms feature antique furniture, 4-poster beds (1 dating back to 1730) & excellent en-suite bathrooms. Plus, of course, tea/coffee-making facilities & T.V.. There is also a comfortable lounge with a small bar where you can relax after spending the day exploring historic York. Delicious breakfasts served in the attractive dining room. Ideal centre for visiting the Dales, Moors & coast. Children over 8. **E-mail: stansue@grasmeadhouse.freeserve.co.uk**	£35.00 to £40.00 *see PHOTO over* *p. 481* VISA: M'CARD: AMEX:	Y	N	N
Mr & Mrs David Reynard **Arndale Hotel** **290 Tadcaster Road** **York** **YO24 1ET** **Tel: (01904) 702424** **Open: ALL YEAR (Excl. Xmas & New Year)** **Map Ref No. 38**	Nearest Road: A.64, A.1036 A delightful Victorian house, directly overlooking York's famous race course, with beautiful enclosed walled gardens giving a country-house atmosphere within the city. There is a spacious, elegant lounge, complete with antiques, fresh flowers, paintings & a small bar. The 10 outstanding & thoughtfully equipped bedrooms are all en-suite. Many bathrooms are Victorian in style, with modern whirlpool baths. Antique half-tester/4-poster beds. Delicious quality breakfasts. Friendly, attentive service. Large enclosed gated car park. Children over 7 years.	£26.00 to £37.50 *see PHOTO over* *p. 483* VISA: M'CARD:	Y	N	N
Richard & Wendy Wood **Curzon Lodge & Stable Cottages** **23 Tadcaster Road** **Dringhouses** **York YO24 1QG** **Tel: (01904) 703157** **Fax 01904 703157** **Open: ALL YEAR (Excl. Xmas)** **Map Ref No. 38**	Nearest Road: A.64, A.1036 A charming 17th-century Grade II listed house & oak-beamed stables within city conservation area overlooking the racecourse. Once a home of renowned York chocolate makers, guests are now invited to share the unique atmosphere in 10 delightful & fully-equipped en-suite rooms. Some 4-poster & brass beds. Country antiques, old prints, books, maps, fresh flowers & sherry in the sitting room lend traditional ambience. Warm & informal. Delicious English breakfasts. Parking. Restaurants within 1-min walk. Children over 7.	£27.50 to £37.50 *see PHOTO over* *p. 484* VISA: M'CARD:	Y	N	N

Visit our website at:
http://www.bestbandb.co.uk

Arndale Hotel. York.

Curzon Lodge. York.

Holmwood House Hotel.   York.

Yorkshire

		rate £ from - to per person	children taken	evening meals	animals taken
Rosie Blanksby & Bill Pitts **Holmwood House Hotel** **114 Holgate Road** **York YO24 4BB** **Tel: (01904) 626183** **Fax 01904 670899** **Open: ALL YEAR** **Map Ref No. 38**	Nearest Road: A.59 The conversion of 2 listed, early-Victorian town houses has created an elegant hotel that offers guests a feeling of home with a touch of luxury. All rooms, of course, have en-suite facilities but are very different in both size & decoration. There are 3 honeymoon rooms (2 with 4-poster beds) & 1 with a spa bath. 3 family suites are available. The guest sitting room, with an open fire, is on the ground floor. Children over 8 welcome. **E-mail: holmwood.house@dial.pipex.com**	£27.50 to £45.00 *see PHOTO over* *p. 485* VISA: M'CARD: AMEX:	Y	N	N
Mr & Mrs Magson **Bishops Hotel** **135 Holgate Road** **York** **YO24 4DF** **Tel: (01904) 628000** **Fax 01904 628181** **Open: ALL YEAR** **Map Ref No. 38**	Nearest Road: A.59 Bishops Hotel is a traditional Victorian villa beautifully restored throughout. Close to the city's main attractions, railway station & racecourse, with its own private car park. Individually designed en-suite bedrooms. Sumptuous 4-poster suite & canopy bed, ideal for romantic breaks. Families are very welcome in the spacious family rooms. Also there are attractive single rooms. Enclosed garden. Bishops Hotel is family-run & offers friendly personal service.	£27.00 to £35.00 VISA: M'CARD:	Y	N	N
Mrs Yvonne Thompson **Brentwood Cottage** **Main Street** **Shipton-by-Beningbrough** **York YO30 1AB** **Tel: (01904) 470111** **Fax 01904 426384** **Open: ALL YEAR** **Map Ref No. 40**	Nearest Road: A.19 A warm & friendly welcome awaits all guests at Brentwood Cottage. Located 5 miles outside the historic city of York, it offers guests a choice of 5 very pleasant bedrooms, 2 with en-suite/private facilities & amenities, & each with tea/coffee makers. There is also a comfortable residents' lounge & garden available. Brentwood Cottage makes a good base for touring York & the surrounding countryside. A large car park. **E-mail: yvonne@yorkcity.co.uk**	£18.00 to £22.50 VISA: M'CARD:	Y	N	N
Mr & Mrs Roe **Four Seasons Hotel** **7 St. Peters Grove** **Bootham** **York** **YO30 6AQ** **Tel: (01904) 622621** **Fax 01904 620976** **Open: FEB - DEC** **Map Ref No. 38**	Nearest Road: A.19 An elegant Victorian residence. Ideally situated in a peaceful cul-de-sac only 7 mins' stroll from the Minster & York's many other historic attractions. Accommodation is in 6 beautifully appointed & tastefully furnished en-suite bedrooms, all fully equipped. A 4-course English breakfast is served. Residential licence & private car parking. The Four Seasons Hotel is an ideal base to explore York, & is within easy reach of Harrogate & the beautiful Yorkshire Dales. **E-mail: roe@fourseasons.netlineuk.net**	£27.00 to £30.00 *see PHOTO over* *p. 487* VISA: M'CARD:	Y	N	N
Keith & Jacqueline Jessop **Bloomsbury Hotel** **127 Clifton** **York** **YO30 6BL** **Tel: (01904) 634031** **Fax 01904 676789** **Open: ALL YEAR** **Map Ref No. 38**	Nearest Road: A.1237 The Bloomsbury is a beautiful large Victorian town house with adequate car parking. Situated in a conservation area only a 12-minute walk from York Minster in the historic centre of York. Each of the 9 guest rooms in this delightful family-run establishment has been individually designed by the owners for your comfort. The proprietors will gladly give assistance & advice to ensure your stay is enjoyable & successful. Children over 7.	£23.00 to £32.50 *see PHOTO over* *p. 488* VISA: M'CARD:	Y	N	N

Four Seasons Hotel. York.

Bloomsbury Hotel. York.

Arnot House. York.

	rate £ from - to per person	children taken	evening meals	animals taken

Mrs Ann & Miss Kim Sluter-Robbins
Arnot House
17 Grosvenor Terrace
Bootham
York YO30 7AG
Tel/Fax: (01904) 641966
Open: ALL YEAR
Map Ref No. 38

Nearest Road: A.19
Overlooking Bootham Park, only 5 mins' walk from the York Minster & city centre. Arnot House is a Victorian town house built for a wealthy merchant in 1865. The house is beautifully decorated, & there are fine antiques & paintings. Many of its original features have been retained including marble fireplaces & ornate coving. The 4 attractive bedrooms have either Victorian brass or wooden beds & every facility. An excellent location. Children over 12 years.

£25.00 to £28.00 — Y — N — N

see PHOTO over
p. 489
VISA: M'CARD:

Will & Penny Lefebve
The Bentley
25 Grosvenor Terrace
Bootham
York YO30 7AG
Tel: (01904) 644313
Fax 01904 644313
Open: FEB - DEC
Map Ref No. 38

Nearest Road: A.19
Relax in an elegant Victorian town house, furnished with quality, care & comfort in mind for the really discerning guest. Enjoy the spacious en-suite rooms (with T.V., tea/coffee facilities, etc.), most of which have a fine view across parkland to the beautiful York Minster. The Bentley is just a few mins' stroll from the city centre & its many historical treats, yet in a quiet one-way street, with parking. York is also a unique shopping experience. Children over 10 years.

£21.00 to £26.00 — Y — N — N

see PHOTO over
p. 491

Mrs Susan Taylor
Alcuin Lodge Guest House
15 Sycamore Place
Bootham
York
YO30 7DW
Tel: (01904) 632222
Fax 01904 626630
Open: ALL YEAR
Map Ref No. 38

Nearest Road: A.19
A fine old Edwardian house, Alcuin Lodge is situated in a quiet cul-de-sac, overlooking a bowling green. Offering 5 attractively furnished bedrooms, each with en-suite/private facilities. The house is only 5 mins walk through the Yorkshire Museum Gardens to the heart of this historic city. The splendours of the Yorkshire countryside - the Dales, the Moors - are all within an hours' drive. A warm welcome is assured to make your stay memorable. Children over 10.
E-mail: alcuinlodge@aol.com

£18.00 to £25.00 — Y — N — N

VISA: M'CARD:

Tony & Tricia Styan
Primrose Cottage
Lime Bar Lane, Grafton
York YO51 9QJ
Tel: (01423) 322711
Tel/Fax 01423 322835
Fax 01423 323985
Open: ALL YEAR (Excl. Xmas)
Map Ref No. 39

Nearest Road: A.1 M.
A warm friendly welcome awaits you at Primrose Cottage, in a quiet picturesque village 1 mile east of the A.1. Comfortable bedrooms with washbasins & tea/coffee facilities. 2 bath/shower rooms. Spacious T.V. lounge, & sheltered patio garden with barbecue for guests' use. 2 local inns serving excellent food. Ideally situated 15 mins north of York. Ripon, Harrogate & Yorkshire Dales within easy distance.

£19.00 to £19.00 — Y — N — Y

Chris & Sarah Braithwaite
Plumpton Court
High Street
Nawton, Helmsley
York
YO62 7TT
Tel: (01439) 771223
Open: ALL YEAR
Map Ref No. 43

Nearest Road: A.170
Plumpton Court is a family-run 17th-century guest house set in the foothills of the North Yorkshire Moors, & is ideally situated for York & exploring the east coast. Offering 7 en-suite, comfortable & well-appointed bedrooms, all with clock/radio, tea/coffee-making facilities & colour T.V.. There is a comfortable lounge in which guests may relax, with real fire, small bar & T.V.. Delicious evening meals served using fresh local produce. Secure, gated car park & garden. A charming home. Children over 12 years.

£20.00 to £25.00 — Y — Y — N

The Bentley. York.

Yorkshire

		rate £ from - to per person	evening meals children taken	animals taken	

Sam & Annie Atcherley-Key
Laurel Manor Farm
Helperby - Brafferton
York
YO61 2NZ
Tel: (01423) 360436
Fax 01423 360437
Open: ALL YEAR
Map Ref No. 42

Nearest Road: A.1, A.19

Hidden up a lane, beside the village church, is Laurel Manor Farm, its 28 acres running down to the River Swale. The recently refurbished bedrooms have en-suite/private bathrooms & are furnished with antiques, a 4-poster, family portraits, beams & open fireplaces. Dine with your hosts or walk 2 mins to one of 4 inns. The Keys have a tennis court, croquet lawn & river walks, & are licensed. Situated only 4 miles from the A.1M. 12 miles York/Harrogate.
E-mail: laurelmf@globalnet.co.uk

£25.00 to £30.00

see PHOTO over
p. 493

£25.00 to £30.00	Y	Y	Y

**All the establishments mentioned in this guide
are members of
The Worldwide Bed & Breakfast Association**

**When booking your accommodation please
mention
The Best Bed & Breakfast**

Laurel Farm. Brafferton.

Scotland

Scotland

Scotland's culture & traditions, history & literature, languages & accents, its landscape & architecture, even its wildlife set it apart from the rest of Britain. Much of Scotland's history is concerned with the struggle to retain independence from England.

The Romans never conquered the Scottish tribes, but preferred to keep them at bay with Hadrian's Wall, stretching across the Border country from Tynemouth to the Solway Firth.

Time lends glamour to events, but from the massacre of Glencoe to the Highland Clearances, much of Scotland's fate has been a harsh one. Robert the Bruce did rout the English enemy at Bannockburn after scaling the heights of Edinburgh Castle to take the city, but in later years Mary, Queen of Scots was to spend much of her life imprisoned by her sister Elizabeth I of England. Bonnie Prince Charlie (Charles Edward Stuart) led the Jacobite rebellion which ended in defeat at Culloden.

These events are recorded in the folklore & songs of Scotland. The Border & Highland Gatherings & the Common Ridings are more than a chance to wear the Tartan, they are reminders of national pride.

Highland Games are held throughout the country where local & national champions compete in events like tossing the caber & in piping contests. There are sword dances & Highland flings, the speciality of young men & boys wearing the full dress tartan of their clan.

Scotland's landscape is rich in variety from the lush green lowlands to the handsome splendour of the mountainous Highlands, from the rounded hills of the Borders to the far-flung islands of the Hebrides, Orkney & Shetland where the sea is ever-present.

There are glens & beautiful lochs deep in the mountains, a spectacular coastline of high cliffs & white sandy beaches, expanses of purple heather moorland where the sparkling water in the burns runs brown with peat, & huge skies bright with cloud & gorgeous sunsets.

Argyll & The Islands

This area has ocean & sea lochs, forests & mountains, 3000 miles of coastline, about 30 inhabited islands, the warming influence of the Gulf Stream & the tallest tree in Britain (in Strone Gardens, near Loch Fyne).

Sites both historic & prehistoric are to be found in plenty. There is a hilltop fort at Dunadd, near Crinan with curious cup-&-ring carvings, & numerous ancient sites surround Kilmartin, from burial cairns to grave slabs.

Kilchurn Castle is a magnificent ruin in contrast to the opulence of Inveraray. Both are associated with the once-powerful Clan Campbell. There are remains of fortresses built by the Lords of the Isles, the proud chieftains who ruled the west after driving out the Norse invaders in the 12th century.

Oban is a small harbour town accessible by road & rail & the point of departure for many of the islands including Mull.

Tobermory. Isle of Mull.

Scotland

Mull is a peaceful island with rugged seascapes, lovely walks & villages, a miniature railway & the famous Mull Little Theatre. It is a short hop from here to the tiny island of Iona & St. Columba's Abbey, cradle of Christianity in Scotland.

Coll & Tiree have lovely beaches & fields of waving barley. The grain grown here was once supplied to the Lords of the Isles but today most goes to Islay & into the whisky. Tiree has superb windsurfing.

Jura is a wilder island famous for its red deer. The Isles of Colonsay & Oronsay are joined at low water.

Gigha, 'God's Isle', is a fertile area of gardens with rare & semitropical plants. The Island of Staffa has Fingal's Cave.

The Borders, Dumfries & Galloway

The borderland with England is a landscape of subtle colours & contours from the round foothills of the Cheviots, purple with heather, to the dark green valley of the Tweed.

The Lammermuir Hills sweep eastwards to a coastline of small harbours & the spectacular cliffs at St. Abbs Head where colonies of seabirds thrive.

The Border towns, set in fine countryside, have distinctive personalities. Hawick, Galashiels, Selkirk & Melrose all played their parts in the various Border skirmishes of this historically turbulent region & then prospered with a textile industry which survives today. They celebrate their traditions in the Common Riding ceremonies.

The years of destructive border warfare have left towers & castles throughout the country. Roxburgh was once a Royal castle & James II was killed here during a seige. Now there are only the shattered remains of the massive stone walls. Hermitage Castle is set amid wild scenery near Hawick & impressive Floors Castle stands above Kelso.

At Jedburgh the Augustine abbey is remarkably complete, & a visitors centre here tells the story of the four great Border Abbeys; Jedburgh itself, Kelso, Dryburgh & Melrose.

The lovely estate of Abbotsford where Sir Walter Scott lived & worked is near Melrose. A prolific poet & novelist, his most famous works are the Waverley novels written around 1800. His house holds many of his possessions, including a collection of armour. Scott's View is one of the best vantage points in the borderlands with a prospect of the silvery Tweed & the three distinctive summits of the Eildon Hills.

Eildon Hills.

There are many gracious stately homes. Manderston is a classical house of great luxury, & Mellerstain is the work of the Adam family. Traquair was originally a Royal hunting lodge. Its main gates were locked in 1745 after a visit from Bonnie Prince Charlie, never to be opened until a Stuart King takes the throne.

Dumfries & Galloway to the southwest is an area of rolling hills with a fine coastline.

Plants flourish in the mild air here & there are palm trees at Ardwell House & the Logan Botanic Garden.

Scotland

The gardens at Castle Kennedy have rhododendrons, azaleas & magnolias & Threave Gardens near Castle Douglas are the National Trust for Scotland's School of gardening.

The Galloway Forest Park covers a vast area of lochs & hills & has views across to offshore Ailsa Craig. At Caerlaveroch Castle, an early Renaissance building near the coast of Dumfries, there is a national nature reserve.

The first church in Scotland was built by St. Ninian at Whithorn in 400 on a site now occupied by the 13th century priory. The spread of Christianity is marked by early memorial stones like the Latinus stone at Whithorn, & the abbeys of Dundrennan, Crossraguel, Glenluce & Sweetheart, named after its founder who carried her husband's heart in a casket & is buried with it in the abbey.

At Dumfries is the poet Burns' house, his mausoleum & the Burns Heritage Centre overlooking the River Nith.

In Upper Nithsdale the Mennock Pass leads to Wanlockhead & Leadhills, once centres of the lead-mining industry. There is a fascinating museum here & the opportunity of an underground trip.

Lowland

The Frith of Clyde & Glascow in the west, & the Firth of Forth with Edinburgh in the east are both areas of rich history, tradition & culture.

Edinburgh is the capital of Scotland & amongst the most visually exciting cities in the world. The New Town is a treasure trove of inspired neo-classical architecture, & below Edinburgh Castle high on the Rock, is the Old Town, a network of courts, closes, wynds & gaunt tenements around the Royal Mile.

The Palace of Holyrood House, home of Mary, Queen of Scots for several years overlooks Holyrood Park & nearby Arthur's Seat, is a popular landmark.

The City's varied art galleries include The Royal Scottish Academy, The National Gallery, Portrait Gallery, Gallery of Modern Art & many other civic & private collections.

The Royal Museum of Scotland displays superb historical & scientific material. The Royal Botanic Gardens are world famous.

Cultural life in Edinburgh peaks at Festival time in August. The official Festival, the Fringe, the Book Festival, Jazz Festival & Film Festival bring together artistes of international reputation.

The gentle hills around the city offer many opportunities for walking. The Pentland Hills are easily reached,

Inverary Castle.

with the Lammermuir Hills a little further south. There are fine beaches at Gullane, Yellowcraigs, North Berwick & at Dunbar.

Tantallon Castle, a 14th century stronghold, stands on the rocky Firth of Forth, & 17th century Hopetoun House, on the outskirts of the city is only one of a number of great houses in the area.

North of Edinburgh across the Firth of Forth lies the ancient Kingdom of Fife. Here is St. Andrews, a pleasant town on the seafront, an old university

Scotland

town & Scotland's ecclesiastical capital, but famous primarily for golf.

Glasgow is the industrial & business capital of Scotland. John Betjeman called it the 'finest Victorian city in Britain' & many buildings are remarkable examples of Victorian splendour, notably the City Chambers.

Many buildings are associated with the architect Charles Rennie MacKintosh; the Glasgow School of Art is one of them. Glasgow Cathedral is a perfect example of pre-Reformation Gothic architecture.

Glasgow is Scotland's largest city with the greatest number of parks & fine Botanic Garden. It is home to both the Scottish Opera & the Scottish Ballet, & has a strong & diverse cultural tradition from theatre to jazz. Its museums include the matchless Burrell Collection, & the Kelvingrove Museum & Art Gallery, which houses one of the best civic collections of paintings in Britain, as well as reflecting the city's engineering & shipbuilding heritage.

The coastal waters of the Clyde are world famous for cruising & sailing, with many harbours & marinas. The long coastline offers many opportunities for sea-angling from Largs to Troon & Prestwick, & right around to Luce Bay on the Solway.

There are many places for birdwatching on the Estuary, whilst the Clyde Valley is famous for its garden centres & nurseries.

Paisley has a mediaeval abbey, an observatory & a museum with a fine display of the famous 'Paisley' pattern shawls.

Further south, Ayr is a large seaside resort with sandy beach, safe bathing & a racecourse. In the Ayrshire valleys there is traditional weaving & lace & bonnet making, & Sorn, in the rolling countryside boasts its 'Best Kept Village' award.

Culzean Castle is one of the finest Adam houses in Scotland & stands in spacious grounds on the Ayrshire cliffs.

Robert Burns is Scotland's best loved poet, & 'Burns night' is widely celebrated. The region of Strathclyde shares with Dumfries & Galloway the title of 'Burns Country' . The son of a peasant farmer, Burns lived in poverty for much of his life. The simple house where he was born is in the village of Alloway. In the town of Ayr is the Auld Kirk where he was baptised & the footbridge of 'The Brigs of Ayr' is still in use. The Tam O'Shanter Inn is now a Burns museum & retains its thatched roof & simple fittings. The Burns Trail leads on to Mauchline where Possie Nansie's Inn remains. At Tarbolton the National Trust now care for the old house where Burns founded the 'Batchelors Club' debating society.

Perthshire, Loch Lomond & The Trossachs

By a happy accident of geology, the Highland Boundary fault which separates the Highlands from the Lowlands runs through Loch Lomond, close to the Trossachs & on through Perthshire, giving rise to marvellous scenery.

In former times Highlanders & Lowlanders raided & fought here. Great castles like Stirling, Huntingtower & Doune were built to protect the routes between the two different cultures.

Stirling was once the seat of Scotland's monarchs & the great Royal castle is set high on a basalt rock. The Guildhall & the Kirk of the Holy Rude are also interesting buildings in the town, with Cambuskenneth Abbey & the Bannockburn Heritage Centre close by.

Perth 'fair city' on the River Tay,

Scotland

has excellent shops & its own repertory theatre. Close by are the Black Watch Museum at Balhousie Castle, & the Branklyn Gardens, which are superb in May & June.

Scone Palace, to the north of Perth was home to the Stone or Scone of Destiny for nearly 500 years until its removal to Westminster. 40 kings of Scotland were crowned here.

Pitlochry sits amid beautiful Highland scenery with forest & hill walks, two nearby distilleries, the famous Festival theatre, Loch Faskally & the Dam Visitor Centre & Fish Ladder.

In the Pass of Killiecrankie, a short drive away, a simple stone marks the spot where the Highlanders charged barefoot to overwhelm the redcoat soldiers of General MacKay.

Queens View.

Famous Queen's View overlooks Loch Tummel beyond Pitlochry with the graceful peak of Schiehallion completing a perfect picture.

Other lochs are picturesque too; Loch Earn, Loch Katrine & bonnie Loch Lomond itself, & they can be enjoyed from a boat on the water. Ospreys nest at the Loch of the Lowes near Dunkeld.

Mountain trails lead through Ben Lawers & the 'Arrocher Alps' beyond Loch Lomond. The Ochils & the Campsie Fells have grassy slopes for walking. Near Callander are the Bracklinn Falls, the Callander Crags & the Falls of Leny.

Wooded areas include the Queen Elizabeth Forest Park & the Black Wood of Rannoch which is a fragment of an ancient Caledonian forest. There are some very tall old trees around Killiecrankie, & the world's tallest beech hedge - 26 metres high - grows at Meikleour near Blairgowrie.

Creiff & Blairgowrie have excellent golf courses set in magnificent scenery.

The Grampians, Highlands & Islands

This is spacious countryside with glacier-scarred mountains & deep glens cut through by tumbling rivers. The Grampian Highlands make for fine mountaineering & walking.

There is excellent skiing at Glenshee, & a centre at the Lecht for the less experienced, whilst the broad tops of the giant mountains are ideal for cross-country skiing. The chair-lift at Glenshee is worth a visit at any season.

The Dee, The Spey & The Don flow down to the coastal plain from the heights. Some of the world's finest trout & salmon beats are on these rivers.

Speyside is dotted with famous distilleries from Grantown-on-Spey to Aberdeen, & the unique Malt Whisky Trail can be followed.

Royal Deeside & Donside hold a number of notable castles. Balmoral is the present Royal family's holiday home, & Kildrummy is a romantic ruin in a lovely garden. Fyvie Castle has five dramatic towers & stands in peaceful parkland. Nearby Haddo House, by contrast, is an elegant Georgian home.

There is a 17th century castle at Braemar, but more famous here is the Royal Highland Gathering. There are wonderful walks in the vicinity -

Scotland

Morrone Hill, Glen Quoich & the Linn O'Dee are just a few.

The city of Aberdeen is famed for its sparkling granite buildings, its university, its harbour & fish market & for North Sea Oil. It also has long sandy beaches & lovely year-round flower displays, of roses in particular.

Around the coast are fishing towns & villages. Crovie & Pennan sit below impressive cliffs. Buckie is a typical small port along the picturesque coastline of the Moray Firth.

The Auld Kirk at Cullen has fine architectural features & elegant Elgin has beautiful cathedral ruins. Pluscarden Abbey, Spynie Palace & Duffus Castle are all nearby.

Dunnottar Castle.

Nairn has a long stretch of sandy beach & a golf course with an international reputation. Inland are Cawdor Castle & Culloden Battlefield.

The Northern Highlands are divided from the rest of Scotland by the dramatic valley of the Great Glen. From Fort William to Inverness, sea lochs, canals & the depths of Loch Ness form a chain of waterways linking both coasts.

Here are some of the wildest & most beautiful landscapes in Britain. Far Western Knoydart, the Glens of Cannich & Affric, the mysterious lochs, including Loch Morar, deeper than the North Sea, & the marvellous coastline; all are exceptional.

The glens were once the home of crofting communities, & of the clansmen who supported the Jacobite cause. The wild scenery of Glencoe is a favourite with walkers & climbers, but it has a tragic history. Its name means 'the glen of weeping' & refers to the massacre of the MacDonald clan in 1692, when the Royal troops who had been received as guests treacherously attacked their hosts at dawn.

The valleys are empty today largely as a result of the infamous Highland Clearances in the 19th century when the landowners turned the tenant crofters off the land in order to introduce the more profitable Cheviot sheep. The emigration of many Scots to the U.S.A. & the British Colonies resulted from these events.

South of Inverness lie the majestic Cairngorms. The Aviemore centre provides both summer & winter sports facilities here.

To the north of Loch Ness are the remains of the ancient Caledonian forest where red deer & stags are a common sight on the hills. Rarer are sightings of the Peregrine Falcon, the osprey, the Golden Eagle & the Scottish wildcat. Kincraig has excellent wildlife parks.

Inverness is the last large town in the north, & a natural gateway to the Highlands & to Moray, the Black Isle & the north-east.

The east coast is characterised by the Firths of Moray, Cromarty & Dornoch & by its changing scenery from gentle pastureland, wooded hillsides to sweeping coastal cliffs.

On the Black Isle, which is not a true island but has a causeway & bridge links with the mainland, Fortrose & Rosemarkie in particular have lovely beaches, caves & coastal walks. There is golf on the headland at Rosemarkie & a 13th century cathedral of rosy pink sandstone stands in Fortrose.

Scotland

Scotland Gazeteer

Areas of outstanding natural beauty

It would be invidious, not to say almost impossible, to choose any particular area of Scotland as having a more beautiful aspect than another - the entire country is a joy to the traveller. The rugged Highlands, the great glens, tumbling waters, tranquil lochs - the deep countryside or the wild coastline - simply come & choose your own piece of paradise.

Historic Houses & Castles

Bowhill - Nr. Selkirk
18th-19th century - home of the Duke of Bucceleugh & Queensberry. Has an outstanding collection of pictures by Canaletto,Claude, Gainsborough, Reynolds & Leonardo da Vinci. Superb silver, porcelain & furniture.16th & 17th century miniatures.

Traquair House - Innerleithen
A unique & ancient house being the oldest inhabited home in Scotland. It is rich in associations with every form of political history & after Bonnie Prince Charlie passed through its main gates in 1745 no other visitor has been allowed to use them. There are treasures in the house dating from 12th century, & it has an 18th century library & a priest's room with secret stairs.

Linlithgow Palace - Linlithgow
The birthplace of Mary, Queen of Scots.

Stirling Castle - Stirling
Royal Castle.

Drumlanrigg Castle - Nr. Thornhill
17th century castle of pale pink stone - romantic & historic - wonderful art treasures including a magnificent Rembrandt & a huge silver chandelier. Beautiful garden setting.

Braemar Castle - Braemar
17th century castle of great historic interest. Has round central tower with spiral staircase giving it a fairy-tale appearance.

Drum Castle - Nr. Aberdeen
Dating in part from 13th century, it has a great square tower.

Cawdor Castle - Nairn
14th century fortress - like castle - has always been the home of the Thanes of Cawdor - background to Shakespeare's Macbeth.

Dunvegan Castle - Isle of Skye
13th century - has always been the home of the Chiefs of McLeod.

Hopetoun House - South Queensferry
Very fine example of Adam architecture & has a fine collection of pictures & furniture. Splendid landscaped grounds.

Inverary Castle - Argyll
Home of the Dukes of Argyll. 18th century - Headquarters of Clan Campbell.

Burn's Cottage - Alloway
Birthplace of Robert Burns - 1659 - thatched cottage - museum of Burns' relics.

Bachelors' Club - Tarbolton
17th century house - thatched - where Burns & friends formed their club - 1780.

Blair Castle - Blair Atholl
Home of the Duke of Atholl, 13th century Baronial mansion - collection of Jacobite relics, armour, paintings, china & many other items.

Glamis Castle - Angus
17th century remodelling in Chateau style - home of the Earl of Strathmore & Kinghorne. Very attractive castle - lovely grounds by Capability Brown.

Scone Palace - Perth
has always been associated with seat of Government of Scotland from earliest times. The Stone of Destiny was removed from the Palace in 1296 & taken to Westminster Abbey. Present palace rebuilt in early 1800's still incorporating parts of the old. Lovely gardens.

Edinburgh Castle
Fortress standing high over the town - famous for military tattoo.

Culzean Castle & Country Park - Maybole
Fine Adam house & spacious gardens perched on Ayrshire cliff.

Dunrobin Castle - Golspie
Ancient seat of the Earls & Dukes of Sutherland.

Eilean Donan Castle - Wester Ross
13th century castle, Jacobite relics.

Manderston - Duns
Great classical house with only silver staircase in the world. Stables, marble dairy, formal gardens.

Scotland

Cathedrals & Churches

Dunfermline Abbey - Dunfermline
Norman remains of beautiful church.
Modern east end & tower.

Edinburgh (Church of the Holy Rood)
15th century - was divided into two in 17th
century & re-united 1938. Here Mary,
Queen of Scots was crowned.

Glasgow (St. Mungo)
12th-15th century cathedral - 19th century
interior. Central tower with spire.

Kirkwall (St. Magnus)
12th century cathedral with very fine nave.

Falkirk Old Parish Church - Falkirk
The spotted appearance (faw) of the
church (kirk) gave the town its name. The
site of the church has been used since 7th
century, with succesive churches built
upon it. The present church was much
rebuilt in 19th century. Interesting
historically.

St Columba's Abbey - Iona

Museums & Galleries

Agnus Folk Museum - Glamis
17th century cottages with stone slab
roofs, restored by the National Trust for
Scotland & houses a fine folk collection.

Mary, Queen of Scots' House - Jedburgh
Life & times of the Queen along with
paintings, etc.

Andrew Carnegie Birthplace -
Dunfermline
The cottage where he was born is now
part of a museum showing his life's work.

Aberdeen Art Gallery & Museum -
Aberdeen
Sculpture, paintings, watercolours, prints
& drawings. Applied arts. Maritime
museum exhibits.

Provost Skene's House - Aberdeen
17th century house now exhibiting local
domestic life, etc.

Highland Folk Museum - Kingussie
Examples of craft work & tools - furnished
cottage with mill.

West Highland Museum - Fort William
Natural & local hsitory. Relics of Jacobites
& exhibition of the '45 Rising.

Clan Macpherson House - Newtonmore
Relics of the Clan.

Glasgow Art Gallery & Museum -
Glasgow
Archaeology, technology, local & natural
history. Old Masters, tapestries, porcelain,
glass & silver, etc. Sculpture.

Scottish National Gallery - Edinburgh
20th century collection - paintings &
sculpture - Arp, Leger, Giacometti,
Matisse, Picasso. Modern Scottish
painting.

**National Museum of Antiquities in
Scotland** - Edinburgh
Collection from Stone Age to modern
times - Relics of Celtic Church, Stuart
relics, Highland weapons, etc.

Gladstone Court - Biggar
Small indoor street of shops, a bank,
schoolroom, library, etc.

Burns' Cottage & Museum - Alloway
Relics of Robert Burns - National Poet.

Inverness Museum & Art Gallery -
Inverness
Social history, archaeology & cultural life
of the Highlands. Display of the Life of the
Clans - good Highland silver - crafts, etc.

Kirkintilloch - Nr. Glasgow
Auld Kirk Museum. Local history,
including archaeological specimens from
the Antonine Wall (Roman).   Local
industries, exhibitions, etc

Pollock House & Park - Glasgow
18th century house with collection of
paintings, etc. The park is the home of the
award-winning Burrell Collection

The foregoing are but a few of the many
museums & galleries in Scotland - further
information is always freely available from
the Tourist Information.

Historic Monuments

Aberdour Castle - Aberdour
14th century fortification - part still roofed.

Balvenie Castle - Duffton
15th century castle ruins.

Cambuskenneth Abbey - Nr. Stirling
12th century abbey - seat of Bruce's
Parliament in 1326. Ruins.

Dryburgh Abbey - Dryburgh
Remains of monastery.

Loch Leven Castle - Port Glasgow
15th century ruined stronghold - once lived
in by Mary, Queen of Scots.

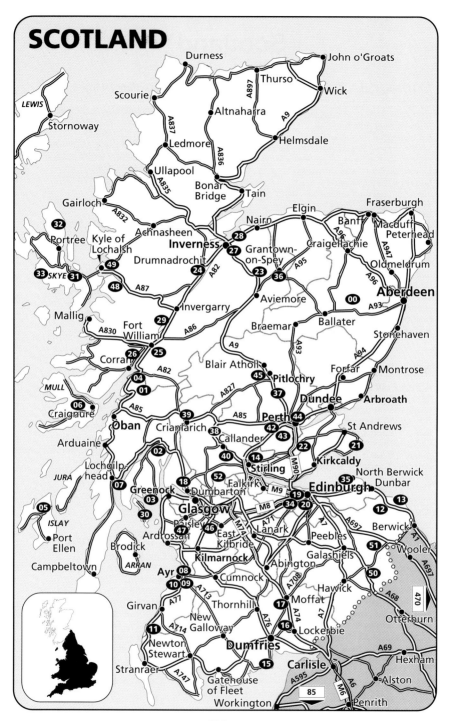

SCOTLAND

LEWIS

Durness   John o'Groats
Thurso   A897   Wick
Scourie   Altnaharra   A9
Stornoway   A837   Helmsdale
Ledmore   A836
Ullapool   A835
Bonar   Tain
Bridge   Elgin   Fraserburgh
Gairloch   A832   Nairn   Banff   Macduff
32   Achnasheen   28   Peterhead
Portree   Kyle of   Inverness   27   Grantown-   Craigellachie
Lochalsh   Drumnadrochit   on-Spey   A947   Oldmeldrum
33   SKYE   49   24   A82   23   36   A95   A96
31   48   A87   Aviemore   00   Aberdeen
Mallig   Invergarry   A93
A830   29   A86   Braemar   Ballater   Stonehaven
Fort   A9   A493   A94
William   26   25   Blair Atholl   Forfar   Montrose
Corran   A82   45   Pitlochry
04   A827   37   Dundee   Arbroath
MULL   01   Perth   44
06   A85   42   St Andrews
Craignure   39   A85   43   21
Oban   Crianlarich   38   Callander   22
Arduaine   02   40   14   Kirkcaldy
Lochgilp-   52   Stirling   M90
JURA   head   07   18   Falkirk   35   North Berwick
Greenock   M9   Edinburgh   Dunbar
05   03   Dumbarton   19   34   20   12   13
ISLAY   Glasgow   M8   A697   Berwick
Port   30   Paisley   M74   A7   A68
Ellen   47   46   East   Lanark   Peebles
Brodick   Ardrossan   Kilbride   Galashiels   Wooler
ARRAN   Kilmarnock   Abington   51   50
Campbeltown   Ayr   08   A708   470
10   09   Cumnock   Hawick
Girvan   A713   Thornhill   17   Moffat   A68
11   A714   New   16   A74   Otterburn
Newton   Galloway   Lockerbie   A7
Stewart   Dumfries   A76
Stranraer   15   Carlisle   Hexham
Gatehouse   A595   85   Alston
of Fleet   M6
Workington   Penrith

502

SCOTLAND

Map references

00 **Strachan**
00 **D. White**
01 **Broadbent**
02 **Mercer**
02 **Cameron**
03 **Dick**
04 **MacArther**
04 **Rice-Garwood**
04 **Sutherland**
05 **Rozga**
06 **Wagstaff**
07 **McKay**
08 **C.McDonald**
09 **Martin**
10 **Gemmell**
11 **Crosthwaite**
11 **Beale**
12 **Taylor**
13 **Brown**
14 **O'Dell**
15 **Jefferies**
16 **Pearson**
17 **M. White**
18 **S. MacDonald**
19 **Baird**
19 **Sandeman**
19 **El-Ghamri**
19 **Femister**
19 **W.Clark**
19 **J.Cairns**
19 **Turner**
19 **D.Vidler**
19 **Urquhart**
19 **Redmayne**
19 **Alexander**
19 **Walton**
19 **Deacon**
19 **Della-Porta**
19 **A. Hamilton**
19 **Hill**
19 **Leishman**
19 **G. Stuart**
19 **Conway**
19 **Stark**
19 **Welch**
19 **Maguire**
19 **C. Hamilton**
19 **Berkengoff**
19 **Fraser**
19 **Drummond**
19 **Telfer**
19 **A.Vidler**
19 **Colville**
19 **Invernizzi**
20 **Donaldson**
21 **McFarlane**
21 **Anderson**
22 **Steven**
23 **Rawson**
24 **MacDonald-Haig**
25 **J.Campbell**
25 **Waugh**
25 **Henderson**
26 **Marshall**
27 **Ozmus**
27 **Parsons**
27 **Hall**
27 **Kinnear**
28 **Pottie**
29 **Cairns**
30 **D. Cameron**
31 **Wilcken**
32 **Booth**
33 **Wathen**
34 **D. Scott**
35 **J. Scott**
36 **Bouchard**
37 **Lumsden**
37 **Buxton**
38 **Gunn**
39 **R. McDonald**
39 **Ferries**
39 **Chisholm**
40 **Graham**
42 **Niven**
43 **Straker**
44 **Stiell**
45 **Sanderson**
45 **Mathieson**
46 **Allison**
47 **Anderson**
48 **Kempthorne**
49 **Franchi**
50 **Irvine**
51 **B.Smith**
52 **Haslam**

OUTER HEBRIDES
WESTERN ISLES
LEWIS
SKYE
HIGHLANDS
INNER HEBRIDES
MULL
JURA
ISLAY
ARRAN
MORAY
ABERDEENSHIRE
ABERDEEN
PERTHSHIRE & KINROSS
ANGUS
DUNDEE
ARGYLL & BUTE
STIRLING
FIFE
EAST LOTHIAN
NORTH AYRSHIRE
SOUTH LANARKSHIRE
EAST AYRSHIRE
SOUTH AYRSHIRE
BORDERS
DUMFRIES & GALLOWAY
1 INVERCLYDE
2 DUNBARTON & CLYDEBANK
3 RENFREWSHIRE
4 EAST RENFREWSHIRE
5 GLASGOW
6 EAST DUNBARTONSHIRE
7 NORTH LANARKSHIRE
8 FALKIRK
9 CLACKMANNAN
10 WEST LOTHIAN
11 EDINBURGH
12 MID LOTHAIN

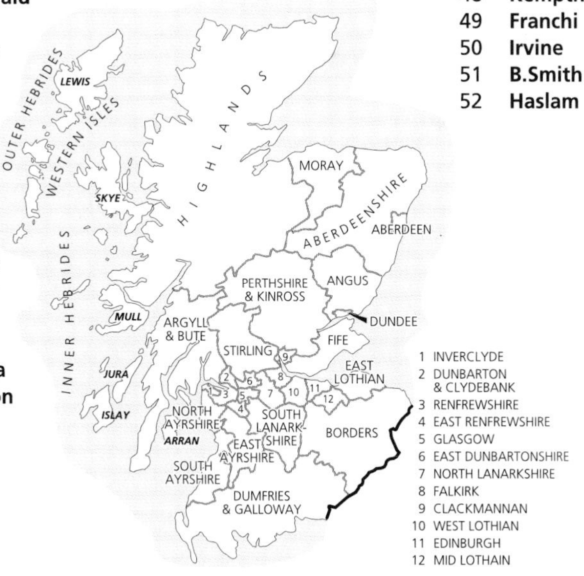

Scotland
Aberdeenshire & Argyll

		rate £ from - to per person	evening meals	children taken	animals taken
Anne & Eddie Strachan **Hazlehurst Lodge** **Ballater Road** **Aboyne** **AB34 5HY** Tel: (013398) 86921 Fax 013398 86660 Open: ALL YEAR Map Ref No. 00	Nearest Road: A.93 Hazlehurst is set in a wooded old-world garden, & was once the coachman's lodge to Aboyne Castle. Now, the interior is an expression of the best in Scottish design & art, & Scottish music, also from traditional roots, is played. Art from the Strachan's own collection & the sculptures & works of invited artists are shown throughout the 7 en-suite bedrooms, lounge areas & dining rooms. Anne is an outstanding chef with a reputation for imaginative cooking. Meals are served in the licensed restaurant. Hazlehurst is different & an intriguing place to stay in the heart of beautiful Royal Deeside. **E-mail: hazleartshotel@btinternet.com**	£27.00 to £44.00 VISA: M'CARD: AMEX:	Y	Y	Y
David & Meg White **Lys-Na-Greyne House** **Rhu-Na-Haven Road** **Aboyne** **AB34 5JD** Tel: (013398) 87397 Fax 013398 86441 Open: ALL YEAR Map Ref No. 00	Nearest Road: A.93 Lys-Na-Greyne is a beautiful Edwardian mansion situated in idyllic surroundings on the banks of the River Dee on the outskirts of Aboyne in Royal Deeside, standing in grounds of around 3 acres. This is a perfect place for exploring the surrounding countryside where there are many castles & places of historic interest. Golf, riding, gliding, fishing, hill-walking, tennis all available locally. Shooting, stalking available by arrangement with hosts. All rooms with en-suite/private bathroom & breathtaking views over the garden or river. **E-mail: DWhite7301@aol.com**	£27.00 to £35.00	Y	Y	Y

Argyll

		rate £ from - to per person	evening meals	children taken	animals taken
Earle & Stella Broadbent **Lochside Cottage** **Fasnacloich** **Appin** **PA38 4BJ** Tel: (01631) 730216 Fax 01631 730216 Open: ALL YEAR Map Ref No. 01	Nearest Road: A.828 Total peace on the shore of Loch Baile Mhic Chailen, in an idyllic glen of outstanding beauty. There are many walks from the cottage garden; or, visit Fort William, Glencoe & Oban, from where you can board a steamer to explore the Western Isles. At the end of the day, a warm welcome awaits you: delicious home-cooked dinner, a log fire & the certainty of a perfect night's sleep in one of 3 en-suite bedrooms.	£22.00 to £30.00	Y	Y	Y
Bill & Maisie Mercer **Arnish Cottage** **Christian Guest House** **Poll Bay** **St. Catherine's** **By Cairndow PA25 8BA** Tel: (01499) 302405 Fax 01499 302405 Open: ALL YEAR Map Ref No. 02	Nearest Road: A.815 Situated across the Loch from Inveraray, a truly idyllic setting on a private road 20 feet from the Lochside, & approx. 1 hr's drive from Glasgow Airport. A T.V. lounge & viewing conservatory are available to relax in. All of the attractive & comfortably furnished bedrooms are en-suite. Non-smoking throughout. Loch fishing, hill & forest walks, pony trekking, etc., are all readily organised. Arnish Cottage is a charming home, ideal for a relaxing break in this lovely part of Scotland.	£25.00 to £££	N	N	N

Abbot's Brae. Dunoon.

Scotland
Argyll

		rate £ from - to per person	children taken	evening meals	animals taken
Gavin & Helen Dick **Abbot's Brae Hotel** **West Bay** **Dunoon** **PA23 7QJ** **Tel: (01369) 705021** Fax 01369 701191 **Open: ALL YEAR** **Map Ref No. 03**	Nearest Road: A.815 Friendly, family-run Victorian country house hotel in secluded 2-acre woodland glen, with breathtaking views of the sea & hills. 7 tastefully furnished, spacious bedrooms, all en-suite with T.V., radio, 'phone & tea/coffee facilities. Unwind with a drink by the fire in the comfortable lounge or dine in the cosy dining room with delicious a la carte menu & select wine list. An ideal base for exploring Argyll & the Western Highlands. 1 hr from Glasgow Airport. Licensed. **E-mail: enquiry@abbotsbrae.ndirect.co.uk**	£27.00 to £33.00 *see PHOTO over* *p. 505* VISA: M'CARD:	Y	Y	Y
Flavia J. MacArthur **Ardsheal Home Farm** **Kentallen** **Duror in Appin** **PA38 4BZ** **Tel: (01631) 740229** Fax 01631 740229 **Open: APR - OCT** **(& New Year)** **Map Ref No. 04**	Nearest Road: A.828 A charming Scottish hill farm of 1,000 acres, surrounded by breathtaking scenery on the shores of Loch Linnhe, overlooking the Morvern Hills. A warm welcome is assured from the friendly hosts. 3 attractive bedrooms, comfortable & well-furnished, with tea/coffee-making facilities, electric blankets, etc. Seafood & other eating places nearby. Convenient for touring & sailing to the inner Isles. An idyllic holiday retreat, there is even 1 mile of private beach. Riding & tennis nearby. Single supplement.	£18.00 to £19.00 (no smoking)	Y	N	N
R. W. Rice-Garwood **The House of Keil** **Duror of Appin** **PA38 4BW** **Tel: (01631) 740255** Fax 01631 740365 **Open: ALL YEAR** **Map Ref No. 04**	Nearest Road: A.828 The House of Keil sits on the shores of Loch Linnhe, where guests have direct access to 1 1/2 miles of private foreshore, from where they can fish, bird watch, or just walk & enjoy the stunning scenery. 2 bedrooms look out over the Loch & battlements & the third overlooks the gardens. It is a warm & comfortably furnished house & being an old Stewart house, has many unusual features. A charming home.	£19.00 to £25.00 (no smoking)	Y	N	N
Mrs Margaret Rozga **Kilmeny Country Guest House** **Ballygrant** **Isle of Islay PA45 7QW** **Tel: (01496) 840668** Fax 01496 840668 **Open: ALL YEAR** **Map Ref No. 05**	Nearest Road: A.846 Islay is well-known for its abundant & wonderful wildlife & its many malt-whisky distilleries. Kilmeny Country Guest House, in the heart of a 300-acre beef farm, commands magnificent views of the surrounding hills & glen. This family-run business places emphasis on quality & personal service. The exquisite en-suite bedrooms, with country views, are elegantly furnished. The public rooms are charming, with a country-house influence. A 4-course dinner menu. Children over 8 years.	£32.00 to £32.00 (no smoking)	Y	Y	Y
John & Eleanor Wagstaff **Red Bay Cottage** **Deargphort** **Fionnphort** **Isle of Mull** **PA66 6BP** **Tel: (01681) 700396** **Open: ALL YEAR** **Map Ref No. 06**	Nearest Road: A.849 A really warm welcome awaits the visitor to this charming modern house, offering 3 very comfortable rooms with modern facilities. Situated only 20 metres from the sea, & overlooking Iona Sound & the white sandy beaches on the Isle of Iona, this surely must be the ideal base for a relaxing & peaceful holiday. Mr Wagstaff offers superb food. Eleanor is a qualified, practising silversmith, so why not enjoy a winter break on their residential silversmithing course?	£16.50 to £16.50	Y	Y	Y

Ardsheal House. Kentallen of Appin.

Scotland
Argyll & Ayrshire

		rate £ from - to per person	evening meals children taken	animals taken

Neil & Philippa Sutherland **Ardsheal House** **Kentallen of Appin** **PA38 4BX** **Tel: (01631) 740227** Fax 01631 740342 **Open: ALL YEAR** **Map Ref No. 04**	Nearest Road: A.828 Ardsheal House is spectacularly situated on the shores of Loch Linnhe, in 800 acres of woodlands, fields & gardens. It is a wonderful place for a relaxing holiday. This historic mansion is elegantly furnished throughout with family antiques & pictures, & offers 6 en-suite bedrooms which are attractive & well-appointed. The food at Ardsheal is excellent. It delights the eye & pleases the palate, & includes local fresh produce & home-made bread & preserves. A lovely home. **E-mail: info@ardsheal.co.uk**	£39.00 to £42.00 *see PHOTO over* *p. 507* VISA: M'CARD: AMEX:	Y Y Y
Mrs Margaret McKay **Allt-na-Craig** **Tarbert Road** **Ardrishaig** **By Lochgilphead** **PA30 8EP** **Tel: (01546) 603245** **Open: ALL YEAR (Excl.** **Xmas & New Year)** **Map Ref No. 07**	Nearest Road: A.83 The McKays warmly welcome all their guests to Allt-na-Craig, a lovely old Victorian mansion set in picturesque grounds overlooking Loch Fyne. Accommodation in 6 comfortable en-suite bedrooms with tea/coffee makers. A guests' lounge with open fire & dining room is also available. This is a perfect base for outdoor activities, like hill-walking, fishing, golf, riding & windsurfing, or for visiting the islands. Delicious evening meals are available by arrangement.	£30.00 to £35.00	Y Y Y
Mrs Sandra Cameron **Thistle House** **St. Catherines** **PA25 8AZ** **Tel: (01499) 302209** Fax 01499 302531 **Open: APR - OCT** **Map Ref No. 02**	Nearest Road: A.815 Superbly situated Victorian country house retaining many original features. Surrounded by 2 acres of mature garden, commanding spectacular views of Loch Fyne & sitting directly across the Loch from Inverary & its famous castle. 4 en-suite bedrooms with tea/coffee-making facilities & colour T.V.. Lounge with open fire. Good eating place in village & other restaurants nearby for evening meals. The Cowal Peninsula is well located for exploring Argyll & the Loch Lomond area. 1 hr's drive from Glasgow Airport.	£23.50 to £27.00 VISA: M'CARD:	Y N N

Aryshire

Caroline McDonald **The Crescent** **26 Bellevue Crescent** **Ayr** **KA7 2DR** **Tel: (01292) 287329** Fax 01292 286779 **Open: Mid JAN - NOV** **Map Ref No. 08**	Nearest Road: A.70 Elegant Victorian terraced house set in the heart of Ayr. All rooms are comfortable & individually styled including 1 with 4-poster bed. Each has a private bathroom. Within 5 minutes' walk, guests can enjoy a leisurely stroll along the promenade or a relaxing drink in one of Ayr's cosy pubs. Ideal location for golf, Burns Heritage, Culzean Castle & the Galloway Forest. Children over 8. **E-mail: CARRIE@26crescent.freeserve.co.uk**	£24.00 to £32.00 VISA: M'CARD:	Y N N

Visit our website at:
http://www.bestbandb.co.uk

		rate £ from - to per person	children taken	evening meals	animals taken
Helen Martin **Brenalder Lodge** 39 Dunure Road Doonfoot Ayr KA7 4HR Tel: (01292) 443939 Open: ALL YEAR Map Ref No. 09	Nearest Road: A.719 A warm welcome is assured at Brenalder Lodge. Located on the coastal route yet only 2 miles from Ayr town centre & 1 1/2 miles from the A.77. Set in the heart of Burns country, a perfect base for Turnberry, Troon & Prestwick golf courses & nearby Culzean Castle. All rooms are en-suite with T.V. & tea/coffee makers. After a day touring, relax & unwind in the comfort of the spacious lounge & enjoy breakfast in the conservatory style dining room. An excellent location for a relaxing break. Children over 7.	£25.00 to £30.00	Y	N	Y
Mrs Agnes Gemmell **Dunduff House** Dunure Ayr KA7 4LH Tel: (01292) 500225 Fax 01292 500222 Open: FEB - NOV Map Ref No. 10	Nearest Road: A.77 A warm friendly welcome awaits you at Dunduff House. Situated just south of Ayr at the coastal village of Dunure, this family-run beef & sheep unit of some 600 acres, is only 15 mins from the shore. Excellent accommodation, yet homely & comfortable. Bedrooms have panoramic coastal views over Arran, the Holy Isle, Mull of Kintyre & Ailsa Craig. Each is well-equipped & has beverage facilities, T.V. & an en-suite or private bathroom. Good location for exploring south-west Scotland & ideal for Culzean Castle, Robert Burns' Cottage & the Heritage Trail. VISA: M'CARD:	£22.00 to £35.00	N	N	N
Susan & Robin Crosthwaite **Cosses Country House** Ballantrae KA26 0LR Tel: (01465) 831363 Fax 01465 831598 Open: MAR - NOV Map Ref No. 11	Nearest Road: A.77 A former shooting lodge (1800s) & home farm (1900s), set in a secluded valley of garden & woodland. Superb accommodation, en-suite facilities, T.V., a hospitality tray & a roaring log fire on chilly evenings. A good base for exploring this delightful part of Scotland. The kitchen & herb garden supplement local produce for you to enjoy the taste of Scotland dinners. Castles (incl. Culzean), gardens, Burns's birthplace, golf courses, fishing, walks & cycling within easy reach. Irish ferry terminals 30 mins' drive. Children over 6 years welcome. **E-mail: cosses@compuserve.com**	£32.00 to £48.00 *see PHOTO over p. 510* VISA: M'CARD:	Y	Y	Y
Janet Beale **Balkissock Lodge** Ballantrae Girvan KA26 0LP Tel: (01465) 831200 Fax 01465 831537 Open: ALL YEAR Map Ref No. 11	Nearest Road: A.77 Janet offers bed & breakfast in her lovely Georgian home, quietly situated amid superb countryside. Comfortable beds, full en-suite facilities & a choice of delicious breakfasts. Peace & quiet combine to make a stay at the lodge memorable. Ideally situated for touring Burns country, Culzean Castle & the Irish ferries. Numerous golf courses within easy reach. **E-mail: accom@greenarrow.demon.co.uk**	£22.50 to £26.50 VISA: M'CARD:	Y	Y	Y

When booking your accommodation please mention
The Best Bed & Breakfast

Cosses. Ballantrae.

Scotland
Berwickshire & Clackmannanshire

		rate £ from - to per person	children taken	evening meals	animals taken
Martin & Libby Taylor **Kirkside House** **Bonkyl** **Duns** **TD11 3RJ** **Tel: (01361) 884340** **Fax 01361 884340** **Open: ALL YEAR** **Map Ref No. 12**	Nearest Road: A.1, A.6112 Kirkside House is an early-Victorian former manse, situated in a peaceful rural location. The spacious bedrooms have lovely views to the hills & are well-equipped. Guests are welcome to relax in the charming walled garden with its herbaceous borders, old roses & ornamental pond. Ideally located for exploring the Borders area, & wonderful hill & coastal walks. Edinburgh approx. 1 hr. Children over 12 years welcome.	£22.00 to £22.00	Y	N	N
Mr & Mrs Ronald Brown **Dunlaverock Country** **House** **Coldingham Bay** **Eyemouth** **TD14 5PA** **Tel: (018907) 71450** **Fax 018907 71450** **Open: ALL YEAR (Excl.** **Xmas & New Year)** **Map Ref No. 13**	Nearest Road: A.1 This spacious late Victorian villa is spectacularly situated on cliffs overlooking Coldingham Sands & the rugged surrounding coastline. The magnificent scenery & beautiful gardens offer true peace & serenity. Large, warm en-suite bedrooms, log fires & award-winning meals all add to your comfort & enjoyment. Activities include birdwatching, walking, fishing, boat cruises & an excellent 18-hole golf course. (Your hosts have 2 sets of clubs for guests' use.) Edinburgh is 1 hour away. A warm welcome awaits you. Children over 10. **E-mail: dunlaverock@lineonenet**	£26.00 to £38.00 VISA: M'CARD:	Y	Y	Y

Clackmannanshire

Jane O'Dell **Westbourne House B & B** **10 Dollar Road** **Tillicoultry** **Stirling** **FK13 6PA** **Tel: (01259) 750314** **Fax 01259 750642** **Open: ALL YEAR** **Map Ref No. 14**	Nearest Road: A.91 A Victorian mill-owner's mansion set in wooded grounds beneath Ochil Hills, in excellent walking country with numerous golf courses. Warm, friendly atmosphere, delicious home-cooking including vegetarian dishes. Log fires, croquet lawn, T.V., radio & tea/coffee-making facilities in all rooms (en-suite is on the ground floor). Centrally situated for Edinburgh, Glasgow, Perth & Stirling, home of 'Braveheart'. Secure off-street parking. **E-mail: odellwestbourne@compuserve.com**	£21.00 to £26.00	Y	N	Y

Visit our website at:
http://www.bestbandb.co.uk

Kirkton House. Cardross.

Scotland
Dumfriesshire & Dunbartonshire

		rate £ from - to per person	children taken	evening meals	animals taken
F. D. & J. Jeffries **Cavens House** **Kirkbean** **By Dumfries** **DG2 8AA** **Tel: (01387) 880234** **Fax 01387 880234** **Open: ALL YEAR** **Map Ref No. 15**	Nearest Road: A.710 Formerly an old mansion with a strong American historical connection, this charming guest house offers 6 really comfortable rooms with modern facilities, including a private bath or shower. Tea-making facilities & colour T.V. in each room. Standing in 11 acres of mature gardens & woodland, it makes a perfect base for those wishing to explore the joys of the Solway Coast, with its beautiful scenery & excellent beaches. Sailing, fishing, walking, golfing & riding all local. An excellent cuisine here. A friendly atmosphere. Animals by arrangement.	£26.00 to £32.00 *see PHOTO over* *p. 514* VISA: M'CARD:	Y	Y	N
Mrs Jane Pearson **Applegarth House** **Lockerbie** **DG11 1SX** **Tel: (01387) 810270** **Fax 01387 811701** **Open: ALL YEAR** **Map Ref No. 16**	Nearest Road: M.74 Applegarth House is a delightful former manse in a peaceful situation overlooking the River Annan, yet only 3 miles from Lockerbie & Jt. 17 on the M.74. It is the perfect centre from which to explore the beautiful Border country, or an ideal overnight stop. Shooting, stalking, fishing & wildfowling can be arranged locally. Jane is an excellent cook, & you are assured a warm welcome in their relaxed family home with its comfortable, sunny & spacious rooms. Children over 10. 'Phone for directions. Animals by arrangement. **E-mail: frank@applegarthtown.demon.co.uk**	£30.00 to £37.00 VISA: M'CARD:	Y	Y	Y
Margaret White **Hartfell House** **Hartfell Crescent** **Moffat** **DG10 9AL** **Tel: (01683) 220153** **Open: MAR - OCT** **Map Ref No. 17**	Nearest Road: A.701 Hartfell House is a splendid Victorian manor house located in a rural setting overlooking the hills, yet only a few mins' walk from the town. A listed building known locally for its fine interior woodwork. Offering 8 spacious bedrooms, 7 with en-suite facilities. Standing in landscaped gardens of approximately 2 acres of lawns & trees, & providing an atmosphere of peaceful relaxation. **E-mail: robert.white@virgin.net**	£23.00 to £25.00	Y	Y	Y

Dunbartonshire

		rate £ from - to per person	children taken	evening meals	animals taken
Stewart & Gillian Macdonald **Kirkton House** **Darleith Road** **Cardross** **Dumbarton** **G82 5EZ** **Tel: (01389) 841951** **Fax (01389) 841868** **Open: FEB - NOV** **Map Ref No. 18**	Nearest Road: A.814 Experience a blend of olde worlde charm, modern amenities & superb views at this converted 18/19th-century farmhouse, set in a tranquil location & yet handy for Glasgow Airport (20/25 mins), Loch Lomond, The Trossachs & most West Highland routes. All the spacious bedrooms have full en-suite facilities. The cosy lounge has a roaring fire on chilly evenings. Enjoy home-cooked food & savour a glass of wine at dinner by oil lamplight. Like the lounge, the convivial dining room has the original stone walls & a rustic fireplace, with the old swee from which the cooking pots were hung. **E-mail: info@kirktonhouse.co.uk**	£28.50 to £42.50 *see PHOTO over* *p. 512* VISA: M'CARD: AMEX:	Y	Y	Y

Cavens House.   Kirkbean-by-Dumfries.

Scotland
Edinburgh

		rate £ from - to per person	children taken	evening meals	animals taken
Helen Baird **Arisaig** **64 Glasgow Road** **Corstorphine EH12 8LN** **Tel: (0131) 3342610** **Fax 0131 3341800** **Open: APR - OCT** **Map Ref No. 19**	Nearest Road: M.8, M.9, A.720 A warm Scottish welcome awaits you here at this luxury detached bungalow, situated only 3 miles from the city centre. There are 2 beautiful bedrooms, all with modern amenities, & all kept to a very high standard. Tea/coffee-making & en-suite facilities. Parking. Excellent bus service. An ideal base from which to explore Edinburgh. Children over 12. Brochures available. **E-mail: helen_baird@hotmail.com**	£23.00 to £26.00 🚭	Y	N	N
Joyce Sandeman **Sandeman House** **33 Colinton Road** **Edinburgh** **EH10 5DR** **Tel: (0131) 4478080** **Fax 0131 4478080** **Open: ALL YEAR** **Map Ref No. 19**	Nearest Road: A.702 Built in 1860, Sandeman House is a charming family home which has been sympathetically restored by Neil & Joyce Sandeman. The 3 bedrooms are individually furnished & are bright & tastefully decorated to a very high standard. Each has an en-suite/private bathroom, T.V., tea/coffee facilities, hairdryer etc. A full traditional Scottish breakfast is served including home-made preserves. Many shops, bars & restaurants close by. Sandeman House is centrally situated & within easy reach of most of the city's attractions.	£26.00 to £40.00 🚭	Y	N	N
Mr & Mrs Magid El-Ghamri **Ashgrove House** **12 Osborne Terrace** **Edinburgh EH12 5HG** **Tel: (0131) 3375014** **Fax 0131 3135043** **Open: ALL YEAR** **Map Ref No. 19**	Nearest Road: A.8, M.9 Heather & Magid warmly invite you to their recently refurbished Victorian guest house. Most rooms are en-suite. Ashgrove House is only 1 mile from the heart of Edinburgh. There is a car park, & it is conveniently situated on the A.8 near Murrayfield & the Edinburgh International Conference Centre. An ideal base for exploring historic Edinburgh & the surrounding countryside.	£25.00 to £35.00 🚭 VISA: M'CARD:	Y	N	N
Brian & Fiona Femister **Kingsburgh House** **2 Corstorphine Road** **Murrayfield** **Edinburgh EH12 6HN** **Tel: (0131) 3131679** **Fax 0131 3460554** **Open: ALL YEAR** **Map Ref No. 19**	Nearest Road: A.8 Kingsburgh House is a detached Victorian villa situated in Murrayfield, one of Edinburgh's most desirable areas. This is a charming guest house 1 1/2 miles from Edinburgh's city centre. If you enjoy comfort in delightful surroundings make this your base for exploring Edinburghs' many attractions. Bedrooms are all en-suite with T.V. & hospitality tray. Start your day with a delicious breakfast served from the extensive menu. **E-mail: BOOKINGS@THEKINGSBURGH.COM**	£25.00 to £40.00 *see PHOTO over* *p. 516* VISA: M'CARD:	Y	N	N
William & Eleanor Clark **Tudorbank Lodge** **18 St. John's Road** **Corstorphine** **Edinburgh** **EH12 6NY** **Tel: (0131) 3347845** **Fax 0131 3345386** **Open: ALL YEAR** **Map Ref No. 19**	Nearest Road: A.8 An enchanting Tudor-style house (Historic Scotland listed building) set in private gardens with parking. Come & enjoy the warmth of Scottish hospitality. Superb breakfasts are freshly cooked to order with an ample choice for vegetarians. Colour T.V., hospitality tray, washbasins in all rooms, some en-suite. Ideal for touring, business, golf & especially the Festival, Fringe & Tattoo. Easy access to city centre, zoo, Murrayfield, airport & motorways. **E-mail: tudorbank@cwcom.net**	£25.00 to £35.00 VISA: M'CARD:	Y	N	N

Kingsburgh House. Edinburgh.

Scotland
Edinburgh

		rate £ from - to per person	children taken	evening meals	animals taken
Mrs J. Cairns **Cairn Lodge Guest House** **2 Downie Terrace** **Murrayfield** **Edinburgh** **EH12 7AU** Tel: **(0131) 5392117** Fax **0131 5398117** Open: **ALL YEAR** Map Ref No. 19	Nearest Road: A.8 Cairn Lodge is an elegant Victorian house, conveniently situated for Murrayfield, the airport, motorways & the city. A warm, friendly Scottish welcome awaits you in this charming house, which has been lovingly restored. Excellent bedrooms with marble fireplaces & original cornices, en-suite facilities, colour T.V. & hospitality trays in all rooms. Superb breakfasts. Private parking & an excellent bus service. An ideal base from which to explore Edinburgh. E-mail: janice@cairnlodge.demon.co.uk	£20.00 to £35.00 (no smoking)	Y	N	N
Lois-May & David Donaldson **Newmills House** **1 Newmills Road** **Balerno** **Edinburgh** **EH14 5AG** Tel: **(0131) 4494279** Fax **0131 4492919** Open: **ALL YEAR (Excl. Xmas)** Map Ref No. 20	Nearest Road: A.70 Only 7 miles from Edinburgh, Newmills House is a charming Georgian family house built in about 1780 & set in an acre of secluded gardens with an historic yew hedge. Lois-May & David offer a warm welcome in an informal atmosphere. The house is full of interesting paintings. Also, many period features remain including a large, comfortable drawing room. 4 attractive bedrooms with en-suite/private facilities etc. Breakfast is served in the sunny conservatory. Children over 2. E-mail: donaldson@newmills.demon.co.uk	£25.00 to £35.00 VISA: M'CARD:	Y	N	Y
Susan Turner **Camus Guest House** **4 Seaview Terrace** **Joppa** **Edinburgh EH15 2HD** Tel/Fax: **(0131) 6572003** Open: **ALL YEAR** Map Ref No. 19	Nearest Road: A.1 A Victorian, terraced villa overlooking the Firth of Forth, Camus House enjoys the peace of the seaside, along with an excellent bus service to the city centre, with its cultural, historical and leisure interests. The 5 guest rooms are comfortably furnished, and have wash basins, colour T.V., radio alarms & tea/coffee facilities. 4 are en-suite. A genuine and friendly welcome is assured.	£18.00 to £25.00 VISA: M'CARD:	Y	N	Y
Mrs Dorothy Vidler **Kenvie Guest House** **16 Kilmaurs Road** **Edinburgh** **EH16 5DA** Tel: **(0131) 6681964** Fax **0131 6681964** Open: **ALL YEAR** Map Ref No. 19	Nearest Road: A.7, A.68, A.1 Kenvie Guest House is charming, comfortable, warm, friendly & inviting. This small Victorian town house is situated in a quiet residential street, 1 small block from the main road, leading to the city centre (an excellent bus service) & the bypass to all routes. Offering, for your comfort, lots of caring touches, including complimentary tea/coffee, colour T.V. & no-smoking rooms. Private facilities available. You are guaranteed a warm welcome from Richard & Dorothy.	£26.00 to £30.00 (no smoking) VISA: M'CARD:	Y	N	N
Maggie Urquhart **Kildonan Lodge Hotel** **27 Craigmillar Park** **Edinburgh** **EH16 5PE** Tel: **(0131) 6672793** Fax **0131 6679777** Open: **ALL YEAR** Map Ref No. 19	Nearest Road: A.701 Ideally situated in central Edinburgh, Kildonan Lodge is an outstanding example of Victorian elegance providing the perfect setting for your visit to Scotland's capital. Relax & enjoy a 'dram' at the Honesty bar. Each of the well-appointed non-smoking en-suite bedrooms have T.V., 'phone, radio/alarm & tea/coffee trays. Spa bath & 4-poster beds available in selected rooms. Car park. Delicious wholesome Scottish breakfasts are served. A warm friendly welcome awaits you. E-mail: kildonanlodge@compuserve.com	£35.00 to £49.00 *see PHOTO over* p. 518 VISA: M'CARD: AMEX:	Y	Y	N

Kildonan Lodge Hotel. Edinburgh.

Scotland
Edinburgh

Lyn Redmayne **Kingsley Guest House** **30 Craigmillar Park** **Newington** **Edinburgh EH16 5PS** **Tel/Fax: (0131) 6678439** **Open: ALL YEAR** **Map Ref No. 19**	Nearest Road: A.701 A warm, friendly welcome awaits you at this Victorian terraced villa. Offering 5 comfortably furnished bedrooms, each with either en-suite or private facilities, T.V. & tea/coffee-making facilities. A full English or Continental breakfast is served. Kingsley Guest House is conveniently situated in the south of the city with an excellent bus service at the door to & from the city centre with its many tourist attractions. Private parking.	£18.00 to £30.00	Y	N	N
Norah Alexander **Tiree Guest House** **26 Craigmillar Park** **Edinburgh EH16 5PS** **Tel: (0131) 667 7477** **Fax 0131 662 1608** **Open: ALL YEAR** **Map Ref No. 19**	Nearest Road: A.701 Situated on the south side of Edinburgh, about 1 1/2 miles from the city centre. Offering accommodation in 6 comfortable rooms, all with en-suite facilities. All rooms have colour T.V. & tea/coffee makers. Conveniently located for Edinburgh University, Holyrood Palace & the shopping centre. Children are very welcome here, & are given reduced rates. (Min. age 6 years.) A full Scottish breakfast is served.	£18.00 to £36.00	Y	N	N
Ms Emily Walton **Frederick House Hotel** **42 Frederick Street** **Edinburgh** **EH2 1EX** **Tel: (0131) 2261999** **Fax 0131 6247064** **Open: ALL YEAR** **Map Ref No. 19**	Nearest Road: A.7 Frederick House Hotel is perfectly situated in the very heart of Edinburgh's city centre, a stones' throw from Princes Street. All of the 44 newly refurbished & tastefully decorated bedrooms feature en-suite bathrooms (with bath & shower); breakfast is served in your room. Your hosts' aim is to make your stay as comfortable & relaxing as possible, with all modern conveniences combined together with an 'olde worlde' atmosphere. **E-mail: frederickhouse@ednet.co.uk**	£25.00 to £55.00 VISA: M'CARD: AMEX:	Y	Y	N
Annie Deacon **53 Eskside West** **Musselburgh** **Edinburgh** **EH21 6RB** **Tel: (0131) 6652875** **Open: ALL YEAR** **Map Ref No. 19**	Nearest Road: A.1 A warm & helpful hostess awaits you at this stone-built terraced cottage on the bank of the River Esk. Charmingly decorated to a high standard. Double room en-suite & a twin-bedded room with a luxurious private bathroom. Fresh flowers, T.V., radio & tea/coffee-making facilities in all rooms. A professional cook, Annie provides excellent breakfasts. A super base, only 15 mins' from Holyrood & 20 mins' from the centre of Edinburgh. Children over 6 years welcome.	£16.00 to £18.00	Y	N	N
Gerald Della-Porta **Gerald's Place** **21B Abercromby Place** **Edinburgh** **EH3 6QE** **Tel: (0131) 5587017** **Fax 0131 5587014** **Open: ALL YEAR** **Map Ref No. 19**	Nearest Road: A.1 Your host Gerald, welcomes you to his delightful home full of character, colour & comforts. The accommodation includes 2 double bedrooms (each with one king-size bed or 2 3ft beds of supreme comfort & quality) with 2 private bathrooms (each with power shower & bath tub). It is ideal for 2 couples travelling together. The full Scottish breakfast is a feast whether hot, cold or vegetarian. Abercromby Place is at the very centre of the city, only 6 mins' walk from Waverley station & is one of the finest streets in Edinburgh. **E-mail: gerald@geraldsplace.com**	£34.50 to £34.50 *see PHOTO over* p. 520	N	N	N

Gerald's Place. Edinburgh.

Ellesmere Guest House. Edinburgh.

Scotland
Edinburgh

		rate £ from - to per person	children taken	evening meals	animals taken
Mr & Mrs Andrew Hamilton **16 Lynedoch Place** **Edinburgh** **EH3 7PY** **Tel: (0131) 2255507** **Fax 0131 2264185** **Open: ALL YEAR** **Map Ref No. 19**	Nearest Road: A.74 A beautiful, listed Georgian terraced house, built in 1821 & situated in the heart of the Georgian New Town. This elegantly furnished house, though modernised to the highest of standards, still retains all its original features including sash windows, cornices & marble fireplaces. 3 attractive & well-appointed en-suite bedrooms. Situated within 2 mins' walk of Princes Street, this is the perfect spot for exploring this vibrant city with shops, restaurants & places of historic interest. **E-mail: Susie.Lynedoch@BTinternet.com**	£35.00 to £45.00 🚭 VISA: M'CARD:	Y	N	Y
Mrs C. Leishman **Ellesmere Guest House** **11 Glengyle Terrace** **Edinburgh** **EH3 9LN** **Tel: (0131) 229 4823** **Fax 0131 229 5285** **Open: ALL YEAR** **Map Ref No. 19**	Nearest Road: A.702 Guests are made welcome at this very elegant tastefully restored Victorian town house, quietly situated overlooking golf links in the centre of Edinburgh. Rooms are all en-suite & decorated to a very high standard & well-equipped with every comfort in mind. Delicious breakfasts are served. 'A home away from home.' Convenient for castle, Princes Street, Royal Mile, International Conference Centre, theatres & restaurants. Children over 10 years welcome.	£25.00 to £35.00 *see PHOTO over* *p. 521*	Y	N	N
Marny Hill **Elmview** **15 Glengyle Terrace** **Edinburgh EH3 9LN** **Tel: (0131) 2281973** **Fax 0131 2297296** **Open: ALL YEAR** **Map Ref No. 19**	Nearest Road: A.702 Marny Hill's luxurious bed & breakfast is situated in the heart of Edinburgh within easy walking distance of Edinburgh Castle & Princes Street (1 km). Elmview is a wonderful base from which to enjoy your stay in Edinburgh. Each bedroom has been elegantly furnished & all are en-suite. Direct-dial 'phones, fridges, fresh flowers are but a few of the thoughtful extras in each bedroom. **E-mail: marny@elmview.co.uk.**	£35.00 to £50.00 🚭 *see PHOTO over* *p. 523* VISA: M'CARD:	N	N	N
Leonard & Suzanne Welch **Ravensdown Guest House** **248 Ferry Road** **Edinburgh** **EH5 3AN** **Tel: (0131) 5525438** **Fax 0131 5527559** **Open: ALL YEAR** **Map Ref No. 19**	Nearest Road: A.1 Built at the beginning of the 1900s, Ravensdown offers unsurpassed panoramic views of the Edinburgh skyline. 6 spacious, individually decorated rooms with T.V. & coffee/tea facilities & an en-suite or private bathroom. Guests may socialise in the lounge, with a bar service on the premises. Your friendly hosts can offer advice about local attractions & tours. A delicious breakfast sets you up for a day of sightseeing. An excellent bus service means you can leave the car in the car park & commute the 2 miles to the centre.	£22.50 to £35.00 🚭	Y	N	N
Mrs Moira Conway **Crannoch But & Ben** **467 Queensferry Road** **Edinburgh EH4 7ND** **Tel: (0131) 3365688** **Fax 0131 3365688** **Open: ALL YEAR** **Map Ref No. 19**	Nearest Road: A.90 Warm Scottish welcome at this delightful private house. Offering 2 attractive ground-floor bedrooms with en-suite facilities & tea/coffee makers. The comfortable guest lounge has T.V. & information packs on Edinburgh & the surrounding area. On-site private parking. Easy access to the airport & an excellent bus service to the city centre (just 3 miles journey). **E-mail: crannoch@conway58.freserve.co.uk**	£25.00 to £27.00 🚭	Y	N	N

Elmview. Edinburgh.

Scotland
Edinburgh

		rate £ from - to per person	children taken	evening meals	animals taken
Jon & Gloria Stuart **The Stuarts** **17 Glengyle Terrace** **Edinburgh** **EH3 9LN** **Tel:** (0131) 2299559 Fax 0131 2292226 **Open: ALL YEAR** **Map Ref No. 19**	Nearest Road: A.702 Quietly situated overlooking a park, Stuarts is warm, comfortable & spacious, with a friendly atmosphere. 3 attractive rooms, all with colour T.V. & tea/coffee-making facilities & an en-suite bathroom. Jon & Gloria will welcome you, & help you with where to go, what to do & where to eat. Bookings of 3 nights or more taken in advance. Centrally located & within easy reach of the Castle, Princes St., shops, theatres & restaurants. **E-mail: reservations@the-stuarts.com**	£45.00 to £60.00 🚭 *see PHOTO over* *p. 525* VISA: M'CARD: AMEX:	Y	N	N
Mrs Nan Stark **Ben Cruachan** **17 McDonald Road** **Edinburgh** **EH7 4LX** **Tel:** (0131) 5563709 **Open: APR - OCT** **Map Ref No. 19**	Nearest Road: A.1 Guests are assured of a warm welcome & a friendly atmosphere at this attractive house, situated 1 km from Princes Street. Offering comfortable en-suite bedrooms, well-equipped with every comfort in mind & serving an excellent breakfast. Centrally situated within easy reach of the castle, Royal Mile, Holyrood Palace, shops, theatres & restaurants. Unrestricted parking & on all main bus routes. Children over 5 years.	£25.00 to £35.00 🚭	Y	N	N
Alan Maguire **Greenside Hotel** **9 Royal Terrace** **Edinburgh EH7 5AB** **Tel/Fax:** (0131) 5570022 **Tel:** (0131) 5570121 **Open: ALL YEAR** **Map Ref No. 19**	Nearest Road: A.1 Built in 1820, the Greenside Hotel is an elegant Georgian town-house hotel situated in the city centre & surrounded by peaceful garden settings in one of Edinburgh's most prestigious terraces. A few mins' walk from Waverly Station, Princes St., tourist attractions, local restaurants & theatre. 16 tastefully decorated rooms with all facilities. Large family rooms also available. Full Scottish Breakfast is served each morning. **E-mail: greensidehotel@ednet.co.uk**	£22.50 to £47.50 VISA: M'CARD: AMEX:	Y	Y	N
Cathie Hamilton **Ailsa Craig Hotel** **24 Royal Terrace** **Edinburgh** **EH7 5AH** **Tel/Fax:** (0131) 5566055 **Tel:** (0131) 5561022 **Open: ALL YEAR** **Map Ref No. 19**	Nearest Road: A.1 Ailsa Craig Hotel is situated in the heart of Edinburgh near the city centre in one of the most prestigious terraces. This elegant Georgian town house hotel is situated only 10 mins' walk from Princes Street, Waverly Station & many attractions. 17 tastefully furnished & decorated bedrooms, 14 with en-suite facilities, & all with 'phone, hairdryer, colour T.V. & tea/coffee-making facilities. A delicious breakfast & good evening meals are served. A perfect base for exploring Edinburgh. **E-mail: ailsacraig@ednet.co.uk**	£22.50 to £47.50 VISA: M'CARD: AMEX:	Y	Y	N
Susie Berkengoff **Barony House** **4 Queens Crescent** **Edinburgh** **EH9 2AZ** **Tel:** (0131) 6675806 Fax 0131 6676833 **Open: ALL YEAR (Excl. Xmas)** **Map Ref No. 19**	Nearest Road: A.74 A fine detached Victorian house situated in a select residential area just off the main road. Queens Crescent lies between the A.7/A.701 & A.68 main roads coming into the city from the south, but is only 1 1/2 miles from the city centre. Parking. Breakfast is a wonderful buffet experience! Also, guests can enjoy a 3-course evening meal & Susie uses only the finest local produce. All tastes & special requirements catered for. 9 bedrooms (4 en-suite) with 'phones, refreshment facilities, hairdryers & a complimentary sherry. **E-mail: baronyhouse@cableinet.co.uk**	£18.00 to £40.00 🚭	Y	Y	N

The Stuarts. Edinburgh.

Scotland
Edinburgh

		rate £ from - to per person	children taken	evening meals	animals taken
Deb & Dave Fraser **Glenalmond Guest House** **25 Mayfield Gardens** **Edinburgh** **EH9 2BX** **Tel: (0131) 6682392** Fax 0131 6682392 **Open: ALL YEAR** **Map Ref No. 19**	Nearest Road: A.701 Glenalmond is an attractive family-run guest house, situated only 5 mins' from the city centre. The house is beautifully furnished throughout & offers 10 delightful bedrooms, many with either 4-poster or canopy beds. (5 ground floor rooms.) Each bedroom is spacious & has quality furnishings, T.V. & a tea/coffee tray. A full Scottish breakfast is served & includes porridge & home-baked scones. This is an elegant base from which to explore Edinburgh. Parking. Children over 2. **E-mail: glenalmond@dial.pipex.com**	£25.00 to £40.00 VISA:	Y	N	N
Alan Drummond **Parklands Guest House** **20 Mayfield Gardens** **Edinburgh** **EH9 2BZ** **Tel: (0131) 6677184** Fax 0131 6672011 **Open: ALL YEAR** **Map Ref No. 19**	Nearest Road: A.701 Parklands is an attractive Victorian terraced house conveniently located 1 1/2 miles from Princes Street & all the main tourist attractions. Accommodation is in 6 bedrooms, each is furnished to a high standard & is fully equipped with en-suite/private facilities, colour T.V. & tea/coffee makers. A full Scottish breakfast is served. Nearby are many excellent restaurants. Parklands is family-run with a friendly atmosphere. You are assured of a warm welcome.	£20.00 to £30.00	Y	N	N
Mrs A. Helen Telfer **Ard-Thor** **10 Mentone Terrace** **Newington** **Edinburgh EH9 2DG** **Tel: (0131) 6671647** **Open: ALL YEAR** **Map Ref No. 19**	Nearest Road: A.7 A charming, 19th-century Victorian guest house situated only 10 mins from the city centre, castle & Princes Street by a good local bus service. The Ard-Thor is quiet & friendly, & your comfort is ensured by the personal attention of your host. Guests are offered a choice of 3 rooms, all with T.V. & tea/coffee-making facilities. Queens Park & Commonwealth Pool are nearby. This is an ideal place from which to explore Edinburgh.	£21.00 to £35.00	N	N	N
Alan & Angela Vidler **Rowan Guest House** **13 Glenorchy Terrace** **Edinburgh** **EH9 2DQ** **Tel: (0131) 6672463** Fax 0131 6672463 **Open: ALL YEAR** **Map Ref No. 19**	Nearest Road: A.701 Elegant Victorian home in one of the city's loveliest areas with free parking & only a 10-min. bus ride to the centre. The castle, Royal Mile, restaurants & other amenities easily reached. The charmingly decorated bedrooms are comfortably & tastefully furnished with complimentary tea/coffee & biscuits. Breakfast, including traditional porridge & freshly baked scones, will keep you going until dinner! Attentive friendly hosts. Partially non-smoking. **E-mail: rowanhouse@hotmail.com**	£22.00 to £32.00 VISA: M'CARD:	Y	N	N
Mrs Jane E. Coville **Teviotdale House** **53 Grange Loan** **Edinburgh** **EH9 2ER** **Tel: (0131) 6674376** Fax 0131 6674376 **Open: ALL YEAR** **Map Ref No. 19**	Nearest Road: A.7, A.702 Tastefully restored, elegant, Victorian gentleman's town house. Located in a quiet residential conservation area. Lovely original woodwork. All 7 spacious rooms have every modern facility, with private/en-suite bathrooms, T.V., radio & tea/coffee makers. Some rooms have a refrigerator. Breakfast is a banquet. Home-baked scones, jams & bread. Guaranteed to delight the most travelled of guests. Parking. 10 mins town centre. **E-mail: teviotdale.house@btinternet.com**	£28.00 to £45.00 *see PHOTO over* *p. 527* VISA: M'CARD: AMEX:	Y	N	N

Teviotdale House. Edinburgh.

Beaumont Lodge. Anstruther.

	rate £ from - to per person	children taken	evening meals	animals taken

| Maureen & Adolfo Invernizzi
Roselea House
11 Mayfield Road
Edinburgh
EH9 2NG
Tel: (0131) 6676115
Fax 0131 6673556
Open: ALL YEAR
Map Ref No. 19 | Nearest Road: A.701
Always a warm welcome from Maureen & Adolfo at their elegant Victorian house. They have tastefully restored & refurbished their home to a high standard; whilst still retaining the original features. Each room has colour T.V., tea/coffee-making facilities &, of course, an en-suite or private bathroom. Whether on business or on holiday, this is an ideal oasis to return to & relax in. A delightful home, offering easy access to the many attractions & places of historic interest that Edinburgh has to offer. | £30.00
to
£50.00

VISA: M'CARD: | N | N | N |

Fifeshire

Eric & Moyra McFarlane **The Spindrift** **Pittenweem Road** **Anstruther** **KY10 3DT** Tel: (01333) 310573 Fax 01333 310573 Open: ALL YEAR Map Ref No. 21	Nearest Road: A.917 Set in the picturesque fishing village of Anstruther, The Spindrift is an imposing, stone-built Victorian home with many original features carefully re-stored. 6 individually & tastefully furnished bed-rooms with en-suite/private bathrooms, colour T.V., 'phone, hospitality tray & a host of other extras. Delicious evening meals are served. The Spindrift is only 10 mins' from St. Andrews with its world famous golf courses & excellent beaches. It is an ideal base from which to explore the splendours of central Scotland. **E-mail: spindrift@east-neuk.co.uk**	£26.50 to £32.50 🚭 VISA: M'CARD: AMEX:	N	N	N
Julia Anderson **Beaumont Lodge Guest House** **43 Pittenweem Road** **Anstruther KY10 3DT** Tel: (01333) 310315 Fax 01333 310315 Open: ALL YEAR Map Ref No. 21	Nearest Road: A.917 Only 1 hr's drive from Edinburgh Airport & 9 miles from St. Andrews, this family-run guest house offers excellent accommodation & a cosy dining room where food of a high standard is served. The spacious en-suite/private rooms have many extras which you would only find in the best of hotels. Enjoy true Scottish hospitality in this charming home. Private parking. Children over 10 years welcome. **E-mail: reservations@beau-lodge.demon.co.uk**	£25.00 to £30.00 🚭 *see PHOTO over p. 528* VISA: M'CARD:	Y	Y	N
Donald & Isobel Steven **Ardchoille Farmhouse** **Dunshalt** **Nr. Auchtermuchty** **KY14 7EY** Tel/Fax: (01337) 828414 Tel: (01334) 656733 Open: ALL YEAR Map Ref No. 22	Nearest Road: A.91, B.936 Relax & enjoy the warm comfort, delicious Taste of Scotland food & the excellent hospitality at Ardchoille Farmhouse. 2 tastefully furnished twin-bedded rooms, each with an en-suite/private bath-room, colour T.V. & tea/coffee trays offering home-made butter shortbread. Large comfortable lounge, & elegant dining room with fine china & crystal. Dinner by arrangement. Close by the Royal Palace of Falkland, home of Mary Queen of Scots. 20 mins from St. Andrews, & 1 hr Edinburgh. Ideal base for golfing & touring. Children over 12.	£30.00 to £40.00 *see PHOTO over p. 530* VISA: M'CARD:	N	Y	N

Visit our website at:
http://www.bestbandb.co.uk

Ardchoille Farmhouse. Auchtermuchty.

Borlum Farmhouse. Drumnadrochit.

Scotland
Inverness-shire

		rate £ from - to per person	evening meals	children taken	animals taken
Peter & Penny Rawson **Feith Mhor Country House** **Station Road** **Carrbridge** **PH23 3AP** Tel: (01479) 841621 Open: Mid DEC - Mid NOV Map Ref No. 23	Nearest Road: A.9 A warm, friendly atmosphere is found at this charming 19th-century house set in 1 1/2 acres of delightful garden, surrounded by peaceful, unspoilt countryside. Tastefully furnished, & full of character. 6 very comfortable en-suite bedrooms with tea/coffee & T.V.. Excellent views from each room. A pleasant dining room & spacious, comfortable lounge. Super, varied breakfast menu, home-made preserves. Dinner can be arranged at one of the excellent places to eat in the village. Children over 8 yrs. E-mail: feith.mhor@btinternet.com	£26.00 to £27.00	Y	N	Y
Duncan & Vanessa **MacDonald-Haig** **Borlum Farmhouse** **Drumnadrochit** **IV3 6XN** Tel/Fax: (01456) 450358 Open: ALL YEAR Map Ref No. 24	Nearest Road: A.82 This 180-year-old farmhouse has a unique position overlooking Loch Ness. Each year, visitors world-wide are delighted with the fresh, tastefully furnished rooms, good food & very friendly atmosphere. Borlum is an historic working hill farm, dating back to its service to Urquhart Castle in the 16th century. The farm also has its own B.H.S.-approved riding centre, making it the ideal place to spend a riding holiday.	£21.00 to £30.50 *see PHOTO over p. 531* VISA: M'CARD:	Y	N	N
Mrs Joan Campbell **The Grange** **Grange Road** **Fort William PH33 6JF** Tel: (01397) 705516 Fax 01397 701595 Open: MAR - OCT Map Ref No. 25	Nearest Road: A.82 Set in quiet gardens overlooking Loch Linnhe, yet only 10 mins from the town centre. The Grange offers superb accommodation in 4 en-suite rooms, each well-equipped & enhanced by a very relaxed atmosphere. The area is charming & the house is well-situated, only 1 1/2 hrs from Oban, Inverness & the Isles. An ideal base for touring the Highlands, & returning to a comfortable lounge log fire for chilly evenings. Vegetarians catered for.	£38.00 to £47.00 *see PHOTO over p. 533* VISA:	N	N	N
Mrs Vera G. Waugh **Cabana House** **Union Road** **Fort William PH33 6RB** Tel: (01397) 705991 Fax 01397 705991 Open: ALL YEAR Map Ref No. 25	Nearest Road: A.82 This elegant Victorian house has been renovated to an exceptional standard. There are 3 designer-decorated bedrooms, 2 en-suite, 1 with private bathroom. Situated in a prime position 5 mins from the town centre, with private parking & garden. An ideal holiday base for touring the spectacular Highlands & islands. Special interest courses in curtain design & paint effects held during spring & autumn.	£26.00 to £28.00	N	N	N
B. B. Henderson **Ashburn House** **1 Ashburn Lane** **Fort William** **PH33 6RQ** Tel: (01397) 706000 Fax 01397 702024 Open: MAR - NOV Map Ref No. 25	Nearest Road: A.82 Ashburn is a splendid Victorian house personally run by Highland hosts. Quietly situated by the shores of Loch Linhe only 600 yards from the town centre & among others the renowned Crannog Seafood Restaurant. An excellent base for touring the Highlands. Sample an imaginative & real Highland breakfast, served at your own individual table, complemented with freshly baked scones from the aga. 7 attractively furnished, en-suite bedrooms, 3 with king-size beds. Parking. Colour brochure & special weekly rates available. E-mail: ashburn@scotland2000.com	£30.00 to £40.00 *see PHOTO over p. 534* VISA: M'CARD: AMEX:	Y	N	N

The Grange. Fort William.

Ashburn House. Fort William.

	Nearest Road	rate £ from - to per person	children taken	evening meals	animals taken
Graham & Alison Marshall **The Inn at Ardgour** Ardgour Fort William PH33 7AA Tel: (01855) 841225 Fax 01855 841214 Open: FEB - DEC Map Ref No. 26	Nearest Road: A.861 This family-run inn at the entrance to the Great Glen enjoys spectacular sea views from all bedrooms. For centuries, travellers have enjoyed the famous West Highland Welcome. A menu featuring fresh local produce, particularly seafood, & a local bar well-stocked with malts complement modern en-suite bedrooms in this old inn. Ardgour is the gateway to the Ardnamurchan peninsula, the most westerly part of Britain, where there are more deer than people. It is ideal for walking, fishing & touring the West Highlands. Also, daytrips to the islands of Mull, Ions & Skye.	£25.00 to £40.00 VISA: M'CARD: AMEX:	Y	Y	Y
Jane & Ishak Ozmus **The Old Royal Guest House** 10 Union Street Inverness IV1 1PL Tel: (01463) 230551 Fax 01463 711916 Open: ALL YEAR Map Ref No. 27	Nearest Road: A.9 Personally managed by the resident proprietor Jane Ozmus, The Old Royal is conveniently situated in the centre of town, opposite the railway station. Accommodation is in 12 comfortable guest bedrooms, 5 with en-suite facilities. All have colour T.V. & tea/coffee makers. The Old Royal has a home-from-home atmosphere, & provides visitors with a comfortable holiday base from which to tour the locality. Children over 3.	£20.00 to £29.00 VISA: M'CARD:	Y	N	N
Mrs Margaret E. Pottie **Easter Dalziel Farmhouse** Dalcross Inverness IV1 2JL Tel: (01667) 462213 Fax 01667 462213 Open: ALL YEAR (Excl. Xmas & New Year) Map Ref No. 28	Nearest Road: A.96, B.9039 This Scottish farming family offer the visitor a friendly Highland welcome on their 200-acre stock/arable farm. 3 charming bedrooms are available in the delightful early-Victorian farmhouse. The lounge has log fire & T.V.. Delicious home cooking & baking served, including a choice of breakfasts. Evening meals available summer only. Ideal base for exploring the scenic Highlands. Local attractions are Cawdor Castle, Culloden, Fort George, Loch Ness & nearby Castle Stuart.	£17.00 to £20.00 VISA: M'CARD:	Y	Y	Y
Alison Parsons **& Philip Alvy** **Ballindarroch** Aldourie Inverness IV12 6EL Tel: (01463) 751348 Fax 01463 751372 Open: ALL YEAR Map Ref No. 27	Nearest Road: A.9, B.862 Ballindarroch was originally built as a shooting lodge around 1870, & stands in 10 acres of woodland gardens above the Caledonian Canal. Decorated with hand-painted wallpaper & furnished with antiques & an eclectic selection of family pieces, the house offers a totally relaxing & peaceful environment only 10 mins from Inverness. Alison Parsons is an award-winning chef & can also offer gourmet dinners (on request). French, Italian, Spanish & German spoken. **E-mail: alison@ballindarroch.freeserve.co.uk**	£20.00 to £30.00	Y	Y	Y
Mrs Sheila P. Hall **Talisker Guest House** 25 Ness Bank Inverness IV2 4SF Tel: (01463) 236221 Fax 01463 234173 Open: ALL YEAR Map Ref No. 27	Nearest Road: A.9 Talisker was built over 150 years ago & is beautifully & quietly situated on the east bank of the River Ness, just minutes from the town centre & 10 mins' walk from the train & bus stations, parks & theatre. Some of the 5 bedrooms overlook the river. All have central heating, remote colour T.V. & welcome tray, & there is ample private parking & storage for bicycles. **E-mail: 106735.2241@compuserve.com**	£22.00 to £28.00 VISA: M'CARD:	Y	N	N

All the establishments mentioned in this guide are members of the Worldwide Bed & Breakfast Association.

If you have any comments regarding your
accommodation please send them to us
using the form at the back of the book.
We value your comments.

	rate £ from - to per person	children taken	evening meals	animals taken

Barbara J. Kinnear
Glenashdale
Daviot East
Inverness
IV2 5XQ
Tel: (01463) 772221
Fax 01463 772131
Open: ALL YEAR
Map Ref No. 27

Nearest Road: A.9
Glenashdale is a modern country house situated 7 miles south of Inverness in quiet countryside, with lovely views. All the comfortable bedrooms have en-suite facilities, central heating, T.V., radio & tea/coffee tray. Joe & Babs Kinnear invite you to escape the hustle & bustle of everyday living & join them in the beauty of the Scottish Highlands, where making all guests feel welcome is a top priority. Children over 6 years.
E-mail: glenashdale@jkinnear.freeserve.co.uk

£20.00 to £22.00 — Y — N — N
VISA: M'CARD:

Mrs Margaret Cairns
Invergloy House
Spean Bridge
PH34 4DY
Tel: (01397) 712681
Open: ALL YEAR
Map Ref No. 29

Nearest Road: A.82
A really interesting Scottish coach house, dating back 120 years, offering 3 charming, comfortable twin-bedded rooms, with modern facilities, 2 with en-suite shower rooms & 1 with an en-suite bathroom. 5 miles north of the village of Spean Bridge towards Inverness, it is signposted on the left, along a wooded drive. Guests have use of own sitting room, overlooking Loch Lochy in 50 acres of superb woodland of rhododendron & azaleas. Fishing from the private beach & rowing boats, & hard tennis court. Children over 8 welcome.

£22.00 to £22.00 — Y — N — N

Isle of Bute

Donald Cameron & William Jeffery
Ardmory House Hotel & Restaurant
Ardmory Road
Ardbeg PA20 0PG
Tel: (01700) 502346
Fax 01700 505596
Open: ALL YEAR
Map Ref No. 30

Nearest Road: A.844
Built in 1833, Ardmory House sits in its own grounds just over a mile from Rothesay town centre & commands an outstanding view over the bay, Firth of Clyde & Loch Striven. All bedrooms have en-suite facilities, colour T.V., 'phone, radio/alarm clock, hospitality tray, electric blankets & hairdryer. (Bedrooms & restaurant are non-smoking.) Ardmory House Hotel is an ideal base for a relaxing break in this lovely part of Scotland.
E-mail: ardmory.house.hotel@dial.pipex.com

£37.50 to £47.50 — Y — Y — Y
VISA: M'CARD: AMEX:

Isle of Skye

Jane & Anthony Wilcken
Corry Lodge
Broadford
IV49 9AA
Tel: (01471) 822235
Fax 01471 822318
Open: MAR - OCT
Map Ref No. 31

Nearest Road: A.87
Corry Lodge, on the Isle of Skye, is a most attractive period house dating from the late 18th century. It has a fine open outlook over Broadford bay, but with a sheltered location, & approximately 1,150 metres of unspoilt sea frontage. There are 4 comfortable & tastefully furnished bedrooms, each with en-suite bathroom, radio, colour T.V. & tea/coffee-making facilities. Corry Lodge forms an ideal base from which to tour the island either by car or bicycle, or on foot.

£25.00 to £30.00 — Y — Y — Y
VISA: M'CARD:

Ashcroft Farmhouse. East Calder.

Scotland
Isle of Skye & Lothian

		rate £ from - to per person	children taken	evening meals	animals taken
Paul & Cathie Booth **Glenview Inn** **& Restaurant** **Culnacnoc** **Staffin IV51 9JH** **Tel: (01470) 562248** **Fax 01470 562211** **Open: MAR - OCT** **Map Ref No. 32**	Nearest Road: A.855 A traditional island house lying between Trotternish Ridge & the sea & ideally situated for exploring North Skye. All the bedrooms have private facilities & are individually decorated, warm & comfortable, with tea/coffee-making facilities. Glenview offers a relaxed & friendly atmosphere & the best of Scotland's varied larder. Only fresh food is used to create a menu including traditional, ethnic & vegetarian specialities. Glenview is an excellent base for a relaxing break.	£25.00 to £35.00 VISA: M'CARD:	Y	Y	Y
Jon & Ros Wathen **Talisker House** **Talisker** **IV47 8SF** **Tel: (01478) 640245** **Fax 01478 640214** **Open: Mid MAR - OCT** **Map Ref No. 33**	Nearest Road: A.863 Set on Skye's ruggedly beautiful west coast, Talisker House welcomes visitors today as it welcomed Johnson & Boswell during their historic Hebridean tour of 1773. With its fine trees & garden, it offers superb views to the sea & currently accommodates 4 couples in spacious & elegantly appointed comfort. Meals feature the best of local produce, & are complemented by carefully selected wines. **E-mail: jon-and-ros.wathen@virgin.net**	£40.00 to £54.00 VISA: M'CARD:	Y	Y	N

Lothian

		rate £ from - to per person	children taken	evening meals	animals taken
Derek & Elizabeth Scott **Ashcroft Farmhouse** **East Calder** **Edinburgh** **EH53 0ET** **Tel: (01506) 881810** **Fax 01506 884327** **Open: ALL YEAR** **Map Ref No. 34**	Nearest Road: A.71 New farmhouse set in beautifully landscaped gardens, enjoying lovely views of the surrounding farmland. Only 10 miles from Edinburgh city centre, 5 miles from the airport, city bypass, M.8/M.9, Ingliston & Livingston. Parking. Bedrooms, including a 4-poster, are attractively furnished in pine with co-ordinating fabrics. Regular bus/train service to city centre (20 mins), so no parking problems! Choice of breakfasts with home-made sausage, smoked salmon, kippers, local produce & even whisky marmalade. Children over 3. **E-mail: ashcroftfa@aol.com**	£25.00 to £40.00 *see PHOTO over* *p. 538* VISA: M'CARD: AMEX:	Y	N	N
Jake & Gwen Scott **The Glebe House** **Law Road** **North Berwick** **EH39 4PL** **Tel: (01620) 892608** **Fax 01620 892608** **Open: ALL YEAR (Excl. Xmas & New Year)** **Map Ref No. 35**	Nearest Road: A.198 A beautiful listed Georgian manse situated in secluded grounds in the centre of historic North Berwick. It is elegantly furnished with many fine original features. Bedrooms are decorated to a high standard (1 with 4-poster bed). Edinburgh is 30 mins' by car, or there is a regular train service to the heart of the city. Airport is 40 mins away. Many places of interest nearby including castles, museums & a distillery. 13 golf courses within 20 mins' drive, such as Muirfield & Gullane. **E-mail: J.A.Scott@Tesco.net**	£30.00 to £35.00	Y	N	N

Visit our website at:
http://www.bestbandb.co.uk

Ardconnel House. Grantown–on–Spey.

Scotland
Morayshire & Perthshire

Column headers (rotated): rate £ from - to per person | children taken | evening meals | animals taken

		rate £ from - to per person	children taken	evening meals	animals taken
Michel & Barbara Bouchard **Ardconnel House** Woodlands Terrace Grantown-on-Spey PH26 3JU Tel: (01479) 872104 Fax 01479 872104 Open: APR - OCT Map Ref No. 36	Nearest Road: A.95 Built in 1890, during the Victorian era of elegance, Ardconnel House stands in its own spacious grounds overlooking a glorious pine forest, Lochan & Cromdale Hills. 6 bedrooms are en-suite, with quality beds, colour T.V., hairdryer & welcome tray, & are charmingly decorated. A superb 4-poster bedroom. Excellent home cooking is complemented by a well-selected, modestly priced wine list. Taste of Scotland selected member. Children over 8 years. E-mail: ardconnel.grantown@virgin.net	£25.00 to £32.00 🚭 *see PHOTO over* *p. 540* VISA: M'CARD:	Y	Y	N

Perthshire

		rate £ from - to per person	children taken	evening meals	animals taken
Kenneth & Nicolette Lumsden **Marlee House** Kinloch Blairgowrie PH10 6SD Tel: (01250) 884216 Open: ALL YEAR Map Ref No. 37	Nearest Road: A.923 This pretty 16th-century manor house is set in extensive grounds by Marlee Loch which holds one of the largest wintering populations of Grey-lag geese in Britain. The house offers an informal country-house atmosphere with log fires in winter. The charming bedrooms have central heating & en-suite bathrooms. An ideal base for golf, fishing & skiing or simply to rest on your way, in elegant & comfortable surroundings. Children over 12 years welcome.	£30.00 to £40.00	Y	N	N
Gordon & Cherry Gunn **Creagan House** Restaurant with Accommodation, Strathyre Callander FK18 8ND Tel: (01877) 384638 Fax 01877 384319 Open: MAR - JAN Map Ref No. 38	Nearest Road: A.84 A peaceful little gem of comfort surrounded by beautiful scenery. Accommodation is in 5 charming bedrooms with many thoughtful extras & a growing collection of antiques. Friendly perfection is your hosts aim. The baronial dining hall helps make each evening a special occasion, using meat from Perthshire, fruits & vegetables grown locally, herbs from the garden, all complemented by fine wines. Creagan House is the perfect spot for a relaxing break.	£40.00 to £50.00 VISA: M'CARD: AMEX:	Y	Y	Y
Roger McDonald **Allt-Chaorain House** Inverherive Crianlarich FK20 8RU Tel: (01838) 300283 Fax 01838 300238 Open: APR - OCT Map Ref No. 39	Nearest Road: A.82 Allt-Chaorain House is a small family hotel situated in an elevated position, with commanding views of Ben More & Strathfillian from the south-facing sun lounge. Accommodation is in 6 comfortable & tastefully furnished bedrooms, all with en-suite facilities. 'Taste of Scotland' home cooking & packed lunches available on request. The friendly & relaxing atmosphere will unwind you as you sit by the log fire after walking, fishing or touring the central Highlands.	£20.00 to £30.00 🚭 *see PHOTO over* *p. 542* VISA: M'CARD: AMEX:	N	Y	Y

When booking your accommodation please mention
The Best Bed & Breakfast

Allt-Chaorain Country House. Crainlarich.

Scotland
Perthshire

		rate £ from - to per person	children taken	evening meals	animals taken
Peter & Daisy Ferries **The Lodge House** Crianlarich FK20 8RU Tel: (01838) 300276 Open: ALL YEAR Map Ref No. 39	Nearest Road: A.82 Although just by the roadside, The Lodge is secluded & all rooms enjoy an excellent view of the surrounding hills & glens. With only 6 rooms, your hosts aim to provide a personal service & compliment this with good Scottish home-cooking. In the small, informal bar, there is an extensive selection of malts for guests to enjoy both before & after dinner. The Lodge House is the perfect location for a relaxing break. VISA: M'CARD:	£25.00 to £40.00	Y	Y	Y
Janice & Sandy Chisholm **Tigh Na Struith** **Guest House** Crianlarich FK20 8RU Tel: (01838) 300235 Fax 01838 300268 Open: MAR - OCT Map Ref No. 39	Nearest Road: A.82 Alongside the River Fillan, & 200 yds from the main road, this friendly family home guarantees a quiet night's sleep. In the same hands for 15 years, this guest house has earned itself high praise for realistic prices together with clean, smoke-free accommodation. Still the best value for money, as awarded in 1984 by the Guild of Travel Writers. All rooms with h/c, colour T.V., tea/coffee-making, central heating & superb views. Party-goers please note: no licence.	£16.00 to £22.00	Y	N	Y
Fiona J. R. Graham **Mackeanston House** Doune FK16 6AX Tel: (01786) 850213 Fax 01786 850414 Open: ALL YEAR Map Ref No. 40	Nearest Road: A.84 Here you will find a touch of luxury in a peaceful rural setting. A 17th-century family home with stylish en-suite bedrooms set in a mature garden looking south to Stirling Castle & the Wallace monument, within sight of Rob Roy country & the Trossachs. 1 hr's drive from Glasgow, Perth & Edinburgh & easy reach of airports. Home-baked bread, fresh fruit & vegetables from the garden feature in gourmet menus. A pretty traditional cottage is available as an annexe. E-mail: mackean.house@cwcom.net *see PHOTO over* *p. 544*	£30.00 to £35.00	Y	Y	Y
Patricia Buxton **Bheinne Mhor** Perth Road Birnam Dunkeld PH8 0DH Tel: (01350) 727779 Open: FEB - NOV Map Ref No. 37	Nearest Road: A.9 A warm welcome awaits you at this comfortable, Victorian, detached house, with turret & private garden, ideally situated for lovely walks both in Macbeth's Birnam Woods & alongside the rivers Tay & Braan. Many places of historic interest & beauty nearby, including Dunkeld Cathedral, the Scottish N.T.'s 'The Hermitage' & the Loch of Lowes Wildlife Reserve. Boundless opportunities for anglers & golfers. 3 en-suite/private bedrooms with modern amenities. E-mail: p.buxton@ukonline.co.uk VISA: M'CARD:	£22.00 to £25.00	N	N	N
Alison & Ian Niven **Gloagburn Farm** Tibbermore Perth PH1 1QL Tel: (01738) 840228 Fax 01738 840228 Open: ALL YEAR Map Ref No. 42	Nearest Road: A.9 A spacious & attractively furnished family farmhouse set on a 450-acre working farm in beautiful open countryside. There are 3 stylish bedrooms with pretty linens, 2 with excellent private bathrooms. Suppers available by prior arrangement. Full breakfast is served, including home-made preserves & home-produced fresh eggs. Within 3 miles of the A.9, & within easy reach of many golf courses & sites of historic interest. A relaxed & friendly home. Children over 8 years welcome. VISA: M'CARD: AMEX:	£26.00 to £28.00	Y	N	N

Mackeanston House. Doune .

Scotland
Perthshire

		rate £ from - to per person	children taken	evening meals	animals taken
D. C. Straker **Dupplin Castle** **Aberdalgie** **Perth** **PH2 0PY** **Tel: (01738) 623224** **Fax 01738 444140** **Open: ALL YEAR** **Map Ref No. 43**	Nearest Road: A.9 Dupplin, a rare mid-20th-century Scottish mansion, stands in 30 acres of private parkland, with views over the River Earn valley to the hills beyond. Bedrooms are individually appointed with en-suite facilities. It is a country house of the highest quality, with all the sophistication & relaxed informality of an old-fashioned house party. Shooting, fishing & golf are within easy reach, & available from Dupplin by arrangement. Perth 15 mins' drive. Edinburgh & Glasgow 1 hour. Children over 12. Animals by arrangement.	£55.00 to £110.00 VISA: M'CARD:	Y	Y	Y
Tricia & John Stiell **Kinnaird Guest House** **5 Marshall Place** **Perth PH2 8AH** **Tel: (01738) 628021** **Fax 01738 444056** **Open: ALL YEAR** **Map Ref No. 44**	Nearest Road: A.85, M.90 Would you like to relax in comfort? Then the warm, friendly atmosphere at Kinnaird is just the place. John & Tricia aim for high standards & traditional home comforts & cater for individual needs. Beautifully situated overlooking a leafy park to the south, & the charming town centre is within easy walking distance. Buses & trains are also within easy reach. An ideal base for exploring this lovely region & many historical attractions.	£23.00 to £££ 🚭 VISA: M'CARD:	N	N	N
Elizabeth Sanderson **Tigh Dornie** **Aldclune** **Killiecrankie** **Pitlochry PH16 5LR** **Tel: (01796) 473276** **Fax 01796 473276** **Open: ALL YEAR** **Map Ref No. 45**	Nearest Road: A.9 Tigh Dornie is situated amid beautiful Perthshire scenery, approx. 5 miles north of Pitlochry. Offering attractive accommodation in 3 very comfortable & tastefully furnished guest bedrooms, each with an en-suite bathroom, T.V. & tea/coffee-making facilities. A warm & friendly welcome is assured from your hosts, who will ensure that your stay is a memorable one. An ideal spot for touring Scotland. Parking. Children over 10.	£22.00 to £24.00 🚭	N	N	N
Mrs Sue Mathieson **Easter Dunfallandy** **Country House B & B** **Logierait Road** **Pitlochry PH16 5NA** **Tel: (01796) 474128** **Fax 01796 473994** **Open: ALL YEAR (Excl. Xmas & New Year)** **Map Ref No. 45**	Nearest Road: A.9 A delightful Victorian country house quietly situated 2 miles south of Pitlochry, off the road to Logierait with wonderful views. 3 twin/double rooms with en-suite bath/shower, T.V. & complimentary toiletries. Each room individually decorated & furnished. Breakfast includes porridge made from local stoneground oats, fresh cream & heather honey & scrambled free-range eggs with cream & smoked salmon - delicious! An elegant home, perfectly situated for a relaxing break. **E-mail: info@westlandshotel.co.uk**	£27.00 to £27.00 🚭 *see PHOTO over* *p. 546*	N	N	N

Visit our website at:
http://www.bestbandb.co.uk

Easter Dunfallandy Country House. Pitlochry.

Scotland
Renfrewshire (Glasgow) & Ross-shire

		rate £ from - to per person	children taken	evening meals	animals taken
Mrs Fiona Allison **New Borland** **Glasgow Road** **Eaglesham** **Glasgow** **G76 0DN** **Tel: (01355) 302051** **Fax 01355 302051** **Open: ALL YEAR** **Map Ref No. 46**	Nearest Road: A.77, A.726 Near the picturesque village of Eaglesham, yet only 9 miles from Glasgow, a warm Scottish welcome is assured at this converted barn. 2 twin rooms (en-suite) & 2 single rooms sharing a bathroom. All rooms have T.V., radio & hostess tray, & have been refurbished to a high standard. Lounge (log fire) & games room Hearty Scottish breakfasts are served in the dining room. Convenient for Glasgow, M.74, Loch Lomond, The Trossachs, Burns Country & the Burrell. Golf & fishing nearby. Private parking. Children over 12. **E-mail: newborland@dial.pipex.com**	£22.50 to £25.00 🚭	Y	N	N
Janet Anderson **East Lochhead** **Largs Road** **Lochwinnoch** **PA12 4DX** **Tel: (01505) 842610** **Fax 01505 842610** **Open: ALL YEAR** **Map Ref No. 47**	Nearest Road: A.760 East Lochhead is a large 100-year-old Scottish farmhouse commanding beautiful views to the south east over Barr Loch & the Renfrewshire hills. 2 beautifully furnished bedrooms with panoramic views, an en-suite/private bathroom, T.V. & tea/coffee facilities. Janet is an enthusiastic cook & breakfast & dinner are delicious. (Vegetarian & special diets catered for.) East Lochhead is an ideal base for visiting Glasgow & touring Ayrshire, the Clyde coast, the Trossachs (Rob Roy country) & Loch Lomond. **E-mail: winnoch@aol.com**	£32.00 to £32.00 🚭 VISA: M'CARD: AMEX:	Y	Y	Y

Ross-shire

		rate £ from - to per person	children taken	evening meals	animals taken
Ms Anne Kempthorne **Duich House** **Letterfearn** **Glenshiel** **IV40 8HS** **Tel: (01599) 555259** **Fax 01599 555259** **Open: ALL YEAR (Excl. Xmas & New Year)** **Map Ref No. 48**	Nearest Road: A.87 A warm welcome & personal service is assured from your hosts at Duich House. A finely furnished 1800s home with beautifully appointed bedrooms & a log fire in the lounge. Nearby is Eilean Donan Castle, other historical sites, wild mammals, birds, seals & otters, & all around there is superb walking. There are outstanding loch & mountain views. Duich House is a perfect base for exploring north-west Scotland & the Isle of Skye. Evening meals & animals by arrangement. **E-mail: duich@cwcom.net**	£33.00 to £35.00 🚭	N	Y	N
John & Ariana Franchi **The Manse** **Innes Street** **Plockton** **IV52 8TW** **Tel: (01599) 544442** **Fax 01599 544442** **Open: ALL YEAR** **Map Ref No. 49**	Nearest Road: A.87 Situated in the picturesque village of Plockton, called 'the Jewel of the Highlands'. The T.V. series 'Hamish Macbeth' was filmed in & around the village. The Manse was converted from the Free Church of Scotland Manse, & it now offers a range of accommodation - a large Victorian suite with bathroom & antiques/Chesterfield etc., a modern 4-poster room with en-suite shower room, & 2 smaller rooms with handbasins, tea/coffee & T.V.. All rooms have a view of Loch Carron. **E-mail: JFran97271@aol.com**	£20.00 to £30.00	Y	N	Y

Scotland
Roxburghshire & Stirlingshire

		rate £ from - to per person	children taken	evening meals	animals taken
Mrs H. Irvine **Froylehurst** **Friars** **Jedburgh** **TD8 6BN** **Tel: (01835) 862477** **Fax 01835 862477** **Open: MAR - NOV** **Map Ref No. 50**	Nearest Road: A.68 An attractive Grade 'B' listed late-Victorian sandstone townhouse retaining most original features, offering 4 comfortable guest bedrooms & residents lounge. All rooms have washbasins with h & c, tea/coffee-making facilities, colour T.V. & radio/alarms. Two shared bathrooms & toilets. Situated in a large garden overlooking the town in a quiet residential area but within 2 mins' walking distance of many good pubs & restaurants. Ample parking. Children over 5 welcome. An ideal base from which to explore this region.	£18.00 to £20.00	Y	N	N
Mrs Betty Smith **Whitehill Farm** **Nenthorn** **Kelso** **TD5 7RZ** **Tel: (01573) 470203** **Fax 01573 470203** **Open: ALL YEAR (Excl.** **Xmas & New Year)** **Map Ref No. 51**	Nearest Road: A.6089 A comfortable & peaceful farmhouse with a large garden standing on a 455-acre, mixed farm 4 miles from Kelso. 4 attractive bedrooms - 2 single & 2 twin, 1 with en-suite shower room - have superb views over rolling countryside. All have central heating & washbasins. A pleasant sitting room with log fire is available to guests. An ideal base for touring this glorious region; maps available. Good home cooking. Dinner by arrangement. (Smoking restricted.) **E-mail: besmith@whitehillfarm.freeserve.co.uk**	£22.00 to £23.00	Y	Y	Y

Stirlingshire

Laird Andrew Haslam **Culcreuch Castle &** **Country Park** **Fintry** **Loch Lomond** **Stirling** **G63 0LW** **Tel: (01360) 860555** **Fax 01360 860556** **Open: ALL YEAR** **Map Ref No. 52**	Nearest Road: A.811 Retreat to 700 years of history at magical Culcreuch, the ancestral fortalice & clan castle of the Galbraiths, home of the Barons of Culcreuch, & now a country house hotel where the Laird and his family extend an hospitable welcome. Set in 1,600 spectacular acres, yet only 19 miles from central Glasgow & 17 miles from Stirling. 8 handsome, well-appointed bedrooms with en-suite or private facilities, 4-poster bedroom supplement of £12 per person per night. Elegant period-style decor & antiques, log fires, the romance of dining by candlelight. Prices £43.00 Apr & Oct, £48.00 May-Sept p.p.p.n..	£38.00 to £65.00 *see PHOTO over* *p. 549* VISA: M'CARD: AMEX:	Y	Y	N

When booking your accommodation please mention
The Best Bed & Breakfast

Culcreuch Castle.   Fintry.

Wales

Wales is a small country with landscapes of intense beauty. In the north are the massive mountains of the Snowdonia National Park, split by chasms & narrow passes, & bounded by quiet vales & moorland. The Lleyn peninsula & the Isle of Anglesey have lovely remote coastlines.

Forests, hills & lakeland form the scenery of Mid Wales, with the great arc of Cardigan Bay in the west.

To the south there is fertile farming land in the Vale of Glamorgan, mountains & high plateaux in the Brecon Beacons, & also the industrial valleys. The coastline forms two peninsulas, around Pembroke & the Gower.

Welsh, the oldest living language of Europe is spoken & used, most obviously in the north, & is enjoying a resurgence in the number of its speakers.

From Taliesin, the 6th century Celtic poet, to Dylan Thomas, Wales has inspired poetry & song. Every August, at the Royal National Eisteddfod, thousands gather to compete as singers, musicians & poets, or to listen & learn. In the small town of Llangollen, there is an International Music Eisteddfod for a week every July

North Wales.

North Wales is chiefly renowned for the 850 miles of the Snowdonia National Park. It is a land of mountains & lakes, rivers & waterfalls & deep

The Snowdon Mountain Railway.

glacier valleys. The scenery is justly popular with walkers & pony-trekkers, but the Snowdon Mountain Railway provides easy access to the summit of the highest mountain in the range with views over the "roof of Wales".

Within miles of this wild highland landscape is a coastline of smooth beaches & little fishing villages.

Barmouth has mountain scenery on its doorstep & miles of golden sands & estuary walks. Bangor & Llandudno are popular resort towns.

The Lleyn peninsula reaches west & is an area of great charm. Abersoch is a dinghy & windsurfing centre with safe sandy beaches. In the Middle Ages pilgrims would come to visit Bardsey, the Isle of 20,000 saints, just off Aberdaron, at the tip of the peninsula.

The Isle of Anglesey is linked to the mainland by the handsome Menai Straits Suspension Bridge. Beaumaris has a 13th century castle & many other fine buildings in its historic town centre.

Historically North Wales is a fiercely independent land where powerful local lords resisted first the Romans & later the armies of the English Kings.

The coastline is studded with 13th century castles. Dramatically sited Harlech Castle, famed in fable & song, commands the town, & wide sweep of the coastline.

The great citadel of Edward I at Caernarfon comprises the castle & the encircling town walls. In 1969 it was the scene of the investiture of His Royal Highness Prince Charles as Prince of Wales.

There are elegant stately homes like Plas Newydd in Anglesey & Eriddig House near Wrexham, but it is the variety of domestic architecture that is most charming. The timber-frame buildings of the Border country are seen at their best in historic Ruthin set in the

Wales

beautiful Vale of Clwyd. Further west, the stone cottages of Snowdonia are built of large stones & roofed with the distinctive blue & green local slate. The low, snow-white cottages of Anglesey & the Lleyn Peninsula are typical of the "Atlantic Coast" architecture that can be found on all the western coasts of Europe. The houses are constructed of huge boulders with tiny windows & doors.

By contrast there is the marvellous fantasy of Portmeirion village. On a wooded peninsula between Harlech & Porthmadog, Sir Clough Williams Ellis created a perfect Italianate village with pastel coloured buildings, a town hall & luxury hotel.

Mid Wales

Mid Wales is farming country where people are outnumbered three to one by sheep. A flock of ewes, a lone shepherd & a Border Collie are a common sight on these green hills. Country towns like Old Radnor, Knighton & Montgomery with its castle ruin, have a timeless quality. The market towns of Rhyader, Lampeter & Dolgellau have their weekly livestock sales & annual agricultural festivals, the largest of which is the Royal Welsh Show at Builth Wells in July.

This is the background to the craft of weaving practised here for centuries. In the valley of the River Tefi & on an upper tributary of the Wye & the Irfon, there are tiny riverbank mills which produce the colourful Welsh plaid cloth.

Towards the Snowdonia National Park in the North, the land rises to the scale of true mountains. Mighty Cader Idris & the expanses of Plynlimon, once inaccessible to all but the shepherd & the mountaineer, are now popular centres for walking & pony trekking with well-signposted trails.

The line of the border with England is followed by a huge earth work of bank & ditch. This is Offa's Dyke, built by the King of Mercia around 750 A.D. to deter the Welsh from their incessant raids into his kingdom. Later the border was guarded by the castles at Hay-on-Wye, Builth Wells, Welshpool, & Chirk which date from mediaeval times.

North from Rhayader, lies the Dovey estuary & the historic town of Machynlleth. This is where Owain Glyndwr's parliament is thought to have met in 1404, & there is an exhibition about the Welsh leader in the building, believed to have been Parliament House.

Wales lost many fine religious houses during the Dissolution of the Monasteries under Henry VIII. The ruins at Cymer near Dolgellau & at Strata Florida were abbeys of the Cistercian order. However, many remote Parish Churches show evidence of the skills of mediaeval craftsmen with soaring columns & fine rood screens.

The Cambrian Coast (Cardigan Bay) has sand dunes to the north & cliffs to the south with sandy coves & miles of cliff walks.

Llangrannog Headland.

Aberystwyth is the main town of the region with two beaches & a yachting harbour, a Camera Obscura on the cliff top & some fine walks in the area. Water-skiing, windsurfing &

Wales

sailing are popular at Aberdovey, Aberaeron, New Quay, Tywyn & Barmouth & there are delightful little beaches further south at Aberporth, Tresaith or Llangrannog.

South Wales

South Wales is a region of scenic variety. The Pembrokeshire coastline has sheer cliffs, little coves & lovely beaches. Most of the area is National Park with an 80 mile foot path running along its length, passing pretty harbour villages like Solva & Broad Haven.

A great circle of Norman Castles stands guard over South Pembrokeshire, Roch, Haverfordwest, Tenby, Carew, Pembroke & Manorbier.

The northern headland of Saint

Tenby.

Brides Bay is the most westerly point in the country & at the centre of a tiny village stands the Cathedral of Saint David, the Patron Saint of Wales. At Bosherton near Saint Govans Head, there is a tiny chapel hidden in a cleft in the massive limestone cliffs.

The Preseli Hills hold the vast prehistoric burial chambers of Pentre Ifan, & the same mountains provided the great blue stones used at faraway Stonehenge.

Laugharne is the village where Dylan Thomas lived & worked in what was a boat-house & is now a museum.

In the valleys, towns like Merthyr Tydfil, Ebbw Vale & Treorchy were in the forefront of the boom years of the Industrial Revolution. Now the heavy industries are fast declining & the ravages of the indiscriminate mining & belching smoke of the blast furnaces are disappearing. The famous Male Voice Choirs & the love of rugby football survives.

The Vale of Glamorgan is a rural area with pretty villages. Beyond here the land rises steeply to the high wild moorlands & hill farms of the Brecon Beacons National Park & the Black Mountains, lovely areas for walking & pony trekking.

The Wye Valley leads down to Chepstow & here set amidst the beautiful woodlands is the ruin of the Great Abbey of Tintern, founded in 1131 by the Cistercian Order.

Swansea has a strong sea-faring tradition maintained by its new Marine Quarter - marina, waterfront village, restaurants, art gallery & theatre.

Cardiff, the capital of Wales, is a pleasant city with acres of parkland, the lovely River Taff, & a great castle, as well as a new civic centre, two theatres & the ultra-modern St. David's Concert Hall. It is the home of the Welsh National Opera & here also is the National Stadium where the singing of the rugby crowd on a Saturday afternoon is a treat.

Pony Trekking

Wales

Wales Gazeteer

Areas of Outstanding Natural Beauty
The Pembrokeshire Coast. The Brecon Beacons. Snowdonia. Gower.'

Historic Houses & Castles

Cardiff Castle - Cardiff
Built on a Roman site in the 11th century.
Caerphilly Castle - Caerphilly
13th century fortress.
Chirk Castle - Nr. Wrexham
14th century Border Castle. Lovely gardens.
Coity Castle - Coity
Mediaeval stronghold - three storied round tower.
Gwydir Castle - Nr. Lanrwst
Royal residence in past days - wonderful Tudor furnishings. Gardens with peacocks.
Penrhyn Castle - Bangor
Neo-Norman architecture 19th century - large grounds with museum & exhibitions. Victorian garden.
Picton Castle - Haverfordwest
12th century - lived in by the same family continuously. Fine gardens.
Caernarfon Castle - Caernarfon
13th century - castle of great importance to Edward I.
Conway Castle - Conwy
13th century - one of Edward I's chain of castles.
Powis Castle - Welshpool
14th century - reconstruction work in 17th century.
Murals, furnishings, tapestries & paintings, terraced gardens.
Pembroke Castle - Pembroke
12th century Norman castle with huge keep & immense walls.
Birthplace of Henry VII.
Plas Newydd - Isle of Anglesey
18th century Gothic style house.
Home of the Marquis of Anglesey.
Stands on the edge of the Menai Strait looking across to the Snowdonia Range. Famous for the Rex Whistler murals.
The Tudor Merchant's House - Tenby
Built in 15th century.
Tretower Court & Castle - Crickhowell
Mediaeval - finest example in Wales.

Cathedrals & Churches

St. Asaph Cathedral
13th century - 19th century restoration. Smallest of Cathedrals in England & Wales.
Holywell (St. Winifred)
15th century well chapel & chamber - fine example.
St. Davids (St. David)
12th century Cathedral - splendid tower - oak roof to nave.
Gwent (St. Woolos)
Norman Cathedral - Gothic additions - 19th century restoration.
Abergavenny (St. Mary)
14th century church of 12th century Benedictine priory.
Llanengan (St. Engan)
Mediaeval church - very large with original roof & stalls 16th century tower.
Esyronen
17th century chapel, much original interior remaining.
Llangdegley (St. Tegla)
18th century Quaker meeting house - thatched roof - simple structure divided into schoolroom & meeting room.
Llandaff Cathedral (St. Peter & St. Paul)
Founded in 6th century - present building began in 12th century. Great damage suffered in bombing during war, restored with Epstein's famous figure of Christ.

Museums & Galleries

National Museum of Wales - Cardiff (also Turner House)
Geology, archaeology, zoology, botany, industry, & art exhibitions.
Welsh Folk Museum - St. Fagans Castle - Cardiff
13th century walls curtaining a 16th century house - now a most interesting & comprehensive folk museum.
County Museum - Carmarthen
Roman jewellery, gold, etc. Romano-British & Stone Age relics.
National Library of Wales - Aberystwyth
Records of Wales & Celtic areas. Great historical interest.
University College of Wales Gallery - AberystwythTravelling exhibitions of painting & sculpture.

Wales

Museum & Art Gallery - Newport
Specialist collection of English
watercolours - natural history, Roman
remains, etc.
Legionary Museum - Caerleon
Roman relics found on the site of
legionary fortress at Risca.
Nelson Museum - Monmouth
Interesting relics of Admiral Lord Nelson &
Lady Hamilton.
Bangor Art Gallery - Bangor
Exhibitions of contemporary paintings &
sculpture.
Bangor Museum of Welsh Antiquities -
Bangor
History of North Wales is shown. Splendid
exhibits of furniture, clothing, domestic
objects, etc. Also Roman antiquities.
Narrow Gauge Railway Museum - Tywyn
Rolling stock & exhibitions of narrow
gauge railways of U.K.
Museum of Childhood - Menai Bridge
Charming museum of dolls & toys &
children's things.

Brecknock Museum - Brecon
Natural history, archaeology, agriculture,
local history, etc.
Glynn Vivian Art Gallery & Museum -
Swansea
Ceramics, old & contemporary, British
paintings & drawings, sculpture, loan
exhibitions.
Stone Museum - Margam
Carved stones & crosses from pre-
historic times.
Plas Mawr - Conwy
A beautiful Elizabethan town mansion
house in its original condition. Now holds
the Royal Cambrain Academy of Art.

Historic Monuments

Rhuddlan Castle - Rhuddlan
13th century castle - interesting diamond
plan.
Valle Crucis Abbey - Llangollen
13th century Cistercian Abbey Church.

Cader Idris.

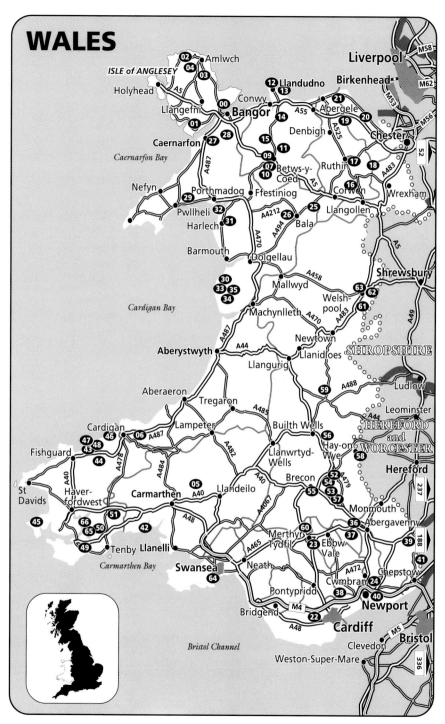

WALES

WALES

Map references

00 **Abas**
01 **M.Roberts**
02 **Hirst**
03 **Brown**
04 **Hughes**
05 **Dent**
06 **Humphreys**
07 **Betteney**
09 **Howard**
09 **D. Jones**
10 **Cutler**
11 **Pitman**
12 **Saunders**
13 **Grimwood**
14 **Marrow**
15 **Nichols**
16 **Harman**
17 **Spencer**
18 **Parry**
19 **A. Roberts**
20 **M. Jones**
21 **Steele-Mortimer**
22 **Renwick**
23 **Hurley**
24 **B. Watkins**
25 **Fullard**
26 **Cunningham**
27 **Bayles**
28 **Kettle**
29 **Murray**
30 **Smyth**
31 **Davies**
32 **Williams**
33 **Sylvester**
34 **Tregarthen**
35 **Corbett**
36 **Harris**
37 **Weatherill**
38 **Price**
39 **Harmston**
40 **C. Park**
41 **Stubbs**
42 **S. Evans**
43 **Cooper**
43 **Williams**
44 **Heard**
45 **Webber**
46 **Phillips**
47 **Rutherford**
48 **Onions**
49 **McHugh**
50 **Fielder**
51 **Gilder**
52 **Gray**
53 **Bradley**
54 **Cole**
55 **P. Jackson**
56 **N. Jones**
57 **C. Jackson**
58 **Roberts**
59 **Millan**
60 **K. Hurley**
61 **Bright**
62 **Thomas**
63 **S. Jones**
64 **Maybery**
65 **Moonie**
66 **Lort-Phillips**

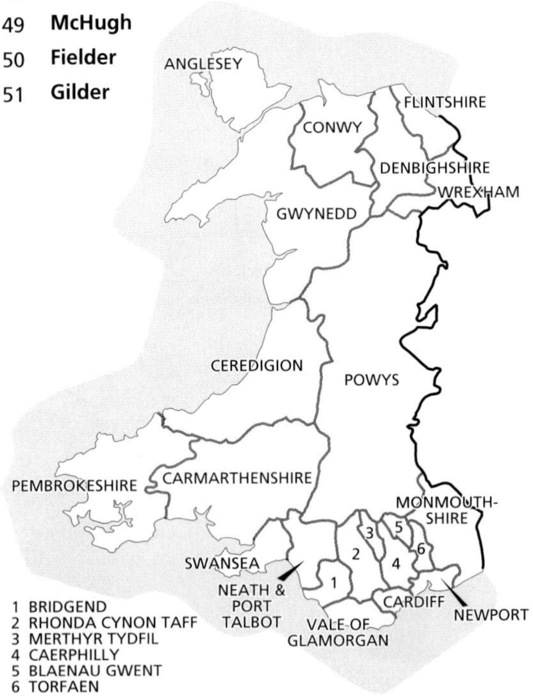

ANGLESEY
CONWY
FLINTSHIRE
DENBIGHSHIRE
WREXHAM
GWYNEDD
CEREDIGION
POWYS
PEMBROKESHIRE
CARMARTHENSHIRE
MONMOUTH-
SHIRE
SWANSEA
NEATH &
PORT
TALBOT
VALE OF
GLAMORGAN
CARDIFF
NEWPORT
1 BRIDGEND
2 RHONDA CYNON TAFF
3 MERTHYR TYDFIL
4 CAERPHILLY
5 BLAENAU GWENT
6 TORFAEN

Llwydiarth Fawr Farm. Anglesey.

Wales
Isle of Anglesey

	rate £ from - to per person	children taken	evening meals	animals taken
Ms. Rosemary Ann Abas **Bwthyn** **5 Brynafon** **Menai Bridge** **Isle of Anglesey LL59 5HA** **Tel: (01248) 713119** **Fax 01248 713119** **Open: ALL YEAR** **Map Ref No. 00**	Nearest Road: A.545 Bwthyn ('dear little house' in Welsh), offering character, comfort & genuine hospitality, is 1 minute from the beautiful Menai Strait, close by Telford's famous suspension bridge, 2 miles A.5/ A.55, Irish Ferry 40 mins. Ideal base for coast, castles & Snowdonia. 2 warm, tastefully fitted en-suite double rooms, each with power shower (& 1 with a bath), colour T.V., tea/coffee makers etc. Scrumptious home-cooking. Over 45's Special - 3 nights Dinner, Bed & Breakfast £79.00 p.p..	£15.00 to £18.00	N	Y	N
Marian Roberts **Plas Trefarthen** **Brynsiencyn** **Isle of Anglesey** **LL61 6SZ** **Tel: (01248) 430379** **Open: ALL YEAR (Excl. Xmas)** **Map Ref No. 01**	Nearest Road: A.4080 A beautiful Georgian house enjoying the most glorious position on the shore of the Menai Straits overlooking Snowdonia mountains & Carnafon Castle. Only 6 miles from the Menai Bridge which makes it ideal for touring Anglesey & the main-land, visiting local N.T. properties & beaches. Elegant bedrooms, some with en-suite bathrooms & all with colour T.V. & beverage facilities. Owned & run by well-known & international soprano Marian Roberts. Excellent self-catering for 6.	£20.00 to £22.00 VISA: M'CARD:	Y	N	N
Mrs G. P. Hirst **Hafod Country House** **Cemaes Bay** **Isle of Anglesey** **LL67 0DS** **Tel: (01407) 710500** **Open: MAR - OCT** **Map Ref No. 02**	Nearest Road: A.5025 A spacious Edwardian house set in an acre of beautiful gardens with wildlife pond, superb sea & mountain views. Peacefully situated on the out-skirts of Cemaes with its picturesque harbour & sandy beach. 3 delightful en-suite, fully-equipped bedrooms. Spacious drawing room with antiques & separate dining room to enjoy a superb break-fast. Homemade preserves, fresh juices when in season. Good pub fayre a short walk away. (M.I.H.Ec.) Licensed. Nearby golf, bird sanctu-ary, lake/sea fishing & wonderful headland walks.	£21.50 to £22.50	Y	N	N
Mrs Jane Bown **Drws Y Coed** **Llannerch-Y-Medd** **Isle of Anglesey** **LL71 8AD** **Tel: (01248) 470473** **Fax 01248 470473** **Open: ALL YEAR (Excl. Xmas)** **Map Ref No. 03**	Nearest Road: A.5025, A.5 Enjoy wonderful panoramic views of Snowdonia & countryside at this beautifully appointed farm-house on a 550-acre working beef, sheep & arable farm. It's situated in peaceful, wooded countryside in the centre of Anglesey. Tastefully decorated & furnished, superb en-suite bedrooms with all facilities. Inviting spacious lounge with antiques & log fire. Excellent breakfasts. Historic farmstead. Lovely private walks. 25 mins to Holyhead Port. A warm Welsh welcome assured.	£21.50 to £23.50 VISA: M'CARD:	Y	N	N
Margaret Hughes **Llwydiarth Fawr Farm** **Llanerchymedd** **Isle of Anglesey** **LL71 8DF** **Tel: (01248) 470321** **Tel: (01248) 470540** **Open: ALL YEAR** **Map Ref No. 04**	Nearest Road: A.5 Secluded Georgian mansion set in 800 acres of woodland & farmland, with lovely open views. Ideal touring base for the island's coastline, Snowdonia & North Wales coast. 5 delightfully furnished bedrooms with en-suite facilities & T.V., & 2 cottage suites. Full central heating, log fires. Enjoy a taste of Wales with delicious country cooking using farm & local produce. Personal attention & a warm Welsh welcome to guests, who will enjoy the scenic walks & private fishing. Convenient for Holyhead-to-Ireland crossings.	£25.00 to £25.00 *see PHOTO over* *p. 557* VISA: M'CARD:	Y	N	N

Plas Allt y Ferin. Nantgaredig.

Wales
Carmarthenshire, Ceredigion & Conwy

		rate £ from - to per person	children taken	evening meals	animals taken
Charlotte & Gerard Dent **Plas Alltyferin** **Pontargothi** **Nantgaredig, Carmarthen** **SA32 7PF** **Tel: (01267) 290662** **Fax 01267 290919** **Open: ALL YEAR (Excl. Xmas)** **Map Ref No. 05**	Nearest Road: A.40 A classic Georgian country house lying in the hills above the beautiful Towy Valley, overlooking a Norman hillfort & the River Cothi - famous for salmon & sea trout. 2 spacious twin bedrooms, each with an en-suite bathroom & stunning views, for guests who are welcomed as friends of the family. Antique furniture & log fires. Good local pubs & restaurants. Totally peaceful. Marvellous touring country for castles, beaches & rural Wales. 5 miles from the National Botanic Garden of Wales - opening 2000. Children over 10.	£22.50 to £25.00 *see PHOTO over* *p. 559*	Y	N	Y

Ceredigion

		rate £ from - to per person	children taken	evening meals	animals taken
G. B. & M. M. Humphreys **Penbontbren Farm Hotel** **Glynarthen** **Cardigan** **SA44 6PE** **Tel: (01239) 810248** **Fax 01239 811129** **Open: ALL YEAR** **Map Ref No. 06**	Nearest Road: A.487 Penbontbren is a rare kind of place: a hotel which offers a genuine taste of Wales accompanied by all the modern comforts. Barrie & Nan Humphreys are your welcoming hosts - & you stay quite literally at their home, for the hotel has been in Nan's family for 4 generations. The accommodation is in a row of converted farmyard barns which have been transformed into rooms finished to extremely high standards, with the full range of facilities. Perfect for a relaxing holiday, tucked away down a country lane & only a few miles from the sandy coves & headlands of Cardigan Bay.	£38.00 to £43.00 *see PHOTO over* *p. 561* VISA: M'CARD: AMEX:	Y	Y	Y

Conwy

		rate £ from - to per person	children taken	evening meals	animals taken
Marion & William Betteney **Bryn Afon Guest House** **Pentre Felin** **Betws-Y-Coed** **LL24 0BB** **Tel: (01690) 710403** **Fax 01690 710989** **Open: ALL YEAR** **Map Ref No. 07**	Nearest Road: A.5 A Victorian stone-built house situated on the banks of the River Llugwy overlooking the Pont-Y-Pair Bridge & waterfall. Well-appointed bedrooms with comfortable beds ensure a good night's sleep. Bryn Afon is central for all tourist attractions & many local walks through the forests. Drying facilities available. Parking for all guests on the premises & a good choice of restaurants within 5-10 mins' walking distance. **E-mail: W.BETTENEY@aol.com**	£18.00 to £26.00	Y	N	N
Kevin & Dianne Jones **Aberconwy House** **Lon Muriau** **Betws-Y-Coed** **LL24 0HD** **Tel: (01690) 710202** **Fax 01690 710800** **Open: ALL YEAR** **Map Ref No. 09**	Nearest Road: A.470 A high standard of comfort & friendly, helpful hosts await you at Aberconwy. This large Victorian home, located in a lovely position above the picturesque village of Betws-Y-Coed, has panoramic views of the Llugney Valley, mountains & the River Conway. Offering 8 very comfortable en-suite bedrooms, with T.V. & tea/coffee makers. Most also have wonderful views. A residents' T.V. lounge & garden are available. This is an ideal centre for touring, walking, fishing & golf. **E-mail: aberconwy@betws-y-coed.co.uk**	£20.00 to £26.00 VISA: M'CARD:	Y	N	Y

Penbontbren Farm Hotel. Glynarthen.

Tan Dinas. Betws-Y-Coed

	rate £ from - to per person	children taken	evening meals	animals taken

Ann Howard **Tan Dinas Country House** **Coed Cynhelier Road** **Betws-Y-Coed** **LL24 0BL** **Tel: (01690) 710635** **Fax 01690 710815** **Open: ALL YEAR** **Map Ref No. 09**	Nearest Road: A.5 A Victorian country house, offering peace, seclusion & a wonderful view. Surrounded by woodland yet only 500 yds from the village. Start with a delicious breakfast & finish your day with a candlelit dinner in the elegant dining room. Relax in the comfortable lounge or retire with a video or book to an attractive, individually furnished bedroom which is appointed for your comfort. Forest walks from house. Ideal touring centre. Ample parking. A delightful home.	£20.00 to £25.00 🚭 *see PHOTO over* *p. 562*	Y	Y	N
Modwena & Ian Cutler **Penmachno Hall** **Penmachno** **Betws-Y-Coed** **LL24 0PU** **Tel: (01690) 760207** **Fax 01690 760207** **Open: Mid JAN - Mid DEC** **Map Ref No. 10**	Nearest Road: A.5 Penmachno Hall was built as a rectory in 1862. Situated on the edge of the village in grounds of 2 1/2 acres, it is ideally located, being peaceful & secluded but enjoying easy access to all the various attractions of North Wales. The aim is to provide an informal, cosy atmosphere, with the very best of home cooking. Accommodation is in 4 delightful en-suite bedrooms. This is the perfect spot for a relaxing break.	£28.00 to £33.00 VISA: M'CARD:	Y	Y	N
P. K. & J. C. Pitman **Tan-Y-Foel Country House Hotel** **Capel Garmon** **Betws-Y-Coed LL26 0RE** **Tel: (01690) 710507** **Fax 01690 710681** **Open: ALL YEAR (Excl. Xmas)** **Map Ref No. 11**	Nearest Road: A.470, A.5 High above the Conwy valley steeped in history, myths & magic lies this Welsh stone country house, transformed inside to sparkle with vibrant fabrics & modern paintwork techniques, a very unique hotel for the area. Top honours have been received for the restaurant's culinary skills. Set in the National Park, only 20 mins' drive from Mount Snowdon. Children over 7 years. **E-mail: tanyfoel@wiss.com.uk**	£38.00 to £75.00 🚭 *see PHOTO over* *p. 564* VISA: M'CARD: AMEX:	Y	Y	N
Peter & Kerry Saunders **Tan Lan Hotel** **Great Ormes Road** **Llandudno** **LL30 2AR** **Tel: (01492) 860221** **Fax 01492 870219** **Open: ALL YEAR** **Map Ref No. 12**	Nearest Road: A.55, A.546 Tan Lan is a warm, welcoming hotel on the edge of town, close to the sea. Service is attentive & is combined with a friendly atmosphere in which you can feel genuinely at home. The hotel is renowned for its excellent food. There are 17 comfortably furnished & well-equipped en-suite rooms, 2 are non-smoking, together with a restaurant & cosy lounge bar. Ideal base to explore castles, Snowdonia & also experience a classic Victorian seaside resort.	£21.00 to £37.00 VISA: M'CARD:	Y	Y	Y
Geoffrey & Carol Grimwood **Bryn-y-Bia Lodge Hotel** **Bryn-y-Bia Road** **Craigside** **Llandudno LL30 3AS** **Tel: (01492) 549644** **Fax 01492 549644** **Open: FEB- NOV** **Map Ref No. 13**	Nearest Road: A.55 A charming spacious Victorian house, Bryn-y-Bia (Magpie Hill) is set in a large & secluded walled garden with parking for every guest. With a sunny aspect it overlooks Llandudno & the sea. A large dining room serves an a la carte breakfast & a delightful guests lounge is avilable for use during the day (books & games supplied). All rooms are en-suite with colour T.V. & hospitality tray. **E-mail: carol@brynybia.demon.co.uk**	£24.00 to £34.00 VISA: M'CARD:	Y	Y	Y

Tan-y-Foel Country House Hotel. Capel Garmon.

		rate £ from - to per person	children taken	evening meals	animals taken

Jack & Mary Marrow
Firs Cottage
Maenan
Llanrwst
LL26 0YR
Tel: (01492) 660244
Open: ALL YEAR (Excl. Xmas)
Map Ref No. 14

Nearest Road: A.470
A 17th-century Welsh cottage & comfortable family home, situated in the beautiful Conway Valley, with excellent views to the hills. Firs Cottage offers 3 attractively furnished rooms, as well as a lovely garden in which to relax & plan visits to the many North Wales attractions, which are all within easy reach. Good food & a warm Welsh welcome will make for a memorable holiday.

£16.50 to £20.00 — Y N Y

Rosina & Christopher Nichols
Hafod Country Hotel
Trefriw
LL27 0RQ
Tel: (01492) 640029
Fax 01492 641351
Open: FEB - DEC
Map Ref No. 15

Nearest Road: A.5
Set in the lovely Conwy Valley, on the edge of Snowdonia, Yr Hafod (The Summer Dwelling) is a former 17th-century farmhouse, extensively furnished with antiques. The bedrooms each offer a highly individual sense of style. Warm hospitality at this award-winning hotel is complimented by outstanding food, while drinks can be enjoyed in the oak-panelled bar or in front of a log fire. Children over 11.

£22.00 to £40.00 — Y Y Y

VISA: M'CARD: AMEX:

Denbighshire

Mrs Mary Harman
Dee Farm
Rhewl
Llangollen
LL20 7YT
Tel: (01978) 861598
Fax 01978 861598
Open: MAR - NOV
Map Ref No. 16

Nearest Road: A.5
Dee Farm is set high in the hamlet of Rhewl, with the River Dee running just below the garden. This charming old stone farmhouse was once a slate-miners inn & now offers attractive & very comfortable accommodtion. 2 pleasant twin-bedded rooms, each with an en-suite/private bathroom. (1 of the rooms has high beams & was the original hayloft, the other has a view over the river & the hills beyond.) Dinner (by arrangement) includes vegetables & herbs from the garden when possible. An ideal base for the attractions of Llangollen.

£20.00 to £23.00 — Y Y Y

Jen & Bert Spencer
Eyarth Station
Llanfair D. C.
Ruthin
LL15 2EE
Tel: (01824) 703643
Fax 01824 707464
Open: ALL YEAR
Map Ref No. 17

Nearest Road: A.525
A warm & friendly reception awaits the visitor to Eyarth Station. A super, converted, former railway station located in the beautiful countryside of the Vale of Clwyd. 6 bedrooms, all en-suite. A comfortable T.V. lounge, & guests are welcome to use the garden, sun patio & outdoor heated pool. Conveniently located for the many historic towns in the region including Conwy, Caernarfon & Ruthin & their castles, with medieval banquet 2 minutes' drive away. The Roman town of Chester is also within driving distance. 1987 winner of Best Bed & Breakfast Award.

£22.00 to £24.00 — Y Y Y

see PHOTO over
p. 566

VISA: M'CARD:

Visit our website at:
http://www.bestbandb.co.uk

Eyarth Station.   Llanfair D.C.

		rate £ from - to per person	children taken	evening meals	animals taken
Elizabeth A. Parry **Llainwen Ucha** **Pentre Celyn** **Ruthin** **LL15 2HL** **Tel: (01978) 790253** **Open: ALL YEAR** **Map Ref No. 18**	Nearest Road: A.525 A working farm set in 130 acres overlooking the very beautiful Vale of Clwyd. Offering 3 pleasantly decorated rooms with modern amenities, & accommodating up to 6 persons. All rooms are centrally heated. Good home cooking made with fresh local produce; vegetarian meals on request. Conveniently situated for visiting Chester, Llangollen, Snowdonia & the coast. Offa's Dyke & fishing nearby. Medieval banquets are held at Ruthin Castle throughout the year.	£17.00 to £18.00	Y	Y	N
Anwen Roberts **Bach-Y-Graig** **Tremeirchion** **St. Asaph** **LL17 0UH** **Tel: (01745) 730627** **Fax 01745 730627** **Open: ALL YEAR** **Map Ref No. 19**	Nearest Road: A.55, A.525 A super 16th-century farmhouse nestling at the foot of the Clwydian range, with undisturbed views of the surrounding countryside. Walk a 40-acre mediaeval woodland trail on the farm where the royal Black Prince once hunted, & enjoy the wealth of rare plants & flowers. All rooms are en-suite/private, with tea/coffee, radio/alarms & colour T.V.. A lounge with colour T.V., an inglenook with log fires (during the colder part of the season) & central heating. Central for Chester, Snowdonia & coastal resorts.	£20.00 to £££	Y	N	N

Flintshire

		rate £ from - to per person	children taken	evening meals	animals taken
Mrs M. Jones **Greenhill Farm** **Bryn Celyn** **Holywell** **CH8 7QF** **Tel: (01352) 713270** **Open: MAR - NOV** **Map Ref No. 20**	Nearest Road: A.55 A 16th-century working dairy farm, overlooking the Dee Estuary, which retains its old-world charm, with a beamed & panelled interior. All bedrooms are tastefully furnished, some having bathroom/shower en-suite. Relax & enjoy typical farmhouse food in the attractive dining room. (Evening meals by prior arrangement.) Children's play area & a utility/games room are also available. A lovely home, within easy reach of both the coastal & mountain areas of North Wales. (UK Freephone 0800 0746857)	£18.00 to £20.00	Y	Y	N
N. & M. Steele-Mortimer **Golden Grove** **Llanasa** **Holywell** **CH8 9NE** **Tel: (01745) 854452** **Fax 01745 854547** **Open: Mid JAN - NOV** **Map Ref No. 21**	Nearest Road: A.5151 Beautiful Elizabethan manor house set in 1,000 acres, close to Chester, Bodnant Gardens & Snowdonia, & en route to Holyhead. The Steele-Mortimer brothers & wives, having returned to the family home from Canada & Ireland, provide a warm welcome for their guests. The menu features home produce, including lamb & game, together with interesting wines & home baking. The atmosphere is friendly & informal. No smoking upstairs. Children over 12 yrs. Licensed. E-mail: golden.grove@lineone.net	£35.00 to £45.00 *see PHOTO over* *p. 568* VISA: M'CARD:	Y	Y	N

When booking your accommodation please mention
The Best Bed & Breakfast

Golden Grove. Llanasa.

Wales
Glamorgan & Gwent

		rate £ from - to per person	evening meals children taken	animals taken
Paul & Monica Renwick **Sant-Y-Nyll** **St. Brides-Super-Ely** **Cardiff** **CF5 6EZ** **Tel: (01446) 760209** **Fax 01446 760897** **Open: ALL YEAR** **Map Ref No. 22**	Nearest Road: A.4232 You can be assured of a friendly welcome to Sant-Y-Nyll, a charming Georgian country residence set in its own extensive grounds, with spectacular views over the Vale of Glamorgan. 6 guest rooms with modern facilities, T.V. & tea/coffee-making. Comfortable, warm & relaxing. Licensed. Children welcome. Cardiff just 7 miles. St. Fagans Welsh Folk Museum 2 miles. Paul & Monica look forward to meeting you. **E-mail: Sant-y-Nyll@msn.com**	£25.00 to £50.00 AMEX:	Y N	Y
Michael & Kathleen Hurley **Tregenna Hotel** **Park Terrace** **Merthyr Tydfil** **CF47 8RF** **Tel: (01685) 723627** **Fax 01685 721951** **Open: ALL YEAR** **Map Ref No. 23**	Nearest Road: A.470 Family-run hotel with high level of comfort & class. 21 bedrooms with bathroom, 7 of which are designated for tourists & family use at special rates (50% reduction for children sharing). Telephone, tea/coffee service tray, colour T.V. in all rooms. Lunch, afternoon tea & dinner served 7 days a week. Brecon Beacons National Park 8 mins' drive. 45 mins Cardiff/Wales Airport, 2 1/4 hours London Heathrow Airport. **E-mail: treghotel@aol.com**	£27.50 to £30.00 VISA: M'CARD: AMEX:	Y Y	Y

Gwent

Mrs Beryl Watkins **The Glebe** **Croes-Y-Ceiliog** **Cwmbran** **Newport** **NP44 2DE** **Tel: (01633) 450251** **Tel: (01633) 450242** **Open: ALL YEAR** **Map Ref No. 24**	Nearest Road: A.4042, M.4 The Glebe overlooking this lovely part of rural Wales is an ideal spot from which to explore this historic region with its numerous castles & abbeys & the book shops of Hay-on-Wye. Your friendly & helpful host is only too happy to help you plan if need be. Cardiff, capital of Wales is 20 mins, London Heathrow Airport 2 1/2 hrs. The tastefully decorated bedrooms are centrally heated & have a hospitality tray. Breakfast menu. In the evening good pub fare is a pleasant country stroll away. Very convenient M.4 & M.5.	£19.00 to £££	Y N	N

Visit our website at:
http://www.bestbandb.co.uk

Melin Meloch Water Mill. Llanfor.

		rate £ from - to per person	children taken	evening meals	animals taken
Richard Fullard & Beryl Gunn Melin Meloch Nr. Llanfor Bala LL23 7DP Tel: (01678) 520101 Mobile 0370 978790 Open: MAR - OCT Map Ref No. 25	Nearest Road: A.494 Just outside Bala, on the B.4401, close to the River Dee, stands this historic Water Mill, its stone walls draped in Virginia creeper. Set in lovely water gardens with a river running through the Victorian turbine. 5-ft-wide doors lead into a unique galleried interior, filled with period furniture & bygones. Pretty en-suite/private facilitie rooms in the Mill cottage & granary, 5 with T.V. & all with hot-drinks trays. Animals & dinner by arrangement. Children over 3. Special rates early Spring/late Autumn (groups of 6 or more).	£22.00 to £25.00 🚭 *see PHOTO over* p.570	Y	Y	Y
Mrs J. M. Cunningham Abercelyn Country House Llanycil Bala LL23 7YF Tel: (01678) 521109 Fax 01678 520556 Open: ALL YEAR (Excl. Xmas) Map Ref No. 26	Nearest Road: A.494 Set in landscaped gardens with its own mountain stream running alongside, this former rectory dates back to before 1721. Situated in the Snowdonia National Park, it is ideally located for walking or touring. Bright & spacious en-suite bedrooms with views over Bala Lake, evenings relaxing before open log fires, & informal conversation over traditional breakfasts with hot home-baked bread, preserves & fresh coffee. E-mail: abercelyn@celtrail.com	£20.50 to £26.50 🚭 *see PHOTO over* p. 572 VISA: M'CARD:	Y	N	N
Mr R. W. Bayles The White House Llanfaglan Caernarfon LL54 5RA Tel: (01286) 673003 Open: MAR - NOV Map Ref No. 27	Nearest Road: A.487 The White House is a large detached house set in its own grounds, overlooking Foryd Bay, & with the Snowdonia mountains behind. There are 4 tastefully decorated bedrooms, all with bath or shower, tea/coffee-making facilities & colour T.V.. Guests are welcome to use the residents' lounge, outdoor pool & gardens. Ideally situated for birdwatching, walking, windsurfing, golf & visiting the historic Welsh castles. E-mail: RWBAYLES@SJMS.CO.UK	£19.00 to £21.00	Y	N	Y
Lynda Kettle Tyn Rhos Country Hotel Seion Llanddeiniolen Caernarfon LL55 3AE Tel: (01248) 670489 Fax 01248 670079 Open: ALL YEAR (Excl. Xmas) Map Ref No. 28	Nearest Road: B.4366 Tyn Rhos is a special place, set in a splendid location on the wide-open plain running between Snowdonia & the sea. Once a working farmhouse, it has now been transformed into a country house of great charm & comfort. Each individually designed bedroom is furnished to a high standard. 2 ground floor rooms have patio doors opening onto the garden. Award-winning Tyn Rhos serves super meals. Quality & exceptional value are the keynotes here. Children over 6. E-mail: enquiries@tynrhos.co.uk	£35.00 to £98.00 VISA: M'CARD: AMEX:	Y	Y	N
Mrs Rita Murray Min-Y-Gaer Hotel Porthmadog Road Criccieth LL52 0HP Tel: (01766) 522151 Fax 01766 523540 Open: MAR - OCT Map Ref No. 29	Nearest Road: A.497 A pleasant, licensed house in a quiet residential area, offering very good accommodation in 10 comfortable rooms, all of which have a bathroom en-suite. All rooms are non-smoking & have T.V. & tea/coffee facilities. The hotel enjoys commanding views of Criccieth Castle & the scenic Cardigan Bay coastline, & is only 2 mins' walk from the safe, sandy beach. Car parking on the premises. An ideal base for touring Snowdonia. E-mail: minygaer.hotel@virgin.net	£21.50 to £24.50 VISA: M'CARD: AMEX:	Y	N	Y

Abercelyn. Llanycil.

Ty Mawr. Llanegryn.

Wales
Gwynedd

Mrs Margaret Smyth Pentre Bach Llwyngwril Nr. Dolgellau LL37 2JU Tel: (01341) 250294 Fax 01341 250885 Open: ALL YEAR (Excl. Xmas) Map Ref No. 30	Nearest Road: A.493 Large, warm, peaceful, award-winning farmhouse in pretty coastal village, with BR station. Delicious food prepared by Mid-Wales Cook of the Year 1994, including free-range eggs, organic produce & herbs. 3 attractive en-suite bedrooms, each with T.V. & easy chairs. In Snowdonia National Park, the adjacent mountains offer walks through history from Stone Age to present day. Also, sea, beaches forests, rivers, steam railways, castles & pony trekking. **Email: smyth@pentrebach.com**	£25.00 to £56.00 *see PHOTO over* *p. 575* VISA: M'CARD:	N	Y	N
Eric & Gillian Newton Davies Noddfa Hotel Ffordd Newydd Harlech LL46 2UB Tel: (01766) 780043 Fax 01766 781105 Open: ALL YEAR Map Ref No. 31	Nearest Road: A.496 A Victorian country house situated within the National Park, with superb views of Snowdon, Tremadog Bay & Harlech Castle. 4 comfortable rooms (2 en-suite, T.V.). Licensed. Gillian & Eric will be delighted to talk about both the medieval weaponry, displayed in the bar, & the history of Harlech Castle, & to give archery lessons in the hotel grounds. Very close to the Castle, beach, indoor swimming pool & theatre. Children over 4. **E-mail: end@lineone.net**	£18.00 to £25.00 VISA: M'CARD: AMEX:	Y	N	N
Deborah Williams Gwrach Ynys Country Guest House Talsarnall Harlech LL47 6TS Tel: (01766) 780742 Fax 01766 781199 Open: MAR - OCT Map Ref No. 32	Nearest Road: A.496 A warm Welsh welcome awaits you at Gwrach Ynys, a 7 bedroom Edwardian country house set in 1 acre of garden, nestled between the sea & the mountains in beautiful Snowdonia National Park. En-suite bedrooms, individually decorated & furnished to a high standard. 2 comfortable guest lounges & a separate dining room. Ideally located for exploring North Wales. Superb area for walkers, birdwatchers & golfers. Children over 3.	£22.00 to £25.00	Y	N	N
Davis & Anne Sylvester Cefn Coch Guest House Llanegryn Tywyn LL36 9SD Tel: (01654) 712193 Fax 01654 712193 Open: MAR - OCT Map Ref No. 33	Nearest Road: A.493 Cefn Coch is an old coaching inn on the edge of the Snowdonia National Park & is surrounded by over an acre of gardens & paddock. It has been tastefully renovated throughout & now provides quality accommodation. 2 attractively furnished bedrooms, each with an en-suite bathroom & tea/coffee-making facilities. Delicious evening meals are served. Guests can enjoy the extensive views of the local countryside. The beautiful Cardigan Bay coast is nearby. A delightful home. **E-mail: david@cefncoch.force9.co.uk**	£22.00 to £24.00	N	Y	N
Lizzie & Richard Tregarthen Ty Mawr Llanegryn Tywyn LL36 9SY Tel: (01654) 710507 Fax 01654 710507 Open: ALL YEAR Map Ref No. 34	Nearest Road: A.493 With mountains to the east & sea to the west, Ty Mawr snugs into the south-facing slope of the Dysnni Valley. Total peace & quiet. There are private entrances to each ground-floor, en-suite bedroom, which are very comfortable & also have tea/coffee-making facilities. Enjoy meals in the conservatory overlooking the garden & valley. Numerous venues of interest, & local heritage. Links golf at Aberdovey.	£22.50 to £33.00 *see PHOTO over* *p. 573*	N	N	N

Pentre Bach. Llwyngwril.

Llanwenarth House. Govilon.

	rate £ from - to per person	evening meals children taken	animals taken

Mr & Mrs N. T. Corbett **Peniarth Uchaf** **Llanegryn** **Tywyn** **LL36 9UG** **Tel: (01654) 710804** **Fax 01654 712044** **Open: APR - OCT** **Map Ref No. 35**	Nearest Road: A.493 Peniarth Uchaf, situated in the Dysynni Valley in the Snowdonia National Park, is surrounded by broadleaved woodlands with rhododendrons, camelias & azaleas. The 18th-century family home has spacious, well-proportioned rooms, plasterwork ceilings & a wealth of period features. A peaceful setting from which to enjoy the countryside, including walking, climbing, sailing, fishing & bird watching. Children over 12. **E-mail: NCorb25486@aol.com**	£30.00 to £30.00 VISA: M'CARD:	Y Y N

Monmouthshire

B. L. Harris **The Wenallt** **Abergavenny** **NP7 0HP** **Tel: (01873) 830694** **Fax 01873 830694** **Open: ALL YEAR** **Map Ref No. 36**	Nearest Road: A.465 A 16th-century Welsh longhouse set in 50 acres of farmland in the Brecon Beacons National Park & commanding magnificent views over the Usk Valley. Retaining all its old charm, with oak beams & inglenook fireplace, yet offering a high standard of accommodation, with en-suite bedrooms, good food & a warm welcome. An ideal base from which to see Wales & the surrounding areas. Licensed.	£20.00 to £25.00 *see PHOTO over* *p. 578*	Y Y Y
Bruce & Amanda Weatherill **Llanwenarth House** **Gofilon** **Abergavenny** **NP7 9SF** **Tel: (01873) 830289** **Fax 01873 832199** **Open: Late FEB - Mid JAN** **Map Ref No. 37**	Nearest Road: A.465 A delightful 16th-century manor house, standing in beautiful grounds & surrounded by the tranquil scenic hills of the Brecon Beacons National Park. Elegantly furnished, tastefully decorated & with superb views, this house is a real pleasure to visit. Dinner, prepared by Amanda, a Cordon Bleu cook, is a delight & is served by candlelight. 4 en-suite bedrooms. Fishing, golf & shooting nearby. No smoking in dining room or bedrooms. Single supplement. Children over 10. Ideal for celebrating your millenium anniversary or birthday.	£38.00 to £41.00 *see PHOTO over* *p. 576*	Y Y Y
Dinah Price **Great House** **Isca Road** **Old Village** **Caerleon** **NP18 1QG** **Tel: (01633) 420216** **Open: ALL YEAR** **Map Ref No. 38**	Nearest Road: B.4596 Great House is an attractive 16th-century house located on the banks of the River Usk. Retaining much of its original character (incl. beams & inglenook fireplaces). 3 very pretty bedrooms with T.V. & tea/coffee facilities. A drawing room with T.V. & woodburner. Garden to rear leads to the riverbank. Golf course, fishing & forest trails nearby. The ancient village of Caerleon is very near with its amphitheatre, museums & Roman Baths. Ideal stop-over for those on the way through Wales or onto Ireland. Children over 12. **E-mail: price.greathouse@tesco.net**	£22.50 to £25.00	Y N N

When booking your accommodation please mention
The Best Bed & Breakfast

The Wenallt. Gilwern.

Wales
Monmouthshire & Pembrokeshire

		rate £ from - to per person	children taken	evening meals	animals taken
Jane Harmston **Llanishen House** Llanishen Chepstow NP16 6QS Tel: (01600) 860700 Open: ALL YEAR Map Ref No. 39	Nearest Road: A.466 17th-century country house set in 5 acres in a beautiful, elevated position. Equidistant between Usk, Chepstow, Tintern & Monmouth. Twin-bedded en-suite room in tranquil converted stables with own sitting room & courtyard. Double-bedded room & private bathroom with stunning views over Usk Valley. Ideal touring centre for Wales & the West Country. 15 mins from Severn Bridge. A walker's paradise. Light meals available by arrangement. Children over 10.	£20.00 to £30.00 🚭	Y	N	N
Mrs C. T. Park **Brick House Country** **Guest House** North Row Redwick, Magor Newport NP6 3DX Tel: (01633) 880230 Fax 01633 882441 Open: ALL YEAR Map Ref No. 40	Nearest Road: M.4 Jt. 23A Brick House is a Grade II listed Georgian country house dating from about 1765, but with up-to-date conveniences. All double bedrooms have an en-suite bathroom. A pleasant T.V. lounge, dining room & bar. Full central heating. There is also a delightful garden where guests may take cream teas, weather permitting. Brick House is ideally situated for touring South Wales & the Wye Valley, or as a stopping-off point just over the Severn Bridge. Single supplement. Children over 10. **E-mail: brickhouse@compuserve.com**	£24.00 to £24.00 🚭	Y	Y	N
Dereck & Vickie Stubbs **Parva Farmhouse Hotel** **& Restaurant** Tintern NP16 6SQ Tel: (01291) 689411 Fax 01291 689557 Open: ALL YEAR Map Ref No. 41	Nearest Road: A.466 A delightful 17th-century stone farmhouse situated 50 yards from the River Wye. The quaint en-suite bedrooms, with their designer fabrics, are gorgeous, & some offer breathtaking views over the River Wye & woodland. The beamed lounge, with log fires, leather Chesterfields & 'Honesty Bar', is a tranquil haven in which to unwind. Mouth-watering dishes, served in the intimate, candlelit Inglenook Restaurant, reflect the owner's love of cooking. A super home, perfect for a relaxing break or for exploring beautiful Wales.	£30.00 to £36.00 *see PHOTO over* *p. 580* VISA: M'CARD: AMEX:	Y	Y	Y

Pembrokeshire

Mrs S. Evans **Merrifields** Amroth SA67 8NW Tel: (01834) 813005 Open: ALL YEAR Map Ref No. 42	Nearest Road: A.477 Merrifields is a modern Scandinavian-style bungalow in an elevated position overlooking Carmarthen Bay. Attractive gardens with patios & parking, give splendid isolation yet easy access to the many tourist attractions of the area. 2 attractive bedrooms, each with an en-suite/private bathroom. Situated on the outskirts of Amroth offering unrivalled views over Carmarthen Bay to the popular resorts of Tenby & Saundersfoot. Merrifields is the ideal place to unwind.	£22.50 to £22.50 🚭	Y	N	N

see PHOTO over p. 580

Visit our website at:
http://www.bestbandb.co.uk

Parva Farmhouse and Restaurant. Tintern.

		rate £ from - to per person	children taken	evening meals taken	animals taken
Mr & Mrs Cooper & Mr & Mrs Lloyd Cnapan East Street, Newport Fishguard SA42 0SY Tel: (01239) 820575 Fax 01239 820878 Open: MAR - DEC Map Ref No. 43	Nearest Road: A.487 Cnapan is a Garde II listed house in the heart of historic Newport. It is beautifully furnished throughout & blessed with character. Bedrooms are spacious, comfortable & individually decorated. (All are en-suite with T.V. & tea/coffee facilities.) Meals are superb from the hearty breakfasts to the mouth-watering dishes served at dinner. Many varied interests & activities are on the doorstep. Parrog Beach & Newport Sands are within a short walk, also the spectacular coastal path.	£28.00 to £35.00 VISA: M'CARD:	Y	Y	N
Peter & Jane Heard Tregynon Country Farmhouse Hotel Gwaun Valley Fishguard SA65 9TU Tel: (01239) 820531 Fax 01239 820808 Open: ALL YEAR Map Ref No. 44	Nearest Road: B.4313 This is a traditional, beamed, award-winning, 16th-century, family-run farmhouse, standing in acres of grounds next to ancient oak woodlands & overlooking the glorious Gwaun Valley in the Pembrokeshire Coast National Park. It is unique, of great natural beauty & quite unspoilt. 6 en-suite ground-floor rooms. Traditional & special diets, wholefood & vegetarian specialities. A range of wines. Own trout ponds, 200ft waterfall & Iron Age fort, abundant wildlife. Children over 6. **E-mail: tregynon@uk-holidays.co.uk**	£30.00 to £37.50 VISA: M'CARD:	Y	Y	N
Mrs E. A. Webber Allenbrook Dale Haverfordwest SA62 3RN Tel: (01646) 636254 Fax 01646 636954 Open: ALL YEAR Map Ref No. 45	Nearest Road: A.40 Allenbrook is a charming country house set in its own grounds. It is adjacent to the beach & situated in the Pembrokeshire National Park on the coastal path. The house is very comfortable with spacious bedrooms fully-equipped with T.V. & tea/coffee-making facilities. All of the bedrooms have en-suite or private bathrooms, & there is a large, comfortable guests' sitting room. A delightful home.	£20.00 to £25.00	N	N	N
Mrs Virgina Lort Phillips Knowles Farm Lawrenny Kilgetty SA68 0PX Tel: (01834) 891221 Fax 01834 891344 Open: EASTER - OCT Map Ref No. 66	Nearest Road: A.4075 Relax, unwind & prepare to be pampered in this lovely south-facing family home overlooking the Milford Haven Estuary. Knowles Farm has access to farmland & ancient woodland & is within 15 mins of the glorious Pembrokeshire coast. There are castles, ancient monuments & theme parks surrounding Knowles Farm, & lovely walks are on the doorstep. Riding, fishing, bird-watching & boating within minutes. After a day out, a special meal (with notice) in the dining room. **E-mail: owenlp@globalnet.co.uk**	£23.00 to £££	Y	Y	Y
Patricia & David Phillips The Old Vicarage Country Guest House Moylegrove SA43 3BN Tel: (01239) 881231 Fax 01239 881341 Open: FEB - NOV Map Ref No. 46	Nearest Road: A.487 Patricia & David welcome you to their elegant Edwardian home set in an elevated position with large lawned gardens & glorious views to the sea. 3 comfortably furnished en-suite bedrooms with tea/coffee-making facilities. Situated in Britain's only coastal National Park, 1 mile from one of the most dramatic sections of the Pembrokeshire Coast Path at Ceibwr Bay, with the Preseli Hills & Teifi Valley nearby. Enjoy the timeless & leisurely tranquillity of north Pembrokeshire. Croeso! **E-mail: oldvic@newport-pembs.co.uk**	£25.00 to £25.00	N	Y	N

Wales
Pembrokeshire

			rate £ from - to per person	children taken	evening meals	animals taken
Mrs R. E. Mooney **The Peacock Tea Garden & Conservatory** **Hoarstone House** **Martletwy** **Narberth SA67 8AZ** **Tel: (01834) 891707** **Fax 01834 891707** **Open: ALL YEAR** **Map Ref No. 65**	Nearest Road: A.40, A.477 Set in its own grounds in the heart of the Pembrokeshire countryside. The Peacock Tea Garden offers 2 prettily furnished guest rooms. 1 double en-suite & 1 twin with private bathroom, each with T.V. & tea/coffee facilities. Excellent breakfasts. Delicious traditional afternoon & cream teas served in the tea garden & conservatory. A lovely base for exploring the glorious Welsh countryside & many attractions. Dinner by arrangement. Licensed. Children over 12. **E-mail: Peacock@jpmarketing.co.uk**		£21.50 to £24.50	Y	Y	N
Barry & Jeannie Rutherford **Trewarren** **Golf Club Road** **Newport** **SA42 0NR** **Tel: (01239) 820455** **Open: ALL YEAR** **Map Ref No. 47**	Nearest Road: A.487 Trewarren is unique. Built on the site of a 300-year-old fisherman's cottage, it is sited on a bluff with fabulous views. Trewarren overlooks the Preseli Hills, the estuary of the River Nevern (with bird sanctuary), the sea & the pretty town of Newport. Its garden slopes down to the coastal path giving easy access to town & the sandy beach. Adjacent to a golf course. There are 2 attractive en-suite rooms.		£20.00 to £25.00	N	N	N
Nina & Hywel Williams **Bettws** **Parrog** **Newport SA42 0RX** **Tel: (01239) 820559** **Open: APR - OCT** **Map Ref No. 43**	Nearest Road: A.470 Superbly renovated & refurbished Victorian house on spectacular Pembrokeshire coastal path. Breakfast in Victorian conservatory feet away from the sea with views across the estuary & bay. There are 3 bedrooms, 2 en-suite, including a family room, 50% reduction for children. Colour T.V. & tea/coffee in 2 of the bedrooms. Set in the Pembrokeshire National Park with facilities for walking, sailing, bird watching, golf & horse riding. A charming home.		£24.00 to £27.00 (non-smoking)	Y	N	N
Mrs Eryl Onions **Bryn Alban House For Guests** **Parrog** **Newport SA42 0RX** **Tel: (01239) 820542** **Open: ALL YEAR** **Map Ref No. 48**	Nearest Road: A.487 A completely refurbished seafarers cottage set at the waters edge, in an Area of Outstanding Natural Beauty & tranquillity. Your hosts offer bed & breakfast, & dinner as an option, in tastefully decorated rooms with a high standard of comfort & service. Tea/coffee-making facilities, central heating & colour T.V. in all rooms. Bryn Alban is conveniently situated for boating, golf, tennis, walking & the Irish ferry.		£25.00 to £28.00	N	Y	N
Mrs Jill McHugh **The Old Vicarage** **Manorbier** **Tenby** **SA70 7TN** **Tel: (01834) 871452** **Fax 01834 871452** **Open: ALL YEAR** **Map Ref No. 49**	Nearest Road: A.4139 Situated in the coastal village of Manorbier with its beautiful beaches & castle, The Old Vicarage offers gracious accommodation with glimpses of Barafundle Bay. The spacious en-suite bedrooms are furnished with antiques & have tea/coffee facilities. Guests are free to enjoy the mature gardens or sit by a log fire in the drawing room. For the more energetic, the renowned Pembrokeshire Coastal Path passes through the village. Beaches a 5-min. walk. Irish ferries from Pembroke (20 mins) & Fishguard (50 mins). (Self-catering accommodation is also available.)		£23.50 to £25.00 (non-smoking)	Y	N	N

Wales
Pembrokeshire & Powys

rate £ from - to per person
children taken
evening meals taken
animals taken

		rate £ from - to per person	children taken	evening meals taken	animals taken
Lionel & Joyce Fielder **Old Stable Cottage** **3 Picton Terrace** **Carew Village** **Tenby** **SA70 8SL** **Tel: (01646) 651889** **Open: APR - OCT** **Map Ref No. 50**	Nearest Road: A.4075, A.477 The Cottage (Grade II listed), with inglenook fireplace & original bread oven, was once a stable & carthouse to 13th-century Carew Castle situated near the entrance & the creek of Carew River with its Tidal Mill. A spiral staircase leads to 3 charming, oak-beamed en-suite bedrooms with colour T.V., home-baked Welsh cakes & tea/coffee. Delicious food is prepared in the farmhouse kitchen on the Aga. Evening meals by arrangement. A conservatory overlooks the garden. Children over 10.	£24.00 to £28.00	Y	Y	N
Margaret & Peter Gilder **Llangwm House** **Whitland** **SA34 0RB** **Tel: (01994) 240621** **Fax 01994 240621** **Open: ALL YEAR** **Map Ref No. 51**	Nearest Road: A.40 Llangwm House is a large, fully modernised farmhouse with glorious panoramic views, ideally situated for the Pembrokeshire Coast, with its beautiful beaches, walks & abundant wildlife. The spacious bedrooms, all of which have en-suite/private facilities, are tastefully furnished with comfort in mind. All have T.V. & tea/coffee-making facilities. Guests are assured of a warm welcome, & may find it interesting to watch Peter train his sheepdogs. Children over 5. Licensed.	£20.00 to £22.00	Y	N	Y

Powys

		rate £ from - to per person	children taken	evening meals taken	animals taken
Mrs Marie Gray **The Laurels** **Church Street** **Bronllys** **Brecon LD3 0HS** **Tel: (01874) 712188** **Fax 01874 712187** **Open: ALL YEAR** **Map Ref No. 52**	Nearest Road: A.438 The Laurels is a comfortable, spacious Victorian house with ample parking, set in a small village surrounded by the glorious countryside of the Brecon Beacons & Black Mountains. It has been modernised with taste & ingenuity reflecting the flair of the owners, John & Marie Gray. Accommodation is in 3 delightful en-suite bedrooms. The village of Bronllys is halfway between Brecon & the fascinating 'Book Town' of Hay-on-Wye. VISA: M'CARD:	£18.00 to £25.00	Y	N	N
Stuart & Ann Bradley **Trewalter** **Llangorse** **Brecon** **LD3 0PS** **Tel: (01874) 658442** **Fax 01874 658442** **Open: ALL YEAR (Excl. Xmas & New Year)** **Map Ref No. 53**	Nearest Road: A.40 Trewalter is perfectly situated in open farmland between the Black Mountains & the Brecon Beacons with far-reaching spectacular views. The delightful Victorian house is elegantly furnished with individually designed & tastefully decorated bedrooms with bath or shower. The family take pride in their reputation for good food & hospitality. Excellent base for walking, riding & watersports & just 10 mins' from Hay-on-Wye. Restaurant licence. No smoking in bedrooms & dining room. Children over 4 years.	£21.00 to £26.00	Y	Y	N

When booking your accommodation please mention
The Best Bed & Breakfast

York House. Cusop.

Wales
Powys

	Nearest Road	rate £ from - to per person	children taken	evening meals	animals taken
Mrs Mary Cole **Dolycoed** **Talyllyn** **Brecon** **LD3 7SY** **Tel: (01874) 658666** **Open: ALL YEAR** **Map Ref No. 54**	Nearest Road: A.40 Dolycoed, built at the turn of the century, retains many of its interesting original features. Standing in a sheltered position in Brecon Beacons National Park, it offers a warm, friendly, homely welcome to all. Accommodation is in 2 comfortable guest bedrooms, with radio & tea/coffee makers, & a guests' lounge with colour T.V.. Many outdoor activities nearby: pony trekking, riding, fishing, watersports & walking.	£18.00 to £18.00	Y	N	Y
Mr & Mrs P. E. Jackson **The Beacons** **16 Bridge Street** **Brecon** **LD3 8AH** **Tel: (01874) 623339** **Fax 01874 623339** **Open: ALL YEAR** **Map Ref No. 55**	Nearest Road: A.40 Recently restored 17th/18th-century house retaining many of its original features. Well-appointed standard, en-suite & luxury period rooms. Enjoy a drink in the original meat cellar (complete with hooks) or relax in a comfortable armchair in front of the fire. The award-winning chef will spoil you with outstanding cuisine freshly cooked to your order. A delightful home & an excellent base for a relaxing break. **E-mail: beacons@brecon.co.uk**	£18.00 to £29.50 (non-smoking) VISA: M'CARD:	Y	Y	Y
Nancy M. Jones **Ty-Isaf Farm** **Erwood** **Builth Wells** **LD2 3SZ** **Tel: (01982) 560607** **Open: ALL YEAR** **Map Ref No. 56**	Nearest Road: A.470 Ty-Isaf Farm, situated in the attractive village of Erwood, offers accommodation in 3 comfortably furnished rooms with modern amenities & tea/coffee-making facilities. Plentiful English or Continental breakfasts are served. Special diets & packed lunches provided by arrangement. Guests may relax in the cosy lounge, with T.V. throughout the day. An ideal base for touring.	£15.00 to £16.00	Y	Y	Y
Christina Jackson **Glangrwyney Court** **Crickhowell** **NP8 1ES** **Tel: (01873) 811288** **Fax 01873 810317** **Open: ALL YEAR** **Map Ref No. 57**	Nearest Road: A.40 Glangrwyney Court is a Georgian mansion set in 4 acres of established gardens & surrounded by parkland. All rooms are comfortably furnished with antiques & fine porcelain & paintings, & there is essentially a welcoming & homely atmosphere. Accommodation is in 5 attractive & well-appointed bedrooms, each with a private or en-suite bathroom. During the winter, log fires burn in all the sitting rooms, & in the summer guests are able to relax with a drink in the gardens. Evening meals are available by arrangement.	£20.00 to £25.00	Y	Y	Y
Peter & Olwen Roberts **York House** **Hardwicke Road** **Cusop** **Hay-on-Wye** **HR3 5QX** **Tel: (01497) 820705** **Open: ALL YEAR** **Map Ref No. 58**	Nearest Road: A.438 Peter and Olwen Roberts welcome you to their traditional Victorian guest house quietly situated in beautiful gardens on the edge of Hay. Sunny mountain views are enjoyed by all the well-appointed en-suite rooms. Ideal for a relaxing holiday spent browsing in the world-famous bookshops, exploring the National Park and Kilvert country, or just enjoying the freshly prepared home cooking. Evening meals by arrangement. Private parking. Children over 8.	£23.00 to £25.00 (non-smoking) *see PHOTO over* *p. 584* VISA: M'CARD: AMEX:	Y	Y	Y

see PHOTO over p. 584

Guidfa House. Llandrindod Wells.

Wales
Powys

Anne & Tony Millan **Guidfa House** **Crossgates** **Llandrindod Wells** **LD1 6RF** **Tel: (01597) 851241** Fax 01597 851875 **Open: ALL YEAR** **Map Ref No. 59**	Nearest Road: A.483, A.44 Licensed Georgian guest house, situated in an ideal location for touring lakes, mountains, national parks & the coast. The bedrooms are all comfortable, non-smoking & spacious, most en-suite, all with colour T.V. & tea/coffee-making facilities. A ground-floor room is also available. Meals are prepared by Anne, who is Cordon-Bleu-trained. Dinner is a set menu, but special diets/requests can always be catered for with a little prior notice. Children over 10 years. **E-mail: guidfa@globalnet.co.uk**	£25.00 to £25.00 *see PHOTO over* *p. 586* VISA: M'CARD:	Y	Y	N
Mrs Kathleen Hurley **Penrhadw Farm** **Pontsticill** **Merthyr Tydfil** **CF48 2TU** **Tel: (01685) 722461** **Tel: (01685) 723481** Fax 01685 721951 **Open: ALL YEAR** **Map Ref No. 60**	Nearest Road: A.470 A wonderful opportunity for you to base yourself deep in the National Park, yet benefit from the high level of service typically afforded of a top grade hotel. Penrhadw Farm has been specially designed to cater for guests wishing to explore the surrounding countryside. The farm allows easy access straight out onto the Beacons. It is proving very popular with artists, photographers, hangliders, pony trekkers & bird watchers. A pair of Red Kites & Perigrine Falcons regularly visit the surrounding farmland. **E-mail: treghotel@aol.com**	£28.00 to £40.00 🚭 VISA: M'CARD: AMEX:	Y	Y	N
Gaynor Bright **Little Brompton Farm** **Montgomery** **SY15 6HY** **Tel: (01686) 668371** Fax 01686 668371 **Open: ALL YEAR** **Map Ref No. 61**	Nearest Road: B.4385, A.489 Robert & Gaynor welcome you to this charming 17th-century farmhouse, situated on this working farm. The house has much original character, with beautiful old oak beams. Pretty bedrooms, with en-suite bathrooms, enhanced by quality antiques. T.V.. Home-cooking is a speciality, although meals are by arrangement. Offa's Dyke runs through the farm. Situated on the B.4385, 2 miles east of the beautiful Georgian town of Montgomery. Come & relax in peaceful, stress-free countryside. Animals by arrangement.	£20.00 to £22.00 🚭	Y	Y	Y
Brian & Jean Thomas **Buttington House** **Buttington** **Welshpool** **SY21 8HD** **Tel: (01938) 553351** **Open: ALL YEAR (Excl. Xmas)** **Map Ref No. 62**	Nearest Road: A.458 A late Georgian former country rectory built of stone & lovingly restored by the owners who wish to share their lovely home with visitors that appreciate a friendly, informal but graceful atmosphere. Set in almost 2 acres of garden. Offering 2 en-suite double bedrooms with tea/coffee-making facilities & radio. Guests' sitting room with T.V.. Ideally situated for the National Trust's Powis Castle (2 miles). For walkers, Offa's Dyke is within yards of the garden. Lakes, mountains & coasts within 50 miles.	£35.00 to £50.00 🚭	Y	N	N

Visit our website at:
http://www.bestbandb.co.uk

Wales
Powys & Swansea

		rate £ from - to per person	evening meals children taken	animals taken

		rate £ from - to per person	children taken	evening meals	animals taken
Mrs Sue Jones Lower Trelydan Farm- house Guilsfield Welshpool SY21 9PH Tel: (01938) 553105 Fax 01938 553105 Open: ALL YEAR Map Ref No. 63	Nearest Road: A.490 Graham & Sue welcome you to their wonderful, award-winning black-&-white farmhouse, set on their working farm & listed for its history & beauty. The bedrooms are tastefully furnished, with en-suite facilities & colour T.V.. An oak-beamed lounge, & a dining room where evening meals are served most nights. Home cooking a speciality. Also, a licensed bar. Powis Castle & many beauty spots are nearby, as well as leisure activities & walks. Relax in this lovely home, & capture the atmosphere of 4 centuries of history in this out-standing house. Self-catering available. **E-mail: lower.trelydan@which.net**	£24.00 to £25.00 *see PHOTO over* *p. 589*	Y	Y	N

Swansea

| Mrs Jan Maybery
Tides Reach
388 Mumbles Road
Mumbles
Swansea
SA3 5TN
Tel: (01792) 404877
Open: MAR - NOV
Map Ref No. 64 | Nearest Road: A.4067
The warmest of welcomes awaits you at Tides Reach, where you will find a lovingly restored early-Victorian town house elegantly furnished with antiques. 6 attractive bedrooms, each with private facilities. Well situated on the seafront in the delightful village of Mumbles (the gateway to Gower), only 4 miles from the city centre. An ideal base for business or pleasure & convenient as a stop on your way to Ireland. | £22.50
to
£35.00 | N | N | Y |

All the establishments mentioned in this guide are members of
The Worldwide Bed & Breakfast Association

When booking your accommodation please mention
The Best Bed & Breakfast

Lower Trelydan Farm. Guilsfield.

Towns & Counties Index

Town	County	Country
Abergavenny	Monmouthshire	Wales
Abingdon	Oxfordshire	England
Aboyne	Aberdeenshire	Scotland
Alcester	Warwickshire	England
Allendale	Northumberland	England
Alnwick	Northumberland	England
Alresford	Hampshire	England
Altrincham	Cheshire	England
Ambleside	Cumbria	England
Ampleforth	Yorkshire	England
Amroth	Pembrokeshire	Wales
Andover	Hampshire	England
Anstruther	Fifeshire	Scotland
Appin	Argyll	Scotland
Ardbeg	Isle of Bute	Scotland
Arundel	Sussex	England
Ashbourne	Derbyshire	England
Ashford	Kent	England
Auchtermuchty	Fifeshire	Scotland
Aylmerton	Norfolk	England
Ayr	Ayrshire	Scotland
Bala	Gwynedd	Wales
Ballantrae	Ayrshire	Scotland
Bamburgh	Northumberland	England
Banbury	Oxfordshire	England
Barnstaple	Devon	England
Bath	Somerset	England
Bath	Wiltshire	England
Bedale	Yorkshire	England
Bedford	Bedfordshire	England
Belper	Derbyshire	England
Berkhamsted	Hertfordshire	England
Betws-Y-Coed	Conwy	Wales
Bideford	Devon	England
Bingley	Yorkshire	England
Bishop Auckland	Durham	England
Bishop's Stortford	Essex	England
Blairgowrie	Perthshire	Scotland
Blidworth	Nottinghamshire	England
Bolney	Sussex	England
Bordon	Hampshire	England
Boroughbridge	Yorkshire	England
Boscastle	Cornwall	England
Boston Spa	Yorkshire	England
Bourne	Lincolnshire	England
Bournemouth	Dorset	England
Bourton-on-the-Water	Gloucestershire	England
Bowness-on-Windermere	Cumbria	England
Bradford-on-Avon	Wiltshire	England
Brampton	Cumbria	England
Braunton	Devon	England
Brecon	Powys	Wales
Bridgnorth	Shropshire	England
Bridgwater	Somerset	England
Bridlington	Yorkshire	England
Bridport	Dorset	England
Brighton	Sussex	England
Bristol	Gloucestershire	England
Bristol	Somerset	England
Broad Campden	Gloucestershire	England
Broadford	Isle of Skye	Scotland
Broadstairs	Kent	England
Broadway	Worcestershire	England
Broadway	Gloucestershire	England
Brockenhurst	Hampshire	England
Brough	Yorkshire	England
Bude	Cornwall	England
Builth Wells	Powys	Wales
Bungay	Suffolk	England
Burford	Oxfordshire	England
Burley	Hampshire	England
Burnley	Lancashire	England
Bury St. Edmunds	Suffolk	England
Buttermere	Cumbria	England
Buxton	Derbyshire	England
Caerleon	Monmouthshire	Wales
Caernarfon	Gwynedd	Wales
Cairndow	Argyll	Scotland
Callander	Perthshire	Scotland
Camberley	Surrey	England
Cambridge	Cambridgeshire	England
Canterbury	Kent	England
Cardiff	Glamorgan	Wales
Cardigan	Ceredigion	Wales
Carlisle	Cumbria	England
Carmarthen	Carmarthenshire	Wales
Carnforth	Lancashire	England
Carrbridge	Inverness-shire	Scotland
Cartmell Fell	Cumbria	England
Chagford	Devon	England
Chard	Somerset	England
Chelmsford	Essex	England
Cheltenham	Gloucestershire	England
Chelwood Gate	Sussex	England
Chepstow	Monmouthshire	Wales
Chester	Cheshire	England
Chichester	Sussex	England
Chippenham	Wiltshire	England
Chipping Camden	Gloucestershire	England
Chipping Norton	Oxfordshire	England
Christchurch	Hampshire	England
Cirencester	Gloucestershire	England
Clitheroe	Lancashire	England
Coalville	Leicestershire	England
Cockermouth	Cumbria	England
Colchester	Suffolk	England
Colchester	Essex	England
Corbridge	Northumberland	England
Corsham	Wiltshire	England
Corstorphine	Edinburgh	Scotland
Crackington Haven	Cornwall	England
Cranbrook	Kent	England
Cranleigh	Surrey	England
Craven Arms	Shropshire	England
Crediton	Devon	England
Crewkerne	Dorset	England
Crewkerne	Somerset	England
Crianlarich	Perthshire	Scotland

Towns & Counties Index

Town	County	Country	Town	County	Country
Criccieth	Gwynedd	Wales	Haverfordwest	Pembrokeshire	Wales
Crickhowell	Powys	Wales	Haverhill	Suffolk	England
Danehill	Sussex	England	Hawes	Yorkshire	England
Darlington	Yorkshire	England	Hawkhurst	Kent	England
Dartmouth	Devon	England	Hay-on-Wye	Powys	Wales
Dereham	Norfolk	England	Heathfield	Sussex	England
Devizes	Wiltshire	England	Helston	Cornwall	England
Didmarton	Gloucestershire	England	Henfield	Sussex	England
Diss	Norfolk	England	Henley	Oxfordshire	England
Dolgellau	Gwynedd	Wales	Henley-on-Thames	Oxfordshire	England
Dorchester	Dorset	England	Henley-on-Thames	Buckinghamshire	England
Dorking	Surrey	England	Hereford	Herefordshire	England
Doune	Perthshire	Scotland	Hexham	Northumberland	England
Dover	Kent	England	Holbeach	Lincolnshire	England
Drumnadrochit	Inverness-shire	Scotland	Holywell	Flintshire	Wales
Dumbarton	Dunbartonshire	Scotland	Honiton	Devon	England
Dumfries	Dumfriesshire	Scotland	Hope Valley	Derbyshire	England
Dunkeld	Perthshire	Scotland	Horley	Surrey	England
Dunoon	Argyll	Scotland	Horsham	Sussex	England
Duns	Berwickshire	Scotland	Hungerford	Berkshire	England
Dunster	Somerset	England	Hunstanton	Norfolk	England
Durham	Durham	England	Hurstpierpoint	Sussex	England
Duror in Appin	Argyll	Scotland	Inverness	Inverness-shire	Scotland
Easingwold	Yorkshire	England	Ipswich	Suffolk	England
East Hoathly	Sussex	England	Ironbridge	Shropshire	England
Eastbourne	Sussex	England	Isle of Anglesey	Anglesey	Wales
Edinburgh	Edinburgh	Scotland	Isle of Islay	Argyll	Scotland
Edinburgh	Lothian	Scotland	Isle of Mull	Argyll	Scotland
Ely	Cambridgeshire	England	Isle of Wight	Hampshire	England
Emsworth	Hampshire	England	Jedburgh	Roxburghshire	Scotland
Exeter	Devon	England	Kelso	Roxburghshire	Scotland
Eyam	Derbyshire	England	Kendal	Cumbria	England
Eyemouth	Berwickshire	Scotland	Kenilworth	Warwickshire	England
Falmouth	Cornwall	England	Kentallen of Appin	Argyll	Scotland
Farnham	Hampshire	England	Keswick	Cumbria	England
Faversham	Kent	England	Keswick-on-Derwentwater	Cumbria	England
Fishguard	Pembrokeshire	Wales	Kettering	Northamptonshire	England
Folkestone	Kent	England	Kidderminster	Shropshire	England
Fordham	Cambridgeshire	England	Kilgetty	Pembrokeshire	Wales
Fordingbridge	Hampshire	England	Kingsbridge	Devon	England
Fort William	Inverness-shire	Scotland	Kington	Herefordshire	England
Gainsborough	Lincolnshire	England	Kirkby Lonsdale	Cumbria	England
Garway	Herefordshire	England	Knebworth	Hertfordshire	England
Girvan	Ayrshire	Scotland	Knutsford	Cheshire	England
Glasgow	Renfrewshire	Scotland	Launceston	Cornwall	England
Glastonbury	Somerset	England	Leamington Spa	Warwickshire	England
Glenshiel	Ross-shire	Scotland	Leeds	Yorkshire	England
Gloucester	Gloucestershire	England	Leek	Staffordshire	England
Grange-over-Sands	Cumbria	England	Leigh	Surrey	England
Grantown-on-Spey	Morayshire	Scotland	Leigh	Gloucestershire	England
Grasmere	Cumbria	England	Leighton Buzzard	Buckinghamshire	England
Great Yarmouth	Norfolk	England	Leominster	Herefordshire	England
Hailsham	Sussex	England	Leyburn	Yorkshire	England
Harlech	Gwynedd	Wales	Lifton	Devon	England
Harrogate	Yorkshire	England	Lincoln	Lincolnshire	England
Hartfield	Sussex	England	Liskeard	Cornwall	England
Haslemere	Surrey	England	Lizard	Cornwall	England
Hassocks	Sussex	England	Llandrindod Wells	Powys	Wales
Hastings	Sussex	England	Llandudno	Conwy	Wales

Towns & Counties Index

Towns & Counties Index

Town	County	Country
Stirling	Clackmannanshire	Scotland
Stoke-on-Trent	Staffordshire	England
Stokesley	Yorkshire	England
Stonehouse	Gloucestershire	England
Storrington	Sussex	England
Stowmarket	Suffolk	England
Stragglethorpe	Lincolnshire	England
Stratford-upon-Avon	Warwickshire	England
Stroud	Gloucestershire	England
Sturminster Newton	Dorset	England
Swadlincote	Derbyshire	England
Swaffham	Norfolk	England
Swansea	Swansea	Wales
Swindon	Wiltshire	England
Talisker	Isle of Skye	Scotland
Tarporley	Cheshire	England
Taunton	Somerset	England
Tavistock	Devon	England
Teignmouth	Devon	England
Tenby	Pembrokeshire	Wales
Tenterden	Kent	England
Tetbury	Gloucestershire	England
Tewkesbury	Gloucestershire	England
Thetford	Norfolk	England
Thirsk	Yorkshire	England
Tintagel	Cornwall	England
Tintern	Monmouthshire	Wales
Tiverton	Devon	England
Tonbridge	Kent	England
Torpoint	Cornwall	England
Totnes	Devon	England
Trefriw	Conwy	Wales
Truro	Cornwall	England
Tunbridge Wells	Kent	England
Twyford	Berkshire	England
Tywyn	Gwynedd	Wales
Uffington	Oxfordshire	England
Uppingham	Rutland	England
Uttoxeter	Staffordshire	England
Wallingford	Oxfordshire	England
Wareham	Dorset	England
Warminster	Wiltshire	England
Warwick	Warwickshire	England
Wells	Somerset	England
Welshpool	Powys	Wales
Welwyn	Hertfordshire	England
Wendling	Norfolk	England
West Lulworth	Dorset	England
Weymouth	Dorset	England
Wheddon Cross	Somerset	England
Whitby	Yorkshire	England
Whitchurch	Shropshire	England
Whitland	Pembrokeshire	Wales
Wimborne	Dorset	England
Winchcombe	Gloucestershire	England
Winchelsea	Sussex	England
Winchester	Hampshire	England
Windermere	Cumbria	England
Witney	Oxfordshire	England
Woking	Surrey	England
Woolacombe	Devon	England
Worcester	Worcestershire	England
Worthenbury	Cheshire	England
Worthing	Sussex	England
Yelverton	Devon	England
York	Yorkshire	England

Recommendation 2000

Thank you for taking the trouble to supply this information .
We value your comments & will take appropriate action where necessary.
We regret that we are unable to reply to you individually.

Proprietors _____

House Name _____

Address _____

_____

_____

Please give some general information about your stay, the house, rooms, food & hosts etc.

Date of stay _____

_____

_____

_____

_____

_____

_____

_____

Your Name _____

Address _____

_____

_____

Reply to: W.W.B.B.A. P.O. Box 2070,
London. W12 8QW

Recommendation 2000

Thank you for taking the trouble to supply this information .
We value your comments & will take appropriate action where necessary.
We regret that we are unable to reply to you individually.

Proprietors _____

House Name _____

Address _____

_____

_____

Please give some general information about your stay, the house, rooms, food & hosts etc.

Date of stay _____

_____

_____

_____

_____

_____

_____

_____

Your Name _____

Address _____

_____

Reply to: W.W.B.B.A. P.O. Box 2070.
London. W12 8QW

Recommendation 2000

Proprietors _____

House Name _____

Address _____

_____

_____

Please give some general information about your stay, the house, rooms, food & hosts etc.

Date of stay _____

_____

_____

_____

_____

_____

_____

_____

Your Name _____

Address _____

_____

Reply to: W.W.B.B.A. P.O. Box 2070.
London. W12 8QW

Complaint 2000

Thank you for taking the trouble to supply this information.
We value your comments & will take appropriate action where necessary.
We regret that we are unable to reply to you individually.

Proprietors _____

House Name _____

Address _____

_____

_____

Please be specific about your complaint. State exactly what was wrong with your stay e.g. the room, food, house keeping etc.

Date of stay _____

_____

_____

_____

_____

_____

_____

_____

Your Name _____

Address _____

_____

Reply to:W.W.B.B.A. P.O. Box 2070,
London. W12 8QW

Complaint 2000

Thank you for taking the trouble to supply this information .
We value your comments & will take appropriate action where necessary.
We regret that we are unable to reply to you individually.

Proprietors _____

House Name _____

Address _____

_____

**Please be specific about your complaint. State exactly what was
wrong with your stay e.g. the room, food, house keeping etc.**

Date of stay _____

_____

_____

_____

_____

_____

_____

_____

Your Name _____

Address _____

_____

**Reply to:W.W.B.B.A. P.O. Box 2070,
London. W12 8QW**

Recommendation 2000

Thank you for taking the trouble to supply this information .
We value your comments & will take appropriate action where necessary.
We regret that we are unable to reply to you individually.

Proprietors _____

House Name _____

Address _____

_____

Please give some general information about your stay, the house, rooms, food & hosts etc.

Date of stay _____

_____

_____

_____

_____

_____

_____

_____

Your Name _____

Address _____

_____

**Reply to: W.W.B.B.A. P.O. Box 2070.
London. W12 8QW**

Notes